FROMMER'S

COMPREHENSIVE TRAVEL GUIDE

New Mexico

3rd Edition

by Lisa Legarde
and Don Laine

MACMILLAN • USA

ABOUT THE AUTHORS

Lisa Legarde (Chapters 1–6) was born in New Orleans and graduated from Wellesley College with a degree in English. She worked as an assistant editor at Macmillan Travel before embarking on her career as a travel writer. Lisa has traveled extensively in Europe and North America and is author or co-author of numerous Frommer's travel guides, including *Frommer's Maui* and *Frommer's New Orleans.*

Don Laine (Chapters 7–10) has written about and traveled extensively throughout the Rocky Mountains and the Southwest. He and his wife, Barbara, have authored a Frommer's guide to Colorado and are the regional editors of *Frommer's America on Wheels: Arizona & New Mexico*. The Laines, who reside in northern New Mexico, are currently at work on *Frommer's Utah.*

MACMILLAN TRAVEL

A Prentice Hall Macmillan Company
15 Columbus Circle
New York, NY 10023

ISBN 0-02-860076-2
ISSN 1053-2455

Design by Michele Laseau
Maps by Geographix Inc. and Ortelius Design

SPECIAL SALES

Bulk purchases (10+ copies) of Frommer's travel guides are available to corporations at special discounts. The Special Sales Department can produce custom editions to be used as premiums and/or for sales promotion to suit individual needs. Existing editions can be produced with custom cover imprints such as corporate logos. For more information write to Special Sales, Simon & Schuster, 1230 Avenue of the Americas, New York, NY 10020.

Manufactured in the United States of America.

Contents

List of Maps

What the Symbols Mean

★ **Frommer's Favorites**   Hotels, restaurants, attractions, and entertainment you should not miss

$ **Super-Special Values**   Really exceptional values

In Hotel and Other Listings

The followings symbols refer to the standard amenities available in all rooms:

A/C   air conditioning
TEL   telephone
TV   television
FRIDGE   refrigerator
MINIBAR   refrigerator stocked with beverages and snacks

The following abbreviations are used for credit cards:

AE   American Express
CB   Carte Blanche
DC   Diners Club
DISC   Discover
EC   Eurocard
ER   enRoute
JCB   (Japan)
MC   MasterCard
V   Visa

Trip Planning with This Guide

USE THE FOLLOWING FEATURES:

Calendar of Events   To plan for or avoid

Suggested Itineraries   For seeing the cities and regions

Easy-to-Read Maps   Regional attractions, city sights, hotel and restaurant locations—all referring to or keyed to the text

Distances and Transportation Information   At the beginning of each town section

Fast Facts   All the essentials at a glance: climate, embassies, emergencies, safety, taxes, tipping, and more

Invitation to the Readers

In researching this book, we have come across many wonderful establishments, the best of which we have included here. We're sure that many of you will also come across appealing hotels, inns, restaurants, guest houses, shops, and attractions. Please don't keep them to yourself. Share your experiences, especially if you want to comment on places that have been included in this edition that have changed for the worse. You can address your letters to:

Lisa Legarde and Don Laine
Frommer's New Mexico
c/o Macmillan Travel
15 Columbus Circle
New York, NY 10023

A Disclaimer

Readers are advised that prices fluctuate in the course of time and travel information changes under the impact of the varied and volatile factors that affect the travel industry. Neither the author nor the publisher can be held responsible for the experiences of readers while traveling. Readers are invited to write to the publisher with ideas, comments, and suggestions for future editions.

Safety Advisory

Whenever you're traveling in an unfamiliar city or country, stay alert. Be aware of your immediate surroundings. Wear a money belt and keep a close eye on your possessions. Be particularly careful with cameras, purses, and wallets, all favorite targets of thieves and pickpockets.

Getting to Know New Mexico

1

Welcome to New Mexico. And prepare yourself for an assault on the senses.

The sights, sounds, smells, and tastes of this remarkable state have enraptured visitors for centuries. Probably no one who has ever trodden New Mexican soil can say they were unchanged.

What is it about the 47th state that is so special?

To some, it's the landscape. The state slopes gently upward from the Texas prairies and the Chihuahuan Desert to a wonderland of contorted canyons and high wilderness peaks, split by the life-sustaining river known as the Rio Grande. The mutable colors of the high plains, the sound of a coyote's howl, the smell of a storm-dampened creosote bush, the taste of a juicy prickly pear fruit—all these things are unforgettable.

Visitors also are entranced by New Mexico's unique blend of peoples and cultures. The most thoroughly tricultural of the contiguous 48 states, New Mexico is an overlay of Native Americans, Hispanics, and Anglos (non-Hispanic Caucasians). The groups live and work side by side, yet each preserves its distinct communities and cultural nuances.

Other visitors may point to its history for what makes New Mexico unique. Prehistoric culture reached its apex with the Anasazi (ca. A.D. 800–1300); when the Spanish first visited in the 16th century, they found a thriving post-Anasazi Pueblo culture. The newcomers built their capital at Santa Fe in 1610, spreading religion and politics across the region. In the 19th century, as the United States moved westward, New Mexico spawned legends like Billy the Kid and Geronimo, Kit Carson and the Cimarron Trail. Today, visitors can descend into the *kivas* of ancient Anasazi at Chaco Canyon and the Aztec Ruins; feel the damp earth at El Santuario de Chimayo, credited by pilgrims for two centuries of medical miracles; and relive the echoes of outlaws' gunfire in melodramatic re-creations at Fort Sumner and elsewhere.

There's something here for everyone. Hiking, skiing, and rafting for the outdoors lover; world-famous artists' and musicians' communities for the culture vulture; innovative and palate-pleasing cuisine for the gourmet; atomic and space museums for the amateur scientist. Excitement and relaxation for all.

1   The Lay of the Land

Dateline

- 3,000 B.C. First evidence of stable farming settlements in region.
- A.D. 700 Earliest evidence of Anasazi presence.
- 1540 Francisco Vásquez de Coronado marches to Cíbola in search of a Native American "city of gold."
- 1542 Coronado returns to Spain, declaring his mission a failure.
- 1610 Immigration to New Mexico increases; ➤

IT WOULD BE EASY—AND ACCURATE—TO call New Mexico "high and dry" and leave it at that. The lowest point in the state, in the southeastern corner, is still over 2,800 feet in elevation, higher than the highest point in at least a dozen other states. The southern Rocky Mountains extend well into NewMexico, rising above 13,000 feet in the Sangre de Cristo range and sending a final afterthought above 10,000 feet, just east of Alamogordo. Most of New Mexico receives fewer than 20 inches of precipitation annually, the bulk of that coming either as summer afternoon thunderstorms or winter snowfall. In an area of 121,666 square miles—the fifth largest American state—there are only 221 square miles of water. Thus rivers and lakes occupy less than 0.2% of the landscape.

But look again: Statistics can lie, and there's a lot to meet the eye. New Mexico is bisected by the Rio Grande, the "Big River" of Hispanic lore. The Rio Grande nourishes hundreds of small farms from the Pueblo country of the north to the bone-dry Chihuahuan Desert of the far south. On either side of the river, sage-speckled plains are interrupted by mountains cloaked in forests of juniper and mesquite, and at higher elevations, denser stands of piñon, ponderosa, and aspen. Six of the earth's seven life zones are represented in New Mexico, from subtropical desert to alpine tundra.

New Mexico is nearly square in shape, about 350 miles north-south and 340 miles east-west, with a small panhandle tagged onto its southwestern corner. It is bordered on the west by Arizona, on the north by Colorado, on the east by Texas and a small piece of Oklahoma, and on the south by Texas and Mexico.

Picture New Mexico divided into vertical thirds. The eastern third of the state is an extension of the Great Plains of the Texas Panhandle. These flat plains, drained by the Pecos and Canadian rivers and widely used for grazing, slope gently upward to meet the Rockies. Climaxing at 13,161-foot Wheeler Peak north of Taos, the range is incised by the Rio Grande: a stark canyon in the north, a wide, gentle stream in the south. New Mexico's western third is predominantly high plateau, including mesa land in the north and the rugged Gila Wilderness farther south.

Words can't do justice to the spectacular colors of the landscape: colors that have drawn contemporary artists from around the world for nearly a century, colors that have made Taos and Santa Fe synonymous with artists' communities. The blues of the sky, browns of the earth, greens of the plants, reds and oranges and yellows of the rock mesas and canyons, all in every imaginable variation and hue, make this land a living canvas. This is truly big sky country, where it seems you can see forever.

Visitors should be aware of New Mexico's high elevation for two reasons. The first is clothing: Don't come at any time of year, even in the middle of summer, without at least a warm sweater and rain gear. The second is health: Don't push yourself too hard during your first few days here. The air is thinner, the sun more direct. You should expect to sunburn more easily and stop to catch your breath more frequently.

Dateline

Don Pedro de Peralta establishes Santa Fe as capital.

- 1680 Pueblo Indians revolt against Spanish.
- 1692 Spanish recapture Santa Fe.
- 1706 Albuquerque established.
- 1739 First French traders enter Santa Fe.
- 1779 Cuerno Verde, leader of rebellious Comanche tribes, falls to Spanish forces.
- 1786 Comanches and Utes sign treaty with Spanish.
- 1821 Mexico gains independence from Spain.
- 1828 Kit Carson, the legendary frontiersman, arrives in Taos.
- 1846 Mexican War breaks out; Gen. Stephen Kearny takes possession of New Mexico for United States.
- 1847 Revolt in Taos against U.S. control; newly appointed governor Charles Bent killed.
- 1848 Under provisions of Treaty of Guadalupe Hidalgo, Mexico officially cedes New Mexico to United States.
- 1861 Victorious Confederate general proclaims all of New Mexico south of the 34th parallel the new, Confederate territory of Arizona.
- 1862 Confederates routed from New Mexico.
- 1864 Navajos relocated to Bosque Redondo Reservation.
- 1868 Navajos return to their homeland.

➤

Dateline

- 1879 Atchison, Topeka & Santa Fe Rail Road routes main line through Las Vegas, Albuquerque, El Paso, and Deming, where connection is made with California's Southern Pacific line.

- 1878–81 Lincoln County War erupts; comes to epitomize the lawlessness and violence of the Wild West.

- 1881 Legendary outlaw Billy the Kid killed by Pat Garrett.

- 1886 Apache chief Geronimo captured; signals end of New Mexico's Indian wars.

- 1898 Painters Ernest Blumenschein and Bert Phillips settle in Taos.

- 1912 New Mexico becomes the 47th state.

- 1914 Blumenschein and Phillips form Taos Society of Artists; Taos becomes a major center of influence in mid-century American art and letters.

- 1916 Construction of Elephant Butte Dam brings irrigation to southern New Mexican farms.

- 1924 Native Americans granted full U.S. citizenship.

- 1943 Los Alamos National Laboratory built; "Manhattan Project" scientists spend two years in complete seclusion developing nuclear weapons.

- 1945 First atomic bomb exploded at Trinity Site.

- 1947 Reports of a flying saucer crash near Roswell make national headlines,

➤

2 New Mexico Past & Present

EARLY CIVILIZATIONS Archaeologists say that humans first migrated to the Southwest, moving southward from the Bering Land Bridge, about 12,000 B.C. Sites such as Sandia Cave and Folsom—where weapon points were discovered that for the first time clearly established that our prehistoric ancestors hunted now-extinct mammals such as woolly mammoths—are internationally known. When these large animals died off during the late Ice Age (about 8,000 B.C.), people turned to hunting smaller game and gathering wild food.

Stable farming settlements, as evidenced by the remains of domestically grown maize, date from about 3,000 B.C. As the nomadic peoples became more sedentary, they built permanent residences—pit houses—and made pottery. Cultural differences began to emerge in their choice of architecture and decoration: The Mogollon people, in the southwestern part of modern New Mexico, created brown and red pottery and built large community lodges; the Anasazi, in the north, made gray pottery and smaller lodges for extended families.

The Mogollon, whose pottery dates from about 100 B.C., were the first of the sophisticated village cultures. They lived primarily in modern-day Catron and Grant counties. The most important Mogollon ruins extant today are in the Gila River Valley, including Gila Cliff Dwellings National Monument north of Silver City.

By about A.D. 700, and perhaps a couple of centuries earlier, the Anasazi of the northwest had absorbed village life and expanded through what is now known as the Four Corners Region (where New Mexico, Arizona, Utah, and Colorado come together). Around A.D. 1000, their culture eclipsed that of the Mogollon. Chaco Canyon National Historic Park, Aztec Ruins National Monument, and Salmon Ruins all exhibit an architectural excellence and skill, and a scientific sensitivity to nature, that marks this as one of America's classic pre-Columbian civilizations.

Condominium-style communities of stone and mud adobe bricks, three and four stories high, were focused around central plazas. The villages incorporated circular spiritual chambers called *kivas*. The Anasazi also developed means to irrigate their fields of corn, beans, and squash by controlling the flow of water from the San Juan River and its tributaries. From

Chaco Canyon, they built a complex system of well-engineered roads leading in four directions to other towns or ceremonial centers. Artifacts found during excavation, such as seashells and macaw feathers, indicate they had a far-reaching trade network. The incorporation of solar alignments into some of their architecture has caused modern archaeoastronomers to speculate on the importance of the equinoxes to their religion.

The disappearance of the Anasazi culture, and the emergence of the Pueblo culture in its place, is something of a mystery today. Those who study such things are in disagreement as to why the Anasazi abandoned their villages around the 13th century. Some suggest drought or soil exhaustion; others, invasion, epidemic, or social unrest. But by the time the first Spanish arrived in the 1500s, the Anasazi were long gone and the Pueblo culture was well established throughout northern and western New Mexico, from Taos to Zuni, near Gallup. Most of the people lived on the east side of the Continental Divide, in the Rio Grande valley.

Certain elements of the Anasazi civilization had clearly been absorbed by the Pueblos, including the apartmentlike adobe architecture, the creation of rather elaborate pottery, and the use of irrigation or flood farming in their fields. Agriculture, and especially corn, was the economic mainstay.

Each pueblo, as the scattered villages and surrounding farmlands were known, fiercely guarded its independence. When the Spanish arrived, there were no alliances between villages, even among those that shared a common language or dialect. No more than a few hundred people lived in any one pueblo, an indication that the natives had learned to keep their population (which totaled 40,000 to 50,000) down in order to preserve their soil and other natural resources. But not all was peaceful: They alternately fought and traded with each other, as well as with nomadic Apaches. Even before the Spanish arrived, a pattern had been established.

- despite U.S. Air Force's denials that it has occurred.
- 1972 Pioneer balloonist Sid Cutter establishes Albuquerque International Balloon Fiesta.
- 1981 The Very Large Array, the world's most powerful radio telescope, begins observations of distant galaxies from the desert west of Socorro.
- 1982 U.S. space shuttle *Columbia* lands at Holloman Air Force Base, near White Sands National Monument.
- 1984 New Mexico's last remaining section of famed Route 66, near San Jon, is abandoned.
- 1990 New Mexico's last uranium mine, near Grants, closes.
- 1992 The 70th anniversary of the Inter-Tribal Indian Ceremonial is held at Gallup.
- 1994 Under pressure from Congress, U.S. Air Force reopens investigation of the 1947 flying saucer crash reports, concluding that the debris found was likely from tests of a secret cold-war spy balloon; UFO believers allege a cover-up.

IMPRESSIONS

For a greatness of beauty I have never experienced anything like New Mexico. . . . Just a day itself is tremendous there.
—D.H. Lawrence, "New Mexico," *Survey Graphic*, 1931

On the license plates in New Mexico it reads: "the Land of Enchantment." And that it is, by God! . . . Everything is hypnagogic, chthonian, and super-celestial. Here Nature has gone Gaga and Dada.
—Henry Miller, *The Air-conditioned Nightmare*, 1945

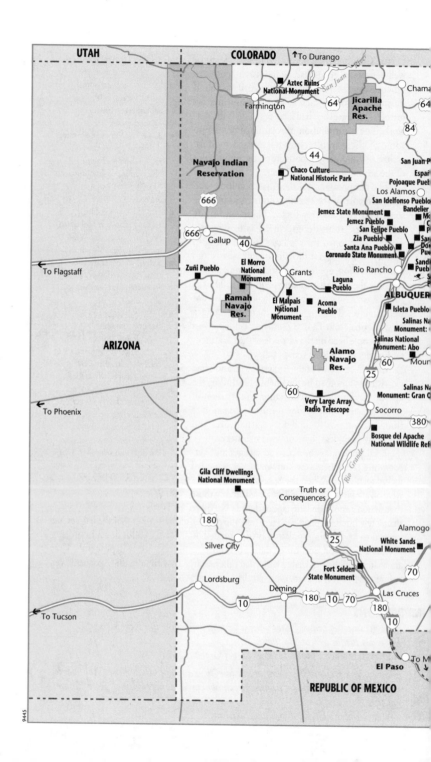

40 mi
0
68 km

N

Raton

Capulin Volcano
National Monument

64

64   Clayton

OKLAHOMA

Red River
Taos Ski Valley

Wheeler Peak

Taos Pueblo

68   Taos   Angel Fire

Picuris Pueblo

Sipapu

Santa Fe
Ski Area

suque Pueblo

anta Fe

Pecos
National
Monument

85

Rio Grande

Canadian River

25

Fort Union
National Monument

Las Vegas

84

Pecos River

Tucumcari

40

Amarillo

Santa Rosa

84

60   Fort Sumner

Fort Sumner
State Monument

Clovis

TEXAS

54

285

70

Lubbock

Apache

Lincoln State
Monument

Ruidoso

70   Roswell

380

**Mescalero
Apache Res.**

Pecos River

Cloudcroft

Artesia

Hobbs

285

Carlsbad

Carlsbad Caverns
National Park

**Guadalupe Mtns.
National Park**

TEXAS

THE ARRIVAL OF THE SPANISH   The Spanish controlled New Mexico for 300 years, from the mid–16th to the mid–19th century. That's twice as long as the United States. The Hispanic legacy in language and culture is stronger today in New Mexico than anywhere else in the Southwest, no doubt a result of the prominence of the Rio Grande valley as the oldest and most populous fringe province of the viceroyalty of New Spain.

The spark that sent the first European explorers into what is now New Mexico was a fabulous medieval myth that seven Spanish bishops had fled the Moorish invasion of the 8th century, sailed westward to the legendary isle of Antilia, and built themselves seven cities of gold. Hernán Cortés's 1519 discovery and conquest of the Aztecs' treasure-laden capital of Tenochtitlán, now Mexico City, fueled belief in the myth. When a Franciscan friar 20 years later claimed to have sighted, from a distance, "a very beautiful city" in a region known as Cíbola while on a reconnaissance mission for the viceroyalty, the gates were open.

Francisco Vásquez de Coronado, the ambitious young governor of New Spain's western province of Nueva Galicia, was commissioned to lead an expedition to the "seven cities." Several hundred soldiers, accompanied by servants and missionaries, marched overland to Cíbola with him in 1540, along with a support fleet of three ships in the Gulf of California. What they discovered, after six hard months on the trail, was a bitter disappointment: Instead of a city of gold, they found a rock-and-mud pueblo at Hawikuh, the westernmost of the Zuni towns. The expedition wintered at Tiguex, on the Rio Grande near modern Santa Fe, before proceeding to the Great Plains seeking more treasure at Quivira, in what is now Kansas. The grass houses of the Wichita Indians were all they found.

Coronado returned to New Spain in 1542, admitting failure. Historically, though, his expedition was a great success, contributing the first widespread knowledge of the Southwest and Great Plains, and discovering en route the Grand Canyon.

By the 1580s, after important silver discoveries in the mountains of Mexico, the Spanish began to wonder if the wealth of the Pueblo country might lie in its land rather than its cities. They were convinced that they had been divinely appointed to convert the natives of the New World to Christianity. And so a northward migration began, orchestrated and directed by the royal government. It was a mere trickle in the late 16th century. Juan de Onate established a capital in 1598 at San Gabriel, near San Juan Pueblo, but a variety of factors led to its failure. Then in 1610, under Don Pedro de Peralta, the migration began in earnest.

It was not dissimilar to America's schoolbook stereotype. Bands of armored conquistadors did troop through the desert, humble robed friars striding by their sides. But most of the pioneers came up the valley of the Rio Grande with oxcarts and mule trains rather than armor, intent on transplanting their Hispanic traditions of government, religion, and material culture to this new world.

Peralta built his new capital at Santa Fe and named it La Villa Real de la Santa Fe de San Francisco de Asis, the Royal City of the Holy Faith of St. Francis of Assisi. His capitol building, the Palace of the Governors, has been continuously occupied as a public building ever since by Spanish, Mexicans, Americans, and for 12 years (1680–92) by the Pueblo Indians. Today it is a museum.

RELIGION & REVOLT   The 17th-century in New Mexico was essentially a missionary era, as Franciscan priests attempted to turn the Indians into model Hispanic peasants. Their churches became the focal points of every pueblo, with Catholic schools a mandatory adjunct. By 1625 there were an estimated 50 churches in the Rio Grande valley. But the Native Americans weren't enthused about doing "God's work"—building new adobe missions, tilling fields for the Spanish, and weaving garments for export to Mexico—so soldiers backed the padres in extracting labor, a system known as *repartimiento*. Simultaneously, the *encomienda* system provided that a yearly tribute in corn and blankets be levied upon each Indian. The Pueblos were pleased to take part in Catholic religious ceremonies and proclaim themselves converts. To them, spiritual forces were actively involved in the material world. If establishing harmony with the cosmos meant absorbing Jesus Christ and various saints into their hierarchy of *kachinas* and other spiritual beings, so much the better. But the Spanish friars demanded they do away with their traditional singing and masked dancing, and with other "pagan practices." When the Pueblo religion was violently crushed and driven literally underground, resentment toward the Spanish grew and festered. Rebellions at Taos and Jemez in the 1630s left village priests dead, but the Pueblos were savagely repressed.

A power struggle between church and state in Nuevo Mexico weakened the hand of the Spanish colonists, and a long drought in the 1660s and 1670s gave the warlike Apaches reason to scourge the Spanish and Pueblo settlements for food. The Pueblos blamed the friars, and their ban on traditional rain dances, for the drought. The hanging of four medicine men as "sorcerers," and the imprisonment of 43 others, was the last straw for the Rio Grande natives. In 1680, the Pueblo Revolt erupted.

Popé, a San Juan shaman, catalyzed the revolt. Assisted by other Pueblo leaders, he unified the far-flung Native Americans, who never before had confederated. They pillaged and burned the province's outlying settlements, then turned their attention upon Santa Fe, besieging the citizens who had fled to the Palace of the Governors. After nine days, having reconquered Spain's northernmost American province, they let the refugees retreat south to Mexico.

Popé ordered that the Pueblos should return to the lifestyle they had had before the arrival of the Spanish. All Hispanic items, from tools to livestock to fruit trees, were to be destroyed, and the blemish of baptism was to be washed away in the river. But the shaman misjudged the influence of the Spanish upon the Pueblo people. They were not the people they had been a century earlier, and they *liked* much of the material culture they had absorbed from the Europeans. What's more, they had no intention of remaining confederated; their independent streaks were too strong.

In 1692, led by newly appointed Gov. Don Diego de Vargas, the Spanish recaptured Santa Fe without bloodshed. Popé had died, and without a leader to reunify them, the Pueblos were no match for the Spanish. Vargas pledged not to punish them, but to pardon and convert. Still, when he returned the following year with 70 families to recolonize the city, he had to use force. And for the next several years, bloody battles persisted throughout the Pueblo country.

By the turn of the 18th century, Nuevo Mexico was firmly in Spanish hands. This time, however, the colonists seemed to have learned from some of their past errors. They were more tolerant in their religion, less ruthless in their demands and punishments.

ARRIVAL OF THE ANGLOS   By the 1700s, there were signals that new interlopers were about to arrive in New Mexico. The French had laid plans to begin colonizing the Mississippi River, and hostile Native American tribes were on the warpath. The Spanish viceroyalty fortified its position in Santa Fe as a defensive bastion, and established a new villa at Albuquerque in 1706.

In 1739, the first French trade mission entered Santa Fe, welcomed by the citizenry but not by the government. For 24 years, until 1763, a black-market trade thrived between Louisiana and New Mexico. It ended only when France lost its toehold on its North American claims during the French and Indian War against Great Britain.

The Native Americans were more fearsome foes. Apache, Comanche, Ute, and Navajo launched repeated raids against each other and the Rio Grande settlements for most of the 18th century, which led the Spanish and Pueblos to pull closer together for mutual protection. Pueblo and Hispanic militias fought side by side in campaigns against the invaders. But by the 1770s, the attacks had become so savage and destructive that the viceroy in Mexico City created a military jurisdiction in the province, and Gov. Juan Bautista de Anza led a force north to Colorado to defeat the most feared of the Comanche chiefs, Cuerno Verde ("Green Horn"), in 1779. Seven years later, the Comanches and Utes signed a lasting treaty with the Spanish, and thereafter helped keep the Apaches in check.

France sold the Louisiana Territory to the young United States in 1803, and the Spanish suddenly had a new intruder to fear. The Lewis and Clark expedition of 1803 went unchallenged, much as the Spanish would have liked to challenge it; but in 1807, when Lt. Zebulon Pike built a stockade on a Rio Grande tributary in Colorado, he and his troops were taken prisoner by troops from Santa Fe. Pike was taken to the New Mexican capital, where he was interrogated extensively, and then to Chihuahua, Mexico. The report he wrote upon his return to the United States was Atlantic America's first inside look at Spain's frontier province.

At first, pioneering American merchants — excited by Pike's observations of New Mexico's economy — were summarily expelled from Santa Fe or jailed, their goods confiscated. But after Mexico gained independence from Spain in 1821, traders were welcomed. The wagon ruts of the Santa Fe Trail soon extended from Missouri to New Mexico, and from there to Chihuahua. (Later, it became the primary southern highway to California.)

As the merchants hied to Santa Fe, Anglo American and French Canadian fur trappers headed into the wilderness. Their commercial hub became Taos, a tiny village near a large pueblo a few days' ride north of Santa Fe. Many married into native or Hispanic families. Perhaps the best known was Kit Carson, a sometime federal agent, sometime Indian scout, whose legend is inextricably interwoven with that of early Taos. He spent 40 years in Taos, until his death in 1868.

In 1846, the Mexican War broke out and New Mexico became a territory of the United States. There were several causes of the war—the U.S. annexation of Texas in 1845, disagreement over the international boundary, unpaid claims owed to American citizens by the Mexican government—but foremost was the prevailing U.S. sentiment of "manifest destiny," the belief that the Union should extend "from sea to shining sea." Gen. Stephen Kearny marched south from Colorado; in the Las Vegas plaza, he announced that he had come to take possession of New Mexico for the United States. His arrival in Santa Fe on August 18, 1846, went unopposed.

An 1847 revolt in Taos resulted in the slaying of the new governor of New Mexico, Charles Bent, but U.S. troops defeated the rebels and executed their leaders. That was the last threat to American sovereignty in the territory. In 1848, the Treaty of Guadalupe Hidalgo officially transferred title of New Mexico, along with Texas, Arizona, and California, to the United States.

Kearny promised New Mexicans that the United States would respect their religion and property rights, and would safeguard their homes and possessions from hostile Indians. His troops behaved with a rigid decorum. The United States upheld Spanish policy toward the Pueblos, assuring the survival of their ancestral lands, their traditional culture, and their old religion—which even three centuries of Hispanic Catholicism could not do away with.

THE CIVIL WAR   As conflict between the North and South flared east of the Mississippi, New Mexico found itself caught in the debate over slavery. Southerners wanted to expand slavery to the western territories, but abolitionists fought a bitter campaign to prevent that from happening. New Mexicans themselves voted against slavery twice, while their delegate to Congress engineered the adoption of a slavery code. In 1861, the Confederacy, after its secession from the Union, laid plans to make New Mexico theirs as a first step toward capturing the West.

In fact, southern New Mexicans, including those in Tucson (Arizona was then a part of the New Mexico Territory), were disenchanted with the attention paid them by Santa Fe and already were threatening to form their own state. So when Confederate Lt. Col. John Baylor captured Fort Fillmore, near Mesilla, and on August 1, 1861, proclaimed all of New Mexico south of the 34th parallel to be the new territory of Arizona, there were few complaints.

The following year, Confederate Gen. Henry Sibley assembled three regiments of 2,600 Texans and moved up the Rio Grande. They defeated Union loyalists in a bloody battle at Valverde, near Socorro; easily took Albuquerque and Santa Fe, which were protected only by small garrisons; and proceeded toward the federal arsenal at Fort Union, 90 miles east of Santa Fe. Sibley planned to replenish his supplies there before continuing north to Colorado, then west to California.

On March 27–28, 1862, the Confederates were met head-on in Glorieta Pass, about 16 miles outside of Santa Fe, by regular troops from Fort Union supported by a regiment of Colorado Volunteers. By the second day, the rebels were in control—until a detachment of Coloradans circled behind the Confederate troops and destroyed their poorly defended supply train. Sibley was forced into a rapid retreat back down the Rio Grande. A few months later, Mesilla was reclaimed for the Union, and the Confederate presence in New Mexico was ended.

THE LAND WARS   The various tribes had not missed the fact that whites were fighting among themselves, and they took advantage of this weakness to step up their raids upon border settlements. In 1864, the Navajos, in what is known in tribal history as "The Long Walk," were relocated to the new Bosque Redondo Reservation on the Pecos River at Fort Sumner, in east central New Mexico. Militia Col. Kit Carson led New Mexico troops in this venture, a position to which he acceded as a moderating influence between the Navajos and those who called for their unconditional surrender or extermination.

It was an ill-advised decision: The land could not support 9,000 people; the government failed to supply adequate provisions; and the Navajo were unable to live peacefully with the Mescalero. By late 1868, the tribes retraced their routes to their homelands, where the Navajos gave up their warlike past. The Mescalero's raids were squashed in the 1870s and they were confined to their own reservation in the Sacramento Mountains of southern New Mexico.

Corraling the rogue Apaches of southwestern New Mexico presented the territory with its biggest challenge. Led by chiefs Victorio, Nana, and Geronimo, these bands wreaked havoc upon the mining region around Silver City. Eventually, however, they succumbed, and the capture of Geronimo in 1886 was the final chapter in New Mexico's long history of Indian wars.

As the Native American threat decreased, more and more livestock and sheep ranchers established themselves on the vast plains east of the Rio Grande, in the San Juan basin of the northwest, and in other equally inviting parts of the territory. Cattle drives up the Pecos Valley, on the Goodnight-Loving Trail, are the stuff of legend; so, too, was Roswell cattle baron John Chisum, whose 80,000 head of beef probably represented the largest herd in America in the late 1870s.

Mining grew as well. Albuquerque blossomed in the wake of a series of major gold strikes in the Madrid Valley, close to ancient turquoise mines; other gold and silver discoveries through the 1870s gave birth to boomtowns—now mostly ghost towns—like Hillsboro, Chloride, Mogollon, Pinos Altos, and White Oak. The copper mines of Santa Rita del Cobre, near Silver City, are still thriving.

In 1879, the Atchison, Topeka & Santa Fe Rail Road sent its main line through Las Vegas, Albuquerque, El Paso, and Deming, where it joined with the Southern Pacific line coming eastward from California. (The Santa Fe station was, and is, at Lamy, 17 miles southeast of the capital.) Now linked by rail to the great markets of America, New Mexico's economic boom period was assured.

But ranching invites cattle rustling and range wars, mining beckons feuds and land fraud, and the construction of railroads has often been tied to political corruption and swindles. New Mexico had all of them, especially during the latter part of the 19th century. Best known of a great many conflicts was the Lincoln County War (1878–81), which began as a feud between rival factions of ranchers and merchants. It led to such utter lawlessness that Pres. Rutherford B. Hayes ordered a federal investigation of the territorial government and the installation as governor of Gen. Lew Wallace (whose novel, *Ben Hur,* was published in 1880).

One of the central figures of the Lincoln County conflict was William "Billy the Kid" Bonney, a headstrong youth (b. 1858) who became probably the best-known outlaw of the American West. He blazed a trail of bloodshed from Silver City to Mesilla, Santa Fe to Lincoln, and Artesia to Fort Sumner, where he was finally killed by Sheriff Pat Garrett in July 1881.

By the turn of the century, most of the violence had been checked. The mineral lodes were drying up, and ranching was taking on increased importance. Economic and social stability were coming to New Mexico.

STATEHOOD, ART & ATOMS   Early in the 20th century, its Hispanic citizens having proved their loyalty to the United States by serving gallantly with Theodore Roosevelt's Rough Riders during the Spanish-American War, New Mexico's long-awaited dream of becoming an integral part of the Union was finally recognized. On January 6, 1912, Pres. William Howard Taft signed a bill making New Mexico the 47th state.

Within a few years, Taos began gaining fame as an artists' community. Two painters from the East Coast, Ernest Blumenschein and Bert Phillips, settled in Taos in 1898, lured others to join them, and in 1914 formed the Taos Society of Artists, one of the most influential schools of art in America. Writers and other intellectuals soon followed, including Mabel Dodge Luhan, novelists D. H. Lawrence and Willa Cather, and poet-activist John Collier. Other artists settled in Santa Fe and elsewhere in northern New Mexico; the best known was Georgia O'Keeffe, who lived miles from anywhere in tiny Abiquiu. Today, Santa Fe and Taos are world renowned for their contributions to art and culture.

The construction in 1916 of the Elephant Butte Dam near Hot Springs (now Truth or Consequences) brought irrigated farming back to a drought-ravaged southern New Mexico. Potash mining boomed in the southeast in the 1930s. Native Americans fared well, gaining full citizenship in 1924, two years after the All Pueblo Council was formed to fight passage in Congress of a bill that would have given white squatters rights to Indian lands. And in 1934, with ex-Taos intellectual John Collier as commissioner of Indian Affairs, tribes were accorded partial self-government. The Hispanics, meanwhile, became the most powerful force in state politics, and remain so today.

But the most dramatic development in 20th-century New Mexico was induced by the Second World War. In 1943, the U.S. government sealed off a tract of land on the Pajarito Plateau, west of Santa Fe, that previously had been an exclusive boys' school. On the site, in utter secrecy, they built the Los Alamos National Laboratory, otherwise known as Project Y of the Manhattan Engineer District—the "Manhattan Project." Their goal: to split the atom and develop the world's first nuclear weapons.

Under the direction of J. Robert Oppenheimer, later succeeded by Norris E. Bradbury, a team of 30 to 100 scientists lived and worked in almost complete seclusion for two years. Their work resulted in the atomic bomb, tested for the first time at the Trinity Site, north of White Sands, on July 16, 1945. The bombings of Hiroshima and Nagasaki, Japan, three weeks later, signaled to the world that the nuclear age had arrived.

Even before that time, New Mexico was climbing the ladder of stature in America's scientific community. Robert H. Goddard, considered the founder of modern rocketry, conducted many of his experiments near Roswell in the 1930s, during which time he became the first person to shoot a liquid-fuel rocket faster than the speed of sound. Clyde Tombaugh, the discoverer of the planet Pluto in 1930, helped establish the department of astronomy at New Mexico State University in Las Cruces. And former Sen. Harrison (Jack) Schmitt, an exogeologist and the first civilian to walk on the moon in 1972, is a native of the Silver City area.

Today the White Sands Missile Range is one of America's most important astrophysics sites, and the International Space Hall of Fame in nearby Alamogordo honors men and women from around the world who have devoted their lives to space exploration. Aerospace research and defense contracts are economic mainstays in Albuquerque, and Kirtland Air Force Base is the home of the Air Force Special Weapons Center. Los Alamos, of course, continues to be a national leader in nuclear technology.

Despite the rapid approach of the 21st century in many parts of the state, there are other areas still struggling to be a part of the 20th. Many Native Americans, be they Pueblo, Navajo, or Apache, and Hispanic farmers, who till small plots in isolated rural regions, hearken to a time when life was slower paced. But life in New Mexico was never simple—for anyone.

3 Art, Architecture & Literature

ART   Since prehistoric times, New Mexico has been a cradle of artistic genius for its native peoples. Prehistoric Mogollon, Mimbres, and Anasazi pottery is unique in its design and color. Today's Pueblo Indians are noted not only for their pottery—each pueblo being distinctive in its touches from the next—but also for their textile crafts. Navajos are renowned for their silver jewelry, often with turquoise, and for their weaving and sand painting; Apaches are master basket makers.

Hispanic art was by nature either religious, rustic, or both. Cut off for centuries from most of the rest of the world, save through the rarely traveled colonial lifeline to Mexico, artisans handcrafted their own ornate furnishings. Paintings (*retablos*) and carved icons (*santos*) underscored the creators' devotion to their Roman Catholic faith. Traditional decorative tinwork and furniture are popular today, along with weaving and silversmithing.

New Mexico wasn't discovered by Anglo-American artists until the end of the 19th century. Two East Coast painters, Ernest Blumenschein and Bert Phillips, happened upon Taos in 1898 and were hypnotized by the dramatic light. They returned to make the valley their home, and in 1914 founded the Taos Society of Artists. The society disbanded in 1927, a victim of its own success—it so widely marketed the works of the town's isolated masters that other artists thronged to Taos. Today, the art community is prolific, indeed: By some estimates, more than 10% of the permanent population of Taos are painters, sculptors, writers, musicians, or others who earn income from artistic pursuits.

New Mexico and Georgia O'Keeffe: The Transformation of a Great American Artist

In June 1917, during a short tour of the Southwest, painter Georgia O'Keeffe (b. 1887) visited New Mexico for the first time. She was immediately enchanted by the place—her mind wandered frequently to the arid land and undulating mesas even after she returned to the vibrant sights and sounds of New York. It wasn't until she was coaxed back by arts patroness and "collector of people" Mabel Dodge Luhan twelve years later, however, that O'Keeffe returned to the multi-hued desert of her daydreams.

When she arrived in Santa Fe in April of 1929, O'Keeffe was reportedly ill, both physically and emotionally. New Mexico seemed to soothe her spirit and heal her physical ailments almost immediately. Only two days after Georgia's arrival, Mabel Dodge convinced the artist to move to her home in Taos. There, she could be free to paint and socialize as she liked.

In Taos, O'Keeffe began painting some of her best-known canvasses—close-ups of desert flowers and objects such as cow and horse skulls. "The color up there is different . . . the blue green of the sage and the mountains, the wildflowers in bloom," O'Keeffe once said of Taos. "It's a different kind of color from any I've ever seen— there's nothing like that in north Texas or even in Colorado." Her personality, as well as her art, was transformed by Taos's influence. She bought a car and learned to drive (in that order). Sometimes, on warm days, she ran stark naked through the sage fields. That August, a new, rejuvenated O'Keeffe rejoined her husband, photographer Alfred Stieglitz, in New York.

The artist returned to New Mexico year after year, spending time with Mabel Dodge as well as staying at the isolated Ghost Ranch. She drove through the countryside in her snappy Ford, stopping to paint in her favorite spots. But, until 1949, O'Keeffe always returned to New York in the fall. Three years after Stieglitz's death, though, she relocated permanently to New Mexico, spending her winters and springs in Abiquiu, summers and falls at Ghost Ranch. Georgia O'Keeffe died in Santa Fe in 1986.

Santa Fe grew as an art community on the heels of Taos. By 1921, Los Cinco Pintores, a group of five avant-garde painters, were establishing names for themselves. The quintet included Jozef Bakos, Fremont Ellis, Walter Mruk, Willard Nash, and Will Shuster. The number of full-time professional artists in Santa Fe today exceeds 700, and that doesn't include writers or musicians. Thousands more dabble in the creative professions.

Santa Fe is home to the School of Indian Art, where many of today's leading Native artists studied, including Apache sculptor Allan Houser. It's also the site of the Institute of American Indian Arts. The best-known Native American painter today is R. C. Gorman, an Arizona Navajo who has made his home in Taos since the 1960s. Now in his early 50s, Gorman is internationally acclaimed for his bright, somewhat surrealistic depictions of Navajo women.

ARCHITECTURE   In a land as dry and treeless as most of New Mexico, it's not surprising that adobe has long been the principal construction material. Clay, mixed with grasses for strength, is placed in a mold and dried in the sun. The bricks are then stacked to create the building and reinforced with more wet clay. Almost every structure in New Mexico prior to 1879, when the railroad arrived, was built in this style by Pueblo Indians, Hispanics, and Anglos.

Architectural elements in adobe buildings usually include a network of *vigas,* long beams supporting the roof, their ends protruding through the facade; *latillas,* smaller stripped crossbeams layered between the vigas; corbels, carved wooden supports for the vertical posts and the vigas; a portal, usually shading a brick floor set into the ground; and a plastered adobe-brick *banco,* or fireplace, set into an outside wall.

The Territorial style of architecture became popular in the late 19th century, when railroads could carry in bricks, large logs, and other building materials. Today, adobe is again in vogue—for aesthetics, for price (it's cheap, and there's no shortage of mud!), and for its ability to retain heat for extended periods.

Modern architectural styles prevalent throughout the Western world are of course seen in New Mexico, especially in innovative downtown Albuquerque. But it's tradition that visitors find stunning. Santa Fe is the center of attention, as strict building codes have maintained the traditional architectural integrity of the city's core since the 1950s.

LITERATURE   Many noted writers have made their homes in New Mexico in the 20th century. In the 1920s, the most noted were D. H. Lawrence and Willa Cather, both short-term Taos residents. Lawrence, the romantic and controversial English novelist, was here for parts of 1922–25, and reflected on that period in *Mornings in Mexico and Etruscan Places.* Though he died in Europe years later, a family shrine north of Taos is a popular place of pilgrimage for Lawrence devotees. Lawrence's Taos period is described in *Lorenzo in Taos,* written by his patron, Mabel Dodge Luhan. Cather, a Pulitzer Prize winner famous for her depictions of the pioneer spirit, penned *Death Comes for the Archbishop,* a fictionalization of the career of 19th-century Santa Fe bishop Jean-Baptiste Lamy, as a result of her stay.

Many well-known contemporary authors live in and write about New Mexico. John Nichols of Taos, whose *The Milagro Beanfield War* was turned into a popular movie in 1987, writes with insight about the problems of poor Hispanic farming communities. Tony Hillerman of Albuquerque is renowned for two decades of weaving mysteries around Navajo tribal police in such books as *Listening Woman* and *Thief of Time.* Hispanic novelist Rudolfo Anaya's *Bless Me, Ultima* and Pueblo writer Leslie

Marmon Silko's *Ceremony* capture the lifestyles of their respective peoples. Of desert environment and politics, no one wrote better than the late Edward Abbey; *Fire on the Mountain,* set in New Mexico, was one of his most powerful works.

4 **Religion & Ritual**

Religion has always been at the heart of Indian life. Throughout the Southwest, the cosmos is viewed as a single whole. Within that whole, all living creatures are seen as mutually dependent, and every relationship, whether with another person, an animal, or even a plant, carries spiritual meaning. A hunter will pray before killing a deer, for instance, to ask the creature to give itself to the tribe. The slain deer is then treated as a guest of honor before the hunter ritually sends its soul back to its comrades to be reborn. Even the harvesting of a plant requires prayer, thanks, and ritual.

Pueblo Indians believe their ancestors originally lived underground, the source of life (and the place from which plants spring). Encouraged by burrowing animals, they entered the world of humans—the "fifth" world—through a hole, a *sipapu,* by clinging to a web woven for them by Spider Woman.

The Pueblo peoples honor Mother Earth and Father Sun. In this dry land, the sun can mean life and death. The tribes watch the skies closely, tracking solstices and planetary movements, to determine the optimum timing for crop planting cycles.

Dances are ritual occasions. Usually held in conjunction with the feast days of Catholic saints (including Christmas Eve for Jesus Christ), the ceremonies demonstrate how the Pueblos absorbed certain aspects of Christianity from the Spanish without surrendering their traditional beliefs.

There are medicine dances, fertility rites, prayers for rain and for good harvests. The spring and summer corn or *tablita* dances are among the most impressive. Ceremonies begin with an early morning mass and procession to the plaza honoring an image of the saint. The rest of the day is devoted to song, dance, and feasting, with performers masked and clad as deer, buffalo, eagles, and other creatures.

The all-night Shalako festival at Zuni Pueblo in late November or early December is the most spectacular of the Pueblo ceremonies. Colorfully costumed *kachinas,* or spirit dancers, act out the Zuni story of creation and evolution. Everyone awaits the arrival of the *shalakos,* 12-foot-tall kachinas who bless new and renovated homes in the village.

Visitors are normally welcome to attend Pueblo dances, but should respect the Native Americans' requests that they not be photographed or tape-recorded.

Navajos believe in a hierarchy of supernatural beings, the Holy Ones, who can travel on a sunbeam, a thunderbolt, or the wind. At their head is Changing Woman, the earth mother, who vigilantly assures humans' well-being by teaching them to live in harmony with nature. Her children, the Hero Twins, ward off our enemies—all but Old Age and Death. Religious symbolism, which pervades art and music, underscores the Navajo belief that their homeland was created by the Holy Ones for them to live in. Typical of Navajo dancing are the *yeibichai* rituals, curative ceremonies marked by circular social dances with long song cycles.

The Apaches have a similar creation belief. They were created by Father Sun and Mother Earth ("the White Painted Lady") to live in the Southwest region, and the Holy Ones' twin sons helped them ward off wicked creatures by teaching them how to ride horses and use a bow and arrow. The most important ceremony among the

Apaches today, including the Mescaleros, is the 4-day puberty ritual for young girls. The colorful masked *gahans,* or mountain spirits, perform to celebrate the subject's womanhood, when the White Painted Lady resides within her body.

Outside the pueblos and reservations, the most visible places of worship are those of the Roman Catholics. Santa Fe's Cathedral of St. Francis is the state's best-known church, but a close second is El Santuario de Chimayo, an hour north of the state capital. Constructed in 1816, it has long been a site of pilgrimage for Catholics who attribute miraculous powers of healing to the earth in the chapel's anteroom. Most Hispanic Catholics believe strongly in miracles.

5 Sports & Recreation Highlights

Whether you're a spectator or a participant, there's year-round action in New Mexico.

SPECTATOR SPORTS   There's professional baseball (the Albuquerque Dukes play in the AAA Pacific Coast League), major college football and basketball, and horse racing at Santa Fe (in summer) and near Las Cruces (in winter).

FISHING & HUNTING   For outdoors lovers, New Mexico is famous for its fishing and hunting. There are German brown, rainbow, cutthroat, and lake trout in the streams and high lakes; bass, crappie, catfish, and pike are denizens of some of the larger bodies of water, like Elephant Butte and Navajo lakes. Fishing licenses, required of anyone 12 or older, cost $41. A 1-day license costs $9, and a 5-day license is $16. A Wildlife Habitat Improvement stamp ($6) must also be purchased for fishing in national forests or Bureau of Land Management–controlled waters. Fishing on an Indian reservation requires a permit from the reservation.

Hunters must also be licensed to hunt game birds—such as ducks, geese, quail, grouse, and wild turkey—and big-game animals, including mule deer, elk, pronghorn antelope, ibex, black bear, mountain lion, and javelina (peccary). For further information on hunting or fishing, contact the New Mexico Department of Game and Fish, Villagra Building, Galisteo Street, Santa Fe, NM 87503 (☎ **505/827-7911**).

BACKPACKING & HIKING   With so much national forest and wilderness, there are unlimited opportunities for backpackers and day hikers. There are 3,000 miles of trails in the 10 million acres of New Mexico national forests. Perhaps the most varied and interesting trails are in the Gila National Forest and Wilderness in southwestern New Mexico. For information, write the U.S. Forest Service, 517 Gold Ave. SW, Albuquerque, NM 87102 (☎ **505/842-3292**); or specific forests: Carson National Forest, P.O. Box 558, Taos, NM 87571 (☎ **505/758-6201**); Cíbola National Forest, 10308 Candelaria Blvd. NE, Albuquerque, NM 87112 (☎ **505/761-4650**); Gila National Forest, 2610 N. Silver St., Silver City, NM 88061 (☎ **505/388-8201**); Lincoln National Forest, 11th and New York streets, Alamogordo, NM 88310 (☎ **505/434-7200**); or Santa Fe National Forest, 1220 St. Francis Dr., Santa Fe, NM 87504 (☎ **505/988-6940**).

The Bureau of Land Management (BLM), P.O. Box 1449, Santa Fe, NM 87504 (☎ **505/438-7400**), administers 13 million acres around the state. Included is the upper Rio Grande, a popular destination for white-water rafting.

SKIING   For winter visitors, Taos Ski Valley is considered one of the leading ski resorts in the United States. There are other ski resorts in the Taos area at Angel Fire, Red River, and Ski Rio; Santa Fe Ski Area; Sandia Peak at Albuquerque; at Ski Apache at Ruidoso. In addition, Cloudcroft, Los Alamos, Penasco, and Raton boast smaller hills. Cross-country skiing is popular on high-elevation trails in the national forests and on BLM land. You can get information from regional convention and visitors bureaus or chambers of commerce. Or contact Ski New Mexico Inc., P.O. Box 1104, Santa Fe, NM 87504 (☎ **505/982-5300**). Check snow conditions by dialing New Mexico Snophone (☎ **505/984-0606**) 24 hours daily.

OTHER ACTIVITIES   Those who prefer less strenuous or time-consuming activities will find golf courses, tennis courts, and swimming pools in communities throughout the state. And then there's ballooning: Albuquerque is the site of the world's largest hot-air balloon extravaganza every October, and trips operate in several cities throughout the year.

6   New Mexican Cuisine

New Mexican cuisine isn't the same as Mexican cooking, or even those American concoctions sometimes called "Tex-Mex" or "Cal-Mex." It's a consequence of southwestern history, a unique blend of Hispanic and Pueblo recipes. As the Native Americans taught the Spanish conquerors about their corn—how to roast it, how to make corn pudding, stewed corn, cornbread, cornmeal, and *posole* (hominy)—the Spanish introduced their beloved chiles, adding spice to the cuisine.

Lovers of tacos, burritos, and enchiladas will find them here, although they may not be quite as you've had them before. Tacos, for instance, are more often served in soft rolled tortillas than in crispy shells. Tamales are made from cornmeal mush, wrapped in husks and steamed. Chile rellenos are stuffed with cheese, deep-fried, then covered with green chile.

Many dishes include unusual local ingredients, such as piñon nuts, jicama, and prickly pear cactus. Here's a sampling of some of the more regional dishes that might be hard to find outside the Southwest:

blue corn   Pueblo vegetable that produces a crumbly flour widely used in tortilla shells, especially for enchiladas

carne adovada   Tender pork marinated in red chile, herbs, and spices, then baked

chorizo burrito   (also called a breakfast burrito) Mexican sausage, scrambled eggs, potatoes, and scallions wrapped in a flour tortilla with red or green chile and melted Jack cheese

empanada   A fried pie with nuts and currants

fajitas   Strips of beef or chicken sautéed with onions, green peppers, and other vegetables, and served on a sizzling platter

green chile stew   Locally grown chiles cooked in a stew with chunks of meat, beans, and potatoes

huevos rancheros   Fried eggs on corn tortillas, topped with cheese and red or green chile, served with pinto beans

pan dulce   Indian sweet bread

posole   A corn soup or stew (called hominy in other parts of the South), sometimes with pork and chiles

sopaipillas   A lightly fried puff pastry served with honey as a dessert, or stuffed with meat and vegetables as a side dish

You Say Chili, They Say Chile

It's never "chili" in New Mexico. New Mexicans are adamant that *chile,* the Spanish spelling of the word, is the only way to spell it—no matter what your dictionary might say.

Go ahead, look up *chile.* It's not in there. I guarantee it. Well, maybe it is, but only as a secondary spelling for the word *chili.* Personally, I think that's only been put there to appease the population of New Mexico.

The peppers that New Mexicans will only identify as chiles are grown throughout the state. The climate is perfect for cultivating and drying the small but powerful red and green New Mexican varieties. The state's residents have such a personal attachment to their most famous agricultural product that in 1983 they directed their senior U.S. Senator, Pete Domenici, to enter New Mexico's official stand on the spelling of *chile* into the Congressional Record.

The town of Hatch, New Mexico bills itself as the chile capital of the world. But wherever you travel, chiles make an appearance on every menu in the state. Just about everything you'll order during your stay in New Mexico will be covered with a sauce made from chiles. As a general rule, green chile sauce is hotter than the red chile sauce, but be sure to ask. No matter which you order, your eyes will start watering, your sinuses will drain, and your palate will be on fire after one heaping forkful. Be warned: No amount of water or beer will take the sting away. (Drink milk. A sopaipilla drizzled with honey also might help, too.)

Don't let my words of caution scare you away from genuine New Mexico chiles. The pleasure of eating them outweighs the pain. Start slow, with salsas and chile sauces first, maybe *rellenos* (stuffed peppers) next, then *rajas* (roasted peeled chiles cut into strips). Before you know it, you'll be buying *chile ristras* (dried chiles strung together for cooking as well as decorative use). You might even buy bags of chile powder and maybe a chile plant to bring home. By then you will have realized that you've never had a chili that tasted quite like this—and you'll know why it's a chile.

7   Recommended Reading

General

Casey, Robert L. *Journey to the High Southwest: A Traveler's Guide* (Pacific Search Press, 1985).

Chilton, Lance and Katherine, et al. *New Mexico: A New Guide to the Colorful State* (University of New Mexico Press, 1984).

Horgan, Paul. *Great River: The Rio Grande in North American History* (Holt, Rinehart and Winston, 1960).

Jenkins, Myra Ellen, and Albert H. Schroeder. *A Brief History of New Mexico* (University of New Mexico Press, 1974).

Nichols, John, and William Davis. *If Mountains Die: A New Mexico Memoir* (Knopf, 1979).

Simmons, Marc. *New Mexico: An Interpretive History* (University of New Mexico Press, 1988).

Native American & Hispanic Culture

Anaya, A. Rudolfo. *Bless Me, Ultima* (Quinto Sol, 1972).

Boyd, E. *Popular Arts of Spanish New Mexico* (Museum of New Mexico Press, 1974).

Dozier, Edward P. *The Pueblo Indians of North America* (Holt, Rinehart and Winston, 1970).

Silko, Leslie Marmon. *Ceremony* (Viking, 1977).

Williamson, Ray A. *Living the Sky: The Cosmos of the American Indian* (University of Oklahoma Press, 1987).

Art & Literature

Cather, Willa. *Death Comes for the Archbishop* (Random House, 1971).

Hillerman, Tony. *Thief of Time* (Harper & Row, 1988).

Lawrence, D. H. *Mornings in Mexico and Etruscan Places* (Penguin, 1967).

Luhan, Mabel Dodge. *Lorenzo in Taos* (Knopf, 1932).

Nichols, John. *The Milagro Beanfield War* (Ballantine, 1988).

O'Keeffe, Georgia. *O'Keeffe* (Viking, 1976).

Planning a Trip to New Mexico

2

As WITH ANY TRIP, A LITTLE PREPARATION IS ESSENTIAL BEFORE YOU START YOUR journey to New Mexico. This chapter will provide you with a variety of planning tools, including information on when to go, how to get there, how to get around once you're there, and some suggested itineraries.

1 Information & Climate

SOURCES OF INFORMATION The best place to obtain detailed information is the **New Mexico Department of Tourism** in the Lamy Building, 491 Old Santa Fe Trail, Santa Fe, NM 87503 (☎ toll free **800/545-2040**).

The various cities and regions of the state are represented by convention and visitors bureaus, and/or chambers of commerce. Their addresses and telephone numbers are listed in the appropriate chapters in this book.

CLIMATE Summers are hot throughout most of the state, though distinctly cooler at higher elevations. Winters are relatively mild in the south, harsher in the north and in the mountains. Spring and fall are pleasant all over. Rainfall is sparse except in the higher mountains; summer afternoon thunderstorms and winter snows account for most precipitation.

Santa Fe and Taos, at 7,000 feet, have midsummer highs in the 80°s, overnight midwinter lows in the teens. Temperatures in Albuquerque, at 5,000 feet, often run about 10° warmer. Snowfall is common from November through March, and sometimes as late as May, though it seldom lasts long. Santa Fe averages 32 inches total annual snowfall. At the high-mountain ski resorts, as much as 300 inches (25 feet) may fall in a season—and stay. The plains and deserts of the southeast and south commonly have summer temperatures in excess of 100°.

New Mexico Temperatures & Precipitation

	Jan High–Low	Apr High–Low	July High–Low	Oct High–Low	Annual Precip. (inches)
Alamogordo	57–28	78–40	95–65	79–42	7.5
Albuquerque	47–28	70–41	91–66	72–45	8.9
Carlsbad	60–28	81–46	96–67	79–47	13.5
Chama	33–3	54–22	73–37	52–18	9.3
Cloudcroft	41–19	56–33	73–48	59–36	25.8
Farmington	44–16	70–36	92–58	70–37	7.5
Las Cruces	56–26	79–45	95–66	82–47	8.6
Roswell	56–24	78–42	91–65	75–45	12.7
Ruidoso	50–17	65–28	82–48	67–31	21.4
Santa Fe	40–18	59–35	80–57	62–38	14.0
Taos	40–10	62–30	87–50	64–32	12.1
Truth or Conseq.	54–27	75–44	92–66	75–47	8.5

New Mexico Calendar of Events

January

- **Three Kings' Day.** Most pueblos honor their new tribal officers with ceremonies. Traditional dancing is held at Cochiti, Jemez, Laguna,

Nambe, Picuris, Sandia, San Felipe, San Ildefonso, San Juan, Santa Ana, Santa Clara, Santo Domingo, Taos, Tesuque, and Zia pueblos. January 6.

February

- **Mount Taylor Winter Quadrathlon.** Bicycling, running, cross-country skiing, and snowshoeing. Near Grants. Third weekend.

March

- **Easter Celebrations.** At Cochiti, Nambe, Picuris, San Felipe, San Ildefonso, Santa Ana, Santo Domingo, and Zia pueblos, with masses, parades, and dances, including the corn dance. There's a street party in the historic district of Silver City, and a balloon rally at Truth or Consequences. Late March or early April.

April

- **Albuquerque Founders' Day.** Parade, auction, and street entertainment in Old Town. Albuquerque. Third weekend.
- **Gathering of Nations Powwow.** Miss Indian World contest, dance competitions, arts and crafts exhibitions, fitness runs and walks. University of New Mexico arena. Albuquerque. Mid–late April.

May

- **Cinco de Mayo Fiestas.** The restoration of the Mexican republic (from French occupation 1863–67) is celebrated at Hobbs, Las Cruces (Old Mesilla Plaza), Silver City, and Truth or Consequences. First weekend.
- **Taos Spring Arts Festival.** Three-week survey of visual, performing, and literary arts. Taos. Third week May to mid-June.
- **Spring Festival of the Arts.** Eleven-day celebration. Santa Fe. Ends Memorial Day weekend.
- **Great Rio Grande Raft Race.** Homemade boats launch from the Corrales and Central bridges. Albuquerque. Third Saturday.
- **Santa Fe Powwow.** Native dances, singing, games, crafts, and food. The Downs at Santa Fe. Memorial Day weekend.

June

- **Rails and Trails Days.** Rodeo, train rides, fiddlers contest, quilt and art shows. Las Vegas. First weekend.
- **Old Fort Days.** Includes world's richest tombstone race. Fort Sumner. Second weekend.

July

- **Fourth of July Celebrations.** Parades, fireworks, and various other events at Albuquerque, Capitan, Carlsbad, Clayton, Farmington, Gallup, Grants, Las Vegas, Lordsburg, Moriarty, Red River, Roswell, and Socorro. July 4.
- **Apache Maidens' Puberty Rites.** Rodeo and ceremonial Dance of the Mountain Spirits, Mescalero. July 4.
- **Waterfall Ceremonial.** Several rarely seen traditional dances are presented at Nambe Falls, Nambe Pueblo. July 4.
- **Rodeo de Santa Fe.** Parade, dance, and four rodeo performances. Santa Fe. Weekend after July 4.
- **Taos Powwow.** Intertribal competitions in traditional and contemporary dances, Taos. Second weekend.

- **Billy the Kid–Pat Garrett Historical Days.** Lectures, tours, stew cook off, western music and dance, at Ruidoso. Second weekend.
- **Eight Northern Pueblos Artist and Craftsman Show.** More than 600 Indian artists exhibit their work. Traditional dances, food booths, and more at San Juan Pueblo. Third weekend.
- **Spanish Market.** Santa Fe Plaza. Last weekend.

August

- **Bat Flight Breakfast.** Carlsbad Caverns National Park. Early August.
- **Old Lincoln Days.** Billy the Kid pageant, Lincoln. First weekend.
- **Inter-Tribal Indian Ceremonial.** Fifty tribes from the United States and Mexico participate in rodeos, parades, dances, athletic competitions, and an arts and crafts show, at Red Rock State Park, east of Gallup. Second week.
- **Connie Mack World Series Baseball Tournament.** Teams of teenagers from throughout the United States and Puerto Rico compete in a 7-day, 17-game series. Ricketts Park, Farmington. Second week.
- **Annual Indian Market.** Juried Native American art competition, musical entertainment, dances, food booths. Santa Fe Plaza. Third weekend.
- **Great American Duck Race.** Parade, ballooning, tortilla toss, dances— and, of course, the duck race. Deming. Fourth weekend.

September

- **International Space Hall of Fame Induction.** Alamogordo.
- **Hatch Chile Festival.** Hatch. Labor Day weekend.
- **Hillsboro Apple Festival.** Crafts, flea market, food, dancing, at Hillsboro, west of Truth or Consequences. Labor Day weekend.
- **New Mexico State Fair.** Third-largest state fair in the United States. Seventeen days of Spanish and Indian villages, midway, livestock exhibits, arts and crafts, country-and-western entertainment. Albuquerque State Fairgrounds. Begins Friday after Labor Day.
- **Fat Tire Fiesta,** Socorro. Last weekend in September.
- **Fiesta de Santa Fe.** Santa Fe Plaza. Second weekend.
- **Stone Lake Fiesta.** Apache festival with rodeo, ceremonial dances, and footrace. Jicarilla Reservation. Dulce. September 14 to 15.
- **Mexican Independence Day.** Parade and dances in Carlsbad (San Jose Plaza) and Las Cruces (Old Mesilla Plaza), with a rodeo in Carlsbad. September 16.
- **Old Taos Trade Fair.** Reenactment of Spanish colonial living in the 1820s, with craft demonstrations, food, and entertainment. Martinez Hacienda, Taos. Third weekend.
- **Taos Fall Arts Festival.** Gallery openings, concerts, crafts fair. Taos. Third weekend to first weekend October.
- **Shiprock Navajo Fair.** Rodeo, traditional dancing and singing, parade, arts and crafts exhibits. Shiprock. Last weekend.

October

- **Fall Festival of the Arts.** Eleven-day event focusing on New Mexican painters, sculptors, and craftspeople. Santa Fe. Ends Columbus Day.
- **Albuquerque International Balloon Fiesta.** World's largest balloon rally,

with races, contests, and special events, including weekend mass ascensions. Albuquerque. First to second weekend.

November

- **Bosque Fall Fest.** Bosque del Apache Wildlife Refuge, San Antonio, Socorro County.
- **Festival of the Cranes.** Socorro. Late November.
- **Indian National Finals Rodeo.** Indian rodeo riders from throughout the United States and Canada compete. Powwow, ceremonial dancing, Miss Indian Rodeo pageant, arts and crafts. Albuquerque State Fairgrounds. Third weekend.

December

- **Shalako Ceremony.** Night-long chanting and dances, Zuni Pueblo. First or second weekend.
- **Yuletide in Taos.** *Farolito* tours, candlelight dinners, dance performances, art events, ski-area activities. Taos. First to third weekends.
- **Our Lady of Guadalupe Fiesta.** Pilgrimage to Tortugas Mountain and torchlight descent, followed by mass and traditional Hispanic dances. Tortugas, near Las Cruces. December 10 to 12.
- **Christmas in Cloudcroft.** Snow Queen contest, skating party, lighting contests, caroling, snowmobile races. Cloudcroft. Weekend before Christmas.
- **Sundown Torchlight Procession of the Virgin.** Vespers and Matachines dance at San Ildefonso, Santa Clara, Taos, and Tesuque pueblos. December 24.

2 Health & Insurance

HEALTH PREPARATIONS One thing that sets New Mexico apart from most other states is its altitude. Most of the state is above 4,000 feet in elevation, and many heavily touristed areas—including Santa Fe—are at 7,000 feet or above. Getting plenty of rest, avoiding large meals, and drinking lots of nonalcoholic fluids (especially water) can help make the adjustment easier for flatlanders.

The reduced oxygen and humidity can bring on some unique problems, not the least of which is acute mountain sickness. Characterized in its early stages by headaches, shortness of breath, appetite loss and/or nausea, tingling in the fingers or toes, and lethargy and insomnia, it ordinarily can be treated with aspirin and a slower pace. If it persists or worsens, you must descend to a lower altitude.

Sunburn and hypothermia are other dangers of higher elevations, and should not be lightly regarded.

INSURANCE Before setting out on your trip, check your medical insurance policy to be sure it covers you away from home. If it doesn't, it's wise to purchase a traveler's policy, widely available at banks, travel agencies, and automobile clubs. Coverage offered by numerous companies is relatively inexpensive. In addition to medical assistance, including hospitalization and surgery, it should include the cost of an accident, death, or repatriation; loss or theft of baggage; costs of trip cancellation; and guaranteed bail in the event of a suit or other legal difficulties.

3 Getting There

BY PLANE   Albuquerque is the hub for travel to most parts of New Mexico. A secondary hub for southern New Mexico is El Paso, Texas. Both airports are served by **American** (☎ toll free **800/433-7300**), **America West** (☎ toll free **800/247-5692**), **Continental** (☎ toll free **800/525-0280**), **Delta** (☎ toll free **800/221-1212**), **Southwest** (☎ toll free **800/435-9792**), and **United** (☎ toll free **800/241-6522**). In addition, Albuquerque is served by **TWA** (☎ toll free **800/221-2000**), and the regional carrier, **Mesa** (☎ toll free **800/637-2247**).

BY TRAIN   **AMTRAK** has two routes through the state. The *Southwest Chief,* which runs between Chicago and Los Angeles, passes through New Mexico once daily in each direction, with stops in Gallup, Grants, Albuquerque, Lamy (for Santa Fe), Las Vegas, and Raton. A second train, the *Sunset Unlimited,* skims through the southwest corner of the state three times weekly in each direction—between Los Angeles and New Orleans—with stops in Lordsburg, Deming, and El Paso, Texas.

You can get a copy of AMTRAK's National Timetable from any AMTRAK station, from travel agents, or by contacting AMTRAK, 400 N. Capitol St. NW, Washington, DC 20001 (☎ toll free **800/USA-RAIL**).

BY BUS   **Greyhound Lines, Inc.** and **TNM&O Coaches** (Texas, New Mexico & Oklahoma) have extensive networks that penetrate every corner of the state, with daily connections virtually everywhere. Call **505/243-4435** for information on schedules and rates.

BY CAR   Three interstate highways cross New Mexico. The north-south I-25 bisects the state, passing through Albuquerque and Las Cruces. The east-west I-40 follows the path of the old Route 66 through Gallup, Albuquerque, and Tucumcari in the north; while I-10 from San Diego crosses southwestern New Mexico until intersecting I-25 at Las Cruces.

Here are the approximate mileages to Albuquerque from various cities around the United States:

Atlanta	1,424	Minneapolis	1,257
Boston	2,248	New Orleans	1,188
Chicago	1,351	New York	2,029
Cleveland	1,616	Oklahoma City	540
Dallas	670	Phoenix	537
Denver	449	St. Louis	1,051
Detroit	1,572	Salt Lake City	617
Houston	907	San Francisco	1,091
Los Angeles	802	Seattle	1,460
Miami	2,018	Washington, D.C.	1,883

PACKAGE TOURS   Tours within the state of New Mexico are offered by the following inbound operators:

Jack Allan Tours Inc., 5921 Lomas Blvd. NE (P.O. Box 11940), Albuquerque, NM 87192 (☎ **505/266-9688**).

Destinations Southwest, 121 Tijeras NE, Suite 1100, Albuquerque, NM 87102. (☎ **505/766-9068** or toll free **800/999-3109**).

Gray Line Tours, 800 Rio Grande NW, Suite 22, Albuquerque, NM 87104 (☎ **505/242-3880** or toll free **800/256-8991**).

Photo Adventure Tours, 2035 Park St., Atlantic Beach, NY 11509-1236 (☎ **516/371-0067**).

Rocky Mountain Tours, 1323 Paseo de Peralta, Santa Fe, NM 87501 (☎ **505/984-1684**).

Rojo Tours & Services, 228 Old Santa Fe Trail, Santa Fe, NM 87501 (☎ **505/983-8333**).

Sun Tours, Ltd., 4300 San Mateo Blvd. NE, Suite B-155, Albuquerque, NM 87110 (☎ **505/889-8888**).

Travel New Mexico, Inc., 3317 Valencia NE, Albuquerque, NM 87110 (☎ **505/883-9718** or toll free **800/333-7159**).

Zia Tours/A to Z Travelink, 6020 Indian School Rd., Albuquerque, NM 87110 (☎ **505/883-5865** or toll free **800/366-0282**).

4 Getting Around

BY PLANE **Mesa Airlines** (☎ toll free **800/637-2247**) flies from Albuquerque to Alamogordo, Carlsbad, Clovis, Farmington, Gallup, Hobbs, Las Cruces, Roswell, Santa Fe, Silver City, and Taos.

BY TRAIN **AMTRAK's** northern New Mexico line, the *Southwest Chief,* runs west-east and east-west once daily, with stops in Gallup, Grants, Albuquerque, Lamy (for Santa Fe), Las Vegas, and Raton. The *Sunset Unlimited* connects Lordsburg and Deming with El Paso, Texas, three times weekly each direction. Greyhound/Trailways bus lines provide through-ticketing for AMTRAK between Albuquerque and El Paso. Call for information (Albuquerque ☎ **505/842-9650** or toll free **800/USA-RAIL**).

BY BUS Service links every sizable city in the state: Alamogordo, Albuquerque, Artesia, Belen, Carlsbad, Clayton, Clovis, Costilla, Cuba, Deming, Espanola, Farmington, Gallup, Grants, Hatch, Hobbs, Jal, Las Cruces, Las Vegas, Lordsburg, Portales, Raton, Roswell, Ruidoso, Santa Fe, Santa Rosa, Shiprock, Silver City, Socorro, Springer, Taos, Truth or Consequences, Tucumcari, and other communities en route.

Service is provided by **Greyhound Lines, Inc.** (Albuquerque ☎ **505/243-4435**) and **TNM&O** (Texas, New Mexico & Oklahoma; ☎ **505/243-4435** in Albuquerque). Many of the two coach companies' routes are now combined.

BY CAR Visitors who plan to drive their own car to and around New Mexico should give their vehicle a thorough road check before starting out. There are lots of wide-open desert and wilderness spaces in New Mexico, and it is not fun to be stranded in the heat or cold with a vehicle that doesn't run. Check your lights, windshield wipers, horn, tires, battery, drive belts, fluid levels, alignment, and other possible trouble spots. Make sure your driver's license, vehicle registration, safety-inspection sticker, and auto-club membership (if you have one) are valid. Check with your auto insurance company to make sure you're covered when out of state, and/or when driving a rental car.

Unless otherwise posted, the speed level on open roads is 65 mph (105 km/h). Minimum age for drivers is 16. Safety belts are required for drivers and all passengers age 5 and over; children under 5 must use approved child seats.

Indian reservations are considered sovereign nations, and they enforce their own laws. For instance, on the Navajo reservation (New Mexico's largest), it is prohibited to transport alcoholic beverages, to leave established roadways, or to travel without a seat belt. Motorcyclists must wear helmets.

Gas is readily available at service stations throughout the state. Prices are cheapest in Albuquerque (about $1.20 a gallon in the fall of 1994), and 10% to 15% more expensive in more isolated communities. All prices are subject to the same fluctuations as elsewhere in the United States.

An excellent state highway map can be obtained from the New Mexico Department of Tourism, Lamy Building, 491 Old Santa Fe Trail, Santa Fe, NM 87503 (☎ toll free **800/545-2040**). More specific county and city maps are available from the State Highway and Transportation Department, 1120 Cerrillos Rd., Santa Fe, NM 87501 (☎ **505/827-5100**).

The State Highway and Transportation Department has a toll-free hot line (☎ **800/432-4269**) providing up-to-the-hour information on road closures and conditions.

In case of an accident or road emergency, contact the New Mexico State Police. District offices are in Alamogordo (☎ **437-1313**), Albuquerque (☎ **841-9256**), Clovis (☎ **763-3426**), Espanola (☎ **753-2277**), Farmington (☎ **325-7547**), Gallup (☎ **287-4141**), Hobbs (☎ **392-5588**), Las Cruces (☎ **524-6111**), Las Vegas (☎ **425-6771**), Raton (☎ **445-5571**), Roswell (☎ **622-7200**), Santa Fe (☎ **827-9300**), Socorro (☎ **835-0741**), and Taos (☎ **758-8878**).

Members of the American Automobile Association can get free emergency road service wherever they are, 24 hours, by calling AAA's emergency number (☎ toll free **800/336-4357**).

Car rentals are available in every sizable town and city in the state, always at the local airport, and usually also downtown. **Payless Car Rental** (☎ **505/247-9255**) has excellent rates. Widely represented agencies include: **Alamo** (☎ toll free **800/327-9633**), **Avis** (☎ toll free **800/331-1212**), **Budget** (☎ toll free **800/527-0700**), **Dollar** (☎ toll free **800/327-7607**), **Hertz** (☎ toll free **800/654-3131**), **National** (☎ toll free **800/227-7368**), and **Thrifty** (☎ toll free **800/367-2277**). Drivers who need wheelchair accessible transportation should call **Wheelchair Gateways of New Mexico,** 1015 Tramway Ln. NE (☎ **505/247-2626** or toll free **800/408-2626**); they rent vans by the day, week, or month.

Words of warning: U.S. 666 between Gallup and Shiprock has been labeled America's "most dangerous highway" by *USA Today.* New Mexico has the highest per capita rate of traffic deaths of any American state. Drive carefully!

Suggested Itineraries

If You Have 1 Week

Days 1–2   Spend your first 2 nights in Albuquerque. Wander around Old Town, visit the Albuquerque Museum and Indian Pueblo Cultural Center, take the tramway up Sandia Peak. Then drive to Santa Fe, not much more than an hour north.

Days 3–5   Stay 3 nights in Santa Fe, and be sure to include a day trip to Los Alamos and Bandelier National Monument.

Days 6–7   Drive to Taos in the morning, taking the "High Road" through Chimayo. Stay overnight in Taos to see the pueblo, the art galleries, and the historic properties.

Day 7   In the afternoon, return to Albuquerque for the flight home.

If You Have 2 Weeks

Spend days 1 to 6 as described above.

Day 7   In the afternoon drive west from Taos on U.S. 64 to Chama to spend the night.

Day 8   Spend the day in Chama on the famous Cumbres & Toltec narrow-gauge steam railroad. After the train trip, continue west on U.S. 64 to Farmington to spend 2 nights.

Day 9   Take an easy day trip from Farmington to Aztec Ruins National Monument, the Salmon Ruins, or Shiprock, on the Navajo Reservation.

Day 10   Start out early to spend most of the day at fascinating Chaco Culture National Historic Park. Then drive to Gallup for 2 nights.

Day 11   Explore the pawn shops of Gallup, and visit Zuni Pueblo, perhaps the most culturally unique pueblo in New Mexico.

Day 12   Drive to Grants for lunch, passing El Morro National Monument on the way. In the afternoon visit historic Acoma Pueblo as you head back to Albuquerque.

Day 13   Do a loop tour of the pueblos north of the city, or to drive to the three divisions of Salinas National Monument southeast of Albuquerque.

Day 14   Day 14 is your departure date from Albuquerque airport.

If You Have 3 Weeks

Spend the first 2 weeks as described above.

Day 15   Drive south from Albuquerque on I-25, stopping en route to explore Socorro and the Bosque del Apache National Wildlife Refuge. Stay the night in Truth or Consequences.

Day 16   Get an early start and visit Gila Cliff Dwellings National Monument. Spend the night in Silver City.

Day 17   Drive to Las Cruces, southern New Mexico's largest city, and its historic suburb of La Mesilla via City of Rocks State Park and Deming.

Day 18   Drive over the Organ Mountains to Alamogordo, being sure not to miss White Sands National Monument or the International Space Hall of Fame.

Day 19   If you get an early start, you can lunch in Carlsbad, check into your hotel, then spend the entire afternoon at Carlsbad Caverns.

Day 20   Take a trip to Ruidoso, a picturesque mountain resort town, via Roswell and the Old West village of Lincoln.

Day 21   Head back to Albuquerque for your departure.

Fast Facts: New Mexico

American Express   Atlas American Express, 1301 Wyoming Blvd. NE, Albuquerque (☎ **505/291-6575**). To report a lost card, call toll free **800/528-4800.** To report lost traveler's checks, call toll free **800/221-7282.**

Banks   Major statewide banks are the Bank of New Mexico, First Interstate Bank, First National Bank in Albuquerque, SunWest Bank, United New Mexico Bank, and Western Bank. They're typically open Monday to Thursday 10am to 3pm and Friday 10am to 6pm. Drive-up windows may be open later. Some may also open Saturday morning. Most branches have cash machines available 24 hours.

Business Hours   In general, Monday to Friday 9am to 5pm, with many stores also open Friday night and Saturday. Some cities may have different hours; in Las Cruces, for instance, many merchants close their doors on Monday but are open all day Saturday.

Camera & Film   Film of all kinds is widely available at camera stores throughout the state, and simple repairs can be handled in the major cities.

Consulates   There is one in New Mexico, the Mexican Consulate, Western Bank Bldg., 401 5th St. NW, Albuquerque, NM 87102 (☎ 505/247-2147 or 247-2139).

Drugstores   24-hour prescription services are available at selected Walgreens Drug Stores around the state. Prices at Thrifty and Wal-Mart outlets might be somewhat less. If you're having trouble getting a prescription filled, call the nearest hospital pharmacy.

Electricity   As throughout the U.S., 110 to 115 volts, 60 cycles.

Emergencies   For emergency medical help or information call the New Mexico Medical Crisis Center toll free at **800/432-6866.** The center is open 24 hours a day. In most cities, for police, sheriff, fire department, or ambulance, dial **911** at any time; otherwise, dial **0,** and ask the operator to connect you.

Hitchhiking   Hitching a ride is legal in New Mexico, and in summer you may find backpack-laden vagabonds at interstate highway entrances, at road junctions, in the Navajo Indian Reservation, and on secondary roads.

Language   English is the lingua franca, but Spanish is almost as frequently spoken. You'll also hear Native American languages—Navajo (the most widely spoken surviving North American Indian dialect), Apache, Zuni, Tanoan, and Keresan.

Liquor Laws   Drinking age is 21. Bars close at 2am; on Sunday they are open noon to midnight. Wine, beer, and spirits are sold at licensed supermarkets and liquor stores. A special allowance must be granted for liquor to be dispensed in proximity to any church. It is illegal to transport liquor through most Indian reservations.

Mail   It takes two to three days for mail from major New Mexico cities to reach other major American cities. Figure an extra day from and/or to smaller communities. Domestic postage for letters is 32¢ for the first ounce, 23¢ per additional ounce, and 20¢ for a postcard. Postage to most foreign countries is 50¢ per half-ounce. (It's 40¢ per ounce to Canada, 35¢ per ounce to Mexico.) Buy stamps and send parcels from post offices in any city, town, or village. Major city post offices are open Monday to Friday 8am to 4pm, Sat 9am to noon; smaller communities often have limited hours.

You can have mail sent to you in any city in New Mexico. Have it addressed to you, c/o General Delivery, Main Post Office, Name of City. The post office will hold it for one month. You must pick it up in person and show proof of identification. A passport will suffice.

Maps   The official state highway map is published by the State Tourism and Travel Division; county and city maps can be obtained from the State Highway and Transportation Department. Many local visitors bureaus or chambers of commerce publish their own city or regional maps. The American Automobile Association (AAA) supplies detailed state and city maps free to members.

Newspapers & Magazines Larger cities and regional hubs have daily newspapers, and many smaller towns publish weeklies. The *Albuquerque Tribune,* published mornings, and the *Albuquerque Journal,* published evenings, are widely available around the state. The *El Paso Times* is favored in southern New Mexico. National newspapers like *USA Today* and the *Wall Street Journal* can be purchased in cities and major hotels. The state's favorite magazine is *New Mexico,* a high-quality monthly published by the State Tourism and Travel Division since 1923.

Pets Dogs, cats, and other small pets are accepted at motels in most parts of the state, though not as universally in Albuquerque and Santa Fe as elsewhere. Some properties require owners to pay a damage deposit in advance. If you bring your pet, keep it well dusted with flea powder: Plague bacilli, a disease borne by fleas, is endemic to New Mexico.

Police In the event of any emergency, contact the New Mexico State Police. Call **911** or **0** for an operator. Regional telephone numbers are listed in "Getting Around," above.

Radio & TV There are 125 AM and FM radio stations in New Mexico, so if you have a car radio or other receiver, you'll never be far from the rest of the world. Albuquerque has five television stations, including ABC, CBS, NBC, FOX, and PBS affiliates. Santa Fe has one station. Southern New Mexico gets reception from El Paso, Texas.

Safety Whenever you're traveling in an unfamiliar city or region, stay alert. Be aware of your immediate surroundings. Wear a money belt and keep a close eye on your possessions. Be particularly careful with cameras, purses, and wallets, all favorite targets of thieves and pickpockets.

Taxes The 6% state tax on gross receipts includes hotel bills. Local governments tack their own lodging tax on top of that, which ranges from 2.75% to 5.812% depending upon the city.

Telephone & Fax The area code for the entire state of New Mexico is **505.** Local calls are normally 25¢. Facsimiles can be transmitted by most major hotels at a nominal cost to guests. As of June 1994, no matter where you are in the state, if you're placing a call outside city limits you must use the **505** area code.

Time New Mexico is on mountain standard time, one hour ahead of the West Coast and two hours behind the East Coast. Daylight saving time is in effect from April to October.

Tipping A tip of $1 per bag is appropriate for hotel valets and airport porters. If you're staying longer than a night or two in a hotel or motel, tip about $1 per night for chamber service. Restaurant servers should get 15% to 20% of your bill for service.

Water You can drink the water everywhere.

3

For Foreign Visitors

A s NEW MEXICO IS A PART OF THE UNITED STATES, ALL FOREIGN VISITORS MUST satisfy the entrance requirements for a visit to the USA before continuing their trip to the Southwest. This chapter is designed to explain the intricacies.

1 Preparing for Your Trip

DOCUMENT REGULATIONS   Canadian citizens may enter the U.S. without visas; they need only proof of Canadian residence.

Citizens of the U.K., New Zealand, Japan, and most western European countries traveling with valid passports may not need a visa for fewer than 90 days of holiday or business travel to the U.S., providing that they hold a round-trip or return ticket and enter the U.S. on an airline or cruise line participating in the visa waiver program.

(Note that citizens of these visa-exempt countries who first enter the U.S. may then visit Mexico, Canada, Bermuda, and/or the Caribbean Islands and then reenter the U.S., by any mode of transportation, without needing a visa. Further information is available from any U.S. embassy or consulate.)

Citizens of countries other than those stipulated above, including citizens of Australia, must have two documents:

- a valid passport, with an expiration date at least six months later than the scheduled end of the visit to the U.S.; and
- a tourist visa, available without charge from the nearest U.S. consulate. To obtain a visa, the traveler must submit a completed application form (either in person or by mail) with a $1^1/_2$-inch square photo and demonstrate binding ties to the residence abroad.

Usually you can obtain a visa at once or within 24 hours, but it may take longer during the summer rush from June to August. If you cannot go in person, contact the nearest U.S. embassy or consulate for directions on applying by mail. Your travel agent or airline office may also be able to provide you with visa applications and instructions. The U.S. consulate or embassy that issues your visa will determine whether you will be issued a multiple- or single-entry visa and any restrictions regarding the length of your stay.

MEDICAL REQUIREMENTS   New arrivals in the United States do not need any inoculations unless they are coming from, or have stopped over in, an area known to be suffering from an epidemic, particularly cholera or yellow fever.

Anyone applying for an immigrant's visa must undergo a screening test for the AIDS-associated HIV virus, under a law passed in 1987. This test does not apply to tourists.

Any visitor with a medical condition that requires treatment with narcotics or other drugs, or with paraphernalia such as syringes, must carry a valid, signed prescription from a physician. This will show Customs officials and others that you are carrying drugs for a legitimate purpose.

TRAVEL INSURANCE   All such insurance is optional in the United States. Medical care is very costly in the United States, however, and every traveler is strongly advised to secure full insurance coverage before starting a trip.

For a relatively low premium, numerous specialized insurance companies will cover (1) loss or theft of baggage, (2) costs of trip cancellation, (3) guaranteed bail in the event of a suit or other legal difficulties, (4) the cost of medical assistance—including surgery and hospitalization—in the event of sickness or injury, and (5) the cost of an accident, death, or repatriation. Travel agencies, automobile clubs, and banks are among those selling travel insurance packages at attractive rates.

2 Getting to & Around the U.S.

Nearly all major airlines, including those of the United States, Europe, Asia, Australia, and New Zealand, offer **APEX (advance purchase excursion) fares** that significantly reduce the cost of transoceanic air travel. This enables travelers to pick their dates and ports, but requires that they prepurchase their ticket, and meet minimum- and maximum-stay requirements—often 15 to 90 days. Season of travel and individual airline discounts also affect fares, but this is the most widely acknowledged means of cheap, flexible travel.

Some large airlines, including Delta, Eastern, Northwest, TWA, and United, have in the past offered foreign travelers special add-on discount fares under the name **Visit USA.** Though not currently available, they may be repeated in the future, and are worth asking a travel agent about. These tickets (which could be purchased overseas only) allowed unlimited travel between U.S. destinations at minimum rates for specified time periods, such as 21, 30, or 60 days. Short of bus or train travel, which can be inconvenient and time-consuming, this was the best way of traveling around the country at low cost.

International visitors can also buy a **USA Railpass,** good for 15 or 30 days of unlimited travel on AMTRAK. The pass is available through many foreign travel agents. Prices in 1994 for a 15-day pass are $208 off-peak, $308 peak; a 30-day pass costs $309 off-peak, $389 peak. (With a foreign passport, you can also buy passes at some AMTRAK offices in the U.S., including locations in San Francisco, Los Angeles, Chicago, New York, Miami, Boston, and Washington, D.C.). Reservations are generally required and should be made for each part of your trip as early as possible.

Visitors should also be aware of the limitations of long-distance rail travel in the U.S. With a few notable exceptions (for instance, the Northeast Corridor line between Boston and Washington, D.C.), service is rarely up to European standards: delays are common, routes are limited and often infrequently served, and fares are rarely significantly lower than discount airfares. Thus, cross-country train travel should be approached with caution.

The cheapest way to travel the U.S. is by bus. Greyhound, the nation's nationwide bus line, offers an **Ameripass** for unlimited travel for 7 days (for $250), 15 days (for $350), and 30 days (for $450). Bus travel in the U.S. can be both slow and uncomfortable, so this option is not for everyone.

For visitors who plan to rent a car, automobile organizations and auto clubs will supply maps, suggested routes, guidebooks, accident and bail-bond insurance, and emergency road service. The major auto club in the United States, with 955 offices nationwide, is the American Automobile Association (AAA). Members of some foreign auto clubs have reciprocal arrangements with the AAA and enjoy its services at no charge. If you belong to an auto club, inquire about AAA reciprocity before you leave. The AAA can provide you with an International Driving Permit validating your foreign license. You may be able to join the AAA even if you are not a member of a reciprocal club. To inquire, call toll free **800/336-4357.** In addition, some automobile rental agencies now provide these services, so you should inquire about their availability when you rent your car.

For detailed information on travel by car, train, and bus, see "Getting Around," Chapter 2.

Fast Facts: For the Foreign Traveler

Business Hours   Banks open weekdays from 9am to 3pm, although there's 24-hour access to the automatic tellers (ATMs) at most banks and other outlets. Generally, offices open weekdays from 9am to 5pm. Stores are open six days a week with many open on Sundays, too; most department stores usually stay open until 9pm one day a week.

Climate   See "Information & Climate," chapter 2.

Currency Exchange   You will find currency exchange services in major airports with international service. Elsewhere, they may be quite difficult to come by. In New York, a very reliable choice is Thomas Cook Currency Services, Inc., which has been in business since 1841 and covers a wide range of services, among which are commission-free foreign and U.S. traveler's checks, drafts, and wire transfers; they also do check collections (including Eurochecks). Their rates are competitive and service excellent. They maintain several offices in New York City (☎ for the Fifth Avenue office is **212/757-6915**), at the JFK Airport International Arrivals Terminal (☎ **718/656-8444**), and at La Guardia Airport in the Delta terminal (☎ **718/533-0784**).

Traveler's checks in *U.S. dollars* are easily cashed in payment for goods or services at most hotels, motels, restaurants, and large stores. The best rates, however, are given at banks; a major bank is also the only place where you can confidently cash traveler's checks in any currency *but* U.S. dollars. In fact, don't plan on changing any foreign currency here; the foreign-exchange bureaus common in other countries are largely absent from U.S. cities.

Credit Cards   The method of payment most widely used is the credit or charge card: Visa (BarclayCard in Britain), Mastercard (EuroCard in Europe, Access in Britain, Chargex in Canada), American Express, Diners Club, Discover, and Carte Blanche. You can save yourself trouble by using "plastic money" rather than cash or traveler's checks in most hotels, motels, restaurants, and retail stores (a growing number of food and liquor stores now accept credit cards). You must have a credit card to rent a car. It can also be used as proof of identity (often carrying more weight than a passport), or as a "cash card," enabling you to draw money from banks that accept them.

Customs & Immigration   U.S. Customs allows each adult visitor to import the following, duty free: (1) one liter of wine or hard liquor; (2) 1,000 cigarettes or 100 cigars (*not* from Cuba) or three pounds of smoking tobacco; and (3) $400 worth of gifts. The only restrictions are that the visitor must spend at least 72 hours in the United States, and must not have claimed them within the preceding six months. Food and plants are forbidden from import.

Foreign tourists may import or export up to $5,000 in U.S. or foreign currency, with no formalities. Larger amounts of money must be declared to Customs.

Visitors arriving by air, no matter what the port of entry, are well advised to be exceedingly patient and to resign themselves to a wait in the Customs and immigration line. At busy times, especially when several overseas flights arrive within a few minutes of each other, it can take two or three hours just to get a passport stamped for arrival. Allot *plenty* of time for connections between international and domestic flights!

Border formalities by road or rail from Canada are relatively quick and easy.

Electric Current The United States uses 110 to 120 volts, 60 cycles, compared to 220 to 240 volts, 50 cycles, as in most of Europe. Besides a 100-volt converter, small appliances of non-American manufacture, such as hair dryers or shavers, will require a plug adapter with two flat, parallel pins.

Embassies & Consulates All embassies are located in the national capital, Washington, D.C.; some consulates are located in major cities, and most nations have a mission to the United Nations in New York City.

Listed here are the embassies and East and West Coast consulates of the major English-speaking countries. Travelers from other countries can get telephone numbers for their embassies and consulates by calling "Information" in Washington, D.C. (**202/555-1212**).

The **Australian embassy** is at 1601 Massachusetts Ave. NW, Washington, D.C. 20036 (☎ **202/797-3000**). The **consulate** in New York is located at the International Building, 630 Fifth Ave., Suite 420, New York, NY 10111 (☎ **212/245-4000**). The consulate in Los Angeles is located at 611 N. Larchmont, Los Angeles, CA 90004 (☎ **213/469-4300**).

The **Canadian embassy** is at 501 Pennsylvania Ave. NW, Washington, D.C. 20001 (☎ **202/682-1740**). The **consulate** in New York is located at 1251 Avenue of the Americas, New York, NY 10020 (☎ **212/768-2400**). The consulate in Los Angeles is located at 300 Santa Grand Ave., Suite 1000, Los Angeles, CA 90071 (☎ **213/687-7432**).

The **New Zealand embassy** is at 37 Observatory Circle NW, Washington, DC 20008 (☎ **202/328-4800**). The **consulate** in Los Angeles is located at 10960 Wiltshire Blvd., Los Angeles, CA 90024 (☎ **213/477-8241**). There is no consulate in New York.

The **British embassy** is at 3100 Massachusetts Ave. NW, Washington, DC 20008 (☎ **202/462-1340**). The **consulate** in New York is located at 845 Third Ave., New York, NY 10022 (☎ **212/745-0200**). The consulate in Los Angeles is located at 1766 Wilshire Blvd., Suite 400, Los Angeles, CA 90025 (☎ **310/477-3322**).

Emergencies A single emergency telephone number, **911,** will put you in touch with police, ambulance, or fire department in Albuquerque, Santa Fe, and other major New Mexico cities. In Taos and smaller towns without a **911** line, dial **0** (zero) for the operator.

Holidays On the following national and legal holidays, banks, government offices, post offices, and many stores, restaurants, and museums are closed: January 1 (New Year's Day), third Monday in January (Martin Luther King Day), third Monday in February (President's Day), last Monday in May (Memorial Day), July 4 (Independence Day), first Monday in September (Labor Day), second Monday in October (Columbus Day), November 11 (Veteran's Day/Armistice Day), last Thursday in November (Thanksgiving Day), and December 25 (Christmas).

The Tuesday following the first Monday in November, Election Day, is a legal holiday in presidential-election years.

Information See chapter 2, section 1.

Legal Aid Those accused of serious offenses are advised to say and do nothing before consulting a lawyer. Under U.S. law, an arrested person is allowed one telephone call to a party of his or her choice: Call your embassy. If you are pulled up for a minor infraction, such as a traffic offense, never attempt to pay the fine directly to a police officer. You may wind up arrested on the much more serious charge of attempted bribery. Pay fines by mail, or directly into the hands of the clerk of a court.

Mail   If you want your mail to follow you on your vacation and you aren't sure of your address, your mail can be sent to you, in your name, c/o General Delivery at the main post office of the city or region where you expect to be. The addressee must pick it up in person and produce proof of identity (driver's license, credit card, passport, etc.).

Newspapers & Magazines   Foreign publications, other than Spanish-language periodicals from Mexico, may be hard to find in New Mexico. There are newsstands in Santa Fe and Albuquerque that carry a few magazines from overseas, but no newspapers. Your best bet for staying abreast of foreign news is to pick up a copy of the *New York Times* or an American weekly newsmagazine.

Post Office   See "Mail" above or in the individual city and region chapters.

Radio & Television   There are dozens of radio stations (both AM and FM), each broadcasting talk shows, continuous news, or a particular kind of music—classical, country, jazz, pop, gospel—punctuated by frequent commercials. Television, with four coast-to-coast networks—ABC, CBS, NBC, and FOX—joined by the Public Broadcasting System (PBS) and a growing network of cable channels, plays a major part in American life.

Safety   Whenever you're traveling in an unfamiliar city or country, stay alert. Be aware of your immediate surroundings. Wear a money belt and don't flash expensive jewelry and cameras in public. This will minimize the possibility of your becoming a crime victim. Be alert even in heavily touristed areas. You may wish to contact the local tourist information bureau in your destination before you arrive. They may be able to provide you with a safety brochure.

Taxes   In the United States, there is no VAT (Value-Added Tax) or other indirect tax at a national level. New Mexico levies a 6% state tax on gross receipts, including hotel checks and shop purchases. Food is exempt. In addition, each city or county levies an additional lodging tax to support the local tax base.

Telephone, Telegraph, Telex   The telephone system in the U.S. is run by private corporations, so rates, especially for long-distance service, can vary widely—even on calls made from public telephones. Local calls in the U.S. usually cost 25¢.

Generally, hotel surcharges on long-distance and local calls are astronomical. You are usually better off using a public pay telephone, which you will find clearly marked in most public buildings and private establishments as well as on the street. Outside metropolitan areas, public telephones are more difficult to find. Stores and gas stations are your best bet.

Most long-distance and international calls can be dialed directly from any phone. For calls to Canada and other parts of the U.S., dial **1** followed by the area code and the seven-digit number. For international calls, dial **011** followed by the country code, city code, and the telephone number of the person you wish to call.

Time   The United States is divided into six **time zones.** From east to west, they are: eastern standard time (EST), central standard time (CST), mountain standard time (MST), Pacific standard time (PST), Alaska standard time (AST), and Hawaii standard time (HST). Keep time zones in mind when traveling or telephoning long distances in the United States. For example, noon in New York City (EST) is 11am in Chicago (CST), 10am in Salt Lake City (MST), 9am in San Francisco (PST), 8am in Anchorage (AST), and 7am in Honolulu (HST). **Daylight saving time** is in effect from the last Sunday in April through the last Saturday in October; this alters the clock so that sunrise and sunset are an hour later.

Toilets   Some foreign visitors complain that public "johns" are hard to find in the States. There are none on the streets, but most hotels, restaurants, bars, department stores, gasoline stations, museums, and other tourist attractions have them available. In a restaurant or bar, it's usually appropriate to order a cup of coffee or soft drink to qualify you as a customer.

Yellow Pages   There are two kinds of telephone directories available. The general directory is called "white pages," and includes individuals and businesses alphabetically by name. The second directory, called "yellow pages," lists all local services, businesses, and industries alphabetically by category, with an index in the back. Listings include not only the obvious, such as automobile repairs and drugstores (pharmacies), but also restaurants by cuisine and location, places of worship by religious denomination, and other information that a tourist might not otherwise readily find. The yellow pages also include city plans or detailed area maps and often show postal ZIP codes and public transportation routes.

The American System of Measurements

Length

1 inch (in.)	=	2.54cm					
1 foot (ft.)	=	12 in.	=	30.48cm	=	.305m	
1 yard	=	3 ft.			=	.915m	
1 mile (mi.)	=	5,280 ft.				=	1.609km

To convert miles to kilometers, multiply the number of miles by 1.61 (for example, 50mi. × 1.61 = 80.5km). Note that this conversion can be used to convert speeds from miles per hour (mph) to kilometers per hour (km/h).
To convert kilometers to miles, multiply the number of kilometers by .62 (for example, 25km × .62 = 15.5mi.). Note that this same conversion can be used to convert speeds from kilometers per hour to miles per hour.

Capacity

1 fluid ounce (fl. oz.)			=	.03 liter		
1 pint	=	16 fl. oz.	=	.47 liter		
1 quart	=	2 pints	=	.94 liter		
1 gallon (gal.)	=	4 quarts	=	3.79 liter	=	.83 Imperial gal.

To convert U.S. gallons to liters, multiply the number of gallons by 3.79 (example, 12 gal. × 3.79 = 45.58 liters).
To convert U.S. gallons to Imperial gallons, multiply the number of U.S. gallons by .83 (example, 12 U.S. gal. × .83 = 9.95 Imperial gal.).
To convert liters to U.S. gallons, multiply the number of liters by .26 (example, 50 liters × .26 = 13 U.S. gal.).

To convert **Imperial gallons to U.S. gallons,** multiply the number of Imperial gallons by 1.2 (example, 8 Imperial gal. × 1.2 = 9.6 U.S. gal.).

Weight

1 ounce (oz.)			=	28.35 grams			
1 pound (lb.)	=	16 oz.	=	453.6 grams	=	.45 kilograms	
1 ton	=	2,000 lb.			=	907 kilograms	= .91 metric ton

To convert **pounds to kilograms,** multiply the number of pounds by .45 (example, 90 lb. × .45 = 40.5kg).

To convert **kilograms to pounds,** multiply the number of kilos by 2.2 (example, 75kg × 2.2 = 165 lb.).

Area

1 acre			=	.41 hectare		
1 square mile (sq. mi.)	=	640 acres	=	2.59 hectares	=	2.6km²

To convert **acres to hectares,** multiply the number of acres by .41 (example, 40 acres × .41 = 16.4ha).

To convert **square miles to square kilometers,** multiply the number of square miles by 2.6 (example, 80 sq. mi. × 2.6 = 208km²).

To convert **hectares to acres,** multiply the number of hectares by 2.47 (example, 20ha × 2.47 = 49.4 acres).

To convert **square kilometers to square miles,** multiply the number of square kilometers by .39 (example, 150km² × .39 = 58.5 sq. mi.).

Temperature

To convert **degrees Fahrenheit to degrees Celsius,** subtract 32 from °F, multiply by 5, then divide by 9 [example, (85°F – 32) × 5 ÷ 9 = 29.4°C].

To convert **degrees Celsius to degrees Fahrenheit,** multiply °C by 9, divide by 5, and add 32 (example, 20°C × 9 ÷ 5 + 32 = 68°F).

4

Albuquerque

WITH A POPULATION OF ABOUT HALF A MILLION, ALBUQUERQUE IS NEW MEXICO'S largest city. But it holds onto the bustling spirit of western towns of half a century ago when "progress" was a fashionable word and growing bigger was unquestionably synonymous with getting better.

The historic center of Albuquerque is Old Town, where it was founded in 1706. The city jumped away from its origins when the railroad came through in 1880 and caused a new Albuquerque to be planted around the passenger and freight depots. This *Saturday Evening Post*-style center, so reminiscent of hundreds of small plains cities of the thirties and forties, still exists along Central Avenue between Second and Sixth streets. But a new downtown, with an impressive new convention center, luxury hotels, financial district of glass skyscrapers, and underground shopping mall, is emerging just a few steps north. And vast commercial and shopping complexes are part of the urban expanse east of downtown, within quick reach by car via the long, wide, straight, flat streets and avenues of the sprawling grid that reach nearly to the foot of the Sandia Mountains 20 miles east of the old center.

In spite of the leveling, gentrifying effect of the spread of chain restaurants, interchangeable condos, and placeless superhighways, Albuquerque retains strong elements of its original western spirit. It feels somehow closer to the plains to the east, the directness of the Texan, than to the thin, chic optimism and faddishness of California. It is a young city: The people are young in years and in energy. The University of New Mexico plays a central role in life here, both by its geography just east of downtown and for the part it takes in the life of its city through its outstanding museums and cultural programs.

The city does have its unsightly commercial strips along the main east-west highway. The notorious old Route 66, where mid-20th-century pioneers heading west used to "get their kicks," still goes straight through town, though most of its traffic has been diverted to I-40. But it was not all that long ago that Albuquerque had for a main drag a movie set–like row of false-front hotels, bars, and stores lined in front with hitching posts and wooden sidewalks along a muddy, rutted roadway crowded with wagons and buggies and figures on horseback.

That shot-in-the-arm railroad connection a little over a century ago gave Albuquerque the impetus to grow, to build, to move out in every direction without a thought for the future—without any plan at all. The city grew so big and so much, before there was any thought of saving any of its land for public use, that it wasn't until 1975 that any serious attempt at growth control took place. That action has provided citizens (and visitors) with some green spaces, and there are more to come. First-time visitors, viewing the city from a car speeding in over the interstate, which makes a huge cross in the middle of town with its east-west and north-south trajectories meeting and corkscrewing in and around one another, might suppose themselves lost in a Los Angeles–style wasteland of urban sprawl. But parts of Albuquerque are very special indeed—you just have to make sure to find them.

One of these is the plaza of Old Town, which rivals the plazas of Santa Fe and Taos for historical interest, architectural beauty, and lively shopping and restaurant-going scenes. Another is the innovative complex of glass-and-steel bank buildings clustered around a tiled open space, containing a pool and a fountain, terraces and tables with parasols, the whole of which conceals First Plaza—a brightly lighted futuristic warren of underground shops, bars, and eating places that could make you imagine you'd come to Montreal on the Rio Grande. That good old western-style downtown is just outside in case you feel a dire need for a touch of reality.

The city was long a supply center for the region. Today it has added to its original mercantile base by developing supply depots for military bases and building experimental scientific laboratories in a wide variety of specialized fields. Its warm, sunny climate and healthful altitude—varying from 4,200 to 6,000 feet—also bring in many vacationers and retirement residents.

The fairgrounds is the site for the annual state fair and for a colorful and locally renowned annual arts-and-crafts show. Indian pueblos in the area welcome tourists, and along with other pueblos throughout New Mexico have worked together to create the Pueblo Cultural Center, a showplace of Indian crafts of both past and present. The country's longest aerial tramway takes visitors to the top of Sandia Peak, which protects the city's eastern flank.

1 Orientation

Arriving

BY PLANE **Albuquerque International Airport** is in the south central part of the city, between I-25 on the west and Kirtland Air Force Base on the east, just south of Gibson Boulevard. A major renovation and expansion, completed in early 1990, gave the city a sleek and efficient air terminal.

The airport is served by eight national airlines—**America West** (☎ **247-0737**), **American** (☎ toll free **800/433-7300**), **Continental** (☎ **842-8220**), **Delta** (☎ **243-2794**), **Southwest** (☎ **831-1221**), **TWA** (☎ **842-4010**), and **United** (☎ toll free **800/241-6522**)—plus one regional carrier, **Mesa** (☎ **842-4218**).

Most hotels have courtesy vans to take new arrivals to their accommodations. **Shuttlejack** (☎ **243-3244** or toll free **800/452-2665** outside New Mexico) also runs a service to city hotels and on to Santa Fe. **Sun Tran** (☎ **843-9200**), Albuquerque's public bus system, also makes airport stops. There's efficient taxi service to and from the airport, and numerous car-rental agencies.

BY TRAIN **AMTRAK's** *Southwest Chief* arrives and departs daily from and to Los Angeles and Chicago. The station is at 314 First St. SW, two blocks south of Central Avenue (☎ **842-9650**).

BY BUS **Greyhound Lines, Inc.** (☎ **243-4435** for schedules and information) and **TNM&O Coaches** (☎ **242-4998**) arrive and depart from the Albuquerque Bus Transportation Center (☎ **505/842-9188**) adjacent to the train station at 300 Second St. SW.

BY CAR If you're driving yourself, you'll probably arrive in the city either via the east-west Interstate 40 or the north-south Interstate 25. Exits are well marked. For information and advice on driving in New Mexico, see the "Getting Around" section in chapter 2.

Tourist Information

The head office of the **Albuquerque Convention and Visitors Bureau** is at 121 Tijeras Ave. NE, first floor (P.O. Box 26866) (☎ **505/243-3696** or toll free **800/284-2282**). It's open Monday to Friday from 8am to 5pm. In addition, the bureau operates information centers at the airport, bottom of the escalator in the lower level, open from 9:30am to 8pm daily; and in Old Town at 303 Romero Street NW, Suite 107, open Monday to Saturday 9am to 7pm and Sunday 10am to 5pm. The bureau

Greater Albuquerque

To Santa Fe

25

Southern Blvd

Rio Rancho Dr

Angel Rd

Corrales Rd

Rio Grande

Meadowlark La

528

Cibola
National
Forest

448

Tramway Rd   556

Arroyo De Las Calabacilla

Alameda Blvd

Paradise Blvd

Pan-American Frwy

Paseo Del Norte Dr

Balloon
Fiesta Park

Indian
Petroglyph
Nat'l Mon

LOS RANCHOS DE
ALBUQUERQUE

423   541   Paseo Del Norte Dr

Coors Rd

1

303

Rio Grande
Valley
State Park

98

2 JOURNAL CENTER

Montaño Rd

2nd St

La Boca
Negra Park

Rio Grande Blvd

Edith Blvd

556

Atrisco Dr

Unser Blvd

Ladera Rd

Rio Grande
Nature Center
State Park

25

Montgomery Blvd.

Comanche Rd

Candelaria Rd

4th St

San Mateo Blvd.

Tramway Blvd

MIDTOWN

3

Menaul   **4**   Blvd

Chelwood Park Blvd

40   Coronado Frwy **5**

← To Gallup

OLD TOWN

40

UPTOWN

Indian School Rd

Coronado Frwy

Juan Tabo Blvd

Central Av

Lomas   Blvd

8 **9** University of
New Mexico

6

7

Central Av

40

Bridge Blvd

DOWNTOWN

10

U of NM
Stadium

Louisiana

Wyoming

Eubank

To Santa
Rosa

Gibson Blvd

Arenal

Tapia Blvd

Rd

La Vega Dr

45

Pan-American Frwy

11

Albuquerque
International
Airport

USS Bullhead
Memorial Park

Blake Rd

Rio Bravo Blvd 500

303

47

Veterans
Adminstration
Hospital

KIRTLAND AIR
FORCE BASE

Coors Blvd

Broadway

25

Rio Bravo
State Park

Montesa
Park

0   1.5 mi
               2.4 km

N

↓ To Las Cruces

NEIGHBORHOODS

Albuquerque Bus
Transportation Center **10**

Albuquerque Convention
and Visitors Bureau **9**

Albuquerque
Convention Center **8**

Albuquerque
International Airport **11**

Old Town Information Center **6**

Downtown **7**

Journal Center **2**

Los Ranchos de
Albuquerque **1**

Midtown **3**

Old Town **5**

Uptown **4**

publishes a wide variety of visitor information, including the city's official annual visitors guide, brochures about local and regional attractions and accommodations, and quarterly calendars of events.

Tape-recorded information on current local events is available from the bureau Monday to Friday after 5pm and all day Saturday and Sunday. Call **243-3696** or toll free **800/284-2282.**

City Layout

Lay a map of Albuquerque before you and notice how the crossroads of I-40 and I-25 divide the city into four neat quadrants. The southwest quadrant is the location of Downtown and Old Town. Central Avenue (the old "Route 66") and Lomas Boulevard flank downtown on the south and north, respectively; they come together 2 miles west of downtown near the Old Town Plaza. The Rio Grande greenbelt lies about a half mile southwest of Old Town.

Lomas and Central continue east across I-25, staying about a half mile apart as they pass by first the University of New Mexico, then the New Mexico State Fairgrounds. The airport is due south of the UNM campus, about 3 miles via Yale Boulevard. Kirtland Air Force Base—site of Sandia National Laboratories and the National Atomic Museum—is an equal distance south of the fairgrounds on Louisiana Boulevard.

Roughly paralleling I-40 to the north is Menaul Boulevard, focus of the Midtown and Uptown shopping and hotel districts. (Think of Midtown as extending from I-25 to San Mateo Boulevard, about $2^1/2$ miles, and Uptown from there to Eubank Boulevard, another 3 miles.) As Albuquerque expands northward, the Journal Center business park area, about $4^1/2$ miles north of the freeway interchange, is getting more attention. Broad San Mateo Boulevard links Journal Center with Midtown and Uptown. East of Eubank are the Sandia Foothills, where the alluvial plain slants a bit more steeply toward the mountain.

For address purposes, Central Avenue divides the city into north and south, and the railroad tracks—which run just east of First Street, downtown—split it into east and west. Street names are followed by a directional: NE, NW, SE, or SW.

The most comprehensive Albuquerque street map is the one published by Sun West Bank and distributed by the Convention and Visitors Bureau.

2 Getting Around

BY BUS   **Sun Tran of Albuquerque** (☎ 843-9200) cloaks the arterials with its city bus network. Call for information on routes and fares.

BY TAXI   **Albuquerque Cab** (☎ 883-4888), **Checker Cab** and **Yellow Cab** (☎ 247-8888 or 243-7777, for either) serve the city and surrounding area 24 hours a day.

BY CAR   The yellow pages list more than 30 **car-rental** agencies in Albuquerque. **Payless Car Rental** (☎ 247-9255) offers some of the best rates around. It's located one-eighth of a mile from the airport. Among the well-known national firms are **Alamo,** at the airport (☎ 842-4057), **Avis,** airport (☎ 842-4080), **Budget,** airport (☎ 768-5900), **Dollar,** airport (☎ 842-4224), **Hertz,** airport (☎ 842-4235). **Rent-a-Wreck,** 500 Yale Blvd. SE (☎ 242-9556), and **Thrifty,** 2039 Yale Blvd. SE (☎ 842-8733). Those not in the airport itself are nearby, and provide rapid airport pickup and delivery service.

When you return your vehicle to the rental agency, fill the tank before you get directly back to the airport. Service stations near the airport often jack their prices for gasoline up 33% higher than stations a mile or two away.

Parking is generally not difficult in Albuquerque—nor, for that matter, is rush hour a serious problem (yet). Meters operate from 8am to 6pm weekdays and are not monitored at other times. Most hotels do not charge for parking, with the exception of the large downtown properties.

BY BICYCLE   The wide streets and gentle slopes make Albuquerque an ideal city for cycling. There is a large network of designated bike lanes, as well as a citywide system of bike trails. However, be careful to obey all traffic laws when not in an area with designated bike lanes.

Numerous bicycle shops sell bikes and accessories, handle repairs, and supply parts. Among them is centrally located **Two Wheel Drive,** 1706 Central Ave. SE, near University Boulevard (☎ **243-8443**) and **Gardenswartz Sportz,** 2720 San Mateo Blvd. NE (☎ **884-6787**).

Fast Facts: Albuquerque

American Express   A travel service representative is the **Atlas Travel American Express Travel Agency,** 3412 Central Ave. NE (☎ **255-5558**). To report lost cards, call toll free **800/528-4800.** To report lost traveler's checks, call toll free **800/221-7282.**

Area Code   505.

Babysitters   Most hotels can arrange on request. Otherwise, try **Albuquerque Nursery and Kindergarten,** 3740 Eubank Blvd. NE (☎ **298-7564**); or **The Children's Center,** 4001 Montgomery Blvd. NE (☎ **881-9565**). Both offer sitting services from early morning to late night.

Business Hours   In general, Monday to Friday 9am to 5pm, with many stores also open Saturday.

Doctor   Presbyterian Hospital (☎ **841-1234**) makes referrals for visitors.

Drugstores   **Walgreens** offers 24-hour prescription service at 2950 Central Ave. SE (☎ **262-1745**).

Embassies & Consulates   See "Fast Facts: For the Foreign Traveler" in chapter 3.

Emergencies   For police, fire, or ambulance, dial **911.** For nonemergencies call **242-2677.**

Eyeglasses   Look for **LensCrafters,** 133 Winrock Center NE (☎ **889-3464**) or **Lens Express,** 4306 Lomas Blvd. NE (☎ **265-8846**). Both are open daily.

Hairdressers & Barbers   Many of the better hotels have in-house salons or can recommend nearby parlors. For budget watchers, **SuperCuts** has nine locations in Albuquerque, most of them in the northeastern part of the city. Consult your yellow pages.

Hospitals   The major facilities are **Presbyterian Hospital,** 1100 Central Ave. SE (☎ **841-1234,** emergency **841-1111**); and **University of New Mexico Hospital,** 2211 Lomas Blvd. NE (emergency ☎ **843-2411**). **Lovelace Medical Center,** 5400 Gibson Blvd. SE (☎ **262-7000,** emergency **262-7222**) has seven other urgent care facilities around the city, open daily 8am to 8pm year-round.

Information See "Information," chapter 2. The **Albuquerque Convention and Visitors Bureau** head office is at 121 Tijeras Ave. NE, Suite 1000 (P.O. Box 26866), Albuquerque, NM 87102 (☎ **505/243-3696** or toll free **800/284-2282**). Branch centers are at Albuquerque International Airport, at the lower level in front of the escalator, open 9:30am to 8pm daily; and in Old Town on Romero Street NW (in Plaza Don Luis), open Monday to Saturday 9am to 7pm, Sunday 10am to 5pm.

Laundry & Dry Cleaning Virtually all hotels provide either valet and laundry service or guest laundry facilities. A 24-hour self-service laundry is **Harold's Laundries,** 1500 Girard Blvd. NE (☎ **268-9834**).

Libraries The main branch of the **Albuquerque/Bernalillo County Public Library** is downtown at 501 Copper Ave. NW (☎ **768-5140**). There are 13 other branches, including the notable **Ernie Pyle Branch** at 900 Girard Ave. SE (☎ **256-2065**). The **University of New Mexico Libraries** are headquartered on campus near Central Avenue and University Boulevard (☎ **277-5761**).

Lost Property Contact city police (☎ **768-2020**).

Mail The main post office, 1135 Broadway NE (☎ **848-3872**), is open 8am to 4pm daily. There are 14 branch post offices, and another 13 in surrounding communities.

Newspapers & Magazines The two daily newspapers are the *Albuquerque Journal,* published mornings, and the *Albuquerque Tribune,* published evenings. *Albuquerque Monthly* magazine covers many aspects of city life and is widely available.

Photographic Needs **Kurt's Camera Corral,** with three locations, handles sales, repairs, rentals, and processing. Find them at 3417 Central Ave. NE (☎ **266-7766**); 6909 Menaul Blvd. NE, beside the Ramada Hotel Classic (☎ **883-5373**); and 1713 Juan Tabo Blvd. NE (☎ **296-4888**).

Police For emergencies, call **911.** For other business, contact Albuquerque City Police (☎ **768-2020**) or the New Mexico State Police (☎ **841-9256**).

Radio & TV Albuquerque has some 30 local radio stations catering to all musical tastes. Albuquerque television stations include KOB Channel 4 (NBC affiliate), KOAT Channel 7 (ABC affiliate), KGGM Channel 13 (CBS affiliate), KNME Channel 5 (PBS affiliate), and KGSW Channel 14 (FOX and independent). There are, of course, numerous local cable channels as well.

Religious Services **Anglican,** Church of St. Peter, Eubank and Paseo del Norte (☎ **822-1192**). **Assemblies of God,** First Family Church, 4701 Wyoming Blvd. (☎ **299-7202**). **Baptist,** First Baptist Church, 101 Broadway Blvd. NE (☎ **247-3611**). **Church of Christ,** Albuquerque Church of Christ, 1908 Sunshine Terrace SE (☎ **764-9277**). **Episcopal,** Episcopal Diocese of the Rio Grande, 4304 Carlisle Blvd. NE (☎ **881-0636**). **Jewish,** Congregation B'nai Israel, 4401 Indian School Rd. NE (☎ **266-0155**). **Lutheran,** St. Paul Lutheran Church, 1100 Indian School Rd. NE (☎ **242-5942**). **Methodist,** Central United Methodist Church, 1615 Copper Ave. NE (☎ **243-7834**). **Mormon,** 1100 Montano Rd. NW (☎ **345-7642**). **Nazarene,** Sandia Church of the Nazarene, 2801 Louisiana Blvd. NE (☎ **881-0267**). **Presbyterian,** La Mesa Presbyterian Church, 7401 Copper Ave. NE (☎ **255-8095**). **Roman Catholic,** San Felipe Church, 2005 Plaza NW, Old Town (☎ **243-4628**); Immaculate Conception Church, 619 Copper Ave. NW (☎ **247-4271**). **Seventh-day Adventist,** Central Seventh Day Adventist Church,

2201 Estancia Dr. NW (☎ **836-1845**). **United Church of Christ,** First Congregational Church, 2801 Lomas Blvd. NE (☎ **265-5749**).

3 Accommodations

New Mexico's largest city has some 9,000 hotel rooms. Although Albuquerque is growing as a convention destination, a high percentage of the rooms remain vacant during much of the year. That means visitors can frequently request, and obtain, a room rate lower than the one posted. The exceptions would be during peak periods—the New Mexico Arts & Crafts Fair in late June, the New Mexico State Fair in September, and the Kodak Albuquerque International Balloon Fiesta in early October—when hoteliers may raise their rates as much as 50% and still fill every room.

In the listings below, the following categories define price ranges: **very expensive,** over $120 per night double; **expensive,** $90 to $120; **moderate,** $60 to $90; **inexpensive,** $30 to $60; **budget,** less than $30 per night double. An additional 10.8125% tax is imposed on every hotel bill. Parking at most hotels is free (unless otherwise indicated).

Downtown/Old Town

This area is the best location to stay if you want to be close to many of the major sights and attractions. All of the following accommodations are between I-25 and the Rio Grande, and between I-40 and Route 66 (Central Avenue).

VERY EXPENSIVE

Hyatt Regency Albuquerque, 330 Tijeras Ave. NW, Albuquerque, NM 87102.
☎ **505/842-1234** or toll free **800/233-1234.** Fax 505/842-1184. 395 rms, 14 suites. A/C TV TEL

Rates: $115–$130 single; $140–$155 double; $310–$725 suite. Weekends $85 single or double. AE, CB, DC, DISC, MC, V. **Parking:** $7 self-parking; $11 valet.

This 20-story, $60-million property became a city landmark the day it opened in August 1990. The boldly appointed Hyatt makes a statement unlike any other in New Mexico. Marble pillars, Irish carpets, and an extensive use of mahogany contribute to the feeling of opulence. A pyramid skylight nourishes palms surrounding a fountain in the lobby. The hotel boasts a $500,000 collection of public art in contemporary and western genres, including an original sculpture by Frederic Remington.

Spacious rooms, decorated in mauves and forest greens, feature such touches as remote-control television, clock radios, full-length mirrors, mahogany desks, even data-port jacks for business travelers. In southwestern fashion, each boasts a potted cactus.

Dining/Entertainment: McGrath's, open daily from 6:30am to 2:30pm and 5 to 10pm, offers a gourmet grill menu in a rich atmosphere of black cherry and mahogany. A casual lounge adjoins the restaurant. A lobby bar has whimsical oil paintings on its walls, depicting saloons where the deer and the antelope play.

Services: Room service from 6am to midnight, concierge, valet laundry, courtesy van.

Facilities: Rooms for nonsmokers and the disabled, heated outdoor swimming pool, health club with massage service and large weight and exercise room, gift shop, several upscale art galleries, Delta airlines desk, Budget auto rental desk, hair salon, florist, optician, travel agency.

EXPENSIVE

Casas de Sueños, 310 Rio Grande Blvd. SW, Albuquerque, NM 87102.
☎ **505/247-4560** or toll free **800/CHAT-W/US.** 15 rms. TV TEL
Rates: $85–$200 single or double. AE, CB, DC, DISC, MC, V.

You'll know Casas de Sueños by the bright sign and the snail-shaped front of the main building (you'll know exactly what I mean when you see it, and you can't miss it). The buildings that comprise Casas de Sueños were once private homes—apparently they were something of an artists' colony. Most of them face a courtyard that was co-operatively maintained for many years by the residents. In the spring and summer, the gardens, filled with roses, are maintained by today's owners of Casas de Sueños, making the place a kind of oasis right in the middle of Albuquerque.

Each of the rooms has an individual theme: For instance, Cupid is done in black, white, and pink and has a claw-foot bathtub—a nice romantic getaway. La Cascada, so named because of the fountain outside its door, has a Monet theme with its pastel colors, Monet posters, and a Monet print comforter. The Kachina room has many little *kachinas* (storyteller dolls) scattered about. Some of the rooms have kitchens, and La Miradora has two bedrooms (with king- and queen-size beds), a living room with a fireplace, a full bath with a two-person Jacuzzi, and a back porch with a swing over-looking a golf course. All the rooms have private entrances.

Gordon and Maggie Johnston, the managers, serve a delicious full breakfast in the main building every morning. Works by local artists are displayed in the breakfast room. Guests have sports club privileges, and there is a massage therapist on premises. No smoking is permitted indoors. Pets are not accepted, but children 12 and older are welcome.

Doubletree Hotel, 201 Marquette St. NW, Albuquerque, NM 87102.
☎ **505/247-3344** or toll free **800/528-0444.** Fax 505/247-7025. 294 rms, 13 suites. A/C TV TEL
Rates (including breakfast): $74–$124 single; $84–$134 double. AE, CB, DC, DISC, ER, MC, V.

A pillared lobby with a marble floor—as well as a plateful of chocolate chip cookies—greets arrivals to this elegant property. But perhaps the most remarkable feature of the Doubletree, which adjoins the Albuquerque Convention Center, is the two-story waterfall that cascades against a marble backdrop from the lobby to the restaurant and lounge below. An underground passageway links the hotel to the convention center and a shopping mall.

All rooms in this 15-story hotel are decorated in pastel shades and southwestern designs, including custom-made furnishings. Each has a cable TV (with in-house mov-ies) hidden in an armoire, a clock radio, full mirror on the bathroom door, and a good-sized desk for business travelers.

Dining/Entertainment: La Cascada Restaurant is an airy coffee shop, with trees and mirrors making it appear larger than it is, open from 6am to 11pm daily. A vari-ety of food is served, from sandwiches and pastas to New Mexican specialties and meat, fish, and chicken main courses. Drinks are served in the Bistro Bar, adjacent to the waterfall; the Lobby Lounge, with its marble-top bar, has live music daily during happy hour (4:30–6:30pm).

Services: Room service from 6am to midnight, valet laundry, airport courtesy van.

Facilities: Rooms for nonsmokers and the disabled, swimming pool, weight room, gift/sundry shop, American Airlines ticket counter.

Central Albuquerque Accommodations

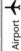 Airport

ALBUQUERQUE AREA

Hotel	No.
Albuquerque Central KOA	24
Albuquerque Hilton Hotel	8
Amberley Suite Hotel	2
Best Western Airport Inn	17
Best Western Fred Harvey	18
Best Western Winrock Inn	22
Casas de Sueños	11
Clubhouse Inn	9
Courtyard by Marriott	20
Doubletree Hotel	12
Hampton Inn	1
Holiday Inn Midtown	6
Holiday Inn Pyramid	3
Howard Johnson Plaza Hotel	4
Hyatt Regency Albuquerque	13
La Posada de Albuquerque	14
La Quinta Motor Inn	19
Le Baron Inn	5
Motel 6	7
Palisades RV Park	23
Plaza Inn	15
Radisson Inn	16
Sheraton Old Town	10
University Lodge	21

★ **La Posada de Albuquerque,** 125 2nd St. NW (at Copper St.), Albuquerque, NM 87102. ☎ **505/242-9090** or toll free **800/777-5732.** Fax 505/242-8664. 114 rms, 5 suites. A/C TV TEL

Rates: $88–$98 single; $98–$110 double; $180–$275 suite. AE, CB, DC, DISC, MC, V. **Parking:** Complimentary valet.

Built in 1939 by Conrad Hilton as the famed hotelier's first inn in his home state of New Mexico, this hotel is listed on the National Register of Historic Places. The atmosphere is of a 19th-century hacienda courtyard in old Mexico. In the center of the tile floor is an elaborate Moorish brass-and-mosaic tile fountain, and beyond it, a piano bar surrounded by plush leather-upholstered seating. Tin chandeliers hang from the two-story-high ceiling.

The guest rooms are somewhat outdated but equally charming. As in the lobby, all furniture is handcrafted, but here it's covered with cushions of stereotypically southwestern design. There are limited-edition lithographs by R. C. Gorman and Amado Pena on the white walls, and an ample desk opposite the wood-shuttered windows.

Dining/Entertainment: Conrad's Downtown features contemporary interpretations of traditional Spanish and Mexican recipes. You can dine in Conrad's casual art deco setting from 6:30am to 10pm everyday. In the evening, the Lobby Bar is a nice spot for a cocktail or after-dinner drink. On weekdays a pianist entertains during happy hour, and on Friday and Saturday you can enjoy the sounds of a jazz combo.

Services: Room service, valet laundry, 24-hour courtesy van.

Facilities: Rooms for nonsmokers and the disabled, gift shop.

Sheraton Old Town, 800 Rio Grande Blvd. NW, Albuquerque, NM 87104. ☎ **505/843-6300** or toll free **800/237-2133** or **800/325-3535.** Fax 505/842-9863. 190 rms, 20 suites. A/C MINIBAR TV TEL

Rates: $100–$110 single; $110–$120 double; $140 suite. Children free with adult. AE, CB, DC, MC, V.

Within five minutes' walk of the Old Town Plaza and overlooking two of Albuquerque's major museums, the Sheraton is an ideal spot for visitors without their own vehicles who don't want to be at the mercy of taxis or rental cars. Mezzanine-level windows light the adobe-toned lobby, which is separated from the Fireside Lounge by a double-sided fireplace.

Each guest room is characterized by a Pueblo Indian craft on the wall over the beds. Southwest colors are the preferred shades of decoration. All furniture, including dressers, desks, and chairs, is handmade. Southside rooms, facing Old Town, have private balconies.

Dining/Entertainment: The Customs House Restaurant, designed with a southwestern flair, is the main dining room. It specializes in seafood and regional cuisine, with dinner main courses priced in the $10 to $17 range. Open for lunch weekdays from 11:30am to 2pm; dinner daily from 5:30 to 10:30pm; Sunday champagne brunch from 11:30am to 2pm. Cafe del Sol is the Sheraton's coffeehouse; open daily from 6am to 9pm, its dinner main courses are priced from $6 to $12. Taverna Don Alberto, serving drinks off the main lobby, features dance bands Friday and Saturday nights.

Services: Room service, concierge, valet laundry, 24-hour courtesy van, secretarial, babysitting.

Facilities: Rooms for nonsmokers and the disabled, outdoor swimming pool and Jacuzzi, exercise room. Sheraton owns and operates Old Town Place, a shopping center to which it is directly connected. Shops include art dealers, bookstore, beauty salon, and manicurist.

MODERATE

The W. E. Mauger Estate, 701 Roma Ave. NW, Albuquerque, NM 87102.
☎ **505/242-8755.** 8 rms, 1 suite.

Rates (including full breakfast): $65–$95 single; $75–$115 double. AE, DC, MC, V.

A restored Queen Anne–style residence constructed in 1897, this former residence of wool baron William Mauger is listed on the National Register of Historic Places. Today it is a wonderfully atmospheric bed-and-breakfast, with high ceilings and rich brass appointments. It's located close to downtown, just five blocks from the convention center and only 5 miles from the airport. All rooms feature period furnishings, private baths and showers. Some also have a fireplace or balcony. A full breakfast is served each morning, in indoor and outdoor dining rooms, that includes tea or coffee, juice, freshly baked pastries, a hot egg dish, and a breakfast meat.

Midtown/Uptown

This area, which extends from I-25 to Eubank Boulevard, and between Central Avenue and Montgomery Boulevard, is a popular resting place for business travelers, shoppers, and other visitors seeking a central location. It includes Freeway Loop, which surrounds the interchange of I-25 and I-40; several major hotels are on Menaul or University boulevards nearby.

EXPENSIVE

Albuquerque Hilton Hotel, 1901 University Blvd. NE, Albuquerque, NM 87102.
☎ **505/884-2500** or toll free **800/27-HOTEL.** Fax 505/889-9118. 250 rms, 2 suites. A/C TV TEL

Rates: $91–$105 single; $95–$105 double; $375–$400 suite. AE, CB, DC, DISC, MC, V.

White stucco corridors with petroglyph-style paintings are a trademark of this hotel. Many of the rooms are in a high-rise tower which underwent a multimillion-dollar renovation in 1988. Two floors of rooms comprise a VIP level for business travelers; cabana rooms with 15-foot cathedral ceilings surround the outdoor pool.

Standard rooms, if there is such a thing, typically have maroon carpeting and peach walls with limited-edition prints by Susan Brooke. Furnishings include a queen-size bed, sofa bed, desk, dresser, satellite TV, full-wall mirror, radio/alarm clock, and two telephones—desk and bedside. No pets are allowed.

Restaurant/Entertainment: The Ranchers Club (see "Dining," below) is considered by many to be Albuquerque's number one restaurant. A less formal mealtime option is Casa Chaco, open daily from 6am to 10pm for coffee shop–style breakfasts and lunches, and highly regarded contemporary southwestern dinners. The Cantina, with its fajitas grill and piano bar, serves as the hotel lounge.

Services: Room service during restaurant hours, valet laundry, courtesy van.

Facilities: Rooms for nonsmokers and the disabled, indoor and outdoor swimming pools, whirlpool, saunas, tennis courts. Gift shop.

Holiday Inn Express, 10330 Hotel Ave. NE, Albuquerque, NM 87123.
☎ **505/275-8900.** Fax 505/275-6000. 104 rms, 7 suites. A/C TV TEL

Rates: $67.50–$125 single; $72.50–$125 double; $85–$135 suite for one; $90–$140 suite for two. AE, DC, DISC, V.

This souped-up version of the traditional Holiday Inn opened in February of 1994. Its primary focus is on the business traveler. Rooms have either two double beds or a king-size bed, and all come equipped with desks, phones with fax and data ports and voice mail, clock radios, and coffeepots for those who don't have time for breakfast but can't make it without their morning coffee. For those with time for breakfast, there's a complimentary breakfast bar in the lobby/breakfast room every morning. Laptop computers are available for rental at the front desk, and facilities include a fitness center with StairMasters and treadmills, an indoor pool, a Jacuzzi, and a sauna. Additionally, there's a courtyard with a gazebo for those who would like spend their free time relaxing out of doors. Smoking is not permitted in the rooms, and there are 15 different handicapped-accessible rooms, each of which is designed to cater to guests with specific disabilities. Pets are permitted at a charge of $5.

Residence Inn, 3300 Prospect Ave. NE, Albuquerque, NM 87107. ☎ **505/881-2661** or toll free **800/331-3131.** Fax 505/884-5551. 112 rms, all suites. A/C FRIDGE TV TEL

Rates (including continental breakfast): Weekdays $109 studio suite, $135 penthouse suite; weekends $89 studio suite, $114 penthouse suite. Weekly and monthly rates on request. AE, CB, DC, DISC, JCB, MC, V.

Located just off I-40 at its Carlisle Boulevard exit, this Marriott property caters to those planning extended stays. The average guest, in fact, makes the inn home for 10 nights. It's constructed like a condominium complex, with 8 units in each of 14 different buildings.

The suites are entirely residential, with full kitchens (refrigerator, stove, microwave, dishwasher, coffeemaker, toaster, and the like) and all utensils provided. Every living room has a wood-burning fireplace; each unit has its own water heater and air conditioner. Decor has a southwestern theme. Bedrooms contain either two queen-size beds or a king-size bed and a full working desk. Penthouse units feature a bedroom in a loft above the living area.

Dining/Entertainment: Continental breakfast is served in Gatehouse room off lobby. Social hour weekdays from 5:30 to 7pm, also in Gatehouse, includes complimentary buffet. No alcohol is served.

Services: Valet laundry, courtesy van, complimentary grocery-shopping service, free daily newspaper.

Facilities: Rooms for nonsmokers and the disabled, outdoor swimming pool, Jacuzzi, weight/exercise room, sports court, guest Laundromat.

MODERATE

Best Western Winrock Inn, 18 Winrock Center NE, Albuquerque, NM 87110. ☎ **505/883-5252** or toll free **800/866-5252.** Fax 505/889-3206. 174 rms, 4 suites. A/C TV TEL

Rates (including breakfast buffet): $55–$78 single or double; $85–$110 suite. AE, CB, DC, DISC, MC, V.

Located just off I-40 at the Louisiana Boulevard interchange, the Winrock is attached to Albuquerque's second-largest shopping center, Winrock Center. A hotel with prime appeal to international visitors, its two separate buildings are wrapped around a private lagoon and garden featuring Mandarin ducks, giant *koi* (carp), and an impressive waterfall.

The comfortable rooms, many of which have private patios overlooking the lagoon, feature a pastel southwestern-motif decor. There are rooms for nonsmokers and the disabled. The Club Room offers a breakfast buffet each morning and complimentary happy-hour drinks each evening. The hotel offers valet laundry, 24-hour courtesy van, a heated outdoor swimming pool, and guest Laundromat.

$ **Clubhouse Inn,** 1315 Menaul Blvd. NE at I-25, Albuquerque, NM 87107. ☎ **505/345-0010** or toll free **800/258-2466**. Fax 505/344-3911. 137 rms, 17 suites. A/C TV TEL

Rates (including breakfast): $63 single; $73 double; $80–$90 suite. Extra person $10. Children under 11 free with parent. AE, CB, DC, DISC, MC, V. **Parking:** Free.

The Clubhouse lobby sets the tone for the rest of the inn by looking just like a living room, complete with fireplace, sofas, and lush plants. Furnishings in each of the brightly appointed, oversized rooms include a freestanding desk with phone (free local calls), cable TV, and sofa or easy chair with ottoman. The suites include kitchenettes and numerous other special touches. Complimentary buffet breakfast served from 6:30 to 9am, and coffee, tea, and hot chocolate are available 24 hours a day. The hotel provides valet laundry service, rooms for nonsmokers and the disabled, a swimming pool, Jacuzzi, guest laundry, and barbecues.

Holiday Inn Midtown, 2020 Menaul Blvd. NE, Albuquerque, NM 87107. ☎ **505/884-2511** or toll free **800/545-0599** or **800/HOLIDAY**. Fax 505/881-4806. 363 rms. A/C TV TEL

Rates: $79–$89 single; $89–$99 double. Extra person $10. Children under 18 free in parents' room. AE, CB, DC, DISC, JCB, MC, V.

Nicely appointed rooms have all standard furnishings, including satellite television and radio/alarm clocks. The larger "king leisure" rooms are designed to accommodate business travelers. The Sandia Springs Restaurant, famous for its frequent all-you-can-eat buffets, is open daily from 6:30am to 2pm and 4 to 10pm. Lunches run $6.09 to $10.98; dinners, $6.95 to $13.95. It's adjoined by the popular Sandia Springs Lounge, featuring live country-and-western music nightly except Sunday. The Springwater Deli (open from 6am to 11pm daily) serves sandwiches and snacks under the atrium roof, and the adjacent Conversations Lounge offers drinks. The hotel has room service during restaurant hours, valet laundry, courtesy van, and rooms for nonsmokers; pets are permitted. Facilities include an indoor swimming pool, weight/exercise room, sauna, whirlpool, games room, guest Laundromat, gift shop.

INEXPENSIVE

Le Baron Inn, 2120 Menaul Blvd. NE, Albuquerque, NM 87107. ☎ **505/884-0250** or toll free **800/444-7378**. Fax 505/883-0594. 200 rms, 33 suites. A/C TV TEL

Rates: $55 single; $65 double; $85–$125 suite. AE, CB, DC, DISC, MC, V.

Of special note at this large, recently renovated motel are two dozen two-room suites, all of which have microwaves and refrigerators. A rich color scheme dominates the other rooms, which have standard furnishings including satellite TV and two phones, one in the bath; local calls are free. Free continental breakfast is served in the lobby each morning. The Village Inn, a 24-hour restaurant, is on adjoining property. The hotel offers valet laundry and 24-hour courtesy van service; 60% of rooms are designated for nonsmokers. No pets are permitted. Facilities include a swimming pool and a coin-op laundry.

Plaza Inn, 900 Medical Arts Ave. NE (at Lomas Blvd. and I-25), Albuquerque, NM 87102. ☎ **505/243-5693** or toll free **800/237-1307**. Fax 505/843-6229. 120 rms. A/C TV TEL

Rates: $50–$55 single, $60–$80 double. AE, CB, DC, DISC, MC, V.

Centrally located just east of downtown and west of the University of New Mexico campus, the Plaza offers amenities of larger, pricier hotels with the rates and convenience of a motel. Services include round-the-clock airport shuttle and lobby coffee service, secretarial assistance, meeting space for up to 60 people, and valet laundry. The inn has a heated outdoor swimming pool, a coin-op guest Laundromat, and pay in-house movies. Rooms are average size, with pastel decor and standard furnishings, including a working desk. Parking is free, and pets are accepted. JB's Restaurant and Lounge is adjacent.

BUDGET

Motel 6, 1701 University Blvd. NE at I-40, Albuquerque, NM 87102. ☎ **505/843-9228** or **505/891-6161.** 118 rms. A/C TV TEL

Rates: May–Oct $27.95 single, $39.95 double; Nov–Apr $23.95 single, $29.95 double. AE, DC, DISC, MC, V.

Typical of the 16 other members of this chain scattered around New Mexico, the midtown Motel 6 is a no-frills accommodation with the essentials for a comfortable stay. It's just big enough, it's clean, it has a phone and television, and there's even a swimming pool for summer afternoon dips.

Other Motel 6s in Albuquerque are at 13141 Central Ave. NE, I-40 at Tramway Boulevard Exit 67 (☎ **505/294-4600**), and 6015 Iliff Rd. NW, I-40 at Coors Road Exit 155 (☎ **505/831-3400**).

University Lodge, 3711 Central Ave. NE, Albuquerque, NM 87108.
☎ **505/266-7663.** 53 rms. A/C TV TEL

Rates: $19.95 single, $24.95 double. AE, CB, DC, DISC, ER, MC, V.

This Nob Hill property, a former TraveLodge six blocks east of UNM, is average in every way. Its pastel-decor rooms are adequate in size, clean, and comfortable, with standard motel furnishings. Complimentary morning coffee is available in the lobby, and there's an outdoor swimming pool, open seasonally. Rooms for nonsmokers and the disabled are available. Pets are discouraged.

Airport

This district lies south of Central Avenue (Route 66) and primarily east of I-25, and includes Kirtland Air Force Base and Albuquerque International Airport. Most accommodations here are along Yale or Gibson boulevards near the airport entrance.

MODERATE

Best Western Fred Harvey, 2910 Yale Blvd. SE, Albuquerque, NM 87106.
☎ **505/843-7000** or toll free **800/227-1117.** Fax 505/843-6307. 266 rms, 13 suites. A/C TV TEL

Rates: $80–94 single, $95–$104 double, $150–$300 suite. AE, CB, DC, DISC, MC, V.

No accommodation is closer to the airport than this Best Western, which is literally a stone's throw north of the main terminal. It caters to air travelers with a 24-hour desk and shuttle service, and overnight valet laundry.

Rooms are appointed in pastel decor with a southwestern flavor and are furnished with king-size or double beds, four-drawer dressers, leather easy chairs with ottomans, cable TV/radios, and phones (local calls are 50¢).

Lil's is an exclusive Victorian restaurant serving continental cuisine beneath crystal chandeliers. The Harvey House Restaurant offers breakfast, lunch, and dinner for more reasonable prices. Room service, courtesy van, valet laundry, complimentary shoeshine, and rooms for nonsmokers and the disabled are available. Pets are not permitted. Facilities include an outdoor swimming pool, coed sauna, two all-weather tennis courts, and a gift shop.

⭐ **Courtyard by Marriott,** 1920 Yale Blvd. SE, Albuquerque, NM 87106. ☎ **505/843-6600** or toll free **800/321-2211**. Fax 505/843-8740. 136 rms, 14 suites. A/C TV TEL

Rates: $79 single; $89 double; $84–$103 suite. Weekend packages available. AE, CB, DC, DISC, MC, V.

Opened in 1990, this four-story member of the Marriott family is built around an attractively landscaped courtyard reminiscent of a village green, complete with shake-roofed bandstand. The white-marbled lobby floor is also filled with greenery. Families appreciate the security system: Access is by key card only between 11pm and 6am.

The rooms feature walnut furniture and decor in pastel tones. Among the nicer touches are coffee and tea service from a 190-degree faucet, full-length mirrors, full-size writing desks, voice mail, clock radios, and massage showerheads. Refrigerators are available by request at no charge in any room.

The coffee shop, separated by planter boxes from the main lobby, is open Monday through Friday from 6 to 10am for breakfast and 5 to 10pm for dinner; Saturday and Sunday from 7 to 11am and 5 to 10pm. It features breakfast and lunch buffets, and a variety of all-American dinners priced from $6.95 to $12.50. An adjacent lounge opens from 4 to 11pm daily. The hotel provides valet laundry, courtesy van, and rooms for nonsmokers. Guest facilities include an indoor swimming pool, whirlpool, exercise room, and Laundromat.

Radisson Inn, 1901 University Blvd. SE, Albuquerque, NM 87106. ☎ **505/247-0512** or toll free **800/333-3333**. Fax 505/843-7148. 148 rms. A/C MINIBAR TV TEL

Rates: $75–$85 single; $85–$95 double. AE, CB, DC, DISC, MC, V.

The Spanish colonial–style Radisson is a mile from the airport. It's nice to be away from the hubbub, especially lounging on the spacious deck of the swimming pool in the center of the landscaped grounds. The newly renovated rooms are decorated in emerald green and navy blue, and are furnished with king- or queen-size beds, two-drawer credenzas, tables and chairs, and cable TV/radios.

Diamondback's Restaurant, open daily from 6am to 2pm and 5 to 10pm, specializes in steaks and regional dishes like pollo a la parrilla and trout Rio de Pecos. Breakfasts run from $4.75 to $7.50; lunches, $6.75 to $10.95; dinners, $9.95 to $15.95. The restaurant features live classical guitar Thursday through Saturday evenings. Coyote's Cantina is a popular watering hole.

The hotel offers room service from 6am to 10pm, valet laundry, and a 24-hour courtesy van. Rooms for nonsmokers are available; small pets are accepted. Guests enjoy a year-round outdoor swimming pool, whirlpool, lobby art gallery, and free use of a nearby health club.

INEXPENSIVE

Best Western Airport Inn, 2400 Yale Blvd. SE, Albuquerque, NM 87106. ☎ **505/242-7022** or toll free **800/528-1234**. Fax 505/243-0620. 120 rms. A/C TV TEL

Rates (including breakfast): $52–$59 single; $62–$69 double. AE, CB, DC, DISC, MC, V.

A landscaped garden courtyard behind the hotel is a lovely place to relax on cloudless days. The rooms, with dark brown carpets and beige-checkered bedspreads, contain standard furnishings and cable TV; local phone calls are free. Deluxe units have refrigerators and other special touches. Breakfast is served free in rooms, or guests can get a coupon good for $3 off their morning meal at the adjacent Village Inn. The hotel has a courtesy van on call from 6am to midnight, valet laundry, and nonsmoking and handicapped rooms. No pets are accepted. Guests may use the outdoor swimming pool and Jacuzzi, or a nearby health club.

La Quinta Motor Inn, 2116 Yale Blvd. SE, Albuquerque, NM 87106.
☎ **505/243-5500** or toll free **800/531-5900.** Fax 505/247-8288. 105 rms. A/C TV TEL

Rates: $58 single; $66 double. AE, CB, DC, DISC, ER, JCB, MC, V.

A *quinta* (pronounced "*keen*-ta") is a villa in the Spanish language, and like vacation homes, La Quinta motels—a 240-strong Texas-based chain—are friendly and gracious toward visitors.

Rooms are appointed in pleasant modern tones. Each has one king-size or two extra-long double beds, a credenza, a table and chairs, a satellite TV/radio with pay in-house movies, and individually controlled heating and air conditioning. Local phone calls are free. Rooms for nonsmokers and the disabled are available, and small pets are permitted. La Quinta has an outdoor swimming pool. Coffee is on 24 hours in the lobby, and Goody's restaurant is adjacent to the motel.

Other La Quinta Motor Inns in Albuquerque are located at 5241 San Antonio Dr. NE, off I-25 at Journal Center (☎ **505/821-9000,** fax 505/821-2399; 130 rooms); and at I-40 and San Mateo Boulevard (☎ **505/884-3591**; 106 rooms). All have the same rates and facilities, including adjacent restaurants.

Journal Center/North City

North of Montgomery Boulevard, the focal point is the I-25 interchange with Osuna Road and San Mateo Boulevard. On the west side of the freeway, the Journal Center business park is dominated by the giant pyramid of the Holiday Inn. East of the freeway, at San Mateo and Academy boulevards, numerous hotels, restaurants, and shopping complexes dominate.

EXPENSIVE

 Holiday Inn Pyramid, 5151 San Francisco Rd. NE, Albuquerque, NM 87109.
☎ **505/821-3333** or toll free **800/544-0623** or **800/HOLIDAY.**
Fax 505/828-0230. 312 rms, 60 suites. A/C TV TEL

Rates: $100–$130 single; $110–$140 double; $115–$300 suite. AE, CB, DC, DISC, JCB, MC, V.

Driving north from Albuquerque toward Santa Fe, you can't help being startled by the spectacular stepped Aztec pyramid that seems to rise from nowhere on the west side of the I-25 freeway. It's meant to catch your attention: This is a major hotel and convention complex. Reached via the Paseo del Norte Exit 232 from I-25, it's a monument to the possibilities of modern-day hotel architecture.

The 10 guest floors focus around a "hollow" skylit core. Vines drape from planter boxes on the balconies, and a fountain falls five stories between the two glass elevators to a pool below. The Aztec theme is perpetuated in the sand-and-cream-colored decor and the figures etched into the glass facing the fountain, opposite the entrance. The color scheme extends to the spacious rooms, furnished with king- or queen-size beds, two easy chairs, a desk, a four-drawer dresser, a fully lit dressing table, cable television with in-room movies, and a radio/alarm clock. Rooms with kitchenettes are available.

Dining/Entertainment: The Pyramid has two restaurants and two lounges. The Gallery is open for fine dining from 5:30 to 10pm nightly except Sunday. Main courses, priced from $12.50 to $24.25, include oysters Tasso in cream, boneless duck breast Chambord, and fresh salmon in raspberry and green-peppercorn sauce. The Terrace, an atrium cafe surrounded by greenery, is open from 6am to 2pm and 5 to 10pm daily; dinner prices top out at $23. The Palm Court, next to the Terrace, has a baby grand piano bar open until 10pm every day. The Pyramid Club attracts the younger set with a disc jockey providing video music for dancing until 2am Monday through Saturday nights.

Services: Room service, full-service concierge, 24-hour courtesy car, valet laundry.

Facilities: Rooms for nonsmokers and the disabled, indoor/outdoor swimming pool, sauna, two whirlpools, health club with weights and exercise room. Jogging trails wind through the 313-acre Journal Center business park.

Amberley Suite Hotel, 7620 Pan American Fwy. NE, Albuquerque, NM 87109. ☎ **505/823-1300** or toll free **800/333-9806**. Fax 505/823-2896. 170 rms, all suites. A/C FRIDGE TV TEL

Rates: $94–$104 single or double, $20 higher during balloon fiesta. Discounts for longer stays, weekend arrivals, or corporate or government travelers. Extra person $10. AE, CB, DC, DISC, MC, V.

Every room in the recently renovated Amberley Suite Hotel is a one- or two-room suite. They're fully carpeted units, most with a living room/kitchenette and separate bedroom; the deluxe king is an efficiency studio with a kitchen area. Kitchen facilities include a refrigerator filled with complimentary beverages, microwave oven, coffeemaker, pots, pans, and utensils. Each living room has a swivel rocker with an ottoman and cable television. Every bathroom is provided with a built-in hairdryer. Watson's Cafe and Deli, open from 6am to 10pm daily, serves an all-you-can-eat breakfast buffet ($5.95) until 10am and a summer patio barbecue Tuesday through Thursday from 5 to 9pm. The hotel manager hosts a happy-hour reception Wednesday at 5:30pm with cocktails, hors d'oeuvres, live music, and trivia games. The hotel also provides a 24-hour courtesy car (within 2-mile radius), free airport shuttle, valet laundry, rooms for nonsmokers and the disabled. Guest facilities include an outdoor swimming pool, sauna, hot tub, weight/exercise room, and Laundromat.

MODERATE

Howard Johnson Plaza Hotel, 6000 Pan American Fwy. NE at San Mateo Blvd., Albuquerque, NM 87109. ☎ **505/821-9451** or toll free **800/446-4656**. Fax 505/858-0239. 150 rms, 12 suites. A/C TV TEL

Rates: $48–$110 single; $58–$145 double; $75–$145 suite. Various discount packages available. AE, CB, DC, DISC, MC, V.

Howard Johnson's doesn't try to be as grand as the Pyramid, but it does have a five-story lobby atrium with fountains of its own. A three-story-high tapestry reminds visitors of Albuquerque's obsession with hot-air ballooning, and there are old-fashioned flower-topped lampposts on the mezzanine deck.

Private balconies are an outstanding feature of every room. They've got all standard furnishings, including remote-control cable TV. Earl's Cafe, open from 6am to 2pm and 5 to 9pm daily, offers southwestern meals ($5 to $14). The Atrium Lounge has a big-screen TV for watching sports events and a top-40 DJ for dancing. The hotel offers room service during restaurant hours, a 24-hour courtesy van, valet laundry, and rooms for nonsmokers and the disabled. Pets are permitted with manager's prior approval. Facilities include an indoor/outdoor swimming pool, sauna, Jacuzzi, weight/ exercise room, guest laundry, and gift shop.

INEXPENSIVE

Hampton Inn, 5101 Ellison NE, Albuquerque, NM 87109. ☎ **505/344-1555** or toll free **800/HAMPTON.** Fax 505/345-2216. 125 rms. A/C TV TEL

Rates (including continental breakfast): $54–$56 single; $59–$63 double. Children under 18 stay free in parents' room. AE, CB, DC, DISC, MC, V.

These sound-insulated rooms offer cost-conscious travelers standard furnishings, remote-control cable TV, and free local phone calls. The inn has an outdoor swimming pool, and guests have free use of health club located one mile away. This hotel is a particularly good choice for those attending the annual balloon fiesta in October, or for people who are planning trips to Santa Fe. It's okay to bring your pet. The coffeepot is on in the lobby 24 hours.

Bed & Breakfasts on the Outskirts ─────────────────────

Casa del Granjero, 414 C de Baca Ln. NW, Albuquerque, NM 87114.
☎ **505/897-4144.** 3 rms (all with bath).
Rates: $87–$107 double. Extra person $20. MC, V.

From the potbelly pig to the old restored wagon out front, Casa del Granjero, meaning "the Farmer's House," is true to its name. It might come as more of a surprise, however, that the innkeepers actually are the Farmers—Butch and Victoria Farmer—and they have transformed their home into an exquisite bed and breakfast. The great room has an enormous sculpted adobe fireplace, comfortable bancos for lounging around, a library, and scores of Old West and Native American artifacts. As a guest at Casa del Granjero, you might want to curl up in front of the fire and read a book or listen to Butch's stories about a Native American fighter relative who was a scout for George Washington. If you'd rather spend a couple of hours watching a movie but are too tired to head back into downtown Albuquerque, the 52-inch television in the den fills the bill. The three guest rooms all have *kiva* fireplaces and are beautifully furnished. Cuarto del Rey, with queen-size and day beds, features Mexican furnishings and handmade quilts and comforters. Cuarto de Flores has French doors that open onto a portal, and Cuarto Alegre (the largest of the rooms) has a king-size canopy bed done up in lace and satin. All the bathrooms are unique and quite beautiful. The one in Cuarto Alegre has wooden beams, corbels, and handmade Mexican tiles. In the morning, breakfast is served at the spectacular dining room table or on the portal. It includes fresh fruit, homemade pastries and breads, and a hot main course. There is an outdoor hot tub available for guest use. Smoking is permitted outdoors only, and pets are not permitted.

La Hacienda Grande, 21 Baros Ln., Bernalillo, NM 87004. ☎ **505/867-1887.**
6 rms (all with bath).
Rates: $79–$110 double. Extra person $15. MC, V.

La Hacienda Grande, run by brother-and-sister team Daniel Buop and Shoshana Zimmerman, opened in October of 1993. The inn has a wonderful history: Situated on 4 acres of land that were once part of the original 100-square-mile Spanish land grant, the completely restored adobe home is over 250 years old and has two-foot-thick walls. It was one of two original stagecoach stops and is said to have had the very first adobe stables and corral (built to prevent Native Americans from stealing the horses). Today's kitchen served as a chapel before any churches were built, and the courtyard, surrounded by high adobe walls, has a vortex that once had special significance to the Native Americans who came here often to pray and hold ceremonies. The owners recently learned that during the Civil War gold and silver were often stored here—the walled courtyard, with a roofline that could be easily patrolled, was a perfect fortress.

All of the guest-room furnishings were custom-crafted for the inn. Much of the furniture is made of bent willow, which lends a rustic air to the hacienda. One room has a queen-size wrought-iron canopy bed; all rooms have small sitting areas and southwestern-style armoires, and four have wood-burning *kiva* fireplaces. Brick or tile floors are covered with throw rugs. Every morning at 7:30, thermoses of coffee are left outside guest-room doors. Breakfast is served between 8 and 8:45am and usually consists of homemade breads, specialty honeys, fresh-ground coffees, egg dishes, fruit, and granola—the emphasis here is on healthy eating. Guests may make use of the living room, which has a TV and VCR available for use. Tea and snacks are served in the afternoon. Children under 11 are not permitted, and smoking is prohibited except on the patio.

Hacienda Vargas, El Camino Real (P.O. Box 307), Algodones, NM 87001.
☎ **505/867-9115.** 4 rms (all with bath).
Rates: $69–$129 double. Extra person $15. MC, V.

Unassuming in its elegance, Hacienda Vargas is located right on old Route 66. Owned and operated by the DeVargas family, the inn is situated in the small town of Algodones, about 20 miles from Albuquerque. It's a good place to stay if you're planning on spending time in both Santa Fe and Albuquerque, but don't want to stay in one of the downtown hotels in either city. The walls in the entry hallway are hung with the works of local artists (for sale), and each of the guest rooms has a private entrance. All rooms are furnished with New Mexican antiques; each is individually decorated, and all have handmade *kiva* fireplaces. The Wagner Room, the largest of the four, looks out onto the courtyard and features a Jacuzzi tub with a skylight view. The Pinon Room has direct access to the outdoor hot tub in addition to having it's own beautiful antique claw-foot bathtub. The main attraction in the Pena Room is the unique bed and headboard, and the Pueblo Room has authentic adobe walls. Hosts Julie and Paul DeVargas are extremely gracious, friendly, and helpful—they'll make you feel right at home in their home. A full breakfast is served every morning in the dining room. The only drawback here is that train tracks run directly parallel to the back of the house—during my stay the last train went by at around midnight. At all other times, the inn is very quiet and restful.

Camping

Albuquerque Central KOA, 12400 Skyline Rd. NE, Albuquerque, NM 87123.
☎ **505/296-2729.**

200 sites, bathhouse, guest laundry, outdoor swimming pool (open summers only), convenience store. Cabins available.

Albuquerque North KOA, 555 Hill Rd., Bernalillo, NM 87004. ☎ **505/867-5227.**

101 sites, laundry, outdoor swimming pool (open May to October), playground, convenience store, cafe, free outdoor movies. Free pancake breakfast daily. Reservations recommended.

American RV Park of Albuquerque, I-40 west at Exit 149, Albuquerque, NM 87121. ☎ **505/831-3545.**

186 sites, picnic area, bathhouse, guest laundry, heated swimming pool, playground, outdoor games area, movies, convenience store.

Palisades RV Park, 9201 Central Ave. NW, Albuquerque, NM 87121.
☎ **505/831-5000.**

110 sites, bathhouse, guest laundry, recreation room, small convenience store, propane available. Near Old Town.

4 Dining

In these listings, the following categories define price ranges: **very expensive**—most dinner main courses over $20; **expensive**—most dinner main courses $15 to $20; **moderate**—most dinner main courses $10 to $15; **inexpensive**—most dinner main courses $6 to $10; **budget**—most dinner main courses under $6.

Downtown/Old Town

MODERATE

Artichoke Cafe, 424 Central Ave. SE. ☎ **243-0200.**

> **Cuisine:** CONTINENTAL. **Reservations:** Recommended.
> **Prices:** Appetizers $4.50–$5.95; dinner $8.95–$19.95. AE, CB, DC, MC, V.
> **Open:** Lunch Mon–Fri 11am–2:30pm; dinner Mon–Sat 5:30–10pm.

The no-frills decor is clean and tasteful, with modern-art prints on azure walls, white linens on tables shaded by standing plants, and classical music playing in the background. Start your meal with an artichoke appetizer, then go on to a main dish like baked chicken stuffed with goat cheese, spinach, and roasted red pepper, or New Zealand mussels with sweet Italian sausage in white wine. Crêpes, pastas, salads, and sandwiches are popular at lunch. The cafe has an excellent list of California and French wines.

High Noon, 425 San Felipe St. NW. ☎ **765-1455.**

> **Cuisine:** STEAKS, SEAFOOD & NEW MEXICAN. **Reservations:** Recommended.
> **Prices:** Appetizers $3–$7.95; main courses $8.50–$18.50. AE, CB, DC, DISC, MC, V.
> **Open:** Mon–Sat 11am–3pm and 5–10pm, Sun noon–9pm.

One of Albuquerque's oldest existing buildings, this restaurant boasts a 19th-century saloon atmosphere with stucco walls, high and low ceiling beams, and historical photos on the walls. One photo depicts the original 1785 structure, which now comprises the building's foyer and *santo* room. Additional rooms were added in the late 1960s.

The dinner menu offers a choice of beef dishes, like the house-specialty pepper steak sautéed with brandy; fish dishes, including red trout with avocado margarita salsa; game dishes, including buffalo, venison, and caribou; and regional favorites, among

Central Albuquerque Dining

them burritos and enchiladas. Sandwiches dominate the lunch menu, along with fine salads and pastas.

La Hacienda Restaurant, 302 San Felipe St. NW, at North Plaza. ☎ 242-3131.

Cuisine: NEW MEXICAN & AMERICAN. **Reservations:** For large parties.
Prices: Appetizers $3.50–$6.25; main courses $8.95–$16.95. AE, DC, MC, V.
Open: Daily, lunch 11am–4pm; dinner 4–9pm.

A mural on La Hacienda Restaurant's outer wall tells of the establishment of the city of Albuquerque and the construction of this Villa de Albuquerque at the turn of the 18th century. The cozy restaurant within is approached through a large and interesting gift shop; adorned with hanging plants and chile *ristras*, the room has an intimate, laid-back atmosphere. Outside seating faces the San Felipe de Neri church.

The menu is predominantly regional, with house specialties including beef or chicken fajitas, carne adovada, tostadas compuestas, and tortilla-chile soup. Steaks, shrimp, and other American meals also are offered. Guitarists play daily beginning at noon. La Hacienda has a full-service bar.

★ **Maria Teresa**, 618 Rio Grande Blvd. NW. ☎ 242-3900.

Cuisine: CONTEMPORARY AMERICAN. **Reservations:** Recommended.
Prices: Appetizers $3.95–$7.25; main courses $10–$21. AE, MC, V.
Open: Daily 11am–9pm.

The city's most beautiful and classically elegant restaurant, Maria Teresa is located in the 1840s Salvador Armijo House, a national historic property furnished with Victorian antiques and paintings. Built with 32-inch adobe bricks, the house exemplifies 19th-century New Mexico architecture, when building materials were few and defense a prime consideration. The house had 12 rooms, 7 of which (along with a large patio) are now reserved for diners. Another room is home to the 1840 Bar and Lounge.

The menu features salads, pastas, and sandwiches for lunch. A wide range of gourmet dinners is available, from raspberry chicken to fresh salmon with tequila lime butter, and from baby back ribs to regional dishes like carne y pollo asada burrito. Dinner is usually $16.25, including cover charge.

Stephen's, 1311 Tijeras Ave. NW (at 14th and Central). ☎ 842-1773.

Cuisine: CONTEMPORARY AMERICAN. **Reservations:** Recommended.
Prices: Appetizers $4.95–$8.95; main courses $15.95–$24.95. AE, MC, V.
Open: Lunch Mon–Fri 11am–2pm; dinner Sun–Thurs 5:30–9:30pm, Fri–Sat 5:30–10:30pm.

Big bay windows face Central Avenue, and foliage shades an enclosed patio. This modern, open, airy restaurant was inspired by Mexico City's Hacienda Angel and features interior decor by the noted designer Richard Worthen.

The eclectic menu is described as "fresh American and southwestern ingredients prepared with continental inspiration." Dishes include everything from scallops Provençale to braised lamb shank, veal schnitzel to stuffed tortellini, poached trout with piñon nuts to New York strip steak. Homemade pastas, salads, and Mexican foods are served at lunch. Stephen's also has a full bar.

INEXPENSIVE

$ **Catalina's**, 400 San Felipe St. NW. ☎ 842-6907.

Cuisine: NEW MEXICAN.
Prices: $3.50–$7.95. MC, V.

Open: Breakfast Mon–Sat 8–11am; lunch daily 11am–2pm; dinner daily (summer only) 4–8pm; open Sun 8am–4pm. **Closed:** Usually mid-Jan to Mar.

Right in the heart of Old Town in an old adobe home, set back in the rear of the Patio San Felipe del Norte courtyard, is this oft-overlooked gem. The white stucco interior, covered with Mexican handcrafts, still has its original log beams. All meals are homemade by Catalina Walsh; the chile rellenos are superb, as are the tacos, tostadas, enchiladas, and other New Mexican specialties.

La Placita, 208 San Felipe St. NW at South Plaza. ☎ **247-2204.**

Cuisine: NEW MEXICAN & AMERICAN. **Reservations:** For large parties.
Prices: Lunch $4.25–$6.95; dinner $5.25–$13.25. AE, DISC, MC, V.
Open: Daily 11am–9pm. (Hours vary according to business.)

Native American artisans spread their wares on the sidewalk outside here, the old Casa de Armijo, built by a wealthy Hispanic family in the early 18th century. The adobe hacienda, which faces the Old Town Plaza, features hand-carved wooden doorways, sunken windows, and an ancient patio. Fine regional art and furnishings decorate the five dining rooms and an upstairs gallery.

The house favorite is a full Mexican dinner ($9.35) that includes an enchilada Colorado de queso, chile relleno, taco de carne, frijoles con queso, arroz español, ensalada, and two sopaipillas. There is also a variety of beef, chicken, and fish main courses, including a 14-ounce New York–cut steak ($13.25) and sandwiches. Children's plates are available. The restaurant is licensed to serve beer and wine only.

Midtown/Uptown

EXPENSIVE

Nob Hill Bistro, 3118 Central SE. ☎ **255-5832.**

Cuisine: CONTINENTAL. **Reservations:** Recommended.
Prices: Appetizers $5.95–$6.50; main courses $14.50–$19.50.
Open: Lunch Mon–Fri 11:30am–2pm; dinner Mon–Thurs 5:30–9pm, Fri–Sat 5:30–10pm. DISC, MC, V.

For fine dining in an intimate bistro setting, Nob Hill Bistro, located in historic Nob Hill, is a perfect choice. The small dining room is bright and comfortable, with no more than a dozen white-clothed tables, and the service is extremely attentive. I recommend that you start with the classic French onion soup. With a puff pastry topping, it's like no other you've ever had. The peppered beef carpaccio or creamed leek and crab baked in phyllo and served with a lemon chervil hollandaise are also excellent ways to start your meal. For a main course I had the sautéed sterling salmon with a lemon dill compound butter, which was excellent. Other offerings include chicken breast stuffed with goat cheese, basil, and a Mediterranean sauce; sautéed pork chop with herb jus lié; and sautéed duck breast and duck leg confit with marjoram glace de canard. Dessert selections vary daily, but I had a delightfully light (but very rich) flourless chocolate torte with a raspberry coulis. The wine list is excellent.

 Ranchers Club, in the Albuquerque Hilton Hotel, 1901 University Blvd. NE. ☎ **884-2500.**

Cuisine: CONTINENTAL. **Reservations:** Recommended, especially at dinner.
Prices: Appetizers $5.95–$9.95; lunch $5.95–$10.95; dinner $18.95–$28. AE, CB, DC, DISC, MC, V.

Open: Lunch Mon–Fri 11:30am–2pm; Sun brunch buffet 10am–2pm; Dinner Mon–Thurs 5:30–10pm, Fri–Sat 5:30–10:30pm, Sun 5:30–9pm.

Like a British hunting lodge transplanted to the high plains, the Ranchers Club creates a mood of western elegance with its polished oak decor, flagstone fireplace, and remarkable longhorn chandelier. Established in 1986 to offer Albuquerque "something unique and different," the Club consistently ranks number one in the list of the city's favorite restaurants.

But the food outdoes the atmosphere, thanks in part to its unique preparation over aromatic woods. Dilled cucumber complements swordfish, for instance, and garlic butter is great with lobster or steak. Then there's the "small" (14-ounce) New York sirloin, grilled over sassafras with wild mushroom sauce, and Norwegian salmon, grilled over mesquite with curried apple chutney. All main courses are served with a choice of vegetables.

MODERATE

Cafe Oceana, 1414 Central Ave. SE. ☎ **247-2233.**

Cuisine: SEAFOOD. **Reservations:** Recommended.
Prices: Appetizers $3.95–$6.95; main courses $11.95–$13.95. Oysters $4.75 per half dozen, $8.95 per dozen. AE, MC, V.
Open: Lunch Mon–Fri 11am–3pm; dinner Mon–Thurs 5–11pm. Fri–Sat 5–11:30pm. Oyster hour Mon–Thurs 3–6:30pm and 10–11pm Fri 3–6:30pm and 10:30–11:30pm, Sat 5–7pm and 10:30–11:30.

Cafe Oceana is and has been Albuquerque's favorite oyster bar and fresh seafood cafe for years. In a New Orleans–style atmosphere in a dining room with high ceilings and hardwood floors, you can enjoy fresh oysters, fresh fish daily, scallops, crab rellenos (for the New Mexican touch), and the house special, shrimp Oceana (beer-batter fried shrimp). If you're really in the mood for New Orleans cuisine, you can also get some red beans and rice here.

Cooperage, 7220 Lomas Blvd. NE. ☎ **255-1657.**

Cuisine: STEAKS & SEAFOOD. **Reservations:** Recommended.
Prices: Lunch $4–$8; dinner $9–$22. AE, CB, DC, DISC, MC, V.
Open: Lunch Mon–Fri 11am–2:30pm, Sat noon–2:30pm; dinner Mon–Thurs 5–10pm, Fri–Sat 5–11pm, Sun noon–9pm. **Closed:** Christmas Day.

The Cooperage is shaped to make you feel as if you're in a gigantic beer barrel. Circular and wood paneled, its walls are decorated with reproductions of 19th-century paintings and depictions of coopers at work making barrels.

The dinner menu features a variety of seafood and beef dishes, including trout parmesan and prime rib. The restaurant also has a great 30-item salad bar, and is fully licensed. There's live music for dancing Wednesday through Saturday nights.

Cooperage West is at 10200 Corrales Rd. NW, in Corrales (☎ **898-5555**).

★ **Monte Vista Fire Station,** 3201 Central Ave. NE, Nob Hill. ☎ **255-2424.**

Cuisine: CONTEMPORARY AMERICAN. **Reservations:** Recommended.
Prices: Appetizers $4.95–$6.95; main courses $8.95–$19.95. AE, MC, V.
Open: Lunch Mon–Fri 11am–2:30pm; dinner Sun–Thurs 5–10:30pm, Fri–Sat 5–11pm. Bar open to 2am Mon–Sat, to midnight Sun.

The Fire Station has been a city landmark since it was built in pure Pueblo Revival style in 1936. Its occupants no longer make fire calls, however—they concentrate instead on serving a unique menu in an art deco setting. Both the lunch and dinner menus focus on creative cookery. Luncheon diners can start with crab cakes and goat cheese, then go on to sliced sirloin with green peppercorn and cognac cream. Popular dinner appetizers are zucchini squash blossoms filled with ricotta and sun-dried tomatoes served with baby greens, pancetta, and balsamic vinaigrette; and grilled duck and pepper sausage with zinfandel sauce. Main courses include grilled marinated lamb chops with a cucumber-yogurt sauce, and quail with wild mushrooms in a tawny port sauce. Try the tiramisu for dessert.

There's a popular singles bar on the fourth-story landing.

Scalo, 3500 Central Ave. SE, Nob Hill. ☎ **255-8782.**

Cuisine: NORTHERN ITALIAN. **Reservations:** Recommended.
Prices: Appetizers $2.50–$7.50; main courses $6.95–$15.95. AE, MC, V.
Open: Lunch Mon–Fri 11:30am–2:30pm; dinner Mon–Sat 5–11pm. Bar open Mon–Sat 11am–1am.

Scalo has a simple bistro-style elegance, with white linen–covered indoor tables and outdoor seating on a covered, temperature-controlled patio. The kitchen, which makes its own pasta and breads, specializes in contemporary adaptations of classic northern Italian cuisine. Featured appetizers are calamaretti fritti (fried baby squid with garlic aioli) and caprini con pumante (goat cheese with toast, sun-dried tomatoes, capers, and roasted garlic). There's a fine selection of pastas for both lunch and dinner, and a choice of meat, chicken, and fish dishes—among them pollo casino (grilled chicken with prosciutto, provolone, tomato, and arugula served on focaccia) and filetto con salsa balsamica (grilled filet of beef with fresh garlic, green peppercorns, and balsamic sauce). Dessert selections change daily. The wine list focuses on Italian imports and California wines.

INEXPENSIVE

Adam's Table, 3619 Copper NE. ☎ **266-4214.**

Cuisine: VEGETARIAN. **Reservations:** Not required.
Prices: Main courses $5.50–$7.50.
Open: Sun–Thurs 7am–9pm, Fri 7am–3pm. DISC, MC, V.

Located in the historic Nob Hill district, just off Central Avenue, Adam's Table bills itself as "a true vegetarian restaurant," whose aim is "to educate [diners] on the wonderful principles of health: proper diet, rest, exercise, pure water, sunshine, temperance, and trust in divine power." After a meal there, I can honestly say that they truly succeed in the area of "proper diet." Mexican specialties include whole wheat quesadillas smothered with sour cream, guacamole, cheese, and tomato; chile rellenos (not fried) with cashew cheese; and Adam's burrito (fried potato, tomato, green pepper, and onions, served with avocado or guacamole). All Mexican specialties are served with beans and rice and red or green chile. Other menu items include spinach or sesame noodles with pesto; pizza with bell peppers, onions, soy sauce, and olives; and an oat burger (a blend of brown rice, rolled oats, and sunflower seeds). There's an "all-you-should-eat" breakfast, lunch, and dinner buffet as well as a salad bar. Adam's offers a nice selection of natural juices, sodas, and teas, as well as tofu milk and fruit smoothies.

Chili's Grill & Bar, 6909 Menaul Blvd. NE. ☎ **883-4321.**

Cuisine: TEX-MEX.
Prices: Appetizers $2.25–$5.25; main courses $4.95–$9.95. AE, CB, DC, DISC, MC, V.
Open: Mon–Thurs 11am–10:30pm, Fri–Sat 11am–11:30pm, Sun 11:30am–10pm.

A casual bar and grill adjacent to the Ramada Classic Hotel, Chili's is like a small greenhouse. There are plants in baskets and pots, standing and hanging, dispersed among the antique bric-a-brac suspended from the ceilings or on shelves high above the red tile floors. The menu focuses on hamburgers (like the verde burger, with guacamole) and southwestern grill—fajitas, chicken, ribs, steaks, and the like. There are also salads, sandwiches, and chili. The bar, which has a happy hour from 3 to 6pm weekdays, is noted for its margaritas.

$ **India Kitchen,** 6910 Montgomery Blvd. NE. ☎ **884-2333.**

Cuisine: INDIAN. **Reservations:** Suggested at dinner.
Prices: Dinner $6.95–$9.95. AE, CB, DISC, MC, V.
Open: Dinner Mon–Thurs and Sun 5–9pm, Fri–Sat 5–9:30pm.

In a shopping strip near Louisiana Boulevard you'll find this little restaurant, the pride and joy of Ajay Gupta, a 20-year U.S. resident who left his job as a Chicago engineer to start cooking. And he does it well! Main courses, all served with *pullao* (rice), *puri* (wheat bread), and *bhujia* (mixed vegetables), include *korma* (beef with almonds, pecans, and sour cream) and shrimp curry in coconut-cream sauce. There are also vegetarian dishes like jackfruit *vindaloo* or chickpea curry. Wash your meal down with a yogurt *lassi*. Raga music from sitars plays continuously in the background as you dine, and there are Mogul-style paintings and batiks on the walls.

BUDGET

Double Rainbow, 3416 Central Ave. SE. ☎ **255-6633.**

Cuisine: CAFE/BAKERY. **Reservations:** Not accepted.
Prices: All items under $10.
Open: Mon–Sat 6:30am–midnight, Sun 6:30am–11pm.

If you're a people watcher worth your salt, you can't miss a visit to the Double Rainbow, located in Albuquerque's historic Nob Hill district. Of course, that's not the only reason to stop in—Double Rainbow has great sandwiches, ice cream, and coffee, too. And, one of the best things about this place is its enormous selection of magazines. In fact, there are over 700 titles, ranging from comic books to film and fashion magazines to a travel magazine for gays and lesbians. Not only will you find architectural magazines, but you'll also find *Tricycle* (a Buddhist review), and *Blues Review Quarterly*. A selection of newspapers spans the globe as well. No one will feel out of place here!

$ **ej's,** 2201 Silver Ave. SE. ☎ **268-2233.**

Cuisine: VEGETARIAN/NATURAL FOOD.
Prices: Breakfast $2.50–$5.95; lunch $3.95–$7.50; dinner $5.25–$8.75. MC, V.
Open: Mon–Thurs 7am–11pm, Fri 7am–midnight, Sat 8am–midnight, Sun 8am–9:30pm.

A popular coffeehouse just a couple of blocks from the UNM campus, ej's roasts its own specialty coffees—and also caters to natural-foods lovers. Breakfasts include granola and croissants from ej's own bakery. Lunch features homemade vegetarian soups, tempeh burgers, organic turkey sandwiches, and cheese enchiladas. The gourmet dinner menu lists shrimp linguine, spinach fettuccine Alfredo, Monterey chicken, and a vegetarian stir-fry.

$ **66 Diner,** 1405 Central Ave. NE. ☎ **247-1421.**

Cuisine: AMERICAN.
Prices: $3–$5.95. AE, DISC, MC, V.
Open: Mon–Thurs 9am–11pm, Fri 9am–midnight, Sat 8am–midnight, Sun 8am–10pm.

Like a trip back in time to the days when Martin Milner and George Maharis got "their kicks on Route 66," this thoroughly 1950s-style diner comes complete with Seeburg jukebox and full-service soda fountain. The white caps make great hamburgers, along with meat-loaf sandwiches, grilled liver and onions, and chicken-fried steaks. Ham-and-egg and pancake breakfasts are served every morning. Beer and wine are available.

Airport

MODERATE

Rio Grande Yacht Club, 2500 Yale Blvd. SE. ☎ 243-6111.
> **Cuisine:** SEAFOOD. **Reservations:** Suggested at dinner.
> **Prices:** Appetizers $1.95–$8.95; main courses $4.50–$7.95 at lunch; $9.95–$14.50 at dinner. AE, CB, DC, MC, V.
> **Open:** Lunch Mon–Fri 11am–2pm; dinner daily 5:30–10:30pm.

Red-white-and-blue sails are draped beneath the skylight of this large room, which is dominated by a tropical garden. The walls are of wood strips like those of a ship's deck, and yachting prints and photos hang on the walls. The intercom pipes the music of Jimmy Buffett and other soft-rock performers. Buffett, the contemporary sailor's chanteur, couldn't have created a better milieu for the Caribbean yachtsman–wannabe.

Fresh fish, of course, is the order of the day. Catfish, whitefish, bluefish, salmon, grouper, sole, mahimahi, and other denizens of the deep are prepared in a variety of ways—broiled, poached, blackened, teriyaki, Veracruz, au gratin, Mornay, amandine, and more. Diners can also opt for shrimp, steaks, ribs, chicken, and seafood-and-steak or prime rib combinations. Sandwiches and salads are served at lunch. Desserts include the Aspen snowball and frozen mud pie. The cozy lounge has a full bar and an outdoor courtyard.

INEXPENSIVE

Cervantes, 5801 Gibson Blvd. at San Pedro Blvd. ☎ 262-2253.
> **Cuisine:** NEW MEXICAN. **Reservations:** Suggested at dinner.
> **Prices:** Lunch $3.50–$6.25; dinner $5.75–$12.95. AE, CB, DC, MC, V.
> **Open:** Daily 11am–10pm. **Closed:** Major holidays.

An impressive classical Spanish decor hides behind Cervantes' rather unimpressive exterior, near Kirtland Air Force Base. A portrait of Miguel Cervantes, author of the classic *Don Quixote,* holds a place of honor, though he only shares a name with the owners. New Mexican dinners with all the trimmings are extremely reasonably priced: A combination plate of a taco, tamale, enchilada, and carne adovada, for instance, is just $5.75, including beans, rice, chile, and sopaipillas.

There's another Cervantes—this one with a piano bar—at 10030 Central Ave. NE, near Manzano Mesa (☎ 275-3266).

Hunan Chinese Restaurant, 1218 San Pedro Blvd. SE. ☎ 266-3300.
> **Cuisine:** CHINESE (HUNAN & PEKING).
> **Prices:** Individual dishes $4.25–$22.95; lunch buffet $6.50; dinner buffet $7.95. AE, MC, V.
> **Open:** Daily 11am–9:30pm.

The atmosphere here, a garish overload of red-and-gold decor, reflects the spiciness of the cuisine in what may be Albuquerque's most authentic Chinese restaurant. You can start with hot-and-sour soup, then try sizzling beef (sautéed with peanuts, water chestnuts, and green onions) or whole fish with hot bean sauce. The lunch and dinner buffets offer a variety of spicy and not-so-spicy options. Chinese wine is served.

Journal Center/North City

EXPENSIVE

High Finance Restaurant & Tavern, 40 Tramway Rd., atop Sandia Peak. ☎ **243-9742.**

Cuisine: CONTINENTAL. **Reservations:** Requested.
Prices: Appetizers $3–$7; main courses $13.95–$35. Tramway $9.50 with dinner reservations ($12.50 without). CB, DC, DISC, MC, V.
Open: Lunch daily 11am–4pm; dinner daily 5–9:30pm.

Perched atop Sandia Peak, two miles above Albuquerque and the Rio Grande valley, diners at High Finance have a breathtaking panorama of New Mexico's largest city. The atmosphere inside is elegant yet casual. The menu focuses on prime rib, steaks (including a wonderful steak Diane), and fresh seafood, from fresh fish to crab and lobster. Diners can also choose pasta or Mexican main courses. Many tram riders just drop in for the view and a drink at the casual full-service bar. Smoking is permitted only in the bar.

★ **Le Marmiton,** 5415 Academy Blvd. NE. ☎ **821-6279.**

Cuisine: FRENCH. **Reservations:** Highly recommended.
Prices: Appetizers $3–$5.95; lunch $5.75–$7.95; dinner $13.95–$19.95. AE, DC, MC, V.
Open: Dinner daily 5–9:30pm.

The name means "the apprentice," but there's nothing novice about the food or presentation. The 15 tables seat 40 people in a romantic French provincial atmosphere, with lace curtains and antique plates on shelves.

Recommended main courses include *fantaisie aux fruits de mer*, a mixture of shrimp, scallops, and crab in a mushroom-cream sauce on pastry, and *cailles*, two whole quail finished with a shallot sherry-cream sauce. If you arrive early for dinner (between 5 and 6pm) Monday through Thursday you can take advantage of the prix-fixe light dinners, which include soup or salad, a choice of main course, and coffee or tea for $7.95. There's a long wine list and great cinnamon-apple crêpes for dessert.

MODERATE

The Firehouse Restaurant at the Tram, 38 Tramway Rd. ☎ **292-3473.**

Cuisine: STEAKS & SEAFOOD. **Reservations:** Highly recommended.
Prices: Main courses $12–$18. AE, MC, V.
Open: Daily 11am–10pm. Bar open daily from noon.

Located at the bottom of the Sandia Peak Tramway, the Firehouse has an old steam-powered fire engine serving as its bar and windows on all sides: The views of the city and the Rio Grande valley are great. Seafood, steaks, chicken, and baby pork ribs get special treatment on the mesquite grill. Of particular note are the lime chicken scallops with toasted piñon and white wine, and the peppered steak. There's nightly entertainment; guests with reservations get a discount on tram tickets.

Seagull Street Fish Market, 5410 Academy Blvd. NE. ☎ **856-0020.**

Cuisine: SEAFOOD. **Reservations:** Recommended at dinner.
Prices: Lunch $3.95–$7.95; dinner $11.95–$21.95. AE, DC, DISC, MC, V.

Open: Lunch Mon–Fri 11am–2:30pm; dinner Mon–Thurs 5–10pm, Fri–Sat 5–11pm. Open Sun noon–9pm.

An average of 15 different selections of fresh mesquite-grilled fish are available here on any given day. If the weather is fine, seafood lovers can dine in true maritime fashion on an outdoor dock. Steaks are also on the menu, and there's full bar service.

Out of Town

Some of Albuquerque's finest restaurants are outside the city. Prairie Star is about 20 miles north, via I-25 and N.M. 44, near Bernalillo; the Luna Mansion is about 24 miles south, also via I-25.

EXPENSIVE

⭐ **Prairie Star**, 1000 Jemez Canyon Dam Rd., Bernalillo. ☎ **867-3327.**
Cuisine: CONTEMPORARY REGIONAL. **Reservations:** Required.
Prices: Appetizers $3.50–$8; main courses $12–$23. AE, MC, V.
Open: Dinner Sun–Thurs 5–10pm, Fri–Sat 5–11pm; Sun brunch 10:30am–2:30pm.

A sprawling adobe home, with a marvelous view across the Valle Grande Golf Course and the high plains to Sandia Peak, is host to this intimate dining experience. The 6,000-square-foot house, on a rural site leased from Santa Ana Pueblo, was built in the 1940s in Mission architectural style. Exposed *vigas* and full *latilla* ceilings, hand-carved fireplaces and *bancos* complement the thick adobe walls in the dining room. All art displayed on the walls is for sale.

Diners can start with smoked quail or baked cheese in puff pastry (a blend of mascarpone and gruyere cheese scented with toasted hazelnuts and fresh tarragon). Main courses include shrimp margarita (shrimp sautéed and flambéed with tequila, fresh tomatoes, roasted poblano chilis, and finished with lime juice and butter), veal sweetbreads (served in puff pastry with a tarragon and wild mushroom cream sauce), lamb loin stuffed with garlic, pine nuts, and goat cheese, and pan-fried Truchas trout with piñon nuts. There are daily specials and a lounge at the top of a circular stairway. Private parties often reserve the patio and tiled swimming pool.

MODERATE

The Luna Mansion, Hwys. 6 and 85, Los Lunas. ☎ **865-7333.**
Cuisine: STEAK & SEAFOOD. **Reservations:** Required.
Prices: Appetizers $3–$8.50; main courses $9.95–$20.95. AE, MC, V.
Open: Brunch Sun 11am–2pm; dinner daily 5–10:30pm.

A mile and a half east of I-25 is this national historic landmark, built in 1881 by the Santa Fe Railroad as compensation to the Don Antonio Jose Luna family when the railroad built a track through their existing hacienda. While the two-story mansion is Southern Colonial in style, its basic construction material is adobe. A solarium, a front portico, and impressive ironwork were added in the 1920s.

The menu offers such gourmet dishes as blackened prime rib, Sonoma stuffed chicken breasts (with sun-dried tomatoes, goat cheese, and fresh parsley), the Mansion steak (a 9-ounce filet topped with king crab and béarnaise), and lamb loin medallions with two sauces. There are fresh seafood specials daily and a full bar.

Specialty Dining

Local favorites, all of them specializing in New Mexican cuisine, include **La Hacienda Restaurant** (p. 62) and **La Placita** (p. 63).

The best hotel dining is found at **the Ranchers Club** in the Albuquerque Hilton (p. 63) and **Conrad's** in La Posada de Albuquerque (p. 50).

For dining with a view, head for the Sandia Peak Tramway, where you can choose between the **Firehouse Restaurant** (p. 68) at the base or **High Finance** (p. 68) at the summit.

Light, casual, and fast food is readily found throughout the city. Personal favorites include **ej's** (p. 66) and the **66 Diner** (p. 66).

Good spots for breakfast include **ej's** (p. 66) and **Catalina's** (p. 62).

Late-night dining (after 10pm) is available at **Cafe Oceana** (p. 64), **Chili's** (p. 65), **ej's** (p. 66), the **Rio Grande Yacht Club** (p. 67), and **Scalo** (p. 65), among others.

For 24-hour dining, your best bet may be **Village Inn Pancake House,** 2437 Central Ave. NW (☎ **247-2579**), where most main courses are $3 to $10. It's not flashy, but it serves good American food at reasonable prices. Seven other locations around the city include: 5505 Central Ave. NE (☎ **265-2811**); 2039 Fourth St. NW (☎ **242-3440**); 800 Juan Tabo Blvd. NE (☎ **298-3444**); 2118 Menaul Blvd. NE (☎ **884-0316**); 6300 San Mateo Blvd. NE (☎ **821-5900**); 2240 Wyoming Blvd. NE (☎ **294-6191**); and 2340 Yale Blvd. SE (☎ **243-5476**).

5 **Attractions**

Albuquerque's original town site, today known as Old Town, is the central point of interest for visitors to the city today. Here, centered around the plaza, are the venerable Church of San Felipe de Neri and numerous restaurants, art galleries, and crafts shops. Several important museums stand nearby.

But don't get stuck in Old Town. Elsewhere in the city are the Sandia Peak Tramway, Kirtland Air Force Base and the National Atomic Museum, the University of New Mexico with its museums, and a number of natural attractions. Within day-trip range are several Native American pueblos and a trio of national monuments.

Suggested Itineraries

If You Have 1 Day

Focus your attention on Old Town. Take in the ambience of the plaza, the old church, and the numerous shops and galleries. Don't miss the nearby Albuquerque Museum, and if time permits (or you have the kids along), the New Mexico Museum of Natural History. Late in the day, head for Sandia Peak and its justly famed tramway. Watch the sun set while dining or sipping an apéritif at High Finance.

If You Have 2 Days

Spend the morning at the Indian Pueblo Cultural Center. After lunch there, spend the rest of the day in the anthropological past (Indian Petroglyphs State Park, the Maxwell Museum at the University of New Mexico), in the nuclear future (National Atomic Museum at Kirtland Air Force Base), or in the environmental present (Rio Grande Nature Center State Park, Rio Grande Zoological Park).

If You Have 3 Days

Get out of town, ideally to the Acoma Pueblo, a little over an hour's drive west via I-40. Here you'll get a true taste of the Pueblo life that you merely sampled at the

Cultural Center. There are numerous other pueblos in the Albuquerque area. If history intrigues you, Coronado State Monument, near Bernalillo, and the three divisions of Salinas National Monument, near Mountainair, are all within 90 minutes' drive.

If You Have 5 Days or More

Spend at least one of them in Santa Fe, traveling either there or back via N.M. Highway 14, the "Turquoise Trail" of all-but-abandoned mining metropolises. The more time you have, the more of New Mexico you can uncover—the mountain mecca of Taos, the gripping ruins of Chaco Canyon, hypnotizing White Sands, awesome Carlsbad Caverns, and so on.

The Top Attractions

★ **Old Town,** northeast of Central Ave. and Rio Grande Blvd. NW.

A maze of cobbled courtyard walkways lead to hidden patios and gardens where many of Old Town's 150 galleries and shops are located. Adobe buildings, many refurbished in Pueblo Revival style in the 1950s, focus around the tree-shaded **Old Town Plaza,** created in 1780. Pueblo and Navajo Indian artisans often display their pottery, blankets, and silver jewelry on the sidewalks lining the plaza.

The buildings of Old Town once served as mercantile shops, grocery stores, and government offices. But the importance of Old Town as Albuquerque's commercial center declined after 1880, when the railroad came through 1.2 miles east of the plaza and businesses relocated nearer the tracks. Old Town clung to its historical and sentimental roots, but the quarter was disintegrating until it was rediscovered in the 1930s and 1940s by artisans and other shop owners and tourism took off.

The first structure built when colonists established Albuquerque in 1706 was the **Church of San Felipe de Neri,** facing the plaza on its north side. The house of worship has been in almost continuous use for 285 years. When the original building collapsed about 1790, it was reconstructed and subsequently expanded several times, all the while remaining the spiritual heart of the city. The windows are some 20 feet from the ground and its walls are four feet thick—structural details needed to make the church also serviceable as a fortress against Indian attack. A spiral stairway leading to the choir loft is built around the trunk of an ancient spruce. Confessionals, altars, and images are hand carved; Gothic spires, added in the late 19th century, give the church a European air from the outside. The church's annual parish fiesta, held the first weekend in June, brings food and traditional dancing to the plaza.

Next door to the church is the **Rectory,** built about 1793. Also on the north plaza is **Loyola Hall,** the Sister Blandina Convent, built originally of adobe in 1881 as a residence for Sisters of Charity teachers who worked in the region. When the Jesuit fathers built **Our Lady of the Angels School,** 320 Romero St., in 1877, it was the only public school in Albuquerque.

The **Antonio Vigil House,** 413 Romero St., is an adobe-style residence with traditional *viga* ends sticking out over the entrance door. The **Florencio Zamora Store,** 301 Romero St., was built in the 1890s of "pugmill" adobe for a butcher and grocer. The **Jesus Romero House,** 205 Romero St., was constructed by another grocer in 1915 in "Prairie-Mediterranean" style. Just down the street, the **Jesus Romero Store,** built in 1893, has Territorial and Queen Anne structural features. On the south plaza, the **Manuel Springer House** had a hipped roof and bay windows, still visible under its commercial facade of today. The adjacent **Cristobal Armijo House,** a banker's two-story adobe, was completed in 1886 in combined Italianate and Queen Anne architectural styles.

Casa Armijo, in the 200 block of San Felipe Street, dates from before 1840; it was a headquarters for both Union and Confederate troops during the Civil War days. The nearby **Ambrosio Armijo House and Store,** also in San Felipe, an 1882 adobe structure, once had the high false front of wooden boards so typical of Old West towns in movies. The **Herman Blueher House,** at 302 San Felipe St., built by a business-man in 1898, is a three-story Italianate mansion with fancy porches on two levels, now obscured by storefronts.

The Albuquerque Museum conducts guided **walking tours** of Old Town's historic buildings during the summer at 11am Tuesday through Friday and 1pm Sat-urday and Sunday. The $2-per-person price includes museum admission. For visitors who don't find those times convenient, the museum publishes a brochure for a self-guided walking tour of Old Town.

The Old Town Easter Parade, held annually on the Saturday preceding Easter, brings the Easter Bunny to the streets of the quarter, along with a variety of floats and marching bands. On Christmas Eve, thousands of *luminarias* or *farolitos*—brown paper bags filled with sand and lighted candles—line the narrow streets and flat-roofed build-ings surrounding the plaza.

★ **Sandia Peak Tramway,** 10 Tramway Loop NE. ☎ **856-7325** or **856-6419.**

The world's longest tramway extends 2.7 miles from Albuquerque's northeastern city limits to the summit of 10,378-foot Sandia Peak. A 15-minute ride up the tram is a memorable experience, rising from urban desert at its base to lush mountain foliage in the Cíbola National Forest at its peak—and dropping about 20 degrees in tem-perature in the process. Animals viewed on the wild slopes from the tram occasionally include bears, bighorn sheep, deer, eagles, hawks, and a rare mountain lion. The view from the observation deck encompasses more than 11,000 square miles, well beyond Santa Fe and Los Alamos to the north.

Winter skiers often take the tram to the **Sandia Peak Ski Area,** where visitors can couple their trip with a ride on the resort's 7,500-foot double-chair lift through the spruce and ponderosa pine forests on the mountain's eastern slope. (A single ride costs $4; the chair operates from 10am to 3pm in summer, 9am to 4pm in winter.)

The Sandia Peak tram is a "jigback"; in other words, as one car approaches the top, the other nears the bottom. The two pass halfway through the trip, in the midst of a 1.5-mile "clear span" of unsupported cable between the second tower and the upper terminal.

There is a popular and high-priced restaurant at the tramway's summit, **High Finance** (☎ **243-9742;** p. 68); at the base is the **Firehouse** (☎ **856-3473;** p. 68) another upscale eatery. Special tram rates apply with dinner reservations.

To reach the base of the tram, take I-25 north to the Tramway Road Exit 234 then proceed east about five miles on Tramway Road (N.M. 556); from I-40 take Exit 167 (Tramway Blvd.) and go north for approximately 9 miles.

Admission: Adults $12.50, seniors and children 5–12 $9.50.

Open: Memorial Day–Labor Day daily 9am–10pm; spring and fall Thurs–Tues 9am–9pm, Wed 5–9pm; ski season Mon–Tues and Thurs–Fri 9am–9pm, Wed noon–9pm, Sat–Sun 8am–9pm.

 Indian Pueblo Cultural Center, 2401 12th St. NW. ☎ **843-7270** or toll free **800/766-4405.**

Owned and operated as a nonprofit organization by the 19 pueblos of northern New Mexico, this is a fine place to begin an exploration of Native American culture. Located about a mile northeast of Old Town, this museum—modeled after Pueblo Bonito, a spectacular 9th-century ruin in Chaco Culture National Historic Park—consists of several parts.

In the basement, a permanent exhibit depicts the evolution from prehistory to present of the various pueblos, including displays of the distinctive handcrafts of each community. Note, especially, how pottery differs in concept and design from pueblo to pueblo. The displays include a series of remarkable photographs of Pueblo people taken between 1880 and 1910, a gift of the Smithsonian Institution. The Pueblo House Children's Museum, also located on premises, is a hands-on museum that gives children the opportunity to learn about and understand the evolution of Pueblo culture.

Upstairs is an enormous (7,000-square-foot) gift shop—a fine place to price the Pueblos' colorful creations of art before bartering with private artisans. The code of ethics of the Indian Arts and Crafts Association guarantees work here to be stylistically authentic. A gallery displays a variety of ancient and modern works from different pueblos, with exhibits changing monthly.

Every weekend throughout the year, Native American dancers perform and artisans demonstrate their crafts expertise in an outdoor arena surrounded by original murals. An annual craft fair is held on the July 4 holiday weekend, the first weekend in October, and Thanksgiving weekend.

A restaurant, open from 7:30am to 4pm, emphasizes the cornmeal-based foods of the Pueblo people. Daily specials are priced at $4; an ample meal is *posole,* treated dried corn with beef, chili, and oven bread.

Admission: Adults $3, seniors $2, students $1; free for children 4 and under.

Open: Daily 9am–5:50pm; restaurant 7:30am–4pm. **Closed:** New Year's Day, Thanksgiving Day, and Christmas.

★ **Albuquerque Museum,** 2000 Mountain Rd. NW. ☎ **243-7255** or **242-4600.**

Among objects held in the museum's collection are arms and armor used during the Hispanic conquest, medieval religious artifacts and weavings, maps from the 16th to 18th centuries, and coins and domestic goods traded during that same period. Of special note is a 17th-century *repostero,* or tapestry, once belonging to the Spanish House of Albuquerque. It was given to the city in 1956 by the 18th duke of Albuquerque to commemorate the 200th anniversary of the founding of the Spanish settlement here. Made of silk with gold and silver thread, it is 12 feet square and displays a dragon.

A permanent exhibit, *Four Centuries: A History of Albuquerque,* chronicles the city's evolution from the earliest 16th-century forays of Coronado's *conquistadores* to its present-day status as a center of military research and high-technology industries.

An accompanying multimedia audiovisual presentation depicts the history of the mid–Rio Grande region from the Spanish conquest to the present. *History Hopscotch* is a hands-on history exhibition designed specifically for children.

There's also a gallery of early and modern New Mexico art, housing permanent and changing exhibits, and a major photo archive. Lectures and workshops are offered in an auditorium and classroom. A gift shop offers souvenirs and other wares.

Admission: Free; donation appreciated.

Open: Tues–Sun 9am–5pm. **Closed:** Holidays.

More Attractions

University of New Mexico, Yale Blvd. NE north of Central Ave. ☎ 277-0111.

The state's largest institution of higher learning stretches across an attractive 700-acre campus about two miles east of downtown Albuquerque, north of Central Avenue and east of University Boulevard. The six campus museums, none of which charge admission, are constructed (like other UNM buildings) in a modified pueblo style. Popejoy Hall, in the south-central part of campus opposite Yale Park, hosts many performing arts presentations, including those of the New Mexico Symphony Orchestra; other public events are held in nearby Keller Hall and Woodward Hall.

The **Maxwell Museum of Anthropology** (☎ 277-4405), an internationally acclaimed repository of southwestern anthropological finds, is situated on the west side of campus on Redondo Drive at Ash Street NE. Permanent galleries include *Ancestors,* describing 4 million years of human evolution, and *Peoples of the Southwest,* a 10,000-year summary. Mimbres and Pueblo pottery, Hopi *kachina* dolls, Navajo weavings, and a variety of regional jewelry, basketry, and textiles are on display. The collections support education and research in anthropology, archaeology, and ethnology. Native American art and books about the state's cultural heritage are on sale in the museum's gift shop. It's open Monday through Friday from 9am to 4pm, Saturday from 10am to 4pm, and Sunday from noon to 4pm. Closed holidays.

The **University Art Museum** (☎ 277-4001), in the Fine Arts Center adjoining Popejoy Hall on Cornell Street, just north of Central Avenue, is a multilevel museum focusing on 19th- and 20th-century American and European artists. The prides of its permanent collection are an exhibit of early modernist work and exhibitions covering the history of photography and prints. It's open from September through May, Tuesday from 9am to 4pm and 5 to 9pm, Wednesday through Friday from 9am to 4pm, and Sunday from 1 to 4pm; closed holidays. A gift shop offers many art books and periodicals, as well as some prints of the works displayed.

The intimate **Jonson Gallery** (☎ 277-4967), at 1909 Las Lomas Blvd. NE on the north side of the central campus, features more than 2,000 works by the late Raymond Jonson, a leading modernist painter in early 20th-century New Mexico, as well as works by contemporary artists. The gallery is open Tuesday 9am to 4pm and 5 to 8pm, Wednesday to Friday 9am to 4pm.

Located in Northrop Hall (☎ 277-4204), about halfway between the Maxwell Museum and Popejoy Hall in the southern part of campus, the adjacent **Geology Museum** and **Meteoritic Museum** (☎ 277-1644) cover the gamut of recorded time from dinosaur bones to meteorites. The 3,000 meteorite specimens held here comprise the sixth-largest collection in the United States. The Geology Museum is open Monday through Friday from 8am to 5pm; the Meteoritic Museum, Monday through Friday from 9am to noon and 1 to 4pm.

Finally, the **Museum of Southwestern Biology** (☎ 277-5340) in the basement of Castetter Hall (the biology building next to Northrop Hall) has few displays, but has an extensive research collection of global flora and fauna. The holdings especially represent southwestern North America, Central America, South America, East Asia, and parts of Europe. Visitors must call ahead for an appointment.

⭐ **National Atomic Museum**, Wyoming Blvd. and K St., Kirtland Air Force Base. ☎ 845-6670.

This museum is the next best introduction to the nuclear age after the Bradbury Science Museum in Los Alamos. It traces the history of nuclear-weapons development

Central Albuquerque Attractions

ALBUQUERQUE AREA

Albuquerque Children's Museum **6**
Albuquerque Museum **4**
American International Rattlesnake Museum **7**
Cliff's Amusement Park **15**
Ernie Pyle Memorial Library **13**
Explora! Science Center **9**
Indian Pueblo Cultural Center **3**
Maxwell Museum of Anthropology **10**
National Atomic Museum **14**
New Mexico Museum of Natural History and Science **5**
Petroglyph National Monument **1**
Rio Grande Nature Center State Park **2**
Rio Grande Zoological Park **8**
Sandia Peak Tramway **16**
University Art Museum **12**
University of New Mexico **11**

Airport ✈

9449

beginning with the top-secret Manhattan Project of the 1940s, including a copy of the letter Albert Einstein wrote to Pres. Franklin D. Roosevelt suggesting the possible development of an atomic bomb. A 50-minute film, *Ten Seconds That Shook the World*, is shown four times daily, at 10:30 and 11:30am, and 2 and 3:30pm. There are full-scale models of the "Fat Man" and "Little Boy" bombs, displays and films on peaceful applications of nuclear technology and other alternative energy sources. Fusion is explained in a manner that a layperson can begin to understand; other exhibits deal with the problem of nuclear waste. Outdoor exhibits include a B-52 "Stratofortress," an F-1015D "Thunderchief," and a 280 mm atomic cannon. A tour that lasts about an hour takes visitors through the development of the first nuclear weapons to today's technology. You'll also see a solar-powered TV and be able to test your budgeting skills as you use the Energy-Environment Simulator to manipulate energy allocations to make the planet's supplies last longer. The museum is directly across the street from the International Nuclear Weapons School, adjacent to Sandia National Laboratory.

Admission: Free. Visitors must obtain passes at the Wyoming or Gibson gate of the base. Children under 12 not admitted without parent or adult guardian.

Open: Daily 9am–5pm. **Closed:** New Year's Day, Easter Day, Thanksgiving Day, and Christmas.

Rio Grande Nature Center State Park, 2901 Candelaria Rd. NW. ☎ 344-7240.

Located on the Rio Grande Flyway, an important migratory route for many birds, this wildlife refuge extends for nearly a mile along the east bank of the Rio Grande. Numerous nature trails wind through the cottonwood *bosque,* where a great variety of native and migratory species can be seen at any time of year. The center publishes a checklist to help visitors identify them, as well as several self-guiding trail brochures. Housed in a unique building constructed half aboveground and half below, the visitor's center contains classrooms, laboratory space, a library, and exhibits describing the history, geology, and ecology of the Rio Grande valley. Films and interpreted hikes are scheduled every weekend.

Admission: $1 adults, 50¢ children 6 and older.

Open: Daily 10am–5pm. **Closed:** New Year's Day, Thanksgiving Day, and Christmas.

Petroglyph National Monument, 6900 Unser Blvd. NW, west of Coors Rd. ☎ 839-4429.

Albuquerque's western city limits are marked by five extinct volcanoes. The ancient lava flows here were a hunting ground for prehistoric Native Americans, who camped among the rocks and left a cryptic chronicle of their lifestyle etched and chipped in the dark basalt. Some 10,500 of these petroglyphs have been found in several concentrated groups at this archaeological preserve. Plaques interpret the rock drawings—animal, human, and ceremonial forms—for visitors, who may take four hiking trails, ranging from easy to moderately difficult, winding through the lava. The 45-minute Mesa Point trail is the most strenuous, but also the most rewarding.

Camping is not permitted in the park; it is strictly for day use; picnic areas, drinking water, and rest rooms are available.

Admission: $1 per vehicle.

Open: Summer daily 9am–6pm; winter 8am–5pm. **Closed:** State holidays.

Spanish History Museum, 2221 Lead St. SE. ☎ 268-9981.

This exclusive gallery features *From Kingdom to Statehood,* an exhibit outlining Hispanics' role in New Mexico's pursuit of statehood from 1848 to 1912. There's also documentation of Spain's assistance to the 13 original colonies during the American Revolution, information about New Mexico's founding Hispanic families and their heraldic coats of arms, and family history booklets. The Columbus display is an in-depth study of the great navigator's life.

Admission: $1 donation requested.

Open: Summer 10am–5pm; rest of year 1–5pm. **Closed:** Major holidays.

Los Colores Museum, 4499 Corrales Rd., Corrales. ☎ **898-5077.**

If you're staying in a bed and breakfast on the outskirts of Albuquerque, take some time to stop by Los Colores Museum. Housed in the historic Alejandro Gonzales House, the museum is dedicated to the weaving traditions of New Mexico. The focal point of the museum is a collection of approximately 200 antique Mexican serapes that represent over two hundred years of weaving tradition. You'll also see exhibits of traditional and contemporary New Mexican folk art.

Admission: Free.

Open: Weekends 1–4pm, other days by appointment.

Ernie Pyle Memorial Library, 900 Girard Blvd. NE. ☎ **256-2065.**

The 1940 home of America's favorite war correspondent is now a library. Memorabilia and poignant exhibits recalling the Pulitzer Prize–winning journalist, killed in action during World War II, stand in display shelves between the book stacks.

Admission: Free.

Open: Tues and Thurs 12:30–9pm; Wed and Fri–Sat 9am–5:30pm.

Cool for Kids

If you're traveling with children, you'll be happy to know that there are a number of Albuquerque attractions that are guaranteed to keep the kids interested. One of the city's best child-oriented activities takes place on Sundays year-round on Romero Street in the Old Town, where costumed actors re-create **Wild West shoot-outs.** On weekends, there are also regular puppet plays at the **Old Town Puppet Theatre** (☎ **243-0208**).

★ **New Mexico Museum of Natural History & Science,** 1801 Mountain Rd. NW. ☎ **841-8837.**

Two life-size bronze dinosaurs stand outside the entrance to this modern museum, opposite the Albuquerque Museum. The pentaceratops and albertosaur greeting them are only the first of the museum's displays that kids will love.

When the museum opened in 1986, on money drawn mostly from taxes on oil, gas, and coal produced in the state, it began nearly from scratch, without any major collections of artifacts or other materials. Today it contains permanent and changing exhibits on regional zoology, botany, geology, and paleontology.

Innovative video displays, polarizing lenses, and black lighting enable visitors to stroll through geologic time. You can walk a rocky path through the Hall of Giants, as dinosaurs fight and winged reptiles swoop overhead; step into a seemingly live volcano, complete with simulated magma flow; or share an Ice Age cave, festooned with stalagmites, with saber-toothed tigers and woolly mammoths. Hands-on exhibits in the Naturalist Center permit use of a video microscope, viewing of an active beehive, and participation in a variety of other activities. An atrium in the lobby features a 22-foot relief map of the earth showing the surfaces of continents and seabeds; a network of 2,500 fiber-optic elements monitors the pulse of the planet, flashing wherever earthquakes or eruptions occur—about every three seconds. The giant-screen

Dynamax Theater features large-format films on natural history topics. Shows are every hour on the hour from 10am to 5pm.

There's a gift shop on the ground floor, and the Museum Cafe is on the mezzanine.

Admission: Museum only, adults $4, seniors $3, children 3–11 $2. Museum and Dynamax, $7 adults, $5 seniors, $3 children 3–11. Children under 12 must be accompanied by an adult.

Open: Daily 9am–5pm, to 6pm May–Sept. **Closed:** Christmas and Mon in Jan and Sept.

Albuquerque Children's Museum, 800 Rio Grande Blvd. NW. ☎ 842-5525.

At the Albuquerque Children's Museum, there's something for everyone: bubbles, whisper disks, a puppet theater, a giant loom, a dress-up area, zoetropes, a capture-your-shadow wall, art activities, science demonstrations, even a giant pinhole camera. The museum also sponsors wonderful educational workshops. *The Me I Don't Always See* was a health exhibit designed to teach children about the mysteries of the human body, and recently, the museum sponsored a "Great Artists" series that featured live performances depicting artists' lives and work followed by an art activity.

Admission: $3 children 2–12, $1 13 and up, under 2 free.

Open: Tues–Sat 10am–5pm, Sun noon–5pm.

American International Rattlesnake Museum, 202 San Felipe St. NW. ☎ 242-6569.

This unique museum has living specimens—in naturally landscaped habitats—of common, not so common, and rare rattlesnakes of North, Central, and South America. Over 20 species can be seen, including such oddities as albinos and patternless rattlesnakes. Especially popular with the kids are the baby rattlesnakes. A 7-minute film explains the rattlesnake's contribution to the ecological balance of our hemisphere. Throughout the museum are rattlesnake artifacts from early American history, Native American culture, medicine, the arts, and advertising. A gift shop sells southwestern jewelry, T-shirts, and other mementos—with an emphasis on rattlesnakes, of course.

Admission: $2 adults, $1 children.

Open: Daily 10am–6:30pm.

Explora! Science Center, 401 1st Plaza, Suite 68. ☎ 842-6188.

Children and adults alike will enjoy a trip to Explora! Science Center, a hands-on science and technology museum. The flight demonstrator captures the imaginations of all museum goers, while the gravity well both entertains and fascinates. Kids won't soon forget time spent in the echo tube, either.

Admission: $2 adults, $1 ages 5–17 and 62 and older, children under 5 free.

Open: Wed–Sat 10am–5pm, Sun noon–5pm.

Rio Grande Zoological Park, 903 10th St. SW. ☎ 843-7413.

Open-moated exhibits with animals in naturalized habitats are a treat for zoo goers. Highlight exhibits include the giraffes, sea lions (with underwater viewing), the catwalk, the bird show, and ape country, with its gorillas and orangutans. More than 1,200 animals of 300 species live on 60 acres of riverside *bosque* among ancient cottonwoods. The zoo has an especially fine collection of elephants, reptiles, and native southwestern species. There are numerous snack bars on the zoo grounds, and La Ventana Gift Shop carries film and souvenirs.

Admission: Adults $4.25, children and seniors $2.25. Children under 12 must be accompanied by an adult.

Open: Daily 9am–5pm, with extended hours in summer. **Closed:** New Year's Day, Thanksgiving Day, and Christmas.

Cliff's Amusement Park, 4800 Osuna Rd. NE. ☎ **883-9063.**

This is New Mexico's largest amusement park. Children of all ages love the 23 rides, video arcades, recording studio, picnic ground, and live entertainment.

Admission: $8.

Open: May Fri 7–11pm, Sat 1–11pm, Sun 1–7pm; Memorial Day–Labor Day Fri 2–11pm, Sat 1–11pm, Sun 1–9pm, Mon–Thurs 6–10pm (1–7pm Mon holidays); Sept Sat 1–10pm, Sun 1–6pm.

Tours

Albuquerque is very spread out and doesn't lend itself to **walking tours**—except in Old Town. The Albuquerque Museum, 2000 Mountain Rd. NW (☎ **243-7255** or **242-4600**), publishes a brochure for self-guided walking tours of Old Town and conducts guided tours during the summer, Tuesday through Friday at 11am and Saturday and Sunday at 1pm. Many of the buildings included on that tour are discussed above, in this chapter's treatment of Old Town.

Consult any of the following **tour operators** for city and regional tours: **Jack Allen Tours,** P.O. Box 11940, Albuquerque, NM 87192 (☎ **505/266-9688**); **Discover Travel,** 6303 Indian School Rd. NE, Albuquerque, NM 87110 (☎ **505/888-2444**).

6   Sports & Recreation

Spectator Sports

BASEBALL   The Albuquerque Dukes, 1990 champions of the Class AAA Pacific Coast League, are the number one farm team of the Los Angeles Dodgers. They play 72 home games from mid-April to early September in the city-owned 30,000-seat Albuquerque Sports Stadium, 1601 Stadium Blvd. SE at University Boulevard (☎ **243-1791**). Among the former Dukes now playing major-league baseball are John Franco, Sid Fernandez, Pedro Guerrero, Orel Hershiser, Candy Maldonado, and Dave Stewart.

BASKETBALL   The University of New Mexico team, nicknamed the Lobos, plays an average of 16 home games from late November to early March. Capacity crowds cheer the team at the 17,121-seat University Arena (fondly called "the Pit") at University and Stadium boulevards. The arena was the site in 1983 of the annual National Collegiate Athletic Association championship tournament.

BOXING   Albuquerque has several professional boxing gyms. Local bouts, whose sites have varied, have featured top contenders in various weight divisions. Several nationally ranked boxers live and train in the Albuquerque area.

FOOTBALL   The UNM Lobos football team plays a September-to-November season, usually including five home games, at the 30,000-seat University of New Mexico Stadium, opposite both Albuquerque Sports Stadium and University Arena at University and Stadium boulevards.

HORSE RACING   **The Downs at Albuquerque,** 201 California St. (☎ **265-1188** for post times), is in the State Fairgrounds near Lomas and Louisiana boulevards NE.

Racing and betting—on thoroughbreds and quarter horses—take place Wednesdays, Fridays, and Saturdays from late January to June and during the state fair in September. The Downs has a glass-enclosed grandstand, exclusive club seating, valet parking, complimentary racing programs, and tip sheets.

RODEO   The All-American Pro Rodeo, a key event on the national professional rodeo circuit, takes place the second through third weekends of September each year as a part of the New Mexico State Fair. Tickets—at $5 general, $9 reserved—must be ordered from fair officials (☎ toll free **800/235-FAIR**).

Recreation

 BALLOONING   Visitors not content to watch the colorful craft rise into the clear blue skies have a choice of several hot-air balloon operators from whom to get a ride, with rates starting at about $85–$125 per person. They include: **Braden's Balloons Aloft,** 9935-B Trumbull Ave. SE (☎ **281-2714** or toll free **800/367-6625**); **Cameron Balloons,** 2950 San Joaquin Ave. SE (☎ **265-4007**); **Rainbow Ryders, Inc.** 430 Montclaire Dr. SE (☎ **268-3401**); **World Balloon Corporation,** 4800 Eubank Blvd. NE (☎ **293-6800**).

BICYCLING   Albuquerque is a major bicycling hub in the summer, both for road racers and mountain bikers. Full information on competitive events and touring, as well as rentals, can be obtained from **Gardenswartz Sportz,** 2720 San Mateo Blvd. NE (☎ **884-6787**), or **R.E.I.,** 1905 Mountain Rd. NW (☎ **247-1191**).

BOWLING   There are 10 bowling alleys in Albuquerque. They include the 40-lane **Fiesta Lanes,** 6001 Menaul Blvd. NE, at San Pedro Boulevard (☎ **881-4040**), open daily from 8am to midnight, with a pro shop, private locker rooms, child care, and a restaurant; and the 32-lane **Leisure Bowl,** 7400 Lomas Blvd. NE, near Louisiana Boulevard (☎ **268-4371**), open daily from 9am to 1am, with a 15-minute break from 5:45 to 6pm, with a pro shop, sports bar, and "bumper bowling" for children.

FISHING   Although most avid anglers head for high-mountain lakes or outlying streams, the Rio Grande, even as it flows through Albuquerque, remains an attraction to some fishermen. Youngsters may catch their first trout or crappie at **Shady Lakes,** 11033 Fourth St. NW (☎ **898-2568**). Licenses, equipment, and bait can be purchased from numerous sporting goods outlets, including **Charlie's Sporting Goods,** 7401-H Menaul Blvd. NE (☎ **884-4545**), and **Quality Baits,** 4257 Isleta Blvd. SW (☎ **877-0780**).

GOLF   There are 11 public and private courses in Albuquerque, all of them open year-round, sunrise to sunset. Clubhouses will make arrangements for partners on request. Public courses include: **Arroyo del Oso Golf Course** (18 holes), 7001 Osuna Blvd. NE (☎ **884-7505**); **Los Altos Golf Course** (18 holes), 9717 Copper St. NE (☎ **298-1897**); **Puerto del Sol Golf Course** (9 holes), 1600 Girard Blvd. SE (☎ **265-5636**); **Ladera Golf Course** (18 holes), 3401 Ladera Dr. NW (☎ **836-4449**); **University of New Mexico South Course** (18 holes), 3601 University Blvd. SE (☎ **277-4546**); **University of New Mexico North Course** (9 holes), Yale Boulevard at Tucker Road (☎ **277-4146**). Private courses offering reciprocity include: **Albuquerque Country Club** (18 holes), 601 Laguna Blvd. SW (☎ **247-4111**); **Four Hills Country Club** (18 holes), 911 Four Hills Rd. SE (☎ **299-9555**); **Paradise Hills Country Club** (18 holes), 10035 Country Club Lane NW (☎ **898-0960**); **Rio Rancho Country Club** (18 holes), 500 Country Club Dr,

SE, Rio Rancho (☎ **892-5813**); **Tanoan Country Club** (18 holes), 10801 Academy Blvd. NE (☎ **822-0433**). There's miniature golf at **Highland Swing,** 312 Adams St. SE off Zuni Avenue (☎ **255-9992**). Located near Highland High School, it's a tree-shaded course.

HIKING & BACKPACKING   The 1.6-million-acre **Cíbola National Forest** offers ample opportunities. In the Sandia Mountain section alone are 18 recreation sites, though only one—Cedro Peak, four miles southeast of Tijeras—allows overnight camping. For details, contact Sandia Ranger Station, NM-337, south toward Tijeras (☎ **381-3304**).

Elena Gallegos/Albert G. Simms Park, near the base of the Sandia Peak Tramway at 1700 Tramway Blvd. NE (☎ **291-6224** or **768-3550**), is a 640-acre mountain picnic area with hiking trail access to the Sandia Mountain Wilderness. Nature programs and hikes are guided during the summer.

Llama pack trips, guided backpacking trips, and gourmet day hikes are offered by **Southwest Wilderness Trails,** Star Route Box 303, Placitas, NM 87043 (☎ **505/867-3442**). Trips into Bandelier National Monument and the Pecos Wilderness are regularly scheduled and cost as little as $65 per person per day.

Sporting goods stores specializing in this type of outdoor equipment include **R.E.I.,** 1905 Mountain Rd. NW (☎ **247-1191**) and **Sandia Mountain Outfitters,** 1700 Juan Tabo Blvd. NE (☎ **293-9725**).

HORSEBACK RIDING   Many urban riders make use of the 20-mile path along the irrigation ditches flanking the Rio Grande from Bernalillo through Albuquerque to Belen. Others head up the slopes of Sandia Mountain. Local stables rent horses, offer instruction, and provide outfitters as required. Try **Los Amigos Stables,** 10601 Fourth St. NW, Alameda (☎ **898-8173**), with more than 300 acres of trails on the Sandia Indian Reservation; or **Turkey Track Stables,** 1306 U.S. Hwy. 66 East, Tijeras (☎ **281-1772**).

HUNTING   In the Albuquerque area, **Cíbola National Forest** is popular among hunters for game birds and some big-game animals, including mule deer, bear, and mountain lion. Licenses and information can be obtained from **Charlie's Sporting Goods,** 7401-H Menaul Blvd. NE (☎ **884-4545**), or **Los Ranchos Gun & Tackle Shop,** 6542 Fourth St. NW (☎ **345-4276**).

Bow hunters can practice their craft indoors at the **Albuquerque Archery** shooting range, 5000-B Menaul Blvd. NE (☎ **881-0808**), open daily until 9pm.

RIVER RAFTING   This mainly takes place farther north, in the Santa Fe and especially Taos areas. Check with **Wolf Whitewater Kayak Canoe School & River Tours,** P.O. Box 666, Sandia Park, NM 87047 (☎ **281-5042** or toll free **800/552-0070**), or **Rio Grande Rapid Transit,** Box A Pilar, NM 87571 (☎ **758-9700** or toll free **800/222-RAFT**).

In mid-May each year, the **Great Race** takes place on a 14-mile stretch of the Rio Grande through Albuquerque. Eleven categories of craft, including rafts, kayaks, and canoes, race down the river. Call **768-3490** for details.

RUNNING   Albuquerque Park & Recreation (☎ **768-3550**) maintains numerous recreational trails. Bicyclists and walkers enjoy them, too, but they're ideal for runners. They include **Paseo del Nordeste,** a 6.1-mile asphalt trail beginning at Tucker Avenue, north of the UNM campus, and ending at Sandia High School on Pennsylvania Boulevard NE; **Paseo del Bosque,** a 5-mile trail running parallel to the irrigation ditch on the east side of the Rio Grande, with access from Candelaria Road NW, Campbell Road NW, Mountain Road NW, Central Avenue SW, and other streets; **Paseo de las Montanas,** following Embudo Arroyo 4.2 miles from Pennsylvania Boulevard NE, east of Winrock Center, to Lynnwood Park near Tramway Boulevard NE; **Tramway,** 4 miles, along the east side of Tramway Boulevard from Montgomery Boulevard to I-40; **La Mariposa,** 1.5 miles, between Montano Road NW and Dellyne Avenue NW, west of Taylor Ranch Road NW; and **Jefferson-Osuna,** 0.4 mile, following the Bear Arroyo between Jefferson Street NE and Osuna Boulevard NE.

SKATING   The **Outpost Ice Arena,** 9530 Tramway Blvd. NE (☎ 856-7595), has a year-round rink, with instructors and a hockey league. There's also a fitness center and a restaurant. Skaters who prefer a maple floor can try the **Rainbow Garden Roller Drome,** 204 San Mateo Blvd. SE (☎ 255-2480), an enormous air-conditioned facility with a pro shop.

SKIING   The **Sandia Peak Ski Area** has twin base-to-summit chair lifts to its upper slopes at 10,378 feet and a 1,700-foot vertical drop. There are 25 trails, (35% beginner, 55% intermediate, 10% advanced) serviced by four double chairs and two surface lifts. There's a full rental shop, skier's cafe, outdoor grill, and ski boutique. All-day lift tickets are $30 for adults, $21 for children; rental packages are $14 for adults, $11 for kids. The season usually runs from the Christmas holidays through March. Contact the ski area's offices at 10 Tramway Loop NE (☎ 856-6419) for more information, or call the hot line for ski conditions (☎ 242-9052).

Cross-country skiers can enjoy the trails of the **Sandia Wilderness** from the ski area or can go an hour north to the remote **Jemez Wilderness** and its hot springs.

Among the many shops in Albuquerque renting full ski equipment are **R.E.I.,** 1905 Mountain Rd. NW (☎ 247-1191), and **Ski Systems,** 1605 Juan Tabo Blvd. NE, Suite A (☎ 296-9111).

SWIMMING   There are five indoor and nine outdoor swimming pools in Albuquerque, allowing year-round swimming in all parts of the city. Open 12 months a year are the following pools: **Highland,** 400 Jackson St. SE (☎ 256-2096), **Los Altos,** 10300 Lomas Blvd. NE (☎ 291-6290), **Sandia,** 7801 Candelaria Blvd. NE (☎ 291-6279), and **Valley,** 1505 Candelaria Blvd. NW (☎ 761-4086). Among those open summers only are **Sierra Vista West,** 5001 Montano Rd. NW (☎ 897-4517), **South Valley,** 3912 Isleta Blvd. SW (☎ 877-3959), and **West Mesa,** 6705 Fortuna Rd. NW (☎ 836-0686). For more information, call **Albuquerque Culture and Recreational Services** (☎ 768-3520).

Slightly more off-beat water entertainment is available at the **Beach,** I-25 and Montano Road (☎ 344-6111). This 15-acre water park, including a wave pool, five water slides, and two restaurants, is open daily in summer from 11am to 8pm.

TENNIS   There are some 140 public tennis courts at 29 parks in and near Albuquerque. Many of them can be reserved in advance. There are tennis complexes at **UNM South Campus,** 1903 Stadium Blvd. SE (☎ 848-1389), and **Jerry Cline Park,** Louisiana Boulevard NE and Constitution Avenue NE, at I-40 (☎ 256-2032).

7 Savvy Shopping

Nowhere in the state could one get a better shopping "fix" . The city has the two largest shopping malls in the state within two blocks of one another, both on Louisiana Boulevard just north of I-40—Coronado Center and Winrock Center.

Visitors interested in regional specialties will find many artists and galleries, although they're not as concentrated as in Santa Fe and Taos. The galleries and regional fashion designers around the plaza in Old Town make a sort of shopping center of their own for tourists, with more than 40 merchants represented. The Sandia Pueblos run their own crafts market on their reservation land off I-25 at Tramway Road, just beyond Albuquerque's northern city limits.

Business hours vary from store to store and from shopping center to shopping center. In general, it's safe to say that shops will be open Monday through Saturday from 10am to 6pm, but many have extended hours; some have reduced hours; and a few, especially in shopping malls or during the high tourist season, are open Sunday.

Best Buys

Look for southwestern regional items in Albuquerque. These include arts and crafts of all kinds, from traditional Native American and Hispanic to contemporary works. In Native American art, look for silver and turquoise jewelry, pottery, weavings, baskets, sand paintings, and Hopi *kachina* dolls. Hispanic folk art, including handcrafted furniture, tinwork and *retablos,* religious paintings, is worth seeking out. Contemporary art focuses primarily on painting, sculpture, jewelry-making, ceramics, and fiber art, including weaving. By far the greatest concentration of galleries is in Old Town; others are spread around the city, with smaller groupings in the university district and the northeast heights. Consult the brochure published by the Albuquerque Gallery Association, *A Select Guide to Albuquerque Galleries,* or Wingspread Communications' annual *The Collector's Guide to Albuquerque,* widely distributed at shops.

You should note that every week ArtsCrawl organizes art exhibits, artist receptions, and demonstrations in a convenient geographic area. Galleries in that area stay open late during the ArtsCrawl, and all events are free. The Albuquerque Art Business Association (☎ 842-9918) prepares maps for walking and driving; you can also get one from the Albuquerque Convention and Visitors Bureau.

Other things to keep your eyes open for are fashions in southwestern print designs; gourmet items, including blue-corn flour and chile *ristras;* and other souvenirs unique to the region, especially Native American and Hispanic creations.

Shopping A to Z

ANTIQUES

Andrew Nagen Old Navajo Rugs, 14 Corrales Rd., Corrales. ☎ 345-4599.

Very much a specialty dealer, Nagen buys, sells, and appraises historic Navajo, Pueblo, and Hispanic weavings. He opens by appointment only.

Brandywine Galleries, 120 Morningside Dr. SE. ☎ 255-0266.

In an elegant setting of period furniture, porcelain, and silver are displayed some of the outstanding representational works of art of 19th- and 20th-century New Mexico, including pieces by the original Taos and Santa Fe schools. The gallery specializes in art and antique appraisals and restorations.

Classic Century Square, 4616 Central Ave. SE. ☎ 265-3161.

More than 100 individual dealers in antiques, collectibles, and arts and crafts exhibit here, between the University of New Mexico and the State Fairgrounds. Jewelry, china, crystal, silver, books, dolls, home accessories, and other items are available.

A second location, **Classic Century Square II,** is at 3100 Juan Tabo Blvd. NE (☎ **294-9904**), in the eastern foothills. Both centers are open Monday through Saturday from 10am to 6pm and Sunday from noon to 5pm.

ART

Absolutely Neon, 3903 Central NE. ☎ **265-6366.**

Southwestern, one-of-a-kind neon art pieces.

Adobe Gallery, 413 Romero St. NW, Old Town. ☎ **243-8485.**

Art of southwestern Native Americans is featured here. The gallery also carries numerous contemporary and antique Indian items, including pottery, weavings, pawn jewelry, baskets, paintings, and *kachina* dolls. There is a large selection of books on Southwest Native American and Hispanic culture, and the gallery also features a small selection of American arts and crafts and Mission Oak antique furniture. Open Monday through Saturday from 10am to 6pm, Sunday from 1 to 4pm.

Andrews Pueblo Pottery & Art Gallery, 400 San Felipe NW. ☎ **243-0414.**

Traditional Pueblo pottery, fetishes, baskets, and *kachinas,* as well as southwestern landscapes by Doug West.

Dartmouth Street Gallery, 3011 Monte Vista NE. ☎ **266-7751.**

Vapor mirage works of Larry Bell, paintings by Angus Macpherson, tapestries, sculpture, and works on paper by contemporary New Mexico artists.

Hernandez Fine Art, 404 San Felipe NW. ☎ **242-9557.**

Hand-pulled serigraphs by internationally known artist, Fermin Hernandez.

Michael C. McCullough Fine Arts, 323 Romero NW. ☎ **242-8667.**

Fine quality southwestern artwork, including works by local artists. Bronze sculptures by Ken Payne, and originals by Amado Pena.

R. C. Gorman Navajo Gallery Old Town, 323 Romero St. NW, Old Town. ☎ **843-7666.**

The painting and sculpture of famed Navajo artist Gorman, a resident of Taos, are shown here daily from 11am to 5pm. Most works are available in limited-edition lithographs.

Weyrich Gallery (Rare Vision Art Galerie), 2935-D Louisiana Blvd. at Candelaria Rd. ☎ **883-7410.**

Contemporary paintings, sculpture, textiles, jewelry, and ceramics by regional and nonregional artists are exhibited at this spacious midtown gallery. Open Monday through Saturday from 10am to 5:30pm.

BOOKS

In addition to the independent bookstores in Albuquerque, the nationwide chain stores B. Dalton and Waldenbooks are represented. Among the most interesting bookstores are:

Bookworks, 4022 Rio Grande Blvd. NW. ☎ **344-8139.**

This store, selling both new and used books, has one of the most complete southwestern nonfiction and fiction sections. Recently enlarged, Bookworks carries major offerings in children's books, gift books, travel, art, literature, gardening, cooking, and architecture.

Corner Bookstore, 3500 Central Ave. SE. ☎ **266-2044.**

Located in the nostalgic Nob Hill section, Corner Bookstore has an especially fine collection of nonfiction and fine arts books. A superb source for a wide collection of travel, language, and Southwest books.

Cantwell's Books & Fine Papers, 8236 Menaul Blvd. NE. ☎ **294-4454.**

Cantwell's is noteworthy as the center for codependency books and serious modern fiction, as well as a large selection of children's books. Their gift and paper sidelines are worth checking out.

Footsteps Across New Mexico, 303 Romero NW, Suite 205. ☎ **243-4656.**

Located in Old Town Plaza, Footsteps Across New Mexico is a bookstore and a theater. The bookstore has the most comprehensive selection of books, maps, and guidebooks about New Mexico. The theater features a multimedia show that explains the history of New Mexico. Shows begin at 9am and run continuously throughout the day.

★ **Page One,** 11018 Montgomery Blvd. NE. ☎ **294-2026.**

New Mexico's largest bookstore has more than 135,000 titles in stock, close to 5,000 foreign and domestic magazines, and more than 150 out-of-state and foreign news-papers. It also carries road maps, computer books and software, and compact discs. Open daily from 8am to 10pm.

Tom Davies Bookshop, 414 Central Ave. SE. ☎ **247-2072.**

A specialist in rare and out-of-print books, maps, and documents since 1956, they carry a fine collection of hard-to-find southwestern regional literature. Open Monday through Saturday from 12:30 to 5pm, or by appointment.

Other specialty bookstores include **Birdsong Used Books & Records,** 139 Harvard Ave. SE, near the University of New Mexico (☎ **268-7204**), for used books and records; **Blue Eagle Book Shoppe,** 4807 Central Ave. NE, Suite B (☎ **268-3682**), for New Age materials; **Holman's,** 401 Wyoming Blvd. NE (☎ **265-7981**), for professional and technical texts; **Hosanna,** 2421 Aztec Blvd. NE, at Girard Boulevard (☎ **881-3321**), for Christian literature; **Murder Unlimited,** 2510 San Mateo Blvd. NE (☎ **884-5491**), for mystery titles; and **Trespassers William,** 5003 Lomas Blvd. NE (☎ **268-4601**), for children's books.

COOKING SCHOOL

Jane Butel's Cooking School, 800 Rio Grande NW, #14.
☎ toll free **800/473-TACO,** fax 505/243-8297.

If you've fallen in love with New Mexican and southwestern cooking during your stay in New Mexico (or even before you've arrived), you might like to sign up for cooking classes with Jane Butel, a leading southwestern cooking authority and author of 12 cookbooks. You'll learn the history and techniques of southwestern cuisine, and you'll develop cooking techniques through hands-on preparation. If you opt for the weeklong session, you'll start by learning about chiles. The second and third days you'll try your hand at native breads and dishes; the fourth day focuses on more innovative dishes, and the final day centers on appetizers, beverages, and desserts. There are also week-end sessions available. Call, write, or fax for current schedules and fees.

CRAFTS

Andrews Pueblo Pottery & Art Gallery, 303 Romero NW, Plaza Don Luis, Old Town. ☎ 243-0414.

Probably nowhere in New Mexico has a wider selection of contemporary and Pre-Columbian Pueblo pottery. The gallery also carries baskets, serigraphs, fetishes, and *kachina* dolls. Open daily from 10am to 6pm, until 8pm in summer.

Bien Mur Indian Market Center, I-25 at Tramway Rd. NE. ☎ 821-5400.

The Sandia Pueblos' crafts market is on their reservation, just beyond Albuquerque's northern city limits. The market sells turquoise and silver jewelry, pottery, baskets, *kachina* dolls, handwoven rugs, sand paintings, and other arts and crafts. The market is open Monday through Saturday from 9am to 5:30pm and Sunday from 11am to 5pm.

Gallery One, in the Nob Hill Shopping Center 3500 Central SE. ☎ 268-7449.

Folk art, jewelry, contemporary crafts, cards and paper, and natural fiber clothing.

House of the Shalako, First Plaza Galeria no. 65. ☎ 242-4579.

Traditional and contemporary Southwest Native American art—including Pueblo pottery, Navajo rugs, fetishes, jewelry, sand paintings, baskets, *kachinas*, and miniatures—can be found here. Open Monday through Friday from 10am to 5:30pm and Saturday from 10am to 5pm.

Mariposa Gallery, 113 Romero St. NW, Old Town. ☎ 842-9097.

Five rooms of contemporary crafts display everything from small-scale regional works to major national acquisitions. The collection includes fine jewelry, porcelain, tapestries, mixed-media works, and an otherwise eclectic variety of pieces. Mariposa's second location is at 303 Romero NW; it features a selection of contemporary American artwear, jewelry, and craft objects.

Nizhoni Moses Ltd., 326 San Felipe St. NW, Old Town. ☎ 842-1808.

Fine Native American art is featured here, including Pueblo pottery, Navajo weavings and mud toys, and a variety of contemporary and antique jewelry. Open daily from 10am to 7pm, later in spring and summer.

The Pueblo Loft, in the Nob Hill Shopping Center, 3500 Central SE. ☎ 268-8764.

All items featured here are crafted by Native Americans.

Tanner Chaney Gallery, 410 Romero St. NW, Old Town. ☎ 247-2242.

Contemporary and traditional Native American art, jewelry, weavings, sculpture, pottery, and baskets are displayed in this gallery, one of New Mexico's oldest. Lodged in a Civil War–era adobe hacienda, it also has notable historic collections. Open Monday through Saturday from 10am to 6pm and Sunday from noon to 6pm.

⭐ **Wright's Collection of Indian Art**, Park Square, 6600 Indian School Rd. NE. ☎ 883-6122.

This free private museum, first opened in 1907, carries fine handmade Native American arts and crafts, both contemporary and traditional. Open Monday through Friday from 10am to 6pm, Saturday 10am to 5pm.

FASHIONS

Fashion Square, San Mateo and Lomas Blvds. NE.

Upscale boutique lovers congregate at this award-winning midtown shopping area. The various shops feature retail fashions, jewelry, gift items, home furnishings, and luggage. There's also a florist, a beauty salon, and restaurants. Most shops are open Monday through Saturday from 10am to 6pm; some remain open Monday and Friday until 8pm and Sunday from noon to 5pm. Extended holiday hours are in effect Thanksgiving through Christmas.

Shops include **Kistler Collister,** with retail men's and women's fashions, shoes, accessories, furs, lingerie, cosmetics, and fragrances; **Ashlynn Fine Lines,** contemporary fashions and accessories; and **Santa Fe Pendleton,** with men's and women's clothing, Native American trade blankets, sweaters, and accessories.

Western Warehouse, 6210 San Mateo Blvd. NE. ☎ **883-7161** or toll free **800/214-7731.**

Family western wear, including an enormous collection of boots, is retailed here. Open Monday through Friday from 9:30am to 8pm, Saturday from 9:30am to 6pm, and Sunday from 11am to 5pm.

FOOD

The Candy Lady, 524 Romero St. NW, Old Town. ☎ **243-6239.**

What a fun place to visit, even if you're not a chocoholic! Chocolate candies and cakes of all kinds are made on the premises, and there's a side room "for over 18 only" with more ribald chocolate delights. Open Monday through Saturday from 10am to 6pm and Sunday from 10am to 5pm. Opposite the intersection of Mountain Road and Rio Grande Boulevard NW.

Chili Pepper Emporium, 328 San Felipe St. NW, Old Town. ☎ **242-7538.**

Old Town's "Hot Spot" carries everything to do with chili and chiles, from ground powders to the hottest chili pods in the world. You'll find all sorts of salsas and jams, as well as chile ceramics, jewelry, T-shirts, aprons, and oven mitts. They'll ship it home for you, too.

My Santa Fe Connection, 517 1/2 Central Ave. NW. ☎ **842-9564.**

This mail-order company specializes in native New Mexican food and gift items, including decorated chile *ristras,* and ships them anywhere. Open Monday through Friday from 8:30am to 5pm.

FURNITURE

Ernest Thompson Furniture, 2618 Coors Blvd. SW. ☎ **873-4652.**

Original design, handcrafted furniture is exhibited in the factory showroom. Thompson is a fifth-generation furniture maker who still uses traditional production techniques. Open Monday through Friday from 8am to 5pm and Saturday from 10am to 4pm. **Note:** At press time Ernest Thompson was moving to a new location. Call ahead for new address.

Schelu Interiors Gallery, 306 San Felipe St. NW, Old Town. ☎ **765-5869.**

Featured is the American Southwest Home Collection—weavings, rugs, handcrafted pottery, stoneware, and designer sculpture for contemporary homes. Open Monday through Saturday from 10am to 6pm and Sunday from 11am to 6pm.

Strictly Southwestern, 1321 Eubank Blvd. NE. ☎ **292-7337.**

Solid oak southwestern-style furniture is manufactured and sold directly to the buyer. Lighting, art, pottery, and other interior items are available. Open Monday through Saturday from 9am to 5pm.

GIFTS/SOUVENIRS

Casa de Avila, 324 San Felipe St. NW, Old Town. ☎ **242-3753.**

Southwest contemporary gifts, jewelry, and interior decor are retailed here. Open in summer weekdays from 9am to 9pm, weekends from 9am to 8pm; in winter, weekdays from 10am to 7pm, weekends from 10am to 6pm.

Elaine's Candles & Gifts, 1919 Old Town Rd. NW, Old Town. ☎ **242-2608.**

Native American pottery, sand paintings, chimes, bells, southwestern prints, T-shirts, and other popular souvenirs are sold. Open Monday through Saturday from 10am to 5pm and Sunday from 11am to 5pm.

La Piñata, 2 Patio Market NW, Old Town. ☎ **242-2400.**

Piñatas and paper flowers are the specialty here; they can be custom ordered and shipped. Open in winter daily from 10am to 5pm; in summer, daily from 9:30am to 8:30pm.

New Mexico's Own Bernalillo Store, 925 Camino del Pueblo, Bernalillo. ☎ **867-3004.**

Just north of Albuquerque in the town of Bernalillo is this wonderful store, which showcases a large selection of cottage-industry products—all of which were made in New Mexico. Inside you'll find gourmet food products, furniture, handmade clothing, cosmetics, and artwork.

Treasure House, 2012 S. Plaza NW, Old Town. ☎ **242-7204.**

Decorative tiles, ironwood carvings, Navajo sand paintings, Native American and gemstone jewelry, and other interesting items are available. The shop has been open since the 1940s. Open daily.

JEWELRY

Estevan's Custom Jewelry, 2 Patio Market NW, Old Town. ☎ **247-4615.**

Master goldsmith Estevan B. Garcia designs and handcrafts his own contemporary southwestern pieces. Open daily from 10am to 5pm (longer in summer).

Felipe's Indian Jewelry, 2038 S. Plaza NW, Old Town. ☎ **242-4784.**

Turquoise-and-silver jewelry isn't the only thing Felipe sells—he's also got a fine selection of gold and diamond jewelry. Open Monday through Saturday from 9am to 9pm and Sunday from 9am to 6:30pm.

Gus's Trading Company, 2026 Central Ave. SW, Old Town. ☎ **843-6381.**

Gus sells and repairs Hopi, Navajo, Zuni, and Santo Domingo Indian jewelry. He also carries *kachina* dolls, pottery, and original Native American paintings. Open Monday through Saturday from 9am to 5:30pm and Sunday from 10am to 5pm.

Jeweler's Repair Shop, 6910 Central Ave. SE. ☎ **266-9057.**

Besides repairs, this excellent shop opposite the State Fairgrounds sells diamonds, gold and silver jewelry, pottery, and *kachinas*. Open Monday through Friday from 9am to 5:30pm and Saturday from 9am to 3pm.

⭐ **Ortega's Indian Arts and Crafts,** 726 Coronado Center NE. ☎ **881-1231.**

An institution in Gallup, adjacent to the Navajo Reservation, Ortega's now has this Albuquerque store. They do sales, repairs, engravings, and appraisals of silver and turquoise jewelry. Open Monday through Friday from 10am to 9pm, Saturday from 10am to 6pm, and Sunday noon to 6pm.

⭐ **The Silver Bird,** 3821 Menaul Blvd. NE, at Carlisle Blvd. ☎ **881-2780.**

Visitors can make appointments to view the factory workshop, where Native Americans make jewelry and concho belts. Pottery, ceramics, paintings, mandalas, storytellers, sand paintings, and other crafts are also sold here. Open Monday through Friday from 8:30am to 6pm and Saturday from 9am to 5pm. A second location is at 2436 Menaul Blvd. NE.

Skip Maisel's Wholesale Indian Jewelry & Crafts, 510 Central Ave. SW, downtown. ☎ **242-6526.**

The largest selection of Native American jewelry, along with other arts and crafts, can be found at this downtown outlet. Zuni, Hopi, Navajo, and Santo Domingo Pueblo jewelry is featured. Open Monday through Friday from 9am to 5:30pm and Saturday from 9am to 5pm.

MARKETS

Flea Market, New Mexico State Fairgrounds.

Every Saturday and Sunday, year-round, the fairgrounds hosts this market from 8am to 5pm. There's no admission; just come and look around.

WINERIES

In addition to everything else New Mexico has to offer its visitors, wineries seem to be springing up all over the state. Wineries in Albuquerque or within short driving distance of the city include **Anderson Valley Vineyards** at 4920 Rio Grande Blvd. NW, Albuquerque, NM 87107 (☎ **505/344-7266**); **Sandia Shadows Vineyard & Winery,** 11704 Coronado NE, Albuquerque, NM 87122 (☎ **505/856-1006**); **Las Nutrias Vineyard & Winery,** 4627 Corrales Rd., Corrales, NM 87048 (☎ **505/897-7863**); and **Gruet Winery,** 8400 Pan-American Freeway NE, Albuquerque, NM 87113 (☎ **505/344-4453**).

8   Evening Entertainment

Albuquerque has an active performing arts and nightlife scene, as befits a city of half a million people. The performing arts are naturally multicultural, with Hispanic and (to a lesser extent) Native American productions sharing time with Anglo works; they include theater, opera, symphony, and dance. In addition, many national touring companies appear in the city. Country music predominates in nightclubs, though aficionados of rock, jazz, and other forms of music can find them here as well.

Full information on all major cultural events can be obtained from the Albuquerque Convention and Visitors Bureau (☎ **243-3696,** with a tape recording of local events after business hours). Current listings can be found in the two daily newspapers: Detailed weekend arts calendars can be found in the Thursday evening *Tribune* and the Friday morning *Journal.* The weekly *Albuquerque Voice,* launched in 1990, and the monthly *On the Scene* also carry entertainment listings.

Tickets for nearly all major entertainment and sporting events can be obtained from **TicketMaster,** 4004 Carlisle Blvd. NE (☎ **884-0999** for information, or **842-5387** to place credit-card orders on American Express, MasterCard, or VISA). This computerized ticket service is located in Smith's Food & Drug Stores, with 10 outlets in the greater Albuquerque area, and at the box offices of the New Mexico Symphony Orchestra, the Albuquerque Civic Light Opera Association, and Popejoy Hall on the University of New Mexico campus.

Discount tickets are often available for midweek and matinee performances. Check with specific theaters or concert halls.

Don't miss the free entertainment from May to August on Civic Plaza, at Third and Marquette streets NW. Musicians serenade outdoor diners during the Friday noon hour, while ethnic performers take to the plaza every Saturday evening, from 5 to 10pm, as part of Summerfest.

The Performing Arts

MAJOR PERFORMING ARTS COMPANIES

Classical Music & Opera

 New Mexico Symphony Orchestra, 3301 Menaul Blvd. NE, Suite 4, Albuquerque, NM 87107. ☎ **881-9590,** or **800/251-6676** for tickets.

NMSO musicians may be the busiest performing artists in New Mexico. As the orchestra enters its 63rd season in 1994–95, and its 18th as the official state symphony orchestra, it continues a hectic agenda, with approximately 60 performances of classics, pops, and chamber concerts scheduled in a September to May season.

Nine pairs of classics and six pops concerts are presented at Popejoy Hall. A chamber series is heard on six Sunday afternoons at the Sunshine Music Hall, 120 Central Ave. SW. In addition, the NMSO tours frequently: Another 10 dates are set in cities throughout the state.

Prices: Popejoy Hall concerts, adults $15–$25.50, students $12–$21, $5 Hot Tix (available 15 minutes prior to Popejoy Hall concerts). Symphony in the Sunshine, adults $10, students and seniors $6.

Chamber Orchestra of Albuquerque, 2730 San Pedro Dr. NE, Suite H-23.
☎ **881-2078.**

The 31-member professional orchestra, conducted by music director David Oberg, performs an October to June season, primarily at St. John's United Methodist Church, 2626 Arizona St. NE. The concerts include a subscription series of six classical concerts (in October, November, January, March, May, and June); an all-baroque concert in February; concerts for children in February and April; a joint concert with the University of New Mexico Chorus; and outreach programs for seniors in December. The orchestra regularly features guest artists of national and international renown.

Prices: $12–$21, depending on seating and performance.

Albuquerque Civic Light Opera Association, 4201 Ellison Rd. NE.
☎ **345-6577.**

Five major Broadway musicals are presented each year at Popejoy Hall during a March to December season. Each production is staged for three consecutive weekends, including two Sunday matinees.

In 1994, in its 27th season, ACLOA presented *South Pacific, The Fantasticks, Chicago, Big River, and The Music Man.*

Prices: Adults $9–$17.50, students and seniors $7–$15.50.

Opera Southwest in Albuquerque, 809 Morningside Dr. NE. ☎ 243-0591.

Most years, this regional company, established in 1972, presents three European operas (with English lyrics) between October and May. Performances are at the KiMo Theatre on Saturday, Tuesday, and Friday evenings, followed by a Sunday matinee.

Prices: Adults $8–$25, student rush (day of performance) $3.

Theater Companies

La Compañia de Teatro de Albuquerque, 518 1st St. NW. ☎ 242-7929.

One of only 10 major professional Hispanic companies in the United States and Puerto Rico, this company presents four productions at the KiMo Theatre in October, December, April, and June. It also does barrio tours and takes its productions to local community centers and churches. The semiprofessional company's mix of contemporary and classic comedies, dramas, and musicals includes one Spanish play a year; others are in English or bilingual.

Prices: Thurs and Sun, adults $8, students and seniors $7; Fri–Sat, adults $9, students and seniors $8.

Dance Companies

The New Mexico Ballet Company, 3620 Wyoming Blvd. NE, Suite 105D. (P.O. Box 21518), Albuquerque, NM 87154. ☎ 299-7798.

Founded 1972, the state's oldest ballet company performs an October-to-April season at Popejoy Hall. Its schedule typically includes a fall production like *Legend of Sleepy Hollow,* a December performance of *The Nutcracker* or *A Christmas Carol,* and a contemporary spring production. Professional guest artists fill the leading roles in some productions, but most of the cast of 60 to 150 are local and amateur. The New Mexico Symphony Orchestra sometimes provides the music.

Prices: Adults $10–$20, students $5–$10.

MAJOR CONCERT HALLS & ALL-PURPOSE AUDITORIUMS

Keller Hall, Cornell St. at Redondo Dr. S, University of New Mexico, ☎ 277-4402.

The fine arts department's main auditorium, with seating for 336, hosts numerous musical concerts throughout the year, including student recitals and concerts. It's best known for its two annual distinguished faculty and guest artist series, with seven chamber music and solo concerts each from August to December and from January to June.

Tickets: General admission $6; students $3, faculty, staff, and seniors $2.50.

★ **KiMo Theatre,** 419 Central Ave. NW at 5th St. ☎ 848-1370 for information, 764-1700 for tickets (Mon–Fri 11am–5pm).

Albuquerque's historic showcase of the performing arts is a tribute to the region's Native American cultures. Opened in 1927, the KiMo's architecture is a colorful adaptation of an adobe pueblo, and its interior decor emphasizes Native American motifs. Handmade tiles adorn the lobby; wall paintings simulate Navajo sand paintings; murals of the legendary "Seven Cities of Cíbola" stand outside the balcony seating area; even the design of the box office is based on a *kiva.* And then there's the remarkable lighting: White plaster buffalo heads with lights in their eye sockets adorn the mezzanine columns and outline the ceiling of the theater itself.

The 750-seat theater, owned by the city of Albuquerque, is the home of Opera Southwest and La Compañia de Teatro de Albuquerque. In addition, it hosts numerous dance, music, and theater groups. The KiMo and the city also sponsor a series of touring shows of national and international importance.

Prices: $5–$25 depending on seating and performance. Series tickets are available at a discount, and there are discounts for children.

Popejoy Hall, Cornell St. at Redondo Dr., University of New Mexico. ☎ **277-3121.**

A multipurpose performing arts facility, Popejoy Hall is Albuquerque's leading venue for major musical entertainment. Seating 2,094, it is the home of the New Mexico Symphony Orchestra, the Albuquerque Civic Light Opera Association, the New Mexico Ballet Company, and UNM's highly popular September to April "Broadway" series, featuring major New York productions. For information on each of the local companies, see the descriptions above and below.

Adjacent Woodward Hall is the site of Albuquerque's **June Music Festival** (☎ **888-1842**), a series of five concerts, featuring nationally and internationally known string quartets with guests artists from leading symphony orchestras, during the first two weeks following Memorial Day. The festival celebrated its 50th anniversary year in 1991. Season subscription tickets are $65 to $80; single tickets, $16 to $20 for adults, $10 for students.

Tickets: Broadway series, $20–$38 general admission (depending upon production), with discounts for students, faculty, staff, and seniors. For prices of other events, see descriptions of specific companies.

South Broadway Cultural Center, 1025 Broadway Blvd. SE. ☎ **848-1320.**

Funded by the city of Albuquerque, SBCC presents a diversity of multicultural programming in the performing arts—from blues singers to avant-garde comedy, Mexican dance theater to medieval troubador melodies. The center, which seats 315, includes a 3,000-square-foot gallery space and a 2,000-square-foot multipurpose room. There is also a large, well-stocked branch library. Open Monday through Saturday from 9am to 5:30pm. It's located on the northwest corner of Broadway and Garfield SE, three blocks north of Stadium Boulevard.

Tickets: Adults $5, children 12 and under $2 for touring shows.

THEATERS

Albuquerque Little Theatre, 224 San Pasquale Ave. SW. ☎ **242-4750.**

The 65-year-old amateur theater presents six plays annually during a September-to-May season. Each year, productions cover the gamut from classic to contemporary, comedy to mystery, drama to musical. The 1994–95 calendar included *A Chorus Line, Count Dracula, The Best Christmas Pageant Ever, You Can't Take It with You, Steel Magnolias,* and *Lend Me a Tenor.*

The 570-seat Little Theatre Building, a masterpiece of Territorial architecture, was designed by noted regional architect John Gaw Meem and built in the 1930s with WPA funds. It's located just south of Old Town.

Prices: Adults $9–$11, seniors and students $7–$9.

Rodey Theatre and Experimental Theatre, Fine Arts Center, University of New Mexico. ☎ **277-4332.**

Major student dramatic productions and dance recitals, from classical ballet to modern jazz dance, hold forth at the 440-seat Rodey Theatre. The adjacent Experimental

Theatre, which seats 75 to 150 (depending upon configuration), hosts a variety of unique productions, from one-acts to dance recitals.

Prices: General admission $8, faculty $6, students $4.50.

The Vortex Theatre, Buena Vista (just South of Central Ave.) ☎ **247-8600.**

An 18-year-old community theater known for its innovative productions, the Vortex is Albuquerque's "Off Broadway," presenting plays ranging from classic to original scripts. The company mounts 10 shows a year, including (in 1993–94) the Tony Award–winning *Dancing at Lughnasa,* the bawdy Greek comedy *Lysistrata,* and Shakespeare's *Macbeth.* Performances take place Friday and Saturday at 8pm and Sunday at 6pm. The black-box theater seats 90.

Prices: Adults $7, students and seniors $6, children 13 and under $5. All tickets $5 Sun.

Albuquerque Children's Theatre, 4139 Prospect Ave. NE. ☎ **888-3644.**

Playwright Bill Hayden established this troupe at his ballet school in the late 1950s, and it has grown to become one of the country's most unique children's theaters. Hayden's philosophy was to produce shows for children, by children, and to give the participating kids a nonstressful introduction to theater: just 90 minutes of rehearsal each week. When he died in 1989, after three decades of instruction, he left a legacy of original plays and adaptations of such classics as *Cinderella, Snow White,* and *Puss in Boots.* There are three companies: seniors (ages 12 to 16) do January and July shows at Popejoy Hall or Rodey Theatre at UNM. Juniors (ages 8 to 11) and play actors (ages 4 to 7) also do two shows a year, but theirs are at the Hayden School of Ballet.

Prices: $4 for public (senior) shows.

LOCAL CULTURAL ENTERTAINMENTS

Attracted in large part by its Hispanic heritage, there are several local **flamenco** troupes, and others of national renown often visit Albuquerque. Eva Encinias's **Ritmo Flamenco Dance Company** is among the outstanding local troupes.

The Rodey Theatre (see above) at the University of New Mexico hosts an annual **Flamenco Festival** in late June, with four performances in one long weekend. Tickets run $15 to $20 per show. Call **277-6122** for information.

THE CLUB & MUSIC SCENE

Comedy Clubs/Dinner Theater

Laffs Comedy Caffe, 3100 Juan Tabo Blvd., at Candelaria Rd. NE. ☎ **296-JOKE.**

Top acts from each coast, including comedians who have appeared on the *Tonight Show, The Late Show with David Letterman,* and HBO, also appear at Albuquerque's top comedy club. Show times are Tuesday through Thursday and Sunday at 8pm, with second shows Friday and Saturday at 10:30pm.

Tuesday is "Best of Albuquerque" night. Wednesday is smokefree night; Thursday and Sunday are Laff's T-shirt nights. The cafe serves dinner nightly from 6pm.

Admission: Cover varies.

Downtown Funnies, 407 Central NW. ☎ **247-8727.**

A "cappuccino comedy club," Downtown Funnies is a popular place for live entertainment on Wednesday through Saturday nights.

Admission: Cover varies.

Mystery Cafe, 125 Second NW. (in La Posada de Albuquerque) ☎ **237-1385.**

If you're in the mood for a little dinner theater, the Mystery Cafe might be just the ticket. You'll help the characters in this ever-popular, delightfully funny show solve the mystery as they serve you a four-course meal. Reservations are a must. Call for show times and prices.

Country Music

Caravan East, 7605 Central Ave. NE. ☎ **265-7877.**

"Always a dance partner," boasts this large country-and-western club, located east of the State Fairgrounds. Two bands share stage time Monday through Saturday from 5pm to 2am and Sunday from 4:30pm to midnight; there are occasional national acts. Tuesday is ladies' night. Happy hour is from 4:30 to 7pm, and there's a free dinner buffet from 5 to 7pm.

Admission: Fri–Sat $3; free other nights.

Midnight Rodeo, 4901 McLeod Rd. NE, near San Mateo Blvd. ☎ **888-0100.**

The Southwest's largest nightclub of any kind, Midnight Rodeo not only has bars in all corners of its enormous domicile, it even has its own shopping arcade, including a boutique and gift shop. A DJ spins records daily until closing; the 5,000-square-foot hardwood dance floor is so big it resembles an indoor horse track. Free dance lessons are offered Sunday from 5:30 to 7pm and Tuesday from 7 to 8pm. A busy kitchen serves simple but hearty meals to dancers who work up appetites, and there's a $3 buffet Monday to Friday from 5 to 7pm.

Admission: Fri–Sat $3.

Rock/Jazz

Beyond Ordinary, 211 Gold SW. ☎ **764-8858.**

Albuquerque's alternative rock hangout has live music, including reggae, and a DJ spinning progressive disks Friday and Saturday from 7pm to 1:30am and Sunday from 7pm to midnight. An art gallery exhibits equally alternative paintings. Happy hour is Wednesday through Friday from 4 to 8pm.

Admission: $4.

Brewsters Pub, 312 Central SW. ☎ **247-2533.**

Wednesday through Saturday nights, Brewsters Pub offers live entertainment in a sports-bar setting. There are 24 beers on tap, as well as a wide variety of bottled beer. Sports fans can enjoy the day's game on a big-screen TV. Barbecue is served at lunch and dinner.

Admission: Cover varies.

The Cooperage, 7220 Lomas Blvd. NE. ☎ **255-1657.**

Jazz, rhythm-and-blues, rock, and salsa keep dancers hopping Friday and Saturday nights inside this gigantic wooden barrel (see "Dining" above).

Admission: $3–$5.

Dingo Bar, 313 Gold SW. ☎ **243-0663.**

The Dingo Bar is one of Albuquerque's premier rock clubs. The nightly live entertainment runs from punk rock to classic rock-and-roll to jazz.

Admission: Cover varies according to performers.

MORE ENTERTAINMENT

Albuquerque's best nighttime attraction is the **Sandia Peak Tramway** (see "Attractions" above), and its two restaurants, **High Finance** at the summit and the **Firehouse** at the base (see "Dining" above). Both offer a view nonpareil of the Rio Grande valley and the city lights.

The best place to catch foreign films, art films, and limited-release productions is the **Guild Cinema,** 3405 Central Ave. NE (☎ 255-1848). For film classics, check out the **UNM SUB Theater,** on the UNM campus, with double features Wednesday through Sunday, changing nightly.

Major Albuquerque first-run theaters include **Coronado Six Theater,** 6401 Uptown Blvd. NE (☎ 881-5266); **Del Norte Cinema Four,** 7120 Wyoming Blvd. NE (☎ 823-6666); **United Artists Four Hills 12 Theater,** 13160 Central Ave. SE, at Tramway Blvd. (☎ 275-2114); **Ladera Six Cinema,** 3301 Coors Blvd. NW (☎ 836-5606); **Montgomery Plaza-5,** San Mateo Boulevard at 165 Montgomery Plaza NE (☎ 881-1080); **San Mateo Cinema 8,** 631 San Mateo Blvd. NE (☎ 889-3051); **United Artists 8 at High Ridge,** Tramway Boulevard at Indian School Road (☎ 275-0038); and **Winrock 6 UA Cinema,** 201 Winrock Center NE (☎ 883-6022). **The Albuquerque Drive-In Theatre,** Montgomery Boulevard NE and I-25 (☎ 345-8641), has six theaters, all showing double features beginning at 8pm.

Isleta Gaming Palace, 11000 Broadway Blvd. SE (☎ 869-2614).

A luxurious, air-conditioned bingo parlor with a full-service restaurant, nonsmoking section, and free bus transportation on request. Doors open (7 days a week) at 9pm for the video casino, and bingo begins at noon and 6:30pm on Saturday and Sunday; weekdays gaming begins at 6:30pm.

9 Easy Excursions

Pueblos

Ten Native American pueblos are located within an hour's drive of central Albuquerque. Two of them, Acoma and Laguna, are discussed in chapter 8, "Northwestern New Mexico." The others, from south to north, are discussed here along with Coronado and Jemez state monuments, which preserve ancient pueblo ruins.

In visiting pueblos, remember to respect them as people's homes. Don't peek into doors and windows, and don't climb on top of buildings. Stay out of cemeteries and ceremonial rooms, such as *kivas,* as these are sacred grounds. Do not speak during dances or ceremonies, nor applaud after their conclusions: Silence is mandatory. Most pueblos require a permit to carry a camera or to sketch or paint on location. Many pueblos prohibit picture taking at any time.

Isleta Pueblo, P.O. Box 1270, Isleta, NM 87022. ☎ **869-3111.**

Just 14 miles south of Albuquerque, off I-25 or U.S. 85, is the largest of the Tiwa-speaking pueblos, comprising several settlements on the west side of the Rio Grande. The largest village, Shiaw-iba, contains the Mission of San Agustin de Isleta, one of the few mission churches not destroyed in the 17th-century Pueblo rebellion. Grasslands and wooded *bosque* along the river are gradually becoming part of Albuquerque's growing urban sprawl; already, some governmental agencies and commercial interests are leasing property from the Isleta. Most of the pueblo's 3,000 residents work in Albuquerque; others are employed in farming and ranching or private business.

Isleta women potters make red wares distinctive for their red-and-black designs on white backgrounds. The tribe operates a modern bingo hall at 11000 Broadway Blvd. SE (☎ 869-2614), and fishing and camping areas at Isleta Lakes. Permits ($2 to $7 daily) can be purchased at the recreation area.

The Isleta hold an evergreen dance in late February, and stage a Spanish fiesta with a carnival, food stands, and religious events on August 28. The big day of the year is the feast day honoring St. Augustine, September 4, when a midmorning mass and procession are followed by an afternoon harvest dance.

Admission: Free. Photography limited to church only.

Open: Daylight hours, seven days a week.

Sandia Pueblo, P.O. Box 6008, Bernalillo, NM 87004. ☎ 867-3317.

Established about 1300, this was one of the few pueblos visited by Coronado's contingent in 1540. Remains of that village, known as Nafiat, or "sandy," are still visible near the present church. The Sandia people temporarily fled to Hopi country after the Pueblo rebellion of 1680, but returned to the Rio Grande in 1742. Many of today's 300 Tiwa (Tanoan) speaking inhabitants work in Albuquerque or at Pueblo Enterprises. They also run the bingo hall (sessions Monday to Thursday 12:30 and 6:30pm) and the Bien Mur Indian Market Center on Tramway Road (☎ 821-5400). Both are about 14 miles north of Albuquerque off I-25.

The pueblo celebrates its St. Anthony feast day on June 13 with a midmorning mass, procession, and afternoon corn dance. Another dance honors newly elected governors in January.

Admission: Free. No photography, recording, or sketching allowed.

Open: Daylight hours.

Coronado State Monument, N.M. 44 (P.O. Box 95), Bernalillo, NM 87004. ☎ 867-5351.

When the Spanish explorer Coronado traveled through this region in 1540–41 while searching for the Seven Cities of Cíbola, he wintered at a village on the west bank of the Rio Grande—probably one located on the ruins of the ancient Anasazi pueblo known as Kuaua. Those excavated ruins have been preserved in this state monument. Hundreds of rooms can be seen, and a *kiva* has been restored so that visitors may descend a ladder into the enclosed space, once the site of sacred rites. Unique multi-colored murals, depicting human and animal forms, were found on successive layers of wall plaster in this and other kivas here; some examples are displayed in the monument's small archaeological museum.

An adjacent state park has sheltered campsites, hot showers, and RV hookups. The site is 20 miles north of Albuquerque, via I-25 to Bernalillo and N.M. 44 west.

Admission: Adults $2.10. Children 15 and under free.

Open: May 1–Sept 15 9am–6pm; Sept 16–Apr 30 8am–5pm; closed major holidays.

Santa Ana Pueblo, Star Route, Box 37, Bernalillo, NM 87004. ☎ 867-3301.

Though partially abandoned and closed to visitors except for ceremonial events, this pueblo on the lower Jemez River claims a population of about 550. Many "residents" who maintain family homes at the pueblo actually live nearer the stream's confluence with the Rio Grande, in a settlement known as Ranchos de Santa Ana near Bernalillo, where farming is more productive.

Pottery, wood carvings, ceremonial bands, red cloth belts, and unique wooden crosses with straw inlay are produced in the old village by a handful of craftspeople. Marketing is handled by the Ta-Ma-Myia Co-operative Association.

Guests are normally welcomed only on ceremonial days. Pueblo members perform the turtle and corn dances on New Year's Day; the eagle, elk, buffalo, and deer dances on January 6, Three Kings Day; the spring corn basket dance at Easter; various dances for St. Anthony's Day on June 29 and St. Anne's Day on July 26; and several days of dances at Christmastime.

The pueblo is about 30 miles north of Albuquerque, reached via I-25 to Bernalillo, then 8 miles northwest on N.M. 44.

Admission: Free. No photography is permitted.

Open: Daylight hours, certain ceremonial days only.

Zia Pueblo, San Ysidro, NM 87053. ☎ 867-3304.

This pueblo of 720 inhabitants blends in so perfectly with the soft tans of the stone and sand of the desertlike land around it that it's very hard to see—it's like a chameleon on a tree trunk. The pueblo is best known for its famous sun symbol—now the official symbol of the state of New Mexico—adapted from a pottery design showing three rays going in each of the four directions from a sun, or circle. It is hailed in the pledge to the state flag as "a symbol of perfect friendship among united cultures."

Zia has a reputation for excellence in pottery making. Zia pottery is identified by its unglazed terra-cotta coloring and traditional geometric designs and plant and animal motifs painted on a white slip. Paintings, weaving, and sculptures are also prized products of the artists of the Zia community; their work can be viewed and purchased at the Zia Cultural Center located at the pueblo. Our Lady of the Assumption, the patron saint, is given a celebratory corn dance on her day, August 15.

The pueblo is about eight miles northwest of the Santa Ana Pueblo, just off N.M. 44.

Admission: Free. No photography is permitted.

Open: Daylight hours.

Jemez Pueblo, P.O. Box 78, Jemez, NM 87024. ☎ 834-7359.

The 2,400 Jemez natives—including descendants of the Pecos Pueblo, east of Santa Fe, abandoned in 1838—are the only remaining people to speak the Towa dialect of the Tanoan group. The Jemez are famous for their excellent dancing and feast-making—their feast days attract residents from other pueblos, turning the celebrations into multitribal fairs. Two rectangular *kivas* are central points for groups of dancers. Try to attend the Feast of Our Lady of Angels on August 12; the Feast of San Diego on November 12, when the Pecos bull dance is performed; or the Feast of Our Lady of Guadalupe on December 12 for the Matachines dance, based on a Spanish morality play.

Woven belts, plaited yucca-fiber baskets, and cloth for garments are the primary crafts. A famous native potter who lives at Jemez Pueblo is Estella Loretto (☎ 834-7444), who has studied ceramics from Italy to Japan, the South Pacific to the Himalayas.

There is fishing and picnicking along the Jemez River, and camping at the Dragonfly Recreation Area. Pueblo stores fishing permits at $2 to $5 daily, and permits for game hunting may be bought from the pueblo governor's office.

The pueblo is 42 miles northwest of Albuquerque via I-25 to Bernalillo, N.M. 44 to San Ysidro, and N.M. 4 for 43 final miles.

Admission: Free. No photography is permitted.

Open: Daylight hours daily. (May be closed certain ceremonial days.)

Jemez State Monument, N.M. 4, (P.O. Box 143) Jemez Springs, NM 87025. ☎ **829-3530.**

All that's left of the Mission of San Jose de los Jemez, founded by Franciscan missionaries in 1621, is preserved at this site. Visitors find the mission's massive walls standing alone, its sparse, small door and window openings underscoring the need for security and permanence in those times. The mission was excavated between 1921 and 1937, along with portions of a prehistoric Jemez pueblo. The pueblo, near the Jemez Hot Springs, was called Giusewa—"place of the boiling waters."

A small museum at the site exhibits artifacts found during the excavation, describes traditional crafts and foods, and weaves a thread of history from Anasazi to the 21st century in a series of displays. An interpretive trail winds through the ruins. The monument is located about 18 miles north on N.M. 4 from N.M. 44.

Admission: $2.10 per person 16 and over, 15 and under free.

Open: May 1–Sept 15 9:30am–5:30pm, Sept 16–Apr 30 8:30am–4:30pm. **Closed:** Thanksgiving, Christmas, and New Year's Day.

San Felipe Pueblo, P.O. Box A, San Felipe, NM 87001. ☎ **867-3381.**

This conservative pueblo of 2,400 people, located on a mesa on the west bank of the Rio Grande, is known for its beautiful ritual ceremonies. The plaza has been worn into the shape of a bowl by the feet of San Felipe's dancers over the centuries. In the grandest of these dances, hundreds of men, women, and children move through their rhythmic steps all day long in the spring corn dance on May 1, performed in honor of the pueblo's patron, St. Philip (San Felipe). The dancing is done to a great chorus of male singers intoning music that reaches back into prehistory and evokes strong emotions in participants and in visitors, too. Other ceremonial events here are a January 6 corn dance, a February 2 buffalo dance for Candelaria Day, and many dances over several days around Christmastime.

San Felipe is 30 miles northeast of Albuquerque via I-25 and an access road.

Admission: Free. Photography is not permitted.

Open: Daylight hours.

Santo Domingo Pueblo, P.O. Box 99, Santo Domingo, NM 87052. ☎ **465-2214.**

One of New Mexico's largest pueblos with 3,450 residents, this farming community on the east bank of the Rio Grande is also one of the state's most traditional. Craftspeople are known for their beautiful silver jewelry, unique necklaces of *heishi* (shell fragments), innovative pottery, and fine weaving. They are renowned as astute traders and often will swap with visitors for the value of their crafts rather than selling them for cash.

At the dramatic Santo Domingo Pueblo feast day, August 4, the corn dance is performed as it is done nowhere else. It is a lavish production involving clowns, scores of singers and drummers, and 500 tireless and skilled dancers in imaginative traditional costumes. Other festive occasions during the year include Three Kings Day, January 6, with elk, eagle, buffalo, and deer dances; Candelaria Day, February 2, with the buffalo dance; the Easter spring corn dance and basket dance; the San Pedro's Day corn dance, June 29; and many traditional dances in the Christmas season.

Santo Domingo is 50 miles northeast of Albuquerque via I-25 north to N.M. 22.

Admission: Free. No photography or sketching is permitted.

Open: Daylight hours.

Cochiti Pueblo, P.O. Box 70, Cochiti Pueblo, NM 87041. ☎ **465-2244.**

Occupied continuously since the 14th century, the northernmost of the Keresan-speaking pueblos (pop. 920) stretches along the Rio Grande. Its Church of San Buenaventura, though rebuilt and remodeled since, still contains sections of its original 1628 structure.

Cochiti is well known for its pottery, especially the famous "storyteller" figures created by Helen Cordero. Beadwork and soft leather moccasins are other craft specialties. The pueblo's double-headed dance drums, made from hollowed-out cottonwood logs and covered with leather, are used in ceremonies throughout the Rio Grande area.

San Buenaventura Feast Day is July 14, when the corn and rain dances are performed. Other events include a New Year's Day turtle dance and corn dance; eagle, elk, buffalo, and deer dances on January 6, Three Kings Day; the spring corn dance and basket dance for Easter; more such dances on May 3, Santa Cruz Day; and ceremonies for several days around Christmas.

Fishing and bird hunting on pueblo grounds requires purchase of a permit from the pueblo governor for $2 to $7. Cochiti Lake is popular for water sports among Albuquerque citizens.

The pueblo is about 40 miles north of Albuquerque, via U.S. 85, then north on N.M. 22 and N.M. 16.

Admission: Free. No photography or sketching is permitted.

Open: Daylight hours daily.

The Turquoise Trail

New Mexico Highway 14 begins 16 miles east of downtown Albuquerque, at I-40's Cedar Crest exit, and winds 46 miles to Santa Fe along the east side of the Sandia Mountains. Best known as the Turquoise Trail, this state-designated scenic and historic route traverses the revived "ghost towns" of Golden, Madrid, and Cerrillos, where gold, silver, coal, and turquoise were once mined in great quantities. Modern-day settlers, mostly artists and craftspeople, have brought a renewed frontier spirit to these old mining towns.

Before reaching the first of these towns, however, travelers can make a turn at **Sandia Park,** 6 miles north of the I-40 junction, to begin climbing 10,678-foot **Sandia Crest** on N.M. 536. The road is paved, well maintained, and wide enough to accommodate tour buses, with no severe hairpin turns; there is parking at the summit overlook. Sandia Crest is the high point of the Sandia Mountains and, like Sandia Peak, offers a spectacular panoramic view in all directions. Many miles of Cíbola National Forest trails, including the popular north-south Sandia Crest Trail, run through here; box lunches can be provided for day hikers by the **Sandia Crest House Restaurant & Gift Shop** (☎ **243-0605**). The restaurant is open daily May to October from 10am to 9pm, 10am to one hour after sunset the rest of the year.

En route to the summit, on N.M. 536 in Sandia Park, is the **Tinkertown Museum** (☎ **281-5233**), a miniature wood-carved western village with more than 10,000 objects on display, including 500 animations—among them a turn-of-the-century circus. There are also antique dolls and old-time music machines. In 1994 a 45-foot antique wooden sailing ship (built in England in 1936) was added to the museum collection. Tinkertown is open April 1 to October 31 daily from 9am to 6pm. Admission is $2.50 for adults, $2 for seniors, and $1 under 16.

If you turn north off N.M. 536 onto the unpaved N.M. 165, and proceed about 5 tortuous miles on the rough, narrow byway, you'll come to **Sandia Cave,** a short walk from the road. Artifacts identified as those of "Sandia Man," dating back to 23,000 B.C. were found in this cave. They are some of the oldest evidence of humankind ever discovered in the United States.

Golden is 10 miles north of the Sandia Park junction on N.M. 14. Its sagging houses, with their missing boards and the wind whistling through their broken eaves, make it a purist's ghost town. There is a general store open, though, as well as a bottle seller's "glass garden." Nearby are ruins of an Indian pueblo called Paako, abandoned around 1670. Such communities of mud huts were all the Spaniards ever found on their avid quests for the gold of Cíbola.

Madrid (pronounced with the accent on the first syllable) is 12 miles north of Golden. Madrid and neighboring Cerrillos were in a fabled turquoise-mining area dating back into prehistory. This semiprecious stone, known in the Old World since 4000 B.C., got its name from the French for "Turkish." In Mexico it was sacred to the Aztec royal house and was forbidden to commoners; it was believed to have an affinity to its owner, to grow pale in prophecy of a coming misfortune, or to glow richly with its wearer's good health. A visitor might still find a bit of raw turquoise in the tailings of an ancient pit mine. The Spanish worked these mines, using local Native American slave labor, until 1680, when a rockfall killed 30 of the miners. Their lack of concern was one of the final sparks contributing to the Pueblo revolt of that year.

Gold and silver mines followed, and when they faltered, there was still coal. The Turquoise Trail towns supplied fuel to locomotives of the Santa Fe Railroad until the 1950s, when the railroad converted to diesel fuel. Madrid used to produce 100,000 tons of coal a year.

In 1919, an idealistic mine owner named Huber transformed a gloomy scene into a showcase village with a new recreation center, hotel, hospital, school, church, post office, department store, drugstore, auto showroom, beauty shop, fire station, dental office, tennis and basketball courts, golf course, shooting range, a brass band, and a Christmas light show; early transcontinental planes used to detour over the town for a look. But the town emptied when the mine closed in 1956.

Twenty years later, the owner's son sold everything at auction: tipple, breaker, tavern, church, store, houses, roads—the lot. A handful of diehards, many of them artists and craftspeople, bought property and stayed on. Today the village seems stuck in the 1960s: Its funky, ramshackle houses have many counterculture residents, the "hippies" of yore, who operate several crafts stores and import shops.

Madrid's **Old Coal Mine Museum** (☎ 473-0743) is an on-site museum that features mining and railroad relics, including antique cars, tools, workshops, and a fully restored 1900 Baldwin Steam Locomotive—you can even climb aboard and ring the bell! The museum is open daily, weather permitting, and the admission price is $2.50 for adults.

Next door, the **Mine Shaft Tavern** continues its lively career with buffalo steaks on the menu and live music daily, attracting folks from Santa Fe and Albuquerque. It's adjacent to the **Madrid Opera House,** claimed to be the only such establishment on earth with a built-in steam locomotive on its stage. (The structure was an engine repair shed; the balcony is made of railroad track.)

Cerrillos, 3 miles north of Madrid, is a village of dirt roads that sprawls along Galisteo Creek. It appears to have changed very little since it was founded during a lead strike in 1879; the old hotel, the saloon, even the sheriff's office have a flavor very much like an Old West movie set.

Cerrillos once had eight daily newspapers, several hotels, and two dozen saloons, serving miners from 30 mines. Today only the Palace Hotel stands, in ruins, used as a stable for llamas that go on backcountry pack trips. The general store sells flea-market items, antiques, and some old turquoise. The Cerrillos Bar—part of the original Tiffany Saloon, founded by the New York jewelry family—has billiard tables in an ornate Victorian setting. And an old adobe house called Casa Grande shelters an unusual trading post.

I-25 at Santa Fe is 15 miles on.

Salinas Pueblo Missions National Monument, P.O. Box 496, Mountainair, NM 87036. ☎ 847-2585.

The Spanish conquistadors' Salinas Jurisdiction, on the east side of the Manzano Mountains (southeast of Albuquerque), was an important 17th-century trade center because of the salt extracted by the Native Americans from the salt lakes. Franciscan priests, utilizing Native American labor, constructed missions of adobe, sandstone, and limestone for their converts. The ruins of some of the most durable—along with evidence of preexisting Anasazi and Mogollon cultures—are highlights of a visit to Salinas Pueblo Missions National Monument. The monument consists of three separate units: the ruins of Abo, Quarai, and Gran Quivira. They are centered around the quiet town of Mountainair, 75 miles southeast of Albuquerque at the junction of U.S. 60 and N.M. 55.

Abo (☎ 847-2400) boasts the 40-foot-high ruins of the Mission San Gregorio de Abo, a rare example of medieval architecture in the United States. Quarai (☎ 847-2290) preserves the largely intact remains of the Mission of La Purisima Concepción de Cuarac (1630). Its vast size—100 feet long and 40 feet high—contrasts with the modest size of the pueblo mounds. A small museum in the visitor center has a scale model of the original church, with a selection of artifacts found at the site. Gran Quivira (☎ 847-2770) once had a population of 1,500. Las Humanes has 300 rooms and 7 *kivas*. Rooms dating to 1300 can be seen. There are indications that an older village, dating to A.D. 800, may have previously stood here. Ruins of two churches (one almost 140 feet long) and a convent have been preserved. At the visitor center, you'll be able to view many artifacts from the site, a 40-minute movie showing the excavation of some 200 rooms, and a short history video of Las Humanes.

All three pueblos and the churches that rose above them are believed to have been abandoned in the 1670s. Self-guided tour pamphlets can be obtained at the units' respective visitor centers and at the Salinas Pueblo Missions National Monument Visitor Center in Mountainair, one block west of the intersection of U.S. 60 and N.M. 55 on U.S. 60. This main visitor center offers an audiovisual presentation on the region's history, a bookstore, and an art exhibit.

Admission: Free.

Open: Sites, daily 9am–5pm. Visitor center in Mountainair, daily 8am–5pm. **Closed:** Christmas and New Year's Day. **Directions:** Abo is 9 miles west of Mountainair on U.S. 60. Quarai is 9 miles north of Mountainair on N.M. 55. Gran Quivira is 25 miles south of Mountainair on N.M. 55. All roads are paved.

5

Santa Fe

THE NEW MEXICO STATE CAPITAL IS CAUGHT IN A TIME WARP BETWEEN THE 17TH and 21st centuries, between traditional Native American and Hispanic cultures and the modern onslaught of tourism. The longest continuously occupied capital city in the United States, it has been under the rule of five governments: Spain (1610–80 and 1692–1821), the Pueblos (1680–92), Mexico (1821–46), the United States (since 1846), and the Confederacy (for a short time in 1862).

Nestled at 7,000 feet in the pastel foothills of the Sangre de Cristo Mountains is this community of 60,000 people. Residents call it "The City Different."

A carefully considered plan to preserve and perpetuate pre-20th-century architecture has made downtown Santa Fe look like an adobe enclave. Much of the rest of the city has followed suit. For miles in all directions, flat-topped, earth-colored homes, many of them valued in the millions of dollars, speckle the hills amid sparse piñon and mesquite forests. Most of the construction is actually stuccoed concrete. A standing joke in Santa Fe art circles is that the city sanctions the use of 42 shades of brown.

But therein lies much of its charm. Santa Fe is nothing if not aesthetically pleasing and artistically involved. It has a famous art colony, larger (though not as historically rich, perhaps) than that of Taos; the world-renowned Santa Fe Opera and other acclaimed performing-arts companies; a highbrow literary segment; an active festival life; and more than its fair share of energetic, creative citizens in all pursuits.

Santa Fe has always been close to the earth. For its first two centuries and longer, it was a town of one- and two-story adobes. When the United States took over the territory from Mexico in 1846 and trade began flowing from the eastern states, new tools and materials began to change the face of the city. The old adobe took on brick facades and roof decoration in what became known as the Territorial style. But the flat roofs were retained so that the city never lost its unique, low profile, creating a sense of serenity to be found in no other American city, and only in a few of the smaller towns of the Southwest, such as Taos.

Bishop Jean-Baptiste Lamy, the inspiration for the character of Bishop Latour in Willa Cather's *Death Comes for the Archbishop,* built the French Romanesque St. Francis Cathedral shortly after he was appointed to head the diocese in 1851. Other structures still standing include what is claimed to be the oldest house in the United States, built of adobe by Native Americans an alleged 800 years ago. The San Miguel Mission is the oldest mission church in the country, while the state capital, built in the circular form of a ceremonial Indian *kiva,* is among the newest in the United States.

The city was originally named La Villa Real de la Santa Fe de San Francisco de Asis (The Royal City of the Holy Faith of St. Francis of Assisi) by Spanish governor Don Pedro de Peralta, who founded it. Peralta built the Palace of the Governors as his capitol on the north side of the central Plaza, where it stands today as an excellent museum of the city's four centuries of history. It is one of the major attractions in the Southwest, and under its portico, Pueblos sit cross-legged, hawking their crafts to eager tourists, as they have done for decades.

The Plaza is the focus of Santa Fe's mid-September fiesta, celebrated annually since 1770 to commemorate the reconquest of the city by Spanish governor Don Diego de Vargas in 1692, following the years of the Pueblo revolt. It was also the terminus of the Santa Fe Trail from Missouri, and of the earlier Camino Real (Royal Road) up from Mexico, when the city thrived on the wool and fur of the Chihuahua trade.

1 Orientation

Part of the charm of Santa Fe is that it's so easy to get around. Like most cities of Hispanic origin, it was built around a parklike central plaza, with its centuries-old adobe buildings and churches lining the narrow streets. Many of them now house shops, restaurants, art galleries, and museums.

Santa Fe sits high and dry at the foot of the Sangre de Cristo range. Santa Fe Baldy rises to more than 12,600 feet a mere 12 miles northeast of the Plaza. The city's downtown straddles the Santa Fe River, a tiny tributary of the Rio Grande that is little more than a trickle for much of the year. North is the Espanola valley (a beautiful view of which is afforded from the Santa Fe Opera grounds) and beyond that, the village of Taos, 66 miles distant. South are ancient Indian turquoise mines in the Cerrillos Hills; southwest is metropolitan Albuquerque, 58 miles away. To the west, across the Caja del Rio Plateau, is the Rio Grande, and beyond that, the 11,000-foot Jemez Mountains and Valle Grande, an ancient and massive volcanic caldera. Native American pueblos dot the entire Rio Grande valley an hour's drive in any direction.

Arriving

BY PLANE The **Santa Fe Municipal Airport** (☎ **473-7243**), just outside the southwest city limits on Airport Road off Cerrillos Road, is primarily used by private planes. Commercial service is offered by **Mesa Airlines** (☎ toll free **800/637-2247**), which shuttles up to seven times a day between Albuquerque and Santa Fe and has direct flights to Taos and Denver. The nine-passenger Cessna Caravans have a 25-minute flying time to Albuquerque International Airport, with interline connections with all major carriers. Charter services include **Capital Aviation** (☎ **471-2525**) and **Santa Fe Aviation** (☎ **471-6533**).

Typically, air travelers to Santa Fe arrive in Albuquerque and either rent a car there or take the **Shuttlejack** bus (☎ **982-4311** in Santa Fe, **243-3244** in Albuquerque). This express service travels direct from the Albuquerque airport to central Santa Fe hotels and back. The fare is $20, payable to the driver, and there's service every $2^{1}/_{2}$ hours or so between 5am and 10:15pm. **Greyhound Lines, Inc.** (☎ **471-0008**) also runs two round-trips daily between the Albuquerque airport and the Santa Fe bus station at 858 St. Michael's Dr. **Faust's Transportation** (☎ **758-3410**) shuttles between Albuquerque and Taos with a stop in Santa Fe each direction.

BY TRAIN **AMTRAK** (☎ **842-9650** or toll free **800/872-7245**) runs the *Southwest Chief* between Los Angeles and Chicago, making a stop at the frontier village of Lamy, 14 miles southeast of Santa Fe. (Lamy ticket office phone: **988-4511**). There is one arrival and one departure in each direction daily, each arriving about 2:45pm. A shuttle van leaves for Santa Fe at 3:30pm, for a charge of $12.

BY BUS **Greyhound Lines, Inc.** and **TNM&O Coaches** (☎ **471-0008**) offer regular daily service between Santa Fe and Albuquerque, Taos, Denver, Phoenix, Dallas, and points around the state and the country. The Santa Fe bus station is at 858 St. Michael's Dr.; fare to or from Albuquerque runs around $12. Because the bus station is several miles south of the city center, travelers often need a taxi to get to their hotels. It may be more convenient to pay a few extra dollars for an airport-to-hotel shuttle.

BY CAR I-25 skims past Santa Fe's southern city limits, connecting it north and south with points from Billings, Montana, to El Paso, Texas. I-40, the state's major east-west thoroughfare that bisects Albuquerque, affords coast-to-coast access to "The City Different." (From the west, motorists leave I-40 in Albuquerque and take I-25 north; from the east, travelers exit I-40 at Clines Corners, an hour's drive east of Albuquerque, and continue 52 miles to Santa Fe via U.S. 285.) For travelers coming from the northwest, the most direct route is via Durango, Colorado, entering Santa Fe on U.S. 84.

Tourist Information

The **Santa Fe Convention and Visitors Bureau** is located at 201 W. Marcy St., in Sweeney Center at the corner of Grant Street downtown (P.O. Box 909), Santa Fe, NM 87504-0909 (☎ 505/984-6760 or toll free **800/777-CITY**). The **New Mexico Department of Tourism** is in the Lamy Building, 491 Old Santa Fe Trail (☎ toll free **800/545-2040**). The **Santa Fe Chamber of Commerce** is at 510 N. Guadalupe (☎ **505/988-3279**).

City Layout

The limits of downtown Santa Fe are demarcated on three sides by the horseshoe-shaped **Paseo de Peralta,** and on the west by **St. Francis Drive,** otherwise known as U.S. 84/285. **Alameda Street** follows the north shore of the Santa Fe River through downtown, with the State Capitol and other federal buildings on the south side of the stream, and most buildings of historic and tourist interest on the north, east of Guadalupe Street.

The **Plaza** is Santa Fe's universally accepted point of orientation. Its four diagonal walkways meet at a central fountain, around which a strange and wonderful assortment of people, of all ages, nationalities, and lifestyles, can be found at nearly any hour of the day or night.

If you stand in the center of the Plaza looking north, you're gazing directly at the Palace of the Governors. In front of you is Palace Avenue; behind you, San Francisco Street. To your left is Lincoln Avenue and to your right **Washington Avenue,** which divides downtown avenues into "East" and "West." St. Francis Cathedral is the massive Romanesque structure a block east, down San Francisco Street. Alameda Street is two blocks behind you.

Streaking diagonally to the southwest from the downtown area, beginning opposite the state office buildings on Galisteo Avenue, is **Cerrillos Road.** Once the main north-south highway connecting New Mexico's state capital with its largest city, it is now a 6-mile-long motel and fast-food "strip." St. Francis Drive, which crosses Cerrillos Road three blocks south of Guadalupe Street, is a far less pretentious byway, linking Santa Fe with I-25 four miles southeast of downtown. The **Old Pecos Trail,** on the east side of the city, also joins downtown and the freeway. **St. Michael's Drive** interconnects the three arterials.

Free city and state maps are easily obtained at tourist information offices. Other good regional maps can be purchased at area bookstores. Gousha publishes a laminated "Fast Map" of Santa Fe and Taos that has proved indispensible during my travels.

2   Getting Around

BY BUS   In 1993, Santa Fe opened **Santa Fe Trails** (☎ **984-6730**), its first public bus system. There are six routes, and visitors may pick up a map from the Convention and Visitors Bureau. Buses operate from 6:30am to 7:30pm Monday through

Friday and from 7am to 7pm on Saturdays. There is no service on Sundays or holidays. Call for current schedule and fare information.

BY TAXI   It's best to telephone for a cab, for they are difficult to flag from the street. Taxis have no meters; fares are set for given distances. Expect to pay an average of about $2.50 per mile. **Capital City Cab** (☎ **982-9990**) is the main company in Santa Fe.

BY CAR   Cars may be rented from any of the following firms in Santa Fe: **Adopt-a-Car,** 3574 Cerrillos Rd. (☎ **473-3189**); **Agency Rent-A-Car,** 3347 Cerrillos Rd. (☎ **473-2983**); **Avis,** Garrett's Desert Inn, 311 Old Santa Fe Trail (☎ **982-4361**); **Budget,** 1946 Cerrillos Rd. (☎ **984-8028**); **Capitol Ford,** 4490 Cerrillos Rd. (☎ **473-3673**); **Enterprise,** 1911 Fifth St. (☎ **473-3600**); **Hertz,** 100 Sandoval St. (☎ **471-7189**); and **Snappy Car Rental,** 3012 Cielo Court (☎ **473-2277**).

If you're having car trouble **Payne Bros. Automotive,** 1121 Calle La Resolana (☎ **471-8958**), is well-established. Many other garages, including import specialists, are listed in the telephone directory. For **AAA Towing Service,** call **471-6620.**

Street parking is difficult to find during the summer months. There is a parking lot near the Federal Courthouse, two blocks north of the Plaza; another one behind Santa Fe Village, a block south of the Plaza; and a third at Water and Sandoval streets.

BY BICYCLE   A bicycle is a perfect way to get around town. Check with **Palace Bike Rentals** at 409 E. Palace Avenue (☎ **984-2151**) about rentals.

Fast Facts: Santa Fe

American Express   There is no representative in Santa Fe. To report lost cards, call toll free **800/528-4800.** To report lost traveler's checks, dial toll free **800/221-7282.**

Area Code   505.

Babysitters   Most hotels can arrange on request. Alternatively, call the **Santa Fe Kid Connection,** 1015 Valerie Circle (☎ **471-3100**).

Business Hours   In general, Monday to Friday 9am to 5pm, with many stores also open Saturday and Sunday in the summer season. Most banks are open Monday to Thursday 9am to 3pm and Friday 9am to 6pm.

Currency Exchange   Four banks in Santa Fe will exchange foreign currency. **SunWest Bank,** 1234 St. Michael's Dr. (☎ **471-1234**) offers same-day sales of 20 different currencies. **First Interstate Bank,** 150 Washington Ave. (☎ **982-3671**), **First National Bank of Santa Fe,** Plaza (☎ **984-7500**), and the **Bank of Santa Fe,** 241 Washington Ave. (☎ **984-0500**), as well as SunWest, will buy currencies—but this usually takes two to three days.

Dentist   Most work in the medical office area several miles south of downtown. Among those near downtown, **Dr. Leslie E. La Kind,** 400 Botulph Lane (☎ **988-3500**), offers 24-hour emergency service. You might also call the **Dental Referral Service** (☎ **989-9158**) for help in finding a dentist.

Doctor   The **Lovelace Alameda** clinic, 901 W. Alameda St. (☎ **986-3666** for urgent care, **986-3600** for family care) is in the Solano Center near St. Francis Drive. It's open every day of the year 8am to 8pm for urgent care, with no appointments required.

Drugstores   Frasier Pharmacy is located downtown at 501 Old Santa Fe Trail (☎ **982-5524**), open Monday through Friday from 8:30am to 6:30pm, and Saturday from 9am to 6pm. The emergency and delivery service can be arranged with the **Medical Center Pharmacy** (☎ **983-4359**), adjacent to St. Vincent Hospital at 465 St. Michael's Dr., open 8:30am to 6pm, Monday through Friday, and 9am to 12:30pm on Saturday.

Emergencies   For police, fire or ambulance emergency, dial **911.**

Eyeglasses   Quintana Optical Dispensary, 109 E. Marcy St. (☎ **988-4234**), offers 1-hour prescription service Monday to Friday 9am to 5pm and Saturday 9am to noon.

Hairdressers & Barbers   You can get your hair cut in the Inn at Loretto, the La Fonda Hotel, or numerous other locations throughout the city. Santa Fe's **Supercuts** franchise is at 1936 Cerrillos Rd. (☎ **988-7559**). Your best bet for finding a good hairstylist is to ask locals who they'd recommend.

Hospitals   The **St. Vincent Hospital,** 455 St. Michael's Dr. (☎ **983-3361**), is a 268-bed full-service medical center. Patient services include 24-hour urgent and emergency-room care, ambulatory surgery, diagnostic radiology, cancer diagnosis and treatment, behavioral sciences, and a family recovery center for adolescent substance abuse. **Lovelace Health Systems** has two walk-in offices, one at 901 W. Alameda, the other at 440 St. Michaels Drive.

Hot lines   Battered Families, 473-5200. Poison Control, toll free **800/432-6866. Psychiatric Emergencies, 983-3361. Sexual Assault, 473-7818. Teen Suicide, 989-5242. Emergency Lodging, 988-4252** after 4pm daily.

Information   The **Santa Fe Council on International Relations,** P.O. Box 1223, Santa Fe, NM 87504 (☎ **982-4931**), assists foreign visitors by providing community information. An office in Room 281 of La Fonda Hotel on the Plaza is open Monday to Friday 9am to noon.

Laundry & Dry Cleaning   Just outside the downtown perimeter is **Shockey's Coin-op Laundry,** 755 Cerrillos Rd. (☎ **983-9881**), open daily 6am to 10pm. You can drop off laundry ($5 a load) at **Adobe Laundromat,** 411 W. Water St. (☎ **982-9063**). **Solano Center Laundromat & Dry Cleaners,** 949 1/2 W. Alameda (☎ **989-8905**), offers drop-off service, as well as dry cleaning service daily from 7am to 9:30pm.

Libraries   The **Santa Fe Public Library** is a block from the Plaza at 145 Washington Ave. (☎ **984-6780**). There are branch libraries at Villa Linda Mall and at 1713 Llano St., just off St. Michael's Drive.

Lost Property   Contact city police at **473-5000.**

Newspapers & Magazines   The *New Mexican,* a Gannett property, is Santa Fe's daily newspaper. Offices are at 202 E. Marcy St. (☎ **983-3303**). The weekly *Santa Fe Reporter,* published on Wednesdays, is often more willing to be controversial; its entertainment listings are excellent. Regional magazines published locally are *New Mexico Magazine* (monthly, statewide interest), the *Santa Fean Magazine* (monthly, local interest), *Santa Fe Lifestyle* (quarterly, local interest), and *Southwest Profile* (eight times a year, regional art).

Photographic Needs   Everything from film purchases to camera repairs to 1-hour processing can be handled by the **Camera Shop,** 109 E. San Francisco St.

(☎ **983-6591**). **Camera & Darkroom,** 216 Galisteo St. (☎ **983-2948**) also processes film.

Police   In case of emergency, dial **911.** All other inquiries should be directed to the main **Santa Fe Police Station,** 2515 Camino Entrada (☎ **473-5000** or **473-5080** after 5pm and weekends). The **Santa Fe County Sheriff's Office** is in the county courthouse, Grant Avenue and Johnson Street (☎ **984-5060**). The **New Mexico State Police** search-and-rescue line is **827-9300.**

Postal Services   The Main Post Office (**988-6351**) is at 120 South Federal Place, two blocks north and a block west of the Plaza. The branch Coronado Station is at 541 W. Cordova Rd. (☎ **438-8452**). Most of the major hotels have stamp machines and mailboxes with twice-daily pickup.

Radio   Santa Fe's radio stations include KMIK-AM 810 (all-news CBS affiliate), KTRC-AM 1400 (nostalgia music and early radio dramas), KSFR-FM 90.7 (classical), KNYN-FM 95.5 (country), KBAC-FM 98.1 (adult contemporary), KLSK-FM 104.1 (adult alternative), KBOM-FM (Spanish), and KVSF-AM 1260 (news and talk). Albuquerque stations are easily heard from Santa Fe.

Religious Services   Roman Catholics are the highest-profile group in Santa Fe, with eight churches and the venerable **St. Francis Cathedral.** Visitors may attend services at the Franciscan cathedral, 131 Cathedral Place, one block east of the Plaza (☎ **982-5619**).

Other denominations active in Santa Fe include Anglican, Assembly of God, Baptist, Charismatic, Christian and Missionary Alliance, Christian Science, Church of Christ, Church of God, Disciples of Christ, Episcopal, Foursquare Gospel, Friends, Jehovah's Witnesses, Lutheran, Methodist, Mormon, Nazarene, Seventh-day Adventist, and United Church of Christ. There is also a Jewish synagogue. The **Galisteo News & Ticket Center,** 201 Galisteo St. (☎ **984-1316**), is a good clearinghouse of information on metaphysical pursuits.

Shoe Repairs   Most convenient to downtown Santa Fe is the **Jacobs Shoe Repair Shop,** 646 Old Santa Fe Trail (☎ **982-9774**).

Taxes   A city lodging tax of 3.875% is added onto all lodging bills, over and above the gross receipts tax of 6.25%.

Telephone, Telegrams/Fax   Telegrams can be sent through **Western Union,** 519 Airport Rd. (☎ **438-3141**). Numerous agencies, including most hotels, will send and receive faxes, among them **Kinko's Copies,** 333 Montezuma Ave. (☎ **982-6311**). **Note:** As of June 1994, if you're calling from Santa Fe to anywhere else in the state you must use the 505 area code.

Television   Two local independent television stations are KKTO-TV (Channel 2) and KCHF-TV (Channel 11), the latter offering Christian programming. The three Albuquerque network affiliates—KOB-TV (Channel 4, NBC), KOAT-TV (Channel 7, ABC) and KQRE-TV (Channel 13, CBS)—all have offices at the state Capitol.

Useful Telephone Numbers   Information on road conditions in the Santa Fe area can be obtained from the state police (☎ **827-9300**). For time and temperature, call **473-2211.**

Weather   For weather forecasts, call **988-5151.**

3 Accommodations

Although Santa Fe has over 50 hotels, motels, bed-and-breakfast establishments, and other accommodations, rooms can still be hard to come by at the peak of the tourist season. You can get year-round assistance from **Santa Fe Central Reservations,** 320 Artist Road, no. 10 (☎ **505/983-8200** or toll free **800/776-7669.** Fax 505/984-8682). The service will also book transportation and activities. **Emergency Lodging Assistance**—especially helpful around Fiesta time in September—is available free after 4pm daily at **988-4252.**

Accommodations are often booked solid through the summer months, and most establishments raise their prices accordingly. Rates are usually increased further for Indian Market, the third weekend of August. But there's little agreement on the dates marking the beginning and end of the tourist season; whereas one hotel may not raise its rates until July 1 and may drop them again in mid-September, another may have higher rates from May to November. Some hotels recognize a shoulder season or increase rates again over the Christmas holidays. It pays to shop around during these "in-between" seasons of May–June and September–October.

In any season, senior, group, corporate, and other special rates are often available. If you have any questions about your eligibility for these rates, be sure to ask.

In these listings, the following categories define midsummer price ranges: **very expensive,** most rooms over $150 per night double; **expensive,** $110 to $150; **moderate,** $75 to $110; **inexpensive,** $45 to $75; **budget,** less than $45 per night double. Remember that an additional 10.125% tax is imposed on every hotel bill. Parking is usually free, unless otherwise indicated.

Downtown

Everything within the horseshoe-shaped Paseo de Peralta, and east a few blocks on either side of the Santa Fe River, is considered downtown Santa Fe. None of these accommodations is beyond walking distance from the Plaza.

VERY EXPENSIVE

Eldorado Hotel, 309 W. San Francisco St., Santa Fe, NM 87501. ☎ **505/988-4455** or toll free **800/955-4455.** Fax 505/982-0713. 219 rms, 18 suites. A/C MINIBAR TV TEL

Rates: July–Aug and major holidays $239 single or double; $349–$750 suite; Mar–June and Sept–Oct $209 single or double, $319–$700 suite; Nov–Feb excluding holidays $169 single or double, $279–$500 suite. AE, DC, DISC, MC, V. **Parking:** Free for guests, 24-hour valet.

With five-story pueblo architecture built around a lovely courtyard two blocks west of the Plaza, the luxurious Eldorado boasts a southwestern interior with an art collection appraised at more than $500,000, including antique furniture, Native American pottery, carved animals, and other works mainly by Santa Fe artists.

The guest rooms continue the regional theme. Many of them have traditional *kiva* fireplaces, handmade furniture, and decks or terraces. The upper rooms in particular afford outstanding views of the surrounding mountains. Each room—tastefully appointed in southwestern colors—has one king-size bed or two double beds, easy chairs, a double closet, a remote-control TV in an armoire, and a minirefrigerator with an honor bar. Rooms on the fifth floor have the added luxury of butler service. Additionally, just down the street from the main hotel is Zona Rosa, which houses two-, three-, and four-bedroom suites.

Dining/Entertainment: The innovative and elegant Old House restaurant was built on the preserved foundation of a Santa Fe house that was originally built in the early 1800s. Its *vigas* and *latilla* ceiling, polished wood floor, and pottery and *kachinas* in niches give it a distinct regional touch that is also present in its creative continental cuisine. Open for dinner from 6pm Tuesday through Sunday, its main courses are in the $14 to $21 price range. The Old House Tavern is open from 6 to 11pm Tuesday through Sunday. More casual meals are served in the spacious Eldorado court, open for breakfast 7am to 11pm and lunch 11:30am to 2pm. Dinner is served from 5:30pm to 9:30pm Monday through Saturday, and Sunday brunch is offered from 11:30am to 2pm. Dinner prices range from $6 to $16 for anything from cheese enchiladas to seared filet of salmon. The lobby lounge has low-key entertainment.

Services: Room service, concierge, butler, laundry, twice-daily maid service, and safe-deposit boxes. Pets are welcome.

Facilities: Rooms for nonsmokers and the handicapped; heated rooftop swimming pool and Jacuzzi, exercise rooms, his-and-hers saunas; professional masseuse; beauty salon; free membership in Santa Fe Spa; shopping arcade with Southwest artifacts, jewelry, gifts, apparel, news, and a real-estate showcase.

Hilton of Santa Fe, 100 Sandoval St. (P.O. Box 25104), Santa Fe, NM 87504-2387.
☎ **505/988-2811** or toll free **800/336-3676** or **800/HILTONS.** Fax 505/988-1730. 158 rms, 6 suites. A/C MINIBAR TV TEL

Rates: (based on single or double occupancy) Jan 1–May 1 $100–$200; May 2–June 29 $130–$230; June 30–Sept 3 $150–$250; Sept 4–Oct 28 $130–$230; Oct 29–Dec 21 $100–$200; Dec 22–Dec 31 $150–$250. Suites $375–$500. Extra person $20. AE, CB, DC, DISC, MC, V. **Parking:** Free for guests.

With its city-landmark bell tower, the Hilton covers a full city block two blocks west of the Plaza, between Sandoval, San Francisco, Guadalupe, and Alameda streets. It's built around a central pool and patio area. There's cozy lobby seating around a traditional fireplace, flanked on one side by a cactus, on the other by a folk-art sculpture of a howling coyote.

The units are clean and spacious, furnished with king-size, queen-size, or double beds. Each room—with forest-green carpets and drapes, pastel-patterned bedspreads, and potted plants—has a deck or balcony, couch or two easy chairs and a table, four-drawer credenza, in-room movies, modern-art prints, and a mirror on the walls. There are two sinks, one inside the bathroom, one outside at a dressing table; every room has a coffeepot.

In June of 1994 the Hilton opened Casa Ortiz de Santa Fe, a small building located adjacent to the main hotel, which houses three exclusive guest houses. Casa Ortiz was once the coach house (1625) of Nicholas Ortiz III, but today, the thick adobe walls hold two one-bedroom units and one two-bedroom suite. Each unit has a living room with a *kiva* fireplace, a fully stocked kitchenette, and a bathroom with a whirlpool tub. One of the one-bedroom units has an additional fireplace in the bedroom.

Dining/Entertainment: Two restaurants occupy the premises of Casa de Ortiz. In the Piñon Grill, with its intimate candlelight dinner service from 5 to 11pm daily, you'll see ancient beams and pillars similar to those of the main house construction. Lunch is served from 11am to 5pm. All main courses are prepared on the wood-fired grill, including fresh wild game, chile-marinated lamb, and Rocky Mountain trout; dinner prices range from $14.95 to $19.95. The Chamisa Courtyard serves breakfast

Downtown Santa Fe Accommodations

Alexander's Inn **21**
Dancing Ground
  of the Sun **19**
Eldorado Hotel **5**
El Farolito **9**
Four Kachinas Inn **10**
Grant Corner Inn **4**
Hilton of Santa Fe **6**

Homewood Suites **1**
Hotel Plaza Real **15**
Hotel Santa Fe **8**
The Inn at Loretto **12**
Inn of the Anasazi **14**
Inn of the Animal Tracks **18**
Inn on the Alameda **11**
Inn on the Paseo **16**

La Fonda **13**
La Posada de Santa Fe **20**
The Preston House **17**
Santa Fe Motel **7**
Spencer House
  Bed & Breakfast Inn **3**
A Starry Night Bed
  & Breakfast **2**

Information ☉   Post Office ✉

daily from 6:30 to 11am; featuring casual garden-style tables amid lush greenery under a large skylight, the Chasima is built on the home's enclosed patio. El Cañon wine and coffee bar specializes in fine wines by the glass and gourmet coffees. Open from 7am to midnight El Cañon also serves house-baked breads and pastries as well as tapas (from 5pm).

Services: Room service, concierge, courtesy car, valet laundry.

Facilities: Outdoor swimming pool, Jacuzzi, gift shop, car-rental agency. Rooms for nonsmokers and the disabled.

Homewood Suites, 400 Griffin St., Santa Fe, NM 87501. ☎ **505/988-3000** or toll free **800/225-5466.** Fax 505/988-4700. 105 suites. A/C TV TEL

Rates: Jan 1–June 25 and Oct 31–Dec 15 $145–$165 one-bedroom suite, $255 two-bedroom suite; June 26–Oct 30 and Dec 16–Dec 31 $155–$175 one-bedroom suite, $310 two-bedroom suite. AE, DC, DISC, MC, V.

Homewood Suites is downtown Santa Fe's only all-suite hotel. The apartment-style units are perfect for families or travelers who prefer having the option to cook for themselves occasionally while on vacation. The Homewood suite has a living room, bedroom, kitchen, and bathroom with a separate dressing area. The Master suite is a larger version of the Homewood suite, and there are a few suites with two bedrooms and two baths. Kitchens are fully equipped and have microwaves, two-burner stoves, and full-size refrigerators with ice makers. Both living and bedrooms have televisions, and living-room couches convert into full-size beds (perfect for the kids). Each suite has a recliner chair with an ottoman. Many of the suites have fireplaces, and all have VCRs. All come equipped with ironing boards and irons. Video rentals are available in the "Suite Shop" on the lobby level. Business travelers enjoy the convenience of the business center—use of the computer, copier, and typewriter are free of charge. A complimentary continental breakfast is served in the Lodge daily, and there's a free social function on Monday through Thursday evenings.

Services: Concierge, complimentary shopping service.

Facilities: Outdoor pool, outdoor hot tubs, exercise center with bikes, weights, a step machine, and a rower; activity court; guest laundry; business center; Suite Shop for purchase of sundries, food, and video rentals.

⭐ **Inn of the Anasazi,** 113 Washington Ave., Santa Fe, NM 87501. ☎ **505/988-3030** or toll free **800/688-8100.** Fax 505/988-3277. 59 rms, all with bath. A/C MINIBAR TV TEL

Rates: Jan–Apr and Nov–Dec $180–$245 single or double, $305–$335 suite; May–Oct $230–$260 single or double, $390–$415 suite. Holiday and festival rates may be higher. AE, CB, DC, DISC, MC, V. **Parking:** $10 per night.

Located near the Palace of the Governors, this luxury hostelry is currently one of *Condé Nast Traveler*'s "best places to stay in the world." The inn is named in a celebration of the "enduring and creative spirit" of the Native Americans known as the Anasazi. It opened in July 1991 and is one of the projects of Robert Zimmer, who is well known for his exciting concepts in hotels like this one, which is "committed to ecological and environmental awareness, the interconnectedness and diversity of all people, land, heritage, and sentient beings, and makes every effort to operate in a sound and conscious manner." Every piece of paper used in the inn is recycled; the fireplaces are gas, rather than wood burning; linens, soaps, and shampoos are all natural, and the food in the restaurant is chemical free and organic.

None of this is to say that the hotel skimps on amenities—there are TVs, VCRs, and stereos in all the rooms, as well as minibars, private safes, coffeemakers, telephones in the bathrooms, and walk-in closets. The artwork is original, and there is a living room with a fireplace, as well as a library where you can sit and relax before dinner.

Dining/Entertainment: The Inn of the Anasazi restaurant serves breakfast, lunch, and dinner every day, and it features Native American and northern New Mexican dishes (see "Santa Fe Dining," below).

Services: Room service, twice-daily maid service, complimentary newspaper, tours of galleries and museums, concierge, massage and aromatherapy treatments, stationary bicycles available for use in guest rooms. Access to spas and fitness centers can be easily arranged through the hotel.

⭐ **Inn on the Alameda,** 303 E. Alameda St., Santa Fe, NM 87501.
☎ **505/984-2121** or toll free **800/289-2122.** Fax 505/986-8325, 66 rms, (8 suites). A/C TV TEL

Rates (including breakfast): Nov–Mar $130–$170 single, $140–$180 double, $190–$335 suite; Apr–Oct $155–$200 single, $170–$215 double, $245–$350 suite. Holiday and special events rates may be higher. AE, CB, DC, MC, V.

This might be just the ticket for visitors who prefer more intimacy than large hotels can offer. Just two blocks from the Plaza and one block from gallery-intense Canyon Road, opposite the Santa Fe River at the corner of Paseo de Peralta, the Inn on the Alameda preserves the spirit of old Santa Fe behind an exterior of adobe and adzed-wood pillars. You'll catch the flavor as soon as you enter the lobby, with its traditional *viga-latilla* ceiling construction. Just past the unobtrusive reception desk is a sitting room/library with handcrafted furnishings, soft pillows, and a rocking chair placed around an inviting fireplace.

The mood continues to the guest rooms, which are characterized by the warm pastel shades of contemporary southwestern decor. Each features a king-size bed or two queen-size beds, a desk with three-drawer credenza, an additional table and chairs, and cable TV with built-in AM/FM radio. Freshly cut flowers brighten each room, charming prints hang on the walls, and wood-slat blinds add warmth and privacy. Heating and air conditioning are individually controlled. Some rooms have outdoor patios or private balconies, refrigerators, and *kiva* fireplaces.

A new wing has recently been added to this inn. It includes 19 more rooms, a guest laundry, a fitness facility, and a massage room. Eight individually designed suites have such luxuries as traditional kiva fireplaces, TVs in both the living room and bedroom, and minirefrigerators. Their furnishings are much the same as the rest of the hotel, but they are set away from the main building and have their own parking areas.

Dining/Entertainment: An elaborate complimentary "Breakfast of Enchantment" is served each morning in the outdoor courtyard, Agoyo Room, or in the privacy of your own room. A full-service bar is open nightly.

Services: Room service 7 to 11am, concierge, valet laundry, complimentary morning newspaper. Child care can be arranged. Small pets are accepted.

Facilities: Two open-air Jacuzzi spas, fitness facility, massage room, guest laundry. Rooms for nonsmokers and the disabled.

⭐ **La Fonda,** 100 E. San Francisco St. (P.O. Box 1209), Santa Fe, NM 87501.
☎ **505/982-5511** or toll free **800/523-5002**. Fax 505/982-6367. 153 rms, 21 suites. A/C TV TEL

Rates: $150–$185 single or double; $165–$200 deluxe or minisuite; $225–$500 suite. Extra person $15. Children under 12 free with parent. AE, CB, DC, MC, V. **Parking:** $2 a day in three-story garage.

"The Inn at the End of the Trail" occupies a full block between the southeast corner of the Plaza, where a marker denotes the terminus of the Santa Fe Trail and Bishop Lamy's St. Francis Cathedral. When the first Americans to pioneer the trail arrived in Santa Fe in 1821, they found an inn—a *fonda*—on this site. As trappers, traders, and merchants began flocking to Santa Fe, a saloon and casino were added. Among the inn's 19th-century patrons were Pres. Rutherford B. Hayes, Gen. Ulysses S. Grant, and Gen. William Tecumseh Sherman. The original inn was dying of old age in 1920 when it was razed and replaced by what is today La Fonda. Its architecture is Pueblo revival, imitation adobe with wooden balconies and beam ends protruding over the tops of windows.

Every room is a bit different from the next. Each piece of hand-carved Spanish-style furniture is painted in a Hispanic folk motif color coordinated to other pieces in the room (but to nothing outside the room). Beds are king, queen-size, or double. Suites and deluxe rooms have minirefrigerators, tiled baths, and sophisticated artwork, including etched tin and stonework. Some have fireplaces, private balconies, antique furniture, Oriental carpets, and a large amount of closet and shelf space.

Dining/Entertainment: La Plazuela Restaurant, a tiled skylit garden patio, is open for three meals daily from 7am to 10pm. Furniture is solid-wood Spanish colonial, and the waiters and waitresses are garbed accordingly. Cuisine is regional with contemporary flair, ranging at dinner from blue-corn enchiladas to shrimp scampi cilantro. The adjacent La Fiesta Lounge, open Mon to Sat from 11am to 1am and Sun noon to midnight, has nightly entertainment. La Terraza, an enclosed outdoor patio on the third floor, offers lunches daily in summer. The Bell Tower Bar, at the southwest corner of the hotel, is the highest point in downtown Santa Fe; it's a great place from which to view the city.

Services: Room service, concierge, tour desk, valet laundry.

Facilities: Rooms for nonsmokers and the disabled, outdoor swimming pool, two indoor Jacuzzis, cold plunge, massage room. Shopping arcade, galleries, leather shop, boutique, French pastry shop, and newsstand with sundries.

EXPENSIVE

Hotel Plaza Real, 125 Washington Ave., Santa Fe, NM 87501. ☎ **505/988-4900,** or toll free **800/279-REAL.** 56 rms, 44 suites. A/C FRIDGE TV TEL

Rates: Nov 1–Apr 30 $130–$209 double; May 1–June 30 $139–$219 double; July 1–Oct 31 $159–$249 double; suites $295–$475 all year. Extra person $15. Children under 12 free with parent. AE, DC, MC, V. **Parking:** $5 per day.

This three-story hotel opened in August 1990 and is located a half-block north of the Plaza. It is built in traditional Territorial style, complete with red-brick coping along the roof lines and windows trimmed in white. Native American designs and wood beams complement the Santa Fe–style furnishings in the rooms, most of which have fireplaces and outdoor patios. Rooms overlook a peaceful inner courtyard, away from the bustle of the Plaza. Complimentary breakfast is served in the Santa Clara Room and patio or delivered to the guest rooms with the daily paper. La Piazza is the hotel's sidewalk cafe, where guests may enjoy pastries, cappuccino, sandwiches, and cocktails. An intimate lounge also serves cocktails in the evening. Services include a concierge, a complimentary walking tour, a 24-hour desk, valet laundry, and rooms for the disabled.

Hotel Santa Fe, 1501 Paseo de Peralta at Cerrillos Rd., Santa Fe, NM 87501. ☎ **505/982-1200** or toll free **800/825-9876.** Fax 505/984-2211. 131 rms, 91 suites. A/C MINIBAR TV TEL

Rates: May–Oct 15, Thanksgiving, and Christmas $139 single; $159 double; $139–$169 junior suite; $185–$210 deluxe suite. Rest of year $95 single; $115 double; $125–$145 junior suite; $165–$185 deluxe suite. Extra person $20. Children 17 and under stay free with parents. AE, CB, DC, DISC, MC, V.

Open since March 1991, this is the first-ever partnership in New Mexico between a Native American tribe—in this case, Picuris Pueblo—and private business located off reservation trust land. The three-story, pueblo-style building, cruciform in shape and featuring Picuris tribal motifs throughout, is about a half mile south of the Plaza.

The hotel has 40 superior rooms (30 with king-size beds), 51 junior suites (all with kings), and 40 deluxe suites (30 with kings). All rooms are furnished with Taos-style furnishings, remote-control television, and fully stocked minibars. Each of the suites has a microwave oven. Each suite has a separate living room and bedroom, with a TV and phone in each room.

Dining/Entertainment: The hotel offers an extensive continental breakfast and a deli on the lobby level. The Lobby Lounge serves complimentary hors d'oeuvres from 5pm to 7pm daily.

Services: Valet laundry, courtesy shuttle to Plaza and Canyon Rd., 24-hour security, safe-deposit boxes.

Facilities: Rooms for nonsmokers and the disabled, massage room, guest Laundromat, Picuris Pueblo gift shop, outdoor pool and hot tub. Access to Club International fitness center can be arranged through the hotel.

⭐ **The Inn at Loretto,** 211 Old Santa Fe Trail (P.O. Box 1417), Santa Fe, NM 87501. ☎ **505/988-5531** or toll free **800/528-1234.** Fax 505/984-7988. 137 rms, 3 suites. A/C FRIDGE TV TEL

Rates: $95–$195 single; $125–$210 double; $300–$550 suite. Extra person $15. Children 12 and under free with parent. AE, CB, DC, DISC, MC, V.

This handsome, pueblo revival–style building was originally the Loretto Academy, a Catholic girls' school built in the late 19th century under the direction of Bishop Lamy. Although the building—which reopened as a hotel in 1975—has been fully renovated and expanded, bits and pieces of the original academy remain, including the famous chapel of Our Lady of Light with its mysterious spiral staircase (see "Attractions," below). Another unique element of the Inn at Loretto is the use of hand-painted Mimbres designs. There are about 1,000 of these colorful motifs, all different, on lobby, corridor, guest room, meeting room, and restaurant walls throughout the building. Artist Ross Martinez re-created work found on pottery of the 11th- and 12th-century Mimbres people of southwestern New Mexico.

The hotel, a little over one block from the southeast corner of the Plaza, is horseshoe-shaped, with room balconies or patios surrounding a landscaped outdoor courtyard with a pool. Half of the guest rooms have a single king-size bed, the remainder, a pair of double beds. Southwest decor dominates with etched-tin shades on intricate pottery-style lamps, Mexican tiles inset in writing and bedside tables, and colorful patterned comforters. All rooms have either a sofa or an easy chair or an activity table with two chairs.

Dining/Entertainment: Bimi's, styled after the rambling haciendas of northern New Mexico, is open daily from 6:30am to 9pm with extended summer hours. On warm summer days, service is extended to the courtyard. Breakfasts run $5.95 to $8.50; lunches, $6.25 to $9. Dinners, including pastas, regional specialties, and continental cuisine, range from $7.50 to $17. The warm, mezzanine-ringed hotel lounge has live entertainment nightly, and complimentary chips and salsa are available daily at 4pm.

Services: Room service, concierge, valet laundry.

Facilities: Outdoor swimming pool. Shopping arcade with an art gallery, four boutiques, a gold designer, a bookstore, gift shops, a sundries shop, and a hair salon. Rooms for nonsmokers and the disabled are available.

★ **La Posada De Santa Fe**, 330 E. Palace Ave., Santa Fe, NM 87501.
☎ **505/986-0000** or toll free **800/727-5276**. Fax 505/982-6850. 119 rms, 40 suites.
$ A/C TV TEL

Rates: May–Oct. Thanksgiving, and Christmas seasons, $115–$295 single or double, $195–$397 suite; Nov–Apr except holidays $88–$215 single or double, $125–$285 suite. Various packages available. AE, CB, DC, MC, V.

This lovely hotel has 19 adobe-style buildings spread across six acres of thoughtfully landscaped grounds. It is built around the Staab House, a historic mansion built two blocks east of the Plaza in 1882 by Abraham Staab, a German immigrant, for his bride, Julia. Santa Fe's first brick building was equally well known for its richly carved walnut interior woodwork and the decorative scrolls and fluting on its doors and windows. Today, several rooms of the house have been fully restored in classical fashion as a Victorian lounge, with period furnishings and museum-quality 19th-century art. Julia Staab, who died in 1896 at the age of 52, continues to haunt a half-dozen upstairs sleeping rooms. Mischievous but good-natured, she is Santa Fe's best-known and most frequently witnessed ghost.

Each of the hotel's charming rooms is a little different from the next, with variations in size, shape, layout, and detail. Many objets d'art are one of a kind—something which inspires repeat visitors to request "their" room year after year. But the *casitas*, "little houses," share many common traits: outside entrances with wood-carved portals, handcrafted furniture and wrought-iron garden chairs, wood floors with throw rugs, painted tiles built into walls. Eighty-six rooms have fireplaces or wood stoves; piñon firewood is provided daily. Some larger units have wet bars or refrigerators, walk-in closets, and dressing tables. Suites have full kitchenettes. Be aware that finding your way around the hotel grounds may be confusing: Get a map from the desk. The room numbers are in no particular order. No. 143, for instance, is between nos. 195 and 196 and across from 116.

Dining/Entertainment: The Staab House Restaurant, open for three meals daily from 7am to 2pm and 6 to 10pm, has been fully restored with ceiling *vigas* and Pueblo weavings and tinwork on the walls. From spring to early fall, food is also served outside on a big patio. New Mexico cuisine is a house specialty, with breakfasts like eggs Robles (with chorizo sausage and cactus chile), lunch including fresh fish in corn husks and a jicama chicken salad, dinner featuring scallops Encinada, pork Mezcal, and prime rib. The lounge has frequent happy-hour entertainment (usually local musicians).

Services: Room service, valet laundry, concierge.

Facilities: Rooms for nonsmokers and the disabled. Outdoor swimming pool, guest use of local health club, boutique, beauty salon.

INEXPENSIVE

Santa Fe Motel, 510 Cerrillos Rd., Santa Fe, NM 87501. ☎ **505/982-1039** or toll free **800/999-1039.** 22 rms. A/C TV TEL

Rates: May–Oct $75–$85 single, $80–$90 double, $155 Thomas House; Nov–Apr $65–$75 single, $70–$80 double, $160 Thomas House. AE, MC, V.

One of the bonuses of staying at this adobe-style motel is that most rooms have kitchenettes, complete with two-burner stoves and minirefrigerators, fully stocked with pans, dishes, and utensils. Southwestern motifs predominate in the rooms, which are spread across four turn-of-the-century buildings. Fresh-brewed coffee is served each morning in the office, where a bulletin board posts listings of Santa Fe activities. The nearby Thomas House, on West Manhattan Drive, is a fully equipped rental home with living and dining rooms and off-street parking. If you're planning to stay here I'd recommend that you call ahead to see if the hotel has completed renovations that are scheduled as this book goes to press. Otherwise, expect very outdated decor.

Northside

This area, within easy reach of the Plaza, includes accommodations that lie beyond the loop of the Paseo de Peralta to the north.

VERY EXPENSIVE

The Bishop's Lodge, Bishop's Lodge Rd. (P.O. Box 2367), Santa Fe, NM 87504. ☎ **505/983-6377.** Fax 505/989-8739. 74 rms and suites. A/C TV TEL

Rates: European Plan (meals not included): Mar 25–May 26 and Sept 6–Dec 31 $140 standard (for two), $170 standard suite (for two), $215 deluxe room, $245 super deluxe room, $285 deluxe suite; May 27–June 30 $160 standard, $210 standard suite, $245 deluxe, $275 super deluxe, $315 deluxe suite; July 1–Sept 5 $195 standard, $245 standard suite, $295 deluxe, $325 super deluxe, $355 deluxe suite. Modified American Plan (includes breakfast and lunch or dinner daily; available May 27–Labor Day) $236–$271 standard, $286–$321 standard suite, $321–$371 deluxe, $351–$401 super deluxe, $391–$431 deluxe suite. No credit cards, but out-of-state personal checks accepted.

More than a century ago, when Bishop Jean-Baptiste Lamy was the spiritual leader of northern New Mexico's Roman Catholic population, he often escaped clerical politics by hiking 3¹/₂ miles north over a ridge into the Little Tesuque Valley. There he built a retreat he named Villa Pintoresca (Picturesque Villa) for its lovely vistas and a humble chapel (now on the National Register of Historic Places) with high-vaulted ceilings and a hand-built altar. Today Lamy's 1,000-acre getaway has become the Bishop's Lodge. Purchased in 1918 from the Pulitzer family (of publishing fame) by Denver mining executive James R. Thorpe, it has remained in his family's hands for more than seven decades. That gives the lodge a sense of continuity in theme and direction not often found in the visitor industry.

The guest rooms are spread through 10 buildings. All feature handcrafted cottonwood furniture, regional artwork, and etched-tin trim. Guests receive a complimentary fruit basket upon arrival. Standard rooms have balconies and king-size or two twin beds. Deluxe rooms have traditional *kiva* fireplaces, private decks or patios, and walk-in closets; some older units have flagstone floors and *viga* ceilings. Super deluxe rooms have a combination bedroom/sitting room. Deluxe suites are extremely spacious; they have living rooms, separate bedrooms, private patios and decks, and artwork of near-museum quality throughout. All units classified as deluxe have fireplaces, refrigerators, and in-room safes.

Dining/Entertainment: Three large adjoining rooms with wrought-iron chandeliers and wall-size Native American–themed oil paintings comprise the Bishop's Lodge dining room. Santa Feans flock here for breakfast ($12) 7:30 to 10am, lunch ($7 to $12) noon to 1:30pm, Sunday Brunch ($20) 11:30am to 2pm, and dinner (main courses $12 to $25), creative regional cuisine with continental flair, served from 6:30 to 9pm daily. Attire is casual at breakfast and lunch but more formal at dinner, when men are asked to wear a sport coat and women a dress or pants suit. There's a full vintage wine list, and El Charro Bar serves pre- and post-dinner drinks.

Services: Room service, seasonal cookouts, valet laundry.

Facilities: Daily guided horseback rides, introductory riding lessons, children's pony ring: four surfaced tennis courts, pro shop, and instruction; exercise room; supervised skeet and trap shooting; outdoor pool with lifeguard, saunas, and whirlpool; stocked trout pond for children; shuffleboard, croquet, ping-pong; summer daytime program with counselors for children 4 to 12.

EXPENSIVE

Picacho Plaza Hotel, 750 N. St. Francis Dr., Santa Fe, NM 87501. ☎ **505/982-5591** or toll free **800/441-5591.** Fax 505/988-2821. 127 rms, 13 suites, and 34 condominium units. A/C TV TEL

Rates: Jan 2–Feb 28 and Nov 18–Dec 21 $78–$133 single, $88–$133 double; Mar 1–Apr 30 $88–$143 single, $98–$143 double; May 1–Nov 17 and Dec 22–Jan 1 $108–$178 single, $123–$178 double. Children 12 and under free with parent. AE, DC, MC, V.

If you're in town for the Santa Fe Opera, you'll have a hard time finding an accommodation closer than this one. The amphitheater is only three miles north up U.S. 84/285; the Picacho Plaza provides free drop-off and pickup. In fact, there's complimentary shuttle service anywhere within the city limits—including the Santa Fe Plaza, 1¼ miles southeast—from 6am to 10pm daily. Once you're in this landscaped garden-style hotel, though, you may find it hard to leave. You can have free run of facilities at the adjacent Santa Fe Spa, the city's top health club. Standard rooms, with soft southwestern decor, have king-size or two double beds and other typical hotel furnishings. Minisuites are more spacious, with Santa Fe–style furnishings—including an armoire containing the TV—and private balconies. In addition to all the above, each parlor suite has a Murphy bed and traditional *kiva* fireplace in the living room, a big dining area, a wet bar and refrigerator, and a jetted bathtub. Cielo Grande condo units have fully equipped kitchens, fireplaces, and private decks.

Dining/Entertainment: The Petroglyph Bar and Restaurant serves three meals a day from 6:30am to 10pm amid antique local crafts and reproductions of rock drawings. Dinner main courses ($9.95 to $21) are international dishes with a bit of southwestern flair, like grilled chicken jalapeño marinated in olive oil and fresh herbs, grilled and basted with orange jalepeño marmalade; or shrimp spaghetti with mussels, crushed red peppers, and "lots of garlic." A jazz combo plays Thursday through Saturday in the Petroglyph Bar, and the nightclub features the Spanish quicksteps of New Mexico's best-known flamenco dancer and her Estampa Flamenco troupe.

Services: Room service, complimentary shuttle, valet laundry, complimentary *USA Today.* Child care can be arranged.

Facilities: Rooms for nonsmokers and the disabled, outdoor swimming pool, hot tub, Santa Fe Spa (indoor pool, racquetball courts, weights, massage, steamrooms, aerobics, dance, yoga, and karate classes), coin-op guest Laundromat, gift and sundries shop.

Southside

Santa Fe's major commercial strip, Cerrillos Road, is U.S. 85, the main route to and from Albuquerque and the I-25 freeway. It's about 5¼ miles from the Plaza to the Villa Linda Mall, which marks the southern extent of the city limits. Most motels are on this strip, although one—the Residence Inn—is a couple of miles east, closer to St. Francis Drive (U.S. 84).

MODERATE

Best Western High Mesa Inn, 3347 Cerrillos Rd., Santa Fe, NM 87501.
☎ **505/473-2800** or toll free **800/777-3347.** Fax 505/473-5128. 210 rms, 33 suites. A/C FRIDGE TV TEL

Rates (Including buffet breakfast): high season $99–$139 double, $115–$300 suites; low season $69–$85 double, $89–$129 suite. Guests over 55 get 10% discount; children 12 and under stay free with parent. AE, CB, DC, DISC, MC, V.

The High Mesa wins kudos as one of the city's better properties. In the user-friendly lobby is a message board with information on current local events. The rooms feature Southwest regional decor, with a king-size or two queen-size beds, plush carpeting, wet bar and refrigerator, desk/dresser, and satellite TV with in-room movies. Suites have a separate sitting room with a couch and TV and each suite also comes equipped with a microwave and coffeemaker. Five luxury suites have full kitchens and huge desks. Salsa's is the hotel's restaurant, and it's open daily from 8am to 10pm. Kids' menus are available. Room service, courtesy car, valet and coin-op guest laundry, child care, rooms for nonsmokers and the disabled are all available. Facilities include a skylit indoor pool, two Jacuzzis, a weight/exercise room, and a gift shop.

 El Rey Inn, 1862 Cerrillos Rd. (P.O. Box 130), Santa Fe, NM 87504.
☎ **505/982-1931** or toll free **800/521-1349.** Fax 505/989-9249. 85 rms, 8 suites.
A/C TV TEL

Rates (including continental breakfast): July–Aug $54–$92, depending upon size and type of room required; $85–$130 suite. Rest of year $47–$83; $75–$110 suite. AE, CB, DC, MC, V.

"The King" is notable for its carefully tended, shaded grounds and thoughtfully maintained recently renovated units. The white-stucco buildings are adorned with bright trim around the doors and hand-painted Mexican tiles in the walls. No two rooms are alike. Most have *viga* ceilings and Santa Fe–style wood furnishings, a walk-in closet, and a handsome blue-and-white tiled bathroom. Some have kitchenettes, others refrigerators and/or fireplaces. Eight stylish poolside terrace units feature private outdoor patio areas. Facilities include a Territorial-style sitting room with library and game tables, a swimming pool, hot tub, picnic area, children's play area, and coin-op laundry.

BUDGET

Cactus Lodge, 2864 Cerrillos Rd., Santa Fe, NM 87501. ☎ **505/471-7699.** 25 rms, 4 suites. A/C TV TEL

Rates: Mar 15–Oct 31 $48–$68 double with one bed, $68–$75 double with two beds; Nov 1–Mar 14 $32–$48 double with one bed, $38–$58 double with two beds. Extra person $4. AE, DISC, MC, V.

Typical of many small, privately owned motels on the Cerrillos Road strip, the Cactus Lodge includes four two-bedroom suites that can sleep up to seven people. Each room is furnished with a queen-size or double beds, a desk or three-drawer dresser, and a table and chairs. Each has cable TV. Pets are accepted with certain restrictions.

Super 8 Motel, 3358 Cerrillos Rd., Santa Fe, NM 87501. ☎ **505/471-8811** or toll free **800/800-8000**. Fax 505/471-3239. 96 rms. A/C TV TEL

Rates: May–Sept $39.88 single; $45.88 double. Rest of the year $36.88 single; $41.88 double. AE, CB, DC, DISC, MC, V.

It's nothing flashy, but this box-like hotel attracts a regular following as a known quantity: Clean, comfortable rooms with standard furnishings, each including a double bed, a working desk, and free local calls. Rooms for nonsmokers are available. The motel has a 24-hour desk and a coin-op guest laundry.

Bed & Breakfasts

A Starry Night Bed & Breakfast, 324 McKenzie St., Santa Fe, NM 87501. ☎ **505/820-7117.** 1 rm, 1 suite. TV TEL

Rates: $96 double; $116 suite. MC, V.

If you're looking for a small, private place near the center of Santa Fe at which you'll want for nothing, A Starry Night Bed and Breakfast might be just the place for you. Both rooms in this historic adobe home have private entrances off the inn's beautiful flower and herb gardens (frequented by hummingbirds); innkeeper and novelist Lee Purcell has taken great pains to make them comfortable for her guests. One room features a queen-size brass bed covered with a lovely quilt, while the other has an antique four-poster bed. Lace curtains add charm, and books line the walls. The suite has a comfortable sitting area with a TV and coffeemaker as well as a gaslit fireplace. Both rooms have private baths (for which plush terry robes are supplied) and telephones. A continental breakfast is included in the rates and is served in the common room.

Alexander's Inn, 529 E. Palace Ave., Santa Fe, NM 87501. ☎ **505/986-1431.** 6 rms (3 with bath). A/C

Rates: $80–$120 double. MC, V.

Located not too far from the center of downtown Santa Fe in a quiet residential area, Alexander's Inn is unlike most of the other places in town because it isn't done in Southwest decor. Instead, the eight-year-old inn is done in a Victorian/New England style with stenciling on the walls, pastel dhurrie rugs, muted apricot and lilac tones, and white-iron or four-poster queen-size beds. You might begin to think you're in a country inn in Vermont. One of the rooms has a private deck. There's also a new cottage, complete with kitchen, living room (with a *kiva* fireplace), and a porch. All guests can enjoy privileges at El Gancho Tennis Club. Mountain bikes are available for guest use. A continental breakfast of homemade baked goods is served every morning, and every afternoon tea and cookies are available to guests.

Dancing Ground of the Sun, 711 Paseo de Peralta, Santa Fe, NM 87501.
☎ **505/986-9797** or toll free **800/645-5673**. 5 rms (all with bath). TV TEL

Rates: Nov 1–Apr 30 $115–$145 double; May 1–Oct 31 $130–$160 double. MC, V.

Sometimes bed and breakfast owners are able to come up with new and creative theme ideas for their inns: Dancing Ground of the Sun is a case in point. The owners of this bed and breakfast put a great deal of thought and energy into decorating their rooms, and it shows. Each of the five *casitas* has been outfitted with handcrafted Santa Fe–style furnishings made by local artisans; the decor of each room centers around a mythological Native American figure, the likenesses of which have been hand-painted on the walls of each unit. Corn Dancer represents the anticipation of an abundant harvest and is the motif for the studio casita, which has a queen-size bed. The *Kokopelli* Casita is a one-bedroom unit with a dining room, living room, and king-size bed. Kokopelli is a flute player who is thought to bring good fortune and abundance to the Native American people. The Rainbow Dancer represents power, beauty, and strength through the colors of the rainbow. In the Buffalo Dancer Casita, beautiful Native American drums are used as end tables and are meant to remind visitors of the rhythm of life. The one-bedroom Clown (or *Koshari*) Dancer Casita is delightfully representational of the "spirit of the classic Native American prankster." Four of the rooms have fireplaces. All rooms have fully equipped kitchens, and the Buffalo and Rainbow casitas have washers and dryers. Each morning a breakfast of healthful, fresh-baked goods is delivered (along with the paper) to your front door in a basket for you to enjoy at your leisure. Smoking and pets are not permitted.

El Farolito, 514 Galisteo St., Santa Fe, NM 87501. ☎ **505/988-1631.** 7 casitas. TV TEL

Rates: $110–$125 double. MC, V.

El Farolito is just a five-minute walk from downtown Santa Fe, but it's far enough away from the center of town that its guests will be able to enjoy some peace and quiet after a long day of shopping and sightseeing. All seven of the *casitas* here have *kiva* fireplaces, and all are decorated in true Santa Fe style. The floors in each room are either brick or tile and are covered with Mexican rugs; walls are adobe colored, and bedspreads are southwestern in style. Some rooms have semiprivate patios, some have wet bars, and one of the larger rooms has a kitchenette. A continental breakfast of fruit, pastry, cereals, coffee, and tea is served each morning in the breakfast room (which also has a fireplace).

Four Kachinas Inn, 512 Webber St., Santa Fe, NM 87501. ☎ **505/982-2550** or toll free **800/397-2564**. 4 rms (all with bath). TV TEL

Rates: $88–$113 double. MC, V.

Located on a quiet, residential street, but still well within walking distance of downtown Santa Fe, the Four Kachinas Inn is a wonderful little bed and breakfast. The rooms are decorated with southwestern artwork, including beautiful antique Navajo rugs, *kachinas*, and handmade furniture (in fact, some of the furniture was made from the wood salvaged from the old barn that was once on the property here). As you might have guessed, each of the rooms is named for a Hopi kachina: The *Koyemsi* Room is named for the "fun-loving, mudhead clown kachina"; the *Poko* Room for the dog kachina that "represents the spirits of domestic animals"; the *Hon* Room for the "powerful healing bear kachina"; and the *Tawa* Room for the sun god kachina. Three of the rooms are on the ground floor. The upstairs room has a beautiful view of the Sangre de Cristo Mountains. In a separate building, which is constructed of adobe bricks that were made on the property, there is a guest lounge where guests can gather at any time during the day to enjoy complimentary beverages and snacks. The snacks, whatever they are that day, will be a treat—one of the owners won "Best Baker of Santa Fe" at the country fair a couple of years ago. Also in the guest lounge are pieces of art for sale, and a library of art and travel books. One of the rooms here is completely handicapped accessible.

Grant Corner Inn, 122 Grant Ave., Santa Fe, NM 87501. ☎ **983-6678** for reservations or **984-9001** for guest rooms. 11 rms. A/C TV TEL

Rates (including breakfast): June–Oct and major holidays $85 single, $95–$130 standard double. $130–$140 deluxe double; Nov–May except holidays $50 single, $65–$85 standard double, $115–$125 deluxe double. No children 8 or under. MC, V.

This early 20th-century manor at the corner of Johnson Street is just three blocks west of the Plaza. Each room is furnished with antiques, from brass or four-poster beds to armoires and quilts. Each has a portable cable TV, a clock radio, limited-edition lithographs on the walls, and monogrammed terry-cloth robes. Most rooms also have ceiling fans and small refrigerators, and five have private baths. But each room also has its own character. No. 3, for instance, has a hand-painted German wardrobe closet dating from 1772 and a washbasin with brass fittings in the shape of a fish. No. 8 has an exclusive outdoor deck which catches the morning sun. No. 11 has an antique collection of dolls and stuffed animals. The inn's office doubles as a library and gift shop and has hot coffee and tea available at all hours.

Breakfast is served each morning in front of the living-room fireplace, or on the front veranda during the warm months of summer. The meals are so good that an enthusiastic public pays $10.50 a head ($7 for young children) to brunch here Saturday from 8 to 11am and Sunday from 8am to 1pm. (It's included in the room price for Grant Corner Inn guests, of course.) The menu changes daily, but always includes a fruit frappé, a choice of two gourmet main courses, homemade pastries, and coffee and tea.

Inn of the Animal Tracks, 707 Paseo de Peralta, Santa Fe, NM 87501. ☎ **505/988-1546.** 5 rms (all with bath). A/C TV TEL

Rates: (including breakfast and afternoon refreshments): $90–$130 single or double. AE, MC, V.

Inn of the Animal Tracks is a great little inn. All of the rooms, including the common spaces, are named under the sign of different animals. There are five in all: the sign of the rabbit, the soaring eagle, the gentle deer, the playful otter, and the loyal wolf. They are patron spirits of the different rooms. All of the rooms have queen-size beds (with down comforters) and private baths, and all reflect the presence of the patron animal. The Sign of the Rabbit room, for instance, is just overflowing with rabbits—stuffed rabbits, rabbit paintings, and rabbit books. There are handmade furnishings, and the rooms are all pleasant and bright. The Sign of the Soaring Eagle room is the only one with a fireplace.

The Sign of the Bear room is a wonderful living room with a fireplace and a big overstuffed sofa. There's a small library from which you can borrow a book. Breakfast is served in the Sign of the Buffalo room, and it includes fresh bread, juice, fruit, and a different recipe daily. In the afternoon tea is served. Both breakfast and tea are served on the landscaped patio, weather permitting. The inn is nonsmoking; a dog and two cats are residents of the inn.

Inn on the Paseo, 630 Paseo de Peralta, Santa Fe, NM 87501. ☎ **505/984-8200** or toll free **800/457-9045**. Fax 505/989-3979. 19 rms, 2 suites.

Rates: $99–$190 double. MC, V.

Located just a few blocks from the Plaza, the Inn on the Paseo is a good choice for travelers who want to be able to walk to the shops, galleries, and restaurants, but would rather not stay in one of the larger hotels. When you enter the inn, you'll be welcomed by the warmth of the large fireplace in the foyer. Southwestern furnishings dot the spacious public areas, and the work of local artists adorns the walls. The guest rooms are large, meticulously clean, and very comfortable. Many of the rooms have fireplaces, and the focal point of each room is an original, handmade patchwork quilt. The owner is a third-generation quilter; she made all of the quilts you'll see hanging throughout the inn. A breakfast buffet is served out on the sun deck in warmer weather, indoors by the fire on cooler days. It consists of muffins, breads, granola, fresh fruit, coffee, and tea. Complimentary refreshments are served every afternoon.

$ **The Preston House,** 106 Faithway St., Santa Fe, NM 87501. ☎ **505/982-3465.** 15 rms. A/C TV TEL

Rates: High season $70–$80 double with shared bath, $100–$145 private bath, $140 cottage or adobe home; low season $48–$58 double with shared bath, $78–$98 private bath, $115 cottage or adobe home. Extra person $15. Children over 10 only. MC, V.

This is a different sort of building for the City Different—a century-old Queen Anne home. That style of architecture is rarely seen in New Mexico, especially painted sky blue with white trim. The house's owner, noted silk-screen artist and muralist Signe Bergman, adores its original stained glass.

Located three blocks east of the Plaza, off Palace Avenue near La Posada hotel, the Preston House has several types of rooms. Six in the main house have period antiques and exquisitely feminine decor, with floral wallpaper and lace drapes. Many have brass beds covered with quilts; some have decks, several have fireplaces, and only two must share a bath. Seven more rooms with private baths and TVs are in an adobe building catercorner from the house. Two private cottages in the rear of the Preston House and an adobe home across the street have more deluxe facilities. All rooms are stocked with sherry and terry-cloth robes. A continental buffet breakfast is served daily from 8 to 10am, and full tea and dessert are served every afternoon.

Spencer House Bed & Breakfast Inn, 222 McKenzie St., Santa Fe, NM 87501. ☎ **505/988-3024** or toll free **800/647-0530** (between 7am and 7pm). 3 rms (all with bath).

Rates: $85–$95 double. MC, V.

Spencer House is unique among Santa Fe bed and breakfasts. Instead of southwestern-style furnishings, you'll find beautiful antiques from England, Ireland, and colonial America. One guest room features an antique brass bed, another a pencil-post bed, and all rooms are done in Ralph Lauren fabrics and linens (in fact, Spencer House has recently been featured in Ralph Lauren ads). Each of the beds is also outfitted with a fluffy down comforter. All bathrooms are completely new, modern, and very spacious. Owners Keith and Michael keep the inn spotlessly clean and take great pride in Spencer House. From the old Bissell carpet sweeper and drop-front desk in the reading nook to antique trunks in the bedrooms, no detail has been overlooked. In summer, a full breakfast of coffee, tea, yogurt, cereal, fresh fruit, and a different main course daily is served on the outdoor patio. In winter, guests dine indoors by the wood-burning stove. A full afternoon tea is served in the breakfast room for guests. Keith and Michael, who live next door, recently received an award from the Santa Fe Historical Board for the restoration of Spencer House. They plan to have two more rooms ready by the summer of 1995.

4 Dining

There are literally hundreds of restaurants in Santa Fe, from luxury establishments with strict dress codes right down to corner hamburger stands. This is a sophisticated city, and there is a great variety of cuisines here. Some chefs create new recipes by incorporating traditional southwestern foods with other kinds of ingredients; their restaurants are referred to in this listing as "creative southwestern."

The categories below define a **very expensive** restaurant as one in which most dinner main courses are priced above $25; **expensive,** most main courses $18 to $25; **moderate,** $12 to $18; **inexpensive,** $7 to $12; **budget,** most main courses cost less than $7.

Downtown

EXPENSIVE

Cafe Escalera, 130 Lincoln Ave. ☎ **989-8188.**

> **Cuisine:** CREATIVE CONTINENTAL/SOUTHWESTERN. **Reservations:** Recommended.
> **Prices:** Appetizers $2–$6.50; main courses $8.75–$22.50.
> **Open:** Mon–Sat 8:30am–10pm, Sun 5–9pm.

When Cafe Escalera opened a few years ago, the quality of the food wasn't very consistent; however, it is now, and it has become one of Santa Fe's most popular restaurants. The spacious, open, warehouselike space is bright, airy, and filled with energy. The decor is understated in a modern way, and the focus here is on the food. At lunch I like to start my meal with an order of Mediterranean olives and perhaps an order of roasted almonds. If you're in the mood for something more substantial to start, try the roasted peppers and goat cheese or the vegetarian black bean chile. On my last visit to Cafe Escalera for lunch I enjoyed the grilled tuna salad with arugula, new potatoes, green beans, beets, and aioli. Dinner appetizers are usually the same as at lunch, but the main courses differ greatly. The risotto timbale with summer squash, spinach, and basil pesto is a good choice and so is the grilled king salmon with a tomato basil vinaigrette. Those with a heartier appetite will enjoy the roast New York strip steak with saffron garlic mashed potatoes and summer chanterelles. For dessert I had the Grand Marnier ice, which was delicious. There's also always something for chocoholics. Breakfast is served in the bar Monday through Saturday.

Corn Dance Cafe, 409 W. Water St. ☎ **986-1662.**

> **Cuisine:** CREATIVE NATIVE AMERICAN. **Reservations:** Recommended.
> **Prices:** Appetizers $4.50–$8.50; main courses $13.50–$23.50.
> **Open:** Lunch daily 11am–3pm; dinner daily 5:30–10pm.

The recently opened Corn Dance Cafe is unique to the Santa Fe restaurant scene because it focuses on Native American, rather than New Mexican cuisine, and aims to "promote healthy well-being and ecological respect for Mother Earth." Start with the Potawatomi Little Big Pie (Native American flat bread topped with savory chicken,

0 — 200 m
220 y

N

Rio Grande Ave.

Griffin St.

Arroyo de las Lovantos

Paseo de la Cuma

Old Taos Highway

Washington Ave.

Sunset St.

Artist Rd.

Arroyo Mascras

Paseo de Peralta

N. Guadalupe St.

Jefferson St.

Catron St.

Staab St.

McKenzie St.

Johnson St.

Grant Ave.

Post Office ⊠

N. Federal Pl.

S. Federal Pl.

W. Marcy St.

Sheridan

Lincoln

Ave.

Kearney Ave.

Otero St.

Paseo de Peralta

1

E. Marcy St.

Old Fort Marcy Park

W. San Francisco St.

16

W. Alameda St.

Santa Fe River State Park

St.

W. De Vargas St.

San Francisco St.

Water St.

12

9

14 **13**

15

7
8 **6**

4
5 **3**
2

Palace Ave.

Lust St.

10

11

Shelby St.

Cathedral Pl.

Hillside Park

18

19

Guadalupe

Aztec St.

17

20

Montezuma St.

Sandoval St.

Garfield St.

21

Read St.

W. Manhattan Ave.

Cerrillos Rd.

E. Alameda St.

Santa Fe River

De Vargas Park

E. De Vargas St.

S. Capitol St.

Don Gaspar Ave.

State Capitol Complex

23

24

Paseo de Peralta

22

Galisteo St.

W. Santa Fe Ave.

E. Santa Fe Ave.

Webber St.

Santa Fe Trail

Garcia St.

Delgado St.

Acequia Madre

W. Booth St.

Information ⓘ   Post Office ⊠

The Blue Corn Cafe **14**
The Burrito Co. **5**
Cafe Escalera **8**
Cafe Oasis **22**
Cafe Pasqual's **10**
Carlos Gosp'l Cafe **6**
Corbae **24**
Corn Dance Cafe **11**
Cowgirl Hall of Fame **17**

Coyote Cafe **15**
Guadalupe Cafe **20**
Inn of the Anasazi **4**
La Casa Sena **2**
La Tertulia **18**
O.J. Sarah's **16**
Ore House on the Plaza **9**
The Palace **12**

Paul's **7**
The Pink Adobe **23**
Pranzo Italia Grill **19**
San Francisco Street Bar & Grill **13**
Santacafe **1**
The Shed **3**
Tomasita's Santa Fe Station **21**

grilled mushrooms, and corn chili) or the Kick Ass Buffalo Chili in a jalapeño bread bowl. The alderwood-smoked Chinook salmon on red corn cakes is very tasty. My favorite main course here is the fire-roasted Colorado golden trout with blue corn–wild rice johnnycakes. Other interesting main courses include grilled Pueblo rabbit with Roma tomatoes, cilantro, and hazelnuts; and sassafras wood-smoked bobwhite quails with grilled red banana, papaya, and *achiote crema*. At press time, the restaurant was still awaiting a beer and wine license, so call ahead to see if you'll need to bring your own. The restaurant is smoke free.

Coyote Cafe, 132 W. Water St. ☎ **983-1615.**

Cuisine: CREATIVE SOUTHWESTERN. **Reservations:** Required.
Prices: Appetizers $2.25–$5.95 at lunch; main courses $6.50–$12.50. Prix-fixe dinner $39. MC, V.
Open: Lunch Sat–Sun 11:30am–2pm; dinner daily 5:30–10pm.

This is still the number one "trendy" place to dine in Santa Fe. Owner Mark Miller has talked extensively about his restaurant and cuisine on national television; as a result, he is universally identified with Santa Fe cuisine. Tourists throng here: In summer, in fact, reservations are recommended two to three days in advance. The cafe overlooks Water Street from tall windows on the second floor of a downtown building. Beneath the skylight, set in a cathedral ceiling, is a veritable zoo of animal sculptures in modern folk-art forms. Nonsmokers can breathe freely: The atmosphere is completely smoke free.

The cuisine, prepared on a pecan-wood grill in an open kitchen, is southwestern with a modern twist. The menu changes seasonally, but diners might start with the wild boar bacon and fresh corn tamale with glazed granny apples and corn-cumin coulis or griddled buttermilk and wild rice–corn cakes with chipotle shrimp and salsa fresca. Main courses might include pecan-grilled pork tenderloin or grilled tolenas farm sonoma quail with spicy bourbon apple stuffing and la caretta cider glaze. You can get drinks from the full bar or wines by the glass.

The Coyote Cafe has two adjunct establishments. The Rooftop Cantina (open April through October) serves Mexican fare and cocktails. It's open from 11am to 10pm daily; main course prices range from $5 to $16. On the ground floor is the Coyote Cafe General Store, a retail gourmet southwestern food market, featuring Coyote Cafe's own food line (called Coyote Cocina) and hot sauces and salsas from all over the world.

Encore Provence, 548 Agua Fria. ☎ **983-7470.**

Cuisine: FRENCH. **Reservations:** Recommended.
Prices: Appetizers $4.50–$9; main courses $15–$20.
Open: Mon–Sat 6–10pm. AE, MC, V.

If you've been in Santa Fe long enough to be craving something other than New Mexican cuisine, make a reservation at Encore Provence. It's a charming little three-room restaurant that's "rustic Provençal" in feeling and decorated with antique furnishings, dried flowers, and Provence *santos* dolls. The traditionally French menu changes seasonally and might offer escargots or duck confit (a steamed, boiled leg of duck seasoned with walnut oil) as appetizers. Main courses may include veal sweetbread with creamed leeks, potato Anna, and a sherry-and-wine-vinegar sauce; 7-hour leg of lamb with natural jus and aligot potatoes; or Chilean black bass with a black olive coulis and a zucchini and tomato flan. There is a nice wine list.

Geronimo, 724 Canyon Rd. ☎ 982-1500.

Cuisine: CREATIVE NEW MEXICAN. **Reservations:** Recommended.
Prices: Appetizers $6.50–$8.50; main courses $16.50–$21.50.
Open: Lunch Tues–Sun 11:30am–2:30pm; dinner daily 6–10:30pm. AE, MC, V.

When Geronimo opened in 1991, no one was sure that it would make it because so many other restaurants at this location had failed miserably; but Geronimo has done more than just survive, it has flourished. Located in an old adobe structure known as the Borrego House, the restaurant has been restored, but with its numerous small dining rooms, it still retains the comfortable feel of an old Santa Fe home. On a recent visit the menu appetizer offerings included a barbecue shrimp quesadilla with Bermuda onion, goat cheese, crème fraiche, and yellow tomato salsa; and crispy relleno stuffed with chicken mole and served with a lime crème fraiche and an ancho chile puree. Favorite main courses were the white cornmeal–dusted, pan-seared, free-range chicken served with a fresh peach ginger salsa, baby spinach, and roasted new potatoes; fresh lime grilled halibut with smoky red posole and a blackened tomato and roasted yellow pepper vinaigrette; and the mesquite-grilled Black Angus ribeye steak with a roasted pepper, grilled summer vegetable salsa, and white-cheddar-and-green-chile-layered potatoes. The menu changes seasonally, and there is a well-selected wine list.

Inn of the Anasazi Restaurant, 113 Washington Ave. ☎ 988-3236.

Cuisine: NORTHERN NEW MEXICAN/NATIVE AMERICAN.
Reservations: Highly recommended.
Prices: Breakfast $4–$9; lunch appetizers $6.50–$8, main courses $8.50–$11.95; dinner appetizers $6.50–$9.50, main courses $17.50–$29.
Open: Breakfast Mon–Fri 7–10am, Sat–Sun 7–11am; lunch daily 11:30am–2:30pm; dinner Mon–Fri 5:30–10pm, Sat–Sun 5:30–11pm.

In keeping with the theory behind the Inn of the Anasazi, everything offered in this restaurant is all natural. The meats are chemical free, and fruits and vegetables are organic whenever possible. They even serve water only on request "in the interest of conservation." The setting is comfortable, with an exposed beam ceiling, exposed adobe walls, and traditional southwestern decor—it's not at all kitsch, it's very elegant.

For breakfast you can have anything from fruit to a breakfast burrito with ranchero sauce and chile potatoes or a soft scrambled egg quesadilla with yellow tomatoes, apple-smoked bacon, and fresh avocados. At lunch you might try the Anasazi flat bread with fire-roasted sweet peppers and tomato olive salsa to start, followed by achiote charred rare tuna with wasabi aioli and snow pea slaw. For dinner, try the tortilla soup with barbecue pork pot stickers with chili ancho and red tortillas. Maybe you'd rather have dried guava and citrus seared halibut with apricot essence and green rice.

There are daily specials, as well as a nice list of wines by the glass and special wines of the day.

 ## La Casa Sena, 125 E. Palace Ave. ☎ 988-9232.

Cuisine: CREATIVE SOUTHWESTERN. **Reservations:** Recommended.
Prices: Lunch appetizers $2.25–$6.50, main courses $8–$11; dinner appetizers $5–$8, main courses $18–$24. Cantina $4.50–$18.50; Wine prix-fixe dinner $38.50 ($31.50 without wine). AE, CB, DC, DISC, MC, V.
Open: Lunch Mon–Sat 11:30am–3pm, dinner daily 5:30–10pm; Sun brunch in main dining room only, 11am–3pm.

Opposite St. Francis Cathedral, two restaurants look into a spacious garden patio. The elegant main dining room occupies the Territorial-style adobe house built in 1867 by

Civil War hero Maj. Jose Sena for his wife and 23 children. Today, it's a veritable art gallery, with museum-quality landscapes on the walls and Taos-style handcrafted furniture. In the adjacent La Cantina, waiters and waitresses sing arias and tunes from Broadway shows like *Phantom of the Opera, Les Misérables,* and *Little Shop of Horrors* as they carry platters from kitchen to table.

The cuisine in the main dining room might be described as northern New Mexican with a continental flair. Lunches include chicken enchiladas on blue-corn tortillas and grilled almond-crusted salmon with gazpacho salsa, herbed yogurt sauce, and curried orzo. In the evenings, diners might start with caldo de frijole negro (purée of black beans with amontillado sherry), then move to mesquite-grilled free-range chicken breast with sweetwoods chiva, blue and yellow corn polenta, and grilled vegetable salsa.

The more moderately priced Cantina menu offers the likes of chile-rubbed tenderloin medallions (with tomatillo-chipotle sauce and pan-fried potatoes), and carne adovada burrito (prime pork roasted with red chile, served with Hatch green chiles and cheeses). Both restaurants have exquisite desserts and fine wines by the glass.

The Pink Adobe, 406 Old Santa Fe Trail. ☎ **983-7712.**

Cuisine: CONTINENTAL/SOUTHWESTERN. **Reservations:** Recommended.
Prices: Appetizers $5.75–$7.50; lunch $6.50–$9.50; dinner $10.75–$22.25. AE, CB, DC, DISC, MC, V.
Open: Lunch Mon–Fri 11:30am–2:30pm; dinner daily 5:30–10pm.

San Pasqual, patron saint of the kitchen, keeps a close eye on this popular restaurant, in the center of the 17th-century Barrio de Analco, across the street from the San Miguel mission. A Santa Fe institution since 1946, it occupies an adobe home believed to be at least 350 years old. Guests enter through a narrow side door into a series of quaint, informal dining rooms with tile or hardwood floors. Stucco walls display original modern art or Priscilla Hoback pottery on built-in shelves.

At the dinner hour, the Pink Adobe offers the likes of escargots and shrimp rémoulade as appetizers. Main courses include shrimp creole, poulet Marengo, tournedos bordelaise, lamb curry, and porc Napoleone. Lunch has more New Mexican and Cajun dishes, including a house enchilada topped with an egg, turkey-seafood gumbo, and gypsy stew (chicken, green chile, tomatoes, and onions in sherry broth).

Smoking is allowed only in the charming Dragon Room, the lounge across the alleyway from the restaurant. Under the same ownership, the Dragon Room (which is much more popular with locals than the main dining room) has a separate menu from its parent establishment with traditional Mexican foods. The full bar is open from 11:30am to 2am daily, until midnight Sunday and there is live entertainment Sunday through Thursday.

 Santacafe, 231 Washington Ave. ☎ **984-1788.**

Cuisine: CONTEMPORARY AMERICAN. **Reservations:** Recommended.
Prices: Appetizers $5–$10; main courses, lunch $8–$12, dinner $18–$24. MC, V.
Open: Lunch Mon–Sat 11:30am–2pm; dinner daily 6–10pm (5:30–10:30pm in summer).

A casually formal restaurant in the 18th-century Padre Gallegos House, 2¹/₂ blocks north of the Plaza, the service and presentation here are impeccable. Noted for its minimalist decor, art-free soft white adobe interior, and "zen-inspired" courtyard, Santacafe has been a favorite of tourists and locals alike since 1983. Each room has a fireplace, and the courtyard is available for summer dining. Santacafe's unique modern American cuisine also reveals southwestern and Asian influences. Menus change seasonally, but recent offerings included Dungeness crab cakes with cucumber and carrot salad and house-smoked chicken spring rolls with a three-chile dipping sauce as appetizers. Main courses included red chile ravioli filled with goat and feta cheeses, fresh oregano, sun-dried tomato, and a basil green chile sauce, and Atlantic salmon with roasted new potatoes. All breads and desserts are homemade, and the full bar offers wines by the glass.

MODERATE

Cafe Oasis, 526 Galisteo St. ☎ **983-9599.**

Cuisine: INTERNATIONAL/NATURAL. **Reservations:** Not accepted.
Prices: Breakfast $3.75–$7.75; lunch $2.50–$7.75; dinner $6.75–$10.75.
Open: Sun–Thurs 9am–11:30pm, Fri–Sat 9am–1am.

Located on the corner of Paseo de Peralta and Galisteo, Cafe Oasis advertises itself as "funky and elegant" in atmosphere—the kind of place "for those who want something different." It certainly lives up to its reputation, but I might call it one of the last hippie holdouts of the Southwest. Within the walls of Cafe Oasis there are four rooms, each one unique in its atmosphere. There is a "Mystical Room of blue violet," a "Smoking Room of green," a "Social Room of marigold," and a "Romantic Room." There's no flourescent lighting here; instead, there's an eclectic mix of floor and table lamps. Tables and chairs that look like great garage sale finds come in all different shapes and sizes—there's even a couch or two. The breakfast menu is served all day and includes specialties like blue-corn huevos rancheros with red or green chile, sour cream, black beans, and rice; Amalia's fruit-sweetened, wheat-free blue-corn silver dollar pancakes; a stack of three large buckwheat pancakes; or cinnamon raisin challah french toast. At lunch you can begin your meal with the hummus appetizer with feta, olives, cucumbers, tomatoes, and pita, or cold sesame noodles with tahini sauce and crudités. Sandwiches come with a "side o' homies" and might include blue-corn catfish on a baguette with tartar sauce, an Oasis lamb burger with a choice of one filling or cheese, or a Cajun blackened chicken sandwich on a honey wheat bun with barbecue sauce. The dinner menu features full main courses like blue-corn catfish and potato pancakes or Yaki Soba noodles simmered in ginger soy broth topped with seasonal vegetables and fresh fish yakitori. There are daily specials available.

$ Cafe Pasqual's, 121 Don Gaspar Ave. ☎ **983-9340.**

Cuisine: OLD/NEW MEXICAN/AMERICAN.
Reservations: Highly recommended for dinner.
Prices: Breakfast $4.75–$7.75; lunch $6.25–$8.95; dinner appetizers $4.75–$8.75, main courses $10.50–$19.75. MC, V.
Open: Breakfast Mon–Sat 7am–3pm; brunch Sun 8am–2pm; lunch Mon–Sat 11am–3pm; dinner Sun–Thurs 6–10pm, Fri–Sat 6–10:30pm.

This classic New Mexican–style establishment one block southwest of the Plaza is a big favorite of locals and travelers alike. Not only does it have a common table where solo journeyers can meet locals and get acquainted; it also has an innovative menu, one that especially appeals to budget watchers at breakfast and lunch. Omelets, pancakes, cereals, and huevos motulenos—like rancheros but with fried bananas—are among the breakfast options. Soups, salads, sandwiches, and Mexican dishes are popular at lunch; there's a delectable grilled trout in cornmeal with green chile and toasted piñon. There are also daily specials.

The frequently changing dinner menu offers grilled meats and seafoods, plus vegetarian specials. Oaxacan mango, whole roasted garlic, and corn cakes with squash are typical appetizers. Main courses might include chile-marinated New York steak, rack of lamb with tomato-mint salsa, chipotle shrimp on blue-corn tortillas, or an enchilada with spinach and Jack cheese. Pasqual's also boasts house-made desserts, imported beers, and wine by the bottle or glass.

Corbae, 422 Old Santa Fe Trail. ☎ **983-2422.**
Cuisine: ECLECTIC. **Reservations:** Recommended.
Prices: Breakfast and lunch $4.50–$9.50; dinner $6.50–$19.
Open: Daily 7:45am–closing.

Corbae, formerly Patis Corbae, offers "seasonal eclectic" cuisine in a comfortable atmosphere. In cooler months diners are treated to the warmth of the fireplace, and in the summer the dining room extends to the outdoor patio. Lunch is served all day and includes a green chile stew (with potatoes, pork, and mushrooms) ribboned with sour cream. As a main course, the ruby trout with corn fritters with fresh pico de gallo salsa and pure maple syrup on the side is an excellent choice, as is the vegetarian club (a sandwich of avocado, tomato, onions, greens, with a chipotle mayonnaise). At dinner you might like to start with the sopa de lima (shredded free-range chicken, avocado, tomato, and Mexican herbs in a savory chicken broth with a squeeze of lime) or the gazpacho. Main courses run the gamut from beef tenderloin (sautéed tenderloin medallions with shiitake mushrooms, sherry, and garlic) to citrus marinated chicken (roasted half-breast of free-range chicken served with chayote squash, zucchini, fresh corn, and couscous) and pan-roasted salmon (served with lemon, avocado, and roasted vegetables). Coffees are organically grown, and there is a large selection of freshly baked breads and desserts. The wine list is short but well selected.

Cowgirl Hall of Fame, 319 S. Guadalupe. ☎ **982-2565.**
Cuisine: REGIONAL AMERICAN/BBQ. **Reservations:** Recommended.
Prices: Appetizers $4.25–$4.95; main courses $3.95–$12.95.
Open: Daily 11am–11pm.

Mention the Cowgirl Hall of Fame to any Santa Fean, and you'll hear one word: "fun." Everything at this restaurant has been done with a playful spirit—from the cowgirl paraphernalia that decorates the walls to the menu which features items like "chicken wing dings" (eight chicken wings in a "dandy" citrus-tabasco marinade served with a special dressing). The chuckwagon chili is another house favorite, and so is the honey-fried chicken. The bunkhouse smoked brisket with potato salad, barbecue beans, and coleslaw is excellent, as is the cracker-fried catfish with jalapeño tartar sauce. There's even a special "kid's corral" which has horseshoes, a play area, and pin-the-tail-on-the-cow to keep children entertained during dinner. The dessert specialty of the house is the original ice cream baked potato (ice cream molded into a potato shape, rolled in spices, and topped with green pecans and whipped cream). Happy hour is from 4 to 6pm, and the bar stays open until 2am.

★ **La Tertulia,** 416 Agua Fria St. ☎ **988-2769.**
$ **Cuisine:** NEW MEXICAN. **Reservations:** Recommended.
Prices: Lunch $4.95–$7.25; dinner $7.25–$17.95. AE, MC, V.
Open: Lunch Tues–Sun 11:30am–2pm; dinner Tues–Sun 5–9pm.

Housed in a former 18th-century convent, La Tertulia's thick adobe walls separate six dining rooms, among them the old chapel and a restored *sala* (living room) containing a valuable Spanish colonial art collection. There's also an outside garden patio for summer dining. Dim lighting and *viga*-beamed ceilings, shuttered windows and wrought-iron chandeliers, lace tablecloths and hand-carved *santos* in wall niches lend a feeling of historic authenticity. La Tertulia means "The Gathering Place."

A highlight of the menu is Spanish paella (for two or more), an olio of seafood, chicken, chorizo sausage, vegetables, and rice, served with black bean/jalapeño soup and sopaipillas. Gourmet regional dishes include filet y rellenos, carne adovada, pollo adovo, and camarones con pimientas y tomates (shrimp with peppers and tomatoes). If you feel like dessert, try capirotada (bread pudding) or natillas (custard). Many diners request the bar to bring them a pitcher of the homemade sangría.

Ore House on the Plaza, 50 Lincoln Ave. ☎ 983-8687.

Cuisine: STEAKS & SEAFOOD. **Reservations:** Recommended.
Prices: Appetizers $3.50–$9.75; main courses $12.95–$20. AE, MC, V.
Open: Lunch daily 10:30am–2:30pm; dinner daily 5:30–10pm.

The Ore House's second-story balcony, at the southwest corner of the Plaza, is an ideal spot from which to watch the passing parade while enjoying lunch or cocktails. When the weather gets chilly, radiant heaters keep the balcony warm, and there's a big fireplace indoors. The decor is southwestern, with plants and lanterns hanging from white walls and over booths.

The menu is heavy on fresh seafood and steaks. Daily fresh fish specials include salmon and swordfish (poached, blackened, teriyaki, or lemon), rainbow trout, lobster, and shellfish. Steak Ore House, wrapped in bacon and topped with crabmeat and béarnaise sauce, and chicken Ore House, a grilled breast stuffed with ham, Swiss cheese, green chile, and béarnaise, are local favorites. The Ore House also caters to vegetarians with vegetable platters. Luncheon diners often opt for the spinach salad or the prime rib sandwich.

The bar, with solo music Wednesday through Saturday nights, is proud of its 66 "custom margaritas." It has a selection of domestic and imported beers, and an excellent wine list. An appetizer menu is served from 2:30 to 5pm daily, and the bar stays open until midnight or later (only until midnight on Sunday).

The Palace, 142 W. Palace Ave. ☎ 982-9891.

Cuisine: ITALIAN & CONTINENTAL. **Reservations:** Recommended.
Prices: Lunch $5.25–$10.50; dinner appetizers $5.95–$8.50, main courses $9.50–$18.95. AE, DISC, MC, V.
Open: Lunch Mon–Sat 11:30am–5pm; dinner Mon–Sat 5:45–10pm.

When construction crews in 1959 were excavating the Burro Alley site of Dona Tules's notorious 19th-century gambling hall, they came across an unusual artifact: a brass door knocker, half in the shape of a horseshoe, the other half resembling a saloon girl's leg, complete with stocking and high-heel boot. That knocker today is the logo of the Palace, which maintains the Victorian flavor but none of the ill repute of its predecessor. Red velvet wallpaper, dimly lit chandeliers, marble-topped tables, and high-backed chairs provide a classy yet casual decor for the restaurant.

Brothers Lino, Pietro, and Bruno Pertusini have carried on a long family tradition in the restaurant business: Their father was chef at the famous Villa d'Este on Lake Como, Italy. The Pertusinis' menu is predominantly northern Italian but contains a few French and continental dishes as well. Lunches include Caesar salad, roasted "seven Aromas" chicken salad, bruschetta caprini, ruby trout, house-made pasta, and breads. Dinners include crab-stuffed shrimp, scaloppine fontina, New Mexican lamb, steaks, gnocchi, and a variety of vegetarian dishes. The wine list is long and well considered.

You can see the famous door knocker above the bar of the spiffy saloon, open Monday through Saturday from 11:30am to 2am. There's a nightly piano bar.

Pranzo Italia Grill, 540 Montezuma St., Sanbusco Center. ☎ **984-2645.**
   Cuisine: NORTHERN ITALIAN. **Reservations:** Recommended.
   Prices: Appetizers $4.25–$6.95; lunch $4.50–$7.95; dinner $6.95–$17.95. AE, DC, DISC, MC, V.
   Open: Lunch daily 11:30am–3pm; dinner Sun–Thurs 5–10pm, Fri–Sat 5–11pm.

Housed in a renovated warehouse, this sister to Albuquerque's redoubtable Scalo restaurant caters to local Santa Feans with a contemporary setting filled with modern abstract art. An open grill is the centerpiece: The menu has few fried foods.

Homemade soups, salads, creative pizzas, and fresh pastas mark the low end of the menu. Bianchi e nere al capesante (black-and-white linguine with bay scallops in a light seafood sauce) and the pizza Mediterranea (with shrimp, zucchini, and roasted garlic) are consistent favorites. Steaks, chicken, veal, and fresh seafood grills, heavy on the garlic, dominate the dinner menu.

The bar boasts the Southwest's largest collection of grappa, as well as a wide choice of wines and champagnes by the glass. The restaurant's deli, Portare Via, offers Santa Fe's largest selection of Italian deli meats and cheeses.

INEXPENSIVE

The Blue Corn Cafe, 133 W. Water St. ☎ **984-1800.**
   Cuisine: NEW MEXICAN.
   Prices: Main courses $4.95–$8.25.
   Open: Daily 11am–11pm.

This lively, attractively decorated southwestern-style restaurant, which opened in 1992, is just what downtown Santa Fe needed—great food at inexpensive prices. Your waiter will bring freshly made tortilla chips to your table while you peruse the menu. While you're reading, keep in mind that the Blue Corn Cafe is known for its chile rellenos and its burritos. The mercado burrito (a homemade flour tortilla filled with potatoes, bacon, and red or green chile, served with refried beans and blue-corn posole) is a good choice. So is the carne adovada (marinated pork in red chile). For the more adventurous, the tortilla burger (a beef patty covered with cheeses, red or green chile, wrapped in a flour tortilla, and served with chile fries) is a good bet. And for those who can't decide, the combination plates will satisfy. For dessert try the Mexican brownies, the flan, or the fried ice cream. Prices are the same at dinner as they are at lunch.

 Guadalupe Cafe, 313 Guadalupe St. ☎ **982-9762.**
   Cuisine: NEW MEXICAN.
   Prices: Breakfast $4.25–$7.20; lunch $4.50–$7.95; dinner appetizers $2.50–$5.50, main courses $5.75–$12.95. MC, V.
   Open: Breakfast and lunch Tues–Fri 8am–2pm; brunch Sat–Sun 8am–2pm; dinner Tues–Sat 5:30–10pm.

Santa Feans line up at all hours to dine in this casually elegant cafe with tall potted plants and cushioned seats. Breakfasts include sausage and potato burritos, huevos rancheros, and a new specialty, the Santa Fe breakfast crêpe (a large whole wheat tortilla dipped in an egg and cinnamon batter, grilled, and filled with fresh berries, topped with lowfat yogurt and granola). On the lunch menu are Mexican chicken salad and blue-corn enchiladas. Dinner includes everything from breast of chicken relleno to chile-cheese chimichangas. Daily specials feature fresh fish, crêpes, and pastas; don't miss the famous chocolate-amaretto adobe pie for dessert. Beer and wine are served.

Paul's, 72 W. Marcy St. ☎ **982-8738.**
Cuisine: CREATIVE SOUTHWESTERN. **Reservations:** Recommended for dinner.
Prices: Breakfast $2–$4.25; lunch $5.50–$6.95; dinner appetizers $3.95–$6.50, main courses $10.25–$14.25. MC, V.
Open: Mon–Fri 7am–9pm, Sat lunch and dinner 11am–9pm.

Once just a home-style deli, then a little gourmet restaurant called Santa Fe Gourmet, Paul's (opened in 1990) is a great place for lunch or dinner. The lunch menu offers a few main dishes, like sausage and lentils or fettucine, hot or cold sandwiches, and a short vegetarian menu. At dinner, the lights are dimmed, and the bright Santa Fe interior—with folk art on the walls and colorfully painted screens that divide the restaurant into smaller, more intimate areas—becomes a great place for a romantic dinner. The menu might include a black-bean crêpe filled with curried vegetables to start and, as a main course, stuffed pumpkin bread with pine nuts, corn, green chile, red chile sauce, queso blanco, and caramelized apples. Paul's won the Taste of Santa Fe for best main course in 1992 and best dessert in 1994. A wine list is available. The restaurant is entirely nonsmoking.

★ **San Francisco Street Bar and Grill,** 114 W. San Francisco St. ☎ **982-2044.**
Cuisine: AMERICAN.
$ **Prices:** Lunch $4.50–$6.50; dinner $4.50–$12.95. DISC, MC, V.
Open: Daily 11am–11pm.

This easygoing eatery offers casual dining amid simple decor. There are three seating areas: the main restaurant, an indoor courtyard beneath the three-story Plaza Mercado atrium, and an outdoor patio with its own summer grill.

The grill is perhaps best known for its hamburger, but it offers a variety of daily specials. The lunch menu consists mainly of soups, sandwiches, and salads; dinners include fresh deep-fried catfish, grilled pork tenderloin medallions, and New York strip steak. There are also nightly pasta specials. There's full bar service, with draft beers and daily wine specials.

$ **Tomasita's Santa Fe Station,** 500 S. Guadalupe St. ☎ **983-5721.**
Cuisine: NEW MEXICAN.
Prices: Appetizers $1.95–$4.25; main courses $4.25–$9.25 at lunch, $4.75–$9.75 at dinner. MC, V.
Open: Mon–Sat 11am–10pm.

This may be the restaurant most consistently recommended by local Santa Feans. Why? Some point to the atmosphere; others cite the food and prices. Hanging plants and wood decor accent this spacious brick building adjacent to the old Santa Fe railroad station. Traditional New Mexican main courses like chile rellenos and enchiladas (house specialties), as well as stuffed sopaipillas, chalupas, and tacos are served. Offerings also include vegetarian dishes and daily specials, and there's full bar service.

BUDGET

The Burrito Co., 111 Washington Ave. ☎ **982-4453.**
Cuisine: NEW MEXICAN.
Prices: $1.89–$4.75. MC, V.
Open: Mon–Sat 7:30am–11pm.

This is probably downtown Santa Fe's best fast-food establishment. You can people-watch as you dine on the outdoor patio, or enjoy the garden-style poster gallery indoors. Order and pick up at the counter. Breakfast burritos are popular in the morning; after 11am you can get traditional Mexican meals with lots of chiles.

$ **Carlos' Gosp'l Cafe,** 125 Lincoln Ave. ☎ **983-1841.**
Cuisine: DELI.
Prices: $2.65–$6.65. No credit cards.
Open: Mon–Sat 11am–4pm.

You'll want to sing the praises of the "Say Amen" desserts at this cafe, located in the inner courtyard of the First Interstate Bank Building. First, though, try the tortilla or hangover (potato-corn) soup, or the deli sandwiches. Carlos' has outdoor tables, but many diners prefer to sit indoors, reading newspapers or sharing conversation at the large common table. Gospel and soul music play continuously; oil paintings of churches and of many performers cover the walls.

La Choza, 905 Alarid St. ☎ **982-0909.**
Cuisine: NEW MEXICAN.
Prices: Lunch $4.50–$5.50; dinner $5.50–$6.50. MC, V.
Open: Mon–Thurs 11am–8pm, Fri–Sat 11am–9pm.

The sister restaurant of the Shed (see below) is located near Cerrillos Road's intersection with St. Francis Drive. A casual eatery with round tables beneath a *viga* ceiling, it's especially popular on cold days, when diners gather around the wood-burning stove and fireplace. The menu offers traditional enchiladas, tacos, and burritos on blue-corn tortillas, as well as green chile stew, chili con carne, and carne adovada. Vegetarians and children have their own menus. Beer and wine are served.

O.J. Sarah's, 106 N. Guadalupe St. ☎ **984-1675.**
Cuisine: CREATIVE AMERICAN.
Prices: Breakfast $3–$6; lunch $3.50–$7.75. No credit cards.
Open: Daily 7am–2pm.

Named for a since-departed owner who had a penchant for orange juice and other wholesome foods, this cafe offers such unusual breakfasts as cottage-cheese pancakes topped with hot raspberry sauce and three-egg omelets filled with spinach, avocado, cheese, and mushrooms. For lunch, consider a spinach-artichoke salad, a guacamole burrito, or a sour cream chicken enchilada—or play it safe with sandwiches on home-baked bread and fruit smoothies.

$ **The Shed,** 113 ½ E. Palace Ave. ☎ **982-9030.**
Cuisine: NEW MEXICAN.
Prices: Main dishes $3.50–$6.75. No credit cards.
Open: Mon–Sat 11am–2:30pm.

Queues often form outside the Shed, located a half-block east of the Palace of the Governors. A luncheon institution since 1954, it occupies several rooms and the patio of a rambling hacienda built in 1692. Festive folk art adorns the doorways and walls. The food is basic but delicious, a compliment to traditional Hispanic pueblo cooking. Blue-corn enchiladas, tacos, and burritos, all served on blue-corn tortillas with pinto beans and posoles, are standard courses. The green chile soup is a local favorite. There are dessert specials, and beer and wine are available.

Southside/Cerrillos Road

MODERATE

 Old Mexico Grill, 2434 Cerrillos Rd., College Plaza South. ☎ **473-0338.**

Cuisine: MEXICAN. **Reservations:** Requested for large parties.
Prices: Appetizers $2.95–$6.75; main courses $8.75–$16.95. DISC, MC, V.
Open: Lunch Mon–Fri 11:30am–3pm; dinner Sun–Thurs 5–9pm, Fri–Sat 5–9:30pm.
Extended hours in summer.

Here's something unique in Santa Fe: a restaurant that specializes not in northern New Mexico food, but in authentic regional Mexican cuisine. Waitpersons offer attentive service; the centerpiece is an exhibition cooking area with an open mesquite grill and French rotisserie, behind bright blue tiles and beneath a raft of hanging copperware.

A tempting array of fajitas, tacos al carbón, and other specialties are prepared on the grill. Popular dishes include turkey mole poblano, and costillas de puerca en barbacoa de Oaxaca (hickory-smoked baby back ribs baked in a chipotle and mulato chile, honey, mustard barbecue sauce). There's a good choice of soups and salads at lunch, and a selection of homemade desserts, including hazelnut-apricot torte. A full bar serves Mexican beers and margaritas.

Steaksmith at El Gancho, Old Las Vegas Hwy. ☎ **988-3333.**

Cuisine: STEAKS & SEAFOOD. **Reservations:** Recommended.
Prices: Appetizers $3.95–$5.95; main courses $8.95–$28.95. AE, MC, V.
Open: Daily 5:30–10pm.

Santa Fe's most highly regarded steak house is a 15-minute drive up the Old Pecos Trail toward Las Vegas. Guests enjoy attentive service in a pioneer setting with adobe walls and *viga* ceilings.

New York sirloin, filet mignon, and other complete steak dinners are served, along with barbecued ribs and such nightly fresh seafood specials as oysters, trout, and salmon. A creative appetizer menu ranges from ceviche Acapulco to grilled pasilla peppers and beef chupadero. There are also outstanding salads, homemade desserts and bread, and a full bar and lounge that even caters to cappuccino lovers.

Szechwan Chinese Cuisine, 1965 Cerrillos Rd. ☎ **983-1558.**

Cuisine: NORTHERN CHINESE. **Reservations:** Recommended.
Prices: Lunch $4.50–$5.25; dinner $5.25–$20. AE, MC, V.
Open: Daily 11am–9:30pm.

Spicy northern Chinese cuisine pleases the southwestern palate, and there's plenty of it here. Some diners love the Peking duck, made to order with 24 hours' notice, served with traditional pancakes and plum sauce. Also excellent is the seafood platter of shrimp, scallops, crab, fish, and vegetables stir-fried in a wine sauce. Other specialties include Lake Tung Ting shrimp, sesame beef, and General Chung's chicken. Wine is served, along with Tsingtao beer from China.

INEXPENSIVE

 Maria's New Mexican Kitchen, 555 W. Cordova Rd. near St. Francis Drive. ☎ **983-7929.**

Cuisine: NEW MEXICAN. **Reservations:** Accepted but not essential.
Prices: Lunch $5.25–$8.95; dinner $5.75–$15.95. MC, V.
Open: Mon–Fri 11am–10pm, Sat–Sun noon–10pm.

ATTRACTIONS

El Rancho de las Golodrinas 16
Museum of Indian Arts and Culture 6
Museum of International Folk Art 7
Santa Fe Children's Museum 9
Wheelwright Museum of the American Indian 8

ACCOMMODATIONS

Best Western High Mesa Inn 17
Bishop's Lodge 1
Cactus Lodge 14
El Rey Inn 11
Picacho Plaza Hotel 2
Super 8 Motel 15

DINING

Geronimo 3
Maria's New Mexican Kitchen 5
The Natural Cafe 4
Old Mexico Grill 13
Steaksmith at El Gancho 18
Szechwan Chinese Cuisine 12
Tecolote Cafe 10

Attractions, Accommodations & Dining in Greater Santa Fe

Built in 1949 by Maria Lopez and her politician husband, Gilbert (current owners are Laurie and Al Lucero), this restaurant is a prime example of what charm can come from scavenging: Its bricks came from the old New Mexico State Penitentiary, and most of its furniture was once used in La Fonda Hotel. The five wall frescoes in the cantina were painted by master muralist Alfred Morang (1901–58) in exchange for food.

Maria's boasts an open tortilla grill, where cooks can be seen making flour tortillas by hand. Generous portions are on every plate, from the award-winning beef, chicken, and vegetarian fajitas to blue-corn enchiladas, chile rellenos, green chile and posole stews, and huge steaks. If you're a margarita fan, this is the place to taste a variety of them—Maria's features over 40 "Real Margaritas" ranging in price from $3.75 to $20. Children's plates are available. From September through April, Tuesday is "Twos-day," when diners pay only $2 for a second meal. (To take advantage of "Twos-day" diners must be a member of the restaurant's "$2-Club," which has an annual membership fee of $10.) Strolling mariachi troubadours perform nightly. The restaurant offers patio dining in the summer, and two fireplaces warm the dining room in winter.

 The Natural Cafe, 1494 Cerrillos Rd. ☎ **983-1411.**
Cuisine: CREATIVE INTERNATIONAL. **Reservations:** Recommended.
Prices: Lunch $5–$8; dinner $8.50–$15.
Open: Lunch Tues–Fri 11:30am–2:30pm; dinner Tues–Sun 5–9:30pm.

An international menu of tasty and healthy dishes is served in an artsy garden atmosphere by a competent cosmopolitan staff. No fewer than five national cuisines—Mexican (black-bean enchiladas), Chinese (Szechuan vegetables), Indonesian (tempeh burger), Lebanese (hummus with pita bread), and American—are represented on the everyday menu. There is a small number of seafood and chicken dishes. Daily specials include walnut fettuccine and mushroom Stroganoff. A children's menu is available. Homemade desserts are sweetened with maple syrup, raw sugar, or honey. There are a couple of dozen wines and several beers (including Kaliber nonalcoholic beer), plus herbal teas, grain coffee, and other beverages.

BUDGET

 Tecolote Cafe, 1203 Cerrillos Rd. ☎ **988-1362.**
Cuisine: NEW MEXICAN.
Prices: Main dishes $2.60–$8.50. AE, CB, DC, DISC, MC, V.
Open: Tues–Sun 7am–2pm.

This is a breakfast lovers' favorite. The decor may be simple, but the food is elaborate: eggs any style, omelets, huevos rancheros, all served with fresh-baked muffins or biscuits and maple syrup. Luncheon specials include carne adovada burritos and green-chile stew.

5 Attractions

Suggested Itineraries

If You Have 1 Day

Start at the Palace of the Governors to get a visual grasp of New Mexico's four centuries of Hispanic and American history. As you leave, visit with the Native Americans selling their crafts and jewelry beneath the portal facing the Plaza. After lunch, take a self-guided walking tour of old Santa Fe, starting from the Plaza and including St. Francis Cathedral.

If You Have 2 Days

Devote your second day to the arts. Spend the morning learning about regional masters in the Museum of Fine Arts, and the afternoon browsing galleries, perhaps on Canyon Road.

If You Have 3 Days

Visit the cluster of museums on Camino Lejo—the Museum of International Folk Art, the Museum of Indian Arts and Culture, and the Wheelwright Museum of the American Indian. Then wander through the historic Barrio de Analco, and allow yourself the rest of the afternoon to shop.

If You Have 5 Days or More

You'll definitely want to leave the city and explore the surrounding countryside. One day could be devoted to the pueblos, including San Juan Pueblo, headquarters of the Eight Northern Indian Pueblos Council, and Santa Clara Pueblo, with its amazing Puye Cliff Dwellings. Another could take you along the High Road to Taos, with a stop at the spiritually profound El Santuario de Chimayo, returning down the valley of the Rio Grande. Yet another day trip might include Los Alamos, birthplace of the atomic bomb and home of the Bradbury Science Museum and Bandelier National Monument, where the Anasazi culture thrived more than 500 years ago.

The Top Attractions

Nearly all of Santa Fe's top attractions are directly on or adjacent to the city's bustling, central plaza. **The Plaza** has been the heart and soul of Santa Fe since it was established with the city in 1610. Originally designed as a meeting place, it has been the location of innumerable festivals as well as other historical, cultural, and social events; for many years, it was a dusty hive of activity as the staging ground and terminus of the Santa Fe Trail. Today, those who sit around the Plaza's central fountain are afforded the best people-watching in New Mexico.

For information on what the Plaza has to offer in addition to the points of interest discussed below, visit the historic Tully House, located directly on the Plaza at 136 Grant Avenue and home to the Historic Santa Fe Foundation. There, you can pick up the foundation's publication, *Old Santa Fe Today,* which provides detailed descriptions, accompanied by a map and photos, of 50 sites within walking distance of the Plaza.

⭐ **Palace of the Governors,** North Plaza. ☎ **827-6483.**

Built in 1610 as the original capitol of New Mexico, the Palace has been in continuous public use longer than any other structure in the United States. It was designated the Museum of New Mexico in 1909, two years before New Mexico became a state, and has become (appropriately) the state history museum, with an adjoining library and photo archives. Some cutaways of doors and windows show off early architecture.

A series of exhibits chronicle four centuries of New Mexico's Hispanic and American history, from the 16th-century Spanish explorations through the frontier era to modern times. Among Hispanic artifacts, there are early maps and rare hide paintings—historic chronicles on elk and buffalo hides—from the early 1700s. There's even an entire mid-19th-century chapel, with a simple, brightly colored altarpiece made in 1830 for a Taos church by a folk artist named Jose Rafael Aragon.

Governor's offices from the Mexican and 19th-century American eras have been restored and preserved. Displays out of early New Mexico life include a stagecoach, an early working printing press, and a collection of *mestizajes,* portraits of early Spanish colonists detailing typical costumes of the time. A great door from a jail in the Santa Ana pueblo was apparently used at one time as a testing board for a blacksmith who made branding irons: It has the brands of dozens of all over it.

Also on display are pieces from the silver service used aboard the battleship USS *New Mexico* from 1918 to 1939, and a tiny New Mexico state flag, 3" by 4", that was smuggled to the moon.

There are two shops here that visitors should not miss. One is the museum bookstore, with one of the finest selections of art, history, and anthropology books in the Southwest. The other is the print shop and bindery, in which limited-edition works are produced on hand-operated presses.

One of the most lasting impressions Santa Fe visitors bring home is not of the museum itself, but of the Native American artisans squatting shoulder-to-shoulder beneath the long covered portal facing the Plaza. Here on the shaded sidewalk, several dozen colorfully dressed members of local Pueblo tribes, plus an occasional Navajo, Apache, or Hopi, spread their handcrafts: mainly jewelry and pottery, but also woven carpets, beadwork, and paintings. The museum's Portal Program restricts selling space to Native Americans only. There are over 700 vendors.

Admission: Adults $3.50; free for children under 16. Two-day passes good at all four branches of the Museum of New Mexico cost $6 for those 16 and older.

Open: Mar–Dec daily 10am–5pm. **Closed:** Mon in Jan and Feb; Thanksgiving Day, Christmas, and New Year's Day.

⭐ **Museum of Fine Arts,** Palace and Lincoln Aves. ☎ **827-4455.**

Located catercorner from the Plaza and immediately opposite the Palace of the Governors, this was the first Pueblo Revival–style building constructed in Santa Fe, in 1917. As such, it was a major stimulus in Santa Fe's development as an art colony earlier in this century.

The museum's permanent collection of more than 8,000 works emphasizes regional art and includes landscapes and portraits by all the Taos masters as well as Georgia O'Keeffe, and more recent works by such contemporary greats as R. C. Gorman and Amado Pena, Jr.

The museum also has a collection of Ansel Adams photography. Modern artists, many of them far from the mainstream of traditional southwestern art, are featured in temporary exhibits throughout the year. Two sculpture gardens present a range of three-dimensional art from the traditional to the abstract.

Beautiful St. Francis Auditorium, patterned after the interiors of traditional Hispanic mission churches, adjoins the Museum of Fine Arts. (See "Evening Entertainment," below.) A museum shop sells books on southwestern art, plus prints and postcards of the collection.

Admission: Adults $4; free for children under 16. (3-day passes are available).

Open: Mar–Dec, daily 10am–5pm. **Closed:** Mon Jan–Feb; Thanksgiving Day, Christmas, and New Year's Day.

⭐ **St. Francis Cathedral,** Cathedral Place at San Francisco St. (P.O. Box 2127). ☎ **982-5619.**

Santa Fe's grandest religious structure—named after Santa Fe's patron saint—is just a block east of the Plaza. An architectural anomaly in Santa Fe, it was built between 1869 and 1886 by Archbishop Jean-Baptiste Lamy to resemble the great cathedrals of Europe. French architects designed the Romanesque building and Italian masons assisted with its construction.

The small adobe Our Lady of the Rosary chapel on the northeast side of the cathedral reflects a Spanish style. Built in 1807, it is the only parcel remaining from Our Lady of the Assumption Church, founded with Santa Fe in 1610. The new cathedral was built over and around the old church.

A wooden icon set in a niche in the wall of the north chapel, *La Conquistadora,* "Our Lady of Conquering Love," is the oldest representation of the Madonna in the United States. Rescued from the old church during the 1680 Pueblo rebellion, it was carried back by Don Diego de Vargas on his peaceful reconquest 12 years later, thus the name. Today *La Conquistadora* plays an important part in the annual Feast of Corpus Christi in June and July.

In 1986 a $600,000 renovation project relocated an early 18th-century wooden statue of St. Francis of Assisi to the center of the altar screen. Around the cathedral's exterior are front doors featuring 16 bronze door panels of historic note, and a plaque memorializing the 38 Franciscan friars who were martyred in New Mexico's early years. There's also a large bronze statue of Bishop Lamy himself; his grave is under the main altar of the cathedral.

Admission: Donations appreciated.

Open: Daily. Visitors may attend mass Mon–Sat at 6 and 7am and 5:15pm and Sun at 6, 8, and 10am, noon, and 7pm.

More Attractions

Catholic Museum, 223 Cathedral Place. ☎ **983-3811.**

Housed in a complex of buildings that date from 1832, the Catholic Museum is one of New Mexico's newest museums, where visitors have the opportunity to learn about the development and significance of Catholicism in New Mexico. Opened in 1994 by the Archdiocese of Santa Fe, the museum houses a collection of religious relics that include a book printed by Padre Antonio Jose Martinez of Taos and the Lamy chalice that was given to Archbishop Lamy by Pope Pius IX in 1845, as well as the document that formally re-established royal possession of the Villa and Capital of Santa Fe, signed by Diego de Vargas in 1692. There are also photographs on display that document events pertaining to the 11 archbishops of Santa Fe. The museum shop is stocked with books on New Mexico's religious history.

Admission: Mon–Fri 8:30am–4:30pm (Sat morning hours vary, so call ahead).

Open: $1.50 adults, $1 students and seniors.

Institute of American Indian Arts Museum, 108 Cathedral Place. ☎ **988-6211.**

The Institute of American Indian Arts (IAIA) is the nation's only congressionally chartered institute of higher education devoted solely to the study and practice of the artistic and cultural traditions of all American and Alaskan native peoples. Many of the best Native American artists of the last three decades have passed through the IAIA. Their works can often be seen as part of the many exhibitions offered at the museum throughout the year. The museum's National Collection of Contemporary Indian Art is comprised of painting, sculpture, ceramics, textiles, jewelry, beadwork, basketry, and graphic arts. The museum is the official repository of the most comprehensive collection of contemporary Native American art in the world and has loaned items from its collection to museums all over the world. The museum presents the artistic achievements of IAIA alumni, current students, and other nationally recognized Native American and Alaska Native artists.

Admission: Adults $4 (two-day pass); seniors and students $2 (two-day pass); children 16 and under free.

Open: Mar–Dec Mon–Sat 10am–5pm, Sun noon–5pm. **Closed:** Mon in January and February.

MUSEUMS

 Museum of International Folk Art, 706 Camino Lejo. ☎ **827-8350.**

This property of the Museum of New Mexico may not seem quite as typically southwestern as other Santa Fe museums, but it's the largest of its kind in the world. With a collection of well over 200,000 objects from more than 100 countries, it is my personal favorite of the city museums.

It was founded in 1953 by Chicago collector Florence Dibell Bartlett, who said: "If peoples of different countries could have the opportunity to study each others' cultures, it would be one avenue for a closer understanding between men." That's the basis on which the museum operates today.

The special collections include Spanish colonial silver, traditional and contemporary New Mexican religious art, Native Mexican costumes, Mexican majolica ceramics, Brazilian folk art, European glass, African sculptures, East Indian textiles, and the marvelous Morris Miniature Circus. Particularly delightful are numerous dioramas of people around the world at work and play in typical town, village, and home settings. Recent acquisitions include American weather vanes and quilts, Palestinian costume jewelry and amulets, and Bhutanese and Indonesian textiles. Children love to look at the hundreds of toys on display. About half the pieces comprise the 1982 contribution of Alexander and Susan Girard. A new wing was built to hold the vast assemblage of dolls, animals, and entire towns.

In 1989, the museum opened a new Hispanic Heritage Wing. Folk-art demonstrations, performances, and workshops are often presented here. The 80,000-square-foot museum also has a lecture room, a research library, and a gift shop where a variety of folk art is available for purchase.

The museum is located two miles south of the Plaza, in the Sangre de Cristo foothills off Old Santa Fe Trail.

Admission: Adults $4; free for children under 16.

Open: Mar–Dec daily 10am–5pm; Jan–Feb Tues–Sun 10am–5pm. **Closed:** Thanksgiving Day, Christmas, and New Year's Day.

 Museum of Indian Arts and Culture, 710 Camino Lejo. ☎ **827-6344.**

Next door to the folk-art museum, this new museum opened in 1987 as the showcase for the adjoining Laboratory of Anthropology. Interpretive displays detail tribal history and contemporary lifestyles of New Mexico's Pueblo, Navajo, and Apache cultures. More than 50,000 pieces of basketry, pottery, clothing, carpets, and jewelry—much of it quite ancient—is on continual rotating display.

There are frequent demonstrations of traditional skills by Native American artisans, and regular programs in a 70-seat multimedia theater. Native educators run a year-round shop that encourages visitors to try such activities as weaving and corn

Downtown Santa Fe Attractions

Post Office ⊠

Catholic Museum ➐

Footsteps Across
 New Mexico ➑

Institute of American
 Indian Arts Museum ➏

Loretto Chapel ➑

Mission of San Miguel ➒

Museum of Fine Arts ➋

Palace of the Governors ➌

The Plaza ➍

St. Francis Cathedral ➎

Santuario de Nuestra Señora
 de Guadalupe ➊

State Capitol ➓

grinding. There are also regular performances of Native American music and dancing by tribal groups. Concession booths purvey Native American foods in the summer.

The laboratory is a point of interest in itself, an exquisite example of Pueblo Revival architecture by well-known Santa Fe architect John Gaw Meem. Since the museum opened, the lab has expanded its research and library facilities into its former display wing. It was founded in 1931 by John D. Rockefeller, Jr.

Admission: $4 adults, free for children under 17.

Open: Mar–Dec daily 10am–5pm; Jan–Feb Tues–Sun 10am–5pm. **Closed:** Thanksgiving Day, Christmas, Easter, and New Year's Day.

Wheelwright Museum of the American Indian, 704 Camino Lejo.
☎ 982-4636.

Though not a member of the state museum system, the Wheelwright is often visited on the same trip as the folk-art and Indian arts museums by virtue of its proximity: next door. Once known as the Museum of Navajo Ceremonial Art, it was founded in 1937 by Boston scholar Mary Cabot Wheelwright in collaboration with a Navajo medicine man, Hastiin Klah, to preserve and document Navajo ritual beliefs and practices. Klah took the designs of sand paintings used in healing ceremonies and adapted them into the textiles that are a major part of the museum's treasure.

In 1977 the museum's focus was changed to include the living arts of all Native American cultures. Built in the shape of a Navajo hogan, with its doorway facing east (toward the rising sun) and its ceiling made in the interlocking "whirling log" style, it offers rotating single-subject shows of silverwork, jewelry, tapestry, pottery, basketry, and paintings. There's a permanent collection, of course, plus an outdoor sculpture garden with works by Allan Houser and other noted artisans.

In the basement is the Case Trading Post, an arts-and-crafts shop built in the image of a turn-of-the-century trading post such as was found on Navajo reservations. A storyteller gathers listeners outside a teepee at 7pm on Saturday and Sunday in July and August.

Admission: Free (donations welcomed).

Open: Mon–Sat 10am–5pm, Sun 1–5pm. **Closed:** Thanksgiving Day, Christmas, and New Year's Day.

★ El Rancho de Las Golondrinas, 334 Los Pinos Rd. ☎ 471-2261.

This 200-acre ranch, 15 miles south of the Santa Fe Plaza via I-25, was once the last stopping place on the 1,000-mile El Camino Real from Mexico City to Santa Fe. Today, it is a living 18th- and 19th-century Spanish village, comprising a hacienda, village store, schoolhouse, and several chapels and kitchens. There's also a working molasses mill, wheelwright and blacksmith shops, shearing and weaving rooms, a threshing ground, a winery and vineyards, and four water mills, as well as dozens of farm animals. A walk around the entire property is 1³/₄ miles in length.

Highlights of the year for Las Golondrinas (The Swallows) are the Spring Festival (the first weekend of June) and the Harvest Festival (the first weekend of October). On these festival Sundays, the museum opens with a procession and mass dedicated to San Ysidro, patron saint of farmers. Other festivals and theme weekends are held throughout the summer. Authentically costumed volunteers demonstrate shearing, spinning, weaving, embroidery, wood carving, grain milling, blacksmithing, tinsmithing, soap making, and other activities. There's an exciting atmosphere of Spanish folk dancing, music, and theater, and traditional oven-cooked food.

Admission: Adults $3.50, seniors (62) and teens $2.50, children 5–12 $1.50. Festival weekends, adults $5, seniors (62) and teens $3, children 5–12 $2.

Open: June–Sept Wed–Sun 10am–4pm. Guided tours Apr–Oct by advance arrangement.

CHURCHES

 Loretto Chapel, The Inn at Loretto, 211 Old Santa Fe Trail at Water St. ☎ 984-7971.

Though no longer consecrated for worship, the Loretto chapel is an important site in Santa Fe. Patterned after the famous Sainte-Chapelle church in Paris, it was constructed in 1873—by the same French architects and Italian masons who were building Archbishop Lamy's cathedral—as a chapel for the Sisters of Loretto, who had established a school for young ladies in Santa Fe in 1852.

The chapel is especially notable for its remarkable spiral staircase: It makes two complete 360-degree turns, with no central or other visible support! (A railing was added later.) Legend has it that the building was nearly finished in 1878 when workers realized the stairs to the choir loft wouldn't fit. Hoping for a solution more attractive than a ladder, the sisters made a novena to St. Joseph—and were rewarded when a mysterious carpenter appeared astride a donkey and offered to build a staircase. Armed with only a saw, a hammer, and a T-square, the master constructed this work of genius by soaking slats of wood in tubs of water to curve them, and holding them together with wooden pegs. Then he disappeared without waiting to collect his fee.

Today, the chapel is maintained by the Inn at Loretto Hotel.

Admission: $1 adult, children 6 and under free.

Open: Daily 9am–4:30pm. Entry is through the Inn at Loretto.

Mission of San Miguel, Old Santa Fe Trail at E. De Vargas St. ☎ 983-3974.

This is one of the oldest churches in America, having been erected within a couple of years of the 1610 founding of Santa Fe. Tlaxcala Indians, servants of early Spanish soldiers and missionaries, may have used fragments of a 12th-century pueblo found on this site in its construction. Severely damaged in the 1680 Pueblo revolt, it was almost completely rebuilt in 1710, and has been altered numerous times since.

Because of its design, with high windows and thick walls, the structure was occasionally used as a temporary fortress during times of raiding Native Americans. One painting in the sanctuary has holes that, according to legend, were made by arrows.

The mission and a nearby house—today a gift shop billed as "The Oldest House," though there's no way of knowing for sure—were bought by the Christian Brothers from Archbishop Lamy for $3,000 in 1881; the order still operates both structures. Among the treasures in the mission are the San Jose Bell, reputedly cast in Spain in 1356 and brought to Santa Fe via Mexico several centuries later, and a series of buffalo hides and deerskins decorated with Bible stories.

Admission: Free; donations welcomed.

Open: Mon–Sat 11:30am–4pm, Sun 1–4:30pm. Summer hours start earlier. Mass 5pm daily.

Santuario de Nuestra Señora de Guadalupe, 100 Guadalupe St. at Agua Fria St. ☎ 988-2027.

Built between 1795 and 1800 at the end of El Camino Real by Franciscan missionaries, this is believed to be the oldest shrine in the United States honoring the Virgin of Guadalupe, patroness of Mexico. The sanctuary's adobe walls are almost three feet thick, and the deep-red plaster wall behind the altar was dyed with oxblood in traditional fashion when the church was restored earlier this century.

On one wall is a famous oil painting, *Our Lady of Guadalupe,* created in 1783 by renowned Mexican artist Jose de Alzibar. Painted expressly for the church, it was brought from Mexico City by mule caravan.

Today administered as a museum by the nonprofit Guadalupe Historic Foundation, the sanctuary is frequently used for chamber music concerts, flamenco dance programs, dramas, lectures, and religious art shows.

Admission: Donations accepted.

Open: Mon–Fri 9am–4pm, Sat 10am–3pm. **Closed:** Weekends Nov–Apr.

OTHER ATTRACTIONS

State Capitol, Paseo de Peralta and Old Santa Fe Trail. ☎ **984-9589.**

Some are surprised to learn that this is the only round capitol building in America. It's also the newest. Built in 1966 in the shape of a Pueblo Indian *zia* emblem, it symbolizes the Circle of Life: four winds, four seasons, four directions, and four sacred obligations. Surrounding the capitol is a lush 6^1/$_2$-acre garden boasting more than 100 varieties of plants—roses, plums, almonds, nectarines, Russian olive trees, and sequoias among them. Benches are placed around the grounds for the enjoyment of visitors.

Footsteps Across New Mexico, The Inn at Loretto, 211 Old Santa Fe Trail. ☎ **982-9297.**

This multimedia presentation is an impressive introduction to the state. From pre-Hispanic Pueblo culture to the landing of the space shuttle at White Sands, slides, music, and a sculptured, three-dimensional map combine to tell the New Mexico story. There's a fine bookstore here for browsing before or after the show.

Admission: Adults $3.50, $2.50 children 6–16.

Open: Shows every half hour, Mon–Sat 9:30am–5pm, Sun 9:30am–4pm.

Cool for Kids

Don't miss taking the kids to the Museum of International Folk Art, where they'll love the international dioramas and the toys, and to El Rancho de las Golondrinas, a living Spanish colonial village. Other children's attractions include:

Santa Fe Children's Museum, 1050 Old Pecos Trail. ☎ **989-8359.**

Designed for whole families to share, this museum offers interactive exhibits and hands-on displays in the arts, humanities, science, and technology. Special art and science activities and family performances are regularly scheduled.

Admission: Adults $2.50, children under 12 $1.50.

Open: Thurs–Sat 10am–5pm, Sun noon–5pm (Wed–Sat 10am–5pm in June and Aug).

Organized Tours

CITY TOURS

Chamisa Touring Service, 2076 Calle Ensenada (☎ **438-9656** or toll free **800/631-TOURS**). Chamisa's Nicholas and Sandra Cobb offer customized tours in your private car or rental vehicle. They will plan specific tours based on your interests and at the pace you desire.

Gray Line Tours, 1330 Hickox St. (☎ **983-9491**). The trolleylike Roadrunner departs several times daily in summer (less often in winter) from the Plaza, beginning at 9am, for 2¹/₂-hour city tours. Buy tickets (adults $15, children under 12 $7.50) as you board.

RojoTours & Services Inc. 228 Old Santa Fe Trail, Suite 201 (☎ **983-8333**). Customized private tours.

Santa Fe Detours, La Fonda Hotel, 100 E. San Francisco St. (☎ **983-6565** or toll free **800/338-6877**). Perhaps the city's most extensive booking service.

Studio Entrada Tours, 132 Romero, Santa Fe, NM 87502 (☎ **505/983-8786**). Personalized tours to galleries of leading painters, sculptors, craftspersons, and furniture makers.

WALKING TOURS

Afoot in Santa Fe, The Inn at Loretto, 211 Old Santa Fe Trail (☎ **983-3701**). Twice-daily, 2¹/₂-hour personalized tours.

Ghost Tours of Santa Fe, 142 Lincoln Ave. (☎ **983-0111**). Visits 14 haunted places around the city. Nightly June through August, weekends April and May and September and October.

Historical Walking Tours of Santa Fe, 418 Cerrillos Rd. (☎ **984-8235**). Three basic tours are offered several times daily, from morning to early evening.

Pathways Customized Tours, 161 F. Calle Ojo Feliz (☎ **982-5382**). Don Dietz offers several planned tours, including a downtown Santa Fe walking tour and a full city tour.

Santa Fe Walks, La Fonda Hotel, 100 E. San Francisco St. (☎ **983-6565** or toll free **800/338-6877**). Tours of 2¹/₂ hours leave twice daily in summer.

---

6   Sports & Recreation

Spectator Sports

HORSE RACING   The ponies run at the **Downs of Santa Fe,** 11 miles south of Santa Fe off U.S. 85, near La Cienega, from Memorial Day through September. Post time for 10-race cards is 3:30pm Wed and Fri; for 12-race cards, 1:30pm Saturday and Sunday, plus Memorial Day, the Fourth of July, and Labor Day. Admission starts at $1 and climbs depending upon seating. A closed-circuit TV system shows instant replays of each race's final stretch run and transmits out-of-state races for legal betting.

Recreation

BALLOONING   **Rocky Mountain Tours** at 1323 Paseo de Peralta (☎ **984-1684** or toll free **800/231-7238**) offers hot-air balloon flights daily on a custom basis.

BICYCLING   **Palace Bike Rentals,** 409 E. Palace Ave. (☎ **984-2151**) rents mountain bikes and caters to tourists. Half day, full day, and weekly rentals can be arranged.

FISHING   Rainbow trout are the favorite fish for most high-lakes anglers. High-country lakes, streams, and the waters of the San Juan provide year-round fishing. Check with the **New Mexico Game and Fish Department** (☎ **827-7882**) for specific laws and licenses. **High Desert Angler,** 435 S. Guadalupe St. (☎ **988-7688**), specializes in fly-fishing gear and guide service.

GOLF   There are two public courses in the Santa Fe area. The 18-hole **Santa Fe Country Club,** Airport Road (☎ **471-0601**); and the oft-praised 18-hole **Cochiti Lake Golf Course,** 5200 Cochiti Hwy., Cochiti Lake, 35 miles southwest of Santa Fe via I-25 and N.M. 16 and 22.

HIKING & BACKPACKING   It's hard to decide which of the 900 miles of nearby national forest trails to challenge. Three wilderness areas are especially attractive: **Pecos Wilderness,** with 223,000 acres east of Santa Fe; **Dome Wilderness,** 5,200 acres of rugged canyon land adjacent to Bandelier National Monument; and **San Pedro Parks Wilderness,** 41,000 acres west of Los Alamos. Information on these and other wilderness areas is available from the **Santa Fe National Forest,** 1220 St. Francis Dr. (P.O. Box 1689), Santa Fe, NM 87504 (☎ **988-6940**). If you're looking for company on your trek, contact the Santa Fe group of the **Sierra Club** (☎ **983-2703**), or **Tracks,** P.O. Box 173, Santa Fe, NM 87504 (☎ **505/982-2586**).

HORSEBACK RIDING   Trips ranging in length from a few hours to overnight can be arranged by **Galarosa Stables,** on Hwy 41 in Galisteo (☎ **983-6565** or toll free **800/338-6877**). Rides are also major activities at two local guest ranches, the **Bishop's Lodge** (see "Accommodations," above) and **Rancho Encantado.**

HUNTING   Mule deer and elk are taken by hunters in the Pecos Wilderness and Jemez Mountains, as well as occasional black bear and bighorn sheep. Wild turkey and grouse are frequently bagged in the uplands, geese and ducks at lower elevations. Check with the **New Mexico Game and Fish Department** (☎ **827-7911** for information, **827-7880** for licenses) for specific laws and licenses.

RIVER RAFTING   Although Taos is the real rafting center of New Mexico, several companies serve Santa Fe during the April–October white-water season. They include **Southwest Wilderness Adventures,** P.O. Box 9380, Santa Fe, NM 87504 (☎ **983-7262** or toll free **800/869-7238**); **New Wave Rafting,** 107 Washington Ave. (☎ **984-1444**); and the **Santa Fe Rafting Co.,** 80 E. San Francisco St. (☎ **988-4914**).

RUNNING   Despite its elevation, Santa Fe is popular with runners, and hosts numerous competitions, including the annual Old Santa Fe Trail Run on Labor Day. Fun runs begin from the Plaza at 6pm Wednesday year-round (5:30pm in winter).

SKIING   There's something for all skiing ability levels at the ★ **Santa Fe Ski Area,** 16 miles northeast of Santa Fe via Hyde Park (Ski Basin) Road. Built on the upper reaches of 12,000-foot Tesuque Peak, the area has an average annual snowfall of 250 inches and a vertical drop of 1,650 feet. Six lifts, including a 5,000-foot triple chair and a quad chair, serve 39 runs and 700 acres of terrain; the lifts have a capacity of 7,300 skiers an hour. Base facilities, at 10,350 feet, center around La Casa Mall, with a cafeteria, ski rental shop, and boutique. Another restaurant, Tuttemott's Bar and Grill, has a midmountain patio. The ski area is open daily from 9am to 4pm, often from Thanksgiving to Easter, depending on snow conditions. Rates for all lifts are $35 for adults, $22 for children and seniors, free for kids under 3 feet, 10 inches (in their ski boots) and "super seniors," 72 years plus. For more information, write the Santa Fe Ski Area, 1210 Luisa St., Suite 10, Santa Fe, NM 87505-4126 (☎ **982-4429** or Santa Fe Central Reservations toll free **800/776-7669**). For 24-hour taped reports on snow conditions, call **983-9155**. The New Mexico Snophone (☎ **984-0606**) gives statewide reports.

Cross-country skiers find seemingly endless miles of snow to track in the **Santa Fe National Forest** (☎ **988-6940**). A favorite place to start is at the Black Canyon campground, 9 miles from downtown en route to the Santa Fe Ski Area. In the same area are the Borrega Trail and the Norski Trail. Basic nordic lessons, telemarking instruction, backcountry tours, and overnight packages are all offered by Bill Neuwirth's **Tracks,** P.O. Box 173, Santa Fe, NM 87504 (☎ **982-2586**).

SPAS   A common stop for skiers coming down the mountain road from the Santa Fe Ski Area is ❚ **Ten Thousand Waves,** a Japanese-style health spa 3 miles northeast of Santa Fe on Hyde Park Road (☎ **988-1047** or **982-9304**). This serene retreat, nestled in a grove of piñon, offers hot tubs, saunas, and cold plunges, plus a variety of massage and other bodywork techniques. Bathing suits are optional in the 10-foot communal hot tub, where you can stay as long as you want for $12. Nine private hot tubs cost $15–$20 an hour, with discounts for seniors and children. You can also get therapeutic massage, facials, herbal wraps, and salt glows. The spa is open year-round, Sunday, Monday, Wednesday, and Thursday from 10am to 10pm, Tuesday from 4:30 to 10pm, and Saturday and Sunday from 10am to 11:30pm. Reservations are recommended, especially on weekends.

New to Ten Thousand Waves are the Houses of the Moon, three small overnight lodgings.

SWIMMING   The city operates four indoor pools and one outdoor pool. Nearest downtown is the **Fort Marcy Complex** (☎ **984-6725**) on Camino Santiago off Bishop's Lodge Road. Admission is $1.75 for adults, $1.25 for students, and 75¢ for children 8 to 13. Call the city Swimming Pools Division (☎ **984-6671**) for details.

TENNIS   Santa Fe has 27 public tennis courts and four major private facilities. The City Recreation Department (☎ **984-6862**) can locate all indoor, outdoor, and lighted public courts.

7 Savvy Shopping

From traditional Native American crafts to Hispanic folk art to abstract contemporary works, Santa Fe is the place to shop. Galleries speckle the downtown area, and Canyon Road is well known as an artists' thoroughfare. Of course, the greatest concentration of Native American crafts is displayed beneath the portal of the Palace of theGovernors.

Business hours vary quite a bit between establishments, but nearly everyone is open weekdays *at least* from 10am to 5pm, with mall stores open until 9pm. Most shops are open similar hours Saturday, and many are also open Sunday afternoons during the summer. Winter hours are often more limited.

Best Buys

Few visitors to Santa Fe leave the city without having bought at least one item—and often several—from the Native American artisans at the Palace of the Governors. In considering purchases, keep the following pointers in mind:

Silver jewelry should have a harmony of design, clean lines, and neatness in soldering. Navajo jewelry typically features large stones, with designs shaped around the stone. Zuni jewelry usually has patterns of small or inlaid stones. Hopi jewelry rarely uses stones, instead displaying a darkened motif incised into the top layer of silver.

Turquoise of a deeper color is usually higher quality, so long as it hasn't been color treated. *Heishi* bead necklaces usually use stabilized turquoise.

Pottery is traditionally hand coiled and of natural clay, not thrown on a potter's wheel using commercial clay. It is hand polished with a stone, hand painted, and fired in an outdoor oven rather than an electric kiln. Look for an even shape; clean, accurate painting; a high polish (if it is a polished piece); and an artist's signature.

Navajo rugs are appraised according to tightness and evenness of weave, symmetry of design, and whether natural (preferred) or commercial dyes have been used.

Kachina dolls are more highly valued according to the detail of their carving: fingers, toes, muscles, rib cages, feathers, for example. Elaborate costumes are also desirable. Oil staining is preferred to the use of bright acrylic paints.

Sand paintings should display clean narrow lines, even colors, balance, an intricacy of design, and smooth craftsmanship.

Local museums, particularly the Wheelwright Museum and the Institute of American Indian Art, can give a good orientation to contemporary craftsmanship.

Contemporary artists are mainly painters, sculptors, ceramicists, and fiber artists, including weavers. Peruse one of the outstanding catalogs that introduce local galleries— *The Collector's Guide to Santa Fe & Taos* by Wingspread Communications (P.O. Box 13566, Albuquerque, NM 87192), *Santa Fe & Taos Arts* by the Book of Santa Fe (535 Cordova Rd., Suite 241, Santa Fe, NM 87501), or the *Santa Fe Catalogue* by Modell Associates (P.O. Box 1007, Aspen, CO 81612). They're widely distributed at shops or can be ordered directly from the publishers.

An outstanding introduction to Santa Fe art and artists is the personalized studio tours offered by **Studio Entrada,** P.O. Box 4934, Santa Fe, NM 87502 (☎ **983-8786**). For $50 per person (minimum two), director Linda Morton takes small groups into private studios to meet the artists and learn about their work. Each itinerary lasts about $2^{1}/_{2}$ hours, and includes two or three studio/gallery visits.

Shopping A to Z

ANTIQUES

Adieb Khadoure Fine Art, 610 Canyon Rd. ☎ **820-2666.**

This is a working artist's studio with contemporary artist Hal Larsen and Santa Fe artist Phyllis Kapp. Works are shown in the gallery daily from 10am to 6pm, and Adieb Khadoure also features beautiful rugs from around the world.

Alan Kessler, 836 Canyon Rd. ☎ **986-0123.**

Fine quality antique Native American art of the Plains, Southwest, Woodlands, and Northwest Coast people. Also featured: beadwork, historic *kachinas,* and Southwest pottery.

Blue Door Art & Antiques, 300 Garcia. ☎ **983-9635.**

Specializing in decorative arts, furniture, and antiques as well as painting and sculpture by contemporary artists.

Bobby's Plaza Gallery, 233 Canyon Rd. ☎ **989-7193.**

Beautiful *kachinas,* Native American, New Mexican, and Mexican artworks. The works of artists E. J. Predika, Leroy Metzgar, Marsha Howe, Ann Marie Eastburn, Cruz Flores, Napoleon Montoya, O. T. Bonnet, and Lloyd Pinay are featured, as well as antiques and garden sculpture.

Claiborne Gallery, 558 Canyon Rd. ☎ **982-8019.**

Original Spanish colonial furniture.

Robert F. Nichols Americana, 419 Canyon Rd. ☎ **982-2145.**

Prehistoric pottery and country antiques.

ART

Chuck Jones Showroom—Animation Gallery, 135 W. Palace, Suite 203.
☎ **983-5999.**

A comprehensive representation of animation art work from Warner Bros. director Chuck Jones. Original production cels, lithographs, sculpture, drawings, and limited editions.

El Taller Gallery, 235 Don Gaspar Ave. ☎ **988-9298.**

Southwestern art of many media, with work by the renowned Amado Pena, Jr.

⭐ **Gerald Peters Gallery,** 439 Camino del Monte Sol. ☎ **988-8961.**

Taos school and other classical artists; modern oils, watercolors, and ceramics.

Glenn Green Galleries, 50 E. San Francisco St. ☎ **988-4168.**

Exclusive representatives for Allan Houser, bronze and stone sculptures. Paintings, prints, photographs, and jewelry by other important artists.

Horwitch Lewallen Gallery, 129 W. Palace Ave. ☎ **988-8997.**

Contemporary art gallery exhibiting works done on canvas and paper; sculpture in stone, bronze, and glass; ceramics; southwestern folk art; and jewelry by Native American and contemporary southwestern jewelers.

Linda Durham Gallery, 400 Canyon Rd. ☎ **988-1313.**

Contemporary painting, sculpture, and photography.

Linda McAdoo Gallery, 503 Canyon Rd. ☎ **983-7182.**

Impressionist painters and sculptors.

⭐ **Nedra Matteucci's Fenn Galleries,** 1075 Paseo de Peralta. ☎ **982-4631.**

Early Taos and Santa Fe painters; classic American impressionism, historical western, modernism, as well as contemporary southwestern landscapes and sculpture, including monumental pieces displayed in the sculpture garden.

Night Sky Gallery, 826 Canyon Rd. ☎ **982-1468.**

Works of important emerging artists; impressionistic pastels of Reita Newkirk PSA, dramatic Raku ceramics by Anderson and Mayfield.

Owings-Dewey Fine Art, 74 E. San Francisco St. ☎ **982-6244.**

Specializes in 19th- and 20th-century American art, including works by Georgia O'Keeffe, Charles Russell, Robert Henri, and Andrew Dasburg.

⭐ **Photography: Platinum Plus, Inc.,** 943 Canyon Rd. ☎ **982-8920.**

The world's first gallery to specialize in platinum prints. Works by 19th- and 20th-century masters such as Emerson, Evans, Curtis, Strand, Weston, Bravo, Horst, and Mapplethorpe. This is a wonderful gallery!

Rio Grande Gallery, 80 E. San Francisco St. ☎ **983-2458.**

Exclusively features R. C. Gorman paintings and bronzes.

Santa Fe East, 200 Old Santa Fe Trail, Santa Fe, NM 87501. ☎ **988-3103.**

Across from the Loretto Chapel, this gallery has some great museum-quality artwork, including sculpture, pottery, paintings, and one-of-a-kind pieces of jewelry.

Sena Galleries West, Plaza Mercado, 112 W. San Francisco St. ☎ **982-8808.**

Contemporary painters and sculptors.

⭐ **Shidoni Foundry and Gallery,** Bishop's Lodge Rd., Tesuque. ☎ **988-8001.**

Sculpture garden, with bronze casting. Foundry tour available; call for details.

Sigel & Sigel Fine Art, 403 Canyon Rd. ☎ **983-3348.**

Specializing in limited-edition prints by Georgia O'Keeffe and Eyvind Earle, as we as lithographs of O'Keeffe drawings from 1915. Representation of contemporary ar ists like Warhol, Haring, Peter Max, Thomas McKnight, Erte, and Jennifer Marke There is always an exhibit of local artists as well.

Summerfield Gallery, 1512 Paseo de Peralta. ☎ **820-1427.**

Contemporary art including paintings, sculpture, and an outdoor art garden.

Woodrow Wilson Fine Arts, 319 Read St. ☎ **983-2444.**

High-profile Taos and Santa Fe artists, plus modern impressionism and realism.

BOOKS

In addition to independent bookstores in Santa Fe, the nationwide chains B. Dalto and Waldenbooks are represented. Specialty bookstores include **Cornerstone Boo Etc.,** 1722 St. Michael's Dr. (☎ **473-0306**), for Christian literature and musi **Horizons,** 328 S. Guadalupe St. (☎ **983-1554**), for books on travel, nature, ar science; **Margolis & Moss,** 129 W. San Francisco St. (☎ **982-1028**), for rare book prints, and maps; **Parker Books of the West,** 142 W. Palace Ave. (☎ **988-1076** for new and old books about western history and fiction; **Nicholas Pott** (☎ **983-5434**), 203 E. Palace Ave., for used and rare hardbacks; and **Santa Fe Boo seller,** 203 W. San Francisco St. (☎ **983-5278**), for new and out-of-print art book Among the most interesting stores are:

Caxton Books & Music, 216 W. San Francisco St. ☎ **982-8911.**

Probably downtown Santa Fe's best bookstore. Its collection includes a wide choi of regional works, art books, and music.

Footsteps Across New Mexico, Inn at Loretto, 211 Old Santa Fe Trail.
☎ **982-9297.**

The bookstore here sells only in works about New Mexico and the Southwest. Vi tors can also learn a bit about New Mexico history in the new historical theater.

CRAFTS

Bellas Artes, 653 Canyon Rd. ☎ **983-2745.**

Contemporary sculpture, paintings, drawings, and clay and fiber. Also, pre-Columbi and African.

⭐ **Davis Mather Folk Art Gallery,** 141 Lincoln Ave. ☎ **983-1660** or **988-1218**

New Mexican animal wood carvings. Folk, Hispanic, and unpredictable arts. Arti represented include David Alvarez, Felipe Archuleta, Woody Herbert, Alonzo Jimene Paul Lutonsky, Joe Ortega, Ron Rodriguez, and Lula and Wilfred Yazzie.

Economos Works of Art, 500 Canyon Rd. ☎ **982-6347.**

Classic Native American art, pre-Columbian, and antique Mexican pieces.

★ **Gallery 10,** 225 Canyon Rd. ☎ **983-9707.**

Museum-quality pottery, weavings, and basketry; contemporary paintings and mixed media.

Indian Trader West, 204 W. San Francisco St. ☎ **988-5776.**

Navajo baskets, jewelry, rugs (both old and new), Pueblo pottery, Hopi *kachinas* and baskets, and other handcrafts.

★ **Joshua Baer & Company,** 116 E. Palace Ave. ☎ **988-8944.**

Nineteenth-century Navajo blankets, pottery, jewelry, and tribal art.

Kania-Ferrin Gallery, 662 Canyon Rd. ☎ **982-8767.**

Fine Native American baskets, pottery, *kachinas* jewelry, textiles, and beadwork. Antique *santos, retablos,* and antique oceanic material.

Morning Star Gallery, 513 Canyon Rd. ☎ **982-8187.**

North American Indian artifacts.

★ **Nambe Mills, Inc.,** 924 Paseo de Peralta at Canyon Rd. ☎ **988-5528.**

An exquisite alloy is sand-cast and handcrafted to create cooking, serving, and decorating pieces. Also at Plaza Mercado, 112 W. San Francisco St. (☎ **988-3574**), and 216 Paseo del Pueblo Norte (Yucca Plaza), Taos (☎ **758-8221**).

The Rainbow Man, 107 E. Palace Ave. ☎ **982-8706.**

Photography, trade blankets, pawn jewelry, *kachinas,* folk arts, railroad china, and western memorabilia.

Running Ridge Gallery, 640 Canyon Rd. ☎ **988-2515.**

Ceramics, fiber and paper art, and glass work.

★ **Salon & Gallery of the Frightened Owl,** 1117 Canyon Rd. ☎ **983-7607.**

Spanish colonial art and furniture.

Streets of Taos, 200 Canyon Rd. ☎ **983-8268** or **983-4509.**

Navajo rugs, Pueblo jewelry, pottery, and baskets.

FASHIONS

★ **Origins,** 135 W. San Francisco St. ☎ **988-2323.**

Wearable folk art, including handwoven southwestern apparel and jewelry.

Santa Fe Fiesta Fashions, 651 Cerrillos Rd. ☎ **983-1632.**

Designer and manufacturer of southwestern apparel, created by Just Lindee.

Three Sisters, Inn at Loretto Hotel, 211 Old Santa Fe Trail. ☎ **988-5045.**

Traditional and contemporary Southwest attire and accessories, including ribbon shirts and fiesta wear.

FOOD GOODS & COOKING SCHOOL

★ **Santa Fe School of Cooking,** Plaza Mercado (upper level), 116 W. San Francisco St. ☎ **983-4511.**

A 3-hour demonstration class discusses the flavors and history of traditional New Mexican and contemporary Southwest cuisines; $25 includes a meal and recipes. Specialized classes are well attended; call for schedules and rates. An adjoining market offers a variety of regional foods and cookbooks, with gift baskets available.

FURNITURE

Dell Woodworks, 1326 Rufina Circle. ☎ **471-3005.**

Handcrafted Santa Fe–style furniture.

Doolings of Santa Fe, 525 Airport Rd. ☎ **471-5956.**

Southwestern country furniture.

⭐ **Southwest Spanish Craftsmen**, 328 S. Guadalupe ☎ **982-1767.**

Spanish colonial and Spanish provincial furniture, doors, and home accessories.

GIFTS/SOUVENIRS

El Nicho, 227 Don Gaspar Ave. ☎ **984-2830.**

Affordable handcrafted folk art by local Santa Fe artisans. Metal sculpture, tiles, jewelry, and *kachinas.*

Tin-Nee-Ann Trading Co., 923 Cerrillos Rd. ☎ **988-1630.**

Native American arts, moccasins, T-shirts, and other low-cost souvenirs.

JEWELRY

⭐ **James Reid Ltd.**, 114 E. Palace Ave. ☎ **988-1147.**

Silversmithing, gold jewelry, antique Native American art, contemporary paintings, sculpture, furniture, and folk art.

Things Finer, La Fonda, 100 E. San Francisco St. ☎ **983-5552.**

Estate and antique jewelry and gift items as well as Russian objets d'art and silverwork.

MARKETS

Santa Fe Traders Market, 1241 Siler Rd. ☎ **438-0011.**

This huge indoor flea market, offering new and antique goods, is open Friday through Sunday from 10:30am to 5:30pm.

WINES

⭐ **The Winery**, Sanbusco Center, 510 Montezuma St. ☎ **982-WINE.**

Perhaps the most extensive wine shop in New Mexico, it carries gourmet foods and beers, gift baskets, and publishes a monthly newsletter.

WINERIES

If you enjoy tasting wines of different regions, there are several wineries within driving distance of Santa Fe: **Balagna Winery/San Ysidro Vineyards,** 223 Rio Bravo Drive, Los Alamos, NM 87544 (☎ **505/672-3678**); **Santa Fe Vineyards,** 20 miles north of Santa Fe on Hwy. 285 (☎ **505/753-8100**); **Madison Vineyards & Winery,** Star Route 490, Ribera, NM 87560 (☎ **505/421-8020**); and **Black Mesa Winery,** 1502 Highway 68, Valverde, NM 87582 (☎ **800/852-MESA**).

8   Evening Entertainment

Full information on all major cultural events can be obtained from the Santa Fe Convention and Visitors Bureau (☎ **984-6760** or toll free **800/777-CITY**) or from the City of Santa Fe Arts Commission (☎ **984-6707**). Current listings can be found in Friday's "Pasatiempo" edition of the *New Mexican,* Santa Fe's daily newspaper, and in the *Santa Fe Reporter,* published weekly on Wednesdays.

The **Galisteo News & Ticket Center,** 201 Galisteo St. (☎ **984-1316**), is the primary outlet for tickets to the opera and other major entertainment events. **Nicholas Potter, Bookseller,** 203 E. Palace Ave. (☎ **983-5434**), also has tickets to select events. You can order by phone from **TicketMaster** (☎ **842-5387** for information, **884-0999** to order). Discount tickets may be available on the nights of performances; the opera, for example, makes standing-room tickets available at a greatly reduced rate just one hour ahead of time.

A variety of free concerts, lectures, and other events are presented in the summer, cosponsored by the City of Santa Fe and the chamber of commerce under the name **Santa Fe Summerscene.** From mid-June through August, Tuesday and Thursday at noon and 6pm, they are held on the Plaza, in Fort Marcy Park, and run the gamut from light opera to blues, jazz, Cajun, and bluegrass to hot salsa and New Mexican folk music. There's also a wide-ranging Noon Concert Series on Tuesday and Thursday on the Plaza. Call **983-7317** for more information.

The **Santa Fe Summer Concert Series,** at the Paolo Soleri Outdoor Amphitheatre on the Santa Fe Indian School campus on Cerrillos Road, has brought such name performers as Kenny Loggins, B. B. King, and the late Frank Zappa to the city. More than two dozen concerts and special events are scheduled each summer.

Note: Many companies listed here perform at locations other than their headquarters, so check the site of the performance you plan to attend.

The Performing Arts

MAJOR PERFORMING ARTS COMPANIES

Opera & Classical Music

★ **Santa Fe Opera,** P.O. Box 2408, Santa Fe, NM 87504. ☎ **986-5955** or **986-5900** for tickets.

Even if your visit isn't timed to coincide with the opera season, you shouldn't miss seeing its open-air amphitheater. Located on a wooded hilltop seven miles north of the city off U.S. 84/285, the sweeping curves of this serene structure seem perfectly attuned to the contour of the surrounding terrain. At night, the lights of Los Alamos can be seen in the distance under clear skies.

Many rank the Santa Fe Opera behind only the Metropolitan Opera of New York as the finest company in the United States today. Established in 1957 by John Crosby, still the opera's artistic director, it consistently attracts famed conductors, directors, and singers, the list of whom has included Igor Stravinsky.

The opera is noted for its performances of great classics, little-known works by classical European composers, and American premieres of 20th-century works.

The 9-week, 40-performance opera season runs from the first week in July through the last week in August. All performances begin at 9pm.

Tours: First Mon in July through last Fri in Aug, Mon–Sat at 1pm; $5 for adults, free for children 7 to 15.

Prices: Fri–Sat $102, $77, $66, $56, $40, $25; Mon–Thurs $5 less for all seats. Wheelchair seating $14 Mon–Thurs, $20 Fri–Sat; standing room (sold same performance day beginning at 10am) $15 gala opening night, $8 Fri–Sat, $6 Mon–Thurs.

⭐ **Santa Fe Chamber Music Festival,** 239 Johnson St. (P.O. Box 853), Santa Fe, NM 87501. ☎ **983-2075** or **982-1890** (box office July and August only) or toll free **800/962-7286.**

The festival brings an extraordinary group of international artists to Santa Fe every summer. Its 6-week season of some 50 concerts from the second week of July through the third week of August has been held in beautiful St. Francis Auditorium since its founding in 1973. Each festival season features chamber music masterpieces, new music by a composer in residence, jazz, free youth concerts, preconcert lectures, and open rehearsals. Festival concerts are recorded for broadcast in a 13-week nationally syndicated radio series.

Performances are nightly at 8pm, except Saturday and Sunday when they're at 6pm. Open rehearsals, youth concerts, and preconcert lectures are free to the public.

Prices: $20–$32.

The Santa Fe Symphony Orchestra and Chorus, P.O. Box 9692, Santa Fe, NM 87504. ☎ **983-3530.**

This 60-piece professional symphony orchestra has grown rapidly in stature since its founding in 1984. Matinee and evening performances of classical and popular works are presented in a subscription series at Sweeney Center from August to May. There's a preconcert lecture before each performance. During the spring there are music festivals and in the fall there are free concerts in the park. Call for details.

Prices: Single tickets $12–$30 (six seating categories).

The Orchestra of Santa Fe, 111 N. Guadalupe St. (P.O. Box 2091), Santa Fe, NM 87504. ☎ **988-4640.**

A chamber orchestra founded in 1974, this group is best known for its holiday production of Handel's *Messiah* and its January/February Bach or Mozart festivals. In all, it offers 15 classical concerts a year, between mid-September and early May. Noon lectures are given five times a season at St. Francis Auditorium and in Los Alamos.

All regular concert performances are at the Lensic Theatre, 211 W. San Francisco St. (☎ **988-4640**). This early 20th-century Spanish colonial–style theater, otherwise a United Artists cinema, has a state-of-the-art acoustical sound shell, installed in 1989. It seats about 850.

Prices: Single tickets $6–$27 (five seating categories). Students are half price. Ask about the Sunday family-saver package.

The Ensemble of Santa Fe, P.O. Box 8427, Santa Fe, NM 87504. ☎ **984-2501.**

The ensemble is a professional chamber music group composed of leading musicians from the western United States and guests of national and international acclaim. The ensemble performs monthly public concerts from October through May in the historic Loretto Chapel and the Santuario de Guadalupe. Christmas and Holy Week concerts sell out in advance.

Prices: $12–$20.

Santa Fe Concert Association, P.O. Box 4626, Santa Fe, NM 87502. ☎ **984-8759**

Founded in 1938, the oldest musical organization in northern New Mexico has a September-to-May season that includes more than 20 annual events. Among them are a distinguished artist series featuring renowned instrumental and vocal soloists and ensembles; a free youth concert series; a Christmas Eve special; and occasional master classes. All performances are at St. Francis Auditorium; tickets are sold by Nicholas Potter, Bookseller (☎ **983-5434;** see "Books" above).

Prices: $15–$65.

The Desert Chorale, 219 Shelby St. (P.O. Box 2813), Santa Fe, NM 87501. ☎ **988-7505** or toll free **800/244-4011.**

This 24–30 member vocal ensemble, New Mexico's only professional choral group, recruits members from all over the country. It is nationally recognized for its eclectic blend of both Renaissance melodies and modern avant-garde compositions. During the summer months, the chorale performs both classical concerts at the historic Santuario de Guadalupe and the Saint Francis Auditorium, as well as smaller cameo concerts in more intimate settings throughout Santa Fe and Albuquerque. The chorale also performs a popular series of Christmas concerts during the month of December. Most concerts begin at 8pm (3 or 6pm on Sundays).

Prices: $18–$32 adults; students half price.

Sangre de Cristo Chorale, P.O. Box 4462, Santa Fe, NM 87502. ☎ **505/662-9717.**

This 34-member ensemble has a repertoire ranging from classical, baroque, and Renaissance works to more recent folk music and spirituals. Much of it is presented a cappella. The group gives fall and spring concerts at the Santuario de Guadalupe or St. Francis Auditorium, and its Christmas dinner concerts at St. John's College (1160 Camino Cruz Blanca) are avidly attended.

Prices: $8–$30.

The Santa Fe Women's Ensemble, 424 Kathryn Place, Santa Fe, NM 87501. ☎ **982-4075.**

This choral group of 12 semiprofessional singers sponsored by the Santa Fe Concert Association offers classical works sung a cappella, as well as with a variety of instrumental accompaniments during the spring and fall seasons. "A Christmas Offering" concerts are held in mid-December in the Loretto Chapel, and the annual "Spring Offering" concerts are held there as well. Tickets are sold by Nicholas Potter, Bookseller (☎ **983-5434;** see "Books" above), through mail order, and at the door.

Prices: $15 reserved, $12 open seating.

Theater Companies

⭐ **Santa Fe Community Theatre,** 142 E. De Vargas St. (P.O. Box 2084), Santa Fe, NM 87504. ☎ **988-4262.**

Founded in the 1920s, this is the oldest existing theater group in New Mexico. Still performing in a historic adobe theater in the Barrio de Analco, it attracts thousands for its dramas, avant-garde theater, and musical comedy. Its popular one-act melodramas call upon the public to boo the sneering villain and swoon for the damsel in distress.

Prices: $10 adults, $8 students and seniors; previews require only that you "pay what you like."

Dance Companies

Maria Benitez Spanish Dance Company, Picacho Plaza Hotel, 750 N. St. Francis Dr. ☎ **982-1237.**

The Benitez Company's "Estampa Flamenca" summer series is performed from early July to mid-September at the Picacho Plaza. True flamenco is one of the most thrilling of all dance forms, displaying the inner spirit and verve of the gypsies of Spanish Andalusia.

Prices: $14–$21 (subject to change).

158

Santa Fe

MAJOR CONCERT HALLS & ALL-PURPOSE AUDITORIUMS

Center for Contemporary Arts, 291 E. Barcelona Rd. ☎ 982-1338.

The Center for Contemporary Arts (CCA) presents the work of internationally, nationally, and regionally known contemporary artists in art exhibitions, dance, new music concerts, poetry readings, performance-art events, theater, and video screenings. The CCA Cinematique screens cinema from around the world nightly, with special series occurring regularly. A permanent outdoor James Turrell Skyspace is located on the CCA grounds. The CCA Warehouse/Teen Project is a unique program designed to encourage creativity, individuality, and free expression by giving teens a safe, free place to create programs and events, including workshops, art exhibitions, a radio show and publication, theater ensemble, café (with open mike opportunities), and concerts featuring local teen bands.

Open: CCA's galleries are open Mon–Fri 10am–4pm, Sat noon–4pm.
Tickets: Films $6; prices for other performance events vary.

Paolo Soleri Amphitheatre, 1501 Cerrillos Rd., Santa Fe Indian School. ☎ 989-6310.

This outdoor arena is the locale of many warm-weather events. More than two dozen concerts are presented here each summer, including the Santa Fe Summer Concert Series. In recent years, the series has attracted such big-name acts as Joan Armatrading, the Grateful Dead, B. B. King, Kenny Loggins, Anne Murray, Suzanne Vega, Frank Zappa, and the Reggae Sunsplash. Most are booked by Big River Productions, P.O. Box 8036, Albuquerque, NM 87198 (☎ 505/256-1777).

Tickets: Vary according to performer.

⭐ **St. Francis Auditorium**, Museum of Fine Arts. ☎ 827-4455.

This beautiful music hall, patterned after the interiors of traditional Hispanic mission churches, is noted for its acoustics. It hosts a wide variety of musical events, including the Santa Fe Chamber Music Festival in July and August. The Santa Fe Symphony Festival Series, the Santa Fe Concert Association, the Santa Fe Women's Ensemble and various other programs are also held here.

Tickets: $5–$25, depending upon event; see listings for specific performing arts companies.

Sweeney Convention Center, Marcy and Grant Sts. ☎ 984-6760.

Santa Fe's largest indoor arena hosts a wide variety of trade expositions and other events during the year. It's also the home of the Santa Fe Symphony Orchestra.

Tickets: $10–$30, depending upon seating and performances.

The Club & Music Scene

COUNTRY MUSIC

Rodeo Nites, 2911 Cerrillos Rd. ☎ 473-4138.

There's live country dance music nightly at this popular club. Free dance lessons are offered Monday from 7 to 9pm.

Admission: Fri–Sat $3, Sun $2; free weekdays.

ROCK

The Bull Ring, 414 Old Santa Fe Trail. ☎ **983-3328.**

This restaurant near the State Capitol is also a lively bar with dance music after 9pm Wednesday through Saturday. Bands, normally booked for a week at a time, may be rhythm-and-blues, reggae, rock, or tunes from the sixties and seventies.

Admission: Thurs–Sat $3.

Chelsea Street Pub, Villa Linda Mall, Rodeo and Cerrillos Rds. ☎ **473-5105.**

Burgers and beer are served here during the lunch and dinner hours, but when the shopping mall closes at 9pm, the pub really starts hopping. Top bands from throughout the Southwest play dance music until 2am Monday through Saturday and until 7pm Sunday.

Admission: Free.

Chez What, 213 W. Alameda St. ☎ **982-0099.**

There's original live music here nightly from 11am to 2am. Performers could be local, regional, national, or even international, and the music runs the gamut from rock to reggae and pop to jazz and blues.

Admission: $2–$3 Mon–Thurs, $5–$6 Fri–Sun; $10 or more for major acts.

Edge, 135 W. Palace Ave. ☎ **986-1720.**

Located on the third floor of the Palace Court, Edge is popular with a wide cross-section of the Santa Fe population (including the gay crowd). The nightclub features live entertainment during most of the week and dance music on Friday and Saturday nights. There is an adjoining restaurant with a short but satisfying menu.

Open: Mon–Sat 6pm–2am, Sun 6pm–midnight.

Admission: Cover varies according to performer.

Luna, 519 Cerrillos Rd. ☎ **989-4888.**

Originally built as a movie theater, Luna is a 9,000-square-foot dance club that hosts a range of nationally recognized rock bands throughout the week and features DJ music on Friday and Saturday nights. There's no food available, but the bar is enormous.

Open: Mon–Sat 7pm–2am, Sun 7pm–midnight.

Admission: Cover varies according to performer.

JAZZ, BLUES & FOLK

⭐ **El Farol**, 808 Canyon Rd. ☎ **983-9912.**

The original neighborhood bar of the Canyon Road artists' quarter (its name means the Lantern) is the place to head for local ambience. Its low ceilings and muraled walls are the home of Santa Fe's largest and most unusual selection of *tapas* (bar snacks and appetizers), from stuffed calamari to grilled cactus with ramesco sauce. Jazz, folk, and ethnic musicians, some of national note, perform most nights.

Admission: $2–$6.

Fiesta Lounge, La Fonda Hotel, 100 E. San Francisco St. ☎ **982-5511.**

This lively lobby bar offers live entertainment nightly, including a variety of country, jazz, Latin, and big-band show tunes.

Admission: Free.

160

The Bar Scene

Evangelo's, 200 W. San Francisco St. ☎ **982-9014.**

There's no food offered at Evangelo's, but the decor is unique to Santa Fe, and there are over 250 varieties of imported beer available. Pool tables are an added attraction Evangelo's is extremely popular with the local crowd.

Open: Daily from noon until 1 or 2am.
Admission: Free.

Vanessie of Santa Fe, 434 W. San Francisco St. ☎ **982-9966.**

This is unquestionably Santa Fe's most popular piano bar. The talented Doug Montgomery and Taylor Kundolf have a loyal local following. Their repertoire ranges from Bach to Billy Joel, Gershwin to Barry Manilow. They play nightly from around 8:30 (7 on Friday and Saturday) until closing.

Admission: Free.

More Entertainment

Ever since *The Santa Fe Trail,* a splashy western starring Errol Flynn, Olivia de Havilland, Ronald Reagan, and Raymond Massey, premiered in Santa Fe in 1940 northern New Mexico has been a prime site for major studio movie productions. Films like *Butch Cassidy and the Sundance Kid* (1968), *Easy Rider* (1968), *Billy Jack* (1970) *Silverado* (1984), *Young Guns* (1988), and *The Milagro Beanfield War* (1988) have become big national hits. In fact, an estimated 500 movies have been shot in this region since 1900.

In addition to films shown at the Center for Contemporary Arts, several theaters present first-run movies. They include **Cinema 6,** 4250 Cerrillos Rd. (☎ **471-0666**), the **Coronado Twin Theaters,** 508 Cordova Rd. (☎ **983-3179**), **The Movies,** De Vargas Center (☎ **988-2775**), and the **Yucca Drive-In,** Cerrillos Road (☎ **471-1000**). The **Jean Cocteau Cinema,** 418 Montezuma St. (☎ **988-2711**), and the **Grand Illusion,** St. Michael's Drive and Llano Street (☎ **471-8935**), show selected commercial, foreign, and art films.

9 Easy Excursions

Pueblos

Within easy driving distance of Santa Fe are the "Eight Northern Pueblos." Nambe, Pojoaque, San Ildefonso, San Juan, Santa Clara, and Tesuque are all within about 30 miles. Picuris (San Lorenzo) is on the "High Road to Taos," and Taos Pueblo, of course is just outside of the northern New Mexico town of Taos.

The southern six pueblos of this group can easily be seen in a day's round-trip from Santa Fe. Plan to focus most of your attention on San Juan and Santa Clara, including the former's arts cooperative and the latter's Puye Cliff Dwellings.

Certain rules of etiquette apply in visits to pueblos. These are personal dwellings, and must be respected as such. Don't climb on the buildings or peek into doors or windows. Don't enter sacred grounds, such as cemeteries and *kivas.* If you attend a dance or ceremony, remain silent during it, and refrain from applause when it's over. Many pueblos prohibit photography or sketches; others require you to pay a fee for a permit. If you do not respect pueblo rules and the privacy of the Native Americans who live there you will be asked to leave.

Tesuque Pueblo, Rte. 11, Box 1, Santa Fe, NM 87501. ☎ **983-2667.**

Located eight miles north of Santa Fe on U.S. 84/285, Tesuque's (*teh-SOO-keh*) most visible signs are the unusual Camel Rock and a large roadside Bingo operation (nightly 6:30–11pm; ☎ **984-8414**). Despite this concession to the late 20th century, the 400 pueblo dwellers are faithful to traditional religion, ritual, and ceremony. Excavations confirm that there was a pueblo here in A.D. 1250; a mission church and adobe houses surround the plaza.

Some Tesuque women are skilled potters; Ignacia Duran's black-and-white and red micaceous pottery and Teresa Tapia's miniatures and pots with animal figures are particularly notable. Tesuque Pueblo Bingo is open every night. There is a snack bar on premises.

Admission: Free. Still cameras $10, movie cameras $50, sketching $100.
Open: Daily 9am–5pm.

Pojoaque Pueblo, Rte. 11, Box 71, Santa Fe, NM 87501. ☎ **455-2278.**

Seven miles farther north on U.S. 84/285, at the junction of N.M. 503, is Pojoaque (po-*hwa*-keh). Though small (pop. 125) and without a definable village, Pojoaque is important as a center for traveler services. Indigenous pottery, embroidery, silverwork, and beadwork are available for sale at the Pojoaque Pueblo Tourist Center. Camera and sketching permits must be obtained in advance through the governor's office.

Admission: Free. No photography on feast days. Contact the pueblo governor's office for information about sketching and camera fees.

Open: Daylight hours.

Nambe Pueblo, Rte. 1, Box 117 BB, Santa Fe, NM 87501. ☎ **455-2036.**

Drive east three miles from Pojoaque on N.M. 503, then turn right at the Bureau of Reclamation sign for Nambe Falls. Two miles farther is Nambe, a 700-year-old Tewa-speaking pueblo with a solar-powered tribal headquarters, at the foot of the Sangre de Cristo range. A few of the original pueblo buildings still exist, including a large round *kiva,* used today in ceremonies. Pueblo artisans make woven belts, beadwork, and brown micaceous pottery.

Nambe Falls make a stunning three-tier drop through a cleft in a rock face four miles beyond the pueblo, tumbling into Nambe Reservoir. A recreational site at the reservoir offers fishing, boating, hiking, camping, and picnicking.

Admission: Pueblo free; still cameras $5, movie cameras $10, sketching $10. Recreational site, fishing $6/day adults, $4/day children, camping $8 first night, $15 with hookup.

Open: Pueblo daily 8am–5pm; recreational site Apr–May and Sept–Oct 7am–7pm, June–Aug 6am–9pm.

San Ildefonso Pueblo, Rte. 5, Box 315A, Santa Fe, NM 87501. ☎ **455-3549** or **455-2273.**

If you turn left on N.M. 502 at Pojoaque, it's about six miles to the turnoff to this pueblo, nationally famous for the matte-finish black-on-black pottery developed by tribeswoman Maria Martinez in the 1920s. The pottery-making process is explained at the **San Ildefonso Pueblo Museum,** where exhibits of pueblo history, arts, and crafts are presented on weekdays. Tours of the pueblo (pop. 650) may be arranged with the visitor center, on appointment.

San Ildefonso Feast Day, January 22 to 23, is a good time to observe the social and religious traditions of the pueblo, when buffalo, deer, and Comanche dances are presented. There may be dances scheduled for Easter, the Harvest Festival in early September, and Christmas.

The pueblo has a 4½-acre fishing lake open April through October. Picnicking is encouraged; camping is not.

Admission: $1 for noncommercial vehicles, $10 for commercial vehicles, plus 50¢ per passenger. Still cameras $5, movie cameras and sketching $15. Fishing $5 adults, $3 children 6–12.

Open: Summer Mon–Fri 8am–5pm, Sat–Sun 9am–6pm; winter Mon–Fri 8am–4:30pm. **Closed:** Major holidays and San Ildefonso Feast Day as well as other feast days.

★ **San Juan Pueblo,** P.O. Box 1099, San Juan Pueblo, NM 87566. ☎ **852-4400.**

The largest (pop. 1,950) and northernmost of the Tewa- (not Tiwa-) speaking pueblos and the headquarters of the Eight Northern Indian Pueblos Council, San Juan is located on the east side of the Rio Grande—opposite the 1598 site of San Gabriel, the first Spanish settlement west of the Mississippi River and the first capital of New Spain. The pueblo is reached via N.M. 74, a mile off N.M. 68, four miles north of Espanola.

Past and present cohabit here. San Juan Indians, though Roman Catholics, still practice traditional religious rituals; thus two rectangular *kivas* flank the church in the main plaza, and *caciques* (pueblo priests) share influence with civil authorities.

The **Eight Northern Indian Pueblos Council** (☎ 852-4265) is a sort of chamber of commerce and social-service agency.

Aguino's Indian Arts and Crafts features paintings, wood carvings, rasps, and corn dolls. It is open Saturday from 8am to 5pm and Sunday from 9am to 5pm and by appointment. Call Juan B. Aguino at **667-8175.** Another crafts store, **O'ke Oweenge Arts and Crafts Cooperative** (☎ 852-2372), focuses on local wares: This is a fine place to seek out San Juan's distinctive red pottery, a lustrous ceramic incised with traditional geometric symbols. Also exhibited and sold are seed, turquoise, and silver jewelry, wood and stone carvings, indigenous clothing and weavings, embroidery, and paintings. Artisans often work in the center for visitors to watch. The co-op is open Monday through Saturday from 9am to 5pm; closed San Juan Feast Day.

Right on the main road through the pueblo is the **Tewa Indian Restaurant,** serving traditional Pueblo chile stews, breads, blue-corn dishes, posole, teas, and desserts. It's open weekdays from 9am to 2:30pm, except holidays and feast days.

Fishing and picnicking are encouraged at the **San Juan Tribal Lakes,** open year-round.

Like most of the other pueblos, San Juan also offers bingo. In summer doors are open Wednesday through Sunday at 5:30pm; in winter doors open Sunday afternoons at noon.

Admission: Free. Photography or sketching may be allowed with prior permission from the governor's office. The fee for each is $5. Fishing $7 adults, $4 children and seniors.

Open: Daylight hours.

Santa Clara Pueblo, P.O. Box 580, Espanola, NM 87532. ☎ **753-7326.**

Just across the Rio Grande from Espanola on N.M. 5, Santa Clara has a population of about 1,600, making it one of the larger pueblos. Driving and walking tours are offered weekdays, with a week's notice, and include visits to the pueblo's historic church and artists' studios. Visitors are welcome to enter studios so marked, to watch the artists making baskets and a highly polished red-and-black pottery.

The Puye Cliff Dwellings (see below) are on the Santa Clara reservation.
Admission: Free. Still cameras $5, movie cameras $15, sketching $15.
Open: Daylight hours. Visitor's center open daily 9am–4:30pm.

⭐ **Puye Cliff Dwellings,** Santa Clara Pueblo. ☎ **753-7326.**

The Santa Clara people migrated to their home on the Rio Grande in the 13th century from a former home high on the Pajarito Plateau to the west. The ruins of that past life have been preserved in this site, an 11-mile climb west of the pueblo. Thought to have been occupied from about 1250 to 1577, this site at the mouth of the Santa Clara Canyon is a national landmark.

High on a nearly featureless plateau, the volcanic tuff rises in a soft tan facade 200 feet high. Here the Anasazi found niches to build their houses. Visitors can descend via staircases and ladders from the 7,000-foot mesa top into the 740-room pueblo ruin, which includes a ceremonial chamber and community house. Petroglyphs are evident in many of the rocky cliff walls.

Six miles farther west is the **Santa Clara Canyon Recreational Area,** a sylvan summer setting for camping, open year-round for picnicking, hiking, and fishing in ponds and Santa Clara Creek.

Admission: $5 adults, $4 children and seniors. Guided tours additional $1 charge. Tues–Thurs package tour including pueblo feast and dance, $15–$20. Use of recreational area, $8/day per vehicle; camping $10; fishing $8 adults, $4 children.
Open: Daily 8am–8pm in summer; 9am–4:30pm in winter.

Los Alamos

The atomic bomb was born in Los Alamos, a city of 12,000 spread on the craggy, fingerlike mesas of the Pajarito Plateau, between the Jemez Mountains and Rio Grande valley, 33 miles northwest of Santa Fe. Pueblo Indians lived in this rugged area for well over 1,000 years, and an exclusive boys' school operated atop the 7,300-foot plateau from 1928 to 1943. Los Alamos National Laboratory was founded in secrecy as Project Y of the Manhattan Engineer District, the hush-hush wartime program to split the atom and develop the world's first nuclear weapons.

Project director J. Robert Oppenheimer, later succeeded by Norris E. Bradbury, worked with a team of 30 to 100 scientists in research, development, and production of the weapons. Today 3,000 scientists and another 4,800 support staff work at **Los Alamos National Laboratory,** making it the largest employer in northern New Mexico. Still operated by the University of California for the federal Department of Energy (which provides more than 80% of its $600-million annual budget), its 32 technical areas occupy 43 square miles of mesa-top land.

The laboratory is known today as one of the world's foremost scientific institutions. It's still geared heavily to the defense industry—the Trident and Minuteman strategic warheads were created here, for example—but it has many other research programs, including studies in nuclear fusion and fission, energy conservation, nuclear safety, the environment, and nuclear wastes. Its international resources include a genetic sequence data bank, with wide implications for medicine and agriculture, and an Institute for Geophysics and Planetary Physics, among others.

WHAT TO SEE & DO

⭐ **Bradbury Science Museum,** Los Alamos National Laboratory, 15th and Central (Mail Stop C330) ☎ **667-4444.**

This outstanding museum is the laboratory's public showcase. It offers a glimpse into World War II's historic Manhattan Project as well as today's advanced science and technology.

Visitors may explore the museum, experiment with lasers, use computers, and view laboratory research in energy, defense, environment, and health. The laboratory's weapon research program is displayed with historical and current exhibits. Self-guided exhibits have interesting hands-on features and video monitors to enhance the visitor's understanding. Educational and historical films are shown continuously.

Admission: Free.

Open: Tues–Fri 9am–5pm, Sat–Mon 1–5pm. **Closed:** Major holidays.

Los Alamos Historical Museum, 2132 Central Ave. (P.O. Box 43 Los Alamos). ☎ **662-4493.**

The massive log building that once housed the dining and recreation hall for the Los Alamos Ranch School for boys is now a National Historic Landmark known as the Fuller Lodge. Its current occupants include the museum office and research archives, the Fuller Lodge Art Center (see below), and the **Los Alamos County Chamber of Commerce,** P.O. Box 460, Los Alamos, NM 87544 (☎ **662-8105**), which doubles as a visitor information center. The museum (located in the small log and stone building to the north of Fuller Lodge) recounts area history, from prehistoric cliff dwellers to the present, with a variety of exhibits ranging from Indian artifacts to school memorabilia and wartime displays. The museum sponsors guest speakers and operates a bookstore.

Admission: Free.

Open: Mon–Sat 9:30–4:30pm, Sun 11–5pm in summer; Mon–Sat 10am–4pm, Sun 1–4pm in winter.

Fuller Lodge Art Center, 2132 Central Ave. ☎ **662-9331.**

Works of northern New Mexico artists are displayed here. Two annual arts and crafts fairs are also held here—one on the first full weekend in August, and one on the last Saturday in October.

Admission: Free.

Open: Mon–Sat 10am–4pm, Sun 1–4pm.

WHERE TO STAY

Hilltop House Hotel, Trinity at Central, Los Alamos, NM 87544. ☎ **505/662-2441** or toll free **800/462-0936.** Fax 505/662-5913. 82 rms, 18 suites. A/C TV TEL

Rates: $65 single; $82 double; $95–$230 suite. AE, CB, DC, MC, V.

Recently renovated, this hotel's tastefully furnished rooms include 33 efficiency units with kitchenettes. Each room has standard furnishings, satellite TV, and other modern conveniences. There are rooms for nonsmokers and women travelers.

The third-floor Trinity Sights Restaurant, which affords a stunning view across the Rio Grande to Santa Fe, offers a lengthy dinner menu that includes the likes of Cajun-style prime rib, chicken saltimbocca, and scallops Portofino. Dinner main courses range from about $14 to $17. A full breakfast is included in weekday rates. The restaurant is open from 6:30am to 10pm daily. There's a lounge on the mezzanine level above. The hotel also offers room service, valet laundry, secretarial service, and complimentary coffee 24 hours. Pets are accepted with a $25 deposit. Facilities include an indoor swimming pool, coin-op laundry, Avis car-rental agency, travel agent, realty office, beauty salon, 24-hour convenience store, adjacent gas station and liquor store, and meeting and conference facilities.

Los Alamos Inn, 2201 Trinity Dr., Los Alamos, NM 87544. ☎ **505/662-7211** or toll free **800/279-9279.** Fax 505/662-7211 (ask for fax). 116 rms, suites. A/C TV TEL
Rates: $60 single; $65 double. AE, CB, DC, MC, V.

Located just a few minutes from Los Alamos National Laboratory, the inn's comfortable, spacious rooms, including some for nonsmokers and the disabled, have queen-size or double beds, large writing tables, remote-control satellite TV with in-room movies. Some have minibars. Ashley's restaurant is open for three meals daily from 7am to 2pm and 5 to 9pm, with a big salad bar and dinner main courses like steak Mexicana and teriyaki shrimp and scallops in the $10 to $13 range. Ashley's Pub serves happy-hour hors d'oeuvres and late-night snacks. The hotel has an outdoor swimming pool, hot tub, and meeting facilities. No pets.

Bandelier National Monument

Fewer than 15 miles south of Los Alamos along N.M. 4, this is the nearest major prehistoric site to Santa Fe. It combines the extensive ruins of an ancient cliff-dwelling Anasazi Pueblo culture with 46 square miles of canyon-and-mesa wilderness.

Most visitors, after an orientation stop in the visitor center and museum to learn about the culture that persisted here between A.D. 1100 and 1550, follow a cottonwood-shaded 1¹/₂-mile trail along Frijoles Creek to the principal ruins. The pueblo site, including a great underground *kiva,* has been partially reconstructed. The biggest thrill for most folks, though, is climbing hardy piñon ladders to visit an alcove 140 feet above the canyon floor that was once home to prehistoric people. Tours are self-guided or led by a National Park Service ranger.

At night around a campfire, the rangers or local Native Americans talk to groups of visitors about the history, culture, and geology of the ruins, or about Indian legends. On a moonlit evening, the guided night walks reveal a different, spooky aspect of the ruins and cave houses, outlined in the two-dimensional chiaroscuro of the thin cold light from the starry sky. Daytime, there are nature programs for adults and children. A small museum at the visitor center shows artifacts found in the area.

Elsewhere in the monument, 60 miles of maintained trails lead to more Native American ruins and ceremonial sites, waterfalls, and wildlife habitats. The separate **Tsankawi** section of the monument, reached by an ancient 2-mile trail close to White Rock, contains a large unexcavated ruin on a high mesa overlooking the Rio Grande valley.

Areas are set aside for picnicking and camping. Admission is $5 per vehicle. The national monument—named after Swiss American archaeologist Adolph Bandelier, who explored here in the 1880s—is open year-round during daylight hours, except Christmas and New Year's.

Most people are surprised to learn that the largest volcanic caldera in the world is here in northern New Mexico. **Valle Grande,** a vast meadow 16 miles in diameter and 76 square miles in area, is all that remains of a massive volcano that erupted nearly a million years ago. When the mountain spewed ashes and dust as far as Kansas and Nebraska, its underground magma chambers collapsed, forming this great valley. Lava domes which pushed up after the collapse obstruct a full view across the expanse. N.M. 4 skirts the caldera beginning about 15 miles west of Los Alamos.

High Road to Taos

Unless you're in a hurry to get from Santa Fe to Taos, the "high road"—also called the Mountain Road or the King's Road—is by far the most fascinating route. It transits tiny ridge-top villages where Hispanic lifestyles and traditions persist as they did a century ago.

The historic weaving center of **Chimayo** is 16 miles north of Pojoaque junction, at the junction of N.M. 520 and 76 via N.M. 503. Families like the Ortegas maintain a tradition of handwoven textiles begun by their ancestors seven generations ago, in the early 1800s, in this small village. **Ortega's Weaving Shop** and **Galeria Ortega** are fine places to take a close look at this ancient craft.

Today, however, many more people come to Chimayo to visit **El Santuario de Nuestro Señor de Esquipulas** (the Shrine of Our Lord of Esquipulas), better known simply as **El Santuario de Chimayo.** Attributed with miraculous powers of healing, this church has been the destination of countless thousands of pilgrims since its construction in 1814 to 1816. Some 30,000 people may participate in the annual Good Friday pilgrimage, many of them walking from as far away as Albuquerque.

Although only the earth in the anteroom beside the altar has healing powers ascribed to it, the entire shrine has a special serene feeling that's hard to ignore. It's quite moving to peruse the testimonies of rapid recoveries from illness or injury on the walls of the anteroom, and equally poignant to read the as yet unanswered entreaties made on behalf of loved ones.

Designated a National Historic Landmark in 1970, the church contains five beautiful *reredos,* or panes of sacred paintings, one behind the main altar and two on each side of the nave. Each year during the fourth weekend in July, the 9th-century military exploits of the Spanish saint Santiago are celebrated in a weekend fiesta, supported by the National Endowment for the Arts, including the historic play *Los Moros y Cristianos* (Moors and Christians).

Many travelers schedule their drives to have lunch at the **Restaurante Rancho de Chimayo** (☎ **351-4444**) on N.M. 76 east of the junction. The adobe home, built by Hermenegildo Jaramillo in the 1880s, has been in the food business for nearly three decades. Native New Mexican cuisine, prepared from generations-old Jaramillo family recipes, is served on terraced patios and in cozy dining rooms beneath hand-stripped *vigas.* Dinners run $10 to $17. The restaurant is open daily from noon to 10pm from June through August and Tuesday through Sunday from noon to 9pm the rest of the year.

The Jaramillo family also owns a bed-and-breakfast inn, **Hacienda Rancho de Chimayo,** P.O. Box 11, Chimayo, NM 87522 (☎ **505/351-2222**). Once the residence of Epifanio Jaramillo, Hermenegildo's brother, its seven guest rooms all open onto an enclosed courtyard. Each room, furnished with turn-of-the-century antiques, has a private bath and sitting area. Rates are $60 to $100. The office is open daily from 9am to 9pm.

Lovely **Santa Cruz Lake** has a dual purpose: The artificial lake provides water for Chimayo valley farms, but also offers a recreation site for trout fishing and camping at the edge of the Pecos Wilderness. To reach it, turn south 4 miles on N.M. 503, 2 miles east of Chimayo.

Just as Chimayo is famous for its weaving, the village of **Cordova,** 7 miles east on N.M. 76, is noted for its wood carvers. Small shops and studios along the highway display *santos* (carved saints) and various decorative items.

Anyone who saw Robert Redford's 1988 movie production, *The Milagro Beanfield War,* has seen **Truchas.** A former Spanish colonial outpost built at 8,000 feet atop a mesa 4 miles east of Cordova, it was chosen as the site for filming in part because traditional Hispanic culture remains pervasive. Subsistence *acequia* farming has a high profile here. The scenery is spectacular: 13,101-foot Truchas Peak dominates one side of the mesa, and the broad Rio Grande valley the other.

Las Trampas, 6 miles east of Truchas on N.M. 76, is most notable for its **San Jose Church,** to some the most beautiful church built during the Spanish colonial period. It was placed on the National Register of Historic Places in 1966 through the efforts of preservationists who felt it was threatened by a highway project.

Near the regional education center of **Penasco,** 24 miles from Chimayo near the junction of N.M. 75 and 76, is the **Picuris (San Lorenzo) Pueblo** (☎ 587-2519). The 270 citizens of this 15,000-acre mountain pueblo, native Tiwa speakers, consider themselves a sovereign nation: Their forebears never made a treaty with any foreign country, the United States included. Thus they observe a traditional form of tribal council government. Their annual feast day at San Lorenzo Church is August 10.

Still, the people are modern enough to have fully computerized their public showcase, Picuris Tribal Enterprises. Besides the Hotel Santa Fe in the state capital, components include the **Picuris Pueblo Museum,** where weaving, beadwork, and the distinctive reddish-brown clay cooking pottery are exhibited weekdays from 8am to 4:30pm. Guided tours through the old village ruins begin from the museum; camera fees start at $5. **Hidden Valley Restaurant** serves a native Picuris menu, along with an American menu. There's also an information center, crafts shop, grocery, and other shops. Permits ($4 for adults and children) are available to fish or camp at Pu-Na and Tu-Tah lakes, regularly stocked with trout.

One mile east of Penasco on N.M. 75 is **Vadito,** which early this century was the center for the conservative Catholic brotherhood, the Penitentes.

Taos is 24 miles north of Penasco via N.M. 518. But day-trippers from Santa Fe can loop back to the capital by taking N.M. 75 west from Picuris Pueblo. **Dixon,** 12 miles west of Picuris, and its twin village of **Embudo,** a mile farther on N.M. 68 at the Rio Grande, are the homes of many artists and craftspeople who exhibit their works during an annual autumn show sponsored by the Dixon Arts Association. You can follow signs to **La Chiripada Winery** (☎ 579-4437), whose product is surprisingly good. The winery is open Monday through Saturday from 10am to 5pm. There is a tasting room in Taos at the Plaza Real Building that is open Monday to Saturday from 10am to 5pm and noon to 5pm on Sunday.

Near Dixon is the **Harding Mine,** a University of New Mexico property where visitors can gather mineral specimens without going underground. If you haven't signed a liability release at the Albuquerque campus, ask at Labeo's Store in Dixon. They'll direct you to the home of a local resident who can get you started fossicking almost immediately.

Two more small villages lie in the Rio Grande valley at 6-mile intervals south of Embudo on N.M. 68. **Velarde** is a fruit-growing center; in season, the road here is lined with stands selling fresh fruit or crimson chile *ristras* and wreaths of native plants. **Alcalde** is the location of Los Luceros, an early 17th-century home planned for refurbishment as an arts and history center. The unique Dance of the Matachines, a Moorish-influenced production brought from Spain by the conquistadors, is performed here on holidays and feast days.

The commercial center of **Espanola** (pop. 7,000) no longer has the railroad that was responsible for its establishment in the 1880s, but it does have perhaps New Mexico's greatest concentration of "low riders." Their owners give much loving attention to these late-model customized cars, so called because their suspension leaves them sitting exceedingly close to the ground. You can't miss seeing them cruise the main streets of town, especially on weekend nights.

Significant sights in Espanola include the **Bond House Museum,** a Victorian-era adobe home displaying exhibits of local history and art; and the **Santa Cruz Church,** built in 1733 and renovated in 1979, which houses many fine examples of Spanish colonial religious art. Major events include the July **Fiesta de Oñate,** commemorating the valley's founding in 1596; the **Tri-Cultural Art Festival** in October on the Northern New Mexico Community College campus; and the weeklong **Summer Solstice** celebration, staged in June by the nearby, 200-strong Ram Das Puri ashram of the Sikhs (☎ **753-9438**).

Santa Feans sometimes take the half-hour drive to Espanola simply to dine at **Matilda's Cafe,** Corlett Road (☎ **753-3200**). Open Tuesday through Sunday from 9am to 9pm, it's noted for its New Mexican food, including vegetarian plates. There's also **El Paragua,** 603 Santa Cruz Rd. (☎ **753-3211**).

Full information on Espanola and vicinity can be obtained from the **Espanola Valley Chamber of Commerce,** 417 Big Rock Center, Espanola, NM 87532 (☎ **505/753-2831**).

Pecos National Monument

About 15 miles east of Santa Fe, I-25 meanders through **Glorieta Pass,** site of an important Civil War skirmish. In March 1862 volunteers from Colorado and New Mexico, along with Fort Union regulars, defeated a Confederate force marching on Santa Fe, thereby turning the tide of Southern encroachment in the West.

Take N.M. 50 east to **Pecos,** a distance of about 7 miles. This quaint town, well off the beaten track since the interstate was constructed, is the site of a noted Benedictine monastery. North of here 26 miles on N.M. 63 is the village of **Cowles,** gateway to the natural wonderland of the Pecos Wilderness. There are many camping, picnicking, and fishing locales en route.

Pecos National Monument (☎ **757-6414**), 2 miles south of the town of Pecos off N.M. 63, contains the ruins of a 14th-century pueblo and 17th-century mission. The pueblo was well known to Coronado in 1540: "It is feared through the land," he wrote. With a population of about 2,000, the Native Americans farmed in irrigated fields and hunted wild game. Their pueblo had 660 rooms and many *kivas.* By 1620 Franciscan monks had established a church and convent. Military and natural disasters took their toll, however, and in 1838 the 20 surviving Pecos Indians abandoned their ancestral home and took up residence with relatives at the Jemez Pueblo.

The E. E. Fogelson Visitor Center tells the history of the Pecos people in a well-done, chronologically organized exhibit, complete with dioramas of pre-Hispanic lifestyles. A 1¼-mile loop trail departs from the center and leads through Pecos Pueblo and the Mission de Nuestra Senora de Los Angeles de Porciuncula, as the church was formally known. This excavated structure—170 feet long and 90 feet wide at the transept—was once the most magnificent church north of Mexico City.

Visitors to the national monument are asked to pay $1 admission, which goes to further preservation. Hours are 8am to 6pm from Memorial Day to Labor Day; 8am to 5pm the rest of the year.

Taos

6

Taos IS ONE OF THOSE GEMLIKE LITTLE TOWNS WHERE THE LOCAL REGARD FOR traditional architecture, combined with surrounding natural beauty, has drawn the eye of artists. For nearly a century painters, graphic artists, and sculptors have made Taos an art center, many of them settling here to form a sort of informal colony. It is one of the very oldest American towns: The Tiwas living in the traditional apartment complexes in Taos Pueblo nearby have been in residence for at least 1,000 years, perhaps 5,000; prehistoric ruins exist throughout the Taos Valley. The village itself was settled by the Spanish in 1617.

Taos is just 40 miles south of the Colorado border, 70 miles north of Santa Fe, and 130 miles from Albuquerque. Life here moves in and out of, and around, the Plaza, just as did life in old villages in Spain and Mexico. Although the population is only about 4,500, the summertime scene is one of crowded sidewalks, shops, and restaurants, with a never-ending traffic jam on the main road through town, for Taos has become a major tourist attraction in the Southwest. With several fine museums (and a new one on the way as this book goes to press) and a wide choice of accommodations and restaurants for visitors, it is well worth a visit of two to three days.

Its 6,900-foot elevation and dry climate give Taos sharp, clear air that's mild in summer and invigorating in winter—especially for skiers who since the 1950s have flocked to the Taos area in increasing numbers to take to the slopes at five resorts. The winter season in Taos has become even busier than the summer.

Taos began as the northernmost outpost of Spain's Mexican empire. It was a hotbed of revolutionary activity throughout the late 17th century; the suppression of three rebellions helped spark the Pueblo Revolt of 1680. Through the 18th and 19th centuries Taos was an important trade center: New Mexico's annual caravan to Chihuahua, Mexico, couldn't leave until after the annual midsummer Taos Fair. French trappers began attending the fair in 1739. Plains Indians, even though they often attacked the Pueblos at other times, also attended the market festivals under a temporary annual truce. By the early 1800s Taos had become a headquarters for American "mountain men," the most famous of whom, Kit Carson, made his home in Taos from 1826 until his death in 1868.

Taos was firmly Hispanic, and stayed loyal to Mexico during the Mexican War of 1846. The city rebelled against its new U.S. landlord in 1847, killing newly appointed Gov. Charles Bent in his Taos home. Nevertheless, it became a part of the territory of New Mexico in 1850. It fell into Confederate hands for just six weeks during the Civil War, at the end of which time Carson and two other statesmen raised the Union flag over Taos Plaza and guarded it day and night. Since then, Taos has had the honor of flying the flag 24 hours a day.

The town's international renown as an art center had its start in 1898 when two young eastern artists on a sketching tour through the Rockies had a wheel break on their horse-drawn buggy north of Taos. The pair, Ernest Blumenschein and Bert Phillips, took the wheel in for repairs, and were captivated by the dramatic light changes and their visual effect upon buildings and landscapes. They soon settled in Taos, and by 1912 the Taos Society of Artists had placed the town on the international cultural map. Today, by some estimates, more than 10% of the townspeople are painters, sculptors, writers, musicians, or otherwise earn income from an artistic pursuit.

1 Orientation

ARRIVING IN TAOS • By Plane   Taos Municipal Airport (☎ 758-4995) is about eight miles northwest of town on U.S. 64, en route to the Rio Grande Gorge Bridge. **Horizon Air Services** (☎ toll free **800/547-9308**) provides local Cessna 310 services to communities and national parks of the region.

Pride of Taos (☎ 758-8340) meets incoming flights and provides shuttle-bus service to Taos and the Taos Ski Valley.

• **By Bus**   The **Taos Bus Center,** Paseo del Pueblo Sur at the Chevron Station (☎ 758-1144), is not far from the Plaza. **Greyhound** and **TNM&O Coaches** arrive and depart from this depot several times a day.

Two local bus services provide transportation throughout the region. **Pride of Taos** (☎ 758-8340) offers twice-daily shuttle-bus service to and from Albuquerque airport and downtown Santa Fe. **Faust's Transportation** (☎ 758-3410 or 758-7359) runs a similar service once a day, as well as shuttling to and from Red River, Angel Fire, and other area resort towns. Both services charge similar rates of $25 one-way, $45 round-trip, to Albuquerque.

• **By Car**   Most visitors arrive in Taos either via N.M. 68 or U.S. 64. Northbound travelers exit I-25 at Santa Fe, follow U.S. 285 as far as San Juan Pueblo, and continue on the divided highway when it becomes N.M. 68. Taos is 79 miles from the I-25 junction. Travelers southbound from Denver on I-25 exit 6 miles south of Raton at U.S. 64, and follow it 95 miles to Taos. Another major route is U.S. 64 from the west (214 miles from Farmington).

TOURIST INFORMATION   The **Taos County Chamber of Commerce,** P.O. Drawer I, Taos, NM 87571 (☎ **505/758-3873** or toll free **800/732-TAOS**), is located at the corner of Highways 68 and 64. It's open from 8am to 5pm daily, year-round except major holidays. **Carson National Forest** also has an information center in the same building as the chamber.

CITY LAYOUT   The Plaza is a short block west of Taos's major intersection—where U.S. 64 (**Kit Carson Road**) from the east joins N.M. 68, **Paseo del Pueblo Sur** (also known as South Pueblo Road or South Santa Fe Road). U.S. 64 proceeds north from the intersection as **Paseo del Pueblo Norte** (North Pueblo Road). **Camino de la Placita** (Placitas Road) circles the west side of downtown, passing within a block of the other side of the Plaza. Many of the streets that join these thoroughfares are winding lanes lined by traditional adobe homes, many of them a century or more old.

MAPS   To find your way around town, pick up a copy of the Town of Taos map from the chamber of commerce.

2 Getting Around

BY BUS OR TAXI   Two private companies serve Taos. **Pride of Taos** (☎ 758-8340) operates a summer trolley that runs daily from 9am to 4:30pm from Taos Plaza and the chamber of commerce. The tour is a 50-minute narrated sightseeing trolley tour of historic Taos for $7 ($3 for children). In winter, Pride of Taos's shuttle-bus service links town hotels and Taos Ski Valley four times a day for $7 round-trip. A night bus ($10) brings skiers staying at the ski valley into town for dinner and returns them to their lodgings.

Faust's Transportation (☎ 758-3410) offers town taxi service from 7am to 11pm daily, with fares of $7 anywhere in the city limits for up to two people ($2 per additional person), $12 to the airport, $25 to Taos Ski Valley.

BY CAR   With offices at Taos airport **Payless Rental Cars** (☎ 751-1110) is reliable and efficient. **Hertz** (☎ 776-2229) is located at Taos Mountain Lodge, 1 mile from Taos Ski Valley. **Friday Motors** (☎ 758-2252) at 1040 Paseo del Pueblo Norte is another option.

Parking can be difficult during the summer rush, when the stream of tourists' cars moving north and south through town never ceases. Not everyone knows about all the free parking lots, however, especially about the municipal lot behind Taos Community Auditorium, just off Paseo del Pueblo Norte a block north of the Plaza traffic signal. Another lot just to the north of the Plaza has parking meters. Two commercial lots, one behind the Plaza and another off Kit Carson Road, charge a small fee for all-day parking.

A note for outdoor enthusiasts: Reliable paved roads lead to takeoff points for side trips up poorer forest roads to many recreation sites. Once you get off the main roads, you won't find gas stations or cafés. Four-wheel-drive vehicles are recommended on snow and much of the otherwise-unpaved terrain of the region. If you're doing some off-road adventuring, it's wise to go with a full gas tank, extra food and water, and warm clothing—just in case. At the more-than-10,000-foot elevations of northern New Mexico, sudden summer snowstorms are not unknown.

BY BICYCLE   Rentals are available from **Gearing Up Bicycle Shop** of 129 Paseo del Pueblo Sur (☎ 751-0365); **Hot Tracks Cyclery & Ski Tuning Service** at 729 Paseo del Pueblo Sur (☎ 751-0949); and **Native Sons Adventures** at 715 Paseo del Pueblo Sur (☎ 758-9342).

Fast Facts: Taos

Business Hours   Most businesses are open Monday to Friday 9am to 5pm. Some may open an hour earlier and close an hour later. Many also open on Saturday mornings, and some art galleries are open all day Saturday and Sunday, especially during peak tourist seasons. Call for specific hours.

Drugstores   The **Taos Pharmacy,** in Piñon Plaza on Paseo del Pueblo Sur (☎ 758-3342), next door to Holy Cross Hospital, is open 9am to 6pm Monday to Friday and 9am to 5pm Saturday.

Emergencies   Dial **911** for police, fire, and ambulance.

Hairdressers & Barbers   **Spirits of Beauty,** 223 Paseo del Pueblo Sur (☎ 758-1178), next door to the chamber of commerce, and **Kachina Beauty Salon,** 413 Paseo del Pueblo Norte (☎ 758-8727), welcome drop-ins of either sex. There are numerous other shops in town.

Hospital   The **Holy Cross Hospital,** on Paseo del Pueblo Sur (☎ 758-8883), has 24-hour emergency service.

Hot Lines   **Rape Crisis Center, 758-2910. Battered Women, 785-9888. Environmental Improvement Division, 827-9329. Poison Control Center,** toll free **800/432-6866.**

Laundry & Dry Cleaning   The **Peralta Laundry & Dry Cleaning,** 1018 S. Santa Fe Rd. (☎ **758-0239**), a couple of miles south of downtown, is open daily.

Library   The **Harwood Public Library and Museum,** on Ledoux Street near the Plaza (☎ **758-3063**), has a general collection for Taos residents; a children's library; and special collections featuring the Taos Society of Artists as its permanent collection, and changing exhibitions of contemporary artists.

Mail   The main **Taos Post Office** is on Paseo del Pueblo Norte (☎ **758-2081**), a few blocks north of the Plaza traffic light. There are smaller offices in Ranchos de Taos (☎ **758-3944**) and at El Prado (☎ **758-4810**). The ZIP code for Taos is 87571.

Newspapers   The *Taos News* (☎ **758-2241**) and the *Sangre de Cristo Chronicle* (☎ **377-2358**) appear on Thursday. The *Albuquerque Journal* and *Tribune,* the *New Mexican* from Santa Fe, and the *Denver Post* are easily obtained at the Fernandez de Taos Bookstore on the Plaza.

Photographic Needs   Check **Plaza Photo,** 106B Juan Largo Lane, just off North Plaza (☎ **758-3420**). If you need your film developed in a hurry take your film to **April's One-Hour Photos** at 613 E North Pueblo Road (☎ **758-0515**).

Police   In case of emergency, dial **911**. All other inquiries should be directed to **Taos Police,** Civic Plaza Drive (☎ **758-2216**). The **Taos County Sheriff,** with jurisdiction outside the city limits, is located in the county courthouse on Paseo del Pueblo Sur (☎ **758-3361**).

Radio   Local stations are KKIT-AM (1340) for news, sports, and weather (☎ **758-2231**); and KTAO-FM (101.7), which broadcasts an entertainment calendar at 6pm daily (☎ **758-1017**).

Religious Services   The biggest church in town is **Our Lady of Guadalupe Church,** west of the Plaza on Camino de la Placita (☎ **758-9208**). Visitors often enjoy attending a service at the famous **San Francisco de Asis Church,** four miles south of the Plaza in Ranchos de Taos (☎ **758-2754**). Masses are mainly in English, but each church has a Sunday-morning Spanish-language mass.

Other denominations active in Taos include Assemblies of God, Baptist, Brethren, Church of Christ, Episcopal, Foursquare Gospel, Friends, Jehovah's Witnesses, Methodist, Presbyterian, Mormon, and Jewish.

Taxes   There is a local bed tax of 10.3125% in Taos town and 9.8125% on hotel rooms in Taos County.

Useful Telephone Numbers   For information on **road conditions** in the Taos area, call the state police (☎ **758-8878**) or dial **800/432-4269** (within New Mexico) for the State Highway Department. **Taos County offices** are at **758-8834.** The KKIT 24-hour weather line is **758-4267.**

3 Accommodations

During peak seasons, visitors without reservations may find a vacant room hard to come by. **Taos Central Reservations,** P.O. Box 1713, Taos, NM 87571 (☎ **505/758-9767** or toll free **800/821-2437**) might be able to help. **Affordable Meetings & Accommodations,** P.O. Box 1258, Taos, NM 87571 (☎ **505/751-1292**) is also a good source of lodging information.

There are another 300 or so rooms in 15 condos and lodges at or near the Taos Ski Valley. **Taos Valley Resort Association,** P.O. Box 85, Taos Ski Valley, NM 87525 (☎ **505/776-2233** or toll free **800/776-1111**) can book these as well as unadvertised condominium or lodge vacancies.

Unlike Santa Fe, there are two high seasons in Taos, winter (Christmas-to-Easter ski season) and summer. Spring and fall are shoulder seasons, often with lower rates. The period between Easter and Memorial Day is notoriously slow in the tourist industry here, and many restaurants and other businesses take their annual vacations at this time. Book well ahead during ski holiday periods (especially Christmas) and during the annual arts festivals (late May to mid-June and late September to early October).

In these listings, the following categories describe peak-season price ranges: **expensive,** over $100 per night double; **moderate,** $75 to $100; **inexpensive,** $50 to $75; **budget,** less than $40 per night double. Tax of 10.3125% in Taos town and 9.8125% in Taos County is added to every hotel bill. Parking is usually free, unless otherwise indicated.

EXPENSIVE

★ **The Historic Taos Inn,** 125 Paseo del Pueblo Norte, Taos, NM 87571.
☎ **505/758-2233** or toll free **800/TAOS-INN.** Fax 505/758-5776. 39 rms. A/C
$ TV TEL

Rates: $75–$160, according to type of room and season. AE, CB, DC, MC, V.

The last century of Taos history is alive and well within the walls of this atmospheric inn. The inn is made up of several separate adobe houses dating from the mid-1800s, which then surrounded a small plaza complete with communal town well. Dr. T. Paul Martin purchased the complex in 1895: He was Taos County's first physician, and, for many years, the only one. In 1936, a year after the doctor's death, his widow, Helen, enclosed the plaza (now the inn's magnificent two-story lobby), installed indoor plumbing (the first in Taos!), and opened the Hotel Martin. In 1981 and 1982 the inn underwent restoration; it is now listed on the state and national registers of historic places. Today, hotel visitors find the inn full of hospitality and charm, combining 20th-century elegance with 19th-century ambience. The lobby is graced with interior balconies overlooking the town well, reborn as a tiered fountain; above it rises a stained-glass cupola. Large *vigas* adorn the ceiling, handwoven rugs and outstanding artwork cover the walls, and Taos-style *bancos* face a sunken pueblo-style fireplace in one corner of the room.

No two guest rooms are alike. While all are furnished in regional style, they differ in size, shape, and craft items—and thus each has a distinct personality. All rooms contain Taos-style furniture built by local artisans; original Native American, Hispanic, and New Mexican art decorates the interiors. All have custom handloomed bedspreads and 31 rooms have fireplaces.

Dining/Entertainment: Doc Martin's, with outstanding southwestern cuisine, is one of Taos's leading dining establishments (see "Dining," below). The Adobe Bar, popular among Taos artists and other locals, has live entertainment on select weeknights as well as a late-night food menu.

Services: Room service, valet laundry.

Facilities: Rooms for nonsmokers and the disabled, seasonal outdoor swimming pool, year-round Jacuzzi in greenhouse.

The Brooks Street Inn **5**

Casa de las Chimeneas **10**

Casa Europa **8**

El Monte Lodge **9**

El Pueblo Lodge **3**

The Historic Taos Inn **6**

Holiday Inn Don Fernando de Taos **12**

Kachina Lodge de Taos **2**

Laughing Horse Inn **1**

Orinda B&B **4**

Sagebrush Inn **13**

Sun God Lodge **11**

Taos Hacienda Inn **7**

Quail Ridge Inn, Ski Valley Rd. (P.O. Box 707), Taos, NM 87571. ☎ **505/776-2211** or toll free **800/624-4448**. Fax 505/776-2949. 110 rms (60 suites). FRIDGE TV TEL

Rates: (range covers seasonal variations): $75–$135 single or double; $170–$280 suite. A 2% gratuity is added to all rates. Extra person $10. Children under 18 stay free with parent. DC, MC, V.

This sports-oriented lodge bills itself as a family resort and conference center. Tennis and skiing are the recreations of note at this contemporary pueblo-style hotel, which spreads across several acres of open sagebrush about 4 miles north of Taos and three-quarters of a mile east of U.S. 64, en route to the Ski Valley 14 miles distant.

Four room options are available at the Quail Ridge Inn, which won a *Western Home* magazine award for architect Antoine Predock when it opened in 1978. Smallest are "hotel rooms," which can sleep four on a queen-size bed and queen-size sleeper sofa. Next are studios, actually semisuites with full kitchens and patios or balconies. One-bedroom suites, the most popular accommodations, consist of a studio with a connecting hotel room. A half-dozen separate *casitas* contain spacious two-bedroom suites of about 1,600 square feet each.

Every room, no matter what its size, has a big fireplace, huge closets, and full shower/ baths with private hot-water heaters. Kitchenettes are fully stocked and include a stove, refrigerator, microwave oven, and dishwasher. Decor is breezy southwestern, with light woods, dried-flower arrangements in handcrafted pottery, and various pieces of local art and artifacts.

Dining/Entertainment: Carl's French Quarter (☎ **776-8319**), specializing in Cajun/creole cuisine, is one of the most popular restaurants in the Taos area. Breakfasts are served to hotel guests only, and lunches are strictly group affairs; but dinners and Sunday brunches are when Carl's bounces like Basin Street. Appetizers like seafood filet gumbo or shrimp and artichoke bisque run $3.50 to $7.95; main courses, including shrimp creole, blackened chicken, and Cajun prime rib, are $12.95 to $22.95. Dessert favorites are chocolate marquise cake and key lime pie. There's a kids' menu. The lounge serves authentic New Orleans cocktails, like hurricanes and mint juleps.

Services: Valet laundry.

Facilities: Rooms for nonsmokers, year-round heated swimming pool, hot tubs and saunas. Six outdoor and two indoor tennis courts, four racquetball/squash courts, summer volleyball pit. Fitness center with weights and exercise room.

MODERATE

El Monte Lodge, 317 Kit Carson Rd. (P.O. Box 22), Taos, NM 87571.
☎ **505/758-3171.** 13 rms. TV TEL

Rates: $54–$59 single; $85–$95 double. $10 extra for kitchenette units. AE, DISC, MC, V.

Century-old cottonwood trees stand in a parklike picnic area, complete with barbecue grills and children's playground, outside this friendly 1930s motel. Located four blocks east of the Plaza, it's old-fashioned but homey, built in traditional adobe style with protruding *vigas,* painted yellow and framed by flower gardens. The rooms, many of them with fireplaces, occupy eight small buildings. The eclectic decor features considerable Pueblo art. Many rooms have fully stocked kitchenettes; there's a free guest laundry. Pets are permitted for an extra $5.

Holiday Inn Don Fernando de Taos, Paseo del Pueblo Sur (P.O. Drawer V), Taos, NM 87571. ☎ **505/758-4444** or toll free **800/759-2736.** Fax 505/758-0055. 124 rms, 26 suites. A/C TV TEL

Rates: $79–$95 single; $89–$105 double; $105–$135 suites, depending upon season. Christmas season rates are higher. Children 19 and under stay free with parent. AE, CB, DC, DISC, JCB, MC, V.

Taos's newest major hotel, opened in 1989, is like a modern pueblo village spread across landscaped grounds on the south side of town. A half-dozen adobe-style building clusters, each named for a noted New Mexico artist, surround private courtyards. The two-story structures are linked with one another, and with the main lobby and restaurant, by a web of walkways.

Standard rooms, appointed in a soft Southwest-motif decor with Pueblo paintings on the walls, feature hand-carved New Mexican wood furnishings, two double beds or a king-size bed and sleeper sofa, and a special doorside niche for skis and boots. King suites offer a sitting room, fireplace, and wet bar (not stocked). Rooms for nonsmokers and the disabled are available.

Don Fernando's Restaurant, open daily from 6:30am to 2pm and 5 to 10pm, serves a variety of regional breakfasts and lunches. An all-you-can-eat soup-and-salad lunch buffet ($5.95) is served weekdays from 11:30am to 2pm. Dinner main courses ($6.95–$18.95) include steaks, chicken, pasta, and seafood dishes. A children's menu is available. The Fernando's Hideaway Lounge, built around a large adobe fireplace, has happy hour from 5 to 7:30pm Monday through Friday. The hotel provides room service, valet laundry, courtesy van, and a 24-hour desk, as well as an outdoor swimming pool, hot tub, and tennis court.

Kachina Lodge De Taos, Paseo del Pueblo Norte (P.O. Box NN), Taos, NM 87571. ☎ **505/758-2275** or toll free **800/522-4462.** Fax 505/758-9207. 118 rms, 4 suites. A/C TV TEL

Rates: $85–$145 single or double. Additional person $8. Children under 12 free with parent. AE, DC, DISC, MC, V.

A pueblo-style motel with bright blue trim, this long-established lodge is an art lover's dream. The art gallery, which connects the lobby to the lodge's restaurants, has a changing exhibit of paintings and other works from the Taos Gallery. The Navajo Living Room, a comfortable space for indoor games or fireside reading, is full of valuable antique Navajo rugs.

Rooms—of which there are a wide variety, including nonsmoking—are appointed with custom-made Taoseno furniture, including armoire, headboards, table, and chairs. Many have a couch or love seat; all have huge bathrooms and a second sink at the vanity in an outer dressing area.

The Hopi Dining Room (open daily from 5:30 to 10pm for dinner) is an elegant restaurant with a gourmet family-style menu (steaks, chicken, seafood) priced at $10 to $14. The Kiva Coffee House, open daily (6am to 5:30pm), serves filling breakfasts and Mexican-style lunches for prices under $8. The Zuni Lounge is open nightly, and the Kachina Cabaret (see "Evening Entertainment," below) draws big-name acts. A Taos Pueblo dance troupe performs nightly in summer. The hotel has a guest services desk (in summer), valet laundry, 24-hour desk, an outdoor swimming pool, hot tub, and coin-op laundry. A ski shop is adjacent. No pets are permitted.

Sagebrush Inn, Paseo del Pueblo Sur (P.O. Box 557), Taos, NM 87571. ☎ **505/758-2254** or toll free **800/428-3626.** Fax 505/758-5077. 81 rms, 19 suites. A/C TV TEL

Rates (including breakfast): $75 single; $90–$105 double; $120–$147 suite. Extra person $7. AE, CB, DC, MC, V.

Georgia O'Keeffe, probably the most famous artist to have worked extensively in the Southwest, lived and painted for six months in the 1930s in a third-story room at this venerable hotel. Originally called the Chamisa Inn, the hotel was built in Pueblo Mission style in 1929, three miles south of the Plaza near Ranchos de Taos. You should know that if you decide to stay at the Sagebrush you'll be paying for the hotel's history, not its amenities.

Most of the rooms face either an open grass courtyard, the outdoor swimming pool, or the stables. Traditional *viga* ceilings are complemented by earth-patterned decor and standard furnishings. Suites in "Sagebrush Village" have *kiva* fireplaces and beautiful hand-carved furniture. There's a king-size bed in the bedroom, a Murphy bed in the main living area, two full baths, and charcoal drawings of local Native Americans on the walls. There are rooms for nonsmokers and the disabled.

The Los Vaqueros Room is open for dinner from 5:30 to 10pm daily. A complimentary full breakfast is served to guests daily (6:30 to 11am) in the Sagebrush Dining Room. The lobby bar is one of Taos's most active nightspots for live music and dancing (see "Evening Entertainment," below). Services and facilities include valet laundry, courtesy van, swimming pool, two Jacuzzis, and tennis courts.

INEXPENSIVE

 El Pueblo Lodge, P.O. Box 92, Taos, NM 87571. ☎ **505/758-8700** or toll free **800/433-9612.** Fax 505/758-7321. 42 rms, 4 suites. FRIDGE TV TEL

Rates (including continental breakfast): $43–$48 single; $63 double; $73–$215 suite. Additional person $5–$7. AE, MC, V.

The setting here is special: nicely landscaped 2¹/₂-acre grounds, complete with fir trees, gardens, barbecue pits, lawn furniture, and a slide for children. Throw in a year-round outdoor swimming pool and hot tub and it's no surprise this motel is popular with families. All of the brightly colored rooms have southwestern decor and refrigerators. Rooms with kitchenettes and fireplaces are also available. Laundry facilities are free to guests. A light complimentary breakfast is served daily.

Laughing Horse Inn, 729 Paseo del Pueblo Norte (P.O. Box 4889), Taos, NM 87571. ☎ **505/758-8350** or toll free **800/776-0161.** 11 rms, 3 guest houses. TV.

Rates: $42–$52 single; $48–$65 double; $98–$150 penthouse and guest houses.

Occupying the print shop of the 1920s "Laughing Horse Press," the inn is an unmistakable adobe structure with lilac purple trim. Guests can choose between sunny dorm-type loft rooms, cozy private rooms, a deluxe solar-heated penthouse, spacious private guest houses across the street, or a house on the mesa complete with views of Taos Mountain. All accommodations have cassette decks and VCRs; some have fireplaces. Bathrooms are shared in the lower portion of the inn. The penthouse has a private bedroom, enclosed sleeping loft, and a bunk set with double beds. A private bath, wood stove, big-screen TV, video and audio decks, and a small refrigerator complete the room. The inn has a common room around a *kiva* fireplace where a wide variety of audio- and videotapes are shelved. Breakfasts (which might be continental or full), may be eaten in the kitchen or the dining room. The refrigerator is stocked on the honor system. There's an outdoor hot tub, and mountain bikes are free for guests' use. Psychic readings are available from the innkeepers, and a massage therapist is available by appointment.

Sun God Lodge, 919 Paseo del Pueblo Sur (P.O. Box 1713), Taos, NM 87571.
☎ **505/758-3162.** TV TEL

Rates: Summer and winter $67.65 single; $74.30–$85.40 double; $100.90 suite; $105.35–$138.60 casita.

An adobe structure, this recently renovated motel offers 1¹/₂ acres of landscaped grounds. The rooms are done in Southwest decor; all have ceiling fans, double-, queen-, or king-sized beds (with Navajo-patterned spreads), prints and lithographs by Taos artists on the walls, and complimentary bedside coffee service. There are some new accommodations with kitchenette areas (fully supplied with dishes and utensils), coffeemakers, minirefrigerators, living rooms with *kiva* fireplaces (wood and fire starter are supplied), remote-controlled TVs, and niches with howling coyotes or kachinas in them. There are outdoor grills and a hot-tub room.

BUDGET

Abominable Snowmansion Skiers' Hostel, Taos Ski Valley Rd. (P.O. Box 3271), Taos, NM 87571. ☎ **505/776-8298.** 60 beds.

Rates (including full breakfast in winter): $11.50–$50, depending on size of accommodation and season. No credit cards.

Located in the small community of Arroyo Seco, about 8 miles north of Taos and 10 miles from the Taos Ski Valley, this lodging attracts many young people. It's clean and comfortable for those happy with dormitory-style accommodations. Toilets, shower rooms, and dressing rooms are segregated by sex. A two-story lodge room focuses around a circular fireplace, and features a piano and games area. Lodging is also offered in traditional teepees and smaller bunkhouses in the campfire area. Tent camping is permitted outside. Guests can cook their own meals or indulge in home-cooked fare.

Bed & Breakfasts

Some three dozen bed-and-breakfasts are listed with the Taos Chamber of Commerce. The **Taos Bed & Breakfast Association** (☎ **505/758-4747** or toll free **800/876-7857**), with strict guidelines for membership, will provide information and make reservations for member homes. The following are some of my favorites.

★ **Adobe & Pines Inn,** P.O. Box 837, Ranchos de Taos, NM 87557.
☎ **505/751-0947** or toll free **800/723-8267.** Fax 505/758-8423. 5 rms (all with bath). TV. **Directions:** The inn is located directly off Hwy. 68, about 1¹/₂ miles from the recreation area at Hwy. 570 (driving north from Santa Fe), or 0.3 miles from St. Francis Plaza (driving south from Taos town). Driving from Santa Fe, the Adobe & Pines Inn will be on your right. You can't really see the inn from the street, but you will see the multicolored posts that mark the driveway.

Rates: $95–$145 single or double. MC, V.

After some traveling in Europe, the owners, Chuck and Charil, decided that they wanted to open a bed-and-breakfast inn. Their only problem was that they didn't quite

180

Taos

know where—until they ended up in Taos and fell in love with what, after six months of renovation, is now the Adobe & Pines Inn.

As you drive down to the house you'll see the horses out front, and you'll undoubtedly be awed by the length of the Grand Portal (it's 80 feet long). The inn is a 150-year-old adobe home that has been turned into one of the most beautiful and peaceful guest houses in which I have stayed. The inn rests amid four acres of pine and fruit trees (the land here is sacred to the Native Americans, because their ancestors used to stop here to pray for a good hunt on their way to the hunting grounds, and on the way back to thank the gods for their successes); each room has a private entrance, which affords you all the privacy you could ever need. All five rooms have fireplaces (two even have fireplaces in the bathroom), and they are each decorated uniquely. Puerta Azul is a wonderful little, cozy space with an antique writing desk and royal blue accents. Puerta Verde, done in deep greens, has a wonderful old *retablo* (ask Chuck and Charil about it), a sitting area, and a queen-sized canopy bed. Puerta Turquese, my favorite, is a guest cottage that is separate from the rest of the house, it has a full kitchen and is done in bright pastels. A wonderful "broken tile mosaic" floor, that was done about a hundred years ago by a man who did only a select few in the whole town of Taos, runs throughout the whole guesthouse. The colors (turquoise, yellow, maroon, black, and peach) in the tile floor have been picked up in the rest of the decor. You can get cozy in bed under a down comforter while the bedroom fireplace warms the room, or you can relax in a jet whirlpool bath in front of a blaze in the bathroom fireplace.

Two new rooms, Puerta Violeta and Puerta Rosa, are welcome competition for Puerta Turquese. Chuck and Charil have outdone themselves with the addition of these bright, colorful accommodations. Puerta Rosa, with its two-person soaking tub, cedar sauna, and fireplaced bathroom is a minispa in and of itself. The bedroom has been furnished with a unique, handcrafted wrought-iron bed designed by Charil. Puerta Violeta is the only room on the second floor of the inn; its main attraction is the spectacular view from the picture window which faces the bed. From the bed you'll have a wonderful view of the Taos night sky. In addition to a large bathroom with a two-person jet tub, Puerta Violeta has a private patio, making it a great place for a romantic evening of stargazing and sipping champagne.

In the evening, Chuck, Charil, and Rascal (the dog) serve hors d'oeuvres in front of a roaring fire in the living room, which is decorated with local art (on sale), including paintings, sculptures, and greeting cards. Charil does some of her own work—in fact, the paper sculpture hanging above the reception desk is hers. In the morning you're in for a treat with a delicious full breakfast in front of the fire in the glassed-in breakfast room. Chuck and Charil are very gracious hosts. They will help you plan any activities of interest, and they'll also give you suggestions as to how you might want to spend your time in Taos. You really can't go wrong here. If I could give this place two stars I would!

The Brooks Street Inn, 119 Brooks St. (P.O. Box 4954), Taos, NM 87571.
☎ **505/758-1489** or toll free **800/758-1489.** 6 rms (all with bath).
Rates: $75–$100 double; $5 less for single occupancy. AE, MC, V.

The Brooks Street Inn is located on a quiet, tree-lined street within walking distance from Taos Plaza. You'll recognize the rambling adobe home by the circular driveway out front. Carol Frank and Larry Moll will welcome you into their beautiful home, which is designed to make you completely at ease during your stay in Taos. The living room, the entrance of which is flanked by two beautiful carved giraffes, features a large fireplace, a comfortable sitting area, and high, beamed ceilings. Each of the guest rooms is decorated differently—for instance, the Willow Room has a willow bed, the Aspen Room features a comfortable reading banco, and the Birch, Juniper, and Piñon rooms all have *kiva* fireplaces. Some of the rooms also have skylights, in-room coffee, and minirefrigerators.

Breakfast with Carol and Larry is a treat indeed. First, there's the coffee bar (unique to any bed and breakfast I've ever visited), from which you may choose Taos Magic Caffe Mocha, cappuccino, espresso, or steamed almond hot chocolate. Then there's breakfast. Specialties of the house include blue-corn pancakes and pineapple salsa; white chocolate apricot scones; and stuffed French toast topped with an apricot sauce. In addition, there are other homemade breads and muffins, fresh fruit, and juices. In the summer, breakfast is served in the adobe-walled garden behind the house (where there is a hammock for two); in winter, it is served in the common room in front of a blazing fire. In short, the Brooks Street Inn is a great place to stay during your holiday in Taos—it's a place where you'll forget the pressures of the outside world while Carol and Larry cater to your every need.

★ **Casa de las Chimeneas,** 405 Cordoba Lane at Los Pandos Road (P.O. Box 5303), Taos, NM 87571. ☎ **505/758-4777.** Fax 505/758-3976. 4 rms, 1 suite. TV TEL

Rates: $112 single; $122–$130 double; $148 suite (for two). MC, V.

The "House of Chimneys" qualifies as one of Taos's luxury B&Bs. Its three rooms, each of them a work of art and with its own private entrance, look out on a beautifully landscaped private garden. The two-room suite incorporates an old library and two fireplaces; it is furnished with marble-topped antiques, a comfortable reading couch, a bentwood rocker, and a game table complete with chess and backgammon. Beautiful bed linens over a sheepskin mattress pad guarantee a great night's sleep. The Blue Room and Willow Room have similar charm and amenities. The new Garden Room has a separate entrance off the herb, vegetable, and rose garden and features a fireplace, as well as a skylit bathroom with a tub/shower combination and a deep soaking tub for one. Attention to detail is a top priority here, with plush towels, down pillows, extra firewood, books and magazines for reading, and owners eager to share tips on best restaurants, ski runs, or scenic drives. Room minirefrigerators are stocked with complimentary soft drinks, juices, and mineral water, and a full gourmet breakfast is served daily. Bathrobes are supplied in each room. Guests gather in the main house for complimentary afternoon hors d'oeuvres. A courtesy telephone is in the main dining room and a large hot tub is located adjacent to a well-maintained herb, vegetable, and rose garden. Smoking is not permitted. As we go to press, several improvements have been made to this B&B, and the rates may be restructured, so call ahead.

Casa Europa, 840 Upper Ranchitos Rd. (HC68, Box 3F), Taos, NM 87571. ☎ **505/758-9798** or toll free **800/525-TAOS** for reservations. 6 rms.

Rates: $70–$135. MC, V.

This cream-colored, Mediterranean-style pueblo, 1.7 miles west of the Plaza, was built of adobe and *vigas* two centuries ago. The elegant rooms, each with full private bath, vary in furnishings: One, for example, has a marble whirlpool and enamel wood stove; another has a full-size Jacuzzi and fireplace, with glass doors opening onto a courtyard. In fact, there are eight fireplaces and 14 skylights in Casa Europa. The regional artwork in the rooms can be purchased. There's a sitting room for reading and/or conversation; coffee and pastries are offered here each day between 3 and 4pm and during ski season hors d'oeuvres are served from 5 to 6pm. A full gourmet breakfast is served each morning. Smoking is not permitted.

Hacienda del Sol, 109 Mabel Dodge Luhan Ln. (P.O. Box 177), Taos, NM 87571.
☎ **505/758-0287.** 8 rms (6 with bath).
Rates: $55–$75 single; $65–$120 double.

Not far from the Plaza on the north side of Taos, Hacienda del Sol is a lovely, quiet bed-and-breakfast in a surprising location—directly behind the Lottaburger. Housed within the main building is the original 190-year-old adobe structure, easily recognizable by its low ceilings and pueblo doorways. Like many of the homes in Taos, Hacienda del Sol has a wonderful history. The home was once owned by arts patroness Mabel Dodge Luhan, and it was here that author Frank Waters wrote *The People of the Valley.* On the far side of the inn's well-manicured grounds is the adjoining Taos Pueblo. All the guest rooms are constructed of adobe and many of them feature *kiva* fireplaces built by Carmen Velarde, New Mexico's most sought-after kiva fireplace artist. Each room is furnished with handcrafted southwestern-style furnishings, antiques, and original art (for sale). Down comforters, clock radios with tape decks and a selection of cassettes, refrigerators, terry-cloth robes, and private baths (supplied with a basket of items you might have forgotten to bring with you) are added luxuries here. The spacious Sala del Don, located in the main building and once Tony Luhan's room, features a beautiful screen handcrafted by Lydia Garcia. The Casita is a separate building that houses two guest rooms that can be rented separately or as a unit. Both rooms have fireplaces and mountain-view bathtubs. Los Amantes (The Lovers) is, indeed, for lovers—the two-person black Jacuzzi on a mahogany platform, situated directly beneath a skylight, is the perfect place to spend a romantic evening of stargazing. One room even has a private steam room. The extended continental breakfast here consists of fresh-baked goodies, fresh-squeezed juice, fruit, and the inn's special blend of coffee. Refreshments are also served every evening from 5pm. An outdoor hot tub, which offers spectacular views of Taos Mountain, is available for guest use in half-hour blocks. Hacienda del Sol is an excellent choice for those traveling with children—it's one of only a handful of bed and breakfasts that accepts children of any age.

Little Tree Bed & Breakfast, P.O. Box 960, El Prado, NM 87529.
☎ **505/776-8467.** 4 rms (all with bath).
Rates: $70–$85 double. MC, V (personal checks or money orders preferred).

Little Tree is one of my favorite Taos bed and breakfasts, partly because it's located in a beautiful, secluded setting, and partly because it's built out of real adobe—not stucco like most of the new buildings in the area. The Giddens, who call themselves "refugee Dallasites," came to New Mexico and fell in love with everything about the northern region of the state, especially the architecture. When they decided to move to Taos, Charles began researching authentic adobe architecture, and together he and Kay came up with a floor plan that they discussed with an architect; soon they were on their way to building their own home, along with two women who were expert adobe builders. (It's interesting to note that throughout history women built adobe homes, because working with mud was considered women's—not men's—work.) The rooms are small but charming and very cozy. They all have adobe floors, which are warm in the winter because the heat runs through the floors, making for a much healthier environment. All rooms have queen-size beds, private baths, and access to the portal and courtyard garden, at the center of which is the "little tree" for which the inn is named. The Piñon and Juniper rooms have fireplaces and private entrances. Piñon and Aspen rooms have sunset views. The Spruce Room is western in feeling and is decorated with beautiful quilts. In the main building, the living room has a traditional *viga* and *latilla* ceiling, and *tierra blanca* adobe, which is adobe that is naturally white. If you look closely at it you can see little pieces of mica and straw. If you develop a real interest in adobe architecture, there are a number of books available for your reading pleasure. Three cats, Miss Kitty, Mister Mud, and Fred, entertain, and the hummingbirds that visit captivate guests as they enjoy a healthy breakfast on the portal in warmer months. On arrival, guests are treated to refreshments.

Neon Cactus Hotel, 1523 Paseo del Pueblo Sur (Box 5702), Taos, NM 87571.

☎ **505/751-1258.** 4 rms (all with bath).

Rates: Jan, Apr–June, Sept–Dec 18 $65–$85 double, $105 quad. Rest of year $85–$125 double, $125–$145 quad. MC, V.

The Neon Cactus is a delightful change of pace from some of the other hotels and bed and breakfasts in New Mexico. You won't find one hint of southwestern decor anywhere in this hotel, and if you're a movie fan you're not likely to miss it one bit. Each of the rooms here pays homage to a film star—for instance, the Marilyn Monroe Suite is decorated with photographs that document the "many moods of Marilyn," and authentic period furnishings. The dominant color scheme in the room is black and white. There's a queen-size bed as well as a pullout couch, so this room can sleep up to four. The bathroom in the Marilyn Monroe Suite is something to behold—it features a Roman-style, oversized sunken tub complete with bubble bath. The Rita Hayworth Suite is done in rich reds, has two queen-size beds, and features an inviting reading nook. The Hayworth Suite adjoins the Casablanca Room (the Hayworth Suite may be rented on its own, but the Casablanca Room must be rented in conjunction with the Hayworth Suite), which is my favorite room in the hotel. The small room is filled with Oriental rugs, tapestries, and pillows, but the best part is the built-in Turkish-style, curtained twin bed. It sits a couple of feet above the floor and is surrounded with bookshelves. The reading lamp invites guests to climb into bed, close the curtains, and read themselves to sleep. The other two rooms, the James Dean Room and the Billie Holiday Room, are equally well conceived. Each of the rooms is stocked with biographies of the star for which it is named, and there's a growing film library downstairs in the art deco sitting room. All rooms have private decks, and guests enjoy discounted rates at the adjacent Taos Spa. An extended continental breakfast is included in the rates, and there is a Jacuzzi available for guest use.

Orinda B&B, 461 Val Verde Street (P.O. Box 4451), Taos, NM 87571.

☎ **505/758-8581** or toll free **800/847-1837.** 3 rms, 1 suite.

Rates: $65–$85 double. $10 per additional guest. MC, V.

This B&B has the delightful advantage of being in town as well as in the country: Though only a 10-minute walk from the Plaza, it's tucked beneath huge cottonwood trees and offers views across pastureland of Taos Mountain. Thick adobe walls keep it warm in winter and cool in summer. Innkeepers Cary and George Pratt share their living room, including a TV, sound system, and wood-burning stove, with guests. Works by local artists adorn the walls of the dining room, where a hearty continental breakfast is served daily. Two rooms comprise the Vigil Suite, where a sitting room with a fireplace and refrigerator separates two bedrooms. The Truchas Room, with traditional southwestern decor, has a private entrance, fireplace, and bath. Pets and smoking are not permitted.

Salsa del Salto, P.O. Box 453, El Prado, NM 87529. ☎ **505/776-2422.** 8 rms (all with bath).

Rates: $85–$160 double. Extra person $10. MC, V.

Situated between Taos town and the Taos Ski Valley, Salsa del Salto is the perfect place for those seeking a secluded retreat well within short driving distance of Taos's major tourist attractions. Guest rooms in this New Mexican country lodge are tastefully decorated in pastel shades and a southwestern motif, and beds are covered with cozy down comforters. Each room offers views of the mountains or mesas of Taos, and the private bathrooms are modern and spacious. The Master's Room features a beautiful fireplace with copper detailing as well as a private door to a covered portal; the Lobo Room faces Lobo Peak, one of the largest aspen stands in the Taos area. La Familia, comprised of two connecting rooms, is ideal for— as its name suggests— families. The focus here is on relaxation and outdoor activities. Innkeeper Mary Hockett is a native New Mexican who is extremely knowledgeable about the surrounding area and who enjoys horseback riding, skiing, biking, and tennis. She's happy to share information about her favorite activities with her guests. Mary's partner, Dadou Mayer, was born and raised in Nice, France. An accomplished chef, Dadou was also once a member of the French National Ski Team, and he was recently named "The Fastest Chef in the United States" when he won the Grand Marnier Ski Race. Mayer has authored a cookbook, *Cuisine à Taos,* and has been a supervisor of the Ski School of Taos for over twenty years. Salsa del Salto is the only bed and breakfast in Taos that has a pool and hot tub as well as private tennis courts, and it's the only place in Taos where you'll be treated to a full gourmet breakfast whipped up by a true French chef. Mary bakes the muffins and breads, while Dadou serves up specialties like green chile and brie omelettes served with corn muffins—all of which you can savor each morning in front of the massive fireplace. If you're at Salsa del Salto during the winter, you'll get the added bonus of an early morning briefing about ski conditions as you enjoy your breakfast. In short, you'll want for nothing here.

Taos Hacienda Inn, 102 LaLoma Plaza (Box 4159), Taos, NM 87571. ☎ **505/758-1717** or toll free **800/530-3040.** 7 rms (all with bath). TV TEL

Rates: $95–$125 standard double; $145–$185 artist's studio; $135–$300 suite. Discounts available. AE, MC, V.

As you drive into the parking area, you'll see the Taos Hacienda Inn perched atop a small hill. Upon entering the reception area, you'll be immediately relaxed by the abundance of green plants and the slow, gurgling fountain. Local art (all for sale) is displayed, for sale, in all public spaces of this comfortable, spacious adobe home (some of which was built in the 1800s).

Each room is differently decorated, though all have the same amenities, such as bathrobes, fireplaces, fresh flowers, and queen- or king-size beds. Some rooms have patios, and there are a couple of suites and artists' studios with kitchenettes. Cary's

Studio, named for Cary Moore, who was a longtime resident of the home, has a full kitchenette and sleeps up to six. The Happy Trails Room, which is distinctly different from the rest of the rooms in the house, has wonderful pine paneling, a brass bed, and chaps and spurs hanging decoratively. A couple of the rooms have incredible views of Taos Mountain. All the furniture in the rooms is handcrafted.

In the morning, a breakfast of fresh fruit, different kinds of juice, fresh breads, muffins, croissants, and a daily special hot item, perhaps a breakfast burrito with Jerry's special green chile, is served. In the early evening, you'll find southwestern hors d'oeuvres or homemade cookies and coffee waiting for you to snack on while you're planning your evening.

4 Dining

In the listings below, an **expensive** restaurant is one with most main courses for $15 or higher; **moderate** has main courses for $10 to $15; **inexpensive,** $6 to $10; and **budget,** most main courses cost less than $6.

EXPENSIVE

Doc Martin's, Taos Inn, 125 Paseo del Pueblo Norte. ☎ **758-1977.**
Cuisine: CONTEMPORARY SOUTHWESTERN. **Reservations:** Recommended.
Prices: Breakfast $3.95–$7; lunch $4.50–$8.50; dinner, appetizers $4–$8.25, main courses $14.50–$18.50. AE, CB, DC, MC, V.
Open: Daily 7:30am–2:30pm and 5:30–10pm.

This portion of the Taos Inn comprises Dr. Paul Martin's former home, office, and delivery room. In 1912, painters Bert Phillips (Doc's brother-in-law) and Ernest Blumenschein hatched the concept of the Taos Society of Artists in the Martin dining room. Art still predominates here, from paintings to cuisine. The food here is widely acclaimed, and the wine list has received numerous "Awards of Excellence" from the *Wine Spectator* magazine.

Breakfast may include the local favorites—huevos rancheros, fried eggs on a blue-corn tortilla smothered with chile and jack cheese, or "The Kit Carson," eggs Benedict with a southwestern flair. Light fare for lunch includes a Pacific ahi tuna sandwich and Caesar salad. For the heartier appetite, the northern New Mexican casserole (layers of blue-corn tortillas, pumpkin-seed mole, calabacitas, and cheddar) or Doc's chile rellenos (fresh roasted green chiles stuffed with caramelized onions, herbs, and jack cheese) will do the trick. For dinner, start with the salmon gordita (salmon cake made with fresh salmon and served with a house mustard sauce), or the goat cheese and potato terrine. Follow it with the homemade onion ravioli stuffed with onion compote and served with calabacitas in a roast garlic sauce, or the Southwest lacquered duck (poached, roasted, and grilled duck breast served over julienne duck-leg meat and red chile broth with posole and mango relish). If you've still got room after all this, you can finish your meal with your choice of exquisite desserts.

Lambert's of Taos, 309 Paseo del Pueblo Sur. ☎ **758-1009.**
Cuisine: CONTEMPORARY AMERICAN. **Reservations:** Recommended.
Prices: Main courses $10.50–$18.50. AE, DC, MC, V.
Open: Lunch Mon–Fri 11:30am–2:30pm; dinner daily 6–9pm.

Zeke Lambert, a former San Francisco restaurateur who was head chef at Doc Martin's for four years, opened this fine dining establishment in late 1989 in the historic Randall

Home near Los Pandos Road. Now, in simple but elegant surroundings, he presents a new and different menu every night.

Diners can start with the likes of homemade duck pâté with roasted garlic, a spinach-and-basil salad with sautéed mushrooms, or grilled swordfish niçoise. Main courses always include fresh seafood, such as tuna with yams and garlic butter, or Dungeness crab cakes with dipping sauce and pickled vegetables. Other more-or-less typical main dishes could be pepper-crusted lamb with red wine demiglace and garlic pasta, chicken stewed in green chile and served with black beans, or cassoulet with duck confit and lamb sausage. To accommodate different appetites, all main dishes are offered in two sizes. Desserts, like the chocolate oblivion truffle torte and sour-cream cognac cake, are outstanding. Espresso coffees, beers, and wines are poured.

 Stakeout Grill & Bar, Stakeout Dr. (just off N.M. 68). ☎ **505/758-2042.**
Cuisine: INTERNATIONAL. **Reservations:** Highly recommended.
Prices: Appetizers $4.95–$10.95; main courses $13.95–$26.95. AE, CB, DC, DISC, EURO, MC, V.
Open: Dinner daily 5am–10pm. Brunch Sun 10am–2pm.

I love this restaurant. Maybe it's because you have to drive about a mile up a dirt road towards the base of the Sangre de Cristo Mountains—you'll think I'm insane for sending you up Stakeout Drive in the black of night, and you'll think you're never going to get there—but once you get there you've got one of the greatest views of Taos. Or, maybe it's because after you're inside, you're enveloped in the warmth of its rustic decor (which is a great contrast to the close-to-white exterior), the paneled walls, creaking hardwood floors, and the crackling fireplace in the winter. Or, maybe it's the food: You can start with baked brie with sliced almonds and apples or escargots with walnuts and garlic. Then move on to a wonderful filet mignon wrapped in bacon and cooked to your liking, or—my favorite (and the chef's)—the honey almond duck, which is never fatty and always leaves you feeling a little sticky but *very* satisfied. Finish your meal off with some fresh pastry and a cappuccino. You'll really be missing something if you don't get here while you're in Taos.

 Villa Fontana, Highway 522, 5 miles north of Taos. ☎ **758-5800.**
Cuisine: ITALIAN. **Reservations:** Recommended.
Prices: Appetizers $4–$11.50; main courses $15.25–$24. AE, DC, MC, V.
Open: Mon–Sat 5:30pm–closing.

Carlo and Siobhan Gislimberti like to talk about "peccato di gola"—lust of the palate. The couple brought it with them to Taos when they left their home in the Italian Dolomites, near the Austrian border. They have their own herb garden, and Carlo, a master chef, is a member of the New Mexico Mycological Society, so wild mushrooms are a major element in many of his kitchen preparations.

Meals are truly gourmet. Diners can start with scampi alla veneziana (shrimp in a brandy Aurora sauce) or pâté ricco de fegatini alla moda (homemade chicken liver pâté). Main courses include socliola di Dover alle erbe aromatiche (whole Dover sole with fresh herbs) and filetto di bue al cognac papato alla Verdi (beef tenderloin sautéed with brandy, green peppercorns, cream, and demiglaze). Dinners are served with salad, fresh vegetables, and potatoes or rice.

0   500 m
    550 y

N

Taos

Santa Fe

NEW MEXICO

The Apple Tree **6**
Bent Street Deli & Cafe **5**
Cafe Tazza **9**
Doc Martin's, Taos Inn **8**
Dori and Tony's
  Cafe **1**
Lambert's of Taos **11**

Mainstreet Bakery
  & Cafe **3**
Michael's Kitchen **2**
Ogelvie's Bar & Grill **7**
Roberto's Restaurant **10**
Stakeout Grill & Bar **9**
Tapas de Taos Cafe **4**

MODERATE

The Apple Tree, 123 Bent St. ☎ **758-1900.**

    Cuisine: INTERNATIONAL. **Reservations:** Recommended.
    Prices: Appetizers $2.50–$6.95; main courses $10.95–$18.95. AE, CB, DC, DISC, MC, V.
    Open: Lunch Mon–Fri 11:30am–3pm; brunch Sun 10am–3pm; dinner daily 5:30–9pm.

Classical and baroque music pervades the four elegant adobe rooms of this fine restaurant, locaated a block north of the Plaza. Original paintings by Taos masters overlook the candlelit, white-linen service indoors; outside, diners sit at wooden tables on a graveled courtyard beneath spreading apple trees.

    Daily specials supplement a standing menu with an international flavor. A very popular item is velarde carnitas enchiladas (pork layered between blue-corn tortillas with apple chutney, sour cream, and white cheddar). There's a limited children's menu and the chef will modify dishes to suit special dietary needs whenever possible. Homemade desserts, cappuccinos, and fine wines and beer are offered. Classical guitar, harp, and/or flute music is presented live nightly in the summer.

$ Bent Street Deli & Cafe, 120 Bent St. ☎ **758-5787.**

    Cuisine: DELI.
    Prices: Breakfast $2–$6.50; lunch $2.75–$7; dinner $10–$13. MC, V.
    Open: Mon–Sat 8am–9pm.

This popular cafe is a short block north of the Plaza. Outside, a flower box surrounds sidewalk cafe-style seating beneath large blue-and-white umbrellas. Inside, baskets and jars of homemade jam lend a homey, country feel. The menu features breakfast burritos and homemade granola for the morning hours; 18 deli sandwiches, plus a "create-your-own" column, for lunch; and various quiche, pasta, chicken, and fish dishes for dinner.

Casa de Valdez, Paseo del Pueblo Sur. ☎ **505/758-8777.**

    Cuisine: NEW MEXICAN. **Reservations:** Suggested. **Directions:** Drive south of the plaza for about 2^1/$_2$ miles.
    Prices: Appetizers, dinner, $5.95–$6.50; main courses $7.95–$18.95. AE, DISC, MC, V.
    Open: Mon, Tues, Thurs–Sat 11:30am–9:30pm, Sun 4–9:30pm.

You can't really miss Casa de Valdez—it's the only A-frame building in the area. The interior looks more like a mountain home than a New Mexican restaurant because of the wood paneling, which makes it a cozy environment for a quiet dinner for two. The staff is extremely friendly, and they know many of their customers by name. The menu is predictable in terms of New Mexican cuisine, with blue-corn enchiladas, bean burritos, and tamales. You can also get spare ribs and barbecued chicken. Personally, I think the sopaipillas served at Casa de Valdez are the best around—they practically melt in your mouth.

Ogelvie's Bar & Grill, 1031 E. Plaza. ☎ **758-8866.**

    Cuisine: INTERNATIONAL. **Reservations:** Recommended.
    Prices: Appetizers $2.95–$7.50; lunch $5.50–$9.50; dinner $8.50–$19.50. AE, MC, V.
    Open: Daily 10am–4pm and 5–10pm; from 11am in winter.

Like Ogelvie's in Albuquerque and Santa Fe, this is a casual restaurant with rich wood decor. Homemade soups, burgers and other sandwiches, and huevos (eggs) de casa

Ogelvie's are hits on the lunch menu. Dinner might include shrimp Hawaiian; fresh trout piñon; steaks; regional specialties like fajitas, burritos, and enchiladas; and a few pasta dishes. A lively bar with an outdoor deck overlooks the Plaza.

INEXPENSIVE

⭐ 💲 **Michael's Kitchen,** 305 Paseo del Pueblo Norte. ☎ **758-4178.**
Cuisine: NEW MEXICAN & AMERICAN.
Prices: Breakfast $2.85–$8.45; lunch $2.65–$8.25; dinner $5.25–$10.75. MC, V.
Open: Daily 7am–8:30pm.

A couple of blocks north of the Plaza is this eatery, a throwback to earlier days. Between its hardwood floor and *viga* ceiling are various knickknacks on posts, walls, and windows: a deer head here, a Tiffany lamp there, several scattered antique wood stoves. Seating is at booths and tables. Meals, too, are old-fashioned, as far as quality and quantity for price. Breakfasts, including a great variety of pancakes and egg dishes, are served all day, as are luncheon sandwiches. Dinners range from veal Cordon Bleu to knockwurst-and-sauerkraut, plantation fried chicken to enchiladas rancheros, fish-and-chips to New York steak. There's also a children's menu.

Roberto's Restaurant, 122 Kit Carson Rd. ☎ **758-2434.**
Cuisine: NEW MEXICAN. **Reservations:** Recommended.
Prices: Dinner, appetizers $2.85–$5; main courses $6.50–$11.95. MC, V.
Open: Summer Wed–Mon noon–2:30pm and 6–9pm; most weekends in winter.
Closed: Tues year-round.

Hidden within a warren of art galleries opposite the Kit Carson Museum is this local gem, which for 25 years has focused on authentic native dishes. Within this 160-year-old adobe are three small, high-ceilinged dining rooms, each with hardwood floors, a maximum of five tables, and a corner fireplace in one of them. Everyday dishes include tacos, enchiladas, tamales, and chile rellenos. All meals start with sopaipillas and are accompanied by homemade refried beans with *chicos* (dried kernels of corn). Beer and wine only are served. Please note that Roberto is an avid skier, and as a result, winter hours are unpredictable at best.

Tapas de Taos Cafe, 136 Bent St. ☎ **758-9670.**
Cuisine: NEW MEXICAN/TAPAS. **Reservations:** Not accepted.
Prices: Main courses $2.95–$9.95; tapas $3.75–$7.50. V.
Open: Breakast Mon–Fri 8:30–11am; lunch Mon–Fri 11:30am–3pm; brunch Sat–Sun 10:30am–3pm; dinner Mon–Sat 5:30–9:30pm, Sun 5:30–9pm.

If you're familiar with Mexican culture, you'll recognize the theme decor at Tapas de Taos Cafe. It is representational of the Mexican Day of the Dead (*Día de los Muertos*), a Mexican day of celebration. The rows of black skulls that line the walls of the dining room in this 300-year-old adobe may not be everyone's idea of pleasant decor, but they certainly are unique. Breakfast items here include the traditional huevos rancheros and breakfast burritos, but you can also get hotcakes with maple syrup if you're in the mood for something sweet. Bolillos, pan dulce, empanadas, cookies, and pastries are baked fresh daily. The tapas menu is short but excellent, and includes items such as spicy Vietnamese fried calamari, pork and ginger pot stickers, and a shrimp and vermicelli fritter. Other menu offerings include chile rellenos, fajitas, enchiladas, tacos, and chimichangas. You can get a variety of coffees, including café macchiata, cappuccino, café latte, and espresso. Outdoor patio dining is available during the warmer months. There is a kids' menu.

BUDGET

Caffe Tazza, 122 Kit Carson Rd. ☎ **758-8706.**

> **Cuisine:** CAFE.
> **Prices:** All items under $10. No credit cards.
> **Open:** Mon–Thurs 7:30am–6pm; Fri–Sun 7:30am–10pm.

This cozy three-room cafe is a gathering spot for local community groups, artists, performers, and poets (in fact, it is home to the Society of the Muse of the Southwest, SOMOS). Once a week, plays, films, comedy, and musical performances take place in the cafe's main room. The walls are constantly hung with the works of local emerging artists who have not yet made it to the Taos gallery scene. Locals and tourists alike enjoy sitting in the cafe, taking in the scene while sipping a cappuccino or espresso. The food is quite good as well. Soups, sandwiches, tamales, croissants, and pastries are all popular.

Dori & Tony's Cafe, 402 Paseo del Pueblo Norte. ☎ **758-9222.**

> **Cuisine:** AMERICAN/ITALIAN.
> **Prices:** Breakfast $3.45–$6; lunch $2.50–$6.75; dinner $4.25–$7. No credit cards.
> **Open:** Mon–Sat 7am–10pm; Sun brunch 8am–1pm; dinner daily 5–9pm.

This delightful find, next door to the Taos Post Office, is a gathering place for the Taos literary and artistic crowd. In fact, if you read John Nichols's *Nirvana Blues,* you'll recognize the Prince Whales Cafe as Dori & Tony's. Twenty-two years ago when Dori's opened, bagels were a mainstay on the menu, but they turned out to be a hard sell in the beginning. No one in Taos had ever heard of a bagel before. Now, it's a different story. Dori's regulars come here so regularly that they keep their own personal coffee mugs hanging above the kitchen doorway. The cafe also hosts changing art exhibits and musical performances by local artists. Breakfast burritos are popular in the mornings, as are bagels, eggs, pancakes, and granola. In the afternoon, the menu offers sandwiches, soups, salads, and pizzas. Now that Dori has taken her son Tony into partnership, the cafe offers quite an extensive Italian dinner menu with favorites such as bruschetta, antipasto, lasagna, fettuccine Alfredo, roasted chicken breast with fresh rosemary, and deep dish pizza. Of course, pastries are homemade daily, and espresso coffees are served all day. Beer and wine are available.

Mainstreet Bakery & Cafe, Guadalupe Plaza, 112 Dona Luz. ☎ **758-9610.**

> **Cuisine:** VEGETARIAN/NATURAL FOOD.
> **Prices:** $4.95–$12.95. No credit cards.
> **Open:** Mon–Fri 7:30am–11:30am, Sat–Sun 8am–2pm; bakery open until 3pm.

About a block and a half west of the Plaza, this has become possibly Taos's biggest counterculture hangout. The image is fostered by the health-conscious cuisine and the wide selection of newspapers, magazines, and other reading material advocating alternative lifestyles. Coffee and pastries are served all day; vegetarian breakfasts and (on weekends) lunches are very popular.

Wild & Natural Cafe, 812 Paseo del Pueblo Norte. ☎ **751-0480.**

> **Cuisine:** ORGANIC/VEGETARIAN.
> **Prices:** All items under $10. DISC, MC, V.
> **Open:** Mon–Sat 11am–9pm.

When traveling it's often difficult to find a place to eat if you're a vegetarian, but in Taos the choice is easy. In fact, the Wild & Natural Cafe was voted "Natural Food

Restaurant of the Year" by New Mexico Naturally in 1994. Lunches feature soups, salads, sandwiches, veggie burgers, steamed vegetables, southwestern dishes, and lowfat daily specials. At dinner you might try the Thai green curry, East Indian dal, lemon ginger squash, or a vegetable burrito. There's an espresso bar, as well as organic wine, fresh vegetable juice, local beer, fruit smoothies, and dairy-free desserts. Takeout orders are available.

5   Attractions

Suggested Itineraries

If You Have 1 Day

Spend at least two hours at the Taos Pueblo. You'll also have time to see the Millicent Rogers Museum and to browse in some of the town's fine art galleries. Try, too, to make it to Ranchos de Taos to see the San Francisco de Asis Church.

If You Have 2 Days

Explore the Kit Carson Historic Museums—the Martinez Hacienda, the Kit Carson Home, and the Ernest L. Blumenschein Home. And get out of town for the view from the Rio Grande Gorge Bridge.

If You Have 3 Days or More

Drive the "Enchanted Circle" through Red River, Eagle Nest, and Angel Fire. You may want to leave a full day for shopping, or perhaps drive up to the Taos Ski Valley for a look-see. Of course, if you're here in the winter with skis, that's your first priority.

The Top Attractions

 Taos Pueblo, P.O. Box 1846, Taos Pueblo, NM 87571. ☎ **758-9593.**

No other site in Taos is as important or as famous. The community of 1,500, 2¹/₂ miles north of the Plaza, forms a world of its own. The northernmost of New Mexico's 19 pueblos, it has been the home of the Tiwa people for more than 900 years.

Two massive, multistoried adobe apartment buildings appear much the same today as when a regiment from Coronado's expedition first saw them in 1540. Houses are built one upon another to form porches, balconies, and roofs reached by ancient ladders. The distinctive, flowing lines of shaped mud, with a straw-and-mud exterior plaster, are typical of pueblo architecture throughout the Southwest. The buildings blend in with the land around them, as the houses are made of the earth itself. Bright blue painted doors repeat the clear blue of the sky that frames the brown buildings. Between the complexes trickles a fast-flowing creek, the Rio Pueblo de Taos. A footbridge joins the two shores. To the northeast looms Taos Mountain, its long fir-covered slopes forming a timeless backdrop to the old pueblo.

Though the Tiwa were essentially a peaceful agrarian people, they are better remembered as having spearheaded the only successful revolt by Native Americans in U.S. history. Launched by Pope (po-*pay*) in 1680, the uprising drove the Spanish from Santa Fe until 1692, and from Taos until 1698.

Native American culture and religion have persisted since. Taos is one of the most conservative of all North American Indian communities; existing much as it did since before Columbus's arrival in America, the town still eschews such modern conveniences as electricity and plumbing. Arts and crafts and other tourism-related businesses support the economy, along with government services, ranching, and farming.

As you explore the pueblo and absorb insights into its people's lifestyle, you can visit those studios, munch on homemade oven bread, look into the new **San Geronimo Chapel,** and wander past the fascinating ruins of the old church and cemetery. You're expected to ask permission from individuals before taking their photos; some ask a small payment, but that's for you to negotiate. Photographing *kivas* and other ceremonial underground areas is taboo.

San Geronimo is the patron saint of the Taos Pueblo, and his feast day on September 30 combines Catholic and pre-Hispanic traditions. The **San Geronimo Day Trade Fair** is a joyous occasion, with foot races, pole climbs, and crafts booths. Dances are performed the evening of September 29. Other annual events include a turtle dance on New Year's Day, deer or buffalo dances on Three Kings Day (January 6), and corn dances for Santa Cruz Day (May 3), San Antonio Day (June 13), San Juan Day (June 24), Santiago Day (July 23), and Santa Ana Day (July 24). The **Taos Pueblo Pow Wow,** a dance competition and parade drawing tribes from throughout North America, is held the weekend after July 4 on reservation land off N.M. 522. Christmas Eve bonfires mark the start of the children's corn dance, the Christmas Day deer dance, or the three-day-long Matachines dance.

Admission: $5 per vehicle or $1 per person. Still camera $5, video camera $10, sketching or painting $25. No photography permitted on feast days.

Open: Daily summer 8am–5pm; winter 9am–4:30pm.

Note: Taos Pueblo will be closed to the public for a month in late winter or early spring. Before making travel plans you should call in advance to make sure it will be open when you get there.

 Millicent Rogers Museum, off N.M. 522, 4 miles north of Taos. ☎ **758-2462.**

Taos's most interesting collection is this museum, founded in 1953 by family members after the death of Millicent Rogers. Rogers was a wealthy Taos émigré who, beginning in 1947, compiled a magnificent array of aesthetically beautiful Native American arts and crafts. Included are Navajo and Pueblo jewelry, Navajo textiles, Pueblo pottery, Hopi and Zuni *kachina* dolls, paintings from the Rio Grande Pueblo people, and basketry from a wide variety of southwestern tribes. The collection continues to grow through gifts and museum acquisitions.

Since the 1970s the scope of the museum's permanent collection has been expanded to include Hispanic religious and secular arts and crafts, from Spanish and Mexican colonial to contemporary times. Included are *santos* (religious images), furniture, weavings, *colcha* embroideries, and decorative tinwork. Agricultural implements, domestic utensils, and craftspeoples' tools dating from the 17th and 18th centuries are also displayed.

The museum gift shop has some superior regional art. Temporary exhibits, classes and workshops, lectures, and field trips are scheduled throughout the year.

Admission: Adults $4, children (6–16) $2, seniors $3, families $8.

Open: Daily 9am–5pm. **Closed:** Easter Day, San Geronimo Day (Sept 30), Thanksgiving Day, Christmas, New Year's Day.

Taos Ski Valley Rd.

150

522

64

Taos Municipal Airport

Paseo del Pueblo Norte

64

3

1

2

4

Theodora

Valverde Lund

Hinde

Garcia

Brooks

Kit Carson Park

5

6

Saavedra

Camino de La Placita

Armory

Martyrs

Bent

7

Morada

8

Don Fernando

La Lomita

San Antonio

La Loma

Manzanares

Padre

Quesnel

Las Cruces

11

10

9

Siler

Ranchitos

240

Salazar

Los Pandos

Kit Carson

64

Fred Baca Park

Sipapu

Tewa

Albright

12

Rio Fernando

Frontier

Cervantes

Gusdorf

Rio Pueblo

68

Cruz Alta

Lower Ranchitos

Santiago

Rio Grande del Rancho

240

Paseo del Pueblo Sur

Este Es

3

13

Ernest L. Blumenschein Home & Museum 10	Kit Carson Park and Cemetery 6	Taos Pueblo 3
The Fechin Institute 5	Martinez Hacienda 12	Taos Institute of Arts 9
Governor Bent House Museum 7	Millicent Rogers Museum 2	Van Vechten Lineberry Taos Art Museum 4
Harwood Foundation Museum 11	Rio Grande Gorge Bridge 1	
Kit Carson Home and Museum of the West 8	San Francisco de Asis Church 13	

Kit Carson Historic Museums, Drawer P.O. CCC, Taos, NM 87571. ☎ **758-0505.**
This foundation operates three historical homes as museums, affording glimpses of early Taos lifestyles. The Martinez Hacienda, Kit Carson Home, and the Ernest Blumenschein Home each has its individual appeal.

Martinez Hacienda, Lower Ranchitos Road, Highway 240 (☎ **758-1000**), is one of the only Spanish colonial haciendas in the United States that is open to the public year-round. This was the home of merchant and trader Don Antonio Severino Martinez, who bought it in 1804 and lived there until his death in 1827. Located on the west bank of the Rio Pueblo de Taos about two miles southwest of the Plaza, the hacienda was built like a fortress, with thick adobe walls and no exterior windows to protect against raids by Plains tribes.

Twenty-one rooms were built around two placitas, or interior courtyards. Most of the rooms open today contain period furnishings: They include the bedrooms, servants' quarters, stables, a kitchen, and even a large fiesta room. Exhibits in one newly renovated room tell the story of the Martinez family and life in Spanish Taos between 1598 and 1821, when Mexico assumed control.

Don Antonio Martinez, who for a time was *alcalde* (mayor) of Taos, owned several caravans that he used in trade on the Chihuahua Trail to Mexico. This business was carried on by his youngest son, Don Juan Pascual, who later owned the hacienda. His eldest son was Padre Antonio Jose Martinez, northern New Mexico's controversial spiritual leader from 1826 to 1867.

Kit Carson Historic Museums has developed the hacienda into a living museum with weavers, blacksmiths, and wood carvers. Demonstrations are scheduled daily, including during the Old Taos Trade Fair the last weekend in September, when they run virtually nonstop. The Trade Fair recalls days when Natives, Spanish settlers, and mountain men met here to trade. Hours are daily from 9am to 5pm.

Kit Carson Home and Museum of the West, East Kit Carson Road (☎ **758-4741**), located a short block east on the Plaza intersection, is the town's only general museum of Taos history. The 12-room adobe home with walls $2^1/2$ feet thick was built in 1825 and purchased in 1843 by Carson, the famous mountain man, Indian agent, and scout, as a wedding gift for his young bride, Josefa Jaramillo. It remained their home for 25 years, until both died (a month to the day apart) in 1868.

The living room, bedroom, and kitchen are furnished as they might have been when occupied by the Carsons. The Indian Room contains artifacts crafted and used by the original inhabitants of Taos Valley; the Early American Room has an array of pioneer items, including a large number of antique firearms and trappers' implements; the Carson Interpretive Room showcases memorabilia from Carson's unusual life. In the kitchen is a Spanish plaque that reads: *Nadie sabe lo que tiene la olla más que la cuchara que la menea* (Nobody better knows what the pot holds than the spoon that stirs it).

The museum bookshop, with perhaps the town's most comprehensive inventory of New Mexico historical books, is adjacent to the entry. Hours are daily from 8am to 6pm in summer, 9am to 5pm in winter.

Ernest L. Blumenschein Home & Museum, 222 Ledoux St. (☎ **758-0330**), a block and a half southwest of the Plaza, recalls and re-creates the lifestyle of one of the founders (in 1915) of the Taos Society of Artists. An adobe home with garden walls and a courtyard, parts of which date to the 1790s, it was the home and studio of Blumenschein (1874–1960) and his family beginning in 1919. Period furnishings include European antiques and handmade Taos furniture in Spanish colonial style. Blumenschein was born and raised in Pittsburgh. His arrival in Taos in 1898 came somewhat by accident. After training in New York and Paris, he and fellow painter Bert Phillips were on assignment for *Harper's* and *McClure's* magazines of New York when a wheel of their wagon broke during a mountain traverse 30 miles north of Taos. Blumenschein drew the short straw and carried the wheel by horseback to Taos for repair. He later recounted his initial reaction to the valley he entered: "No artist had ever recorded the New Mexico I was now seeing. No writer had ever written down the smell of this air or the feel of that morning sky. I was receiving . . . the first great unforgettable inspiration of my life. My destiny was being decided."

That spark later led to the foundation of Taos as an art colony. An extensive collection of work by early 20th-century Taos masters is on display in several rooms of the home. Among the modern works are paintings by Blumenschein's daughter, Helen. Hours are daily from 9am to 5pm.

Admission: Three museums, $8 adults, $6 seniors, $5 children (6–16), family rate $15. Two museums, $6 adults, $5 seniors, $4 children, family rate $13. One museum, $4 adults, $3 seniors, $2.50 children, family rate $6.

Open: Summer hours, Kit Carson Home daily 8am–6pm; Martinez Hacienda daily 9am–5pm; Blumenschein Home daily 9am–5pm. In winter all museums are open daily 9am–5pm.

Van Vechten Lineberry Taos Art Museum, 501 N. Pueblo Rd. ☎ 758-2690.

As this book goes to press, Taos's newest museum, the Van Vechten Lineberry Taos Art Museum, is opening its doors. The museum is the brainchild of Ed Lineberry, who lives in the spectacular home adjacent to the museum, and who conceived of the museum as a memorial to his late wife, Duane Van Vechten. An artist in her own right, Duane spent a great deal of time working in her studio, which now serves as the entryway to the 20,000-square-foot main gallery of the museum. The entryway features, among other things, John Dunn's roulette wheel. Lineberry spent time traveling throughout Europe studying the preservation and storage techniques, as well as the display space, climate control, and lighting of fine museums; as a result, the Van Vechten Lineberry Taos Art Museum is state-of-the-art. The museum is slated to display the works of Duane Van Vechten, as well as the art of the 11 original Taos artists. Each artist will be represented by at least one piece. While the initial number of works will be between 130 and 150, Mr. Lineberry hopes to acquire more work in the next few years. In addition to the main gallery space, there are smaller spaces available for traveling exhibitions, and there is a wonderful library that will be open to researchers only, by appointment.

Admission: $5 adults, $3 children.

Open: Call ahead for open hours and days.

More Attractions

San Francisco de Asis Church, Ranchos de Taos. ☎ 758-2754.

From the side of N.M. 68, four miles south of Taos, this famous church appears as a modernesque adobe sculpture with no doors or windows. It's often photographed (as by Ansel Adams) and painted (by the likes of Georgia O'Keeffe) from this angle. Visitors must walk through the garden on the west side of this remarkable two-story church to enter and gain a full perspective on its massive walls, authentic adobe plaster, and beauty.

Displayed on the wall of an adjacent building is an unusual painting, *The Shadow of the Cross* by Henri Ault (1896). In ordinary light, it portrays a barefoot Christ at the Sea of Galilee; in darkness, however, the portrait becomes luminescent and the shadow of a cross forms over the left shoulder of Jesus' silhouette. The artist reportedly was as shocked as everyone else. The reason for the illusion remains a mystery.

The church office and gift shop are just across the driveway to the north of the church. A slide show is also presented here. Several crafts shops surround the square.

Admission: Donations appreciated.

Open: Daily. Visitors may attend mass at 5:30pm Sat and 7am (Spanish), 9am, and 11:30am Sun.

Harwood Foundation Museum of the University of New Mexico,
238 Ledoux St. ☎ **758-9826.**

Some of the finest works of art ever produced in or about Taos hang on the walls of this pueblo-style library-and-museum complex, a cultural and community center since 1923.

The museum shows paintings, drawings, prints, sculpture, and photographs by the artists of the Taos area from 1800 to the present. Featured are paintings from the early days of the art colony by members of the Taos Society of Artists, including Oscar Berninghaus, Ernest Blumenschein, Herbert Dunton, Victor Higgins, Bert Phillips, and Walter Ufer. In addition, there are works by Emil Bisttram, Andrew Dasburg, Leon Gaspard, Louis Ribak, Bea Mandelman, Agnes Martin, Larry Bell, and Thomas Benrimo.

Also on display are 19th-century *retablos,* religious paintings of saints that have traditionally been used for decoration and inspiration in the homes and churches of New Mexico. The permanent collection of art shows sculptures by Patrocinio Barela, one of the leading Hispanic artists of 20th-century New Mexico.

The museum also has five or six changing exhibitions each year, many of which feature the best artists currently working in Taos.

Admission: $2.

Open: Mon–Fri 10am–5pm, Sat 10am–4pm.

Governor Bent House Museum, 117 Bent St. ☎ 758-2376.

A short block north of the Plaza, this was the residence of Charles Bent, the New Mexico Territory's first American governor. Bent, a former trader who established Fort Bent, Colorado, was murdered in the 1847 Indian and Hispanic rebellion as his wife and children escaped by digging through an adobe wall into the house next door. The hole is still visible. Period art and artifacts are displayed.

Admission: Adults $1, children 50¢.

Open: Daily, summer 9:30am–5pm, winter 10am–4pm.

★ The Fechin Institute, 227 Paseo del Pueblo Norte (P.O. Box 832), Taos, NM 87571. ☎ 758-1710.

The home of Russian artist Nicolai Fechin (feh-*sheen*) from 1927 to 1933, this historic house memorializes the career of a 20th-century Renaissance man. Born in Russia in 1881, Fechin came to the United States in 1923, already acclaimed as a master of painting, drawing, sculpture, architecture, and woodwork. In Taos, he built a huge adobe home and embellished it with hand-carved doors, windows, gates, posts, fireplaces, and other features of a Russian country home. The house and adjacent studio are now used for Fechin Institute educational activities, as well as concerts, lectures, and other programs.

Admission: $3.
Open: May–Oct Wed–Sun 1–5pm, other times by appointment.

Kit Carson Park and Cemetery, Paseo del Pueblo Norte.

Major community events are held in the park in summer. The cemetery, established in 1847, contains the graves of Carson and his wife, Gov. Charles Bent, the Don Antonio Martinez family, Mabel Dodge Luhan, and many other noted historical figures and artists. Plaques describe their contributions.

⭐ **Rio Grande Gorge Bridge,** U.S. Hwy. 64, 10 miles west of Taos.

This impressive bridge, west of the Taos Airport, spans the Southwest's greatest river. At 650 feet above the canyon floor, it's one of America's highest bridges. If you can withstand the vertigo, it's interesting to come more than once, at different times of day, to observe how the changing light plays tricks with the colors of the cliff walls.

D. H. Lawrence Ranch, San Cristobal. ☎ **776-2245.**

The shrine of the controversial early 20th-century author is a pilgrimage site for literary devotees. A short uphill walk from the ranch home, it is littered with various mementos—photos, coins, messages from fortune cookies—placed by visitors. The guestbook is worth a long read.

Lawrence lived in Taos off and on between 1922 and 1925. The ranch was a gift to his wife, Frieda, from art patron Mabel Dodge Luhan. Lawrence repaid Luhan the favor by giving her the manuscript of *Sons and Lovers.* Lawrence died in southern France in 1930 of tuberculosis; his ashes were returned here for burial. The grave of Frieda, who died in 1956, is outside the shrine.

The shrine is the only public building at the ranch, operated today by the University of New Mexico as an educational and recreational retreat. To reach the site, head north from Taos 15 miles on N.M. 522, then another 6 miles east into the forested Sangre de Cristo range via a well-marked dirt road.

Taos Institute of Arts, P.O. Box 2429, Taos, NM 87571. ☎ **505/758-2793.**

Perhaps you're visiting Taos because it is so well-known as an art community, but galleries and studio visits just aren't enough to satisfy your urge to create. Well, if you're interested in pursuing an artistic adventure of your own while visiting Taos, you should definitely investigate the weeklong classes in sculpture, painting, jewelry making, photography, clay working, textiles, and quite a few other media. Class sizes are limited, so if you're thinking about giving these workshops a try, you should call for information and prices well in advance. The fees vary from class to class and usually don't include the price of materials; they remain, however, quite reasonable.

Organized Tours

Pride of Taos Tours, P.O. Box 1192, Taos, NM 87571 (☎ **758-8340**). Damaso and Helen Martinez's young company offers several packages, including a historical tour that lasts one hour and takes tourists to the Plaza, Martinez Hacienda, and Ranchos de Taos Church.

6 Sports & Recreation

Skiing

There are numerous popular cross-country skiing trails in Carson National Forest, including some so marked en route to Taos Ski Valley. One of the more popular is

Amole Canyon, off N.M. 518 near Sipapu Ski Area, where the Taos Nordic Ski Club maintains set tracks and signs along a 3-mile loop. It's closed to snowmobiles, a comfort to lovers of serenity.

Just east of Red River, with 18 miles of groomed trails in 600 acres of forest land atop Bobcat Pass, is the ⭐ **Enchanted Forest Cross Country Ski Area** (☎ **505/754-2374**). Full-day trail passes, good from 9am to 4:30pm, are $8 for adults, much less for children. Equipment rentals and lessons can be arranged at **Millers Crossing** ski shop on Main Street in Red River (☎ **754-2374**). Qualified nordic skiers can get further instruction in skating, mountaineering, and telemarking.

The **Southwest Nordic Center,** P.O. Box 3212, Taos, NM 87571 (☎ **505/758-4761**), offers lessons and tours in various locations around northern New Mexico. The center also owns two private Mongolian yurts north of Chama for overnight skiing or (in summer) mountain-biking excursions.

Taos Mountain Outfitters, 114 South Plaza (☎ **758-8125**), offers cross-country sales, rentals, and guide service.

Five alpine resorts are located within an hour's drive of Taos. All offer complete facilities, including equipment rentals. Although opening and closing dates may vary according to snow conditions, it's safe to say that skiing usually begins Thanksgiving weekend and continues into early April.

Ski vacationers who can't decide which area to patronize should look into the Ski-3 Card, which, for $15, gives skiers $5 off regular all-lift ticket prices any day of the week (including weekends) and savings on ski lessons at any Taos Ski Valley, Red River, and Angel Fire ski areas. You must purchase the card prior to December 24, 1995. The Ski-3 card cannot be used between December 26 and 31, January 14 and 16, February 18 and 20, and March 12 and 18. Write to **Ski-3,** P.O. Box 15425, Santa Fe, NM 87506 for more information.

SKI RESORTS

 Taos Ski Valley, Taos Ski Valley, NM 87525. ☎ **505/776-2291.**

The preeminent ski resort in the southern Rocky Mountains was founded in 1955 by a Swiss-German immigrant, Ernie Blake. According to local legend, Blake searched for two years in a small plane for the perfect location for a ski resort equal to his native Alps. He found it at the abandoned mining site of Twining, high above Taos. Ernie died in 1989, aged 76; but the area is still in the family, under the command of two younger generations of Blakes. The resort has become internationally renowned for its light, dry powder (312 inches annually), its superb ski school, and its personal, friendly manner. Even the esteemed London *Times* called the valley "without any argument the best ski resort in the world. Small, intimate and endlessly challenging, Taos simply has no equal."

Of the 72 trails and bowls, more than half are designated for expert or advanced skiers. But between the 11,800-foot summit and the 9,200-foot base, there are also ample opportunities for novice and intermediate skiers. The area has an uphill capacity of 14,000 skiers per hour on its six double chairs, one triple, two quad, and one surface tow.

With its children's ski school Taos Ski Valley has always been an excellent location for skiing families, but with the addition (in 1994) of an 18,000-square-foot children's center (Kinderkäfig Center) skiing with your children in Taos is an even better experience. Kinderkäfig offers every service imaginable, from equipment rental for children to babysitting services. Call ahead for more information.

Taos Ski Valley has 13 lodges and condominiums with nearly 700 beds. All offer ski-week packages; six of them have restaurants. There are two more restaurants on the mountain in addition to the expansive facilities of Village Center at the base. For reservations, call the **Taos Valley Resort Association** (☎ **505/776-2233** or toll free **800/776-1111**).

Tickets: All lifts, adults $37 full day, $24 half day; children (12 or younger) $22 full day, $16 half day; seniors 65–69, $15 full day; seniors over 70, free. Novice lifts, adults $20, children $15. Full rental packages, $12 adults, $5 children.

Open: Daily, Thanksgiving Day–first week of April 9am–4pm.

Red River Ski Area, P.O. Box 900, Red River, NM 87558. ☎ **505/754-2747** or toll free **800/348-6444** for reservations.

Lodgers in Red River can walk out their doors and be on the slopes. Two other factors make this 32-year-old, family-oriented area special: first, its 27 trails are geared to the intermediate skier, though beginners and experts have their share; and second, good snow is guaranteed early and late in the year by snowmaking equipment that can work on 75% of the runs, more than any other in New Mexico. There's a 1,500-foot vertical drop here to a base elevation of 8,750 feet. Lifts include three double chairs, two triple chairs, and one surface tow, with a skier capacity of 6,720 per hour.

Tickets: All lifts, adults $28 full day, $20 half day; children (12 and under) and seniors (60 and over) $17 full day, $11 half day. Full rental packages, from $12 adults, $9 children.

Open: Daily, Thanksgiving Day–Apr 1 9am–4pm.

Angel Fire Ski Area, P.O. Drawer B, Angel Fire, NM 87710. ☎ **505/377-6401** or toll free **800/633-7463.**

The 30 miles of ski runs here are heavily oriented to beginning and intermediate skiers. Still, with a vertical drop of 2,180 feet to a base elevation of 8,500 feet, advanced skiers are certain to find something they like. The area's lifts—four double and two triple chairs—have an hourly capacity of 1,900 skiers.

Tickets: All day, adults $25, children $17.

Open: Daily, in season 8:30am–4:30pm.

Sipapu Ski Area, P.O. Box 29, Vadito, NM 87579. ☎ **505/587-2240.**

The oldest ski area in the Taos region, Sipapu is 25 miles southeast on N.M. 518 in Tres Rios canyon. It prides itself on being a small local area, especially popular with schoolchildren. There are just one triple chair and two tows, with a vertical drop of 865 feet to the 8,200-foot base elevation. There are 18 trails, half classified as intermediate. A bunkhouse provides some overnight lodging.

Tickets: Adults $23, children under 12 $18.

Open: Daily, in season 9am–4pm.

Ski Rio, P.O. Box 59, Costilla, NM 87525. ☎ **505/758-7707** or toll free **800/2 ASK RIO (800/227-5746).**

Just south of the Colorado border is this rapidly expanding area (which until recently has been rapidly going in and out of business—call ahead!). Half of its 64 named trails are for the intermediate skier, 30% for beginners, and 20% for advanced skiers. Also within Ski Rio are Snowboard and Snow Skate parks, as well as 21 kilometers of cross-country trails. Annual snowfall here is about 250 inches, and there are three chairlifts (two triple, one double), and three tows. At the ski base you may rent skis, snowboards, snowshoes, and snow skates, as well as find lodgings, restaurants, and a sports shop. Sleigh rides, dogsled tours, and snowmobile tours are also available. The ski school offers private and group clinics (for adults and children) in cross-country and downhill skiing, snow skating, and snowboarding.

Tickets: $29 adults (value season $24–$21), $19 juniors (ages 7–12), children 6 and under free with paying adult.

Open: In season, daily 9am–4pm.

More Recreation

BALLOONING   The Taos Mountain Balloon Rally, P.O. Box 3096, Taos, NM 87571 (☎ **758-8321**), is held each year the third weekend of October. A hot-air balloon workshop is held in Taos the weekend before the rally. Recreational trips are offered by **Taos Mountain Magic Balloons** (☎ **776-8746**).

BICYCLING   **Taos Mountain Outfitters,** South Plaza (☎ **758-9292**), offer mountain bikes for rent or sale. Carson National Forest rangers recommend several biking trails in the greater Taos area, including Garcia Park and Rio Chiquito for beginner to intermediate mountain bikers, Gallegos and Picuris peaks for experts. Inquire at the U.S. Forest Service office next to the Chamber of Commerce for an excellent handout. Annual touring events include Red River's **Enchanted Circle Century Bike Tour** (☎ **754-2366**) in mid-September.

FISHING   Fishing season in the high lakes and streams opens April 1and continues through December, though spring and fall are known as the best times for success. Rainbow, cutthroat, brown trout, and kokanee (a freshwater salmon), are commonly stocked and caught. The Rio Grande also has pike and catfish. Many experienced anglers prefer fly fishing, but those who don't recommend using jigs, spinners, or woolly worms as lures, or worms, corn, or salmon eggs as bait. A license is required; they are sold, along with tackle, at several Taos sporting-goods shops. For backcountry guides, try **Deep Creek Wilderness Outfitters & Guides** P.O. Box 721, El Prado (☎ **776-8423**) in Red River, **Los Rios Anglers** (☎ **758-2798**) in Taos.

GOLF   The par-72 18-hole course in **Angel Fire** has been endorsed by the Professional Golfers Association. Surrounded by stands of ponderosa pine, spruce, and aspen, it's one of the highest regulation golf courses in the world at 8,600 feet. It also has a driving range and putting green. Carts and clubs can be rented at the course, and the club pro provides instruction. **The Taos Country Club** (☎ **758-7300**) has opened a driving range and a new golf course. Since the summer of 1993 all 18 holes have been open for play. The club is located just four miles south of the Plaza and is a first-rate championship golf course designed for all levels of play.

HIKING & BACKPACKING   There are many hundreds of miles of hiking trails in Taos County's mountain and high-mesa country. They're especially popular in summer and fall, although nights turn chilly and mountain weather fickle by September.

Maps (at $2 each) and free handouts and advice on all **Carson National Forest** trails and recreation areas can be obtained from the Forest Service Building, 208 Cruz Alta Rd. (☎ **758-6200**) and from the office adjacent to the chamber of commerce on Paseo del Pueblo Sur. Both are open Monday through Saturday from 8am to 4:30pm. Detailed USGS topographical maps of backcountry areas can be purchased from **Taos Mountain Outfitters** on the Plaza (☎ **758-9292**). This is also the place to rent camping gear, if you came without your own. Tent rentals are $9 a day or $21 a weekend; sleeping bags, $7.50 a day or $16 a weekend.

Two nearby wilderness areas offer outstanding hiking possibilities. The 19,663-acre **Wheeler Peak Wilderness** is a wonderland of alpine tundra encompassing New Mexico's highest (13,161 feet) peak. The 20,000-acre **Latir Peak Wilderness,** north of Red River, is noted for its high lake country. Both are under the jurisdiction of the Questa Ranger District, P.O. Box 110, Questa, NM 87556 (☎ **505/586-0520**).

HORSE & PACK TRIPS The **Taos Indian Horse Ranch,** on Pueblo land off Ski Valley Road just before Arroyo Seco (☎ **758-3212** or toll free **800/659-3210**), offers a variety of guided rides. Open daily from 10am to 4pm and by appointment, the ranch provides horses for all types of riders (English, western, bareback) and ability levels. Call ahead to reserve. Rates are $55 to $125 for a 2-hour trail ride. Horse-drawn trolley rides are also offered in summer. From late November to March, the ranch offers evening sleigh rides to a bonfire and marshmallow roast at $40 a head.

Horseback riding is also offered by the **Shadow Mountain Guest Ranch,** 6 miles east of Taos on U.S. 64 (☎ **758-7732**). Rates are $17 to $20 per hour for trail rides. **Adventures in the Great Outdoors** (P.O. Box 1618, Ranchos de Taos, NM 87557, ☎ **505/758-7332**) will arrange half-day rides to a viewpoint and back, half-day rides with a campfire lunch at a viewpoint, or an overnight ride that includes a campfire dinner, continental breakfast, and a tent (bring your own sleeping bags, or rent them). Call or write for information and rates.

HUNTING Hunters in Carson National Forest bag deer, turkey, grouse, band-tailed pigeons, and elk by special permit. On private land, where hunters must be accompanied by qualified guides, there is also black bear and mountain lion. Hunting seasons vary year to year, so it's important to inquire ahead with the **New Mexico Game and Fish Department** in Santa Fe (☎ **505/827-7882**).

Several Taos sporting-goods shops sell hunting licenses. Backcountry guides include **Agua Fria Guide Service** (☎ **377-3512**) in Angel Fire, **United States Outfitters** (☎ **758-9774**) in Taos, and **Rio Costilla Park** (☎ **586-0542**) in Costilla.

LLAMA TREKKING El Paseo Llama Expeditions (☎ **758-3111** or toll free **800/455-2627**) utilizes U.S. Forest Service–maintained trails that wind through canyons and over mountain ridges. The llamas will carry your gear and food, allowing you to walk and explore, free of any heavy burdens. They're friendly, gentle animals who have a keen sense of sight and smell. Often, other animals like elk, deer, and mountain sheep are attracted to the scent of the llama and will venture closer to hikers if the llamas are present. Llama expeditions are scheduled from June to early October. Day hikes cost $75 per person. Three- to five-day hikes cost $125 per person per day.

RIVER RAFTING Half- or full-day white-water rafting trips down the Rio Grande and Rio Chama originate in Taos and Red River. The wild **Taos Box,** south of the **Wild Rivers Recreation Area,** is especially popular. Early May, when the water is rising, is a good time to go. Experience is not required, but you should wear a life jacket (provided) and be willing to get wet.

One convenient rafting service is **Rio Grande Rapid Transit,** P.O. Box A, Pilar, NM 87571 (☎ **505/758-9700** or toll free **800/222-RAFT**). Its headquarters is at the entrance to the BLM-administered **Orilla Verde Recreation Area,** 16 miles south of Taos, where most excursions through the Taos Box exit the river. Several other serene but thrilling floats through the Pilar Racecourse start at this point. Other rafting outfitters in the Taos area include **Native Sons Adventures** (☎ **758-9342** or toll free **800/753-7559**) and **Los Rios River Runners** (☎ **758-1550** or toll free **800/338-6877**).

Safety Warning: Taos is not the place to experiment if you are not an experienced rafter. Do yourself a favor and check with the **Bureau of Land Management** (☎ **758-8851**) to make sure that you are fully equipped to go white-water rafting without a guide. Have them check your gear to make sure it's sturdy enough—this is serious rafting!

SPAS   After a day outside, **Taos Water Gardens,** in Pueblo Alegre Mall on Paseo del Pueblo Sur (☎ **758-1669**), can treat the sore muscles of skiers, rafters, and others with private and public hot tubs and massage.

Ojo Caliente Mineral Springs, Ojo Caliente, NM 87549 (☎ **505/583-2233**), is on U.S. 285, 50 miles (a 1-hour drive) southwest of Taos. This National Historic Site was considered sacred by prehistoric Indians. When Spanish explorer Cabeza de Vaca discovered and named the springs in the 16th century, he called them "the greatest treasure that I found these strange people to possess." No other hot spring in the world has Ojo Caliente's combination of iron, soda, lithium, sodium, and arsenic. The resort offers herbal wraps, massages, lodging, and meals. Summer hours are from 10am to 8pm daily; in winter the springs don't open until 1pm on weekdays.

Taos Spa & Court Club, Box 5703, Taos, NM 87571 (☎ **505/758-1980**), is a fully equipped fitness center that rivals any you'd find in a big city. There are treadmills, step machines, versa climbers, rowing machines, exercise bikes, NordicTrack, weight training machines, saunas, indoor and outdoor hot tubs, a steam room, and indoor and outdoor pools. Thirty-five step aerobic classes a week, as well as stretch aerobics, aqua aerobics, and classes specifically designed for senior citizens are also offered. In addition, there are five tennis and two racquetball courts. Therapeutic massage by a licensed masseur and masseuse is available daily by appointment. Children's programs include tennis and swimming camp, and babysitting programs are available in the morning and evening. The spa is open Monday through Friday from 6:30am to 9pm, Saturday from 8:30am to 8pm, and Sunday from 10:30am to 8pm. Monthly, weekly, and daily memberships are available for individuals and families. For visitors there's a daily rate of $10.

Northside Health and Fitness Center at 1307 Paseo Del Pueblo Norte in El Prado (☎ **751-1242**) is also a full-service facility, featuring top-of-the-line Cybex equipment, free weights, and cardiovascular equipment. Aerobics classes are scheduled daily, and there are indoor/outdoor pools, four tennis courts, as well as children's and senior citizens' programs.

SWIMMING   **Don Fernando Pool** on Civic Plaza Drive at Camino de la Placita, opposite the new convention center, admits swimmers over age six without adult supervision.

TENNIS   There are free public courts in Taos at **Kit Carson Park** on Paseo del Pueblo Norte and **Fred Baca Memorial Park** on Camino del Medio south of Ranchitos Road, and indoor courts at the **Quail Ridge Inn** (see "Accommodations," above).

7 Savvy Shopping

Visitors come to Taos to buy fine art. Some 50-odd galleries are located within easy walking distance of the Plaza, and a couple of dozen more are a short drive from downtown. Most artists display in one or more of the galleries, which are generally open seven days a week, especially in high season. Some artists show their work by appointment only.

The best-known Taos artist is R. C. Gorman, a Navajo from Arizona who has made his home in Taos for over two decades. Now in his 50s, Gorman is internationally acclaimed for his bright, somewhat surrealistic depictions of Navajo women. His ⭐ **Navajo Gallery,** next door to the Blumenschein House at 5 Ledoux St. (☎ **758-3250**), is a showcase for his widely varied work: acrylics, lithographs, silk screens, bronzes, tapestries, hand-cast ceramic vases, etched glass, and more.

A good place to start an exploration of galleries is the **Stables Art Center,** operated by the Taos Art Association at 133 Paseo del Pueblo Norte (☎ **758-2036**). A changing series of fine and performing arts exhibits introduce many of Taos's emerging artists on a rotating basis. All types of work are exhibited, including painting (from realism to nonrepresentationalism), sculpture, printmaking, photography, and ceramics. Admission is free; it's open Monday through Saturday from 10am to 5pm and Sunday from noon to 5pm, year-round.

Shopping A To Z

ANTIQUES

Dwellings Revisited, 10 Bent St. ☎ **758-3377.**

Mexican and New Mexican primitive furniture.

Second Phase Gallery, 110 Guadalupe Plaza. ☎ **751-0159.**

Fine antique Native American art, including Navajo rugs and blankets, Pueblo pottery, and Plains beadwork.

Stewart's Fine Art, 102B S. Taos Plaza. ☎ **758-0049.**

Historical paintings for collectors.

ART

Act I Gallery, 226D Paseo del Pueblo Norte. ☎ **758-7831.**

Watercolors, *retablos,* furniture, paintings, wood turnings, pottery, jewelry, and sculpture.

Desurmont-Ellis Gallery, 121 N. Plaza. ☎ **758-3299.**

Abstract and impressionist oils and watercolors, sculpture, ceramics, and jewelry, including Angie Coleman woodcuts.

⭐ **El Taller Gallery,** 119A Kit Carson Rd. ☎ **758-4887.**

Exclusive representation of Amado Pena as well as fine art by an excellent group of southwestern artists.

The Fenix Gallery, 228B North Pueblo Rd. ☎ **758-9120.**

Fine contemporary paintings, prints, and sculpture. Representation of artists such as Cynthia Barber, Jane Ellen Burke, Sas Colby, Brenda Euwer, Gretchen Ewert, Alyce Frank, Jan Janerio, Sandra Lerner, Ginger Mongiello, Lee Mullican, Marcia Olever, Marsha Skinner, Pat Smith, Earl Stroh, Gregory Vose, and Ben Wade.

Magic Mountain Gallery, 107A N. Plaza. ☎ **758-9604.**

Impressionistic paintings, sculpture, ceramics, jewelry, and turned wood bowls.

⭐ **New Directions Gallery,** 107B N. Plaza. ☎ **758-2771.**

Features Larry Bell's latest glass sculptures and "mirage paintings," as well as work by acclaimed Taos sculptor Ted Egri.

★ **Philip Bareiss Contemporary Exhibitions**, 15 Ski Valley Rd. ☎ **776-2284.**

The works of some 30 leading Taos artists, including sculptor Gray Mercer and watercolorist Patricia Sanford. Philip Bareiss also has a three-acre sculpture park.

Quast Galleries, 229 Kit Carson Rd. ☎ **758-7160.**

Representational landscapes and figurative paintings and distinguished sculpture. Rotating national and international exhibits.

Shriver Gallery, 401 Paseo del Pueblo Norte. ☎ **758-4994.**

Traditional paintings, drawings, etchings, and bronze sculpture.

Tally Richards Gallery, Ledoux St. ☎ **758-2731.**

Contemporary art, especially surrealism.

The Taos Gallery, 403 Paseo del Pueblo Sur. ☎ **758-2475.**

Southwestern impressionism, contemporary fine art, and bronze sculpture.

★ **Taos Traditions Gallery**, 221 Paseo del Pueblo Norte. ☎ **758-0016.**

Impressionist still lifes, figures (including nudes), and landscapes by internationally acclaimed and exceptional emerging artists.

BOOKS

Among the most interesting bookstores in Taos are the following: The **Taos Book Shop,** 122D Kit Carson Rd. (☎ **758-3733**), founded in 1947, is the oldest general bookstore in New Mexico. **The Brodsky Bookshop,** 218 Paseo del Norte (☎ **758-9468**), has an exceptional inventory of fiction, nonfiction, southwestern and Native American Studies, and children's books. **Moby Dickens Bookshop,** 124A Bent St., #6 Dunn House (☎ **758-3050**), has a children's as well as an adult collection. The **Kit Carson House** (see "Attractions," above) is well stocked with regional history books. The **Fernandez de Taos Bookstore** is located right on the Plaza (☎ **758-4391**). It carries local and regional newspapers as well as a large array of magazines and a substantial offering of books on various southwestern subjects.

CRAFTS

Brooks Indian Shop, 108G Cabot Plaza Mall, 108 Kit Carson Rd. ☎ **758-9073.**

Jewelry, pottery, artifacts, and accessories.

Clay & Fiber Gallery, 126 West Plaza Dr. ☎ **758-8093.**

Contemporary crafts, ceramics, jewelry, textiles, and sculpture.

Open Space Gallery, 103B E. Taos Plaza. ☎ **758-1217.**

A cooperative gallery of contemporary arts and crafts.

★ **Taos Artisans Coop**, Bent St. ☎ **758-1558.**

Local handmade jewelry and wearables, clay work, glass, drums, and baskets.

Weaving Southwest, 216B Paseo del Pueblo Norte. ☎ **758-0433.**

Contemporary tapestries by New Mexico artists, and one-of-a-kind rugs, blankets, and pillows.

FASHIONS

Bluefish, 140 E. Kit Carson Rd. ☎ **758-3520.**

If you love unique articles of clothing, you'll love Bluefish, where you'll find hand-block-printed pieces of art clothing.

Martha of Taos, 121 Paseo del Pueblo Norte. ☎ **758-3102.**

Southwestern-theme original designs.

Twining Weavers and Contemporary Crafts, 135 Paseo del Pueblo Norte. ☎ **758-9000.**

Handwoven rugs, blankets, and other fabrics by designer and weaver Sally Bachman.

FURNITURE

Country Furnishings of Taos, 534 North Pueblo Rd. ☎ **758-4633.**

Here you'll find unique hand-painted folk-art furniture that has become popular all over the country. The pieces are as unique and individual as the styles of the local folk artists who work on them. There are also home accessories, unique gifts, clothing, and jewelry.

Taos Blue, 101A Bent St. ☎ **758-3561.**

An unusual collection of fine contemporary and Native American crafts and furniture.

GIFTS & SOUVENIRS

Broken Arrow Ltd., 222 N. Plaza. ☎ **758-4304.**

Ceramics, weaving, jewelry, baskets, paintings, and sculpture.

JEWELRY

Art Wares Art Center N. Plaza. ☎ **758-8850.**

Innovative contemporary works, featuring Phil Poirier's one-of-a-kind and limited-edition silverwork.

Taos Gems and Minerals, Paseo del Pueblo Sur. ☎ **758-3910.**

Gems, jewelry, and crystals.

MUSICAL INSTRUMENTS

Southwest Moccasin & Drum, 803 Paseo del Pueblo Norte. ☎ **758-9332** or toll free **800/447-3630.**

Fine instruments handmade by master Native American drum makers from Taos Pueblo and handprinted with designs by artists B. J. Quintana and Carl Winters. The world's second-largest selection of moccasins, plus world instruments and tapes, pottery, jewelry, weavings, rattles, fans, pipes, fetishes, and *kachinas.* Some of the profits go to support Native American causes.

Taos Drums, 5 miles south of Taos plaza off N.M. 68 (Box 1916). ☎ **758-9844** or toll free **800/424-DRUM.**

Drum making is an age-old tradition that local artisans are continuing in Taos. The drums are made of hollowed-out logs stretched with rawhide and they come in all different shapes, sizes, and styles. Taos Drums has the largest selection of Native American log and hand drums in the world. In addition to drums, the showroom displays southwestern and wrought-iron furniture, cowboy art, and lamps, as well as a constantly changing display of primitive folk art, ethnic crafts, Indian music tapes, books, and other information on drumming. To find Taos Drums, look for the teepees and drums off U.S. 68.

8 Evening Entertainment

Many occasional events are scheduled by the **Taos Art Association,** P.O. Box 198, Taos, NM 87571 (☎ **758-2036**), with headquarters at the Stables Art Center on Paseo del Pueblo Norte. The TAA imports local, regional, and national performers in theater, dance, and concerts—Dave Brubeck, the late Dizzy Gillespie, the American String Quartet, and the American Festival Ballet have performed here—and offers two weekly film series, including one for children. The TAA is also the best place to purchase tickets for most events.

You can get details on current events in the weekly *Taos News,* published on Thursday. The Taos County Chamber of Commerce (☎ **505/758-3873** or toll free **800/732-TAOS**) publishes semiannual listings of "Taos County Events."

The Performing Arts

MAJOR ANNUAL PROGRAMS

Taos School of Music, 360 State Rd, Arroyo Seco, NM 87514. ☎ **505/776-2388.**

One of the oldest chamber music programs of its kind in the United States offers an intensive eight week (mid-June to mid-August) chamber music study and performance program to advanced students of violin, viola, cello, and piano. There is daily coaching by the American String Quartet and pianist Robert McDonald. The school is located at the Hotel St. Bernard in Taos Ski Valley in northern New Mexico.

The eight-week Chamber Music Festival is an important adjunct to the school, offering 16 concerts and seminars to the public by the American String Quartet, pianist Robert McDonald, and guest violist Michael Tree of the Guarneri Quartet, as well as concerts by the international young artists in attendance. Concerts are given at the Taos Community Auditorium and the Hotel St. Bernard.

Hosted by the Taos Art Association, the school was founded in 1963.

Fort Burgwin Research Center, State Hwy. 518 (south of Taos). ☎ **758-8322.**

This historic site (of the 1,000 year-old Pot Creek Pueblo), located about 10 miles south of Taos, is a summer campus of Southern Methodist University. From mid-May through mid-August, the SMU-in-Taos curriculum (among other studio arts, humanities, and sciences) includes courses in music and theater. There are regularly scheduled orchestral concerts, guitar and harpsichord recitals, and theater performances that are available to the community, without charge, throughout the summer.

★ **Music From Angel Fire,** P.O. Box 502, Angel Fire, NM 87710. ☎ **377-6932** or **989-4772.**

This acclaimed program of chamber, folk, and jazz music begins in mid-August with weekend concerts and continues up to Labor Day. Based in the small resort community of Angel Fire, about 21 miles east of U.S. 64, it also presents numerous concerts in Taos and Raton.

MAJOR CONCERT HALLS & ALL-PURPOSE AUDITORIUMS

Taos Civic Plaza and Convention Center, 121 Civic Plaza Dr. ☎ **758-5792.**

Taos's pride and joy is this new center, located just three short blocks north of the Plaza. Opened in 1990, it accommodates groups of 610 in Rio Grande Hall and another 500 in adjacent Bataan Auditorium. Major concerts and other entertainment events will be scheduled here.

Taos Community Auditorium, 145 Paseo del Pueblo Norte. ☎ **758-4677.**

The town's primary arts facility before the construction of the Civic Plaza, this auditorium—located behind the Stables Art Center—seats 235 for theater. A film series is offered at 8pm every Wednesday (admission $4).

The Club & Music Scene

Adobe Bar, The Historic Taos Inn, 125 Paseo del Pueblo Norte. ☎ **758-2233.**

A favorite gathering place for locals as well as visitors, the Adobe Bar is known for its live music series (Wednesday and Sunday from 6 to 9pm) devoted to the eclectic talents of Taos musicians. The schedule offers a little of everything—classical, jazz, folk, Hispanic, and acoustic. The Adobe Bar features a wide selection of international beers, wines by the glass, light New Mexican dining, desserts, and an espresso menu.
Admission: Free.

Kachina Cabaret, Kachina Lodge, 413 Paseo del Pueblo Norte. ☎ **758-2275.**

Top-name country and Hispanic acts, including the Desert Rose Band, the Nitty Gritty Dirt Band, and Eddie Rabbit, perform in the cabaret. Saturday night is the big night, starting at 9pm. The adjacent Zuni Lounge has rock bands nightly.
Admission: Varies according to performer. Usually $5 Fri–Sat.

Sagebrush Inn, Paseo del Pueblo Sur. ☎ **758-2254.**

Taos's highest-energy dancing spot has country or rock performers nightly, year-round, from 9pm.
Admission: Dance bands, free.

Thunderbird Lodge, Taos Ski Valley. ☎ **776-2280.**

The first two weeks of January, the Thunderbird Jazz Festival brings leading contemporary jazz musicians to perform weeklong gigs at the foot of the ski slopes. Shows start at 8:30pm; dinner-and-show packages are available. The rest of the ski season, the Twining Tavern has country, soft rock, jazz music, and Warren Miller ski movies. Two-step dance lessons.
Admission: Jazz festival $8–$18 depending on seats.

9 Easy Excursions

The Enchanted Circle

This 90-mile loop, a National Forest Scenic Byway, runs through the towns of Questa, Red River, Eagle Nest, and Angel Fire, incorporating portions of N.M. 522, N.M. 38, and U.S. 64. It can be driven in two hours round-trip from Taos—but most folks take a full day, and many several days, to accomplish it.

Traveling north from Taos via N.M. 522, it's a 24-mile drive to **Questa,** whose residents are mainly employed at a molybdenum mine 5 miles east of town. En route north, the highway passes near **San Cristobal,** where a side road turns off to the D. H. Lawrence Shrine, and **Lama,** site of an isolated spiritual retreat.

If you turn west off N.M. 522 onto N.M. 378 about 3 miles north of Questa, you'll descend 11 miles on a gravel road into the gorge of the Rio Grande at the Bureau of Land Management-administered ◼ **Wild Rivers Recreation Area** (☎ **758-8851**). Here, where the Red River enters the gorge, is the most accessible starting point for river-rafting trips through the infamous Taos Box. Some 48 miles of the Rio Grande, south from the Colorado border, are protected under the national Wild and Scenic River Act of 1968. Information on geology and wildlife, as well as hikers' trail maps, can be obtained at the Visitors Center here. Ask for directions to the impressive petroglyphs in the gorge. River-rafting trips can be booked in Taos, Santa Fe, Red River, and other communities.

The village of **Costilla,** near the Colorado border, is 20 miles north of Questa. This is the turnoff point for four-wheel-drive jaunts into Valle Vidal, a huge U.S. Forest Service–administered reserve with 42 miles of roads.

■ **RED RIVER**   Turn east at Questa onto N.M. 38 for a 12-mile climb to **Red River,** a rough-and-ready 1890s gold-mining town which has parlayed its Wild West ambience into a pleasant resort village. Especially popular with families from Texas and Oklahoma, this community at 8,750 feet is a center for skiing and snowmobiling, fishing and hiking, off-road driving and horseback riding, mountain biking, river rafting, and other outdoor pursuits. Frontier-style celebrations, honky-tonk entertainment, and even staged shoot-outs on Main Street are held throughout the year.

The **Red River Chamber of Commerce,** P.O. Box 868, Red River, NM 87558 (☎ **505/754-2366** or toll free **800/348-6444**), lists more than 40 accommodations, including lodges and condominiums. Some are open winters or summers only.

EAGLE NEST   About 16 miles east of Red River, on the other side of 9,850-foot Bobcat Pass, is the village of **Eagle Nest,** resting on the shore of Eagle Nest Lake in the Moreno Valley. There was gold mining in this area as early as 1866, starting in what is now the ghost town of Elizabethtown 5 miles north; but Eagle Nest itself (pop. 200) wasn't incorporated until 1976. The 4-square-mile lake is considered one of the top trout producers in the United States, and attracts ice fishermen in winter as well as summer anglers. Sailboaters and windsurfers also use the lake, although swimming, waterskiing, and camping are not permitted. The **Laguna Vista Lodge,** P.O. Box 65, Eagle Nest, NM 87718 (☎ **505/377-6522** or toll free **800/821-2093**) is the village's best hotel/restaurant.

If you're heading to Cimarron (see Chapter 7, "Northeastern New Mexico") or Denver, proceed east on U.S. 64 from Eagle Nest. But if you're circling back to Taos, continue southwest on U.S. 38 and 64 to Agua Fria and Angel Fire.

Shortly before the Agua Fria junction, you'll see ■ **DAV Vietnam Veterans Memorial.** It's a stunning structure, its curved white walls soaring high against the backdrop of the Sangre de Cristo range. Consisting of a chapel and underground visitor center, it was built by Dr. Victor Westphall in memory of his son, David, a marine lieutenant killed in Vietnam in 1968. The chapel has a changing gallery of photographs of Vietnam veterans who gave their lives in the Southeast Asian war, and a poignant inscription by young Westphall.

■ **ANGEL FIRE**   The full-service resort community of **Angel Fire,** 12 miles south of Eagle Nest, 21 miles east of Taos, and 2 miles south of the Agua Fria junction on N.M. 38, dates only from the late 1960s, but already has some 30 lodges and condominiums. Winter skiing and summer golf are the most popular activities, but there's also ample opportunity for sailing and fishing on Angel Fire Lake, tennis, racquetball, and horseback riding. The unofficial community center is the **Legends Hotel & Conference Center,** P.O. Drawer B, Angel Fire, NM 87710 (☎ **505/377-6401** or toll free **800/633-7463**), a 157-room inn and restaurant with rates starting at $55.

Taos and Environs

To Alamosa
Antonito

D.H. Lawrence Ranch **1**
Kit Carson State
Park **4**
Rio Grande Gorge
State Park **6**
San Francisco de Asis
Church **5**
Taos Airport **2**
Taos Pueblo **3**

To Colorado Springs

159

0 ━━━ 5 mi
8 km

N

COLORADO
NEW MEXICO

Costilla

196

Ski Rio 🎿

Costilla Lake

Latir Lakes

Valle Vidal

Rio Grande

378

522

Wild & Scenic River Rec. Site

Questa

38

Red River

578

Elizabethtown

Red River Ski
Carson National Forest

To Raton

285

Tres Piedras

522

1
San Cristobal

150

Taos Ski Valley

Eagle Nest

To Farmington and Chama

64

Arroyo Hondo

577

Valdez

Arroyo Seco

Taos Indian Reservation

Eagle Nest Lake

Angel Fire

Carson National Forest

Rio Grande Gorge Bridge

2

TAOS
Ranchos de Taos

3
4

64

Angel Fire Ski Resort

567

Talpa

5

Fort Burgwin Research Center

434

285

68

6

518

Ojo Caliente Hot Springs

Pilar

Picuris Indian Reservation

Vadito

Rio Grande

Embudo

75

Dixon

Picuris Church

Peñasco

518

Tres Ritos

68

Las Trampas

Trampas Church

76

SIPAPU SKI AREA

Carson National Forest

ESPAÑOLA

Chimayo

Truchas

To Las Vegas, NM

To Santa Fe & Albuquerque

Ski Area 🎿 Enchanted Circle ——

SANGRE DE CRISTO MOUNTAINS

For more information and full accommodations listings on the Moreno Valley, contact the **Angel Fire/Eagle Nest Chamber of Commerce,** P.O. Box 547, Angel Fire, NM 87710 (☎ **505/377-6353** or toll free **800/446-8117**).

It's 21 miles back to Taos, over 9,100-foot Palo Flechado Pass, down the valley of the Rio Fernando de Taos, and through the small community of Shady Brook.

Northeastern
New Mexico

The region north from I-40, and east of the Sangre de Cristo Mountains, is a vast prairie that, over many thousands of years, has been trodden by dinosaurs and buffalo, by early humans and Plains people, by pioneers and settlers. Dinosaurs left footprints at Clayton Lake State Park, and Folsom Man roamed this region 12,000 years ago. Coronado passed through during his 16th-century search for Cíbola; some 300 years later, covered wagons followed the Santa Fe Trail west.

Cattle baron Lucien Maxwell controlled most of these prairies as his private empire in the latter half of the 19th century. During his era, this was truly the Wild West. The notorious town of Cimarron attracted nearly every gunslinger of the era, from Butch Cassidy to Clay Allison, Black Jack Ketchum to Jesse James; bullets still decorate the ceiling of the St. James Hotel.

Las Vegas, established long before its Nevada namesake, was the largest city in New Mexico at the turn of the 20th century, with a cosmopolitan population from all over the world. Doc Holliday, Bat Masterson, and Wyatt Earp walked its wild streets in the 1880s. A decade later, it was the headquarters of Teddy Roosevelt's Rough Riders, and early in the 20th century, it was a silent film capital (Tom Mix made movies here) and the site of a world heavyweight boxing match. Today, with a population of 15,000, it is the region's largest city, and the proud home of 900 historic properties. Raton (pop. 7,400), on I-25 in the Sangre de' Cristo foothills, is the gateway to New Mexico from the north. Clayton (pop. 2,400), Tucumcari (pop. 6,700), and Santa Rosa (pop. 2,300) are all transportation hubs and ranching centers.

Two national monuments are particular points of interest. Fort Union, 24 miles north of Las Vegas, was the largest military installation in the Southwest in the 1860s and 1870s. Capulin Volcano, 33 miles east of Raton, last erupted 10,000 years ago; visitors can walk inside the crater. Kiowa National Grasslands preserves 136,000 acres of pure prairie.

Drained by the Pecos and Canadian rivers, northeastern New Mexico is otherwise notable for the number of small lakes that afford opportunities for fishing, hunting, boating, camping, and other recreational pursuits. There are 11 state parks and about a half dozen designated wildlife areas within the region. Philmont Scout Ranch, south of Cimarron, is known by Boy Scouts throughout the world.

Suggested Itinerary: Use Las Vegas, just over an hour's drive east of Santa Fe, as your base for exploring this region. After seeing the sights of this historic city, head north a short distance via I-25 and N.M. Highway 161 to Fort Union National Monument. Then follow state roads up the Mora River valley, turning north at Mora on N.M. 434 to Angel Fire and Eagle Nest. Where U.S. 64 turns east off the Enchanted Circle, follow it to Cimarron. You'll need a day to absorb this frontier village.

U.S. 64 traces the Santa Fe Trail northeast to Raton. Explore the town's historic district, then take U.S. 64/87 east to Capulin Volcano National Monument. Continue east to the ranching center of Clayton, then south on N.M. 402 and southwest on U.S. 54 to Tucumcari. This city and Santa Rosa, an hour west on I-40, are oases in the arid east. Return to Las Vegas via U.S. 84.

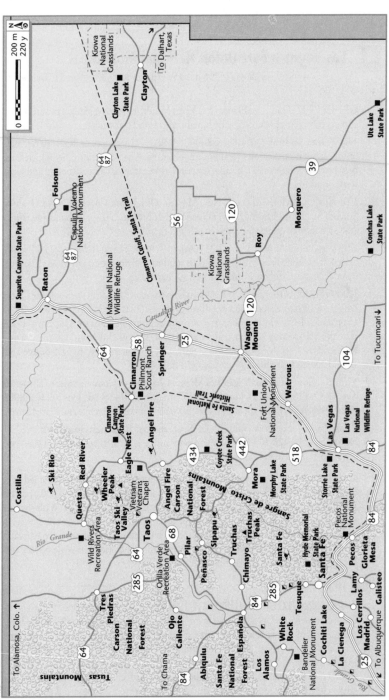

Northeastern New Mexico

1   Las Vegas & Fort Union National Monument

Las Vegas: 64 miles E of Santa Fe; 106 miles W of Tucumcari; 324 miles S of Denver, Colorado

GETTING THERE • **By Plane** Las Vegas Municipal Airport handles private flights and charters. There is no regularly scheduled commercial service.

• **By Train** **Amtrak** (☎ toll free **800/USA-RAIL**) has a depot on Railroad Avenue, but there are no ticket sales: You must book ahead. The *Southwest Chief*, which runs between Los Angeles and Chicago, stops in Las Vegas once daily eastbound and once westbound.

• **By Bus** **Greyhound/Texas, New Mexico, Oklahoma Coach (TNM&O),** 508 Seventh St. (☎ **425-8689**), stops in Las Vegas daily on its Denver–Albuquerque runs. The station may change location, so call ahead.

• **By Car** From Santa Fe, take I-25 north (1¼ hours); from Raton, take I-25 south (1¾ hours); from Taos, follow N.M. 518 southeast 78 miles through Mora (2 hours); from Tucumcari, follow N.M. 104 west (2 hours).

ESSENTIALS • **Orientation** Las Vegas is on the eastern slope of the Sangre de Cristo range, on a Pecos River tributary known as the Gallinas River. Grand Avenue (U.S. 85) parallels I-25, which runs northeast-southwest through the city. Old Town Plaza is at the intersection of four main streets: Hot Springs Boulevard (to the north), Pacific Street (south), Bridge Street (east), and National Street (west). Bridge and Pacific intersect Grand.

• **Information** The **Las Vegas/San Miguel Chamber of Commerce** is at 727 Grand Ave. (P.O. Box 148), Las Vegas, NM 87701 (☎ **505/425-8631** or toll free **800/ 832-5947**). It's at the north end of town, between University Avenue and Bridge Street.

• **Fast Facts** The **area code** is 505. **Northeastern Regional Hospital** is at 1235 Eighth St. (☎ **425-6751**). The main **post office** is located at 1001 Douglas Ave. (☎ **425-9387**). In case of **emergencies,** dial **911.**

Once known as the "gateway to New Mexico," this pleasant town was founded by a land grant in 1835. The Santa Fe Trail came through beginning in the 1850s; nearby Fort Union soon became the southwest's largest military installation. With the advent of the Atchison, Topeka & Santa Fe Railway in 1879, Las Vegas boomed. As prosperity came from shipping cattle raised on millions of acres of surrounding ranch land, Las Vegas put up scores of fancy Queen Anne and Victorian-style houses and hotels that remain today as a visual entry to that lavish era.

What to See & Do

A WALKING TOUR OF HISTORIC LAS VEGAS Start next door to the chamber of commerce on Grand Avenue, at the ∎ **Rough Riders Museum** (☎ 425-8726). About 40% of Teddy Roosevelt's Spanish-American War campaigners in 1898 came from this frontier town, and the museum chronicles their contribution to U.S. history. It's open Monday to Saturday to 9am to 4pm, except holidays.

    Most of the notable structures can be found in the Plaza-Bridge Street historic district. The 1879 **Stern and Nahm Building** has cast-iron columns and pressed and folded sheet-metal ornaments above. Decorative brickwork adorns the 1895 **Winternitz Block.** The Italianate commercial style is exemplified in the fancy arched windows of the 1884 **Anicito Baca Building,** modeled after Italian palazzos. The **E. Romero Hose and Fire Company,** put up in brick in 1909, has banded piers capped by pressed-metal capitals with dentils in a strange neoclassical architecture.

The 1882 Italianate-style **Hedgcock Building** has arched window hoods like those of the Baca building, and has served both as police station and jail as well as shoe factory, saloon, and store.

The **Plaza Hotel** gave the town the finest hotel in the New Mexico Territory back in 1881. Its three-story facade topped with a fancy broken pediment decoration was the town's pride and joy, and it has been happily restored. (See "Where to Stay," below.) The **Charles Ilfeld Building** began as a one-story adobe store in 1867, grew to two stories in 1882, and finally reached three stories with an Italianate facade in 1890. The **Louis Ilfeld Building,** nearby, shows the classic architecture coming into favor at the turn of the century in a storefront now serving as a bookstore.

The town's earlier history, going back to the first Spanish visits in the 16th century, is also seen in adobe architecture still standing alongside the ornate structures of the late 1800s. In addition, there are few places in the West with a better preserved collection of Territorial-style buildings.

OTHER ATTRACTIONS   Las Vegas has two colleges. **New Mexico Highlands University** (☎ 425-7511), 4-year liberal arts school of almost 3,000 students, was established in 1893. In 1971, it hired the nation's first Hispanic college president. Located at Seventh Street and University Avenue, just west of U.S. 85, it is especially strong in its minority education curriculum, and fields outstanding small-college athletic teams.

Armand Hammer United World College of the American West (☎ 454-4200), an international school with students from over 70 countries, is five miles west of Las Vegas via N.M. 65. The campus includes **Montezuma Hot Springs** and the former Montezuma Hotel, a luxury resort built by the Santa Fe Railroad in 1880 and now a historic landmark.

Three U.S. presidents, Germany's Kaiser Wilhelm II, and Japan's Meiji Emperor Mutsuhito stayed in the multistoried, turreted, 270-room "Montezuma Castle," as it came to be known. The hot springs, which are open to the public, have attracted health-seekers for more than 1,000 years; there are legends that ancient Aztecs journeyed here from Mexico long before the arrival of the Spanish in the 1500s. A short drive north of the springs takes you to a pond on the Gallinas River that provides winter skating and summer fishing.

Nearby parklands include **Las Vegas National Wildlife Refuge** (☎ 425-3581), 6 miles southeast via N.M. 104 and N.M. 281, open daily from 8am to 4:30pm, boasting 220 species of birds and animals on 8,750 acres of wetland; and **Storrie Lake State Park** (☎ 425-7278) 4 miles north via N.M. 518, with fishing, swimming, windsurfing, waterskiing, camping, and a visitor center with historic exhibits.

Villanueva State Park (☎ 421-2957), 31 miles southwest via I-25 and N.M. 3, offers hiking, camping, and picnicking between red sandstone bluffs in the Pecos River Valley. Nearby are the Spanish colonial villages of **Villanueva** and **San Miguel del Vado,** the latter a national historic district built around its impressive 1805 church.

NEARBY ATTRACTIONS

Mora, a small village 31 miles north via N.M. 518, is the main center between Las Vegas and Taos, and the seat of sparsely populated Mora County. The 15-mile long

Mora Valley is one of New Mexico's prettiest but most economically depressed regions, where large ranches have more or less pushed out small farmers.

Beautiful and isolated **Morphy Lake State Park** (☎ 387-2328) is reached via N.M. 518 to Mora and N.M. 94 south for 4 miles. The pretty lake is set in a basin of pine forest; it offers primitive camping and trout fishing. Check on road conditions before going. Fourteen miles north via N.M. 434 is another out-of-the-way beauty, **Coyote Creek State Park** (☎ 387-2328), with campsites beside a stream dotted with beaver ponds. The fishing is good, and several well-marked hiking trails head into the mountains.

Thirteen miles south of Mora and 27 miles northwest of Las Vegas, on N.M. 105 off N.M. 94, is the **Pendaries Lodge and Country Club,** P.O. Box 820, Rociada, NM 87742 (☎ **505/425-6076**). This lovely foothills lodge boasts the region's finest 18-hole golf course, tennis courts, stables for horseback riding, and fishing. It also has overnight accommodations and a restaurant/lounge.

Cleveland Roller Mill, P.O. Box 287, Cleveland, NM 87715, N.M. 518, about 2 miles west of Mora. ☎ **387-2645.**

One vestige of a more prosperous past is this two-story adobe mill, which ground out 50 barrels of wheat flour a day, virtually every day from 1901 to 1947. It was the last flour mill to be built in New Mexico, the last to stop running, and is the only roller mill in the state to have its original milling works intact. Today, it's been converted into a museum with exhibits on regional history and culture. The Annual Millfest, on Labor Day weekend, features the mill in operation, dances, arts and crafts, music, and more.

Admission: $2 adults, $1 children 6–17, under 6 free.
Open: Memorial Day to Oct 31 10am–5pm and by appointment.

★ **Fort Union National Monument**, P.O. Box 127, Watrous, NM 87753. ☎ **425-8025.**

Established in 1851 to defend the Santa Fe Trail against attacks from Plains Indians, Fort Union was expanded in 1861 in anticipation of a Confederate invasion, subsequently thwarted at Glorieta Pass. Its location on the Santa Fe Trail made it a welcome way station for travelers, but when the railroad replaced the trail in 1879, the fort was on its way out. It was abandoned in 1891. Today Fort Union, the largest military installation in the 19th-century Southwest, is in ruins. There's little to see but adobe walls and chimneys, but the very scope of the fort is impressive. Santa Fe Trail wagon ruts can still be seen nearby. The national monument visitor center has interpreted the fort's history through exhibits, booklets, and a walking trail.

To reach the site from Las Vegas, drive 18 miles north on I-25 to the Watrous exit, then another 8 miles northwest on N.M. 161.

Admission: $4 per car or $2 per person.
Open: Memorial Day–Labor Day, daily 8am–6pm; rest of year, daily 8am–5pm.
Closed: Christmas and New Year's Day.

Where to Stay

Most motels are on U.S. Highway 85 (Grand Avenue), the main north-south highway through downtown Las Vegas. (An exception is the Plaza Hotel, below.) Local lodging tax is 4%; including state tax (6.375%), a total tax of just over 10% is assessed to each hotel/motel bill. Parking is usually free.

Comfort Inn, 2500 N. Grand Ave., Las Vegas, NM 87701. ☎ **505/425-1100** or toll free **800/716-1103** or **800/228-5151.** 101 rms (all with bath). A/C TV TEL

Rates: $38–$53 single; $42–$59 double. AE, CB, DC, DISC, JCB, MC, V.

This new motel on the outskirts of Las Vegas is clean, comfortable, and very convenient, as well as being reasonably priced. Rooms are done in Southwest decor and have remote-controlled color cable TVs. There's an indoor heated pool, a whirlpool, and washer/dryer available for guests' use.

Inn on the Santa Fe Trail, 1133 Grand Ave., Las Vegas, NM 87701. ☎ **505/425-6791.** 42 rms (all with bath). A/C TV TEL

Rates: $39–$49 single; $44–$54 double; $69 suite. Extra person $5. AE, DC, DISC, MC, V.

Built in the 1920s, the Inn on the Santa Fe Trail has been remodeled in a hacienda style with all rooms looking out onto the central courtyard and sculptured gardens, creating a quiet, intimate retreat just off the busy Grand Avenue. The rooms are small but comfortable and have all the amenities of a major hotel. Done in pink and teal with Southwest furnishings, designed and handcrafted by local artisans, they offer full baths, and cable TV. Every morning a complimentary "sunrise coffee buffet" is served in the fireplace room. There is a heated outdoor pool and spa.

⭐ $ **Plaza Hotel,** 230 Old Town Plaza, Las Vegas, NM 87701. ☎ **505/425-3591** or toll free **800/626-4886.** 36 rms, 2 suites. A/C TV TEL

Rates: $51–$60 single; $55–$65 double; $80–$95 suite. AE, DC, DISC, MC, V.

The windows of this stately old inn look out on the center of Las Vegas life, the Plaza, where in 1846 a ceremony led by Gen. Stephen Kearny marked the takeover of New Mexico by the United States. It was built in Italianate bracketed style in 1882, in the days when western towns, newly connected with the East by train, vied with one another in constructing fancy "railroad hotels," as they were known. Considered the finest hotel in the New Mexico Territory when it was built, it was renovated with a $2 million investment exactly 100 years later. Stately walnut staircases frame the lobby and conservatory (with its piano); throughout the hotel, the architecture is true to its era.

All rooms have antique furnishings, of course, and a queen-size or two double beds. Numerous second- and third-floor units adjoin, and a pair of hexagonal rooms overlook the conservatory. The rooms all open onto spacious hallways with casual seating areas.

Services and facilities include limited room service, courtesy car to/from rail and bus stations, handicapped rooms, and meeting space.

The Plaza Dining Room is considered the fanciest restaurant in town. Notice the walls: The original 19th-century stenciling has been restored. The restaurant is open nightly, from 5 to 9pm (9:30 on Friday and Saturday), as well as for breakfast and lunch from 7am to 2pm. Prices range from $6.95 to $9.95 for New Mexican dishes, $10.95 to $16.95 for continental cuisine. There's often live music in the evenings at Byron T's 19th-century saloon.

Where to Dine

⭐ **El Alto Supper Club,** Sapello St. off New Mexico Ave. ☎ **454-0808.**
Cuisine: STEAKS & NEW MEXICAN. **Reservations:** Recommended.
Prices: $9.95–$23.50. AE, MC, V.
Open: Daily 6–9pm.

Situated atop a hill overlooking the city, El Alto is a local legend: 50 years under one owner. It's known for its steaks—New York, T-bone, sirloin, filet mignon, all guaranteed an inch-and-a-half thick. It also has limited seafood offerings, including lobster, shrimp, trout, and frogs' legs; plus combination New Mexican meals, like enchiladas and tacos. Dinner comes with salad and tortilla chips.

El Rialto Restaurant, 141 Bridge St. ☎ **425-0037.**
Cuisine: NEW MEXICAN. **Reservations:** Suggested weekends.
Prices: Dinner $6.95–$21.69. AE, DISC, MC, V.
Open: Mon–Sat 11am–9pm.

This colorful family restaurant adjacent to the Plaza offers an extensive Mexican-style menu as well as steaks and seafood. Desserts are all homemade, and there's a special children's menu. The Rye Lounge has full bar service.

Hillcrest Restaurant, 1106 Grand Ave. ☎ **425-7211.**
Cuisine: AMERICAN.
Prices: Dinner $6.95–$12.95. DISC, MC, V.
Open: Daily 6am–8:30pm.

Known throughout the city as a "home-style" dining establishment, the Hillcrest has everything from chicken-fried steaks to country-fried chicken to corn-fried catfish. It also has a good selection of Mexican food. The dining room is open for lunch and dinner only; the coffee shop is busy all day. The adjoining Trading Post Saloon offers full bar service. Meeting rooms are available.

2 Raton & Capulin Volcano National Monument

Raton: 95 miles NE of Taos; 165 miles NE of Santa Fe; 220 miles S of Denver, Colo.

GETTING THERE • By Plane Private planes can land at **Raton Municipal Airport,** 10 miles south of Raton (☎ **445-3076**).

• By Train The *Southwest Chief* stops in Raton twice a day—once eastbound toward Chicago, once westbound toward Albuquerque and Los Angeles. Make reservations with **Amtrak** (☎ toll free **800/USA-RAIL**). The 1903 Santa Fe Depot, at First Street and Cook Avenue, still serves passengers.

• By Bus Greyhound (☎ **445-9071**) and **TNM&O Coaches** both serve Raton, making their stops at McDonald's Restaurant, 419 Clayton Hwy. Albuquerque–Denver buses stop in Raton several times daily. Dallas–Denver buses pass through once each day each direction.

• By Car From Santa Fe, take I-25 north (3 hours); from Taos, take U.S. 64 east (2 hours); from Denver, take I-25 south (4 hours).

ESSENTIALS • Orientation Raton is located at the foot of 7,834-foot Raton Pass, the main route into Colorado from the south. Second Street, which runs to the west of north-south I-25, is the main thoroughfare through downtown.

• **Information**   The tourist information center is in the **Raton Chamber and Economic Development Council,** 100 Clayton Hwy. at Second Street (P.O. Box 1211), Raton, NM 87740 (☎ **505/445-3689** or toll free **800/638-6161**).

• **Fast Facts**   The **area code** is 505. Raton's hospital, **Miners Colfax Medical Center,** 200 Hospital Dr. (☎ **445-3661**), is on the south side of town. The main **post office** is at 245 Park Ave. (☎ **445-2681**). In case of **emergencies,** phone **911.**

Raton was founded in 1879 at the site of Willow Springs, a watering stop on the Santa Fe Trail. Mountain man "Uncle Dick" Wooton, a closet entrepreneur, had blasted a pass through the Rocky Mountains just north of the spring, and began charging toll. When the railroad bought Wooton's toll road, Raton developed as the railroad, mining, and ranching center for this part of the New Mexico Territory. Today it has a well-preserved historic district and the finest shooting facility in the United States.

East of Raton is Capulin Mountain, home to Capulin Volcano National Monument. The volcanic crater of the majestic 8,182-foot peak, inactive for 10,000 years, is open to visitors.

What to See & Do

⬛ **A WALKING TOUR OF HISTORIC RATON**   Explore the city's historic district by foot. Five blocks of Raton's original townsite are listed on the National Register of Historic Places, with some 70 significant buildings.

Start at the **Raton Museum,** 216 S. First St. (☎ **445-8979**), where you can pick up a walking tour map. The museum, open Tuesday through Saturday from 10am to 4pm, displays a wide variety of mining, railroad, and ranching items from the early days of the town. It's housed in the Coors Building (1906), previously a Coors Brewing Company warehouse. Next door is the **Haven Hotel** (1913), built of ivory brick with green brick trim, and adorned with a pair of pineapples and three lion heads. At the corner of First and Cook is the **Palace Hotel** (1896), the first three-story building in Colfax County.

The **Santa Fe Depot,** First and Cook, was built in 1903 in Spanish mission revival style. It is still used by Amtrak passengers today. Next door, built in 1910, is the **Wells Fargo Express Company.**

Opposite the station, heading north on First, is the **Roth Building** (1893), whose ornate metal facade boasts Corinthian pilasters and a bracketed cornice; the **Abourezk Building** (1906), with two female figureheads on the upper storefront; the **Marchiondo Building** (1882), a former dry-goods store painted bright yellow with green trim; and the **Joseph Building** (1890s), which still retains the cupids painted on its walls when it was the Gem Saloon.

Walk west 1 block to Second Street, and proceed south. At 131 N. Second St. is the **Shuler Theater** (☎ **445-5528**). Built in 1915, it housed the opera company, fire station, and city offices. The interior of the theater, designed in European rococo style, has superb acoustics. The lobby is decorated with murals recalling local history. It's still in active use year-round. Open Monday to Friday from 8am to 5pm.

At the intersection of Second and Cook are the **Raton Realty Building** (1928), characterized by a red tile roof and terra-cotta trimmed windows; and the **Di Lisio Building** (1918), a former bank with three Doric columns at its entrance and stained glass topping the lower windows. At Third and Cook, the neoclassical U.S. Post Office (1917) is now the **Arthur Johnson Memorial Library,** with a fine collection on southwestern art. The south side of Cook between Second and Third is dominated by the **Swastika Hotel** (1929), now the International State Bank, a seven-story brick building decorated at the roofline with the swastika, a Native American symbol of good luck. The hotel's name was changed to the Yucca Hotel when the German Nazis adopted the swastika as their symbol.

OTHER ATTRACTIONS   The **NRA Whittington Center,** off U.S. Highway 64 about 10 miles south of Raton, is considered the most complete nonmilitary shooting and training facility in the world. Operated by the National Rifle Association, it spans 50 square miles of rolling hills. It has 14 instructional and competitive ranges, a handful of condominium units, and hookups for campers. Classes in pistol, rifle, and shotgun shooting, firearm safety, and conservation are offered. National championship events are held annually. The center is open daily to the public for tours.

Ten miles northeast of Raton via N.M. 526, **Sugarite Canyon State Park** (☎ **445-5607**) offers historic exhibits, camping, boating, and fishing at three trout-stocked lakes.

NEARBY ATTRACTIONS

THE CLAYTON HIGHWAY   There are a number of attractions on the Clayton Highway, U.S. 64/87, running 83 miles east-southeast from Raton to Clayton.

Twenty-seven miles east of Raton in **Capulin,** visitors have the rare opportunity to walk inside a volcanic crater at ⊠ **Capulin Volcano National Monument** (☎ **278-2201**). A 2-mile road spirals up over 600 feet to the crater of the 8,182-foot peak, where two self-guiding trails leave from the parking area: the 1-mile Crater Rim Trail, and the 100-foot descent to the ancient volcanic vent. The mountain was last active about 10,000 years ago, when it exploded and sent out the last of three lava flows. At the Visitor Center, an audiovisual program discusses volcanism, and park personnel will answer questions. A short nature trail behind the center introduces plant and animal life of the area. Admission is $4 per car or $2 per person. The visitor center is open daily from 8:30am to 4:30pm.

Just north of Capulin Mountain, on N.M. 325 off the Clayton Highway, is the tiny town of **Folsom,** the site near where 10,000-year-old "Folsom Man" was discovered by cowboy George McJunkin. The find, excavated by the Denver Museum of Natural History in 1926, represented the first association of the artifacts of prehistoric people (spear points) with the fossil bones of extinct animals (a species of bison). Today the site, on private property, is closed to the public. But artifacts (prehistoric as well as from the 19th century) are displayed at the **Folsom Museum,** Main Street, Folsom (☎ **278-2122**).

Open 10am to 5pm daily in summer, winter by appointment (☎ **278-3616**), the Folsom Museum contains exhibits on prehistoric and historic Native Americans of the area, as well as Folsom's settlement by the white man. Admission is $1 for adults, 50¢ for children 6–12.

Clayton (pop. 2,400) is a ranching center just 9 miles west of the Texas and Oklahoma panhandle borders. Rich prairie grasses, typical of nearby **Kiowa National Grasslands** (☎ **374-9652**), led to its founding in 1887. In New Mexico history, it's known as the town where Thomas "Black Jack" Ketchum, a notorious train robber, was executed and buried in 1901 after a decade of legendary heists.

North of town, near the distinctive Rabbit Ears mountains, tracks from eight species of dinosaurs can be clearly seen at **Clayton Lake State Park** (☎ **374-8808**). The park has a visitor center, and offers fishing and camping.

Information on other area attractions, as well as lodging and dining, can be obtained from the **Clayton-Union County Chamber of Commerce,** 1103 S. First St. (P.O. Box 476) Clayton, NM 88415 (☎ **505/374-9253**).

SOUTH OF RATON   Heading down I-25, **Maxwell National Wildlife Refuge** (☎ 375-2331) on the Canadian River, 24 miles from Raton, has a rich resident and migratory bird population, and numerous native mammals. In the little town of **Springer** (pop. 1,300), 39 miles south of Raton via I-25, the **Santa Fe Trail Museum** (☎ 483-2341) is housed in the three-story 1881 Colfax County Court-house. It contains pioneer artifacts and memorabilia from travelers along the Santa Fe Trail and early residents of the area, as well as a livery stable and New Mexico's only electric chair, which was used to execute seven convicted murderers between 1933 and 1956. Open Monday to Saturday 9am to 4pm, admission costs $1.50 for adults and 75¢ for children under 13. The **Colfax County Fair** takes place in Springer annually in mid-August, with a rodeo and car show.

About 30 miles east of Springer via U.S. 56 is the **Dorsey Mansion,** a two-story log-and-stone home built in the 1880s by U.S. senator and cattleman Stephen Dorsey. With 36 rooms, hardwood floors, Italian marble fireplaces, hand-carved cherry stair-case, and dining-room table that sat 60, it was quite a masterpiece! Public tours are offered by appointment (☎ 375-2222) Monday to Saturday 10am to 4pm, Sunday 1 to 5pm, for an admission charge of $2 adults, $1 for children under 12.

South of U.S. 56 via N.M. 39 is the western of the two parcels that comprise **Kiowa National Grasslands.** Travel this route to reach **Chicosa Lake State Park** (☎ 485-2424), on N.M. 120; 55 miles southeast of Springer, this park has camp-ing, trout fishing, hiking, and historical exhibits on cattle drives along the Goodnight-Loving Trail.

★ **CIMARRON**   Few towns in the American West have as much lore or legend at-tached to them as Cimarron, 41 miles southwest of Raton via U.S. 64. Nestled against the eastern slope of the Sangre de Cristo mountain range, the town (its name is Span-ish for "wild" or "untamed") achieved its greatest fame as an outpost on the Santa Fe Trail between the 1850s and 1880s. Frontier personalities including Kit Carson and Wyatt Earp, Buffalo Bill Cody and Annie Oakley, Bat Masterson and Doc Holliday, Butch Cassidy and Jesse James, painter Frederic Remington and novelist Zane Grey, all passed through and stayed—most of them at the St. James Hotel (see "Where to Stay," below)—at one time or another.

Land baron Lucien Maxwell founded the town in 1848 as base of operations for his 1.7-million-acre empire. In 1857, he built the **Maxwell Ranch,** which he furnished opulently with heavy draperies, gold-framed paintings, and two grand pianos. In the gaming room the tables saw high stakes, as guests bet silver Mexican pesos or pokes of yellow gold dust. Gold was struck in 1867 on Maxwell's land, near Baldy Mountain, and the rush of prospectors that followed caused him to sell out three years later.

The ranch isn't open for inspection today, but Maxwell's 1864 stone grist mill, built to supply flour to Fort Union, is. The **Old Mill Museum** houses an interesting collection of early photos and memorabilia. It's open May to October Monday to Wednesday and Friday and Saturday from 9am to 5pm and Sunday from 1 to 5pm. Admission is $2 adults, $1 seniors and children.

Cimarron has numerous other buildings of historic note, and a walking tour map is included in the Old Mill Museum brochure.

Cimarron is the gateway to the ★ **Philmont Scout Ranch** (☎ 376-2281), a 137,000-acre property donated to the Boy Scouts of America by Texas oilman Waite Phillips in 1938. Scouts from all over the world use it for backcountry camping and leadership training from June through August and for conferences the remainder of the year.

There are three museums on the ranch, all open to the public. **Villa Philmonte,** Phillips's lavish Mediterranean-style summer home, was built in 1927 and remains furnished with the family's European antiques. Four miles south of Cimarron, it's open daily in summer for guided tours, other times by appointment. Admission costs $3. The **Philmont Museum and Seton Memorial Library** commemorates the art and taxidermy of the naturalist and author who founded the Boy Scouts of America, and has exhibits on the varied history of the Cimarron area. It's open year-round, daily from June to August; closed Sunday the rest of the year. Admission is free. The **Kit Carson Museum,** 7 miles south of Philmont headquarters in Rayado, is a period hacienda furnished in 1850s style. Staff in historic costumes lead tours daily June through August. Admission is free.

The **Cimarron Chamber of Commerce,** P.O. Box 604, Cimarron, NM 87714 (☎ 505/376-2417), has complete information on the region.

U.S. 64 from Cimarron leads west 24 miles to Eagle Nest, passing en route **Cimarron Canyon State Park** (☎ 377-6271), a designated state wildlife area at the foot of crenellated granite formations known as the Palisades. Just east of Cimarron, County Road 204 offers access to the Carson National Forest's **Valle Vidal** recreation area, discussed in chapter 6.

Where to Stay

Most motels are found along U.S. 64/87, the Clayton Highway, between Second Street and the I-25 interchange. Local lodging tax is 5%; including the 6.875% state gross receipts tax, each motel bill has almost 12% added tax. Parking is usually free.

Best Western Sands Manor Motel, 300 Clayton Hwy., Raton, NM 87740.
☎ **505/445-2737** or toll free **800/518-2581** or **800/528-1234.** 50 rms. A/C TV TEL
Rates: $42–$67 single, $53–$71 double. Extra person $2. AE, CB, DC, DISC, MC, V.

A rambling, one-story motel, family-owned and operated, the Sands Manor has spacious rooms with a king-size or two queen-size beds and all standard furnishings. Nonsmoking and handicapped rooms are available, as are rooms with coffeemakers and refrigerators. There's an outdoor swimming pool, a playground, a year-round spa, and a gift shop. The coffee shop is open daily, serving three family-style meals from 6am to 10pm.

Harmony Manor Hotel, 351 Clayton Rd., Raton, NM 87740. ☎ **505/445-2763** or toll free **800/922-0347.** 18 rms (all with bath). A/C TV TEL
Rates: Memorial Day–Labor Day $40–$58 single or double; rest of the year $36–$50 single or double. AE, DC, DISC, MC, V.

The Harmony Manor Motel, located just off I-25, is a great buy. The rooms are spotlessly kept by Loyd and Doris Wilkins (the owners) and contain all the amenities you need for a comfortable stay. Each is enormous and has king- or queen-size beds, cable TV, and direct dial phones. Nonsmoking rooms are available. The decor is bright and airy, accented by floral bedspreads. You won't be disappointed with the accommodations at the Harmony Manor.

Melody Lane Motel, 136 Canyon Dr., Raton, NM 87740. ☎ **505/445-3655** or toll free **800/421-5210.** 26 rms. A/C TV TEL
Rates: Mid-May–Labor Day $32–$49 single; $36–$55 double. Labor Day–mid-May $29–$38 single; $33–$45 double. AE, CB, DC, DISC, MC, V.

This nice property on the I-25 business loop (off Exit 454) has a wide variety of room options. Eight rooms have steam baths; many of them have king-size beds. Most have HBO cable reception. All have thermostat-controlled hot-water heating. Pets are permitted here.

IN NEARBY CIMARRON

 St. James Hotel, Rte. 1, Box 2, Cimarron, NM 87714. ☎ **505/376-2664** or toll free **800/748-2694.** Fax 505/376-2623. 26 rms. 2 suites.

Rates: Hotel $75 single or double, $85 suite; motel $45 single, $47 double. AE, DISC, MC, V.

This landmark hotel looks much the same today as it did in 1873, when it was built by Henri Lambert, previously a chef for Napoleon, Abraham Lincoln, and Gen. Ulysses S. Grant. In its early years, as a rare luxury on the Santa Fe Trail, it had a dining room, a saloon, gambling rooms, and lavish guest rooms outfitted with Victorian furniture. Today, the lace and cherry wood have returned to the bedrooms, but without televisions or phones—the better to evoke the days when famous guests such as Zane Grey, who wrote *Fighting Caravans* at the hotel, were residents. Annie Oakley's bed is here, and a glass case holds a register with the signatures of Buffalo Bill Cody and the notorious Jesse James.

Unfortunately, the St. James also was a place of some lawlessness: 26 men were said to have been killed within the two-foot-thick adobe walls, and owner Greg Champion can point out bullet holes in the pressed-tin ceiling of the dining room. The ghosts of some are believed to inhabit the hotel still.

The hotel itself has 15 rooms. There are 11 more in a recently remodeled modern annex; these lack the historic atmosphere of the hotel, but they do provide TV and telephone for those who prefer the late 20th century.

The St. James Dining Room serves the finest meals in this part of New Mexico. The menu is ambitious: main courses like shrimp Diablo, tournedos of beef, and veal marsala, most of them priced from $13 to $22. A separate coffee shop serves three meals daily. The hotel also offers an outdoor patio with bar and grill, gift shop, package store, and meeting room for 30.

Where to Dine

The Capri Restaurant, 304 Canyon Dr. ☎ **445-9755.**

Cuisine: ITALIAN.
Prices: Main courses $4.25–$9.95. AE, DC, DISC, MC, V.
Open: Daily 7am–9pm.

This casual cafe draws rave reviews from locals for its homemade pastas, including stuffed manicotti, and its chicken cacciatore. It also offers a Mexican menu, steaks, and limited seafood, including a popular combination of tenderloin and brook trout.

El Matador, 1012 S. 2nd St. ☎ **445-9575.**

Cuisine: NEW MEXICAN.
Prices: Lunch and dinner $3.25–$12.25.
Open: Tues–Sun 7am–8:30pm.

Festive Mexican decor makes this cafe a lively spot. Tacos, enchiladas, burritos, tostadas, and other menu favorites are prepared à la carte or as part of combination plates. Steaks and other American dishes are also on the menu.

Pappas' Sweet Shop Restaurant, 1201 S. 2nd St. ☎ **445-9811.**

Cuisine: AMERICAN & TEX-MEX. **Reservations:** Suggested at dinner in summer.
Prices: Lunch $3.95–$7.95; dinner $6.95–$27.95. AE, DC, DISC, MC, V.
Open: Daily 9am–2pm and 5–9pm. **Closed:** Sun in winter.

This isn't a bakery, as the name might suggest: It's a fine restaurant, known for its quality beef. Prime rib, filet mignon, and steak-and-seafood combinations are popular, along with broiled breast of chicken and deep-fried shrimp. Across-the-border dishes include Tex-Mex steak, fajitas, and enchiladas. A full-service lounge adjoins the restaurant.

3 The I-40 Corridor

Tucumcari: 172 miles E of Albuquerque; 101 miles W of Amarillo, Texas;
Santa Rosa: 113 miles E of Albuquerque; 170 miles W of Amarillo, Texas

GETTING THERE • By Plane There's no regularly scheduled commercial service into either Tucumcari or Santa Rosa. Private planes can land at **Tucumcari Municipal Airport** (☎ **461-3229**).

• **By Bus** **Greyhound Lines, Inc.** buses pass through both towns several times daily. Coaches stop in Tucumcari at 1st St. and I-40 at McDonald's (☎ **461-1350**) and in Santa Rosa at Mateo's Family Restaurant, 500 W. Coronado Dr. (☎ **472-5720**).

• **By Car** I-40 extends from southern California to North Carolina. Travel time from Albuquerque to Tucumcari is 2 hours, 40 minutes; to Santa Rosa, 1 hour, 45 minutes.

ESSENTIALS • Orientation **Tucumcari** (pop. 6,700), 44 miles from the Texas border, is reached from three freeway exits. Tucumcari Boulevard (east-west U.S. 66) and First Street (north-south N.M. 209, to Clovis) are the principle arteries. **Santa Rosa** (pop. 2,300), situated where I-40 crosses the Pecos River, also is served by three freeway exits. Parker Avenue downtown is the same road as Will Rogers Drive (East Business Loop 40) and Coronado Drive (West Business Loop 40).

• **Information** Contact the **Tucumcari-Quay County Chamber of Commerce,** 404 W. Tucumcari Blvd. (P.O. Drawer E), Tucumcari, NM 88401 (☎ **505/461-1694**) or the **Santa Rosa Chamber of Commerce,** 486 Parker Ave., Santa Rosa, NM 88435 (☎ **505/472-3763**).

• **Fast Facts** The **area code** is 505. Hospitals are **Dr. Dan C. Trigg Memorial Hospital,** 301 E. Liel De Luna Ave. (☎ **461-0141**), in Tucumcari; and **Guadalupe County Hospital,** 535 Lake Dr. (☎ **472-3417**), in Santa Rosa. City **post offices** can be found at First and Aber streets (☎ **461-0370**) in Tucumcari, and at 120 Fifth St. (☎ **472-3743**) in Santa Rosa. In case of **emergency,** dial **911.**

The 216 freeway miles from Albuquerque to the Texas border cross straight, featureless prairie and very few towns. But the valleys of the Pecos River (site of Santa Rosa) and the Canadian River (location of Tucumcari) have several attractions, including natural lakes. There's not a lot to explore here, unless you're a bird hunter or a fisherman, but both towns can make a day's stopover worthwhile.

What to See & Do

The **Tucumcari Historical Museum,** 416 S. Adams, one block east of First Street, is open from 9am to 6pm Monday through Saturday, 1 to 6pm Sunday in summer, and Tuesday through Saturday 9am to 5pm, 1 to 5pm Sunday in winter. An early sheriff's office, an authentic western schoolroom, a hospital room of the early West, a real chuck wagon, a historic windmill, and a barbed-wire collection are among the treasures.

The moonlike **Mesa Redondo,** rising 11 miles south of town via N.M. 209, gives visitors a sense of entering a strange unknown world. To the northwest, 34 miles distant over N.M. 104, is **Conchas Lake State Park** (☎ **868-2270**), with a reservoir 25 miles in length. Two modern marinas provide facilities for boating, fishing, and waterskiing. Camping and picnic areas attract visitors to the south side of the lake—there are full hookups available as well as a nine-hole golf course (☎ **868-2988**). The northern site offers rental cabins, a trailer park with hookups, marina, store, and a restaurant. **Ute Dam** is 22 miles northeast on U.S. 54, near the town of Logan. It has docking facilities on a lake, campsites, and rental boats. Quay County around Tucumcari is noted for its blue-quail hunting, said to be the best anywhere in the United States.

Caprock Amphitheatre (☎ toll free **800/724-0500**), 30 miles southeast of Tucumcari, is a natural amphitheater. Here the New Mexico Outdoor Drama Association presents an outdoor musical drama each summer, Friday and Saturday nights from mid-June to mid-August. *Billy the Kid,* first produced in 1987, is a romantic dramatization of New Mexico's Wild West days. The 2-hour show starts at 8pm, following a 6:30pm barbecue on-site. Show tickets are $10 for adults, $5 for children 6 to 12. Dinner costs $6 for adults, $4 for children. The amphitheater is on N.M. 469, south of San Jon off I-40 (Exit 356). For advance information, write the NMODA, P.O. Box 337, San Jon, NM 88434.

Santa Rosa calls itself "the city of natural lakes." Those bodies of water include **Blue Hole,** a crystal-clear, 81-foot-deep artesian spring just east of downtown. Fed by a subterranean river that flows 3,000 gallons per minute at a constant 64°, it's a favorite of scuba divers. There's a bathhouse on site. **Park Lake,** in the middle of town, offers free swimming, picnicking, and extensive recreational facilities. **Santa Rosa Lake State Park,** P.O. Box 384, Santa Rosa (☎ **472-3110**), on a dammed portion of the Pecos River, has camping, hiking, excellent fishing, and a visitor information center. Ten miles south of town via N.M. 91, the village of **Puerto de Luna** is a 19th-century county seat with a mid-1800s courthouse and church, Nuestra Señora del Refugio.

Where to Stay

In both Tucumcari and Santa Rosa, major hotels are at I-40 interchanges. Smaller "Ma and Pa" motels can be found along the main streets—Tucumcari Boulevard in Tucumcari, Will Rogers Drive in Santa Rosa. All told, there are about 2,000 rooms in Tucumcari and Santa Rosa.

Lodging taxes in Tucumcari are 5% plus gross receipts tax of 6.4375%, for a total hotel tax of about 11$\frac{1}{2}$%. In Santa Rosa, lodger's tax is 3% and gross receipts tax is 6.125%, for a total of 9.125%. Parking is usually free.

TUCUMCARI

Best Western Discovery Motor Inn, 200 E. Estrella Ave. at Exit 332, Tucumcari, NM 88401. ☎ **505/461-4884** or toll free **800/528-1234**. 107 rms. A/C TV TEL

Rates: June–mid-Sept $46–$62 single, $54–$62 double; mid-Sept–May $44–$58 single, $48–$60 double. AE, CB, DC, DISC, MC, V.

This spacious new motor hotel has the advantage of being off the "strip"—it's still central, but it's quieter than many others. Many rooms, all of which have king-size or two queen-size beds, look down upon the outdoor swimming pool. The hotel also has an indoor spa, guest Laundromat, game room, and gift shop. Complimentary morning coffee is an added touch. Nonsmoking and handicapped rooms are available, and small pets are permitted with payment of a damage deposit.

The Headquarters House Restaurant, open from 6am to 10pm, with dinners in the $7 to $13 range, is considered one of Tucumcari's better eating places.

Best Western Pow Wow Inn, 801 W. Tucumcari Blvd. (P.O. Box 1306), Tucumcari, NM 88401. ☎ **505/461-0500** or toll free **800/527-6996** or **800/528-1234.** Fax 505/461-0135. 90 rms, 16 suites. A/C TV TEL

Rates: $40–$50 single; $45–$55 double; $65–$90 suite. AE, CB, DC, DISC, MC, V.

A full-service downtown motor inn, the Pow Wow focuses around its beautiful outdoor swimming pool, with an artificial-turf deck. One-third of the units, including 15 ground-level suites, have kitchens (utensils not provided). Other facilities include a children's playground, a coin-op Laundromat, and a gift shop. Guests get complimentary greens fees at the local golf club. Pets are accepted, but must not be left unattended.

The Pow Wow Restaurant, open from 6am to 10pm, has a daily luncheon buffet; dinners priced from $5 to $12; and a cool, low-lit lounge with live entertainment evenings.

SANTA ROSA

Best Western Adobe Inn, E. Business Loop 40 at I-40 (P.O. Box 410), Santa Rosa, NM 88435. ☎ **505/472-3446** or toll free **800/528-1234.** 58 rms. A/C TV TEL

Rates: May–Oct $48–$52 single, $54–$56 double; Nov–Apr $42–$48 single, $44–$52 double. AE, CB, DC, DISC, MC, V.

This pleasant motel has clean, comfortable rooms with all standard furnishings, including queen-size beds in every room. There's a swimming pool and gift shop, a courtesy car, and an attached coffee shop. Small pets are allowed.

Motel 6, 3400 Will Rogers Dr., Santa Rosa, NM 88435. ☎ **505/472-3045.** 90 rms. A/C TV TEL

Rates: $24.99 single, $30.99 double. Under 18 free with parent. AE, CB, DC, DISC, MC, V.

Rooms are basic but clean; with double beds, table and chairs, three-quarter bath, TV and phones, they meet the needs of many travelers. The motel has an outdoor swimming pool, open seasonally. It's on the north side of I-40, opposite the town.

Super 8 Motel, 1201 Will Rogers Dr., Santa Rosa NM 88435. ☎ **505/472-5388.** Fax 505/472-5388. 88 rms (all with bath). A/C TV TEL

Rates: $34–$36 single; $40–$42 double. AE, CB, DC, MC, V.

Located near the historic Club Cafe, this Super 8 is like other Super 8s in that it's clean and has large rooms with double beds and standard furnishings. The decor is simple—green carpeting and floral bedspreads. There's cable TV with pay movies, a guest laundry, and rooms for nonsmokers. Pets are not permitted.

Where to Dine

TUCUMCARI

Del's, 1202 E. Tucumcari Blvd. ☎ **461-1740.**

> **Cuisine:** AMERICAN & NEW MEXICAN.
> **Prices:** $5.95–$15.95. AE, MC, V.
> **Open:** Mon–Sat 11am–9pm.

The big cow atop Del's neon sign is not only a Route 66 landmark—it also points to the fine steaks inside. T-bones, sirloins, rib eyes, and other cuts highlight the menu. Del's also offers burgers, Mexican plates, and seafood, including an 8-ounce catfish filet. A trip through the large salad bar is a satisfying meal for many. Del's is not licensed for alcoholic beverages.

La Cita, 812 S. 1st St. ☎ **461-3930.**

> **Cuisine:** NEW MEXICAN.
> **Prices:** $2.95–$9.95. MC, V.
> **Open:** Mon–Sun 11am–9pm.

A modern cafe in downtown Tucumcari, La Cita is best known for its tasty fajitas, green chile enchiladas, spicy salsa, and flat enchiladas—served with an egg on top. There's a gift shop attached.

8

Northwestern New Mexico

THIS IS AMERICAN INDIAN COUNTRY, PAST AND PRESENT. PUEBLO, NAVAJO, AND Apache share this colorful area of sandstone bluffs, treading the same ground their Anasazi ancestors did many centuries ago.

The Zuni, Acoma, and Laguna Pueblos make their homes within short distances of I-40. Acoma's "Sky City" has been continually occupied for more than nine centuries. A huge chunk of the northwest is taken up by a part of the Navajo Reservation, the largest in America; and the Jicarilla Apache Reservation stretches 65 miles south from the Colorado border. All share their arts and crafts, and their distinctive cultures with visitors, but ask that their personal privacy and religious traditions be respected.

The past lives here, too, side by side with the present. Chaco Culture National Historical Park, with 12 major ruins and hundreds of smaller ones, represents the highest development of Anasazi civilization in the 11th century. Aztec Ruins National Monument and the nearby Salmon Ruins are similarly spectacular Pueblo preservations.

Two other national monuments in northwestern New Mexico are El Morro and El Malpais—the former a sandstone monolith that bears centuries of inscriptions by passing travelers, the latter a volcanic badlands.

The metropolitan centers of the region are Farmington, center of the fertile San Juan valley and gateway to the Four Corners region, with about 36,500 people; Gallup, self-proclaimed "Indian capital of the world" and a mecca for silver-jewelry shoppers, about 20,000; and Grants, a former uranium-mining boomtown, near 8,500.

Well east of Farmington, about equidistant from Santa Fe, is a fourth regional center of sorts: Chama (pop. 1,000). It's best known as the New Mexico depot for the Cumbres & Toltec Railroad and as a center for hunting and fishing expeditions into New Mexico's high country.

Suggested Itinerary: Albuquerque is your base for exploring northwestern New Mexico. Head west on I-40 via Laguna to Acoma Pueblo to tour the amazing "Sky City." Then proceed west on I-40 to Grants, after another turnoff on N.M. 117 to see El Malpais National Monument. Don't miss the New Mexico Museum of Mining in Grants.

From Grants, head south and west on N.M. 53 to Bandera Volcano and Ice Caves, El Morro National Monument, and the Zuni Pueblo. Then proceed north on N.M. 602 to Gallup, where you'll want to browse in trading posts for Native American jewelry and crafts.

Leaving Gallup, take I-40 east to Thoreau, N.M. 371 north to Crownpoint, and N.M. 57 east and north again to Chaco Canyon National Historical Park, the crown jewel of ancient Anasazi culture in North America. Spend the day here, leaving in time to travel north to Farmington for the night, via N.M. 44 and U.S. 64.

Essential sights in the Farmington area are Aztec Ruins National Monument and the Salmon Ruins, near Bloomfield. Afterward, take U.S. 64 east. Detour briefly to Navajo Lake State Park, then continue to Dulce, in the Jicarilla Apache Indian Reservation. Stay either here or a half-hour down the highway in Chama.

Chama is the home of the Cumbres & Toltec Scenic Railroad, one of New Mexico's premier attractions. When you've waved the train good-bye, follow U.S. 84 south to Santa Fe, leaving time for a midway stop at the Ghost Ranch Living Museum north of Abiquiu. Return to Albuquerque via I-25. This itinerary will take you five to seven days.

1 Grants: Gateway to Acoma, El Morro & El Malpais

78 miles W of Albuquerque; 60 miles E of Gallup

GETTING THERE • By Plane   Private planes are served by **Grants-Milan Municipal Airport,** U.S. 66 west (☎ **287-4700** or after hours **287-4921**). There is no commercial service.

• **By Bus**   The buses of **Greyhound Lines, Inc.,** 1801 W. Santa Fe Ave. (☎ **285-6268**), stop several times a day.

• **By Car**   From Albuquerque, take I-40 west (1¼ hours). From Gallup, take I-40 east (1 hour).

ESSENTIALS • Orientation   Route 66 (Santa Fe Avenue) parallels I-40 as the main street through Grants, on the north side of the east-west freeway. It is bisected by N.M. 547 (First Avenue), which extends north to Roosevelt Avenue and Grants' "second" downtown, where many civic buildings and a large shopping mall are located.

• **Information**   The **Grants/Cíbola Country Chamber of Commerce** is at 100 N. Iron Ave. (P.O. Box 297), Grants, NM 87020 (☎ **505/287-4802** or toll free **800/748-2142**). It's located in the same building as the Mining Museum.

• **Fast Facts**   The **area code** is 505. **Cíbola General Hospital** is at 1212 Bonita St. in Grants (☎ **287-4446**). The main **post office** is located at 120 N. Third St. (☎ **287-3143**). In case of **emergencies,** dial **911**.

Grants, New Mexico's gateway to Acoma Pueblo and El Morro and El Malpais national monuments, was established in the late 19th century as a railroad town and ranching center. It didn't really come of age until 1950, when Paddy Martinez, a Navajo sheep rancher, discovered uranium near Haystack Mountain, northwest of town. Grants has boomed and declined twice since then. Mines remain active today, though in some decline. The city is the seat of expansive Cíbola County, which stretches from the Arizona border nearly to Albuquerque.

WHAT TO SEE & DO

★ **The New Mexico Museum of Mining,** 100 N. Iron St. at Santa Fe Ave. ☎ **287-4802,** or toll free **800/748-2142.**

The world's only uranium-mining museum is structured over a re-creation of an actual underground mine, complete with original machinery and equipment.

Begin your tour on the first level of the museum, following a time line of dinosaur bones and ancient pueblo pottery from the prehistory of the Grants area to the industry of the late 20th century. Then an elevator, representing the "cage" of deep-rock mining, carries you into the mine shaft.

Once underground, you can touch and feel the mining tools, equipment, and cement walls. You'll start at the station, a dimly lit cavern where workers, materials, and yellow uranium ore entered and left the mine. You'll see huge ore cars and actual blasting caps. Deep in the mine, you'll duck into an open "stope," stripped of all ore and off-limits in an actual mine. Retired miners often lead tours—and their memories are worth 10 times the price of admission.

Admission: $2 includes guided tour or self-guiding "sound stick." $1.50 seniors over 60; free for children 8 and under.

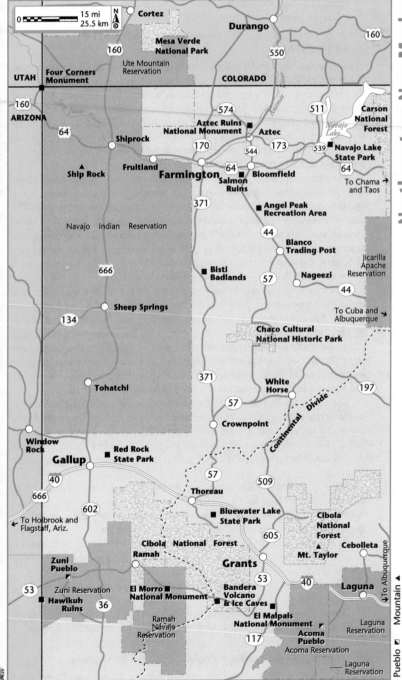

0 15 mi
25.5 km

N

Cortez

Durango

160

Mesa Verde
National Park

160

550

Ute Mountain
Reservation

COLORADO

UTAH

Four Corners
Monument

574

511

Carson
National
Forest

160

ARIZONA

64

Aztec Ruins
National Monument

Aztec

173

Navajo
Lake

539

Navajo Lake
State Park

Shiprock

170

544

Ship Rock

Fruitland

Farmington

64

Bloomfield

64

To Chama
and Taos

Salmon
Ruins

371

Angel Peak
Recreation Area

Navajo   Indian   Reservation

44

Blanco
Trading Post

666

Bisti
Badlands

57

Nageezi

Jicarilla
Apache
Reservation

44

Sheep Springs

To Cuba and
Albuquerque

134

Chaco Cultural
National Historic Park

Tohatchi

371

White
Horse

197

57

Continental   Divide

Crownpoint

Window
Rock

Gallup

Red Rock
State Park

57

509

40

666

602

Thoreau

Bluewater Lake
State Park

605

Cibola
National
Forest

Cebolleta

To Holbrook and
Flagstaff, Ariz.

Cibola   National   Forest

Mt. Taylor

Ramah

Grants

53

Zuni
Pueblo

53

Zuni Reservation

El Morro
National Monument

36

Bandera
Volcano
& Ice Caves

40

Laguna

To Albuquerque

Hawikuh
Ruins

El Malpais
National Monument

Laguna
Reservation

Ramah
Navajo
Reservation

117

Acoma
Pueblo

Acoma Reservation

Laguna
Reservation

Pueblo ◪   Mountain ▲

Open: May–Sept Mon–Sat 9am–6pm, Sun noon–6pm; Oct–Apr Mon–Sat 9am–4pm, Sun noon–4pm.

 Acoma Pueblo, P.O. Box 309, Acoma, NM 87034. ☎ **252-1139** or toll free **800/747-0181.**

The spectacular "Sky City," a walled adobe village perched high atop a sheer rock mesa 367 feet above the 6,600-foot valley floor, is said to have been lived in at least since the 11th century—it's the longest continuously occupied community in the United States. Native legend says it has been inhabited since before the time of Christ. Both the pueblo and its mission church of San Estevan del Rey are National Historic Landmarks. When Coronado visited in 1540, he suggested that Acoma was "the greatest stronghold in the world;" those who attempt to follow the cliffside footpath to the top, rather than take the modern road, might agree.

The Keresan-speaking Acoma (pronounced *Ack*-uh-mah) Pueblo boasts about 4,400 inhabitants, but only about 50 reside year-round on the 70-acre mesa top. Many others maintain ancestral homes and occupy them during ceremonial periods. The terraced three-story buildings face south for maximum exposure to the winter sun. Most of Sky City's permanent residents make livings from tourists who throng here to see the magnificent church, built in 1639 and containing numerous masterpieces of Spanish colonial art, and to purchase the thin-walled white pottery, with brown-and-black designs, for which the pueblo is famous.

Start your tour of Acoma at the visitor center at the base of the mesa. While waiting for your tour to begin, peruse the excellent little museum of Acoma history and crafts, or dine on Native American food in an adjoining cafe. Then board your 13-seat tour bus, which climbs through a rock garden of 50-foot sandstone monoliths and past precipitously dangling outhouses to the mesa's summit. There's no running water or electricity in this medieval-looking village; a small reservoir collects rainwater for most uses, and drinking water is transported up from below. Wood-hole ladders and mica windows are prevalent among the 300-odd adobe structures.

The annual San Estevan del Rey feast day is September 2, when the pueblo's patron saint is honored with a midmorning mass, a procession, an afternoon corn dance, and an arts-and-crafts fair. Traditional "rooster pulls" take place June 24 and 29 and July 25; a Governor's Feast is held annually in February; and four days of Christmas festivals run from December 25 to 28. Cameras are not allowed on the mesa during feast days.

Other celebrations are held in low-lying pueblo villages at Easter (in Acomita), in early May (Santa Maria feast at McCartys), and August 10 (San Lorenzo Day in Acomita). Many Acomas work in Grants, 15 miles west of the pueblo, or in Albuquerque; others are cattle ranchers or operate a tribal bingo parlor.

To reach Acoma from Grants, drive east 15 miles on I-40 to McCartys, then south 13 miles on paved tribal roads to the visitor center. From Albuquerque, drive west 52 miles to the Acoma-Sky City exit, then 12 miles southwest.

Admission: Adults $6, seniors $5, children $4. Still photography $5, sketching or painting $40.

Open: Nov–Mar 8am–4:30pm; Apr–Oct 8am–7pm. One-hour tours every 20 minutes. **Closed:** Easter weekend, long weekend after July 4, and first weekend of Oct.

Laguna Pueblo, P.O. Box 194, Laguna Pueblo, NM 87026. ☎ **552-6654.**

The major Keresan-speaking pueblo consists of a central settlement and five smaller villages some 32 miles east of Grants (46 miles west of Albuquerque) along I-40 and

U.S. 66. Laguna is the youngest of New Mexico's pueblos, and with 6,800 residents, the largest after Zuni. Founded after the 1680 Pueblo Revolt by refugees from the Rio Grande valley, it features the Mission of San Jose de los Lagunas, famous for its interior artwork.

Many Lagunas are engaged in agriculture or private business, including a tribal-operated commercial center.

Pueblo and Navajo people from throughout the region attend St. Joseph's Feast Day (September 19) at Old Laguna Village. The fair begins in the morning with a mass and procession, followed by a harvest dance, sports events, and carnival. New Year's Day (January 1) and Three Kings Day (January 6) are also celebrated at the pueblo with processions and dances. Each smaller village has its own feast day between July 26 and October 17; call the pueblo office for details.

Seboyeta, the oldest Hispanic community in western New Mexico, is 3^1/2 miles north of Paguate, outside Laguna Pueblo. It still shows ruins of adobe fortress walls built in the 1830s to protect the village from Navajo attack. The Mission of Our Lady of Sorrows was built in the 1830s, as was the nearby Shrine of Los Portales, built in a cave north of town.

Admission: Free. No photo fee, but some restrictions apply from village to village.

Open: Daylight hours year-round.

★ **El Malpais National Monument**, 620 E. Santa Fe Ave., Grants, NM 87020. ☎ 285-5406.

Designated a national monument in 1987, El Malpais (Spanish for "badlands") is considered one of the outstanding examples of volcanic landscapes in the United States. El Malpais contains 115,000 acres of cinder cones, vast lava flows, hundreds of lava tubes, ice caves, sandstone cliffs, natural bridges and arches, Anasazi ruins, ancient Native American trails, and Spanish and Anglo homesteads.

There are two approaches to El Malpais, via N.M. 117 and N.M. 53. Route 117 exits I-40 7 miles east of Grants. From **Sandstone Bluffs Overlook** (10 miles south of I-40) many craters are visible in the lava flow, which extends for miles along the eastern flank of the Continental Divide. The most recent flows date back only 1,000 years: Native American legends tell of rivers of "fire rock." Seventeen miles south of I-40, **La Ventana** is the largest accessible natural arch in New Mexico.

From N.M. 53, which exits I-40 just west of Grants, visitors have access to the **Zuni-Acoma Trail,** an ancient Pueblo trade route that crosses four major lava flows in a 7^1/2-mile (one-way) hike. A printed trail guide is available. **El Calderon,** 20 miles south of I-40, is a trailhead for exploration of a cinder cone, lava tubes, and a bat cave (with restricted access).

The largest of all Malpais cinder cones, **Bandera Crater,** is on private property 25 miles south of I-40. The National Park Service has laid plans to absorb this commercial operation, known as **Ice Caves Resort** (☎ 783-4303). Visitors pay $6 to hike up the crater or walk to the edge of an ice cave.

Perhaps the most fascinating phenomenon of El Malpais are the lava tubes, formed when the outer surface of a lava flow cooled and solidified. When the lava river drained, tunnellike caves were left. Ice caves within some of the tubes have delicate ice-crystal ceilings, ice stalagmites, and floors like ice rinks.

Admission: Free.

Open: Daily year-round. Visitor center in Grants open daily 8am–4:30pm.

⭐ **El Morro National Monument,** Rte. 2, Box 43, Ramah, NM 87321. ☎ **783-4226.**

Travelers who like to look history straight in the eye are fascinated by "Inscription Rock," 43 miles west of Grants along N.M. 53. Looming up out of the sand and sage-brush is a bluff 200 feet high, holding some of the most captivating messages in North America. Its sandstone face displays a written record of nearly every explorer, con-quistador, missionary, army officer, surveyor, and pioneer emigrant who passed this way between 1605—when Gov. Don Juan de Onate carved the first inscription—and 1906, when it was preserved by the National Park Service. Onate's inscription, dated April 16, 1605, was perhaps the first graffiti left by any European in America, but El Morro also boasts earlier petroglyph carvings by Native Americans.

A paved walkway makes it easy to walk to the writings, and there is a stone stair-way leading up to other treasures. One reads: "Year of 1716 on the 26th of August passed by here Don Feliz Martinez, Governor and Captain General of this realm to the reduction and conquest of the Moqui." Confident of success as he was, Martinez actually got nowhere with any "conquest of the Moqui," or Hopi, peoples. After a 2-month battle they chased him back to Santa Fe. Another special group was the U.S. Camel Corps, trekking past on their way from Texas to California in 1857. The cam-els worked out fine in mountains and deserts, outlasting horses and mules 10 to 1, but the Civil War ended the experiment. When Peachy Breckinridge, fresh out of the Virginia Military Academy, came by with 25 camels, he noted the fact on the stone here.

El Morro was at one time as famous as the Blarney Stone of Ireland: Everybody had to stop by and make a mark. But when the Santa Fe Railroad was laid 25 miles to the north, El Morro was no longer on the main route to California—and from the 1870s, the tradition began to die out.

Atop Inscription Rock via a short, steep trail are ruins of an Anasazi pueblo occu-pying an area 200 by 300 feet. Its name, Atsinna, suggests that carving one's name here is a very old custom indeed: The word, in Zuni, means "writing on rock."

Self-guided trail booklets are available at the visitor center.

Two private enterprises near El Morro are worthy of special note. **El Morro Lodge,** Route 2, Box 44, Ramah, NM 87321 (☎ **783-4612**), has cabins, and RV and tent camping.

West of El Morro, in Ramah, the **Blue Corn Restaurant,** N.M. 53 (☎ **783-4671**), serves some of the most innovative contemporary American cuisine imaginable in an isolated location like this. Daily specials, in the $10-to-$12 range, include apricot-stuffed chicken breast and red snapper with cilantro cream sauce. It's open from 11am to 8:30pm, Thursday to Sunday in summer.

Admission: $4 per car or $2 per person.

Open: Visitor center, summer 8am–7pm, winter 8am–5pm. Campground ($5) open year-round.

Cíbola National Forest, 1800 Lobo Canyon Rd. ☎ 505/287-8833.

Two major parcels of the forest flank I-40 on either side of Grants. To the northeast, N.M. 547 leads some 20 miles into the San Mateo Mountains. The range's high point, 11,301-foot Mount Taylor, is home of the annual Mount Taylor Winter Quadrathlon in February. The route passes two campgrounds, Lobo Canyon and Coal Mine Can-yon. Hiking, enjoying magnificent scenery, and elk hunting are popular in summer, cross-country skiing in winter.

To the west run the Zuni Mountains, a heavily forested range topped by 9,253-foot Mount Sedgewick. Ask at the convention and visitor bureau or the Forest Service office for the "Zuni Mountain Historic Auto Tour" brochure. This describes a 61-mile loop, including over 45 miles of unpaved road with no gas or water en route, that gives unusual insight into the region's early 20th-century logging and mining activities.

On the northern slope of the Zuni Mountains, but outside of the national forest, is **Bluewater Lake State Park** (☎ **876-2318**). At 7,400 feet, this forested recreational site offers fishing for rainbow trout, boating (rentals available), hiking, picnicking, and camping. There is a cafe and store on the east shore, 7 miles south of I-40 Exit 63 (18 miles west of Grants). Ice fishing is popular in winter.

SPORTS & RECREATION

Grants offers **golf** on the nine-hole city-run Zuni Mountain Golf Course (☎ **287-9239**), open Tuesday through Sunday, with $6 weekday greens fees and $10 on weekends; **swimming** at Grants Swimming Pool (☎ **287-7636**) for $1.50 admission; and **tennis** on 6 city courts (☎ **287-7927**).

Where to Stay

Grants hotels are all on or near Route 66, with major properties near I-40 interchanges, and smaller or older motels nearer downtown. Lodger's tax is 5%, which is added to the gross receipts tax of 6.3125% for a total room tax of just over 11%. Parking is usually free.

Best Western Grants Inn, 1501 E. Santa Fe Ave, I-40 Exit 85 (P.O. Drawer T), Grants, NM 87020. ☎ **505/287-7901** or toll free **800/528-1234** or **800/600-5221.** Fax 505/285-5751. 125 rms. A/C FRIDGE TV TEL

Rates: $56–$87 single. $66–$97 double. AE, DC, DISC, MC, V.

Owned by Maloof Hotels, which operates six others in New Mexico, the inn offers a touch of the tropics to this semiarid land. Skylights nourish a junglelike central courtyard of lush trees and tall plants, which surround an indoor swimming pool and cafe.

Rooms are pleasant and modern. Standard units have king-size or two queen-size beds with southwestern decor, table and chairs, and two sinks: one at the vanity. "King suites" are set up for executive travel with a phone at a working desk, an oversize dresser, and a sleeper sofa in a sitting area. Some rooms are designated for nonsmokers and the disabled.

The inn's cafe offers an outdoor experience indoors beneath the skylight. Umbrellas shade the tables, while silk fuchsias and draping vines lend atmosphere. American fare is served daily for breakfast and dinner. Services and facilities include room service during restaurant hours, valet laundry, 24-hour desk, an indoor swimming pool, men's and women's saunas, hot tub, guest Laundromat, video games area, gift shop, and meeting rooms. Pets are welcome.

$ **Sands Motel,** 112 McArthur St. (P.O. Box 1437), Grants, NM 87020. ☎ **505/287-2996** or toll free **800/424-7679.** 24 rms. A/C FRIDGE TV TEL

Rates: $40 single; $43 double. AE, CB, DC, DISC, MC, V.

A family-style motel set back a block from Highway 66, the Sands has two dozen nicely appointed rooms. Rooms have king, queen, and double beds; some have a dressing area between the bedroom and bathroom. Nonsmoking rooms are available. Fee for pets.

Where to Dine

⭐ **El Jardin Palacios,** 319 W. Santa Fe Ave. ☎ **285-5231.**
$ **Cuisine:** NEW MEXICAN.
Prices: $2.50–$7.95. AE, MC, V.
Open: Mon–Fri 11am–2:30pm, Mon–Sat 5–9pm.

This friendly restaurant, owned and operated by the Palacio family, is located on Route 66. Plants hang in the windows of El Jardin (the garden), and original oils adorn the walls, giving it a homey feeling.

The food is of high quality. Beef is shredded and sautéed for tacos, not ground and fried; the specialty is chimichangas—meat, chicken, or machaca. There is also trout, shrimp, and scampi; shrimp, beef, and chicken fajitas; and chicken enchiladas. If you have room, try the florencita, a dessert special with fruit filling. Beer and wine are served.

Grants Station Restaurant, 200 W. Santa Fe Ave. ☎ **287-2334.**
Cuisine: AMERICAN.
Prices: Breakfast$2.50–$5.50;lunch $2.40–$4.95; dinner $2.75–$11.95. AE,DISC, MC, V.
Open: Daily 6am–11pm.

You can't miss this place: an old red Santa Fe Railroad caboose stands outside on a length of track. And the train theme extends inside with old railroad signs and other memorabilia, donated by numerous aficionados—many of them "just passing through."

This is a great place for breakfast, which is served all day. And you'll find basic American food—chicken-fried steak, sandwiches, salads, fried chicken, top sirloin, and filet of perch. A few Mexican dishes, like tacos, burritos, and fajitas, are also on the menu, and there's an all-you-can-eat Sunday brunch from 8am–2pm (just $5.25). Grants Station is not licensed for alcoholic beverages.

La Ventana, 110½ Geis St., Hillcrest Center. ☎ **287-9393.**
Cuisine: STEAKS. **Reservations:** Recommended.
Prices: Appetizers $2–$5.50; lunch $2.75–$6.75; dinner $3.95–$13.95. AE, CB, DC, DISC, MC, V.
Open: Mon–Sat 11am–11pm.

The newly remodeled southwestern decor displays original Navajo sand paintings and a massive metal sculpture of two horses by John F. Prazen. Prime rib and steaks are the top sellers here and fresh seafood is served weekends. Chicken and beef fajitas are also popular. La Ventana has a full bar.

Monte Carlo Restaurant & Lounge, 721 W. Santa Fe Ave. ☎ **287-9250.**
Cuisine: NEW MEXICAN & STEAKS.
Prices: Appetizers $2.25–$3.50; main courses, breakfast $1.30–$6.60, lunch $2.50–$5.50, dinner $5.75–$12.95. AE, DISC, MC, V.
Open: Daily 7am–10pm.

Open since 1947, this adobe restaurant is one of the few buildings in Grants that predates the uranium boom. The menu hasn't changed a lot over the years: It includes steak Marie (topped with green chile and melted cheese), chile rellenos del mar (with shrimp and crabmeat), even Navajo tacos (frybread with borracho beans, chile, and vegetables) and Mexican pizza. There's live music as well as a full bar in the Cíbola Room. Children's menu available.

2 Gallup, Zuni & the Navajo Reservation

Gallup: 138 miles W of Albuquerque; 122 miles SSW of Farmington; 190 miles E of Flagstaff, Ariz.

GETTING THERE • By Plane   Gallup Municipal Airport, West Highway 66 (☎ **722-4896**), is served several times daily by **Mesa America West Express** (☎ **722-5404** or toll free **800/235-9292**). There are regular connections to and from Farmington and Phoenix, Arizona.

• By Train   AMTRAK stops at the Santa Fe Railroad depot, 201 E. Hwy. 66 at Strong Street (☎ toll free **800/USA-RAIL**). No tickets are sold here; passage must be booked ahead. The *Southwest Chief,* which runs between Los Angeles and Chicago, stops once daily eastbound and once westbound.

• By Bus   Greyhound Lines, Inc., 105 S. Dean St. at Aztec Avenue (☎ **863-3761**), stops several times daily on runs to Albuquerque, Farmington, and Flagstaff, Arizona.

**• By Car   From Albuquerque, take I-40 west (2¹/₂ hours). From Farmington, take U.S. 64 west to Shiprock, then U.S. 666 south (2¹/₂ hours). From Flagstaff, Arizona, take I-40 east (3 hours).

**ESSENTIALS • Orientation   Gallup stretches for about 11 miles east and west along the I-40 corridor. U.S. Highway 66, which parallels the freeway on the south side of the Rio Puerco of the West, is the principal avenue. Through downtown Gallup, it's known as 66 Avenue. Second and Third streets cross 66 as the main north-south arteries of downtown Gallup. A loop bypass is formed by N.M. 564 (east of downtown) and N.M. 602 (west of downtown, extending south to Zuni).

• Information   The Gallup Convention and Visitors Bureau, 701 Montoya Blvd. (P.O. Box 600), Gallup, NM 87305 (☎ **505/863-3841** or toll free **800/242-4282**), is conveniently located in Miyamura Park, just north of the main I-40 interchange for downtown Gallup. Or contact the **Gallup–McKinley County Chamber of Commerce,** P.O. Box 1395, Gallup, NM 87305 (☎ **505/722-2228**).

• Fast Facts   The **area code is 505. **Rehoboth McKinley Christian Hospital** is located at 1901 Red Rock Dr. (☎ **863-7000**). The main **post office** is at 500 S. Second St. (☎ **863-3491**). In case of **emergencies,** dial **911.**

There's more to Gallup than the city's seemingly endless Route 66 neon strip might at first indicate. Founded on the rail line in 1881 as a coal supply town, Gallup has a frontier atmosphere that lingers among the late 19th- and early 20th-century buildings. A proliferation of Native American trading posts and pawnbrokers offers opportunities for shopping and bargaining. The city is the market center for the Navajo Reservation to the north and Zuni Pueblo to the south.

What to See & Do

A WALKING TOUR OF GALLUP

Gallup has 20 buildings that are either listed on, or have been nominated to, the National Register of Historic Places. Start at the **Santa Fe Railroad depot,** East 66 Avenue and Strong Street. Built in 1923 in modified mission style with heavy Spanish–Pueblo revival–style massing, it is earmarked to be renovated into a community transportation and cultural center. Across the highway, the **Drake Hotel** (now the

Turquoise Club), built of blond brick in 1919, had the Prohibition-era reputation of being controlled by bootleggers, with wine running in the faucets in place of water. Two blocks west, the 1928 **White Cafe,** 100 W. 66 Ave., is an elaborate decorative brick structure that catered to the early auto tourist traffic. **Kitchen's Opera House** (now Zimmermans and the Eagle Cafe), 218 W. 66 Ave., dates from 1895; it had a second-floor stage for all kinds of functions and performances, and a first-floor saloon and Cafe. A block farther, the **Rex Hotel,** 300 W. 66 Ave., was constructed of locally quarried sandstone; once known for its "ladies of the night," it's now a police substation.

A block north of the police station, at 101 N. Third St., is the **C. N. Cotton Warehouse** (now Associated Grocers). Built about 1897 in the New Mexico vernacular style, with a sandstone foundation and adobe-block walls, it has a statue in front that is a city landmark: **Manuelito,** the last Navajo chief to surrender to U.S. soldiers. Mr. Cotton, a trader who admired the Navajo's bravery, commissioned the statue.

Reverse course, and head back south two blocks on Third. Turn east on Coal Avenue. The **Grand Hotel** (now Ricca Mercantile), 306 W. Coal Ave., was built about 1925 as the depot for transcontinental buses on Route 66, as well as a travelers' hotel. The **Chief Theater** (now City Electric Shoe Shop), 228 W. Coal Ave., was built in 1920; but in 1936 it was completely redesigned in Pueblo-deco style, with zigzag relief and geometric form, by R. E. "Griff" Griffith, brother of Hollywood producer D.W. Griffith. Almost across the street, the 1928 **El Morro Theater** is of Spanish colonial revival style with an ornate symmetry from the parapet to the corbels. Next door, the **Ruiz Optical Building** has been decorated with Native American *kachinas* between the second-floor windows.

South two blocks at 201 W. Hill Ave., the **McKinley County Court House** was built in 1938 in Spanish Pueblo revival style. The bell tower and upper stories display stylized projecting *vigas,* while wood beams and corbels define the entry. Indian-motif reliefs, tiles, and paintings are found throughout. Back at the corner of First and Coal, the **Old Post Office** (now United Cable Television) is an eclectic mix of Mediterranean, decorative brick commercial, and Spanish Pueblo revival styles. Large carved eagles are used as corbels, and the beams have brightly painted rope molding lines.

OTHER ATTRACTIONS

Red Rock State Park, N.M. 566 (P.O. Box 328), Church Rock, NM 87311.
☎ **722-3829.**

Six miles east of downtown Gallup, this park—with its natural amphitheater—is set against red sandstone buttes. It includes an auditorium/convention center, historical museum, post office, trading post, stables, and modern campgrounds.

An 8,000-seat arena is the site of numerous annual events, including the Inter-Tribal Indian Ceremonial in mid-August. Red Rock Convention Center accommodates 600 for trade shows or concert performances.

The Red Rock Museum has displays on prehistoric Anasazi and modern Zuni, Hopi, and Navajo cultures, and changing art gallery exhibits. From June through September, corns, beans, and squash are grown outside in a traditional Pueblo "waffle garden."

Admission: Museum, adults $1, children 50¢.
Open: Museum, Mon–Fri 8:30am–4:30pm, with extended hours in summer.

⭐ **Navajo Indian Reservation,** P.O. Box 663, Window Rock, AZ 86515.
☎ **602/871-6659** or **871-6436.**

Navajos comprise the largest Native American tribe in the United States, with over 200,000 members. Their reservation, known to them as Navajoland, spreads across 24,000 square miles of Arizona, Utah, and New Mexico. The New Mexico portion, extending in a band 45 miles wide from just north of Gallup to the Colorado border, comprises only about 15% of the total area.

Until the 1920s, the Navajo nation governed itself with a complex clan system. When oil was discovered on reservation land, the Navajos established a tribal government to handle the complexities of the 20th century. Today, the Navajo Tribal Council has 88 council delegates representing 110 regional chapters, some two dozen of which are in New Mexico. They meet at least four times a year as a full body in **Window Rock,** Arizona, capital of the Navajo nation, near the New Mexico border 24 miles northwest of Gallup.

Natural resources and tourism are the mainstays of the Navajo economy. Coal, oil, gas, and uranium earn some $45 million a year, with coal alone providing about two-thirds of that sum. Tourism provides nearly the same amount, especially on the Arizona side of the border, which contains or abuts Grand Canyon and Petrified Forest national parks, Canyon de Chelly, Wupatki, and Navajo national monuments, and Monument Valley Navajo Tribal Park; and in Utah, Glen Canyon National Recreation Area, Rainbow Bridge and Hovenweep national monuments, and Four Corners Monument.

The Navajos, like their linguistic cousins, the Apaches, belong to the large family of Athapaskan Indians found across Alaska and northwestern Canada and in parts of the northern California coast. They are believed to have migrated to the Southwest about the 14th century. In 1864, after nearly two decades of conflict with the U.S. Army, the entire tribe was rounded up and forced into internment at an agricultural colony near Fort Sumner, New Mexico—an event still recalled as "The Long March." Four years of near-starvation later, the experiment was declared a failure, and the now-contrite Navajos returned to their homeland.

Three to four generations later, 320 Navajo young men served in the U.S. Marine Corps as communications specialists in the Pacific during the Second World War. The code they created, 437 terms based on the extremely complex Navajo language, was never broken by the Japanese. Among those heroes still alive is artist Carl Gorman, coordinator of the Navajo Medicine Man Organization and father of internationally famed painter R. C. Gorman.

While Navajos express themselves artistically in all media, they are best known for their work in silversmithing, sand painting, basketry, and weaving. Distinctive styles of handwoven rugs from Two Grey Hills, Ganado, and Crystal are known worldwide.

The place to stay on the reservation is the **Navajo Nation Inn,** Highway 264 (P.O. Box 1687), Window Rock, AZ 86515 (☎ **602/871-4108**). Modern rooms are comfortable and inexpensive, and the restaurant offers Navajo specialties. The inn has an attractive weekend package that for $140 includes two nights' lodging and a Saturday bus trip that takes in **Hubbell Trading Post National Historic Site** at Ganado, 30 miles west of Window Rock; **Canyon de Chelly National Monument,** 39 miles north of Ganado; **Navajo Community College** and its Hatathli Gallery at Tsaile, 28 miles northeast of Chinle; and the 56-mile return to Window Rock.

Attractions in Window Rock itself include the **Navajo Nation Council Chambers,** the **Navajo Nation Arts and Crafts Enterprise,** the **Navajo Museum and Tribal**

Zoo, St. Michael's Mission Museum, and **Window Rock Tribal Park,** containing the natural red-rock arch after which the community is named.

In early September, the annual 5-day **Navajo Nation Fair** attracts more than 100,000 people to Window Rock for a huge rodeo, parade, carnival, Miss Navajo Nation contest, arts-and-crafts shows, intertribal powwow, concerts, country dancing, and agricultural exhibits. Among smaller annual tribal fairs are the traditional October **Shiprock Navajo Fair,** 90 miles north of Gallup, and the **Eastern Navajo Fair** in Crownpoint, 55 miles northeast of Gallup.

The Crownpoint Rug Weavers Association has 12 public auctions a year, normally on Friday evenings, about five weeks apart.

★ **Zuni Pueblo,** N.M. 53 (P.O. Box 339), Zuni, NM 87327. ☎ 782-4481.

The largest of New Mexico's occupied pueblos, Zuni is located about 38 miles south of Gallup via state roads 602 and 53. First seen by Spanish explorers in 1539, the sun reflecting off the adobe buildings created a golden glow, leading to tales of cities of gold and Coronado's search for the fabled Seven Cities of Cíbola. The ruins of **Hawikuh,** believed by historians to be the pueblo first seen by the Spanish, are about 13 miles southwest of the main pueblo.

Today, Zuni tribal members are widely acclaimed for their jewelry, made from turquoise, shell, and jet, set in silver in intricate patterns called "needlepoint." The tribe also does fine beadwork, carving in shell and stone, and some pottery. Jewelry and other crafts are sold at the tribally owned **Pueblo of Zuni Arts and Crafts** (☎ 782-5532).

The **Zuni Museum Project,** open Monday through Friday from 9am to 4pm, displays historical photos and exhibits. **Our Lady of Guadalupe Mission,** originally built in 1629 and then renovated in 1969, is decorated with murals by renowned Zuni artist Alex Seowtewa. The church is open to the public weekday afternoons from 1 to 4pm.

The pueblo is well known for its **Shalako Ceremony,** an all-night celebration with dances, processions, and prayers in late November or early December. Over Labor Day weekend, the pueblo holds a **Fair and Rodeo.**

As at all Indian reservations, visitors are asked to respect tribal customs and individuals' privacy. Photography is strictly prohibited during some ceremonies, and camera permits must be obtained at other times. In addition, some dances may be completely closed to outsiders; it's best to call before going.

Admission: Free.

Open: Daily, dawn to dusk.

INDIAN DANCES

Nightly Native American dance performances take place at the corner of 66 Ave. and First St. in Gallup (☎ 863-1243), each evening at 7pm from Memorial Day through Labor Day.

SPORTS & RECREATION

Fishing and hunting are popular in adjacent national forests and mesa land, and in small lakes and streams in the Chuska and Zuni mountains. Tribal permits may be required.

The 18-hole **Gallup Municipal Golf Course,** 1109 Susan St. (☎ 863-9224), is set on rolling hills and canyonland in the southeastern part of town. It's open year-round, weather permitting, Friday through Sunday and Tuesday and

Wednesday from 6am to dusk, and Monday and Thursday from noon to dusk. Greensfees are $7 weekdays and $10 weekends.

The Fitness Center, 700 Old Zuni Rd. (☎ 722-7271), offers health-club goers a place for aerobics or racquetball. It also has free weights and Nautilus equipment, a gym, an indoor track, sauna, whirlpool, steam room, massage, and tanning.

SHOPPING

Nowhere are the jewelry and crafts of Navajo, Zuni, and Hopi tribes less expensive than in Gallup. The most intriguing places to shop are the trading posts and pawnshops, which provide a surprising range of services for their largely Native American clientele and have little in common with the pawnshops of large American cities.

Navajoland ❏ **pawnbrokers** in essence are bankers, at least from the Navajo and Zuni viewpoint. They're like savings-and-loan institutions, but a lot less likely to fold. In fact, they're an integral part of the economic structure of the Gallup area, providing with such services as the safekeeping of valuable personal goods and the payment of small collateral loans.

Security systems in Navajo hogans and Zuni pueblos are nonexistent. So Native Americans go to the trading post with their turquoise and silver jewelry, ceremonial baskets, hand-tanned hides, saddles, and guns, and "pawn" them for safekeeping. They may accept a payment far less than the value of the goods, because the smaller the amount of the loan, the easier it is to redeem the items when they are needed.

Pawnbrokers are also collateral lenders. Traditionally, Navajos visited trading posts to exchange handmade goods for cash or other products. Today, banks won't take jewelry or guns as loan collateral—but the trading post will. What's more, the trader will hold onto the items for months or even years before deeming it "dead" and putting it up for sale. Less than 5% ever go unredeemed.

Those shopping for jewelry should look for silver concho belts, worn with jeans and southwestern skirts, cuff bracelets, and necklaces, from traditional squash blossoms to silver beads and *heishi,* very fine beads worn in several strands. Earrings may be only in silver, or they may be decorated with varying stones.

For men, bolo ties and belt buckles of silver and/or turquoise are popular. Silver concho hatbands go great on Stetson hats. A silver or gold handcrafted earring, sometimes decorated with turquoise, is a big seller.

Handwoven Native American rugs may be draped on couches, hung on walls, or used on floors. Also look for pottery, *kachinas,* and sculpture.

Most shops are open Monday through Saturday from 9am to 5pm.

ART & CRAFTS   Art-related activities complement exhibits at some of these emporiums: **Gallup Gallery,** 108 W. Coal Ave. (☎ 863-4563); **Kiva Gallery,** 202 E. 66 Ave. (☎ 722-5577); **Red Mesa Art Center,** 105 W. Hill Ave. (☎ 722-4209); and **Windy Mesa Gallery,** 230 W. 66 Ave. (☎ 863-5077).

Two interesting crafts shops are **Denny Pino's Gift Shop,** 116 W. 66 Ave. (☎ 722-6455); and **Pat Yellowhorse Originals,** 1302 S. Second St. (☎ 863-6809).

CLOTHING   For western attire for the whole family, try **Sherman's Boots & Jeans,** 920 E. 66 Ave. (☎ 722-6166); and **Trice's Western Wear,** 210 W. Coal Ave. (☎ 863-4631).

GIFTS/SOUVENIRS   A wide range of items can be found at **The Ceramic Shop,** 502 E. 66 Ave. (☎ 722-4259); and **OB's Indian America,** 3330 E. Hwy. 66 (☎ 722-4431 or toll free **800/545-3819**).

JEWELRY   Prominent local dealers include **Cousins Indian Jewelry,** 2000 E. Hwy. 66 (☎ **722-4471**); **Martinez Indian Jewelry,** 1624 S. Second St., Cedar Hills Plaza (☎ **722-5217**); **Gilbert Ortega's Indian Jewelry,** 3306 E. Hwy. 66 (☎ **722-6666**); **Silver House Trading Company,** 210 W. 66 Ave. (☎ **722-2335**); and **Trailblazer,** 210 W. Hill Ave. (☎ **722-5051**).

PAWNBROKERS   These distinctive area merchants include **Jean's All Indian Pawn Shop,** 2000 E. Hwy. 66 (☎ **722-4471**); **T & R Pawn,** 1300 W. I-40 Frontage Rd., Rio West Mall (☎ **722-3473**); and **Trader Billy K's,** 118 W. 66 Ave. (☎ **722-5151**).

TRADING POSTS   For a look at everything from livestock to unusual souvenirs, visit **Ellis Tanner Trading Company,** Munoz Ave. between I-40 (exit 20) and Zuni Rd. (☎ **863-4434**); **First American Traders of Gallup,** 2201 W. Hwy. 66 (☎ **722-6601**); **Richardson Trading and Cash Pawn, Inc.,** 222 W. 66 Ave. (☎ **722-4762**); **Shi'ma Traders,** 216 W. Coal Ave. (tel. **722-5500**); **Silver Dust Trading Co.,** 120 W. 66 Ave. (☎ **722-4848**); **Tobe Turpen's Indian Trading Company,** 1710 S. Second St. (☎ **722-3806**); and **Turney's Inc.,** 207 S. Third St. (☎ **863-6504**).

Where to Stay

Virtually every accommodation in Gallup is somewhere along Route 66, either near the I-40 interchanges or on the highway through downtown. Local lodging tax is 5%; added to the 6.1875% state tax, a total of just over 11% is levied on hotel bills.

In the listings below the following price ranges apply: **moderate,** over $60 per night double; **inexpensive,** $40–$60; and **budget,** less than $40. Parking is usually free.

MODERATE

Best Western Gallup Inn, 3009 W. Hwy. 66, Gallup, NM 87301. ☎ **505/722-2221** or toll free **800/528-1234.** Fax 505/722-7442. 124 rms, 21 suites. A/C FRIDGE TV TEL

Rates: $54–$82 single; $60–$92 double; $64–$102 suite. AE, CB, DC, DISC, MC, V.

The trademark of this property is its huge central Atrium Courtyard that contains the hotel cafe at one end, the swimming pool at the other, and skylit trees and plants in between. Three 8-foot paintings of Native American dancers dominate the lobby.

The rooms are large and well kept, with one king-size or two queen-size beds and a big desk-dresser combination. The vanity has its own sink in addition to that within the bathroom. There are rooms for nonsmokers and the disabled. The Cafe, under the roof of the Atrium Courtyard, serves breakfast and dinner daily. The lounge serves drinks Monday to Saturday from 2pm. The hotel has room service, valet laundry service, 24-hour desk, an indoor swimming pool, hot tub, men's and women's saunas, weight/exercise room, video games, guest laundry, and gift shop. Meeting facilities accommodate 600. Pets are allowed.

Holiday Inn, 2915 W. Hwy. 66, Gallup, NM 87301. ☎ **505/722-2201** or toll free **800/432-2211.** Fax 505/722-9616. 212 rms. A/C TV TEL

Rates: $49–$87 single or double. AE, CB, DC, DISC, JCB, MC, V.

The spacious lobby of this hotel makes indoors feel like outdoors. A small fountain and various plants stand beneath a high ceiling, while Native American motifs and small murals are painted on some of the walls.

Rooms, many decorated with Southwest decor in tones of purple and rust, contain a king-size or two double beds, a hideabed sofa or leisure chairs, a desk, and a clock radio. Some rooms accommodate nonsmokers or the disabled.

Nicole's offers fine continental cuisine from 5:30 to 10pm Tuesday through Saturday. The specialty in this intimate setting is table-side preparation of dishes like scampi Provençale, steak Diane, and veal scaloppine Nicole. The Cactus Rose serves three meals daily, from 6am to 10pm, in a more casual setting. The City Lights lounge, open from 11:30am to 1:30am Monday to Saturday, has live country-and-western music for dancing nightly. The hotel has room service, valet laundry service, 24-hour desk, courtesy van, an indoor swimming pool, hot tub, sauna, weight equipment, guest laundry, gift shop, and meeting facilities for 800. Pets are allowed.

INEXPENSIVE

Days Inn—West, 3201 W. Hwy. 66, Gallup, NM 87301. ☎ **505/863–6889** or toll free **800/DAYS-INN.** 74 rms, 1 suite. A/C TV TEL

Rates: $35–$55 single; $40–$60 double; $80–$120 suite. AE, CB, DC, DISC, MC, V.

New in September 1990, this handsome two-story pink adobe building is built in Spanish style with a tile roof. Rooms are of average size, but they're nicely done in desert rose color schemes, with prints of regional native crafts on the walls.

Complimentary coffee, donuts, and juice are served in the lobby in the morning. The hotel offers a 24-hour desk, nonsmoking and handicapped rooms, an indoor swimming pool, hot tub, and guest laundry. No pets.

★ **El Rancho Hotel & Motel**, 1000 E. 66 Ave., Gallup, NM 87301. ☎ **505/863-9311** or toll free **800/543-6351.** Fax 505/722-5917. 98 rms, 2 suites. A/C TV TEL

Rates: $41–$53 single; $49–$59 double; $74 suite. AE, CB, DC, DISC, MC, V.

This historic hotel owes as much to Hollywood as to Gallup. Built in 1937 by R. E. "Griff" Griffith, brother of movie mogul D. W. Griffith, it became *the* place for film companies to set up headquarters in the Southwest. Between the 1940s and 1960s, a who's who of Hollywood stayed here. Their autographed photos line the walls of the hotel's cafe mezzanine. Spencer Tracy and Katharine Hepburn stayed here during production of *The Sea of Grass;* Burt Lancaster and Lee Remick were guests when they made *The Hallelujah Trail.* Gene Autry, Lucille Ball, Jack Benny, Humphrey Bogart, James Cagney, Rhonda Flemming, Errol Flynn, Henry Fonda, John Forsythe, Paulette Goddard, Susan Hayward, William Holden, the Marx Brothers, Fred MacMurray, Robert Mitchum, Gregory Peck, Tyrone Power, Ronald Reagan, Rosalind Russell, James Stewart, Robert Taylor, Gene Tierney, John Wayne, and Mae West have all been here—the list goes on and on.

In 1986, Gallup businessman Armand Ortega, a longtime jewelry merchant, bought a run-down El Rancho and restored it to its earlier elegance. The lobby staircase rises to the mezzanine on either side of an enormous stone fireplace, while heavy ceiling beams and railings made of tree limbs give the room a hunting-lodge ambience. The hotel is on the National Register of Historic Places.

Rooms in El Rancho differ one to the next, and are named for the stars who stayed in them. There are ceiling fans, and Southwest art prints on the walls. The corridors bear small paintings of Native American life. Many rooms have balconies.

El Rancho's full-service restaurant, open from 6:30am to 10pm daily, has pleasant hacienda decor. Egg and pancake breakfasts run from $1.75 to $6.95; lunches (salads, burgers, and other sandwiches), from $2.95 to $7.45. Dinner main dishes—standard American meals like steaks, pork chops, and fried chicken—range from $4.50 to $13.95. The '49er Lounge stays lively later. Services and facilities include a 24-hour desk, courtesy car (by request), a seasonal outdoor pool, guest Laundromat, Ortega's Indian Store, and meeting space for 150.

BUDGET

$ **Blue Spruce Lodge,** 1119 E. 66 Ave., Gallup, NM 87301. ☎ **505/863-5211.** 20 rms. A/C TV TEL

Rates: $20 single; $26 double. AE, CB, DC, DISC, MC, V.

This little motel is nothing fancy, but it's clean, hospitable, and a step ahead of others in friendliness. Rooms have standard furnishings; some have shower-bath combinations, others showers only. Small pets are allowed.

El Capitan Motel, 1300 E. 66 Ave., Gallup, NM 87301. ☎ **505/863-6828.** 42 rms, 5 suites. A/C TV TEL

Rates: $26 single; $28–$40 double; $40–$50 suite. AE, CB, DC, DISC, MC, V.

A one-story adobe-style motel, El Capitan has recently been remodeled. Rooms are very spacious, simply but comfortably furnished with full-size beds, desk-dresser, table and chairs, and vanity/dressing area. Family suites that sleep five are a bit more eclectic in appearance than the standard guest rooms. In-room coffee is provided. Pets are accepted.

Where to Dine

Keep in mind that alcoholic beverages cannot be served in Gallup on Sundays.

 Panz Alegra, 1201 E. 66 Ave., Gallup. ☎ **722-7229.**

Cuisine: MEXICAN, STEAK & SEAFOOD. **Reservations:** Recommended.
Prices: Appetizers $2.95–$3.95; lunch $3–$7.95; dinner $4–$12. AE, CB, DC, DISC, MC, V.
Open: Mon–Sat 11am–10pm.

This brown-stone and yellow-adobe building harbors what may be Gallup's finest restaurant. Behind brick arches and planter boxes of silk flowers, diners enjoy steak-and-seafood platters, or opt for the fine New Mexican food. House specialties include carne adovada, arroz con pollo, and the Alegra steak with green chile and cheese. The restaurant has a full bar.

The Ranch Kitchen, 3001 W. Hwy. 66, Gallup. ☎ **722-2537.**

Cuisine: AMERICAN & MEXICAN. **Reservations:** For large parties.
Prices: Appetizers $2.95–$3.75; breakfast $1.95–$5.25; lunch $3.50–$7.95; dinner $5.95–$12.95. AE, CB, DC, MC, V.
Open: Daily, summer 6am–10pm; winter 6am–9pm.

An institution since 1954, the Ranch Kitchen has the perfect location to attract tourists—wedged between Gallup's two largest accommodations at the west end of the city. It takes full advantage of that, with two gift shops flanking the entrance, and a variety of colorful piñatas, *kachinas,* and other folk art hanging everywhere. But come for the food. It's hard to pass up the chicken and ribs, barbecued outside when weather permits. There's great chili, excellent Navajo tacos and rancho grande burritos, fine steaks, and a big soup-and-salad buffet. Children and seniors can order smaller portions from their own menus. The restaurant serves wine and beer.

3 Farmington, Chaco & Aztec Ruins National Monument

Farmington: 182 miles NW of Albuquerque; 122 miles NNE of Gallup; 214 miles W of Taos; 49 miles S of Durango, Colo.

GETTING THERE • By Plane   All commercial flights arrive at busy **Four Corners Regional Airport** on Navajo Drive (☎ 599-1395). The principal carrier is **Mesa Airlines** (☎ 326-3338 or toll free 800/MESA-AIR), with over a dozen daily flights connecting Farmington to Albuquerque and other major cities. **United Express** (☎ 326-4495 or toll free 800/241-6522) links Farmington with Denver and other Colorado communities with several daily flights. **American Eagle,** a division of American Airlines (☎ toll free 800/433-7300), has flights to and from Dallas and Los Angeles.

Car-rental agencies at Four Corners airport include **Avis** (☎ 327-9864), **Budget** (☎ 327-7304), **Hertz** (☎ 327-6093), and **National** (☎ 327-0215).

• By Bus   Farmington is served by **Texas, New Mexico & Oklahoma (TNM&O) Coaches,** 101 E. Animas St. (☎ 325-1009) with daily service to and from Albuquerque, Durango, Salt Lake City, and several Texas cities.

• By Car   From Albuquerque, take N.M. 44 (through Cuba) from the I-25 Bernalillo exit, then turn left (west) on U.S. 64 at Bloomfield (³/₄ hour). From Gallup, take U.S. 666 north to Shiprock, then turn right (east) on U.S. 64 (2¹/₄ hours). From Taos, follow U.S. 64 all the way (4¹/₂ hours). From Durango, take U.S. 500 south (1 hour).

ESSENTIALS • Orientation   Farmington lies at the confluence of the Animas and San Juan rivers, and at the junction of U.S. 64 (from Taos) and U.S. 550 (from Durango). As Highway 64 crosses the Animas and enters downtown Farmington, it becomes Broadway; it is paralleled one block north by Highway 550, here known as Main Street. They join at the west end of downtown. Other main thoroughfares are 20th Street, a quarter mile north of Main, which intersects Highway 550 at its east end; Butler Avenue, a north-south thoroughfare which links Broadway and Main with 20th; and Scott Avenue, a quarter mile east of Butler, where most major accommodations are located.

• Information   The **Farmington Convention and Visitors Bureau,** 203 W. Main St. (☎ 505/326-7602 or toll free 800/448-1240), is the clearinghouse for tourist information. It shares an address with the **Farmington Chamber of Commerce** (☎ 505/325-0279).

• Fast Facts   The **area code** is 505. **San Juan Regional Medical Center,** 801 W. Maple St. (☎ 325-5011), is the principal hospital. The main **post office** is at 2301 E. 20th St. (☎ 325-5047). Taxi service is provided by **K.B. Cab Company** (☎ 325-2999 or toll free 800/765-RIDE). In case of **emergencies,** dial **911.**

A river city of 36,500 residents, Farmington is the gateway to the Four Corners area. Its pride and joy is a system of five parks it's developed along the San Juan River and its tributaries, the Animas and La Plata rivers. In this desert country, it follows that Farmington is an agricultural oasis. It's also an industrial center (for coal, oil, natural gas, and hydroelectricity), and a takeoff point for explorations of the Navajo Reservation, Chaco Culture National Historical Park, Aztec Ruins National Monument, and Mesa Verde National Park in Colorado.

What to See & Do

THE RUINS

 Chaco Culture National Historical Park, Star Rte. 4 (P.O. Box 6500), Bloomfield, NM 87413. ☎ **505/786-7014.**

Chaco represents the high point of pre-Columbian Pueblo civilization. A must-see attraction for any visitor even vaguely interested in ancient Indians, it includes more than a dozen large Anasazi ruins occupied from the early 900s to about A.D. 1200, and hundreds of smaller sites in the wide streambed of the normally dry Chaco Wash.

A series of pueblo ruins stand within 5 or 6 miles of each other on the broad, flat, treeless canyon floor. Pueblo Bonito is the largest. Other ruins accessible directly from an auto road running up and down the canyon are Chetro Ketl, Pueblo del Arroyo, Kin Kletso, Casa Chiquita, Casa Rinconada, Hungo Pavi, and Una Vida. Some ruins demand half-day backcountry hikes to reach; they include Penasco Blanco, Pueblo Alto, Tsin Kletsin, and Wijiji.

Most ruins are on the north side of the canyon. **Pueblo Bonito,** constructed over three acres of land in the 11th century A.D., may have been the largest apartment house built anywhere in the world prior to 1887. It had four stories, 600 rooms, and 40 *kivas,* and may have housed as many as 1,200 people. **Chetro Ketl** had some 500 rooms, 16 kivas, and an impressive enclosed plaza. **Pueblo del Arroyo** was a four-story, D-shaped structure, with about 280 rooms and 20 kivas; **Kin Kletso** had three stories, 100 rooms, and five kivas. **Una Vida,** a short walk from the visitor center, was one of the first pueblos built and has been left only partially excavated; it had 150 rooms and five kivas. **Casa Rinconada,** on the south side of the canyon, is the largest "great kiva" in the park, and is astronomically aligned to the cardinal directions and the summer solstice. It may have been a center for the community at large, used for major spiritual observances.

The Chacoans were skilled masons, building their cities of sandstone blocks mortared with mud, with no metal tools or formal mathematical knowledge. The use of different masonry styles has helped to date the buildings.

The sweeping magnificence of this lost and ruined city, as seen from 100 feet above on the rim of the canyon, impresses visitors most—the outline of Pueblo Bonito, its many kivas forming circles within the great half circle of the community, all of it in the glowing sandstone browns and tans of the land and stone around it. Eventually there were 75 such compact towns all connected with one another in this region of New Mexico.

Aerial photos show hundreds of miles of roads connecting these towns with the Chaco pueblos, one of the longest running 42 miles straight north to Salmon Ruin and the Aztec Ruins (see below). Settlements were spaced along the road at travel intervals of one day. They were not simple trails worn into the stone by foot travel, but engineered roadways 30 feet wide with a berm of rock to contain the fill. Where the road went over flat rock, walls were built along the sides of it. It is this road network that leads some scholars to believe Chaco was the center of a unified Anasazi society.

The Chacoans' trade network, as suggested by artifacts found here, stretched from California to Texas and south into Mexico. Seashell necklaces, copper bells, and the remains of macaws or parrots were found among Chaco artifacts. Some of these items are displayed in the museum at the visitor center. Self-guiding trail brochures are obtained here, as well as permits for the overnight campground (with a water supply, tables, and fireplaces; bring your own wood or charcoal).

The only snag to visiting Chaco is its isolation. Farmington is the nearest population center, and it's still a 75-mile, 2-hour drive to these ruins. N.M. 44 takes you as far as the Nageezi Trading Post, but the final 26 miles are graded dirt—fine in dry weather but dangerous when it rains, and often flooded where arroyos cross it. Inquire before leaving the paved highway. (A turnoff at Blanco Trading Post, 8 miles before Nageezi, cuts 5 miles off the trip, but the road is more subject to hazardous conditions. The park can also be reached from the south via Crownpoint, with the final 19 miles graded dirt.) There's no food, gas, or lodging nearer than Nageezi.

Admission: $4 per car or $2 per person; seniors 62 and older free.

Open: Memorial Day–Labor Day daily 8am–6pm; rest of year daily 8am–5pm. Campground open 24 hours.

★ **Aztec Ruins National Monument,** U.S. Hwy. 550, P.O. Box 640 Aztec. ☎ **334-6174.**

The ruins of a fabulous 500-room Native American pueblo, abandoned by the Anasazi seven centuries ago, make up this site, 14 miles northeast of Farmington in the town of Aztec on the Animas River. Early Anglo settlers, convinced that the ruins were of Aztec origin, misnamed the site. Despite the fact that this pueblo was built long before the Aztecs of central Mexico lived, the name persisted.

The influence of the Chaco culture is strong at Aztec, as evidenced in the preplanned architecture, the open plaza, and the fine stone masonry in the old walls. But Aztec is best known for its Great Kiva, the only completely reconstructed Anasazi great kiva in existence. About 50 feet in diameter, with a main floor sunken eight feet below the surface of the surrounding ground, this circular ceremonial room rivets the imagination. It's hard not to feel spiritually overwhelmed, and perhaps to feel the presence of people who walked here nearly 1,000 years ago.

The visitor center displays some outstanding examples of Anasazi ceramics and basketry found in the ruins.

Admission: $2 per person, children under 17 free.

Open: Daily in summer 8am–6pm in winter 8am–5pm. **Closed:** Christmas and New Year's Day.

★ **Salmon Ruin and San Juan County Archaeological Research Center,** 975 U.S. Hwy. 64 (P.O. Box 125), Bloomfield. ☎ **632-2013.**

This massive C-shaped pueblo, overlooking the San Juan River, was built in the 11th century as a Chacoan colony. A planned community of some 150 rooms, it offers not only a great *kiva* in its plaza, but a remarkable, elevated ceremonial chamber or "tower kiva." Just 11 miles east of Farmington, it is one of the most recently excavated ruins in the West.

The site was actually occupied twice—first, for two generations in the 11th century, by the Chacoans; then, in the 13th century, by emigrants from the great Mesa Verde complex to the north. But they, too, soon abandoned the site.

The site today is only 30% excavated, by design. It's being saved for future generations of archaeologists, who, it's assumed, will be able to apply advanced research techniques. For now, the archaeological research center studies regional sites earmarked for natural-resource exploitation.

In 1990, **Heritage Park** was established on an adjoining plot of land. It comprises a series of reconstructed ancient and historic dwellings representing the area's cultures, from a paleoarchaic sand-dune site to an Anasazi pit house, Apache wickiups and tepees to Navajo hogans, and an original pioneer homestead. Visitors are encouraged to enter the re-creations; several have arts-and-crafts exhibits or living-history demonstrations.

In the visitor center are a museum displaying artifacts found at the site, a gift shop, and a scholarly research library.

Admission: Adults $2, children 6–15 $1, seniors $1.50.

Open: Daily 9am–5pm.

OTHER ATTRACTIONS

Aztec Museum & Pioneer Village, 125 N. Main St., Aztec. ☎ **334-9829.**

The museum contains exhibits depicting local history, and the village includes an old train caboose and 13 authentically furnished buildings, both originals and replicas, from the late 1800s, including a log cabin, blacksmith shop, church, jail, school, and doctor's office. Founder's Day, held the second Saturday of September, turns the village into a living museum with demonstrations, Wild West shoot-outs, and a melodrama.

Admission: $1 donation requested from those 13 to 61 years; free for children and seniors.

Open: Summer Mon–Sat 9am–5pm; winter Mon–Sat 10am–4pm.

Bloomfield Cultural Complex, 333 S. First St., Bloomfield. ☎ **632-2840.**

Changing exhibits of visual arts and area cultural and historical subjects are featured here, along with hands-on programs for children. The complex also contains the community library, senior citizens' center, and a fitness center.

Admission: Free.

Open: Mon–Fri 6am–9pm, Sat 8am–1pm.

Bolack Trophy Museum, 3901 Bloomfield Hwy, Bloomfield. ☎ **325-4275.**

Former New Mexico governor Tom Bolack put together this collection of hundreds of mounted animal trophies from around the world.

Admission: Free.

Open: Mon–Sat by appointment only.

Bolack Eletromechanical Museum, 3901 Bloomfield Hwy., Bloomfield. ☎ **325-7873.**

This museum contains a collection that spans over 30 years and includes early items in the development of electrical power, communications, oil field and farming equipment, and was put together by Tommy Bolack, son of the former governor.

Admission: Free.

Open: Mon–Sat by appointment only.

Farmington Museum, 302 N. Orchard St. ☎ **599-1174.**

This museum offers a variety of exhibits on the history of the area's diverse cultures, including a replica of a 1930s Native American trading post. There are also exhibits on the area's natural environment, including displays portraying this dry, barren land's days as a seacoast. There's a hands-on children's gallery, and a gift shop with educational materials and unique Southwest arts and crafts.

Admission: Free.

Open: Tues–Fri noon–5pm, Sat 10am–5pm.

INDUSTRIAL TOURS

BHP-Utah International Inc. operates three large surface coal mines in the Farmington area. Mine tours of one to two hours are offered weekly at each of them. Appointments are requested for groups of eight or more. Tours of the **Navajo Mine** (☎ 598-5861), the largest open-pit coal mine in the western United States, are 10am Monday. It's 27 miles southwest of Farmington on reservation Road 4048. Tours of the **San Juan Mine** (☎ 598-5871), just north of U.S. 64 about 15 miles west of Farmington, are 10am Wednesday. Tours of **La Plata Mine** (☎ 599-4100), 22 miles north of Farmington via N.M. 170, are 10am Friday. Picnic and barbecue facilities are available in a park near the La Plata Mine.

A minimum of 2 weeks' notice is required for a tour of the **Four Corners Power Plant,** 11 miles west of Farmington on U.S. 64 at the community of Fruitland (☎ 598-8204). Tours describe the plant's use of coal to generate 2 million kilowatts of power. **Morgan Lake,** which provides cooling water for the plant's condenser, has picnic grounds; it's also extremely popular with local windsurfers. Swimming is not allowed, even though the water is 80 degrees year-round. The **San Juan Generating Station,** 15 miles west of Farmington via U.S. 64 (☎ 598-7594), also requests two weeks' notice for tours. Operated by Public Service Company of New Mexico, the plant supplies electricity to much of New Mexico and the Four Corners area.

SPORTS & RECREATION

Auto Racing   **Aztec Speedway,** on Legion Rd. north of Aztec (☎ 334-6629), has racing every Saturday evening April through September, with sprint cars, mini-sprints, IMCA modifieds, and hobby stocks.

Baseball   The **Connie Mack World Series** is held annually in mid-August at Ricketts Park, with top amateur teams from throughout the United States competing in a seven-day, 17-game series. Professional scouts and college coaches come to watch the teenage players, and many current major-leaguers were discovered here.

Fishing & Hunting   The **San Juan River,** fishable year-round, has good fishing for rainbow, brown, and cutthroat trout. A New Mexico fishing license, available at sporting goods stores, is required. There's bass fishing at warm **Morgan Lake,** 15 miles west of Farmington off U.S. 550, with a permit from the Navajo Fish and Wildlife Department (☎ 602/871-6451). Also, see the section on Navajo Lake State Park, below.

Golf   **Piñon Hills Municipal Golf Course,** 2101 Sunrise Pkwy. (☎ 326-6066), was designated "America's best golf bargain" by *Golf Digest* magazine in 1994, a year after the course was rated New Mexico's best by the same magazine. The 18-hole regulation course has desert terrain, and at press time green fees were $11 weekdays and $13 on weekends. Other public courses include the par three **Civitan Municipal,** 2200 N. Dustin St. (☎ 599-1194); and nearby there are two regulation nine-hole courses: **Hidden Valley,** in Aztec at #29 Road 3025 off Southside River Rd. (☎ 334-3248), and **Riverview Golf Course,** County Road 6500 in Kirtland (☎ 598-0140). Fans of miniature golf should head to **Nutty Putty Family Golf and Fun Center,** 7201 E. Main St. (☎ 326-9174).

Rodeo   The **Farmington Pro-Rodeo Roundup** is held the first weekend of April at McGee Park (☎ 325-5415), between Farmington and Bloomfield on U.S. 64. The event draws professionals from throughout the country. The **San Juan County Sheriff Posse Rodeo,** held in early June, is northern New Mexico's largest open rodeo, attracting amateurs as well as pros. It's held at the San Juan County Rodeo Grounds, U.S. 550 east of Farmington.

SHOPPING

Downtown Farmington shops are generally open 10am to 6pm Monday to Saturday. Shops in the **Animas Valley Mall,** in the northeast part of the city on U.S. 550 north of 30th Street, are open from 10am to 9pm Monday through Friday, 10am to 6pm Saturday, and noon to 5pm Sunday. The mall contains five department stores, Beall's, Best, Dillard's, J.C. Penney, and Sears, and 65 smaller stores. It's worth a visit even if you're not shopping, to see the two dozen wall-size American Indian murals that decorate the mall.

Native American arts and crafts are best purchased at trading posts, either downtown on Main or Broadway streets, or west of Farmington on U.S. 64/550 toward Shiprock. Some recommended stores include: **Aztec Ruins Trading Post,** Ruins Road Aztec (☎ 334-2943); **Beasley Manning's Trading Co.,** 704 Orchard Homes Dr. (☎ 327-5580); **Blanco Trading Post,** N.M. 44, 25 miles south of Bloomfield (☎ 632-1597); **Foutz Indian Room,** 301 W. Main St. (☎ 325-9413); **Hogback Trading Co.,** 3221 U.S. 64, Waterflow, 17 miles west of Farmington (☎ 598-5154); and **Navajo Trading Company,** 126 E. Main St. (☎ 325-1685).

EVENING ENTERTAINMENT

The annual **Anasazi Pageant** is a summer musical about the region's multicultural heritage. Presented in the outdoor Lions Wilderness Park Amphitheater (off College Boulevard) against a sandstone backdrop, *Anasazi, the Ancient Ones* weaves a story around the early history of San Juan area settlers through original music and dance. A southwestern-style dinner is also available. The production company also presents other musicals at the amphitheater. For information and tickets contact the Anasazi Reservation Desk at **505/327-9336** or the Farmington Convention and Visitors Bureau at toll free **800/448-1240.**

Admission: Dinner and show, adults $16, seniors $14, children 18 and under $10. Pageant only, adults $10, seniors $8, children $5. Tickets sold at Farmington Convention and Visitors Bureau and at the gate.

Open: Tue–Sun, mid-June to late Aug, dinner 6:30pm, performance 8pm.

NEARBY ATTRACTIONS

Ship Rock, Navajo Indian Reservation southwest of Shiprock, 29 miles west of Farmington via U.S. 64.

This distinctive landmark is known to the Navajo as *Tse bidá hi,* "Rock with wings." Composed of igneous rock flanked by long upright walls of solidified lava, it rises 1,700 feet off the desert floor to an elevation of 7,178 feet. There are viewpoints off U.S. 666, 6 to 7 miles south of the town of Shiprock. You can get closer by taking the tribal road to the community of Red Rock; but to get any nearer this sacred Navajo rock, you must have permission. Climbing is not permitted.

The town named after the rock is a gateway to the Navajo reservation and the Four Corners region. There's a tribal visitor center here.

From Shiprock, it's a 32-mile drive west on N.M. 504 to Teec Nos Pos, Arizona, then north on U.S. 160, to the **Four Corners Monument.** A marker here sits astride the only point in the United States where four states meet—New Mexico, Colorado, Utah, and Arizona. There are no facilities.

Navajo Lake State Park, N.M. 511, 40 miles east of Farmington. ☎ **632-2278.**

Three recreation sites (San Juan River, Pine River, and Sims Mesa) with camping, fishing, and boating make this the most popular water sports destination for residents of northwestern New Mexico. Trout, northern pike, largemouth bass, and catfish are caught in lake and river waters, and the surrounding hills attract hunters seeking deer and elk. A visitor center at Pine River Recreation Area has interpretive displays on natural history and on the construction and purposes of the dam.

Navajo Lake, with an area of 15,000 acres, extends from the confluence of the San Juan and Los Pinos rivers 25 miles north into Colorado. Navajo Dam, an earthen embankment, is three-quarters of a mile long and 400 feet high. It provides Farmington-area cities, industries, and farms with their principal water supply. It's also the main storage reservoir for the Navajo Indian Irrigation Project, designed to irrigate 110,000 acres.

Angel Peak Recreation Area, N.M. 44, 35 miles south of Farmington. ☎ **599-8900.**

The distinctive pinnacle of 6,991-foot Angel Peak can often be spotted from Farmington. This area offers a short nature trail and a variety of unusual, colorful geological formations and canyons to explore on foot. The Bureau of Land Management has developed two campgrounds and picnic area, all with rest rooms. There is no drinking water available. The last 6 miles of access, after turning off from Highway 44, are over a graded dirt road.

Bisti Wilderness, N.M. 371, 37 miles south of Farmington. ☎ **599-8900.**

A federally protected area of weird rock formations, petrified logs, and prehistoric fossils, this wilderness is like an undiscovered planet. Walk among its huge turrets, buttes, spires, and pinnacles. Seventy million years ago, this was a swampland that attracted many dinosaurs and primitive mammals; many fossils remain, and neither fossils nor petrified wood may be removed from the site. There are no facilities here and no motorized vehicles or bicycles are permitted. The site is administered by the BLM.

Where to Stay

There are over 1,500 rooms in about 20 lodging establishments in the Farmington area. Lodging tax is almost 11% (including 5.9375% gross receipts tax).

In the listings below the following price ranges apply: **moderate,** over $55 per night double; **inexpensive,** $35–$55; and **budget,** under $35. Parking is usually free.

MODERATE

Holiday Inn of Farmington, 600 E. Broadway at Scott Ave., Farmington, NM 87401. ☎ **505/327-9811** or toll free **800/HOLIDAY.** Fax 505/325-2288. 150 rms, 5 suites. A/C TV TEL

Rates: $58–$62 single; $64–$68 double; $83–$125 suite. AE, CB, DC, DISC, JCB, MC, V.

The recently renovated lobby is decorated with an Aztec motif. Southwestern decor predominates in the rooms. Standard units have two double beds and normal furnishings. King rooms (with king-size beds, of course) feature a sofa sleeper, leisure chair, and executive desk. There are rooms for nonsmokers and the disabled.

The Brass Apple Restaurant, open daily from 6am to 2pm for breakfast and lunch and 3 to 10pm for dinner, offers southwestern and continental cuisine. A modern dining room with big windows and garden decor, the Brass Apple offers luncheon buffets and full dinners priced from $4.95–$14.50. Save room for the special desserts that are baked fresh daily. The Sportz Club Lounge, open from 3pm to midnight daily, has four TV monitors, two of them big screens. The hotel provides room service during restaurant hours, valet laundry, 24-hour desk, an outdoor swimming pool, sauna, hot tub, fitness center, and meeting space for 200. Pets are accepted; a kennel is also available.

The Farmington Inn, 700 Scott Ave., Farmington, NM 87401. ☎ **505/327-5221** or toll free **800/528-1234** or **800/548-6758.** Fax 505/327-1565. 194 rms. A/C FRIDGE TV TEL

Rates: $59–$84 single; $69–$94 double. AE, CB, DC, DISC, MC, V.

The inn is focused around a skylit central courtyard, with luxuriant trees and plants shading a cafe at one end and a swimming pool at the other.

Pleasant, modern rooms, with king- or two queen-size beds, have rose or lilac decor, serigraph art on the walls, bedside remote controls for TV and lights, and minirefrigerators. All rooms have standard furnishings and two sinks, one outside the toilet at the vanity. Some rooms accommodate nonsmokers or the disabled.

An American menu is served daily from 6 to 10am for breakfast and 5 to 9pm for dinner in the sidewalk-cafe atmosphere of the Coffee Shop. The lounge has live entertainment most nights, and the Sports Room offers big-screen viewing of games and events. The hotel has room service during restaurant hours, valet laundry, 24-hour desk, an indoor swimming pool, sauna, Jacuzzi, weight and exercise room, guest Laundromat, video games area, and gift shop. Pets are welcome.

La Quinta, 675 Scott Ave., Farmington, NM 87401. ☎ **505/327-4706** or toll free **800/531-5900.** Fax 505/325-6583. 106 rms. A/C TV TEL

Rates (including continental breakfast): $47–$62 single; $55–$70 double. AE, CB, DC, DISC, MC, V.

A homey, family-style motel, La Quinta is a purveyor of affordable luxury. Good-sized rooms with southwestern decor have a king-size or two double beds, hardwood furnishings, dressing area (with vanity) behind an accordion door, remote-control television, free local phone calls, clock radios, and reading lamps. The Kettle, a 24-hour restaurant, is next door. Complimentary coffee and tea is always available at the front desk. The hotel also offers valet laundry service, 24-hour desk, nonsmoking and handicapped rooms, and an outdoor swimming pool. Small pets are permitted.

INEXPENSIVE

$ Anasazi Inn, 903 W. Main St., Farmington, NM 87401. ☎ **505/325-4564.** 66 rms, 8 suites. A/C TV TEL

Rates: $37.95 single or double; $45.95–$51.95 suite. AE, CB, DC, DISC, MC, V.

This newly renovated property, built in Pueblo style, is a real bargain. The spacious lobby displays Navajo crafts and gift items. Pastel colors and Navajo motifs brighten the guest rooms, which are decorated with Native paintings and metal sculptures. The rooms each have one king- or two queen-size beds, maple furnishings, a dressing table backed by a large mirror, and a ceiling fan. There's a courtesy car and gift shop. Nonsmoking rooms are available; small pets are permitted.

The ranch-style Coyote Restaurant, with its howling coyote motif, is open 11am to 10pm Sunday through Thursday, and 11am to 11pm on Friday and Saturday.

Steaks, seafood, and Mexican food are offered. The adjoining lounge, done in a sort of "nouveau-rustique" style, sometimes features live solo entertainment.

Enchantment Lodge, 1800 W. Aztec Blvd., Aztec, NM 87410. ☎ **505/334-6143** or toll free **800/847-2194.** Fax 505/334-6144. 20 rms. A/C TV TEL

Rates: $28–$34 single; $38–$44 double. DISC, MC, V.

This pleasant and very reasonable small roadside motel, complete with pink neon lights, is reminiscent of the 1950s. Popular with visiting fishermen, the motel has been recently renovated, and has remote-control color cable television, available refrigerators, an outdoor heated swimming pool, and a grassy picnic area. There is also a gift shop on the premises.

Super 8 Motel, 1601 Bloomfield Hwy. at Carlton Ave., Farmington, NM 87401. ☎ **505/325-1813** or toll free **800/800-8000.** 60 rms. A/C TV TEL

Rates: $29.88 single; $36.50–$54.70 double. Children under 13 free with parent. AE, CB, DC, DISC, MC, V.

A handsome new property on U.S. Highway 64, just across the Animas River from central Farmington, the Super 8 has comfortable, amply sized rooms with standard furnishings, including queen-size or two double beds. Some rooms have water beds. A game room keeps the kids from getting bored. The motel has nonsmoking rooms, a 24-hour desk, and accepts pets (with prior arrangement).

BUDGET

Motel 6, 1600 Bloomfield Hwy. at Cedar St., Farmington, NM 87401. ☎ **505/326-4501.** 134 rms. A/C TV TEL

Rates: $25.95 single; $31.95 double. AE, DC, DISC, MC, V.

This rambling motel on U.S. Highway 64, just east of downtown Farmington, stacks its cubicles in two stories. Rooms are clean but cozy, with all the essentials (double bed, table and chairs, dresser, and wardrobe rack) but none of the luxuries of a more expensive room. An outdoor swimming pool is open seasonally.

Where to Dine

In these listings a moderate restaurant has dinner main courses for $10–$20; inexpensive, under $10.

MODERATE

K.B. Dillon's, 101 W. Broadway at Orchard Avenue. ☎ **325-0222.**

Cuisine: STEAKS & SEAFOOD. **Reservations:** Recommended.
Prices: Appetizers $3–$7.75; lunch $4–$14.25; dinner $10.95–$19.95. AE, MC, V.
Open: Lunch Mon–Fri 11am–2pm; dinner Mon–Sat 5:30–10:30pm. **Closed:** Thanksgiving and Christmas.

Rough wooden walls, brick arches, historical photos, and early 20th-century decor, including signs used in advertising and at railroad crossings, make this downtown restaurant seem like a page out of your grandfather's scrapbook.

The menu, by contrast, is quite modern. Selections include Fracosta (an 8-ounce top sirloin broiled and topped with sautéed sweet peppers, mushrooms, green onions, and white wine); chicken à la Dillon (a sautéed breast topped with fresh tomato, avocado, and melted provolone cheese); and fresh mountain trout amandine, Cajun or Oscar. The restaurant has a full bar that stays open between lunch and dinner.

254

Señor Pepper's Restaurante Y Cantina, Four Corners Regional Airport, Navajo St. ☎ **327-0436.**

Cuisine: NEW MEXICAN.
Prices: Appetizers $3.25–$6.50; breakfast $2.95–$7.50, lunch $1.75–$9.50; dinner $4.95–$16.95. AE, CB, DC, DISC, MC, V.
Open: Sun–Thurs 5am–10pm, Fri–Sat 5am–10:30pm. **Closed:** Christmas and New Year's.

For an airport restaurant and lounge, Señor Pepper's is very "with it." Waitresses in colorful fiesta dress serve diners at booths and tables, beneath hanging lamps and perched tropical birds (not real). Meals are also served in the lounge, where classic rock is piped nonstop and neon lights surround a dance floor that hosts a DJ from 9pm nightly. Painted above the bar is Señor Pepper himself—a reclining red pepper wearing sunglasses.

Meals are very generous, from breakfast burritos to enchiladas de Guaymas (crab) or de Cancùn (shrimp). The steak Mazatlán has drawn raves from *Bon Appetit* readers, and the carne São Paulo (with green chile sauce and cheese) deserves to. Stacked enchiladas, burritos, tacos, tostadas, chile rellenos, tamales, sopaipillas, and every other Mexican standby is also on the menu.

The Trough, U.S. 550, Flora Vista. ☎ **334-6176.**

Cuisine: STEAK & SEAFOOD. **Reservations:** Not accepted.
Prices: Dinners only $10.95–$23.95. AE, DISC, MC, V.
Open: Mon–Thurs 5:30–10:30pm, Fri–Sat 5:30–11:30pm.

Eight miles northeast of central Farmington is this find, tucked behind the often-rowdy Country Palace nightclub. With a rustic, candlelit decor brightened by planter boxes, it feels like a home on the range. Obviously, the staff feels at home here—most of them have been with the restaurant five years or longer.

The oversize menu is your first clue as to the size of the meals. (Everything is for sale here, including the business itself . . . for a price!) Opt for prime rib, steaks, pork chops, ribs, chicken, half duckling, shrimp, lobster, or Alaskan king crab legs. Or choose any of several nightly fresh fish specials. If you still have room, ask to see the dessert tray. There's an extensive Californian and European wine list and a full bar.

INEXPENSIVE

 Clancy's Pub, 2703 E. 20th St. at Hutton Rd. ☎ **325-8176.**

Cuisine: AMERICAN & MEXICAN.
Prices: Appetizers $2.50–$4.95; main courses $3.50–$8. AE, DC, DISC, MC, V.
Open: Mon–Sat 11am–2am, Sun noon–midnight. **Closed:** Christmas, Thanksgiving, and Easter.

The owners of this old adobe building call it "an Irish cantina." The atmosphere is classic pub, with a very attractive enclosed patio and rock music (sometimes live) playing almost continually. Locals love it.

The menu is heavy on sandwiches and finger food, including the Olde English burger (with cheddar cheese and bacon) and the Reuben O'Rourke (with Thousand Island dressing). There's fish-and-chips, of course, Mac McMulligan stew, and "build-your-own" baked potatoes. Enchiladas, burritos, and tacos are also served.

Something Special, 116 N. Auburn Ave. near Main St. ☎ **325-8183.**
Cuisine: GOURMET HOME COOKING.
Prices: Breakfast $3–$6; lunch $7; desserts $2.50. AE, DISC, MC, V.
Open: Tues–Fri 7am–2pm.

If the aroma didn't tip you off, you might walk right past this unimposing white house, with its yellow shutters and yellow door, and not realize it's a bakery and restaurant. It's just like home, or like home ought to be. Dine indoors amid the fresh bakery smells, or outdoors beneath a vine-draped arbor.

A set lunch menu is served daily. It varies from beef Stroganoff to spinach and feta cheese croissants, manicotti to orange-pecan chicken with avocados. Breakfasts also vary, with one criterion: Nothing is ever fried. There's always a difficult choice of nine desserts each day—from butterscotch-pecan pie to ambrosia cake to chocolate-banana torte.

---

4 Chama & the Jicarilla Apache Reservation

Chama: 106 miles N of Santa Fe; 91 miles NW of Taos; 113 miles E of Farmington

GETTING THERE • By Plane   An airport with a 7,200-foot runway was scheduled to open in Dulce, about 25 miles west of Chama, in late 1994, to be operated by the Jicarilla Apache Tribe (☎ 759-3243).

• **By Bus/Shuttle   Twin Hearts Express & Transportation** (☎ 751-1201) operates a shuttle service providing regular transportation to and from Chama, Taos, Española, Ojo Caliente, Santa Fe, and Albuquerque, plus other northern New Mexico and southern Colorado locations on request.

• **By Car**   From Santa Fe, take U.S. 84 north (2 hours). From Taos, take U.S. 64 west (2¹/₂ hours). From Farmington, take U.S. 64 east (2¹/₄ hours).

ESSENTIALS • Orientation   Historic downtown Chama spreads along the west side of N.M. 17 opposite the Cumbres & Toltec railroad depot, 1.4 miles north of the U.S. 64/84 junction (known as the "Y"). N.M. 17 is Terrace Avenue through downtown, Main Street south of there. Various accommodations and restaurants are strung down the highway south for several miles.

• **Information**   The **New Mexico Welcome Center** (☎ 756-2235) is at the south end of town, at the "Y" junction of U.S. 64/84 and N.M. 17. The welcome center is open from 8am to 5pm daily. For complete local information, contact the **Chama Valley Chamber of Commerce,** Cumbres Mall, 499 Main St. (P.O. Box 306), Chama, NM 87520 (☎ 505/756-2306 or toll free 800/477-0149).

• **Fast Facts**   The **area code** is 505. **Dr. J. I. Dunham Memorial Clinic,** Pine Street east of First Street (☎ 756-2143), and **La Clinica** in Tierra Amarilla (☎ 588-7252). The **post office** is at Fifth and Maple streets (☎ 756-2240). In case of **emergencies,** phone police and ambulance (☎ 756-2319), fire (☎ 756-2213), state highway patrol (☎ 756-2343), or the Rio Arriba County sheriff (☎ 588-7271 in Tierra Amarilla).

A village of just 1,000 people, Chama's importance exceeds its small size. It's the largest New Mexico community for two hours in any direction, the head of the fertile Rio Chama valley, and the southern terminal of the world-famous Cumbres & Toltec Scenic Railroad. Lumber and ranching, along with tourism and outdoor recreation, support the economy today. It's a hunting and fishing center in summer, a cross-country skiing and snowmobiling haven in winter. Tierra Amarilla, the Rio Arriba County seat, is 14 miles south; Dulce, governmental seat of the Jicarilla Apache Indian Reservation, is 27 miles west.

What to See & Do

 Cumbres & Toltec Scenic Railroad, P.O. Box 789, Chama, NM 87520. ☎ 505/756-2151.

America's longest and highest narrow-gauge steam railroad, the historic C&T operates on a 64-mile track between Chama and Antonito, Colorado. Built in 1880 as an extension of the Denver & Rio Grande line to serve the mining camps of the San Juan Mountains, it is perhaps the finest surviving example of what once was a vast network of remote Rocky Mountain railways.

The C&T passes through forests of pine and aspen, past striking rock formations, and through the magnificent Toltec Gorge of the Rio de los Pinos. It crests at the 10,015-foot Cumbres Pass, the highest in the United States used by scheduled passenger trains.

Halfway through the route, at Osier, Colorado, the *New Mexico Express* from Chama meets the *Colorado Limited* from Antonito. They stop to exchange greetings, engines, and through passengers. Round-trip day passengers return to their starting point after enjoying a picnic or catered lunch beside the old water tank and stock pens in Osier.

A walking tour brochure, describing 23 points of interest in the Chama railroad yards, can be picked up at the 1899 depot in Chama. A registered National Historic Site, the C&T is owned by the states of Colorado and New Mexico, and operated by a concessionaire, Kyle Railways, Inc.

Fares: Round-trip to Osier and return, adults $32, children 11 and under $16. Through trip to Antonito, return by van (or to Antonito by van, return by train), adults $50, children $26. Reservations highly recommended. MC, V.

Open: Memorial Day weekend to mid-Oct trains leave Chama daily at 10:30am; vans depart for Antonito at 8pm.

Jicarilla Apache Indian Reservation, P.O. Box 507, Dulce, NM 87528. ☎ 759-3242.

About 3,200 Apaches live on this reservation along U.S. Highway 64 and N.M. 537. Its 768,000 acres stretch from the Colorado border south 65 miles to N.M. 44 near Cuba. The word *jicarilla* (pronounced hick-ah-*ree*-ah) means "little basket," so it's no surprise that tribal craftspeople are noted for their basket weaving and beadwork. See their work, both contemporary and museum quality, at the **Jicarilla Apache Arts and Crafts Shop and Museum,** a green building along U.S. 64 west of downtown (☎ 759-3242, ext. 274). Two isolated pueblo ruins, open to the public, are found on the reservation—**Cordova Canyon** ruins on tribal Road 13 and **Honolulu** ruin on Road 63.

This area of New Mexico offers some of the finest hunting in North America. Tribe members guide fishermen and trophy hunters, most of whom seek elk, mule deer, or bear, into the reservation's rugged wilderness backcountry. Just south of Chama on Jicarilla's northeastern flank is **Horse Lake Mesa Game Park,** P.O. Box 313, Dulce, NM 87528 (☎ 505/759-3442), a 20,000-acre reserve surrounded by a predator-proof fence. At an altitude of around 8,500 feet, this is the home of Rocky Mountain elk, mule deer, and countless numbers of bobcat, bear, and coyote.

Fishing permits for seven reservation lakes and the Navajo River run $7 per day for adults, $5 for seniors and children under 12. Rainbow, cutthroat, and brown trout are regularly stocked.

Highlights of the Jicarilla calendar are the Little Beaver Roundup (the second or third weekend in July) and the Stone Lake Fiesta (September 14 to 15 annually).

Admission: Free.

Open: Year-round.

NEARBY ATTRACTIONS

U.S. HIGHWAY 84 SOUTH   Distinctive yellow earth provided a name for the town of **Tierra Amarilla,** 14 miles south of Chama at the junction of U.S. 84 and 64. Throughout New Mexico, this name is synonymous with a continuing controversy over the land-grant rights of the descendants of the original Hispanic settlers. But the economy of this community of 1,000 is dyed in the wool, literally.

The organization Ganados del Valle (Livestock Growers of the Valley) is at work to save the longhaired Spanish churro sheep from extinction through breeding; to introduce other unusual wool breeds to the valley; and to perpetuate a 200-year-old tradition of shepherding, spinning, weaving, and dyeing. Many of the craftspeople work in conjunction with **Tierra Wools,** P.O. Box 118, Los Ojos, NM 87551 (☎ **588-7231**), which has a showroom and workshop in a century-old mercantile building just north of Tierra Amarilla. One-of-a-kind blankets and men's and women's apparel are among the products displayed and sold.

Two state parks are a short drive west from Tierra Amarilla. **El Vado Lake,** 14 miles on N.M. 112 (☎ **588-7247**), offers boating and waterskiing, fishing, and camping in summer: cross-country skiing and ice fishing in winter. **Heron Lake,** 11 miles west on N.M. 95 (☎ **588-7470**), has a no-wake speed limit for motor vessels, adding to its appeal for fishing, sailing, and windsurfing. There's an interpretive center, and camping and picnic sites. The scenic 5^1/$_2$-mile Rio Chama trail connects the two lakes.

East of Tierra Amarilla, the Rio Brazos cuts a canyon through the Tusas Mountains and around 11,403-foot Brazos Peak. From just north of Los Ojos, N.M. 512 heads east 7^1/$_2$ miles up the **Brazos Box Canyon.** High cliffs that rise straight from the valley floor give it a Yosemite-like appearance—one that is made more apparent from an overlook on U.S. 64, 18 miles east of Tierra Amarilla en route to Taos. **El Chorro,** an impressive waterfall at the mouth of the canyon, usually flows only from early May to mid-June, but this is a tremendous hiking area any time of year. There are several resort lodges in the area.

About 27 miles south of Tierra Amarilla on U.S. 84, and 3 miles north of Ghost Ranch, is **Echo Canyon Amphitheater** (☎ **684-2486**), a U.S. Forest Service campground and picnic area. A natural "theater," hollowed out of sandstone by thousands of years of erosion, it is a 10-minute walk from the parking area. Some 13 miles west of here, via a dirt road into the Chama River Canyon Wilderness, is the isolated **Christ-in-the-Desert Monastery** (☎ **843-3049**), built in 1964 by Benedictine monks. The brothers produce crafts, sold at a small gift shop, and operate a guest house.

The ◪ **Ghost Ranch Living Museum** (☎ **685-4312**) is a U.S. Forest Service–operated exhibit of regional plant and animal life, geology, paleontology, and ecology. Short trails lead past re-created marsh, grassland, canyon, and forest land, inhabited by 27 species of native New Mexican animals and birds, most of them brought here injured or orphaned. A miniature national forest, complete with a fire lookout tower, illustrates conservation techniques; a trail through a severely eroded arroyo affords an opportunity to study soil ecology. The new **Gateway to the Past** museum interprets the cultures of the Chama valley. Temporary exhibits from the New Mexico Museum of Natural History are presented in an indoor display hall. It's open May through September (daily 8am to 6pm) and October through April (Tuesday to Sunday 8am to 4:30pm). There's no admission fee, though donations are welcomed.

There's no museum to mark her former residence, but the celebrated artist Georgia O'Keeffe spent most of her adult life in **Abiquiu,** a tiny town in a bend of the Rio Chama 14 miles south of the Ghost Ranch, and 22 miles north of Espanola, on U.S. 84. The inspiration for O'Keeffe's startling landscapes is clear in the surrounding terrain. Many dinosaur skeletons have been found in rocks along the base of cliffs near **Abiquiu Reservoir** (☎ **685-4371**), a popular boating and fishing spot formed by the Abiquiu Dam.

A good place to stay is the **Abiquiu Inn,** a small country inn, restaurant, art gallery, and gift shop, one-half mile north of the village of Abiquiu (☎ **505/685-4378**). Rates are $55 to $125. Heading south from Abiquiu, watch for **Dar al-Islam** (☎ **685-4515**), a spiritual center with a circular Middle Eastern mosque made of adobe; the small community of **Mendanales,** where you'll find the shop of renowned weaver Cordelia Coronado; and **Hernandez,** the village immortalized in Ansel Adams's famous 1941 photograph *Moonrise, Hernandez, New Mexico.*

Where to Stay

Virtually all accommodations in this area are found on N.M. 17 or south of the "Y" on U.S. 64/84. Lodging tax is 9% (including 6% state gross receipts tax). Most lodgings provide free parking.

Best Western Jicarilla Inn, U.S. Highway 64 (P.O. Box 233), Dulce, NM 87528. ☎ **505/759-3663** or toll free **800/742-1938** or **800/528-1234.** Fax 505/759-3170. 42 rms, 6 suites. A/C TV TEL

Rates: $50–$70 single; $60–$80 double; $70–$90 suite. AE, CB, DC, DISC, JCB, MC, V.

Among the best motels in the area, the Jicarilla Inn is 27 miles west of Chama in Dulce, in the northeastern corner of the Jicarilla Apache Indian Reservation. Modern and well maintained, it features a skylit indoor garden down the middle of the corridor between rooms.

Guest units all have queen-size beds and attractive wood furnishings. Upstairs rooms are particularly spacious, with cathedral ceilings. Six suites have kitchenettes; kitchenware is provided on request. Some rooms accommodate nonsmokers or the disabled.

The inn offers a popular "Trains & Indians" package, which combines lodging and meals with a ride on the Cumbres & Toltec Scenic Railroad (see "Attractions" above) for rates starting at $160 double for one night, $240 for two nights.

The Hill Crest Restaurant serves New Mexican and American cuisine in traditional wickiup decor, with historical black-and-white photographs on the walls. It's open from 6:30am to 9pm daily (and from 4:30am during the October-to-December hunting season). Breakfast and lunch run $2.95 to $7.95, dinner $6.95 to $15.95, including the traditional Native American dish, Jicarilla beef-and-potato stew. The cozy Timber Lake Lounge, open at 4pm daily, stages bingo games Thursday and Friday. The hotel also has a tourist information center, 24-hour desk, Apache Mesa Gallery and Gift Shop, video player and tape rental shop, and meeting space for 150.

Branding Iron Motel, West Main St. (P.O. Box 557), Chama, NM 87520. ☎ **505/756-2162** or toll free **800/446-2650.** 41 rms. A/C TV TEL

Rates: $50–$60 single; $65–$75 double. AE, DISC, MC, V.

This modern two-story motel, set back off the highway, has spacious, colorfully appointed motel units with all standard furnishings. Wildlife photos on the walls are reminders of the popularity of hunting in this area. The restaurant/lounge offers coffee-shop fare, three meals a day.

$ Chama Trails Inn, West Main St. at the "Y," Chama (P.O. Box 816). NM 87520. ☎ **505/756-2156** or toll free **800/289-1421.** 16 rms. FRIDGE TV TEL

Rates: $35 single; $41 double. AE, DISC, MC, V.

An art gallery as well as a motel, this white stucco building adorned with chile *ristras* incorporates the work of a different artist into the decor of each room. All rooms have queen-size beds and custom-made pine furnishings. Some units have ceiling fans, gas fireplaces, and/or Mexican-tiled bathroom floors. Several rooms have been designated for nonsmokers and a redwood sauna is available for guest use. The small but impressive art gallery here began as a hobby; now it's a major outlet for local artists' work.

★ Elk Horn Lodge, on Hwy. 84, Chama, NM 87520. ☎ **505/756-2105**, or toll free **800/532-8874.** 33 units. TV TEL

Rates: Rooms $41 single; $57 double; cabins $53–$75 single or double. Extra person $6. DISC, MC, V.

Situated just outside the center of the sleepy little town of Chama, the Elk Horn Lodge is popular with both sportsmen and families. The rooms and cabins are clean and spacious and are done in dark wood paneling with beige carpeting. The furnishings include two double beds, a desk, and a table accompanied by a Naugahyde chair. Outside the door of each room, on the motel-style porch, a folding chair is provided. There are barbecue pits available for guest use, and there is a small cafe.

The Jones House, 311 Terrace Ave. at 3rd St., Chama, NM 87520. ☎ **505/756-2908.** 4 rms.

Rates (including full breakfast): Private bath $55 single, $79 double; shared bath $40 single, $60 double. AE, MC, V.

Phil and Sara Cole's bed-and-breakfast, at the north end of the historic downtown district across from the railroad yard, occupies a 1928 adobe home of Tudor design. It's notable for its pressed-tin ceilings and homey decor. Two guest rooms have private baths; the other two share. Phone and TV are available on request. The living room has a wood stove, games table, and small library, and there's a big yard for bird watching. No smoking or pets are allowed.

CAMPING

Rio Chama RV Campground, N.M. 17, ¼ mile north of C&TSRR depot (P.O. Box 706), Chama, NM 87520. ☎ **505/756-2303.**

Rates: $9–$15.

Within easy walking distance of the Cumbres & Toltec Scenic Railroad depot, this shady campground with 60 sites along the Rio Chama is ideal for RVers and tenters who plan train rides. The campground also offers great photo opportunities of the old steam trains leaving the depot. There are hot showers, a dump station, and complete hookups available. Open mid-May through mid-October only.

Where to Dine

 High Country Restaurant, Main St. (0.1 mile north of "Y"). ☎ **756-2384.**
Cuisine: STEAKS & SEAFOOD.
Prices: Breakfast $1.50–$6.95; lunch $2.50–$7.95; dinner $6.95–$14.95. AE, DISC, MC, V.
Open: Daily 7am–11pm. **Closed:** Thanksgiving and Christmas.

This rustic wood-plank restaurant/saloon is like a country lodge with a big stone fireplace and antique bar. The dinner menu features fried chicken, barbecued pork ribs, a variety of steaks, prime rib, trout, and beer-battered shrimp. Also offered are hamburgers and Mexican food, and about a dozen imported beers on tap.

 Viva Vera's, Main St. (0.2 mile north of "Y"). ☎ **756-2557.**
Cuisine: NEW MEXICAN & AMERICAN.
Prices: Lunch $3.25–$6; dinner $5.50–$9.95. AE, MC, V.
Open: Daily 7am–10pm.

A small white Territorial-style roadside cafe, Vera's may be Chama's most popular hangout. Portions are generous. Try the chile stew and posole. Beer and wine are served with meals.

Southwestern New Mexico

9

THIS REGION BELONGS TO THE OLD WEST. BILLY THE KID LIVED HERE; SO DID Geronimo.

The Rio Grande is southwestern New Mexico's lifeline, throughout history nourishing the Native American, Hispanic, and Anglo settlers who have built their homes beside its banks. It sketches a distinct boundary between the rugged mountains of the Southwest and the desert reaching toward the southeast. The river land was especially fertile around modern Las Cruces; the settlement of La Mesilla was southern New Mexico's major center for three centuries.

West of the river, the Black Range and Mogollon Mountains rise in the area now cloaked by Gila National Forest. This was the homeland of the Mogollon Indians 1,000 years ago; Gila Cliff Dwellings National Monument preserves one of their great legacies. It was also the homeland of the fiercely independent Chiricahua Apaches in the 19th century—considered the last North American Indians to succumb to the whites, they counted Cochise and Geronimo among their chieftains. Mining and outdoor recreation, centered in historic Silver City (pop. 11,200), now are the economic stanchions. But dozens of mining towns have boomed and busted in the past 140 years; a smattering of ghost towns throughout the region are grim reminders.

Las Cruces, at the foot of the Organ Mountains, is New Mexico's second largest city, with 66,500 people. It's a busy agricultural and education center. North up the valley are Truth or Consequences (pop. 6,100), a spa town named for a 1950s radio and TV game show, and Socorro (pop. 8,200), a historic city with Spanish roots. West, on the I-10 corridor to Arizona, are the ranching centers of Deming (pop. 12,000) and Lordsburg (pop. 3,000).

Suggested Itinerary: If you're driving from Albuquerque, follow I-25 south to Socorro. Turn west on U.S. Highway 60 through Magdalena to see the Very Large Array radio telescope. At Datil Well Recreation Area, turn off U.S. 60 onto N.M. 12, which will take you to the Catron County seat of Reserve. Join U.S. 180 just south of Reserve, with stops in Mogollon and the Catwalk near Glenwood. Then proceed to Silver City, a full day's drive from Socorro on this route.

Use Silver City as a base to visit the downtown historic district and Gila Cliff Dwellings National Monument. U.S. 180 continues past City of Rocks State Park to Deming; there, pick up I-10 into Las Cruces, where you'll want to spend time at Old Mesilla Plaza.

Return to Albuquerque from Las Cruces. Head north up I-25, giving yourself a long stop in Truth or Consequences, and returning via Socorro. Ideally, this is a week's journey, with a night in Socorro, two nights each in Silver City and Las Cruces, and a night in T or C.

1 Socorro: Gateway to Bosque del Apache National Wildlife Refuge & the VLA

77 miles S of Albuquerque; 149 miles N of Las Cruces

GETTING THERE • By Plane   There is no direct commercial air service to Socorro. A shuttle service, the **Socorro Roadrunner** (☎ **835-1010**), provides transportation to and from Albuquerque International Airport.

• **By Bus**   Socorro is served by **TNM&O/Greyhound** (☎ **835-1930**) on its Albuquerque–El Paso run. The depot address changes frequently; at this writing, it is at 202 California St. SE. Buses depart twice daily southbound and twice daily northbound.

Southwestern New Mexico

• **By Car**   From Albuquerque, take I-25 south ($1^1/4$ hours). From Las Cruces, take I-25 north ($2^3/4$ hours).

ESSENTIALS • **Orientation**   Socorro is nestled in the valley of the Rio Grande. Highway 85 (California Street) is the main street of Socorro, with access from I-25 at both ends of town.

• **Information**   The **Socorro County Chamber of Commerce,** which is also the visitor information headquarters, is just off North California Street (Highway 85) at 103 Francisco de Avondo (P.O. Box 743), Socorro, NM 87801 (☎ **505/835-0424**).

• **Fast Facts**   The **area code** is 505. **Socorro General Hospital** is located on West Highway 60 (☎ **835-1140**). The **post office** is on the west side of the Plaza (☎ **835-0542**). In case of **emergencies,** dial **911.**

This quiet, pleasant town of 8,200 is an unusual mix of the 19th and 20th centuries. Established as a mining settlement and ranching center, its downtown area is dominated by numerous mid-1800s buildings and the 17th-century San Miguel Mission. The New Mexico Institute of Mining and Technology (New Mexico Tech) is a major research center. Socorro is also the gateway to a vast and varied two-county region that includes the Bosque del Apache National Wildlife Refuge, the Very Large Array national radio astronomy observatory, and three national forests.

What to See & Do

A WALKING TOUR OF HISTORIC SOCORRO

The best introduction to Socorro is a walking tour of the historic district. Start from the parklike **Plaza,** one block west of California Street on Manzanares Street. A brochure published by the chamber of commerce points out several Territorial-style buildings from the mid 1800s, including the **J. N. Garcia Opera House,** the **Juan Nepomoceno Garcia House,** and the **Juan José Baca House.** Several impressive late 19th-century Victorian homes stand in the blocks south of the Plaza.

OTHER ATTRACTIONS

Old San Miguel Mission, 403 El Camino Real, NW, 2 blocks north of the Plaza. ☎ **835-1620.**

Built during the period from 1615 to 1626 but abandoned during the Pueblo Revolt of 1680, this church was subsequently restored, and a new wing built in 1853. It boasts thick adobe walls, large carved *vigas,* and supporting corbel arches. English-language masses are Saturday at 5:30pm and Sunday at 10am and noon.

   Admission: Free.

   Open: Daily 6am–6pm.

New Mexico Institute of Mining and Technology, College St. at Leroy St. ☎ **835-5011.**

Founded in 1889, New Mexico Tech is a highly regarded institution of 1,700 students, whose course work focuses on science and engineering. Its research facilities—including centers for petroleum recovery, explosives technology, and atmospheric research—are internationally acclaimed. Golfers also visit to play the 18-hole university course, considered one of the best in the state. **Macey Center** has a 600-seat auditorium for performing arts and a gallery of rotating art.

Mineral Museum, Campus Rd., New Mexico Tech campus. ☎ **835-5420.**

Run by the New Mexico Bureau of Mines and Mineral Resources, this museum has the largest geological collection in the state. Its more than 10,000 specimens include mineral samples from all over the world, fossils, mining artifacts, and photographs.

Admission: Free.

Open: Mon–Fri 8am–5pm.

New Mexico Firefighters Training Academy, Academy Rd. SW, 2 miles northwest of Socorro via U.S. 60 (P.O. Box 239, Socorro, NM 87801). ☎ **835-7500** or toll free **800/734-6553.**

This school for firefighters, spread over 121 acres, has a three-story control tower, four-story drill tower, and a variety of fire-fighting equipment. Visitors should allow one hour.

Admission: Free.

Open: Tours Mon–Fri 9am–noon and 1–4pm, by appointment only.

Nearby Attractions

SOUTH OF SOCORRO

The village of **San Antonio,** the boyhood home of Conrad Hilton, is 10 miles from Socorro via I-25. During the panic of 1907, his merchant father, Augustus Hilton, converted part of his store into a rooming house. This gave Conrad his first exposure to the hospitality industry, and he went on to worldwide fame as a hotelier. Only ruins of the store/boardinghouse remain.

⭐ **Bosque del Apache National Wildlife Refuge,** 8 miles south of San Antonio via State Hwy. 1 (P.O. Box 1246, Socorro, NM 87801). ☎ **835-1828.**

An estimated 300 permanent and migratory birds and over 100 amphibians, reptiles, and mammals make their homes in the 57,000-acre reserve. It's an especially busy place in winter, when the population includes more than 40,000 snow geese, 30,000 ducks, 15,000 sandhill cranes, and about a dozen endangered whooping cranes. Photographers and nature watchers can start a 15-mile driving tour at the Visitor Center. There are several observation decks and hiking trails.

Admission: $2 per vehicle.

Open: 1 hour before sunrise to 1 hour after sunset, year-round. Visitor center open daily.

NORTH OF SOCORRO

It's about 15 miles to **Sevilleta National Wildlife Refuge** (☎ **864-4021**), the location of one of the National Science Foundation's 17 long-term ecological research sites. Coordinated by the University of New Mexico, it is open only to researchers, by appointment.

WEST OF SOCORRO

U.S. Highway 60, running west to Arizona, is the avenue to several points of interest. **Magdalena,** 27 miles from Socorro, is a mining and ranching town that preserves an 1880s Old West spirit. Its **Woman on the Mountain Inn** (☎ **505/854-2757**) has rooms (from $26) with a country-inn atmosphere. It's popular with families and rock hounds. Three miles south, the ghost town of **Kelly** produced over $40 million worth of lead, zinc, copper, silver, and gold in the late 19th and early 20th centuries.

Thirty-two miles north of Magdalena on a dead-end road is the home of the **Alamo Navajo Nation.** On special occasions, the public may be allowed to visit the band of 1,400 Navajo who live on this reservation: Inquire with the Alamo Chapter Office (☎ **854-2686**).

Southeast of Magdalena, atop 10,783-foot South Baldy Mountain, the **Langmuir Research Laboratory** studies thunderstorms and atmospheric electricity from June through August. There is a visitors' center with exhibits. The research center can be reached by high-clearance and four-wheel-drive vehicles only; would-be visitors should call **835-5423** in advance to check on road conditions.

 Very Large Array National Radio Astronomy Observatory (VLA), 54 miles west of Socorro via U.S. 60 (Socorro office at 1003 Lopezville Rd. NW). ☎ **835-7000.**

Twenty-seven dish-shaped antennae, each 82 feet in diameter, are spread across the plains of San Agustin, forming a single gigantic radio telescope. Photographs taken are similar to the largest optical telescopes, except that radio telescopes are sensitive to low-frequency radio waves. All types of celestial objects are photographed, including the sun and its planets, stars, quasars, galaxies, and even the faint remains of the "big bang" that scientists say occurred some ten billion years ago. The visitors' center contains displays on the VLA and radio astronomy in general, and a self-guided walking tour gives visitors a closer view of the antennae, which resemble giant TV satellite dishes.

Admission: Free.

Open: Daily 8:30am–sunset.

Where to Stay

Most accommodations are along California Street, the main highway through town, or the adjacent I-25 frontage road. Tax on all lodging bills is 10% (6% state gross receipts tax plus 4% local lodger's tax). Most lodgings provide free parking.

The Eaton House, 403 Eaton Ave. (P.O. Box 536), Socorro, NM 87801. ☎ **505/835-1067.** 3 rms and 2 casitas (all with bath). A/C

Rates (including full breakfast): $75–$120 single or double. No credit cards.

This charming bed and breakfast, constructed in 1881 by Col. E. W. Eaton, is on the New Mexico register of historic buildings. Owner Anna Appleby has decorated each room differently, from the early 19th-century Daughters' Room, with twin beds and claw-foot tub and shower, to the Colonel Eaton Room, with queen four-poster bed and Victorian furnishings. The Chavez Casita, which is handicapped accessible, is Pueblo style with a king-size bed and sturdy *vigas;* the Bosque Casita, with its high ceilings and queen-size bed, has 16th-century Spanish colonial–style furnishings. The expertly prepared, generous breakfasts are made of only organic ingredients, and might include an apple-pie pancake with peppered bacon, blueberry French toast, or a fluffy herbed omelet with sliced ham and asparagus. Smoking and pets are not permitted; children 14 and older are welcome. Check-in is from 4 to 6pm.

Sands Motel, 205 California St. NW, Socorro, NM 87801. ☎ **505/835-1130.** 25 rms. A/C TV TEL

Rates: $20 single; $26 double. AE, CB, DC, DISC, MC, V.

Clean, comfortable lodging at very economical rates is what you'll find here; there's color cable television but few other amenities. Centrally located, the Sands is within easy walking distance of several restaurants. Pets are welcome.

Super 8 Motel, 1121 Frontage Rd. NW, Socorro, NM 87801. ☎ **505/835-4626** or toll free **800/800-8000.** Fax 505/835-3988. 63 rms, 8 suites. A/C TV TEL

> **Rates** (including continental breakfast): $43 single; $47 double; $66 suite. AE, DC, DISC, MC, V.

Regular patrons of Super 8 motels return in part because their accommodations are so predictable. Each room here is clean and cozy, with a relaxed atmosphere. Complimentary continental breakfast is served in the attractive lobby. Facilities include a swimming pool, hot tub, and guest laundry.

Where to Dine

Don Juan's Cocina, 118 Manzanares Rd. ☎ **835-9967.**

> **Cuisine:** MEXICAN. **Reservations:** Not necessary.
> **Prices:** Appetizers 95¢–$2.95; Mexican plates $3.60–$6.50. AE, DC, DISC, MC, V.
> **Open:** Mon–Fri 10am–9pm, Sat 10am–3pm.

Located in the 1885 Knights of Pythias Hall, the decor at Don Juan's is simple in the main dining room, but the festive outdoor patio has some extraordinary murals painted on its surrounding walls. If you're not particularly interested in the decor, you'll be very interested in the food—it's excellent, authentic Mexican, and inexpensive. Breakfast is served all day and might consist of the standard huevos rancheros or a breakfast burrito. Appetizers at lunch and dinner include taquitos, chile cheese fries, and sopaipillas. You can order your main course à la carte (tacos, burritos, enchiladas, and tostadas), or you might prefer to get a full Mexican plate with refried beans and rice.

Frank and Lupe's El Sombrero, 210 Mesquite St., Socorro. ☎ **835-3945.**

> **Cuisine:** MEXICAN & AMERICAN.
> **Prices:** Main courses $1.75–$7.25. DC, MC, V.
> **Open:** Daily 11am–9pm. **Closed:** Thanksgiving and Christmas.

Located just out of town on an I-25 frontage road on the east side of the freeway, this popular establishment has a cheerful atmosphere, with a fireplace and a charming atrium with water fountains. It has a wide variety of Mexican cuisine, including chalupas, fajitas, and enchiladas, as well as steaks and burgers. Beer and wine are served. Luncheon buffets are frequently offered.

⭐ **Owl Bar & Cafe,** State Hwy. 1 and U.S. Hwy. 380, San Antonio. ☎ **835-9946.**
> **Cuisine:** AMERICAN.
> **Prices:** Main courses $2.25–$10.95. DISC, MC, V.
> **Open:** Mon–Sat 8am–10pm. **Closed:** Thanksgiving, Christmas, and New Year's.

A low-lit tavern in a one-story adobe building, 7 miles south of Socorro, the Owl has earned a regionwide reputation for "the world's greatest hamburgers." It's especially proud of its green chile cheeseburger. The steak house (open 5 to 10pm Friday and Saturday only) serves T-bones, filet mignon, and catfish.

⭐ **Val Verde Steak House,** 203 Manzanares Ave., Socorro. ☎ **835-3380.**
> **Cuisine:** AMERICAN. **Reservations:** Recommended.
> **Prices:** Appetizers $2.25–$5.75; lunch $4.50–$6.75; dinner $6.75–$32.50. AE, CB, DC, DISC, MC, V.
> **Open:** Mon–Thurs 11am–2pm and 5–9:30pm; Fri 11am–2pm and 5–10pm, Sat 5–9:30pm, Sun noon–9pm. **Closed:** Christmas and July 4.

The horseshoe-shaped Val Verde Hotel is a national historic landmark, built in 1919 in California mission style. The hotel has been converted to apartments, but the public can enjoy the old dining room. The lunch menu is simple but tasty: home-made soups, salads, sandwiches, plus steaks and seafood. Dinner is more elaborate. House specials include beef Stroganoff and pepper steak Capri (in madeira sauce). Gourmet southwestern dishes are also served. The restaurant is about two blocks off California Street (Highway 85), directly east of the Plaza. Beer and wine are served.

2 Truth or Consequences

151 miles S of Albuquerque; 75 miles N of Las Cruces

GETTING THERE • By Plane   Private flights and charters arrive at **Truth or Consequences Municipal Airport,** Old North Highway 85 (☎ **894-6199**).

• **By Bus**   Truth or Consequences is served by **TNM&O/Greyhound,** which stops at 302 S. James St. (☎ **894-3649**), on its Albuquerque–El Paso run. Buses depart twice daily southbound and twice daily northbound. Las Cruces Shuttle (☎ toll free **800/288-1784**) provides service to and from T or C, Las Cruces, and El Paso.

• **By Car**   From Albuquerque take I-25 south (2¹/₂ hours). From Las Cruces take I-25 north (1¹/₄ hours).

ESSENTIALS • Orientation   Best known as "T or C," this year-round resort town and retirement community of 6,100 is spread along the Rio Grande between Elephant Butte and Caballo reservoirs, two of the three largest bodies of water in the state. Business Loop 25 branches off from I-25 to wind through the city, splitting into Main Street (one-way west) and South Broadway (one-way east) in the downtown area. Third Avenue connects T or C with the Elephant Butte resort community, 5 miles east.

• **Information**   The visitor information center is located at the corner of Main Street (Business Loop 25) and Foch Street in downtown T or C. It is administered by the **Truth or Consequences/Sierra County Chamber of Commerce,** P.O. Drawer 31, Truth or Consequences, NM 87901 (☎ **505/894-3536** or toll free **800/831-9487**).

• **Fast Facts**   The **area code** is 505. **Sierra Vista Hospital** is located at 800 E. Ninth Ave. (☎ **894-2111**). The **post office** is downtown, at the corner of Main and Jones streets (☎ **894-3137**). For emergencies, dial **911,** or outside city limits, call **894-6617.**

Originally known as Hot Springs, after the therapeutic mineral springs bubbling up near the river, the town took the name Truth or Consequences in 1950. That was the year that Ralph Edwards, producer of the popular radio and television program "Truth or Consequences," began his weekly broadcast with these words: "I wish that some town in the United States liked and respected our show so much that it would like to change its name to Truth or Consequences." The reward to any city willing to make this change was to become the site of the 10th anniversary broadcast of the program—which would put it on the national map in a big way. The locals voted for the name change, which has survived three protest elections over the years.

Although the "Truth or Consequences" television program was canceled decades ago, Ralph Edwards, now in his 70s, continues to return for the annual T or C Fiesta, the first weekend of May. Another popular annual festival is Geronimo Days, the first weekend of October.

What to See & Do

The Hot Springs

T or C's "original" attraction is its hot springs. The entire downtown area is located over a table of odorless hot mineral water, 98 to 115 degrees, that bubbles to the surface through wells or pools. The first bathhouse was built in the 1880s; most of the half dozen historic spas operating today date from the 1930s. Generally open from morning to early evening, these spas welcome visitors for soaks and massages. Baths of 20 minutes or longer start at $2.50 per person.

The chamber of commerce has information on all the local spas. Among them, **Indian Springs Apartments and Pools,** 200 Pershing St. (☎ 894-3823), has longer hours (7am to 11pm daily) than other spas, naturally flowing pools, a gravel bottom, and payment on the honor system. **The Artesian,** 312 Marr St. (☎ 894-2684), has an RV park on the premises.

★ **Geronimo Springs Museum,** 211 Main St. ☎ 894-6600.

Outside is Geronimo's Spring, where the great Apache shaman is said to have taken his warriors to bathe their battle wounds. Turtleback Mountain, looming over the Rio Grande east of the city, is believed to have been sacred to Native Americans.

Exhibits include prehistoric Mimbres pottery (A.D. 950–1250); the Spanish Heritage Room, featuring artifacts of the first families of Sierra County; and artists' work, including historical murals and sculptured bronzes. Exhibits in the other rooms feature army forts and mining towns; the construction of Elephant Butte Dam; local history, featuring photos and artifacts; Native American artifacts, both prehistoric and of more recent culture; the story of ranching and farming in the county; the rise and fall of mining camps and cattle towns. An authentic miner's cabin has been moved here from the nearby mountains. The Ralph Edwards Wing contains the history and highlights of the annual fiestas, and celebrates the city's name change. Geothermally heated museum. Gift counter.

Admission: Adults $2, students $1; family rates available.

Open: Mon–Sat 9am–5pm.

Elephant Butte Lake State Park, 7 miles north via I-25. ☎ 744-5421.

New Mexico's largest lake, covering 36,000 acres, this state park has 5,000 acres of shoreside land. Fishing for black and white bass, catfish, walleye and Northern pike, and crappie goes on all year long. Trout are stocked in the Rio Grande below Elephant Butte Dam. The park has sandy beaches for tanning and swimming, boating, sailing, waterskiing, and camping. There are frequent regattas. The lake was named for a huge rock formation that makes an island; before the inundation that created the lake, it clearly looked like an elephant! Today, it's partially submerged.

Nearby Attractions

NORTH OF T OR C A couple of so-called ghost towns—abandoned mining centers that nevertheless do have a few live residents—are Winston and Chloride. **Winston,** 37 miles northwest of T or C on N.M. 52, was abandoned in the early 1900s when silver prices dropped and local mining became unprofitable. Some of the original structures are still standing from that era. A similar fate befell **Chloride,** 5 miles west of Winston on a side road off N.M. 52, where famed silver mines had such names as Nana, Wall Street, and Unknown. Chloride also figured in many battles in the turn-of-the-century war between cattle-ranching and sheep-ranching interests.

SOUTH OF T OR C   Twenty miles via I-25 is another recreation area, **Caballo Lake State Park** (☎ 743-3942), which, like Elephant Butte, has year-round water sports, fishing, swimming, and campsites. The lake has the lofty ridge of the Caballo Mountains just to the east to make a handsome backdrop. There is a marina with full service and a shop for boaters, as well as full hookups for recreational vehicles. Reached from the same exit off I-25 is still another area, **Percha Dam State Park** (☎ 743-3942), a lovely shaded spot under great cottonwood trees, part of the ancient *bosque*, or woods, the Spanish found bordering the Rio Grande when they first arrived in this area in the 1530s. The dam here diverts river water for irrigation. There are campsites, rest rooms and showers, hiking trails, and access to fishing here.

Thirty-two miles from T or C, via I-25 south to N.M. 152, then west, is ★ **Hillsboro,** another ghost town fast losing its ghosts to a small invasion of artists and craftspeople, antique shops, and galleries. This town boomed after an 1877 gold strike nearby, and during its heyday produced $6 million in silver and gold. It was the county seat from 1884 to 1938. Its Labor Day–weekend Apple Festival is famous throughout the state.

The **Black Range Historical Museum** (☎ 895-5233 or 895-5685) contains exhibits and artifacts from Hillsboro's mining boom. Located in the former Ocean Grove Hotel, a turn-of-the-century brothel operated by Londoner Sadie Orchard, the museum collection includes some of the madam's effects. The museum is closed Tuesdays and Wednesdays and the entire months of January and February, but open most other afternoons. Local art galleries in Hillsboro include the **Pink Adobe** (☎ 895-5398), and **Chamisa Art Gallery** (895-5201), and you'll find a variety of items at **Hidden Treasures Gift Shop** (☎ 895-5631).

The **Enchanted Villa** bed-and-breakfast inn, P.O. Box 456, Hillsboro, NM 88042 (☎ 505/895-5686), is a 1941 two-story adobe offering five large rooms with king-size beds and private baths. Rates are $35 for singles and $50 for doubles, including full hot breakfasts.

Nine miles west of Hillsboro on N.M. 152, just after you've entered the Gila National Forest, is **Kingston,** born with a rich silver strike in 1880 and locally reputed to have been among the wildest mining towns in the region, with 7,000 people, 22 saloons, a notorious red-light district (conveniently located on Virtue Avenue), and an opera house. Kingston was also once the home of Albert Fall, a U.S. secretary of state who gained notoriety for his role in the Teapot Dome Scandal.

Your headquarters in Kingston should be the **Black Range Lodge,** Star Route 2, Box 119, Kingston, NM 88042 (☎ 505/895-5652), a rustic stone lodge that dates from the 1880s, and over the years has housed miners and soldiers, as well as Pretty Sam's Casino and the Monarch Saloon. There are seven rooms—all with private baths and some with private balconies—a large game room with pool table and video games, a solar-heated hot tub, and family suites. Rates are $35 to $45 single and $55 to $65 double, with multiple-night discounts; both children and pets are welcome.

Among historic buildings in Kingston are the brick assay office, **Victorio Hotel,** and the **Percha Bank,** now a museum open by appointment—ask at the lodge. The town bell in front of the Volunteer Fire Department was first used to warn residents of Native American attacks, until the Apaches' final surrender in 1886. Nearby, **Camp Shiloh** has a public outdoor swimming pool open in summer (again, ask at Black Range Lodge).

EAST OF T OR C   Some 17 miles east via N.M. 51, near the community of Engle, are three wineries producing fine wines in limited quantities. **Domaine Cheurlin**

and **Duvallay Vineyards** (☎ 894-3226 for both), and **Chateau Sassenage** (☎ 894-7244) welcome visitors by appointment.

Where to Stay

There's a wide choice of accommodations in and near T or C. Tax of 11.3125% (5% city, 6.3125% state) is added onto all lodging bills. Parking is usually free.

Best Western Hot Springs Inn, 2270 N. Date St. at I-25 Exit 79, Truth or Consequences, NM 87901. ☎ **505/894-6665** or toll free **800/528-1234.** 40 rms. A/C TV TEL

Rates: $45–$47 single; $50–$52 double. AE, CB, DC, DISC, MC, V.

This freeway-exit motel lives up to the Best Western standard with spacious, comfortable units in a pleasant setting. Rooms are appointed in desert rose and cornflower blue, with large beds, two sinks (one at the full-mirrored vanity), remote-control television, and clock radio. There's an outdoor pool, open seasonally; K-Bob's steak house is adjacent.

⭐ **Elephant Butte Inn**, Hwy. 195 (P.O. Box E), Elephant Butte, NM 87935. ☎ **505/744-5431.** 48 rms. A/C TV TEL

Rates: $49–$59 single; $59–$69 double. AE, CB, DC, DISC, MC, V.

Situated above the shores of Elephant Butte Reservoir, this newly renovated facility caters to boaters, fishermen, and other relaxation lovers. Rooms are furnished with king- or queen-size beds. The restaurant serves American, Italian, and New Mexican meals (dinners $7 to $20) from 6am to 9pm daily, an hour later on Friday and Saturday. The Sports Bar features a lighted volleyball court, horseshoes, and live entertainment. The inn has a swimming pool, tennis courts, and room service.

Rio Grande Motel, 720 Broadway, P.O. Box 67, Williamsburg, NM 87942. ☎ **505/894-9769.** 50 rms. A/C TV TEL

Rates: $24–$34 single; $32–$42 double. DISC, MC, V.

Located in the suburb of Williamsburg near the south access to T or C from I-25, the Rio Grande offers clean, comfortable rooms for a budget price. Some rooms have kitchenettes. There's an outdoor swimming pool, a guest Laundromat, and a restaurant next door.

River Bend Hot Springs Hostel, 100 Austin St., Truth or Consequences, NM 87901. ☎ **505/894-6183.** 16 dormitory beds, 2 apartments.

Rates: Dorm beds $11 for International Youth Hostel Association members, $14 for nonmembers; apartments $35–$42.

This pleasant hostel beside the Rio Grande has the added attraction of hot mineral baths on the premises. There are kitchenette units, family units, and couples can be accommodated. There is also a campground on the property ($7.50 per person), and a small houseboat. A guest laundry is available and day tours of area attractions can be arranged.

Where to Dine

Dam Site Restaurant, Hwy. 177, Elephant Butte. ☎ **894-2073.**

Cuisine: AMERICAN.
Prices: Dinners $7–$11. AE, CB, DC, DISC, MC, V.
Open: Sat–Sun 11am–10pm, Mon–Fri 11am–9pm.

It was inevitable that this lakeside restaurant and lounge would give itself the sobriquet "a dam site better." Part of the Dam Site Recreation Area, it overlooks picturesque Elephant Butte Island and bustling marina. Steaks, fish, and some Mexican dishes are the fare. Also open for breakfast Sat and Sun 7 to 11am, Memorial Day to Labor Day.

K-Bob's Steakhouse, 2260 N. Date St. ☎ 894-2127.

Cuisine: STEAKS/BURGERS.
Prices: Main courses $2.99–$12.99. AE, CB, DC, DISC, MC, V.
Open: Sun–Thurs 7am–9pm, Fri–Sat 7am–10pm. **Closed:** Christmas.

K-Bob's, a New Mexico–wide family steak-house chain, succeeds because it caters to everyone. For example, all meals come with a choice of any of 15 "homestyle veggies." There's a large salad bar; a children's menu; and a selection of beers and wines. Soups, sandwiches, and burgers are always available.

$ La Cocina, 280 Date St. ☎ 894-6499.

Cuisine: NEW MEXICAN.
Prices: Main courses $3.95–$14.50. No credit cards.
Open: Mon–Thurs 11am–9pm, Fri–Sun 11am–10pm. **Closed:** Thanksgiving and Christmas.

This nicely appointed traditional restaurant serves New Mexican and American meals, including excellent compuestas and chile rellenos. The walls are decorated with the work of local artists, and you'll be astonished by the size of their sopaipillas.

La Piñata, 1990 South Broadway. ☎ 894-9047.

Cuisine: MEXICAN/AMERICAN. **Reservations:** Not necessary.
Prices: $1.50–$6.25 main courses. No credit cards.
Open: Mon–Sat 7am–8pm.

For authentic Mexican food at low prices, La Piñata is your best bet. You'll find all the old standbys, including tostadas, chile rellenos, tamales, burritos, and stacked or rolled enchiladas, as well as hamburgers and sandwiches on the menu. The decor is a little more "flashy" than other restaurants in town and the service is fast and friendly. You can order à la carte, or you can get a full meal complete with rice and beans. Portions are large.

★ Los Arcos, 1400 Date St. (Hwy. 85). ☎ 894-6200.

Cuisine: AMERICAN. **Reservations:** Recommended.
Prices: Appetizers $1.95–$8.95; main courses $9–$25.95. AE, CB, DC, DISC, MC, V.
Open: Sun–Thurs 5–10:30pm, Fri–Sat 5–11pm. **Closed:** Thanksgiving Day, Christmas.

A spacious hacienda-style restaurant fronted by a lovely desert garden, Los Arcos offers diners an intimate atmosphere and friendly service, as if you're at an old friend's home. Its steaks are regionally famous, and its fish dishes include fresh local catches like walleye pike and catfish. The restaurant also has a fine dessert list and cordial selection.

3 Las Cruces

225 miles S of Albuquerque; 45 miles N of El Paso, Texas; 272 miles E of Tucson, Ariz.

GETTING THERE • By Plane   Las Cruces International Airport, 8 miles west, has about a dozen arrivals and departures a day to Albuquerque. Contact **Mesa Airlines**

(☎ **526-9743** or toll free **800/MESA-AIR**). El Paso International Airport, 47 miles south, has daily flights to Phoenix, Dallas, and Houston. The **Las Cruces Shuttle Service,** 201 E. University Ave. (☎ **525-1784** or toll free **800/288-1784**), provides continuing service between the El Paso airport and Las Cruces. It leaves Las Cruces twelve times daily between 4:30am and 11:45pm, with a charge of $21 ($35 round-trip). There's a $6 pickup or drop-off charge for service elsewhere than its regular stops at the Las Cruces Hilton and Holiday Inn.

• **By Bus   Greyhound** and **TNM&O** both service Las Cruces from a bus depot at 1150 Hickory Dr. (☎ **524-8518**). The city is a stop on the Denver–Albuquerque–El Paso, Salt Lake–Albuquerque–El Paso, and Los Angeles–El Paso routes, with dozens of departures daily.

• **By Car**   From Albuquerque, take I-25 south (4 hours). From El Paso, take I-10 north (³/₄ hour). From Tucson, take I-25 east (5 hours).

ESSENTIALS • Orientation   New Mexico's second-largest city is beautifully set in the Mesilla Valley with the spectacular Organ Mountains as a backdrop to the east. I-25 from Albuquerque and I-10 from San Diego intersect here.

• **Information**   The **Las Cruces Convention & Visitors Bureau** is at 311 N. Downtown Mall, Las Cruces, NM 88001 (☎ **505/524-8521** or toll free **800/FIESTAS**). The **Las Cruces Chamber of Commerce** is at 760 W. Picacho Ave., Las Cruces, NM 88005 (☎ **524-1968**).

• **Fast Facts**   The **area code** is 505. Public transportation is provided by the **RoadRunner** city bus system (☎ **525-2500**), with seven city routes and one NMSU campus route. One-ride fares start at 50¢ for adults, 25¢ for children 6 to 18 and seniors 60 and over. For a taxi, call **Yellow Cab** (☎ **524-1711**). **Memorial Medical Center** is located at University Avenue and Telshor Boulevard (☎ **522-8641** or for 24-hour emergency service, **521-2286**. The main **post office** is at 201 E. Las Cruces Avenue at Church Street (☎ **524-2841**). In emergency dial **911.**

Established in 1849 on El Camino Real, the "royal highway" between Santa Fe and Mexico City, Las Cruces ("the crosses") was named for the graves of travelers who had been ambushed here a generation earlier by Apaches. It became a supply center for miners prospecting the Organ Mountains and soldiers stationed at nearby Fort Selden. Today, it is New Mexico's second-largest urban area, with 66,500 people in the city and 146,600 in Doña Ana County. It is noted as an agricultural center, especially for its cotton, pecans, and chiles; as a regional transportation hub; and as the gateway to the White Sands Missile Range and other defense installations.

What to See & Do

Las Cruces's early history is the domain of adjacent ⊠ **Mesilla.** This picturesque village on Las Cruces's southwestern flank was established in the late 1500s by Mexican colonists. It became the crossroads of El Camino Real and the Butterfield Overland Stagecoach route. The Gadsden Purchase, which annexed Mesilla to the United States and fixed the current international boundaries of New Mexico and Arizona, was signed in this village in 1854.

Mesilla's most notorious resident, William Bonney—otherwise known as Billy the Kid—was sentenced to death at the county courthouse, but escaped before the sentence was carried out. Legendary hero Pat Garrett eventually tracked down and killed the Kid at Fort Sumner; later, Garrett was mysteriously murdered in an arroyo just outside Las Cruces. He is buried in the local Masonic cemetery.

Thick-walled adobe buildings, which once protected residents against Apache attacks, now house art galleries, restaurants, museums, and gift shops. Throughout Mesilla, colorful red-chile *ristras* decorate homes and businesses.

A WALKING TOUR OF HISTORIC LAS CRUCES

Downtown Las Cruces has numerous historical buildings, which make a walking tour very worthwhile. **Bicentennial Log Cabin,** Main St. and Lucero Ave., Downtown Mall (☎ **524-1422**), is a circa-1850 structure moved to Las Cruces from the Black Range Mountains, containing authentic furnishings and artifacts. This municipal museum is open April through September by appointment. The **Branigan Cultural Center,** 500 N. Water St. (☎ **524-1422**), features traveling and local exhibits of art and local history, and presents performing arts, educational programs, and special events.

The **Old Armijo House,** Lohman Avenue at Main Street, is an 1860s home that was at one time restored with original furnishings and second-floor display rooms. Now Pioneer Savings and Loan, it is open weekdays from 9am to 4pm but the display rooms are no longer open to the public. **Our Lady at the Foot of the Cross Shrine,** near Water Street and Lohman Avenue, is a reproduction of Michelangelo's *Pietà,* dedicated to the Sisters of Loretto. **El Molino,** a grinding wheel from an 1853 flour mill at Water Street and Lohman Avenue, commemorates the work and hardships of early pioneers. The **Amador Hotel,** Amador Avenue and Water Street, built in 1850, once hosted Benito Juarez, Pat Garrett, and Billy the Kid; restored, it now houses county offices, and is not open to the public.

OTHER ATTRACTIONS

San Albino Church, north side of Old Mesilla Plaza.

This is one of the oldest churches in the Mesilla valley. Constructed in 1851, the present structure was built some 55 years later (1906) on its original foundation. It was named for St. Albin, medieval English bishop of North Africa, on whose day an important irrigation ditch from the Rio Grande was completed. The church bells date to the early 1870s; the pews were made in Taos of Philippine mahogany.

Admission: Free; donations appreciated.

Open: For visiting Tues–Sun 1–3pm; English-language masses Sat 6:30pm and Sun 11am, Spanish mass Sun 8am.

Gadsden Museum, Hwy. 28 and Barker Rd. ☎ **526-6293.**

A famous painting of the signing of the Gadsden Purchase is a highlight of this collection, from the Albert Jennings Fountain family. The museum, three blocks east of the Old Mesilla Plaza in the 1875 Fountain family home, also houses Indian and Civil War relics and Old West artifacts. All visitors go on the museum's guided tour.

Admission: Adults $2, children 6–12 $1.

Open: Mon–Sat 9–11am, daily 1–5pm.

New Mexico State University, University Ave. and Locust St. ☎ **646-0111.**

Established in 1888, this institution of 24,000 students is especially noted for its schools of business, engineering, and agriculture. Its facilities include the Solar Energy Institute, the Water Resources Institute of New Mexico, and the New Mexico Environmental Institute.

University Museum in Kent Hall (☎ **646-3739**) has exhibits of historic and prehistoric Native American culture and art; it's open Tuesday through Saturday from 10am to 4pm and Sunday from 1 to 4pm, with free admission. The **Williams Hall Art Gallery** (☎ **646-2545**) features monthly exhibits of contemporary and historical art, and a permanent collection of prints, photographs, and folk art. **Corbett Center Gallery,** in the student center (☎ **646-3200**), has various exhibits throughout the year; a 12-foot copper-alloy triangle outside has a notch that symbolizes the transition from youth to adulthood. **Clyde Tombaugh Observatory,** named for the discoverer of the planet Pluto (who is a current resident of Las Cruces), has a high-powered telescope open for public viewing one evening a month.

COOL FOR KIDS

Las Cruces Museum of Natural History, Mesilla Valley Mall, Telshor Boulevard. ☎ 522-3120.

This small city-funded museum offers a variety of exhibits, changing quarterly, that emphasize zoology, microbiology, meteorology, cartography, and local history. Recent exhibits of live animals have included baby spadefoot toads, leopard frogs, a gopher snake, an aquarium of native fish, and box turtles.

Admission: Free.

Open: Mon–Thurs noon–5pm, Fri noon–9pm, Sat 10am–6pm, Sun noon–6pm.

SPORTS & RECREATION

New Mexico State University football, basketball, baseball, and other teams play intercollegiate schedules in the Big West Conference, against schools from California, Nevada, and Utah. The "Aggies" play their home games on the NMSU campus, south of University Avenue on Locust Street. Football is played in the Chili Bowl, basketball in Pan Am Center arena. For information, call the Athletic Department (☎ 646-1420).

Auto Racing   Fans of motor sports will find sprint and stock car racing at **The Speedway,** at Southern New Mexico State Fairgrounds, 11 miles west of Las Cruces via I-10 (☎ 524-7913), open weekends from April through November.

Fishing   The **Rio Grande** is considered one of the nation's great fishing streams and **Burn Lake,** Amador Avenue at I-10, is also stocked with panfish.

Golf   Two year-round 18-hole public courses are the **Las Cruces Country Club,** Highway 70 East (☎ 526-8731), open daily 7am to 7pm; and the **NMSU Golf Course,** Telshor Boulevard and University Avenue (☎ 646-3219), open dawn to dusk daily. Both courses close for Thanksgiving and Christmas.

Hiking   The most popular spot for day hikes near Las Cruces is **Aguirre Springs Recreation Site** (☎ 525-4300), 20 miles east of the city off U.S. Highway 70, on the eastern flanks of the Organ Mountains.

Horse Racing   New Mexico's longest racing season takes place 45 miles south of Las Cruces at **Sunland Park** (☎ 589-1131). The ponies run Wednesday, Friday, Saturday, and Sunday, October to May.

Swimming   There are public pools at **Apodaca Park,** 801 E. Madrid St. (☎ 524-7008); **Frenger Park,** Parkview and West Park drives (☎ 523-0362); and **Laabs,** 750 W. Picacho Ave. (☎ 524-3168). All are open Memorial Day to Labor

Day. There's also swimming at little **Burn Lake,** Amador Avenue at I-10 (☎ 524-1662).

Tennis   Public courts can be found at **Apodaca Park,** 801 E. Madrid St.; **Frenger Park,** 800 Parkview Dr.; and **Young Park,** 1905 E. Nevada Ave.

SHOPPING

Shoppers should be aware that in Las Cruces, Monday is a notoriously quiet day. Some stores close for the day, and it's best to call ahead before traveling to a specific store.

For **art,** visit **Lundeen Inn of the Arts,** 618 Alameda Blvd. (☎ 526-3327), open from 9am to 6pm daily; **Rising Sky Artworks,** 415 E. Foster (☎ 525-8454), features works in clay by local and western artists, and is open from 9am to 5pm Monday to Saturday; **Universal Community Center of the Arts,** 207 Avenida de Mesilla (☎ 523-0014), from 10am to 5pm Tuesday to Friday, 1 to 5pm Saturday and Sunday; and the **William Bonney Gallery,** 3 Calle Parian, just off the southeast corner of Old Mesilla Plaza (☎ 526-8275), open Monday to Saturday from 10am to 6pm, Sunday noon to 5pm.

For **books,** try **Mesilla Book Center,** in an 1856 mercantile building on the west side of Old Mesilla Plaza (☎ 526-6220), open from 11am to 5:30pm Tuesday to Saturday and 1 to 5pm on Sunday.

For native **crafts and jewelry,** check out **Silver Assets,** Calle de Santiago (☎ 523-8747), 1 1/2 blocks east of San Albino Church in Mesilla.

Got a sweet tooth? **J. Eric Chocolatier** featuring elegant hand-dipped and molded chocolates, is on the east side of Old Mesilla Plaza (☎ 526-2744), and is open Tuesday to Saturday from 10:30am to 5pm and 11am to 5pm on Sunday and Monday.

Mesilla Valley Mall is a full-service shopping center at 700 S. Telshor Boulevard, just off the I-25 interchange with Lohman Avenue (☎ 522-1001), with well over 100 stores. The mall is open Monday to Saturday 10am to 9pm, and Sunday noon to 6pm.

Farmers and Crafts Market operates Wednesday and Saturday mornings (from 7:30am to noon) on the Downtown Mall (☎ 382-0616). Local produce, baked goods, arts, and crafts are commonly available.

There are three **wineries** in the Las Cruces area. **Blue Teal Vineyards** (☎ 524-0390) has a tasting room in the historic Fountain Theater, Calle de Guadalupe, just off the southeast corner of Old Mesilla Plaza, open Tuesday through Sunday from 1 to 5pm. **La Viña Winery** (☎ 882-2092), south of Las Cruces off N.M. 28, welcomes visitors by appointment; and **Mademoiselle de Santa Fe** (☎ 524-0481), has a tasting room at 3910 W. Picacho Avenue, Las Cruces. Call for hours.

EVENING ENTERTAINMENT

National recording artists frequently perform at NMSU's **Pan Am Center** (☎ 646-4413). The NMSU Music Department (☎ 646-2421) offers free jazz, classical, and pop concerts, and the **Las Cruces Symphony** (☎ 646-3709) often performs here as well.

Hershel Zohn Theater (☎ 646-4515), at NMSU, presents plays of the professional/student **American Southwest Theatre Company**—dramas, comedies, musicals, and original works September through May. The highly acclaimed ASTC is headed by Mark Medoff, who won a Tony Award for his play, *Children of a Lesser God.*

The **Las Cruces Community Theatre** (☎ **523-1200**) mounts six productions a year at its own facility on the Downtown Mall.

A popular country-music and dancing club is **Cowboys,** 2205 S. Main St. (☎ **525-9050**), with no cover Sunday through Wednesday, $3 Thursday through Saturday. Free hamburger fry Thursday and Friday. Country dinner on Sundays.

Nearby Attractions

NORTH OF LAS CRUCES

The town of **Hatch,** 39 miles via I-25 or 34 miles via N.M. 185, calls itself the "chile capital of the world." It is the center of a 22,000-acre agricultural belt that grows and processes more chile than anywhere else in the world. The annual Hatch Chile Festival over the Labor Day weekend celebrates the harvest. For information, call the Hatch Chamber of Commerce (☎ **267-3021**).

★ **Fort Selden State Monument,** 15 miles north of Las Cruces between 1-25 (Exit 19) and N.M. 185. ☎ **526-8911.**

Founded in 1865, Fort Selden housed the famous Black Cavalry, the "Buffalo Soldiers" who protected settlers from marauding natives. It was subsequently the boyhood home of Gen. Douglas MacArthur, whose father, Arthur, was in charge of troops patrolling the U.S.–Mexican border in the 1880s. There are only eroding ruins remaining today. Displays in the visitor center tell Fort Selden's story, including photos of young Douglas and his family. The fort closed permanently in 1891. Adjacent to the state monument, **Leasburg Dam State Park** (☎ **524-4068**) offers picnicking, camping, canoeing, and fishing.

Admission: Adults $2, free for children 16 and under.

Open: Daily 9am–6pm in summer; 7am–5pm in winter.

SOUTH OF LAS CRUCES

Stahmann Farms, 10 miles south of La Mesilla on N.M. 28 (☎ **526-2453**), is one of the world's largest single producers of pecans. Several million pounds are harvested annually from orchards in the bed of an ancient lake. Tours are given by appointment. **Stahmann's Country Store** (☎ **526-8974**) sells pecans and pecan candy, other specialty foods, and has a small cafe. It's open weekdays from 9am to 5:30pm, weekends from 10am to 5pm.

✪ **War Eagles Air Museum** (☎ **589-2000**), at the Santa Teresa Airport, about 35 miles south of Las Cruces via I-10 (call for directions), has an extensive collection of historic aircraft from World War II and the Korean conflict, including a beautifully restored P-38 Lightning, P-51 Mustang, F-86 Sabre, and several Russian MIG-15s. Most of the museum's two dozen planes are in flying condition, and are kept inside a large well-lighted hangar. The museum is open Tuesday through Sunday from 10am to 4pm; admission costs $4 for adults, $3 for senior citizens, and children under 12 are admitted free.

EAST OF LAS CRUCES

The **Organ Mountains,** so-called because they resemble the pipes of a church organ, draw inevitable comparisons to Wyoming's Grand Tetons. Organ Peak, at 9,119 feet, is the highest point in Doña Ana County.

The **Aguirre Springs Recreation Area** (☎ **525-4300**), off U.S. Highway 70 on the western slope of the Organ Mountains, is operated by the Bureau of Land

Management. Activities include hiking, camping, and picnicking; there are horse trails here, too.

Where to Stay

Las Cruces has the wide variety of accommodations expected in a town of its size and importance. Local lodging tax of 5% is added to the state tax (6.3125%) for an 11.3125% addition to every hotel bill. Parking is usually free.

Best Western Mesilla Valley Inn, 901 Avenida de Mesilla at I-25, Las Cruces, NM 88005. ☎ **505/524-8603** or toll free **800/327-3314** or **800/528-1234.** Fax 505/526-8437. 166 rms. A/C TV TEL

Rates: $48–$54 single; $52–$58 double. AE, CB, DC, DISC, MC, V.

A large motel set on spacious grounds near the north-south freeway, the Mesilla Valley Inn offers rooms that are comfortably decorated in a southwestern motif. Executive rooms are very spacious and have refrigerators, clock radios, and remote-control televisions. Some rooms have kitchenette facilities.

Eddie's Bar and Grill serves three American or continental-style meals daily (6am to 2pm and 5 to 10pm) in a sidewalk-cafe atmosphere. Lunches (including buffalo burgers) run $3.95 to $7.50, dinners $9.50 to $16.95. There's an enormous soup and salad bar here. The adjacent lounge has a piano bar and sometimes books light jazz combos. The inn has room service, valet laundry, handicapped and nonsmoking rooms, an outdoor swimming pool, Jacuzzi, guest laundry, and meeting space for 350. There is a nominal membership fee to use a nearby health and racquet club.

Best Western Mission Inn, 1765 S. Main St., Las Cruces, NM 88005. ☎ **505/524-8591** or toll free **800/528-1234.** Fax 505/523-4740. 68 rms, 2 suites. A/C TV TEL

Rates (including full breakfast): $48 single; $52 double; $74 suite. AE, CB, DC, DISC, MC, V.

The grounds of this two-story motel have several trees, including a big weeping willow shading a picnic table. Rooms are spacious, with a king or two queen-size beds. Colorful flowers are stenciled on the walls, big mirrors are surrounded by Mexican tiles, and there's a tile shelf behind the beds, giving it the mission look of its name. There are rooms for nonsmokers and the disabled.

Señor Toucan's Coffee Shop is open daily from 6am to 2pm. The Hidden Forest restaurant serves steaks and seafood nightly. The Sports Connection is a big-screen lounge with a deejay dance floor. The inn has a 24-hour desk, same-day laundry, an outdoor swimming pool, and a playground.

★ **Hampton Inn,** 755 Avenida de Mesilla (I-10 Exit 140), Las Cruces, NM 88005. ☎ **505/526-8311** or toll free **800/426-7866.** Fax 505/527-2015. 118 rms. A/C TV TEL

Rates (including continental breakfast): $48–$52 single; $53–$57 double. AE, CB, DC, DISC, MC, V.

This handsome Hampton Inn is in a very good location for vacationers, on the southwest side of Las Cruces near the numerous shops, galleries, restaurants, and attractions of historic Old Mesilla. Rooms are comfortable and quiet, with wood-trimmed furnishings, and refrigerators and microwave ovens are available.

There's a very attractive outdoor swimming pool (unheated), and the continental breakfast is among the best you'll find in town. Handicapped and nonsmoking rooms are available, local phone calls and use of a local health club are free, and pets are permitted.

Hilltop Hacienda, 2520 Westmoreland Rd., Las Cruces, NM 88001.
☎ **505/382-3556.** 3 rms. A/C

Rates (including continental breakfast): $50 single; $65 double. MC, V.

The bed-and-breakfast home of Bob and Teddi Peters is situated on 20 acres of land, 10 minutes' drive north of the city. A two-story, arched-adobe brick dwelling of Spanish-Moorish architectural style, it offers spectacular views of the city, Rio Grande valley, and Organ Mountains. Breakfast is served outdoors on a wide patio or indoors beside a large fireplace. No smoking is allowed. For train enthusiasts, there is a miniature, passenger-carrying, live steam train on the premises.

Lundeen's Inn of the Arts, 618 S. Alameda Blvd., Las Cruces, NM 88005.
☎ **505/526-3327** or toll free **800/553-4ART.** Fax 505/526-3355. 20 rms, 4 suites. A/C

Rates (including breakfast): $58 single; $60 double; $75–$120 suite. AE, CB, DC, DISC, MC, V.

Operated by Gerald Lundeen, an architect and circuit preacher, and his wife, Linda, this bed-and-breakfast establishment is also an art gallery. A late 1890s adobe built in Territorial style, it displays the works of about 30 Southwest painters, sculptors, and potters in its 14,000 square feet of floor space. Outside, guests can help Gerry make adobe bricks for building a large *horno* (outdoor oven) and courtyard with mission archways.

Rooms are named for noted regional artists, including Georgia O'Keeffe, Amado Peña, R. C. Gorman, Frederic Remington, Nicolai Fechin, and Gordon Snidow, and each features the flavor of that artist. Every room is different, but all have wooden floors, tubs or bidets, and regional touches. Two suites have kitchenettes, a private TV, and telephone. Others share the TV and telephone in a downstairs common area. Some rooms have fireplaces. Breakfast includes fresh fruit and eggs, pancakes, strudels, and so forth.

The inn is a popular spot for weddings and artists' workshops including classes in silversmithing, pottery, and painting. The ElderHostel program also stays here. Guests get reduced rates at local health club, and Gerry Lundeen will take them on architectural walking tours of nearby Old Mesilla.

⭐ **Las Cruces Hilton,** 705 S. Telshor Blvd., Las Cruces, NM 88001.
☎ **505/522-4300** or toll free **800/284-0616.** Fax 505/521-4707. 203 rms, 7 suites. A/C TV TEL

Rates: $56–$67 single; $58–$77 double; $90–$165 suite. Weekend packages from $69 for a family, including breakfast. AE, CB, DC, DISC, MC, V.

Las Cruces's finest hotel was built in 1986 on a hill on the east side of the city, across the street from the Mesilla Valley Mall, with an incredible view of the city and the Organ Mountains. Its pleasant tiled lobby has southwestern-style furnishings. That motif carries to the decor of the spacious rooms, each of which has a king- or two queen-size beds, and all standard furnishings, including a working desk. Some rooms accommodate the disabled.

The Ventana Terrace serves breakfast and lunches daily from 6am to 2pm, then does a make-over to fine gourmet dining from 5 to 10pm nightly, with southwestern and continental specialties in the $10.95-to-$15.95 range for main courses.

The hotel offers room service (6am to 10pm), 24-hour desk, courtesy van, valet laundry, an outdoor swimming pool, whirlpool, gift shop, car rental, and an exercise facility. There is meeting space for 700.

 Mesón de Mesilla, 1803 Avenida de Mesilla (P.O. Box 1212), Mesilla, NM 88046. ☎ **505/525-9212**, or toll free **800/732-6025.** Fax 505/525-2380. 13 rms. A/C TV TEL

Rates (including breakfast): $45–$82 single; $52–$82 double. CB, DC, DISC, MC, V.

This large adobe home is a landmark on Highway 28 into Mesilla, and host Chuck Walker likes to say it has the "ambience of a Wine Country inn." Surrounded by beautiful gardens and adjacent to cotton fields, it certainly has the setting.

A portico surrounds the second floor, where the homey guest rooms are located. Appointed in southwestern motifs with clock radios, brass headboards, antiques, and ceiling fans, each room has a private bath. Phones can be used for outgoing calls only; incoming messages are taken at the switchboard. A full breakfast is served in the garden atrium of the gourmet restaurant (see "Where to Dine," below).

Facilities include an outdoor swimming pool, horseshoes, bicycles (including a tandem) free for guests' use.

Where to Dine

In these listings the following categories define price ranges: **expensive**—most dinner main courses are over $15; **moderate**—most dinner main courses are $10 to $15; **inexpensive**—most dinner main courses are under $10.

EXPENSIVE

 Double Eagle, 308 Calle Guadalupe, on the east side of Old Mesilla Plaza. ☎ **523-6700.**

Cuisine: CONTINENTAL. **Reservations:** Recommended.
Prices: Appetizers $3.50–$6.25; lunch $4.95–$9.50; dinner $10.95–$24.95. AE, CB, DC, DISC, MC, V.
Open: Mon–Sat 11am–10pm, Sun 5–9pm.

The recent restoration of this 150-year-old hacienda has put the imposing Territorial-style premises on the National Historic Sites register. Its 30-foot-long bar has Corinthian columns in gold leaf, and there are Gay Nineties oil paintings and 18-armed brass chandeliers hung with Baccarat crystals. A woman's ghost is said to frequent one of the several exquisite small dining rooms. The lush red of carpet and chair upholstery contrasts richly with the dark tones of polished wood in tables, sideboards, and paneling. Specialties of the house include quail, breast of chicken Mesilla, 16-ounce pink mountain trout, and an 18-ounce filet mignon. All portions are generous. There is a lavish salad bar, international-style desserts and coffees, and a good wine and beer list. Sandwiches and light meals are served at lunch.

Mesón de Mesilla, 1803 Avenida de Mesilla, Mesilla. ☎ **525-2380.**

Cuisine: CONTINENTAL. **Reservations:** Required.
Prices: Appetizers $4.95; lunch $4.95–$8.95; Sun brunch $13.95, dinner $17.95–$34.95. AE, CB, DC, DISC, MC, V.
Open: Lunch Wed–Fri 11am–2pm; dinner Tues–Sat 5:30–9pm; champagne brunch Sun 11am–2pm.

Located in an elegant bed-and-breakfast at the northeast gateway to La Mesilla (see "Where to Stay," above), this gourmet restaurant has a Spanish colonial ambience with carved wooden pillars, stained-glass windows, wrought-iron chairs, and a rich burgundy color scheme. Chef Chuck Walker's blackboard menu changes weekly, but always presents several varieties of fresh fish, chicken, beef, and Eastern veal. All meals include soup, salad, main course, vegetables, and dessert. Main courses might be sautéed quail à la meson, black sea bass, shrimp Cardinale, or chateaubriand. Lunches feature salads, sandwiches, quiches, and a buffet. There's an extensive wine and beer list.

MODERATE

Cattle Baron, 709 S. Telshor Blvd. ☎ **522-7533.**

> **Cuisine:** STEAKS & SEAFOOD. **Reservations:** Not taken for parties under 6.
> **Prices:** Appetizers $2.50–$5.75; lunch $3.95–$7.50; dinner $6.95–$20.95. AE, CB, DC, DISC, MC, V.
> **Open:** Sun–Thurs 11am–9:30pm, Fri–Sat 11am–10pm. **Closed:** Christmas.

An attractive and comfortable restaurant with southwestern decor, and suspended brass lamps, the Cattle Baron is within walking distance of the Hilton. Its lounge displays unique works of original southwestern art.

The menu, ranging from filet Oscar to broiled mahimahi, features a wide choice of steaks, chicken, and seafood, including fresh catches of the day. There are homemade soups, a huge salad bar, a children's menu, and desserts such as mud pie.

$ **Peppers**, 306 Calle Guadalupe, on the east side of Old Mesilla Plaza. ☎ **523-4999.**

> **Cuisine:** NEW MEXICAN. **Reservations:** For large parties only.
> **Prices:** Tapas (appetizers) $1.35–$4.95; lunch $4.95–$8.25; dinner $7.95–$13.95. AE, CB, DC, DISC, MC, V.
> **Open:** Mon–Sat 11am–10pm, Sun noon–9pm.

This restaurant shares a building and the same ownership with the Double Eagle, but the resemblance ends there. The Eagle has age and grace; Peppers has youthful exuberance. Hispanic folk art, including traditional masks and *santiagos,* greets guests in the entryway. Music from the sixties and seventies plays continuously. There are cacti on the tables. A regional artist is featured in the gallery.

The cuisine is Santa Fe–style New Mexican, heavy on seafood, such as the seafood chimichanga and blue-corn catfish. Other dishes include the La Fonda strip (sirloin with black beans and a guacamole-and-chipotle sauce), shark fajitas, and shrimp enchiladas. Tapas include green-chile wontons and tortilla-wrapped shrimp with pineapple-chile salsa.

Tatsu, 930 El Paseo Rd. ☎ **526-7144.**

> **Cuisine:** JAPANESE.
> **Prices:** Appetizers $3.50–$6.95; lunch $5.95–$9.50; dinner $9.25–$15.95. AE, DC, MC, V.
> **Open:** Mon–Thurs 11am–9pm, Fri 11am–10pm, Sat noon–10pm, Sun 11am–2pm and 5–9pm.

Tatsu may not be classic Japanese by New York or L.A. standards, but it does well for southern New Mexico. There are no tatami rooms here, but hanging paper lanterns and other designer touches lend a feeling of authenticity. Big windows face the street in the front room. There's somewhat more traditional decor in a rear chamber which houses a Japanese garden.

Sushi, sukiyaki, and soba plates are integral to the menu. The tempura is excellent—seafood, vegetables, and a spicy relleno pepper. "East Meets West" specials include pecan chicken katsu, ginger beef, and soft-shell crab. Imported Japanese beers, sake, and wines are served with meals. There's a children's menu as well.

INEXPENSIVE

$ **Fajitas,** 600 E. Amador Ave. at Tornillo St. ☎ **523-6407.**

Cuisine: NEW MEXICAN.

Prices: Main dishes $4.95–$21.95. AE, CB, DC, DISC, MC, V.

Open: Daily 11am–2pm and 5–9pm. **Closed:** July 4, Thanksgiving, Christmas, and New Year's.

A turn-of-the-century adobe that still has its original *vigas* and hardwood floors, Fajitas also has rebuilt fireplaces and an indoor brick patio. Its mesquite-broiled beef, chicken, pork, or shrimp fajitas are served with grilled, marinated onions and green chile on a sizzling platter, with frijoles, guacamole, pico de gallo, and flour or corn tortillas. Enchiladas, tacos, and nachos are also on the menu, and there's a full bar.

$ **Henry J's Gourmet Hamburgers,** 523 E. Idaho Ave. ☎ **525-2211.**

Cuisine: AMERICAN.

Prices: Sandwiches and hamburgers $2.95–$5; full meals $5.95–$9.95. AE, DISC, MC, V.

Open: Sun–Thurs 10:30am–9pm, Fri–Sat 10:30am–10pm.

Much more than a huge fifties soda fountain—which it incorporates—Henry J's has seating on three levels amidst big bay windows, brass railings, framed period advertisements, and a Wurlitzer jukebox. Besides great hamburgers, Henry J's Gourmet offers beef and chicken tacos, barbecue sandwiches, and a "bottomless" soup bowl priced at just $2.

La Posta, southeast corner of Old Mesilla Plaza. ☎ **524-3524.**

Cuisine: NEW MEXICAN & STEAKS. **Reservations:** Recommended.

Prices: Main courses $2.80–$11.95. AE, CB, DC, DISC, MC, V.

Open: Sun, Tue–Thurs 11am–9pm, Fri–Sat 11am–9:30pm. **Closed:** Thanksgiving and Christmas.

The only surviving stagecoach station of the Butterfield, Overland Mail Route from Tipton, Missouri, to San Francisco, in the late 19th century, La Posta occupies a historic 150-year-old adobe building. Kit Carson, Pancho Villa, and Billy the Kid all ate here. The entrance leads through a jungle of tall plants beneath a Plexiglas roof, past a tank of piranhas and a noisy aviary of macaws, cockatiels, and Amazon parrots, to nine dining rooms with bright, festive decor.

The menu features steaks and such Mexican dinners as "Specialty of La Posta"—chile con queso and corn tortillas, guacamole and salad; rolled red enchiladas, tamale, frijoles, chili con carne, rolled taco, hot corn tortillas; ice cream and coffee. That's a lot of food for one meal! Beer and wine are served with meals.

My Brother's Place, 336 Main St. at Amador Ave. ☎ **523-7681.**

Cuisine: NEW MEXICAN.

Prices: Main courses lunch or dinner $4–$12. AE, CB, DC, DISC, MC, V.

Open: Mon–Thurs 11am–9pm, Fri–Sat 11am–10pm.

Located between the Downtown Mall and the historic Amador Hotel, the Gutierrez brothers' modern adobe hacienda boasts a central fountain, tiled planters, *vigas,* and arches. Mexican menu favorites include fajitas and a hot-hot green enchilada; barbecues and burgers are also popular. Lunch specials are served Monday through Friday.

Three lounges adjoin the restaurant. The Main Street Lounge has an indoor patio overlooking the street from the second story. PM's Billiards Club and the Cantina Game Room have 19 pool tables between them. Margaritas are served by the glass and the pitcher.

Santa Fe Restaurant, 1410 S. Solano Dr., at Foster Rd. ☎ **522-0466.**

Cuisine: SOUTHWESTERN. **Reservations:** Recommended.
Prices: Appetizers $2.50–$5.95; lunch $3.25–$12.50; dinner $4.25–$13.95. AE, DC, DISC, MC, V.
Open: Sun–Thurs 11:30am–2pm and 5–9pm, Fri–Sat 11:30am–2pm and 5–10pm.
Closed: Christmas.

This open Southwest-style restaurant with inlaid-tile tables serves innovative Mexican dishes plus steak, chicken, and fish. Selections include dishes such as pan-fried free-range chicken with smoked chile butter, or filet mignon sautéed in marsala sauce with mushrooms, onions, peppers, and Dijon mustard. There's a very popular weekday lunch buffet ($4.95), and beer and wine are available. The entire restaurant is nonsmoking.

4 Deming & Lordsburg

Deming: 59 miles W of Las Cruces, 213 miles E of Tucson, Ariz.
Lordsburg: 119 miles W of Las Cruces, 153 miles E of Tucson

GETTING THERE • By Plane Deming's **Grant County Airport** serves private planes only. A van line, **Dart Taxi** (☎ 546-6511), shuttles to and from El Paso and Tucson airports on a request basis. **The Las Cruces Shuttle** (☎ toll free **800/288-1784**) has daily runs to El Paso Airport, and Deming, Las Cruces, and Silver City.

• **By Train AMTRAK** trains pass through three times weekly, each direction, on their Los Angeles–El Paso run. The depot in Deming is at 301 E. Railroad Ave.; in Lordsburg on Motel Drive at Main Street. (Neither has a phone.) Tickets must be booked in advance with a travel agent or AMTRAK (☎ toll free **800/USA-RAIL**).

• **By Bus Greyhound** and **Texas, New Mexico, and Oklahoma** buses stop daily in Deming and Lordsburg. The bus station in Deming is at 300 E. Spruce St. (☎ 546-3881); in Lordsburg, buses stop at 112 Wabash Ave. (☎ 542-3412).

• **By Car** From Las Cruces, take I-10 west (1 hour to Deming, 2 hours to Lordsburg). From Tucson, take I-10 east (3 hours to Lordsburg, 4 hours to Deming).

ESSENTIALS • Orientation Both towns are on the northern edge of the Chihuahuan Desert. Deming's downtown area lies just south of I-10, Lordsburg's just north. In each case, the main street parallels the interstate.

• **Information** The **Deming–Luna County Chamber of Commerce,** 800 E. Pine St., Deming, NM 88030 (☎ 505/546-2674 or toll free **800/848-4955**); and the **New Mexico Welcome Center,** Exit 20, I-10, Lordsburg, NM 88045 (☎ 505/542-8149), are the most reliable sources. The **Lordsburg Hidalgo County Chamber of Commerce** is located at 208 Motel Dr. (P.O. Box 699), Lordsburg, NM 88045 (☎ 505/542-9864).

• **Fast Facts** The **area code** is 505. **Mimbres Memorial Hospital** in Deming is located at 900 W. Ash St. (☎ 546-2761). The Deming **post office** is at Spruce and

Copper streets (☎ **546-9461**); in Lordsburg, it's at Third and Shakespeare streets (☎ **542-9601**). In case of **emergency,** dial **911** or **0** for an operator.

New Mexico's least populated corner is this one, which includes the "boot heel" of the Gadsden Purchase that pokes 40 miles down into Mexico. These two railroad towns, an hour apart on I-10, see a lot of traffic; but whereas Deming (pop. 12,000) is thriving as a ranching center, Lordsburg (pop. 3,000) is watching its population dwindle. This is a popular area for rock hounds, aficionados of ghost towns, and history buffs: Columbus, 32 miles south of Deming, was the site of the last foreign incursion on continental American soil, by the Mexican bandit-revolutionary Pancho Villa in 1916.

What to See & Do

DEMING

 Deming Luna Mimbres Museum, 301 S. Silver Ave., Deming. ☎ **546-2382.**
Deming was the meeting place of the second east-west railroad to connect the Pacific and Atlantic coasts, and that heritage is recalled in this museum, run by the Luna County Historical Society. It shows some pioneer-era quilts and laces, a military room containing exhibits from the Indian Wars, Pancho Villa's raid, both world wars, and the Korean and Vietnam Wars, a room featuring the John and Mary Alice King Collection of Mimbres pottery, and a doll room with over 800 dolls. There's a gem and mineral room, a display of ladies' fashions from the Gay Nineties to the Roaring Twenties, a variety of pioneer silver, china, and crystal, and a new Transportation Annex with a chuck wagon—a "traveling kitchen." The museum also houses a collection of 2,200 bells from all over the world, as well as about 1800 liquor decanters.

Admission: By donation.

Open: Mon–Sat 9am–4pm, Sun 1:30–4pm. **Closed:** Thanksgiving Day and Christmas.

Rockhound State Park, 14 miles southeast of Deming via N.M. 11.
☎ **546-6182.**
Here at the base of the Little Florida Mountains is an arid, cactus-covered land with trails leading down into dry gullies and canyons. Visitors are encouraged to pick and take home with them as much as 15 pounds of minerals—jasper, agate, quartz crystal, flow-banded rhyolite, and other rocks. (You may have to walk a bit, as the more accessible minerals have been largely picked out.)

The campground ($7–$11 per night), which has shelters, rest rooms, and showers, gives a distant view of mountain ranges all the way to the Mexican border. The park also has hiking trails and a playground.

Admission: $3.

Open: Year-round.

Pancho Villa State Park, N.M. Highways 9 and 11, Columbus.
☎ **505/531-2711.**
Some 35 miles south of Deming is the tiny border town of Columbus, looking across at Mexico. The state park here marks the last time there was a foreign invasion of American soil. A temporary fort, where a tiny garrison was housed in tents, was attacked in 1916 by 600 Mexican revolutionaries, who cut through the boundary fence at Columbus. Eighteen Americans were killed, 12 wounded; an estimated 200 Mexicans died. The Mexicans immediately retreated across their border. An American

punitive expedition, headed by Gen. John J. Pershing, was launched into Mexico, but got nowhere. Villa restricted his banditry to Mexico after that, until his assassination in 1923.

The state park includes ruins of the old fort and a visitors' center with exhibits and a film. The park also has a strikingly beautiful desert botanical garden, worth the trip alone, plus campsites, rest rooms, showers, an RV dump station, and a playground.

Across the street from the state park is the old Southern Pacific Railroad Depot, which has been restored by the Columbus Historical Society and now houses the **Columbus Historical Museum** (☎ 531-2620), containing railroad memorabilia and exhibits on local history. Call for hours, and write to the historical society at P.O. Box 562, Columbus, NM 88029 for additional information about the community's history.

Three miles south is Las Palomas, Chihuahua (pop. 1,500). The port of entry is open 24 hours. Numerous restaurants and tourist-oriented businesses are located in Las Palomas.

LORDSBURG

Visitors to Lordsburg can go ✪ **rockhounding** in an area rich in minerals of many kinds. Desert roses can be found near Summit, and agate is known to exist in many abandoned mines locally. Mine dumps, southwest of Hachita, contain lead, zinc, and gold. There is manganese in the Animas mountains. Volcanic glass can be picked up in Coronado National Forest, and there is panning for gold in Gold Gulch.

Rodeo, 30 miles southwest via I-10 and U.S. 80, is the home of the **Chiricahua Gallery** (☎ 557-2225), open Monday through Saturday from 10am to 4pm. Regional artists have joined in a nonprofit, cooperative venture to exhibit works and offer classes in a variety of media. Many choose to live on the high-desert slopes of the Chiricahua Range. The gallery is on Highway 80 en route to Douglas, Arizona.

Shakespeare Ghost Town, P.O. Box 253, Lordsburg. ☎ 542-9034.

A national historic site, Shakespeare was once the home of 3,000 miners, promoters, and dealers of various kinds. Under the name "Ralston" it enjoyed a silver boom in 1870. This was followed by a notorious diamond fraud in 1872 in which a mine was salted with diamonds in order to raise prices on mining stock; many notables were sucked in, particularly William Ralston, founder of the Bank of California. It enjoyed a mining revival in 1879 under its new name, Shakespeare. It was a town with no church, no newspaper, and no local law, giving it a reputation for lawlessness. Some serious fights resulted in hangings from the roof timbers in the Stage Station.

Since 1935, it's been privately owned by the Hill family, who have kept it uncommercialized with no souvenir hype or gift shop. They offer 2-hour guided tours on a limited basis, and reenactments and special events four times a year. Six original buildings and two reconstructed buildings survive in various stages of repair.

To reach Shakespeare, drive 1.3 miles south from I-10 on Main Street. Just before the town cemetery, turn right, proceed .6 mile and turn right again. Follow the dirt road .4 mile into Shakespeare.

Admission: $3 adults, $2 children 6–12; for shoot-outs and special events $4 adults, $3 children.

Open: 10am and 2pm second and fourth weekends of every month, except the fourth weekend of December, when it is closed. Special tours by appointment.

Steins Railroad Ghost Town, Exit 3, I-10 (P.O. Box 2185, Roadforks), Steins. ☎ 542-9791.

This settlement 19 miles west of Lordsburg started as a Butterfield Stage stop, then was a railroad town of about 1,000 residents from 1880 to 1955. It was so isolated that water, hauled from Doubtful Canyon, brought $1 a barrel!

Today there remain 10 buildings, with 16 rooms filled with artifacts and furnishings from the 19th and early 20th century. There is also a petting zoo for kids and the Steins Mercantile shop. The owners have plans to build a hotel, free overnight RV dry camping.

Admission: $1.50 over 12 years; under 12, free.

Open: Daily 9am–5pm.

Where to Stay

Lodging tax is 9.25% in Deming, including the 6.25% gross receipts tax. It is 11.125% in Lordsburg, including 6.125% gross receipts tax. Most lodgings provide free parking to guests.

DEMING

Best Western Mimbres Valley Inn, I-10 West Frontage Rd. (P.O. Box 1159), Deming, NM 88030. ☎ **505/546-4544** or toll free **800/528-1234.** 40 rms. A/C TV TEL

Rates: $42–$47 single; $47–$54 double. AE, CB, DC, DISC, MC, V.

This new motel, built in 1993, has very comfortable rooms with Southwest art, pastel-colored walls, and wood furnishings. On the west side of Deming, it is within three miles of a public 18-hole golf course. There's an outdoor heated pool, handicapped and nonsmoking rooms, and pets are welcome.

Chilton Inn, 1709 E. Spruce St. (P.O. Box 790), Deming, NM 88031. ☎ **505/546-8813.** Fax 505/546-7095. 57 rms. A/C TV TEL

Rates: $36–$42 single; $40–$46 double. AE, CB, DC, DISC, MC, V.

Tall pillars, a brick facade, and white-shuttered windows lend an elegant appearance to this main-drag motel, which is more than adequate in many respects. Rooms are clean and comfortable, with a southwestern decor, working desks, and vanities. The Branding Iron restaurant (open 5:30am to 10pm daily) has American-style dinners in the $6.75 to $12.50 range. The property has a swimming pool, and pets are allowed.

Grand Hotel, Hwy. 70/180 east of downtown (P.O. Box 309), Deming, NM 88031. ☎ **505/546-2631.** Fax 505/546-4446. 60 rms. A/C TV TEL

Rates: $38 single; $45–$48 double. AE, CB, DC, DISC, MC, V.

Looking like a redbrick Colonial Williamsburg manor, the Grand is built around a lovely central lawn and shrubbery garden with two outdoor swimming pools. The pleasant rooms have floral decor and standard furnishings, including a large bathroom and an anteroom with a dressing table and wardrobe rack. Refrigerators are available. A restaurant is open from 6am to 9pm daily (full dinners $4.95 to $11.95); a lounge is adjacent. There's courtesy car service to and from the train station. Nonsmoking rooms are available.

★ **Holiday Inn,** off I-10 (P.O. Box 1138), Deming NM 88031. ☎ **505/546-2661** or toll free **800/HOLIDAY.** Fax 505/546-6308. 80 rms. A/C TV TEL

Rates: $48–$58 single; $54–$64 double. AE, CB, DC, DISC, MC, V.

This fully renovated motel is one of Deming's finest. The new owners practically gutted the place, and have done a wonderful job of redecorating and refurbishing the large, comfortable rooms. Many of the guest rooms look out onto the heated outdoor pool, which is open April through October; all are decorated in soft pastels and have cable TV, direct dial phones, and vanity areas separate from the bathroom. The staff is friendly and extraordinarily efficient—which is due in part to the fact that the owners live in an apartment on the premises (a rarity for hotel chains). There is a coin-operated laundry as well as valet laundry.

Fat Eddie's, the hotel's restaurant, is open for breakfast, lunch, and dinner and serves New Mexican and American cuisine. Prices are very reasonable, and there's a children's menu. Room service is available during restaurant hours. The Lazy Lizard Lounge is open for cocktails Monday through Saturday from 4pm to midnight and until 11pm on Sundays. There are rooms for nonsmokers and the disabled. Pets are welcome. You won't find anything to complain about at this Holiday Inn.

$ Wagon Wheel Motel, 1109 W. Pine St., Deming, NM 88030.
☎ **505/546-2681.** 19 rms. A/C TV TEL
Rates: $22–$31 single; $24–$29 double. DISC, MC, V.

You'll find clean, comfortable, and inexpensive lodging in this Mom-and-Pop motel, which is within walking distance of several restaurants. Built in 1958, much renovation has been completed and more was underway in 1994. There is a heated swimming pool open in summer, 30-channel cable television, and guest laundry. Handicapped-accessible and nonsmoking rooms are available, and pets are accepted.

LORDSBURG

Best Western American Motor Inn, 944 E. Motel Dr. (Alt. I-10), Lordsburg, NM 88045. ☎ **505/542-3591** or toll free **800/528-1234.** 92 rms. A/C TV TEL
Rates: $39–$59 single; $44–$59 double. AE, CB, DC, DISC, MC, V.

Located well off I-10 on the old highway through town, the American caters to families by offering an outdoor swimming pool, a small playground with swings, and a handful of family units. Rooms have sturdy maple furnishings and scenic Southwest prints on the walls. Some king-size beds are available, along with nonsmoking rooms. The restaurant, under separate management, serves three American and New Mexican meals daily, with dinner priced from $4.25 to $12.95. It also has kids' menus.

Best Western Western Skies Inn, 1303 S. Main St. at I-10 (Exit 22), Lordsburg, NM 88045. ☎ **505/542-8807** or toll free **800/528-1234.** 40 rms. A/C TV TEL
Rates: $44 single; $49 double. AE, CB, DC, DISC, MC, V.

A newer property at the I-10 interchange, this motel has appointed its spacious rooms in earth tones with southwestern motifs. Each has solid maple furnishings, a large bathroom area, and dressing table/vanity. There's an outdoor pool and free coffee in the lobby beginning at 5:30am. Kranberry's family-style restaurant (see "Where to Dine" below) is next door.

Where to Dine

DEMING

$ Cactus Cafe, 218 W. Cedar St. off I-10 (Exit 82A). ☎ **546-2458.**
Cuisine: AMERICAN & NEW MEXICAN.
Prices: Lunch or dinner $3.90–$9.95. AE, CB, DC, DISC, MC, V.
Open: Daily 7am–9pm. **Closed:** Christmas.

The Perrault family restaurant has a friendly atmosphere that carries into the colorful regional decor. There's a wide choice of menu selections, including chile rellenos, shrimp fajitas, and the popular Tampiqueña steak with green chiles and onions.

K-Bob's, 316 E. Cedar St. off I-10. ☎ **546-8883.**

Cuisine: STEAKS.
Prices: Lunch or dinner $2.99–$14.99. AE, DISC, MC, V.
Open: Daily 10:30am–10pm. **Closed:** Thanksgiving and Christmas.

This family-style steak house offers a wide selection of steaks, chicken, and deep-fried seafood. It is home to the $2.99 chicken-fried steak, and has a large salad bar, a children's menu, and a selection of beers and wines. Soups, sandwiches, and burgers are always available.

LORDSBURG

Kranberry's Family Restaurant, 1405 S. Main St., Lordsburg, NM 88045. ☎ **542-9400.**

Cuisine: AMERICAN & MEXICAN.
Prices: Lunch and dinner main courses $2.69–$13.89. AE, CB, DC, DISC, MC, V.
Open: Daily 6am–10pm.

A friendly, casual family restaurant decorated with Southwest art, Kranberry's offers home-style American favorites including burgers, chicken, beef, and salads, as well as Mexican selections. Baked goods are made on the premises daily, and there's a children's menu.

5 Silver City: Gateway to the Gila Cliff Dwellings

240 miles SW of Albuquerque; 112 miles NW of Las Cruces; 197 miles E of Tucson, Ariz.

GETTING THERE • By Plane Mesa Airlines (☎ **388-4115** or toll free **800/MESA-AIR**) flies daily from Albuquerque to Silver City–Grant County Airport, 15 miles south of Silver City near Hurley. Pick up a car there from **Grimes Aviation and Car Rental** (☎ **538-2142**). **Silver Stage Lines** (☎ toll free **800/522-0162**) offers daily shuttle service to the El Paso and Tucson airports. **The Las Cruces Shuttle** (☎ toll free **800/288-1784**) has daily runs to El Paso Airport, and Deming, Las Cruces, and Silver City.

• **By Bus** There's no regular commercial service into Silver City.

• **By Car** From Albuquerque take I-25 south, 15 miles past Truth or Consequences; then west on N.M. 152 and U.S. 180 (5 hours). From Las Cruces take I-10 west to Deming, then north on U.S. 180 (2 hours).

ESSENTIALS • Orientation Silver City rests in the foothills of the Pinos Altos Range of the Gila National Forest, at 5,900 feet elevation. U.S. Highway 180 is the main east-west artery through town; N.M. 90 (Hudson Street) comes north from Lordsburg and intersects 180 north of downtown. Bullard Street (north-south) and Broadway (east-west) are the main routes in downtown. N.M. 15, the highway to Gila Cliff Dwellings National Monument, turns off U.S. 180 at the east end of Silver City.

• **Information** The **Silver City–Grant County Chamber of Commerce,** at 1103 N. Hudson St., Silver City, NM 88061 (☎ **505/538-3785** or toll free

800/548-9378), maintains a visitor information headquarters on N.M. 90, a few blocks south of U.S. 180. The chamber produces extremely useful tourist publications.

Fast Facts   The **area code** is 505. Medical emergencies are treated at the **Gila Regional Medical Center,** 1313 E. 32nd St. (☎ **538-4000**). The **post office** is located at 500 N. Hudson St. (☎ **538-2831**). In case of **emergencies,** dial **911** or **0** for an operator.

Silver City (pop. 11,200) is an old mining town, located in the foothills of the Pinos Altos Range of the Mogollon Mountains, and gateway to the Gila Wilderness and the Gila Cliff Dwellings. Early Native Americans mined turquoise from these hills, and by 1804 Spanish settlers were digging for copper. In 1870, a group of prospectors discovered silver, and the rush was on. In 10 short months, the newly christened Silver City grew from a single cabin to over 80 buildings. Early visitors included Billy the Kid, Judge Roy Bean, and William Randolph Hearst.

This comparatively isolated community kept pace with every modern convenience: telephones in 1883, electric lights in 1884 (only two years after New York City installed its lighting), and a water system in 1887. Typically, the town should have busted with the crash of silver prices in 1893. But unlike many western towns, Silver City did not become a picturesque memory. Silver City capitalized on its high dry climate to become today's county seat and trade center. Copper mining and processing are still the major industry. But Silver City also can boast that it produces astronauts: Harrison (Jack) Schmitt, the first civilian geologist to visit the moon, and later a U.S. senator, was born and raised in nearby Santa Rita.

What to See & Do

Silver City's downtown ⭐ **historic district,** the first such district to receive National Register recognition, is a must for visitors. The downtown core is marked by the extensive use of brick in construction: Brick clay was discovered in the area soon after the town's founding in 1870, and an 1880 ordinance prohibited frame construction within the town limits. Mansard-roofed Victorian houses, Queen Anne and Italianate residences, and commercial buildings show off the cast-iron architecture of the period. Some are still undergoing restoration.

An 1895 flood washed out Main Street and turned it into a gaping chasm, which was eventually bridged over; finally, the **Big Ditch,** as it's called, was made into a green park in the center of town. Facing downtown, in the 500 block of North Hudson Street, was a famous red-light district from the turn of the century that wasn't shut down until the late 1960s.

Billy the Kid lived in Silver City as a youth. You can see his cabin site a block north of the Broadway bridge, on the east side of the Big Ditch. The Kid (William Bonney) waited tables at the Star Hotel, Hudson Street and Broadway. He was jailed (at 304 N. Hudson St.) in 1875 at the age of 15, after being convicted of stealing from a Chinese laundry, but he escaped—a first for the Kid. The grave of Bonney's mother, Catherine McCarty, is in Silver City Cemetery, east of town on Memory Lane, off U.S. 180. She died of tuberculosis about a year after the family moved here in 1873.

⭐ **Silver City Museum,** 312 W. Broadway. ☎ **538-5921.**

This very well presented museum of city and regional history contains collections of early ranching and mining displays, Native American pottery, and early photographs. Exhibits include a southwest New Mexico history time line; a parlor displaying Victorian decorative arts; and a chronicle of commerce in early Silver City. A local history research library is available to visitors also. The main gallery features changing exhibits.

The museum is lodged in the newly restored 1881 H. B. Ailman House, a former city hall and fire station remarkable for its cupola and Victorian mansard roof. Ailman came to Silver City penniless in 1871, made a fortune in mining, and went on to start the Meredith and Ailman Bank.

Admission: Free.

Open: Tues–Fri 9am–4:30pm, Sat–Sun 10am–4pm. **Closed:** Mondays except Memorial Day and Labor Day.

Western New Mexico University Museum, 1000 W. College Fleming Hall, WNMU. ☎ **538-6386.**

Spread across 80 acres on the west side of Silver City, WNMU celebrated its centennial in 1993. The university boasts a 2,500-student enrollment and 24 major buildings. Among them is historic Fleming Hall, which houses this interesting museum.

The WNMU museum has the largest permanent exhibit of prehistoric Mimbres pottery in the United States. Also displayed are Casas Grandes Indian pottery, stone tools, ancient jewelry, historical photographs, mining and military artifacts. Displays are changed regularly, so there is always something new to see in the museum—such as vanishing Americana, riparian fossils, Nigerian folk art, or a collection of 18th- to 20th-century timepieces. There is a gift shop here.

Admission: By donation.

Open: Mon–Fri 9am–4:30pm, Sat–Sun 10am–4pm.

SPORTS & RECREATION

Scott Park Golf Course, on the south side of town at Silver Acres (☎ **538-5041**), has 18 holes, and is open Mondays 10am to 7pm, and Tuesdays through Sundays 8am to 7pm. **Silver City Municipal Swimming Pool,** 2700 N. Silver St. (☎ **388-4165**), is open daily.

Nearby Attractions

NORTH OF SILVER CITY

The virtual ghost town of ◾ **Pinos Altos,** straddling the Continental Divide, is 6 miles north of Silver City on N.M. 15. Dubbed "Tall Pines" when it was founded in the gold- and silver-rush era, Apache attacks and mine failures have taken their toll.

The adobe **Methodist-Episcopal Church** was built with William Randolph Hearst's money in 1898 and now houses the Grant County Art Guild. The **Pinos Altos Museum** displays a three-quarter-scale reproduction of the Santa Rita del Cobre Fort & Trading Post, built at Santa Rita copper mine in 1804 to protect the area from Apaches. (It was renamed Fort Webster in 1851). It's still possible to pan for gold in Pinos Altos. The town also has the **Log Cabin Curio Shop and Museum** located in an 1866 cabin (☎ **388-1882**), and the Buckhorn Saloon restaurant (see "Where to Dine," below).

★ **Gila Cliff Dwellings National Monument,** Rte. 11, Box 100, Silver City, NM 88061. ☎ **536-9461.**

It takes at least 1¹/₂ hours to reach the Gila Cliff Dwellings from Silver City, 44 miles up narrow, winding N.M. 15 into the Mogollon Mountains. It's definitely worth the trip. First-time visitors are inevitably awed by the sight. At this stone-within-stone-on-stone relic of a long-gone civilization, reality is somehow exaggerated in the dazzling sunlight and contrasting shadow, making the dwellings look, from a distance, as two-dimensional as a stage set. The solid masonry walls are well preserved, even though they've been abandoned for seven centuries.

The cliff dwellings were discovered by Anglo settlers in the early 1870s, near where the three forks of the Gila River rise. Seven natural caves occur in the southeast-facing cliff of a side canyon; six of them contain the ruins of dwellings, which had about 42 rooms. Probably not more than 8 or 10 Mogollon families (40 to 50 people) lived in these dwellings at any one time. Tree-ring dating indicates their residence didn't last longer than 30 to 40 years at the end of the 13th century.

Today, the dwellings allow a rare glimpse inside the homes and lives of prehistoric Native Americans. About 75% of what is seen is original, although the walls have been capped and the foundations strengthened to prevent further deterioration. It took a great deal of effort to build these homes: The stones were held in place by mortar, and all of the clay and water for the mortar had to be carried up from the stream, as the Mogollon did not have any pack animals. The *vigas* for the roof were cut and shaped with stone axes or fire.

The people who lived here were farmers, as shown by the remains of beans, squash, and corn in their homes. The fields were along the valley of the west fork of the Gila River and on the mesa across the canyon. No signs of irrigation have been found.

A 1-mile loop trail, rising 175 feet from the canyon floor, provides access to the dwellings.

Near the visitor center, about a mile away, the remains of an earlier (A.D. 100–400) pit house, built below ground level, and later pit houses (up to A.D. 1000), aboveground structures of adobe or wattle, have been found.

Camping and picnicking are encouraged in the national monument. There are no accommodations here; most visitors stay in Silver City, and the nearby town of Gila Hot Springs has overnight lodging and a grocery store, as well as horse rentals and guided pack trips.

Admission: Free.

Open: Visitor center, Memorial Day—Labor Day daily 8am–7pm; rest of year 8am–5pm. Cliff dwellings, summer daily 9am–7pm; rest of year 9:30am–5pm.

SOUTH OF SILVER CITY

South 12 miles on N.M. 90 is the **Phelps Dodge Open Pit Copper Mine** (☎ **538-5331**). Some 80 million tons of rock are taken out every year. An observation point is open Monday through Friday from 7am to sunset; free guided tours are offered weekdays at 9am, with a day's advance reservation.

Phelps Dodge consolidated its Tyrone holdings in 1909 and hired famous architect Bertram Goodhue to design a "Mediterranean-style" company town. **Tyrone,** later referred to as the Million Dollar Ghost Town, was constructed between 1914 and 1918. A large bank and shop building, administration office, mercantile store, and passenger depot were grouped around a central plaza. Eighty-three single and multiple-unit dwellings, accommodating 235 families, were built on the nearby hillsides; and a school, chapel, garage, restaurant, justice court, hospital, morgue, and recreation building were added. A drop in copper prices caused it to be abandoned virtually overnight.

After a pre–World War II incarnation as a luxurious dude ranch, Tyrone lay dormant for years until the late 1960s, when the town made way for the present-day open pit mine and mill. A new townsite was created 7 miles north. Most of the original homes and major buildings were removed between 1967 and 1969; today, the only remaining structures are Union Chapel, the justice court, and the pump house. The copper mine supplies copper concentrates to the modern Hidalgo Smelter near Playas, southeast of Lordsburg.

EAST OF SILVER CITY

The oldest active mine in the Southwest—and among the largest in America—is the **Chino Mines Co. Open Pit Copper Mine** at Santa Rita, 15 miles east of Silver City via U.S. 180 and N.M. 152. The multicolored open pit is a mile wide and 1,000 feet deep, and can be viewed from a spectacular observation point with a small museum. Apaches once scratched the surface for metallic copper. By 1800, the Spanish, under Col. Jose Manuel Carrasco, were working "Santa Rita del Cobre." Convict labor from New Spain mined the shafts, with mule trains of ore sent down the Janos Trail to Chihuahua, Mexico. An impressive adobe fort was built near the mine, along with smelters and numerous buildings, but Apache raids finally forced the mine's abandonment. In the late 19th century, the mine was reopened, and the town of Santa Rita was reborn. The huge open pit, started around 1910, soon consumed Santa Rita. Giant-sized machines scoop the ore from the earth and huge 175-ton ore trucks transport it to the reduction mill to the southwest of the pit.

■ **City of Rocks State Park** (☎ 536-2800), 30 miles from Silver City via U.S. 180 and N.M. 61, is an area of fantastically shaped volcanic rock formations, formed in ancient times from thick blankets of ash that hardened into tuff. This soft stone, eroded by wind and rain, was shaped into monolithic blocks reminiscent of Stonehenge. For some, the park resembles a medieval village; for others, it is a collection of misshapen, albeit benign giants. Complete with a desert garden, the park offers excellent camping and picnic sites. Hot water is solar heated, while windmills pump it and make electricity; the park is thus self-sufficient.

WEST OF SILVER CITY

U.S. 180, heading northwest from Silver City, is the gateway to Catron County and most of the Gila National Forest, including the villages of Glenwood, Reserve, and Quemado.

■ **Gila National Forest,** with an office at 3005 E. Camino del Bosque, Silver City, NM 88061 (☎ 388-8201), comprises 3.3 million acres in four counties. Nearly one-fourth of that acreage (790,000) comprises the **Gila, Aldo Leopold,** and **Blue Range wildernesses.** Within the forest are 1,490 miles of trails for hiking and horseback riding, and in winter, cross-country skiing and snowmobiling; outside of the wilderness, trail bikes and off-road vehicles are also permitted. The 41-mile Middle Fork Trail, with its east end near Gila Cliff Dwellings, is among the most popular. More than 50 trailheads provide roadside parking.

There are numerous campgrounds in the national forest, although most are undeveloped (no drinking water). Gila National Forest also contains numerous lakes, almost 500 miles of mountain streams, and the country's first designated wilderness area. Its highest peak is Whitewater Baldy, 10,892 feet. Big-game animals found here include mule deer, elk, antelope, black bear, mountain lion, and bighorn sheep.

The ■ **Catwalk National Recreation Trail** (☎ 539-2481), 68 miles north of Silver City on U.S. 180, then 5 miles east of Glenwood via N.M. 174, is reached by foot from a parking area. It follows the route of a pipeline built in 1897 to carry water to the now-defunct town of Graham and its electric generator. About a quarter of a mile above the parking area is the beginning of a striking 250-foot metal causeway clinging to the sides of the boulder-choked Whitewater Canyon, which in spots in 20 feet wide and 250 feet deep. Spectacular vistas are found farther up the canyon, where a suspension bridge spans the chasm. Picnic facilities are located near the parking area.

The scenic ghost town of **Mogollon** is 3¹/₂ miles north of Glenwood on U.S. 180, then 9 miles east on N.M. 159, a narrow mountain road. The village bears witness to silver and gold mining booms beginning in the late 19th century, and to the disastrous effects of floods and fire in later years. Remains of its last operating mine, the Little Fanny (which ceased operation in the 1950s), are still visible, along with dozens of other old buildings, miner's shacks, and mining paraphernalia. An art gallery and museum are found along Mogollon's main street. The movie *My Name Is Nobody*, starring Henry Fonda, was shot here.

Reserve (pop. 300), Catron County seat, is noted as the place where, in 1882, Deputy Sheriff Elfego Baca made an epic stand in a 33-hour gun battle with 80 cowboys. Cochise, Geronimo, and other Apache war chiefs held forth in these mountains in the late 19th century.

Where to Stay

Standard motels are strung along U.S. 180 east of N.M. 90. Some of the more interesting accommodations, however, are not! An 11.375% tax is imposed on all lodging bills (6.375% state tax and 5% city lodging tax). Most lodgings provide free parking.

Bear Mountain Guest Ranch, Bear Mountain Rd., Silver City, NM 88061. ☎ 505/538-2538 or toll free **800/880-2538**. 15 rms, 2 cottages.

Rates (including 3 meals daily): $54 single; $95 double; $105–$195 suites; cottage with kitchenette (meals not included), $55–$80 for 1 to 4 persons. No credit cards.

Spread across 160 acres just 3¹/₂ miles northwest of downtown Silver City, Myra McCormick's ranch has been a New Mexico institution since 1959. This is a nature lover's delight—McCormick hosts birding, wild plant, and archaeological workshops throughout the year, and a "Lodge and Learn" series (for adults of all ages) is a feature every month. The ranch doesn't have horses, but visitors are urged to "bring your own." All rooms have private baths, and home-cooked meals are served in a family-style setting.

To reach the ranch, turn north off Highway 180 on Alabama Street, a half mile west of Route 90 intersection. Proceed 2.8 miles (Alabama becomes Cottage San Road, then Bear Mountain Road) to turnoff; the ranch is another 0.6 miles.

The Carter House, 101 N. Cooper St., Silver City, NM 88061. ☎ 505/388-5485. 5 rms and 20 youth-hostel bunks.

Rates: $50–$70 per room, bed-and-breakfast; $14 per bed ($11 for hostel association members) in youth hostel. MC, V.

The top floor of this renovated 1906 mansion, situated next door to the Grant County Courthouse, is a classic bed-and-breakfast establishment. The lower floor is an official Hostelling International facility. It's a unique combination, but seems to work. B&B patrons feel at home with a living and dining room, library and TV room, all decorated with 19th-century prints—family heirlooms of owner Lucy Dilworth. They also can share the laundry and kitchen facilities with the hostelers in the basement.

Copper Manor Motel, 710 Silver Heights Blvd. (Hwy. 180) (P.O. Box 1405), Silver City, NM 88061. ☎ 505/538-5392 or toll free **800/853-2916**. 67 rms. A/C TV TEL

Rates: $36–$43 single; $43–$48 double. AE, CB, DC, MC, V.

A standard roadside motel, the Copper Manor has the advantage of being part of a one-ownership complex that includes the Red Barn Steak House next door (see "Where to Dine" below) and the Drifter Motel and Restaurant across the street. Room decor is bold; the bathrooms quite small. Facilities include an indoor pool and whirlpool; guests can also use the Drifter's outdoor pool.

Holiday Motor Hotel, 3420 Hwy. 180 E., Silver City, NM 88061.

☎ **505/538-3711,** toll free **800/828-8291.** 80 rms. A/C TV TEL

Rates: $40–$45 single; $46–$58 double. AE, DC, DISC, MC, V.

Located about 3 miles east of downtown near the junction of U.S. 180 and State 15, this motel is a step above the ordinary with its landscaped grounds, attractive outdoor swimming pool, playground, all-night security guard, and guest Laundromat. Rooms are clean and comfortable, with custom-made furnishings. The restaurant serves three meals Monday through Saturday from 6am to 2pm and 5 to 8:30pm, and Sunday, 7am to 3pm and 5 to 8:30pm, with a menu superior to the typical hotel coffee shop.

$ **The Palace Hotel,** 106 W. Broadway (P.O. Box 5093), Silver City, NM 88061.
☎ **505/388-1811.** 13 rms, 7 suites. TV

Rates (including continental breakfast): $29.50–$39.50 single or double; $45–$48 suite. AE, DC, DISC, MC, V.

Old-fashioned elegance and Victorian decor are earmarks of this hotel, first established 1882 and reopened in July 1990 as a historic small European-style hotel. Each of the rooms on the second floor is shaped and decorated differently. All have standard furnishings and steam heat, but bed sizes vary from king to single; some have refrigerators; two share baths; all of the others have bathtubs and showers. That's a sight better than in 1882! The owners provide fresh fruit bread, juice, fruit, coffee, and tea for breakfast, which is served in the upstairs skylit garden room.

Where to Dine

 Buckhorn Saloon and Opera House, N.M. 15, Pinos Altos. ☎ **538-9911.**

Cuisine: CONTINENTAL & STEAKS. **Reservations:** Strongly recommended.
Prices: Main courses $10.95–$26.95. MC, V.
Open: Dinner served Mon–Sat 6–10pm. **Closed:** Thanksgiving and Christmas.

Seven miles north of Silver City in Pinos Altos, the surprising Buckhorn offers elegant dining in 1860s decor. It's noted for its western-style steaks, seafood, homemade desserts, and excellent wine list. There's live entertainment nightly; the saloon opens at 3pm during the week.

The Red Barn Steak House, 708 Silver Heights Blvd. (Hwy. 180). ☎ **538-5666.**

Cuisine: AMERICAN.
Prices: Appetizers $3.25–$7.25; lunch $3.75–$7.95; dinner $6.95–$19.95. AE, CB, DC, DISC, MC, V.
Open: Daily 11am–10pm. **Closed:** Thanksgiving Day, Christmas, and New Year's Day.

This big red barn, with its white silo, is unmistakable on the south side of U.S. 180 as it enters Silver City from the east. The interior is spacious and comfortable, with atmospheric wagon-wheel chandeliers. Steaks are the specialty, from beef teriyaki to steak Oscar. A 20-ounce T-bone is just $18.95. There's a large salad bar. At the rear of the restaurant is the Watering Hole Lounge.

Southeastern New Mexico

10

SOUTHEASTERN NEW MEXICO—THAT PART OF THE STATE EAST OF THE RIO GRANDE (the I-25 corridor) and south of I-40—is a vast and surprising region that in many ways is typical of the "real" West.

Here are the spectacular Carlsbad Caverns and the awesome White Sands National Monument. This is the home of the fierce Mescalero Apaches and of the world's richest horse race. Billy the Kid lived and died in southeastern New Mexico in the 19th century, and the world's first atomic bomb was exploded here in the 20th. From west to east, barren desert gives way to high, forested peaks, snow-covered in winter; to the fertile valley of the Pecos River; and to high plains beloved by ranchers along the Texas border.

The main population center in this section of the state is Roswell, a city of about 45,500. Carlsbad (pop. 26,500), 76 miles south of Roswell, and Alamogordo (pop. 27,500), 117 miles west of Roswell, are of more immediate interest to tourists. Other sizable towns are Clovis (pop. 33,400) and Hobbs (pop. 29,400), both on the Texas border, and Artesia (pop. 11,300), between Roswell and Carlsbad. Ruidoso (pop. 4,900), in the mountains between Alamogordo and Roswell, is a booming resort town.

Suggested Itinerary: A good way to approach the region, if you're coming by car from Albuquerque, is to head south on I-25 to San Antonio, just beyond Socorro, then turn east of U.S. Highway 380 through Carrizozo. This will bring you first to the Ruidoso area, whose major attractions can be defined by a triangle formed by Highway 380, U.S. Highway 70, and N.M. Highway 48.

Drive south on U.S. 70 to explore Alamogordo and White Sands. Then follow U.S. Highway 82 east through the charming mountain village of Cloudcroft and down the valley of the Rio Penasco with its fruit orchards. At Artesia, turn south on U.S. Highway 285 to Carlsbad and its famous caverns.

From Carlsbad, you can either reverse course back up Highway 285 to Roswell and (via N.M. Highway 20) Fort Sumner, site of Fort Sumner State Monument and Billy the Kid's grave, or meander through the Llano Estacado along the Texas border, taking U.S. Highway 62/180 east to Hobbs, then turning north on N.M. 206 to Clovis. From the latter city, Fort Sumner is an hour's drive west on U.S. Highway 60/84. Return to your starting point by heading north from Fort Sumner on U.S. 84 to I-40 at Santa Rosa; it's a 2-hour drive west to Albuquerque.

1 Alamogordo & White Sands National Monument

Alamogordo: 207 miles S of Albuquerque; 68 miles NE of Las Cruces; 87 miles N of El Paso, Texas

GETTING THERE • By Plane **Mesa Airlines** (☎ toll free **800/MESA-AIR**) has connections three times daily with Albuquerque. **Avis** (☎ **437-3140**), **Hertz** (☎ **437-7760**), and **National** (☎ **437-4126**) rent cars at the Municipal Airport.

• By Bus **TNM&O/Greyhound** (☎ **437-3050**) serves Alamogordo from Albuquerque, Las Cruces, Roswell, and El Paso, with arrivals and departures each day from the **Union Bus Station** (☎ **437-3050**).

• By Car From Albuquerque take I-25 south 87 miles to San Antonio; turn east on U.S. 380, 66 miles to Carrizozo; then south on U.S. 54 for 58 miles (4 hours). From Las Cruces, take U.S. 70 northeast (1 1/2 hours). (This road may be closed for up to 2 hours during times of missile testing on White Sands Missile Range.) From El Paso, take U.S. 54 north (1 1/2 hours).

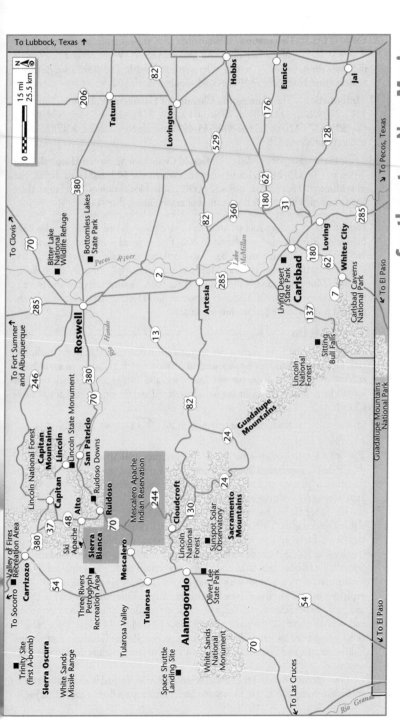

Southeastern New Mexico

ESSENTIALS • **Orientation**   Alamogordo is on the eastern edge of the Tularosa Valley, at the foot of the Sacramento Mountains. U.S. 54 (White Sands Boulevard) is the main street, extending several miles north and south. The downtown district is actually three blocks east of White Sands Boulevard, off 10th Street.

• **Information**   The **Alamogordo Chamber of Commerce** and visitor center is at 1301 N. White Sands Blvd. Write P.O. Box 518, Alamogordo, NM 88311 (☎ **505/437-6120** or toll free **800/545-4021** outside New Mexico, **800/826-0294** within New Mexico).

• **Fast Facts**   The **area code** is 505. **Gerald Champion Memorial Hospital,** 1209 Ninth St. (☎ **439-2100**), has its emergency entrance at 10th and Cuba streets. The **post office,** 900 Alaska Ave. (☎ **437-9390**), is one block south of 10th Street, three blocks east of White Sands Boulevard. For **emergencies,** dial **911.**

Famous for its leading role in America's space research and military technology industries, Alamogordo (population 27,500) first achieved worldwide fame on July 16, 1945, when the first atomic bomb was exploded at nearby Trinity Site. Today, it is home of the Space Center and International Space Hall of Fame, White Sands National Monument, and Holloman Air Force Base. Twenty miles east and twice as high, the resort village of Cloudcroft (elevation 8,650 feet) attracts vacationers to the forested heights of the Sacramento Mountains.

What to See & Do

In addition to the attractions in Alamogordo itself, also enjoyable is the small, historic village of **La Luz,** just 3 miles north of Alamogordo. It has attracted a number of resident artists and craftspeople who live, work, and display some of their products for sale here. Worth seeing are the old adobe corral and the small Our Lady of Light Church.

⭐ **Space Center,** Scenic Dr. and Indian Wells Rd. ☎ **437-2840, 800/545-4021** out-of-state.

The Space Center comes in two parts—the **International Space Hall of Fame** and the **Clyde W. Tombaugh Space Theater.** Both are located on the lower slopes of the Sacramento Mountains, 2 miles east of U.S. Highway 54, and just above New Mexico State University's Alamogordo branch campus.

The Space Hall of Fame occupies the "Golden Cube," a five-story building with walls of golden glass. Visitors are encouraged to start on the top floor and work their way down. En route, they recall the accomplishments of the first astronauts and cosmonauts, including America's Mercury, Gemini, and Apollo programs, and the early Soviet orbital flights. Spacecraft and a lunar exploration module are exhibited. There's a space-station plan, a hands-on cutaway of crew module "Space Station 2001," and explanations of life in space aboard Skylab and Salyut. Other displays tell the history and purposes of rocketry, missiles, and satellites; provide an orientation to astronomy and exploration of other planets; and tell about New Mexico's role in space exploration history, from ancient Indians to rocketry pioneer Robert Goddard to astronauts. Exhibits on the first floor focus on current issues in space, such as the Hubble space telescope.

On adjacent grounds is the "Sonic Wind" sled, which tested human endurance to speeds exceeding 600 m.p.h. in preparation for future space flights; the "Little Joe II" rocket, which tested Apollo launch escape systems; and other historic artifacts of space travel.

Each year, on the first Saturday of October, new members of the Space Hall of Fame are inducted in a special ceremony here. As of 1993, there were 119 members.

At the Tombaugh Theater, OMNIMAX and Spitz 512 Planetarium Systems create earthly and cosmic experiences on a 2,700-square-foot, dome screen. Twenty special-effects projectors can show 2,354 stars, the Milky Way, all the visible planets, the sun and the moon, and can duplicate the night sky anywhere on earth, anytime of the year. Special programs allow visitors to take part in a laser-concert symphony of sight and sound, learn about the cosmos, and share a variety of OMNIMAX experiences.

Admission: Space Hall, adults $2.25, youth (6–12) and seniors (62 and older) $1.75; free for children under 5. Theater, adults $3.75, youths and seniors $2.50. Combined visit, adults $5.25, youths and seniors $3.50.

Open: Daily 9am–6pm summer; 9am–5pm winter. Theater show times Mon–Fri 10am, noon, 2pm, 4pm; Sat–Sun 10am, 11am, noon, 2pm, 3pm, 4pm. **Closed:** Christmas.

★ **White Sands National Monument,** 15 miles southwest of Alamogordo via U.S. Hwy. 70/82. ☎ **505/479-6124.**

Arguably the most memorable natural area in this part of the Southwest, White Sands National Monument preserves the best part of the world's largest gypsum dune field. An area of 275 square miles of pure white gypsum sand reaches out over the floor of the Tularosa Basin in wavelike dunes. Plants and animals have evolved in special ways to adapt to the bright white environment.

The surrounding mountains, the Sacramentos to the east, with their forested slopes, and the serene San Andres to the west, are composed of sandstone, limestone, sedimentary rocks, and pockets of gypsum. Over millions of years, rains and melting snows dissolved the gypsum and carried it down into Lake Lucero. Here the hot sun and dry winds evaporate the water, leaving the pure white gypsum to crystallize. Then the persistent winds blow these crystals, in the form of minuscule bits of sand, in a northeastern direction, adding them to growing dunes. As each dune grows and moves farther from the lake, new ones form, rank after rank, in what seems an endless procession.

Some creatures that have evolved here have a bleached coloration to match the whiteness all around them. Some plants have also evolved means for surviving against the smothering pressures of the blowing sands. The plants and animals together make up a special community of living things adapted to a strange world. The plants and animals, dependent on each other, can thus survive this desert environment.

A 16-mile Dunes Drive loops through the "heart of sands" from the visitor center. Information available at the center will tell you what to look for on your drive. Sometimes the winds blow the dunes over the road, which must then be rerouted around a dune. The dunes are in fact all moving slowly to the northeast, pushed by prevailing southwest winds, some at the rate of as much as 20 feet a year.

In the center of the monument, the road itself is made of hard-packed gypsum. (This part of the road can be especially slick after an afternoon thunderstorm, so drive cautiously!) Visitors are invited to get out of their cars at established parking areas and explore a bit; climb a dune for a better view of the endless sea of sand.

A couple of safety tips are emphasized by the Park Service: one, that tunneling in this sand can be dangerous, for it collapses easily and could suffocate a person; and two, that sand-surfing down the dune slopes, although permitted, can also be hazardous, so it should be undertaken with care, and never near an auto road. Hikers are warned about the possibility of getting lost in a sudden sandstorm should they stray from marked trails or areas.

In summer there are nature walks and evening programs in the dunes. Ranger-guided activities include orientation talks and nature walks. When driving near or in the monument, tune a radio to 1610 AM for information on what's doing.

Admission: $4 per vehicle.

Open: Memorial Day–Labor Day, visitor center 8am–7pm, Dunes Drive 7am–10pm; rest of year, visitor center 8am–4:30pm, Dunes Drive 7am–sunset. Due to missile testing on the adjacent White Sands Missile Range, the drive is sometimes closed for up to 2 hours at a time.

Tularosa Basin Historical Society Museum, 1301 N. White Sands Blvd. ☎ 437-6120.

Located beside the chamber of commerce, this museum displays artifacts and photographs recalling regional history.

Admission: Free.

Open: Mon–Sat 10am–4pm and Sun 1–4pm.

Alameda Park Zoo, 1020 N. White Sands Boulevard. ☎ 439-4290.

Next to the historical society museum is this 7-acre zoo, the oldest zoo in the Southwest. Established in 1898, its collection includes hundreds of mammals and birds from around the world, including a variety of American and African mammals.

Admission: $2 adults, $1 children 3–11 and seniors 62 and older.

Open: Daily 9am–5pm. **Closed:** Christmas and New Year's.

Toy Train Depot, 1991 N. White Sands Blvd. ☎ 437-2855.

A favorite of train buffs, the Toy Train Depot has more than 1,200 feet of model train track, numerous operating electric trains, and even more trains and accessories on display. Exhibits, which are appropriately housed in a genuine 1898 railroad depot, show toy trains dating back to the 1800s, as well as numerous examples from the 1930s through the 1950s. There's even a reproduction of a pink electric train created by the Lionel Corporation in the 1950s as an attempt to lure more girls into the hobby, and the Toy Train Depot has one train layout available for both children and adults who want to run the trains themselves. Rides through the grounds on 12-inch and 16-inch gauge trains are also offered.

Admission: $1.50 adults, $1 children; train rides $2 adults, $1 children.

Open: Wed–Mon noon–5pm. **Closed:** Holidays.

Eagle Ranch Pistachio Groves, 7288 Hwy. 70. ☎ 434-0035.

Believed to be New Mexico's first and largest pistachio groves, Eagle Ranch offers 45-minute tours each weekday at 1:30pm, with a 10am tour added during the summer. There's also a visitors' center with an art gallery displaying the work of local artists, and a gift shop where you can buy pistachio nuts and a variety of other items.

Admission: Free.

Open: Gift shop and gallery daily 9am–6pm.

Oliver Lee Memorial State Park, 15 miles southeast of Alamogordo via U.S. Hwy. 54 and Dog Canyon Rd. ☎ **437-8284.**

Nestled at the mouth of Dog Canyon, a stunning break in the steep escarpment of the Sacramento Mountains, the site has drawn human visitors for thousands of years. Springs and seeps support a variety of rare and endangered plant species, as well as a rich wildlife. Hiking trails into the foothills are well marked; the park also offers a visitor's center with excellent exhibits on local history, and picnic and camping grounds, with showers, electricity, and a dump station.

Dog Canyon was one of the last strongholds of the Mescalero Apache, and was the site of battles between Native Americans and the U.S. Cavalry in the 19th century. Around the turn of the 20th century, rancher Oliver Lee built a home near here and raised cattle; guided tours from the visitor center to his restored house give a taste of early ranch life in southern New Mexico.

Admission: $3 per car.

Open: Daily 7am–sunset; visitor center 9am–4pm. Guided tours Sat–Sun at 3pm, weather permitting.

Trinity Site, west slope of Sierra Oscura, 60 air miles northwest of Alamogordo.

The world's first atomic bomb was exploded in this desert never-never land on July 16, 1945. It is strictly off-limits to civilians—except twice a year, in early April and early October. A small lava monument commemorates the explosion, which left a crater a quarter-mile across, 8 feet deep, and transformed the desert sand into a jade green glaze called "Trinitite" that remains today. The McDonald House, where the bomb's plutonium core was assembled 2 miles from Ground Zero, has been restored to its 1945 condition. Call **White Sands Missile Range,** public affairs office, for details (☎ **505/678-1134**).

NEARBY ATTRACTIONS

✖ Cloudcroft is a picturesque mountain village of 650 people high in the Sacramento Mountains, surrounded by Lincoln National Forest. Though only about 20 miles east of Alamogordo via U.S. Highway 82, it is twice as high, overlooking the Tularosa Valley from a dizzying elevation of about 9,000 feet. It was founded in 1899 when railroad surveyors reached the mountain summit and built a lodge for Southern Pacific Railroad workers. Today, the Lodge is Cloudcroft's biggest attraction and biggest employer (see "A Nearby Place to Stay & Dine," below). There are also other accommodations in town, and lots of recreational opportunities and community festivals. For information, contact the **Cloudcroft Chamber of Commerce,** P.O. Box 1290, Cloudcroft, NM 88317 (☎ **505/682-2733**). It's located in a log cabin in the center of town, on the south side of U.S. 82.

The **Sacramento Mountains Historical Museum,** U.S. 82 east of downtown Cloudcroft (☎ **682-2932**), recalls the community's early days with several pioneer buildings, historic photos, and exhibits of turn-of-the-century railroad memorabilia, clothing, and other artifacts. Call for hours. Nearby, **Lincoln National Forest** (☎ **682-2551**) maintains the unique **La Pasada Encantada Nature Trail,** a short foot path from Sleepygrass Campground, off N.M. 130 south of town, with signs in braille inviting walkers to touch the various plants, leaves, and trees. A new trail, expected to be completed by early 1995, is a several-mile moderate hike to the historic **Mexican Canyon Railroad Trestle.** The trail head is in a U.S. Forest Service picnic area west of the junction of U.S. 82 and N.M. 130, where you'll also find a short walk to an observation point offering spectacular views across White Sands Missile Range and the Tularosa Basin. This picnic area also has tables, grills, drinking water, and rest rooms.

Sunspot National Solar Observatory (☎ **434-7000**), 18 miles south of Cloudcroft via N.M. 6563, a National Scenic Byway, attracts astronomers who come from around the world to study the sun and its effects on planet Earth. There are actually three observatories here, with two open to the public for self-guided tours (allow at least one hour). Free guided tours are offered Saturdays at 2pm from May through October.

Ski Snow Canyon, 2 miles east of Cloudcroft on U.S. Highway 82 (☎ **682-2333** or toll free **800/333-7542**), has 21 runs and a 650-foot vertical, served by two T-bars and two rope tows. It appeals primarily to beginning and intermediate skiers, but has a few advanced pitches. When there's snow (usually December through March), it's open from 9am to 4pm daily. Snowboarding is permitted. Lift rates are $25 for adults, $16 for children.

Where to Stay

All accommodations are along White Sands Boulevard, the north-south highway through town. A tax of just over 9% is imposed on all lodging bills (6.1875% state tax and 3% city lodging tax). Parking is usually free.

Days Inn Alamogordo, 907 S. White Sands Blvd., Alamogordo, NM 88310.
☎ **505/437-5090** or toll free **800/325-2525** or **800/329-7466.** 40 rms. A/C TV TEL
Rates: $38–$45 single; $45–$52 double. AE, CB, DC, DISC, MC, V.

Clean, comfortable rooms with standard furnishings are what you'll find at this Days Inn, which also has an outdoor unheated swimming pool and guest laundry. There are connecting, nonsmoking, and handicapped-accessible rooms available. Pets are not accepted.

Desert Aire Motor Inn, 1021 S. White Sands Blvd., Alamogordo, NM 88310.
☎ **505/437-2110** or toll free **800/528-1234.** Fax 505/437-1898, 102 rms, 5 suites.
A/C FRIDGE TV TEL

Rates (including continental breakfast): $47–$55 single; $52–$60 double; $52–$79 suite.
AE, CB, DC, DISC, MC, V.

This hotel of yellow-and-white concrete-block construction surrounds a huge central parking area. Rooms are cozy, with a king-size or two double beds, photo art posters on the walls, and standard furnishings. There are minirefrigerators in all rooms, microwaves are available, and three-foot-deep Jacuzzis dominate a dozen "spa rooms." The hotel offers a guest recreation room, outdoor swimming pool, hot tub, and sauna.

Holiday Inn, 1401 S. White Sands Blvd., Alamogordo, NM 88310. ☎ **505/437-7100** or toll free **800/HOLIDAY.** Fax 505/437-7100, ext. 299. 106 rms, 1 suite. A/C TV TEL
Rates: $54–$62 single; $62–$70 double; $135 suite. AE, CB, DC, DISC, JCB, MC, V.

A lovely desert garden fronts this single-story hotel, and the dining room has a carving of St. Francis. The newly remodelled rooms have southwestern furnishings, a king-size bed or two doubles, and a full mirror behind the vanity. Room service and many business services are offered; there's an Avis car rental on the premises, plus a hair salon, heated outdoor swimming pool, adjacent children's pool, and guest

Laundromat. Yesterdays, a low-lit restaurant with wooden booths and ceiling fans, serves three meals daily in a moderate price range; cuisine is American with Mexican specials. The lounge has daily hors d'oeuvres and four TVs usually tuned to sports channels.

Where to Dine

Furgi's Pub, 817 Scenic Dr. ☎ **437-9564.**
Cuisine: STEAK & SEAFOOD.
Prices: Appetizers $2.95–$5.95; main courses $7.95–$21.95. DISC, MC, V.
Open: Mon–Sat 11am–10pm. **Closed:** Christmas.

Record albums and photos of classic cars and movie stars decorate the walls of this local favorite, located 1.3 miles south of the Space Center near 10th Street. The menu offers steak and fresh seafood, plus pasta, Mexican dishes, and deli-style sandwiches. The pub section (open until 2am) has a full bar, pool tables, a jukebox, and live rock and country music.

Mt. Carmel Restaurant, 915 Texas Ave. ☎ **434-0722.**
Cuisine: EUROPEAN & AMERICAN.
Prices: Meals $3.95–$6.95; desserts $1.25–$3.75. MC, V for checks of $20 or more only.
Open: Mon–Sat 8am–2:30pm.

This busy little restaurant with an attached religious gift shop is located just south of Tenth Street. Specializing in healthful, everything-from-scratch cooking, you'll find poached or scrambled eggs, pancakes, and biscuits-and-gravy on the breakfast menu; and a variety of specialty sandwiches plus quiche and homemade soup for lunch. There's a daily lunch special, and the popular desserts include Mt. Carmel (caramel) pie and a brownie à la mode.

$ Ramona's, 2913 N. White Sands Blvd. ☎ **437-7616.**
Cuisine: NEW MEXICAN & AMERICAN.
Prices: Appetizers $2.75–$4.95; breakfast $2.25–$6.95; lunch $2.50–$6.50; dinner $4.75–$9.50. AE, MC, V.
Open: Daily 6am–10pm. **Closed:** Thanksgiving.

Huge arched windows face the highway from the indoor patio of this tile-roofed adobe, and a huge wallpaper mural of a Mexican city covers one wall. A favorite meal is Ramona's special: a chicken enchilada, chile relleno, and chicken burrito, with guacamole, sour cream, refried beans, rice, and salad. American dishes include chicken-fried steak and fresh mountain trout. Beer and wine are served.

Yee's Oriental Express, 1115 S. White Sands Blvd. ☎ **437-RICE.**
Cuisine: CHINESE FAST FOOD.
Prices: Appetizers $2.95–$6.95; main courses $4.25–$6.95. No credit cards.
Open: Sun–Thurs 11am–9pm, Fri–Sat 11am–10pm.

Yee's "All-U-Can Eat Buffet" ($5.45) includes 15 Chinese dishes and several American basics such as fried chicken and corn on the cob. The regular menu includes daily specials like Szechuan beef or cashew chicken, and everyday favorites like sweet-and-sour pork, fried wontons, and butterfly shrimp. Yee's makes deliveries, or you can eat inside the bright red building, located between the Holiday Inn and the Desert Aire Motor Inn.

304

A NEARBY PLACE TO STAY & DINE

The Lodge at Cloudcroft, 1 Corona Place (P.O. Box 497), Cloudcroft, NM 88317. ☎ **505/682-2566** or toll free **800/395-6343** in New Mexico. Fax 505/682-2715. 58 rms, 9 suites. TV TEL

Rates: $69–$109 single or double; $99–$189 suite. Tax in Cloudcroft is 9.0625% (including 6.0625% state gross receipts and 3% local lodger's tax). AE, DC, DISC, ER, MC, V.

The only hotel in New Mexico listed in the "Top 100 Hotels in the U.S.," the Lodge is an antique jewel, a well-preserved survivor of another era. From the big fireplace in the lobby to the homey Victorian decor in the guest rooms, this mansion exudes gentility and class. Its nine-hole golf course, one of the nation's highest, challenges duffers across rolling hills between 8,600 and 9,200 feet elevation, and is the site of numerous regional tournaments.

Rooms in the Lodge are filled with antiques, from sideboards and lamps to mirrors and steam radiators. They're decorated in deep burgundy or peach colors; each has a king-size or two double beds. New guests are greeted by a stuffed bear sitting on their bed with a sampler of homemade fudge from the Lodge Mercantile! In 1991 more rooms were added in the form of the Pavilion and the Retreat, which were built adjacent to the Lodge. The Retreat ($249–$309) is an entire house with four bedrooms, kitchen, living room, and dining room. The Pavilion ($49–$89) is an 11-room bed-and-breakfast inn with pine paneled walls, down comforters, and fireplaces. Of course, the guests of the recent additions also have the privilege of enjoying the amenities and facilities of the Lodge.

Rebecca's (☎ **682-2566**) is named for the Lodge's resident ghost, believed to have been a chambermaid in the 1930s who was killed by her lumberjack lover. Breakfast is served from 7 to 10:30am, lunch from 11:30am to 2:30pm, and fine continental cuisine in a moderate-to-expensive price range is offered for dinner from 5:30 to 10pm. The hotel has fax and photocopying services available, a 9-hole golf course, heated outdoor swimming pool, hot tub, sauna, massage, and a gift shop that also sells homemade fudge.

2 Ruidoso, Mescalero & the Lincoln Loop

Ruidoso: 191 miles S of Albuquerque; 46 miles NE of Alamogordo; 71 miles W of Roswell

GETTING THERE • By Plane Ruidoso is served by **Sierra Blanca Regional Airport** (☎ **336-8455**), 17 miles north, near Fort Stanton. **Mesa Airlines** (☎ toll free **800/MESA-AIR**) has daily flights to and from Albuquerque and El Paso.

• By Bus The Ruidoso **bus station** is at 138 Service Rd., one block north of Sudderth Drive (☎ **257-2660**). The town is served by **TNM&O** and **Greyhound Lines, Inc.,** with six stops daily.

• By Car From Albuquerque, take I-25 south 87 miles to San Antonio; turn east on U.S. 380, 74 miles; then south on N.M. 37 and 48 (4 hours). From Alamogordo, take U.S. 70 northeast via Tularosa (1 hour). From Roswell, take U.S. 70 west (1¹/₂ hours).

ESSENTIALS • Orientation Ruidoso (most New Mexicans pronounce it Ree-uh-*do*-so) is situated at 6,900 feet in the timbered Sacramento Mountains, the southernmost finger of the Rockies. N.M. 48 is the main artery through the sprawl-ing town; it's called Sudderth Drive west of its junction with U.S. 70, and Mechem Drive when it turns suddenly north a few miles later.

• **Information**   The **Ruidoso Valley Chamber of Commerce** and visitor center is at 720 Sudderth Dr. Write P.O. Box 698, Ruidoso, NM 88345 (☎ **505/257-7395** or toll free **800/253-2255**).

• **Fast Facts**   The **area code** is 505. **Lincoln County Medical Center** is at 211 Sudderth Drive near the U.S. 70 junction, at Nob Hill (☎ **257-7381**). The **post office** is at Hollywood Station on Sudderth Drive just west of its junction with Mechem Drive. In case of **emergencies,** dial **911,** county wide.

Ruidoso is a mountain resort town named for its site on a noisy stream. It is most famous for the nearby racetrack, where the world's richest race is run for a $2.5-million purse. Outdoors lovers, hikers, horseback riders, fishermen, and hunters are drawn to the surrounding Lincoln National Forest. Southern New Mexico's most important ski resort, Ski Apache, is just out of town. The nearby Mescalero Apache Indian Reservation includes the magnificent Inn of the Mountain Gods resort hotel. Not far away, the historic village of Lincoln recalls the Wild West days of Billy the Kid.

What to See & Do

Ruidoso itself, while a lovely town for wandering, shopping, and enjoying outdoor pursuits, doesn't have any sightseeing attractions *per se*—no museums, no Native American ruins, no astounding sights. Its surrounding area, however, has plenty.

NEARBY ATTRACTIONS

Ruidoso Downs

In nearby Ruidoso Downs, 2 miles east on U.S. 70, is the famous **Ruidoso Downs racetrack** (see "Sports and Recreation," below) with its **new Museum of the Horse** (☎ **378-4142**), which contains a collection of over 10,000 horse-related items, in-cluding saddles from all over the world, a Russian sleigh, a horse-drawn "fire engine," and an 1860 stagecoach. Several great American artists including Frederic Remington, Charles M. Russell, Frank Tenney Johnson, and Henry Alkins are represented here as well. The Anne C. Stradling Collection, also housed here, is composed of family memorabilia that spans six generations. There is a gift shop with some interesting books and curios. Admission is $4 for adults, $3 for seniors, and $2.50 for children 5 to 18 (under 5, free).

Mescalero

Mescalero Apache Indian Reservation, P.O. Box 176, Mescalero, NM 88340.
☎ **505/671-4494.**

Immediately south and west of Ruidoso, the reservation covers over 460,000 acres (719 square miles) and is home to about 2,800 members of the Mescalero, Chiricahua, and Lipan bands of Apaches. Established by order of Pres. Ulysses S. Grant in 1873, it sustains a profitable cattle-ranching industry and the Apache-run logging firm of Mescalero Forest Products.

Even if you're not staying or dining there, don't fail to visit the **Inn of the Moun-tain Gods,** a luxury four-seasons resort owned and operated by the tribe (see "Nearby

Places to Stay," below). It's the crowning achievement of Wendell Chino, president of the Mescalero Apache tribe for all but four years since 1952.

Also on the reservation, on U.S. Highway 70 about 17 miles southwest of Ruidoso, is the ◘ **Mescalero Cultural Center,** open from 8am to 4:30pm Monday through Friday. Photos, artifacts, clothing, craftwork, and other exhibits demonstrate the history and culture of the tribe. Throughout the year, the center hosts powwows of colorful dancing and traditional drumming, open to the public and unrestricted as far as photography.

Restrictions do apply, however, to the annual **Coming of Age Ceremony,** held over four days in early July. A traditional rite reenacted in the tribal community of Mescalero, it includes an Apache maidens' puberty rites ceremony at dawn and a mountain spirits dance at night. Check ahead to learn what you can and can't see, and what you can and can't photograph.

St. Joseph's Church, just off Highway 70 in Mescalero, on a hill overlooking the reservation, is a Gothic-style structure with walls eight feet thick, built between the two world wars. The interior has the symbols of Apache mountain gods along with Roman Catholic saints in paintings and carvings (see "The Lincoln Loop" below).

Lincoln

 Lincoln State Monument, P.O. Box 36, Lincoln, NM 88338. ☎ **505/653-4372.**

One of the last historic yet uncommercialized 19th-century towns remaining in the American West, this tiny community lies 37 miles northeast of Ruidoso on U.S. Highway 380, in the valley of the Rio Bonito. Only 70 people live here today, but it was once the seat of the largest county in the United States, and the focal point of the notorious Lincoln County War of 1878–79. The entire town is now a New Mexico State Monument and a National Historic Landmark.

The bloody Lincoln County War was fought between various ranching and merchant factions over the issue of beef contracts for nearby Fort Stanton. A sharpshooting teenager named William Bonney—soon to be known as "Billy the Kid"—took sides in this issue with "the good guys," escaping from the burning McSween House after his employer and colleague were shot and killed. Three years later, after shooting down a sheriff, he was captured in Lincoln and sentenced to be hanged. But he shot his way out of his cell in the **Old Courthouse,** now a state museum which still has a hole made by a bullet from the Kid's gun. Today's visitors can hear a talk on this famous jail escape, by request, at the Old Courthouse.

Many of the original structures from that era have been preserved and restored by State Monuments, under the aegis of the Museum of New Mexico, the Lincoln County Historical Society, or the Lincoln County Heritage Trust (☎ **653-4025**).

At the trust's **Historical Center,** exhibits explain the role in Lincoln's history of Apaches, Hispanics, Anglo cowboys, and the black Buffalo Soldiers, and detail the Lincoln County War. A brief slide show on Lincoln history is presented in an old-fashioned theater. Start your visit here and either join a tour, included in the admission cost, or pick up a brochure describing the trust's self-guided walking tour (50¢). Across the courtyard is the **Luna Museum Store.**

An annual folk pageant, *The Last Escape of Billy the Kid,* has been presented outdoors since 1949 as a highly romanticized version of the Lincoln County War. It's staged Friday and Saturday nights and Sunday afternoon during the first full weekend in August as part of the **Old Lincoln Days** celebration. The festival also includes living-history demonstrations of traditional crafts, musical programs, and food booths throughout the village. From mid-June to mid-August, other weekend activities, including Apache dancing, historical dramas, and lectures, are scheduled.

Admission: May–Sept (includes entry to 5 buildings) adults $4.50; Oct–Apr (includes entry to 3 buildings) adults $4; children 16 and under free.

Open: Daily May 1–Sept 15 9:30am–5:30pm, rest of year 8:30am–4:30pm.

The Lincoln Loop

An enjoyable way to see many of the sights of the area while staying in Ruidoso is on a one- or two-day 162-mile loop tour.

Heading east from Ruidoso on U.S. 70, about 18 miles past Ruidoso Downs, is the small community of **San Patricio,** where you'll find (watch for signs) the **Hurd– La Rinconada Gallery** (☎ **653-4331**). Late artist Peter Hurd, a Roswell native, flunked out of West Point before studying with artist N. C. Wyeth and marrying Wyeth's daughter, Henriette, and eventually returning with her to New Mexico. This gallery shows and sells works by Peter Hurd, Henriette Wyeth, their son Michael Hurd, Andrew Wyeth, and N. C. Wyeth. In addition to original works, signed reproductions are available. The gallery is open Monday through Saturday from 9am to 5pm, and Sunday from 10am to 4pm. Several rooms and guest houses are also available by the night or for longer periods (see "Nearby Places to Stay," below).

From San Patricio, continue east on U.S. 70 for 4 miles to the community of Hondo, at the confluence of the Rio Hondo and Rio Bonito, and turn west onto U.S. 380. From here it's about 10 miles to **Lincoln,** a fascinating little town that is also a National Historic Landmark (see "Lincoln State Monument," above). From Lincoln, continue west on U.S. 380 about a dozen miles to **Capitan** and **Smokey Bear Historical State Park,** 118 First St. (☎ **354-2748**), open daily 9am to 5pm. Smokey, the national symbol of forest fire prevention, was born near here and found as an orphaned cub by firefighters in the early 1950s. This state park (admission 25¢) has exhibits on Smokey's rescue and life at the National Zoo in Washington, D.C., as well as fire prevention from World War II to the present. Visitors can also stop at Smokey's grave, and explore a nature path that represents six vegetation zones of the area.

Heading west from Capitan about 20 miles takes you to **Carrizozo,** the Lincoln County seat since 1912. For a quick sandwich or burger, stop at **Barb's East Coast Subs,** Twelfth St. and S. U.S. 54 (☎ **648-2155**), before continuing west on U.S. 380 for 4 miles to **Valley of Fires Recreation Area** (☎ **648-2241**), where you'll find what is considered one of the youngest and best-preserved lava fields in the United States. Among the black lava formations there's a ³/₄-mile self-guided nature trail, and a small visitors' center and bookstore in the park campground. Admission costs $3 per person or $5 per car for day use, and camping costs $5–$11. The park is open year-round.

To continue the loop tour, return 4 miles to Carrizozo, turn south onto U.S. 54, and go about 28 miles to the turnoff to **Three Rivers Petroglyph National Recreation Area** (☎ **525-4300**), which is about 5 miles east on a paved road. There are some 20,000 individual rock art images here, carved by Mogollon peoples who lived in the area centuries ago. A trail about eight-tenths of a mile long links many of the more interesting petroglyphs. The park also includes the partially excavated ruins of an ancient Native American village, including a multiroom adobe building, pit house, and masonry house that have been partially reconstructed. Administered by the U.S.

Bureau of Land Management, the park has facilities for picnicking and camping. Day use or camping fee is $2 per vehicle. The U.S. Forest Service also has a campground in the area, about 5 miles east via a gravel road.

From the recreation area, return 5 miles to U.S. 54 and continue south about 15 miles to **Tularosa Vineyards** (☎ **585-2260** or **585-4414**), which offers free tours and tastings daily from noon until 5pm. Using all New Mexico grapes, the winery is especially known for its award-winning reds. Wines can be purchased by the bottle, with prices ranging from $5.50 to $12.

Continuing south from the winery, drive about 2 miles to Tularosa and turn east onto U.S. 70, which you take for about 16 miles to the village of **Mescalero** on the Mescalero Indian Reservation. From U.S. 70, turn south onto Eagle Drive to get to the imposing **St. Joseph Church,** standing over 100 feet tall to the tip of the cross, with stone walls up to 4 feet thick. Built between 1920 and 1939, the mission church also contains an icon of the Apache Christ, with Christ depicted as a Mescalero holy man. Local arts and crafts and religious items are for sale at the parish office. Mass is celebrated Sundays at 10:30am. From the church go south to Apache Boulevard and then east to the **Mescalero National Fish Hatchery** (☎ **671-4401**), which has displays on the life cycle of trout and a self-guided walking tour through the tank house and raceway. The hatchery, which raises and distributes almost half a million trout annually, is open Monday through Friday from 8am to 4pm. Call for weekend hours and to arrange guided tours. Admission is free.

Returning to U.S. 70, it's about 19 miles back to Ruidoso.

SPORTS & RECREATION

CAMPING   Lincoln National Forest has over a dozen campgrounds in the region; four of them are within the immediate area. Maps (at $2) and details can be obtained from all campground offices, including the **Smokey Bear Ranger Station,** 901 Mechem Dr., Ruidoso (☎ **257-4995**), open from Memorial Day to Labor Day, Saturday 7:30am to 4:30pm.

FISHING   Bonito Lake and Rio Ruidoso are popular destinations. A New Mexico fishing license is required (see "Sports and Recreation," in chapter 1), **Seeping Springs Trout Lakes and Campground** (☎ **378-4216**), 4 miles east of Ruidoso Downs on U.S. 70, is privately owned, and state fishing licenses are not required. A family fishing permit costs $1, including poles, bait, and cleaning. You pay for what you catch at 35¢ an inch. The lake is open 8am to 5pm daily.

FITNESS CLUB   **Ruidoso Athletic Club,** 415 Wingfield St. (☎ **257-4900**), has Nautilus equipment and free weights, Lifecycles, racquetball, aerobics, hot tub, sauna, and massage. Day visits are $5 for nonmembers. It's open Monday through Saturday except major holidays.

GOLF   There are plenty of opportunities here. **Cree Meadows Country Club,** Country Club Drive off Sudderth Drive (☎ **257-5815**), is an 18-hole public course. Also public are the 18-hole courses at the **Inn of the Mountain Gods,** Carrizo Canyon Road (☎ **257-5141**); **The Links at Sierra Blanca,** 105 Sierra Blanca Drive (☎ **258-5330**); and the nine-hole **Carrizozo Golf Course** (☎ **648-2451**) in Carrizozo. **Alto Lakes Golf and Country Club,** High Mesa Drive, Alto Village (☎ **336-4231**), is an 18-hole private course. Miniature golf can be played at **Pan-O-Rama Mini Golf,** Eagle Drive at Rio Ruidoso (☎ **257-7164**).

HIKING   More than 225 miles of trails weave a web through Smokey Bear Ranger District of the Lincoln National Forest. From Ruidoso, a favorite destination of hikers is the **White Mountain Wilderness,** with nine trailheads, and the **Capitan Mountains Wilderness,** with 11 trails. Smokey Bear Ranger District office, 901 Mechem Dr., Ruidoso, has excellent maps of each wilderness area at $4 each. **Monjeau Lookout** is a popular destination off Ski Run Road (NM. 532).

HORSE RACING   The world's richest quarter-horse race, the $2.5 million All-American Futurity, is run each year on Labor Day at **Ruidoso Downs** racetrack (☎ **378-4431**). Seventy-seven other days of quarter-horse and thoroughbred racing lead up to the big one, beginning the second week of May. Post time in May and June is 1pm Thursday through Sunday. Grandstand admission is free. Call for reserved seating ($2.50 up, plus boxes seating 4 to 6 persons).

HORSEBACK RIDING   Numerous private stables in the area offer trail rides between 8am and 6pm, at rates from $10 per hour. Stables include **Buddies** (☎ **258-4027**), the **Grindstone Stables** (☎ **257-2241**), and the **Inn of the Mountain Gods** (☎ **257-5141**).

SKIING   Southern New Mexico's premier ski resort is **Ski Apache** (snow report ☎ **257-9001,** information ☎ **336-4565**), only 20 miles northwest of Ruidoso in the Mescalero Apache Reservation. Situated on an 11,500-foot ridge of 12,003-foot Sierra Blanca, the resort boasts a gondola, one quad chair, five triple chairs, two double chairs, a day lodge, sport shop, rental shop, ski school, first-aid center, four snack bars, and a lounge. Ski Apache has 52 trails and slopes (25% beginner, 30% intermediate, and 45% advanced), with a vertical drop of 1,900 feet and a total skier capacity of 15,300 an hour. All-day lift tickets for adults cost $34–$37, and $21–$23 for children (12 and under). The mountain is open Thanksgiving to Easter daily from 8:45am to 4pm. Lift-and-lodging packages can be booked through the Inn of the Mountain Gods (☎ toll free **800/545-9011**).

SWIMMING   Ruidoso Municipal Swimming Pool, 515 Sudderth Dr. (☎ **257-2795**), is open in summer, 11:30am to 4:45pm daily; admission is $2.25 for use of the pool only, and $6 for use of the pool and water slide.

SHOPPING

Many noted artists—among them Peter Hurd, Henriette Wyeth, and Gordon Snidow—have made their homes in Ruidoso and the surrounding Lincoln County. Dozens of other art-world hopefuls have followed them here, with the result that there is a proliferation of galleries in town. Among them are: **California Colors,** 201 Country Club Rd., open Tuesday to Sunday from 11am to 5pm; the **Camel House,** 714 Mechem Dr., open Wednesday to Monday from 10am to 5pm; **Crucis Art Bronze Foundry & Gallery,** 524 Sudderth Dr., open from 10am to early evening daily; **Fenton's Gallery,** 2629 Sudderth Dr., open daily from 10am to 6pm; **Grace's Art & Frame Chalet,** 2206 Sudderth Dr., open Monday to Saturday from 10am to 5pm; **Buckhorn Gallery,** Glencoe, open by appointment (☎ **378-4126**); **Hurd–La Rinconada,** in San Patricio, 20 miles east of Ruidoso on U.S. 70 (see "Lincoln Loop," above), open Monday to Saturday from 10am to 5pm; **McGary Studios,** a bronze foundry at 819 Gavilan Canyon Rd. (☎ **258-4450**); and **Mountain Arts,** 2530 Sudderth Dr., open Monday to Saturday from 10am to 6pm and from 10am to 4pm on Sunday.

Where to Stay

A tax of almost 11% is imposed on all lodging bills (6.8125% state tax and 4% city lodging tax). The only exception is the Inn of the Mountain Gods, governed by Mescalero Apache Reservation laws (7.5% tax). Parking is usually free.

Best Western Swiss Chalet Inn, 1451 Mechem Dr. (P.O. Box 759), Ruidoso, NM 88345. ☎ **505/258-3333** or toll free **800/47-SWISS** or **800/528-1234.** Fax 505/258-5325. 81 rms, 2 suites. A/C TV TEL

Rates: $62–$82 single; $69–89 double; $96 suite. AE, CB, DC, DISC, MC, V.

This blue-and-white chalet-style motel, with Swiss flags hanging outside its entry, looks right at home in a mountain resort. The spacious rooms are very comfortable and decorated in soft colors.

In Ahna-Michelle's Restaurant, Swiss and American food is served in an alpine atmosphere of Swiss bells and other souvenirs. The menu includes the likes of Wiener schnitzel, wursts, Luzern Cordon Bleu, and Davos Platz (peppered beef tips). Prices range from $4.95 to $14.95 for dinner main courses. The restaurant is open for breakfast daily from 7:30am to 11am, and for dinner daily, except Tuesday, from 6pm to 9pm. The inn has room service, connecting and nonsmoking rooms, an indoor swimming pool, Jacuzzi, and guest Laundromat. VCRs and videos are available at the front desk.

The Historic Carrizo Lodge and Condominiums, Carrizo Canyon Rd. (P.O. Drawer A), Ruidoso, NM 88345. ☎ **505/257-9131** or toll free **800/227-1224,** 84 rms. A/C TV TEL

Rates: $49–$79 single or double; efficiencies begin at $79. AE, CB, DC, DISC, MC, V.

Nestled among the pines beside a stream flowing east toward Ruidoso from Lake Mescalero, this lodge, on 7^1/$_2$ acres, is the home of the Carrizo Art School, one of America's oldest. Built in 1879 on a natural river-rock foundation, Carrizo has been designated a New Mexico cultural property and is on the National Register of Historic Places. The lodge, a rose-colored building with stucco walls, and its renovated bungalows retain their original *viga* ceilings, hardwood floors, and brass fixtures. Modern luxury condominium suites all have fireplaces.

The original lodge houses the Carrizo Cafe. Facilities include a swimming pool, sauna, hot tub, video arcade, and convenience store.

Dan Dee Cabins Resort, 310 Main Rd., Upper Canyon (P.O. Box 844), Ruidoso, NM 88345. ☎ **505/257-2165** or toll free **800/345-4848.** 12 cabins. FRIDGE TV

Rates: June 15–Labor Day $77 1 bedroom, $96 2 bedrooms, $115 3 bedrooms; Dec 15–Easter $72 1 bedroom, $89 2 bedrooms, $107 3 bedrooms; rest of year $62 1 bedroom, $79 2 bedrooms, $94 3 bedrooms. DISC, MC, V.

Rustic, woodsy, back-to-nature—these adjectives apply to the Dan Dee Cabins, some of which date back to 1940. Built beside a stream in five acres of forest, the cabins all have sitting porches, fireplaces, kitchens with gas stoves, and their own water heaters. They're popular with honeymooners who don't want to be disturbed: The only phone is in the office. For families, there's a barbecue area and children's playground.

Enchantment Inn, 307 U.S. 70 (P.O. Box 4210), Ruidoso, NM 88345. ☎ **505/378-4051** or toll free **800/435-0280.** Fax 505/378-5427. 50 rms, 30 suites. A/C TV TEL

Rates: $50–$80 single or double; $60–$175 suites. AE, DC, DISC, MC, V.

Completely redecorated in the fall of 1992, this handsome and well-kept motel has southwestern decor, with Mexican tiles and an abundance of wood and glass. Guests have use of an outdoor patio with barbecue grills, video game room, guest laundry, and indoor pool and whirlpool. The Screaming Eagle Restaurant and Lounge serves three meals daily, with most main courses priced under $10. There's also a gift shop on the premises. Nonsmoking and handicapped-accessible rooms are available.

Inn at Pine Springs, off U.S. Hwy. 70 (P.O. Box 2100), Ruidoso Downs, NM 88346. ☎ **505/378-8100** or toll free **800/237-3607**. Fax 505/378-8215. 100 rms, 4 suites. A/C TV TEL

Rates (including continental breakfast): Memorial Day–Labor Day $60–$73 single, $70–$83 double, $160–$169 suite; Labor Day–Memorial Day $40–$55 single, $50–$61 double, $115 suite. Children 12 and under free with parent. AE, CB, DC, DISC, MC, V.

High on a hill overlooking the racetrack, this motel is set on beautifully manicured grounds sprinkled with flowers and pine, spruce, and juniper trees. The rooms are almost too spacious; they're nicely appointed with standard furnishings and many have terrific views of the surrounding hills. A big Jacuzzi on an open-air deck is a favorite of guests.

⭐ **Pines Motel,** 620 Sudderth Dr., Ruidoso, NM 88345. ☎ **505/257-4334** or toll free **800/257-4334**. 10 rms. TV

💲 **Rates:** $32–$50 single; $36–$60 double. AE, DISC, MC, V.

This meticulously maintained family-owned-and-operated motel has six older but completely refurbished rooms, plus four new, more luxurious units overlooking the Rio Ruidoso. Rooms have color cable television and small refrigerators, but no telephones. Nonsmoking and connecting rooms are available. Pets are not accepted. There is no air conditioning, but it is rarely needed at this elevation. Guests can fish for trout in the river at the back of the property, and play horseshoes in a shady area along the river.

Shadow Mountain Lodge, 107 Main Rd., Upper Canyon (P.O. Box 1427), Ruidoso, NM 88345. ☎ **505/257-4886** or toll free **800/441-4331**. 19 rms. FRIDGE TV TEL

Rates: Memorial Day–Labor Day $68–$83 single or double; Labor Day–Memorial Day $53–$68 single or double. Ski and golf packages. AE, CB, DC, DISC, MC, V.

Advertising "luxury lodging for couples," this property doesn't accept children, let alone pets. It's a place of rustic elegance, an outstanding spot for a romantic getaway. Each unit has a king-size bed, a fireplace (wood is provided), and a coffeemaker (with complimentary coffee and tea). Ten rooms have full kitchens; the other nine have a wet bar and microwave. There's a barbecue area outside.

NEARBY PLACES TO STAY

Casa de Patron Bed and Breakfast, on U.S. 380 (P.O. Box 27), Lincoln, NM 88338. ☎ **505/653-4676**. 3 rms, 2 casitas.

Rates (including breakfast): $69 single; $79 double, $87–$97 casita. DISC, MC, V.

The main building of Casa de Patron, an adobe, was built around 1860 and is said to have housed Juan Patron's old store. It is also thought that Billy the Kid used part of the house as a hideout at some point during his time in the Lincoln area.

Jeremy and Cleis Jordan have created some lovely rooms in the main house and two wonderful casitas. The Tunstall Room is the only one with twin beds and is ideal for single travelers. The McSween Room and Juan's Old Store both have queen-size beds, and the latter has a patio and private entrance. People traveling with children are encouraged to take advantage of the casitas. Casita de Paz has two bedrooms, a full bath, front portal, redwood deck, and a sitting area. Casita Bonita was built with adobe bricks by the Jordans and is a small house with a full kitchen, a loft bedroom with a queen-size bed, bathroom, and living room (with a futon that sleeps two). The cathedral ceiling in Casita Bonita gives it a spacious feeling although it is quite small. If you choose to stay in a casita, a continental-plus breakfast is delivered to your door, but if you stay in the main house, Cleis and Jeremy will prepare a full breakfast with a hot dish, sausage, homemade granda, fresh baked muffins or coffee cake, juice, fresh fruit, and coffee or tea.

Ellis Store & Co. Bed & Breakfast, U.S. 380 (P.O. Box 14), Lincoln, NM 88338. ☎ **505/653-4609** or toll free **800/653-6460.** 8 rms (2 with bath).

Rates (including breakfast): $79–$89 single or double. MC, V.

With part of this house dating to 1850, this is believed to be the oldest existing residence in Lincoln County. The notorious Billy the Kid spent several weeks here, although somewhat unwillingly, according to court records that show payment of $64 for two weeks' food and lodging for the Kid and a companion held under house arrest. Today, guests of innkeepers Virginia and David Vigil can come and go as they please, wandering over the inn's 6 quiet acres, or using the inn as a base while exploring Lincoln and nearby attractions.

Four rooms in the main house are a step back into the 1800s, with wood-burning fireplaces or stoves, antique furnishings, and handmade quilts. Two have private baths (including one that is handicapped accessible), and two share baths. The separate Mill House, built of adobe and hand-hewn lumber in the 1880s, has one bath and a complete kitchen for its four bedrooms, and is excellent for a large family or small group. Rooms have no televisions or telephones, but a phone is available for guest use and the Vigils are happy to take messages.

Gourmet breakfasts are cooked to order from an extensive menu, and lunches and dinners are also available by reservation. Nonguests are also welcome for meals, by reservation. Pets are not permitted inside, but kennels are available, and those with horses are invited to use the property's stables.

Hurd Ranch Guest Homes, P.O. Box 100, San Patricio, NM 88348. ☎ **505/653-4331** or toll free **800/658-6912.** Fax 505/653-4218. 4 casitas (all with bath). TV TEL

Rates: $100–$250 per casita (two night minimum). AE, DISC, MC, V.

Located about 20 miles east of Ruidoso on 2,500-acre Sentinel Ranch, these attractive casitas are part of the Hurd–La Rinconada Gallery, which displays the work of well-known artists Peter and Michael Hurd, Henriette Wyeth Hurd, N. C. Wyeth, and Andrew Wyeth. The grounds also include the San Patricio Polo Fields, where matches take place from Memorial Day to Labor Day.

There are two older one-bedroom casitas, built in the early part of the century, and two new and much larger units. All have completely equipped kitchens, fireplaces, and comfortable living areas, and are decorated with antiques, primitives, and art by the Hurd-Wyeth family. The one-bedroom casitas also have private patios with barbecue grills. Pets are welcome.

⭐ **Inn of the Mountain Gods,** Carrizo Canyon Rd. (P.O. Box 269), Mescalero, NM 88340. ☎ **505/257-5141** or toll free **800/545-6040.** Fax 505/257-6173. 250 rms, 10 suites. A/C TV TEL

Rates: June 1–Labor Day $120 single or double, $130 suite; Apr–May and Sept–Oct $95 single or double. $105 suite; Nov–Mar $80 single or double, $90 suite. Golf, tennis, and ski packages. AE, CB, DC, DISC, MC, V.

Southern New Mexico's most luxurious resort is this impressive property on the Mescalero Apache Reservation, 3$^{1}/_{2}$ miles southwest of Ruidoso. It is the successful dream of the tribal president, Wendell Chino, who wanted to help his people get into the recreation and tourism business. They picked a spectacularly beautiful location, overlooking pristine Lake Mescalero and, behind it, 12,003-foot-high Sierra Blanca.

Nine interconnected brown-shake buildings comprise the hotel and an associated convention center. Guests cross a covered wooden bridge over a cascading stream to reach the three-story lobby, dominated by a huge, coneshaped, copper fireplace. Modern tribal art and trophies of wild animals bagged on the reservation are on display. The property includes an 18-hole golf course designed by Ted Robinson, whose work includes the famed course at the Princess in Acapulco; eight tennis courts; horseback riding stables; boating and fishing; and many other recreations. In winter, buses shuttle skiers to the Ski Apache resort, also owned by the tribe.

The guest rooms are spacious and sophisticated, with high ceilings and tasteful furnishings. All are appointed in shades of desert rose or mesquite green. Lithographs on the walls depict typical 19th-century tribal scenes. Each room has a big closet, two sinks, and a dressing table with mirrors. There are rooms for nonsmokers and the disabled.

The Dan Li Ka Room (open 7am to 2:30pm and 6 to 10pm daily) is a huge dining room with a view of lake and mountain beyond. The menu features steak, poultry, seafood, and pasta, plus reservation specialties like Southwest sautée (venison, chicken breast, and beef medallions with marsala-cilantro sauce) and broiled fresh mountain trout. Appetizers run $4.95 to $7.95, dinner main courses $12.95 to $17.95. The Apache Tee Restaurant by the golf course offers casual dining from 6:30am to 10pm. Ina Da Lounge has ample seating and a big floor for dancing and drinks. There's a piano bar off the lobby.

The hotel offers room service (7am to 10pm), valet laundry, a gift shop, and Casino Apache. Facilities include a golf course, stables, outdoor tennis courts, swimming pool, whirlpool, saunas, fishing lake stocked with rainbow trout, trap and skeet shooting, archery, boating (rowboats, pedal boats, and canoes rented), and a base for hunting trips. A convention center is attached. No pets.

⭐ **Sierra Mesa Lodge,** Fort Stanton Road (P.O. Box 463), Alto, NM 88312. ☎ **505/336-4515.** 5 rms.

Rates (including full breakfast): $80 single; $90 double. DISC, MC, V.

Southern California transplants Larry and Lila Goodman operate what may be Ruidoso's friendliest and most elegant B&B for nonsmokers. Each room is faithful to its particular theme. The Country Western Room, for instance, has a huge step-up bed and steamer trunk; the Victorian Room boasts an eagle-claw bathtub/shower. There's also the Oriental Room, the Queen Anne Room, and the French Country Room. All have private baths, period furnishings, comforters and goose-down pillows on the brass and/or four-poster beds, rocking chairs and chaise longues. The lodge has a large private spa and each afternoon offers silver tea service. The rates include high tea as well as a full gourmet breakfast.

Where to Dine

In these listings, the following categories define price ranges: **expensive**—the average meal costs more than $25; **moderate**—the average meal costs $10 to $25; **inexpensive**—the average meal costs less than $10.

EXPENSIVE

 Victoria's Romantic Hideaway, 2103 Sudderth Dr. ☎ **257-5440** or toll free **800/959-1328.**

Cuisine: SICILIAN. **Reservations:** Required (one day in advance suggested).
Prices: $50 prix fixe (including tax). DISC, MC, V.
Open: Daily 6pm–close.

To say one goes to Victoria's Romantic Hideaway for dinner would be a gross understatement. You go to Victoria's for a wonderful 3-to-4-hour dining experience, perhaps a romantic evening by soft candlelight to celebrate a special occasion. Hosts Don and Pat Baker have created a unique restaurant where guests are outrageously pampered during a relaxed eight-course meal. Although the restaurant will seat up to 28, no more than four couples are usually served on any given evening, each couple in a private, elegantly decorated section of the restaurant.

One basic meal is served each night; however, dishes are customized for each particular diner, and dining partners never receive quite the same meal. Everything is homemade, and the Bakers grow many of the herbs themselves. Pat, the chef, learned many of the classic dishes from her Sicilian grandmother, and some of the ingredients and wines are imported from Sicily. Dress is casual, except shorts are not permitted, and smoking is allowed only on an outdoor porch. Victoria's does not welcome children.

MODERATE

Cattle Baron Steak House, 657 Sudderth Dr. ☎ **257-9355.**

Cuisine: STEAK & SEAFOOD. **Reservations:** Recommended.
Prices: Appetizers $2.75–$5.95; lunch $3.95–$6.50; dinner $6.95–$20.95. AE, DISC, MC, V.
Open: Sun–Thurs 11am–9:30pm, Fri–Sat 11am–10:30pm. **Closed:** Christmas.

A casually elegant restaurant with several levels of seating in a white adobe-style interior, the Cattle Baron serves up a variety of fine steaks and chicken dishes. It also boasts an extensive seafood menu, including fresh catches from the Atlantic, Pacific, and Gulf of Mexico. Prime rib is the house specialty. There's a large salad bar and a great lounge. In summer, dine in the waterfall room: Just outside the wall of windows is a lovely cascading (manmade) waterfall.

 La Lorraine, 2523 Sudderth Dr. ☎ **257-2954.**

Cuisine: FRENCH. **Reservations:** Recommended.
Prices: Appetizers $4.95–$6.25; lunch $5.95–$12.95; dinner $13.95–$23.95. AE, MC, V.
Open: Lunch Mon–Sat 11am–2pm; dinner Mon–Sat 6–9:30pm.

This piece of Paris is a bit hard to imagine in a New Mexico mountain town, but here it is, in an adobe building on the main street. Inside, there's French provincial decor, with lace curtains and candlelight; diners can also opt for outdoor courtyard service.

Le menu? Pâtés, bisques, salades . . . and wonderful dishes like canard (duck) à l'orange, rack of lamb, Angus rib-eye, chateaubriand, and salmon with shallots.

Michelena's Italian Restaurant, 2703 Sudderth Dr. ☎ 257-5753.

Cuisine: ITALIAN. **Reservations:** Accepted.
Prices: Appetizers $1.50–$4.25; sandwiches $3.25–$5.50; dinner main courses $6.95–$12.95; pizzas $9.75–$15.95. DISC, MC, V.
Open: Daily 11am–9pm (closed Mon during Apr and Nov). **Closed:** Thanksgiving and New Year's Day.

This pleasant Italian bistro has Chianti bottles hanging from the ceiling and traditional red-and-white checked tablecloths. All the Italian standards are offered, including chicken Alfredo, spaghetti, lasagna, ravioli, manicotti, fettuccine; or you can order a sampler plate. There are also 20 varieties of pizza, and a good selection of Italian-style sandwiches. Luncheon specials are offered Monday through Friday.

INEXPENSIVE

★ Cafe Rio, 2547 Sudderth Dr., Ruidoso. ☎ 257-7746.

$
Cuisine: INTERNATIONAL/PIZZA. **Reservations:** Not accepted.
Prices: Lunch and dinner $3.95–$8.95. No credit cards.
Open: Daily 11am–8:30pm. **Closed:** Dec 1–21 and for one month after Easter.

This unpretentious pizzeria-style restaurant is a lot more than it appears to be, offering a wide selection of dishes from around the world, plus a very good pizza, with everything made from scratch. There's also an extensive selection of domestic and imported beers, including seasonal beers.

Casa Blanca, 501 Mechem Dr. ☎ 257-2495.

Cuisine: NEW MEXICAN.
Prices: Appetizers $1.95–$5.95; main courses $4–$10. AE, MC, V.
Open: Daily 11am–10pm. **Closed:** Christmas.

This large white-stucco building, a half mile north of the Sudderth/Mechem junction toward Alto, commands a lovely valley view from its hilltop garden location. Contemporary regional art hangs on the walls inside, and a large beer garden/patio, shaded by ponderosa pines, is the location of afternoon "jams" from 2 to 6pm every summer Sunday. There's a small cantina downstairs. The menu features a wide variety of southwestern favorites, include chimichangas and green-chile enchiladas.

Hummingbird Tearoom, 2306 Sudderth Dr., Village Plaza. ☎ 257-5100.

Cuisine: AMERICAN.
Prices: $3.25–$5.75. MC, V.
Open: Tues–Sat 11am–2:30pm (afternoon tea served until 5pm in summer). **Closed:** Thanksgiving, Christmas, New Year's.

A delightful little dessert and ice cream shop, the Hummingbird also serves excellent sandwiches, salads, and homemade soups. Afternoon tea is particularly popular. Smoking is permitted only on the patio, open during the summer.

Nearby Places to Dine

 Chango's, Smokey Bear Blvd., Capitan. ☎ **354-4213.**

Cuisine: INTERNATIONAL. **Reservations:** Strongly recommended.
Prices: $12.95–$15.95. MC, V.
Open: Wed–Sat 5pm–close.

Jerrold Donti Flores, the owner of Chango's, left San Francisco in the late 1970s to return to the land of his birth, and after several other ventures found his calling in this small (24-seat) and highly rated restaurant in a turn-of-the-century adobe building. Flores, an accomplished avant-garde sculptor and painter, also displays his art, works by other artists, plus international primitives, in changing exhibits at the restaurant.

A choice of four-to-six gourmet dinners changes every other week, with selections such as fresh poached salmon with chipotle sauce, beef bourguignon, whitefish in an asparagus-pistachio sauce, or pesto chicken. An excellent wine list includes a 26-year old port plus Italian, Spanish, French, Australian, German, and domestic wines.

 Flying J Ranch, Hwy. 48, 1 mile north of Alto. ☎ **336-4330.**

Cuisine: CHUCK WAGON. **Reservations:** Highly recommended.
Prices: $12.50 adults; reduced children's rates. MC, V.
Open: May–Labor Day, Mon–Sat 7:30pm.

A treat for the whole family, this ranch is like a western village, complete with staged gunfights and pony rides for the kids. Gates open at 6pm; a chuck-wagon dinner of beef, baked potato, beans, biscuit, applesauce cake, and coffee or lemonade is served promptly at 7:30. Then, at 8:15pm, the Flying J Wranglers present a fast-paced stage show with western music, a world champion fiddle player, and a world champion yodeler.

Inncredible Restaurant & Saloon, Hwy. 48 North at Ski Run Rd., Alto Village. ☎ **336-4312.**

Cuisine: STEAKS & SEAFOOD. **Reservations:** Recommended.
Prices: Appetizers $3.95–$7.95; dinner $7.95–$18.95. AE, DISC, MC, V.
Open: Daily 5pm–close (bar opens 3:30pm).

Old West–style art hangs on the walls of this modern yet rustic restaurant, with fine etched glass and stained glass accented by large skylights. Especially known for its prime rib and Australian cold water lobster, the menu also includes steaks such as pepper steak in brandy sauce, shrimp and crab au gratin, chicken and pasta. There are special children's meals, and munchies are served in the bar.

Tinnie Silver Dollar, Restaurant and Saloon Hwy. 70 E., Tinnie. ☎ **653-4425.**

Cuisine: STEAKS & SEAFOOD. **Reservations:** Recommended.
Prices: Appetizers $3.95–$8.95; main courses $9.95–$24.50. MC, V.
Open: Lunch Sat–Sun 11:30am–4:30pm; dinner Wed–Sun 5–10pm.

Housed in a Territorial–style building dating from the 1880s, this Victorian eatery is truly a relic from another era. An ornate 19th-century European music box still plays tunes on ancient metal disks. Four stained-glass windows from an old El Paso church cover the entire wall of one room; above the fireplace in another, Neptune is attended by mermaids in an 1880s stained-glass window from a San Francisco seafood restaurant. The restaurant has a massive oak bar, milkglass gaslights, a bell tower, and a veranda offers a fine view of the Rio Hondo valley.

For an appetizer, you can't miss with the layered brie, with pesto and piñon nuts. Selections include everything from rib-eye steak, grilled lamb chops, and lobster tail, to Silver Dollar prawns (basted in drawn butter), pasta Scandiffio, and enchiladas suizas. Tinnie serves espresso coffees.

3 Roswell

199 miles SE of Albuquerque; 185 miles NE of Las Cruces; 76 miles N of Carlsbad.

GETTING THERE • By Plane   Roswell Airport, at Roswell Industrial Air Center on South Main Street (☎ 347-5703), is served commercially by **Mesa Airlines** (☎ 347-5501 or toll free **800/MESA-AIR**). Mesa flies to Albuquerque almost hourly throughout the day and direct to Dallas, Texas, twice daily.

• **By Bus   Texas, New Mexico & Oklahoma (TNM&O) Coaches** serve Roswell with connections to and from Alamogordo, Ruidoso, Albuquerque, Las Cruces, and Carlsbad. The **bus station** is at 1100 N. Virginia Ave. (☎ **622-2510**).

• **By Car**   From Albuquerque take I-40 east 59 miles to Clines Corners; turn south on U.S. 285, 140 miles to Roswell (4 hours). From Las Cruces, take U.S. 70 east (4 hours). From Carlsbad, take U.S. 285 north (1¹/₂ hours).

ESSENTIALS • Orientation   Roswell is at the intersection of east-west U.S. Highway 380, which runs through the city as Second Street, and north-south U.S. Highway 285, known here as Main Street. City streets east and west of Main, and north and south of First (just south of Second), are so designated. On the south side of the city, Main Street branches, with South Main heading due south to the airport and U.S. 285 heading southeast to Carlsbad.

• **Information**   The **Roswell Chamber of Commerce** is at 131 W. Second St. (P.O. Drawer 70), Roswell, NM 88201 (☎ **505/623-5695**).

• **Fast Facts**   The **area code** is 505. The main **hospital,** Eastern New Mexico Medical Center, is at 405 W. Country Club Rd. (☎ **622-8170**) and ENM Medical Center South is on South Main at Chisum Street (☎ **622-1110**). The **post office** is located at 415 N. Pennsylvania Ave., at West Fifth Street (☎ **622-3741**). **Eastern New Mexico University-Roswell** is located at Roswell Industrial Air Center on South Main Street (☎ **624-7000**). In the event of an **emergency,** dial **911** or "0" for operator.

Roswell (pop. 45,500) dominates a vast, sparsely populated prairie of ranch land. From its founding in 1871, it has been a center for farming, and cattle and sheep ranching. It has also become a major industrial center, with plants that produce clothing, food, airplanes, and buses. Its elevation of 3,650 feet gives it a hot climate in summer, mild in winter. The city has a very active cultural life, and a visit to its museums and nearby natural areas make it worth spending some time.

What to See & Do

 Roswell Museum and Art Center, 100 W. 11th St., Roswell. ☎ **624-6744.**
This highly acclaimed small museum is deservedly Roswell's number one attraction. Established in the 1930s through the efforts of city government, local archaeological and historical societies, and the WPA, the museum proclaims this city's role as a center for the arts and a cradle of America's space industry.

The art center contains the world's finest collection of works by Peter Hurd and his wife, Henriette Wyeth, as well as representative works by Georgia O'Keeffe, Ernest Blumenschein, Joseph Sharp, and others famed from the early 20th-century Taos and Santa Fe art colonies. There are also permanent and temporary exhibits of late 20th-century works, as well as Native American and Hispanic art. The museum has an early historical section, but its pride and joy is the Robert Goddard Collection, which presents actual engines, rocket assemblies, and specialized parts developed by Goddard in the 1930s, when he lived and worked in Roswell. Goddard's workshop has been re-created for the exhibit. A special display commemorates the Apollo XVII, which undertook the last manned lunar landing in 1972; it includes the spacesuit worn on the moon by New Mexican Harrison Schmitt. The Goddard Planetarium is used as a science classroom for local students and for special programs. Ask about "the Roswell Incident," an alleged UFO crash near here in 1947.

Admission: Free.

Open: Mon–Sat 9am–5pm, Sun and holidays 1–5pm. **Closed:** Thanksgiving, Christmas, and New Year's Day.

★ **Historical Center for Southeast New Mexico,** 200 N. Lea Ave. at W. 2nd St., Roswell. ☎ **622-8333.**

The handsome mansion that houses this historical collection is as much a part of the museum as the collection itself. A three-story yellow-brick structure built between 1910 and 1912 by rancher J. P. White, its gently sweeping rooflines and large porches reflect the prairie style of architecture made popular by Frank Lloyd Wright. The White family lived here until 1972; today this home, on the National Register of Historic Places, is a monument to turn-of-the-century lifestyles.

First- and second-floor rooms, including the parlor, bedrooms, dining room, and kitchen, have been restored and furnished with early 20th-century antiques. The kitchen includes such vintage appliances as a wood-burning cookstove, an icebox, and a pie safe. The second floor has a gallery of changing historic exhibits, from fashions to children's toys. The third floor, once White's private library, now houses the Pecos Valley Collection and the archives of the Historical Center for Southeast New Mexico.

Admission: $2.

Open: Fri–Sun 1–4pm.

New Mexico Military Institute, 101 W. College Blvd. at N. Main St., Roswell. ☎ **622-6250** or **624-8100.**

"West Point of the West" celebrated its centennial in 1991. Considered one of the most distinguished military schools in the United States, it is the alma mater of luminaries as disparate as football star Roger Staubach and network newsman Sam Donaldson. The state-supported, coeducational institute includes a 4-year college preparatory high school and a 2-year junior college, and is the only J.C. in the country that offers graduates an Army ROTC commission in just two years.

On campus is the **General Douglas L. McBride Military Museum,** with a fine collection of artillery and artifacts that document New Mexico's role in America's wars. Among the memorabilia are items from the Bataan Death March. **Godfrey Athletic Center** is open to Roswell visitors with payment of a small fee; in fact, the whole campus is open. Tours are offered by appointment.

Admission: Free.

Open: Daily (museum hours) 8am–4pm.

Spring River Park and Zoo, 1400 E. College Blvd. at Atkinson Ave., Roswell.
☎ **624-6760.**

This lovely park, covering 48 acres on either side of a stream a mile east of NMMI,
incorporates a miniature train, antique carousel, large prairie-dog town, children's
fishing pond, picnic ground, and playgrounds. There's also a children's petting zoo,
and Texas longhorns.

Admission: Free. Rides 25¢.

Open: Zoo, year-round, daily 10am–sunset, weather permitting. Rides and con-
cessions, June–Labor Day daily 1–6pm; Apr–May and Sept–Oct, Sat–Sun 1–6pm.

NEARBY ATTRACTIONS

★ **Bitter Lake National Wildlife Refuge,** Pecos River, off U.S. 380 and N.M.
265, 15 miles NE of Roswell. ☎ **622-6755.**

A great variety of waterfowl—including cormorants, herons, pelicans, sandhill cranes,
and snow geese—find a winter home on these 24,000 acres of river bottomland, marsh,
stands of salt cedar, and open range. Seven gypsum sinkhole lakes, covering an area of
700 acres, are of a peculiar beauty. If you're here between December and February,
don't miss this place: The sky actually darkens with birds. Once threatened with extinction, the sandhill crane now appears, along with puddle and diving ducks every
winter. Snow geese were unknown here 20 years back, but now turn up to the tune of
some 40,000 every winter. All told, over 300 species of birds have been sighted. You
can get information at the headquarters building at the entrance.

Admission: Free.

Open: Dawn to dusk year-round.

Bottomless Lakes State Park (HC 12 Box 1200), N.M. Highway 409 off U.S. Hwy.
380, 16 miles east of Roswell.

This chain of seven lakes, surrounded by rock bluffs, got its name from early cowboys, who tried to fathom the lakes' depth by plumbing them with lariats. No matter
how many ropes they tied together and lowered into the limpid water, they never
touched bottom. In fact, no lake is deeper than 100 feet. The largest, Lea Lake, is so
clear that skin divers frequent it. Another is so shaded by surrounding bluffs that the
sun rarely reaches it, so its name is Devil's Inkwell. Mirror, Cottonwood, Pasture, and
Figure 8 lakes got their monikers with similar logic; No Name Lake, which apparently didn't have anything to distinguish it, has been renamed Lazy Lagoon.

This park is a popular recreation site for Roswell residents. There's fishing for rainbow trout, swimming and windsurfing, campsites for trailers or tents, and shelters,
showers, a dump station, and a snack bar (open 9am to 6pm Memorial Day to Labor
Day).

Admission: $3 per vehicle.

Open: Daily 6am–9pm year-round.

★ **Dexter National Fish Hatchery,** 1¹/₂ miles east of Dexter on N.M. 190, about
16 miles southeast of Roswell via N.M. 2. ☎ **734-5910.**

Originally built to raise bass and catfish, this national fish hatchery is now a center for
the study and raising of threatened and endangered fish species, such as the razorback
sucker, Colorado squawfish, Chihuahuan chub, and Mexican Yaqui. Year-round, visitors can take self-guided tours among the hatchery's ponds; and from late March

through October the visitors' center is open, with exhibits and an aquarium containing endangered fish. A short film is also shown.

Admission: Free.

Open: Daily 7am–4pm.

⭐ **Fort Sumner,** 84 miles north of Roswell via U.S. Hwy. 285 and N.M. Hwy. 20.

This little town of 1,300 people is important in New Mexico history for two big reasons: It's the site of Fort Sumner State Monument and the burial place of the notorious Billy the Kid.

Fort Sumner State Monument (☎ 355-2573) recalls a tragic U.S. Army experiment (1864–68) to create a self-sustaining agricultural colony for captive Navajos. That native tribe still recalls it as the "Long March," the saddest chapter in their noble history. Today, a visitor center (open daily 9am to 5pm) tells the story of the fort, and the **Old Fort Sumner Museum** (☎ 355-2942) displays artifacts, pictures, and documents. It's located 7 miles southeast of the modern town, via U.S. 60/84 and N.M. 272.

Behind the museum is the **Grave of Billy the Kid,** a 6-foot tombstone engraved to "William H. Bonney, alias 'Billy the Kid,' died July 16, 1881," and to two previously slain comrades with whom he was buried. Those curious about the notorious young outlaw, just 21 when Sheriff Pat Garrett shot him in Fort Sumner, can learn more at the **Billy the Kid Museum** (☎ 505/355-2380), 2 miles east of downtown Fort Sumner on U.S. Highway 60/84. It contains more than 60,000 relics of the Old West, including some recalling the life of young Bonney himself.

The **Old Fort Days** celebration, the second week of June, is Fort Sumner's big annual event. It includes the World's Richest Tombstone Race (inspired by the actual theft of Billy's tombstone, since recovered), two nights of rodeo, a country music show, barbecue, and parade.

Sumner Lake State Park (☎ 355-2541), 16 miles northwest of Fort Sumner via U.S. Highway 84 and N.M. Highway 203, is a 1,000-acre property with a campground and cabin sites. Boating, fishing, swimming, and waterskiing are popular recreations.

For more information on the town, write or phone the **De Baca County Chamber of Commerce,** P.O. Box 28, Fort Sumner, NM 88119 (☎ 505/355-7705). To learn more about Billy the Kid and Pat Garrett, write **Billy the Kid Outlaw Gang Inc.,** P.O. Box 1881, Taiban, NM 88134 (☎ 505/355-9935).

Clovis/Portales, 110 miles northeast of Roswell via U.S. Hwy. 70.

Clovis is a major market center on the Texas border. Founded in 1906 as a railway town, it is now the focus of an active ranching and farming region, with about 33,400 population. **Cannon Air Force Base,** a part of the Tactical Air Command, is just northwest of the city. The **Lyceum Theatre,** 411 Main St. (☎ 763-6085), is a magnificent restoration of a former vaudeville theater; it's now the city's center for performing arts. The **H. A. "Pappy" Thornton Homestead and Museum** in Ned Houk Park (no phone) displays antique farming equipment in a prairie farmhouse. A major rodeo on the national circuit is held the first weekend in June. "Clovis Man," who hunted mammoths in this region about 10,000 B.C., was first discovered at a site near the city.

South of Clovis 19 miles is **Portales,** a town of 11,300 people that is the home of the main campus of **Eastern New Mexico University.** On campus are the **Roosevelt County Historical Museum** (☎ 562-2592) of regional ranching history and the

Natural History Museum (☎ 562-2174), with wildlife exhibits, including a bee colony. There are anthropology and paleontology exhibits at the **Blackwater Draw Museum** (☎ 562-2202), 7 miles northeast of Portales on U.S. Highway 70 toward Clovis.

For lodging in the Clovis/Portales area, try the **Best Western LaViata Inn,** 1516 Mabry Dr. (U.S. Highway 60/70/84), Clovis, NM 88101 (☎ **505/762-3808** or toll free **800/528-1234**), or the **Holiday Inn,** 2700 Mabry Dr., Clovis, NM 88101 (☎ **505/762-4491**). Clovis is the flagship of the **K-Bob's Steakhouse** chain, when you're hungry. The restaurant is at 1600 Mabry Dr. (☎ **763-4443**).

SPORTS & RECREATION

Roswell has 24 parks and playgrounds, 30 tennis courts, three golf courses, and numerous other recreational facilities. For full information, check with the **City of Roswell Recreation & Park Departments,** 1101 W. Fourth St. in Cahoon Park (☎ **624-6721**).

Racquetball courts, weights, and full health-club facilities are available at the **Roswell Racquet Club & Spa,** 200 E. Mescalero St. (☎ **622-0962**).

Most spectator events take place at the **Roswell Sports Complex,** including the Wool Bowl football stadium, east of NMMI on College Boulevard at Garden Avenue.

SHOPPING

Nearly every need can be met at the **Roswell Mall,** 4501 N. Main St. (☎ **623-8553**), a modern 300,000-square-foot complex with a wide choice of stores.

EVENING ENTERTAINMENT

The **Roswell Symphony Orchestra,** 3201 N. Main St. (☎ **623-5882**), a 65-member professional orchestra founded in 1959, gives an annual October-to-April series of five concerts at NMMI's Pearson Auditorium. Tickets are $8 to $17 for adults, $4 to $8.50 for students, depending upon seating. Orchestra members also present a three-part chamber series at the Roswell Museum; tickets are $10 adults, $5 students. There is an annual free Labor Day concert at Spring River Park and Zoo.

The **Roswell Community Little Theatre** (☎ **622-1982**), also founded in 1959, presents five productions a year. The season runs from September to June. All performances are in the troupe's own 142-seat theater at 1101 N. Virginia St., a block east of Main at 12th. Recent works have included Neil Simon's *The Good Doctor,* Jack Sharkey's *The Murder Room,* and musicals such as *Man of La Mancha.* Tickets are $5 adults, $2.50 students; productions usually run four nights over two weekends.

Where to Stay

An 11.375% tax is imposed on all lodging bills (6.375% state tax and 5% city lodging tax). Parking is usually free.

Days Inn, 1310 N. Main St., Roswell, NM 88201. ☎ **505/623-4021.** 62 rms. A/C TV TEL

Rates (including continental breakfast): $34–$38 single; $38–$46 double. AE, CB, DC, DISC, MC, V.

A colonial-style inn with a redbrick and white-wood facade, Days Inn is located on the north side of town. Guest rooms have comfortable southwestern furnishings, king-size or two double beds, desk, and cable TV. There is a full service restaurant and lounge on the premises, and they offer limited room service. Pets are allowed. Outdoors are a large swimming pool and hot tub.

Frontier Motel, 3010 N. Main St., Roswell, NM 88201. ☎ **505/622-1400** or toll free **800/678-1401.** Fax 505/622-1405. 38 rms and suites. A/C TV TEL

Rates (including continental breakfast): $34–$43 single; $38–$47 double; $50 suites. AE, CB, DC, DISC, MC, V.

This comfortable motel just north of the center of town offers clean and attractive rooms in a variety of sizes and decors. Some of the smaller rooms have showers only, while larger rooms have shower and bath combinations. Refrigerators are available and there is an outdoor, unheated pool. Handicapped-accessible and nonsmoking rooms are available, and pets are accepted.

Sally Port Inn, 2000 N. Main St., Roswell, NM 88201. ☎ **505/622-6430** or toll free **800/548-5221** or **800/528-1234.** Fax 505/623-7631. 124 rms. A/C TV TEL

Rates: $52–$54 single; $62–$64 double. Summer weekend specials. AE, CB, DC, DISC, MC, V.

A Best Western property, this two-story white-brick building adjacent to NMMI boasts a huge atrium courtyard. A cafe and swimming pool are at opposite ends of this skylit area, which gives a feeling of being outside while actually being inside.

Guest rooms, all of which have interior access, have double and queen-size beds and blue or green pastel decor. Each has two sinks (one at the vanity), brass fixtures, and a working table. Executive king units have a refrigerator as well as a king-size bed. Some rooms are designated for nonsmokers and the disabled.

The atrium cafe serves three meals daily, and there's also a separate bar. The inn has room service, courtesy van, valet laundry, swimming pool, whirlpool, sauna, weight room, coin-op laundry, hair salon, and gift shop.

Where to Dine

El Toro Bravo, 102 S. Main St. at 1st St. ☎ **622-9280.**

Cuisine: NEW MEXICAN.
Prices: Lunch $2.95–$6.95; dinner $5.75–$10.95. AE, MC, V.
Open: Lunch Mon–Fri 11am–2:30pm, Sat 11am–5pm; dinner Mon–Sat 5–9pm.

Mexican souvenirs adorn the walls of this dimly lit restaurant, which occupies two large rooms. Plants hang from the high ceiling. The menu has a wide selection of regional dishes, including stuffed sopaipillas, chalupas, chile Colorado, and carne asada. There's a $4.95 luncheon buffet Monday through Friday.

Keuken Dutch Restaurant, 12th and N. Main Sts. ☎ **624-2040.**

Cuisine: DUTCH & AMERICAN.
Prices: Appetizers $1.50–$4.30; breakfast $3–$6.50; lunch $2.70–$6; dinner $4.99–$10.99. AE, CB, DC, DISC, MC, V.
Open: Daily 5am–11pm.

This restaurant is straight from New Holland. Blue-and-white delft pottery and Dutch dolls brighten the decor of this family restaurant, while servers in traditional outfits, wearing bonnets and aprons, provide attentive service. Standard American dishes share the menu with Dutch specialties like eggs hollandaise and fruit koeken (pancakes) for breakfast, a Dutch burger with Gouda cheese for lunch, and Metworst sausage with warm red cabbage and German potato salad for dinner. There's free coffee for early risers (5 to 6am).

 Mario's, 200 E. 2nd St. ☎ **623-1740.**

Cuisine: AMERICAN.
Prices: Appetizers $3.95–$5.95; lunch $3.70–$4.95; dinner $4.95–$12.95. AE, MC, V.
Open: Mon–Thurs 11am–9pm, Fri–Sat 11am–10pm. **Closed:** Thanksgiving and Christmas.

The works of regional artists like Peter Hurd and R. C. Gorman hang on the walls, while stained-glass lamps/ceiling fans are suspended above the booths and tables. Dinners include prime rib and New York strip steak, country chicken, and blackened or southern (cornmeal-fried) catfish. "Heart Smart" (low fat, low cholesterol) items are indicated on the menu. All dinners include the expansive salad bar and a miniloaf of bread. An adjoining lounge has complimentary hors d'oeuvres and a big-screen TV. In fine weather you can enjoy dining on the patio.

$ Nuthin' Fancy Cafe, 2103 N. Main St. ☎ **623-4098.**

Cuisine: AMERICAN.
Prices: Breakfast main courses $1–$3.60; lunch and dinner main courses $3.75–$7.50. DISC, MC, V.
Open: Daily 6am–9pm.

This large comfortable room with western decor has tables and booths, and seems just right for a restaurant with the motto "Home cooking without the mess." The menu is basic American diner, prepared better than most. There are also a few Mexican dishes, such as huevos rancheros and breakfast burritos, which join the standard eggs, pancakes, and waffles on the breakfast menu. Lunch and dinner selections include sandwiches, burgers, chicken-fried steak, meat loaf, and grilled chicken and fish.

Pepper's Grill & Bar, Sunbank Building, 500 N. Main St. (off 6th St.). ☎ **623-1700.**

Cuisine: NEW MEXICAN & AMERICAN.
Prices: Appetizers $1.45–$5.95; main courses $3.90–$11.95. AE, DISC, MC, V.
Open: Mon–Thurs 11am–9pm, Fri–Sat 11am–10pm.

It's hard to take too seriously a restaurant with cartoon mariachi chile characters painted on its walls, including one cute little jalapeño pulling a burro. But the frivolous decor is merely a reminder to have fun. And eating here is certainly fun! The menu offers a variety of salads, soups, burgers and other sandwiches, including a charbroiled tuna-steak sandwich. It also features standard Mexican main courses plus regional specialties: steak or chicken fajitas, southwestern chicken or shrimp, country-fried steak, and barbecued baby back ribs. There's a patio for outdoor dining, and a full bar.

4 Carlsbad & Carlsbad Caverns National Park

Carlsbad: 275 miles SE of Albuquerque; 164 miles E of El Paso, Texas; 180 miles W of Lubbock, Texas

GETTING THERE • By Plane   Cavern City Air Terminal (☎ **885-5236**) is 4 miles south of the city via National Parks Highway (U.S. 62/180). **Mesa Airlines** (☎ **885-0245** or toll free **800/MESA-AIR**) provides commercial service with four flights to and from Albuquerque and two flights to and from Dallas, Texas. You can rent a car at the airport from **Hertz** (☎ **887-1500**).

• **By Bus** From Carlsbad's **Union Bus Depot,** 1000 S. Canyon St. near Pompa Street (☎ **887-1108**), there's daily service aboard **Texas, New Mexico & Oklahoma Coaches.** Three buses pass through daily each way on TNM&O's Oklahoma City–El Paso route and one daily each way on the Albuquerque–Roswell–Fort Stockton, Texas, run. From White's City, south of Carlsbad, van service to Carlsbad Caverns National Park is provided by **Sun Country Tours** (☎ **785-2291**).

• **By Car** From Albuquerque take I-40 east 59 miles to Clines Corners; turn south on U.S. 285, 216 miles to Carlsbad via Roswell (6 hours). From El Paso, take U.S. 62/180 east (3 hours).

ESSENTIALS • Orientation Carlsbad straddles the Pecos River, a beautiful stream which gives it its particular character. Downtown spreads along the west side of the river, with the primary artery, Canal Street (U.S. 285), about three blocks from the Pecos. Carlsbad is located at the crossroads of Highway 285, a north-south route linking Albuquerque with southern Texas, and Highway 62/180, an east-west highway connecting El Paso and Dallas.

• **Information** The **Carlsbad Chamber of Commerce,** 302 S. Canal Street (Highway 285) at Green Street (Highway 62/180), P.O. Box 910 Dept. B, Carlsbad, NM 88221-0910 (☎ **505/887-6516** or toll free **800/221-1224**), is open from 8am to 5pm Monday to Friday.

• **Fast Facts** The **area code** is 505. **Guadalupe Medical Center** provides full hospital services at 2430 W. Pierce St., U.S. Highway 285 north (☎ **887-4100**). The **post office** is located at 301 N. Canyon St. (☎ **885-5717**). In case of **emergency,** dial **911.**

Carlsbad is a city of 26,500 on the Pecos River. Founded in the late 1800s, its area was controlled by Apaches and Comanches until just a little over a century ago. Besides a good tourist business from Carlsbad Caverns, the town thrives on farming, with irrigated crops of cotton, hay, and pecans. Pecans grow so well in Carlsbad that it is said the nuts from just two trees in your yard will pay your property taxes. The area is the largest producer of potash in the U.S. The town was named for the spa in Bohemia of the same name.

The caverns are the big attraction, having drawn more than 33 million visitors since opening in 1923. A satellite community, Whites City, was created 20 miles south of Carlsbad at the park entrance junction. The family of Jack White, Jr., owns all of its motels, restaurants, gift shops, and other attractions.

What to See & Do

Carlsbad's pride and joy is its river, with a 3¹/₂-mile **Riverwalk** along both banks of the pretty Pecos River, beginning near the north end of Riverside Drive. Annual **Christmas on the Pecos** pontoon boat rides take place each evening from Thanksgiving to New Year's Eve (except Christmas Eve), past a fascinating display of Christmas lights on riverside homes and businesses. Advance reservations are required, available from the Chamber of Commerce (**887-6516**). Cost is $5 per person; lap tickets are available free for children under three.

The **Carlsbad Museum and Art Center,** 418 W. Fox Street, one block west of Canal Street (☎ **887-0276**), contains Apache relics, pioneer artifacts such as

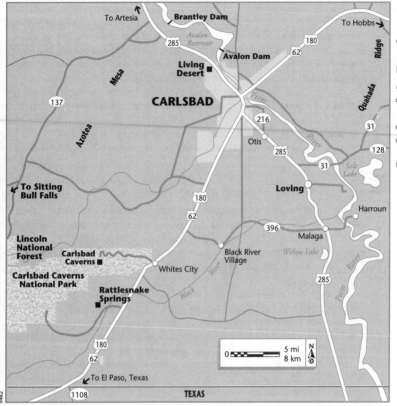

guns and saddles, and an impressive art collection. Open Monday through Saturday from 10am to 6pm, admission is free, although donations are welcome.

About 26 miles southeast of Carlsbad is the **Waste Isolation Pilot Plant (WIPP),** a U.S. Department of Energy facility for the disposal of low-level defense-related radioactive waste. A downtown **WIPP Visitor Center,** 101 W. Greene St. (☎ **234-7200**) has hands-on demonstrations and exhibits on why and how the radioactive waste is to be stored in underground salt beds. It's open Monday through Friday from 8am to 4pm. Tours of the actual plant can also be scheduled.

Recreational facilities in the Carlsbad area include some two dozen parks, several golf courses, numerous tennis courts and swimming pools, a municipal beach, and a shooting and archery range. Contact the **City of Carlsbad Recreation Department** (☎ **887-1191**).

★ **Living Desert Zoo & Gardens State Park,** Skyline Dr. (P.O. Box 100), Carlsbad, NM 88221-0100. ☎ **887-5516.**

Situated within 1,200 acres of authentic Chihuahuan Desert, this park contains more than 50 species of desert mammals, birds, and reptiles, and almost 500 varieties of plants. Paved walkways lead through a variety of habitats past native plants, and into a greenhouse which shelters unusual cacti and exotic succulents from around the world.

Rehabilitation programs provide the park's animals, who have been sick or injured and could no longer survive in the wild. You'll see golden eagles and great horned owls among the birds of prey in the aviary, and large animals such as deer, antelope, elk, and bison in large outdoor pastures. An arroyo exhibit houses javelina, and you'll also see bears, bobcats, and cougars. A prairie dog town is a children's favorite, and a visitors' center houses additional exhibits and a gift shop.

The view from the park, high atop the Ocotillo Hills on the northwest side of Carlsbad, is superb. To reach it, take Skyline Drive off U.S. 285 west of town and proceed just over a mile.

Admission: $3, children 6 and under free. Group rates are available.

Open: Mid-May to Labor Day 8am–6:30pm; rest of year 9am–3:30pm. **Closed:** Christmas.

 Carlsbad Caverns National Park, 3225 National Parks Hwy., Carlsbad, NM 88220. ☎ **785-2232** or **785-2107** (recorded information).

One of the largest and most spectacular cave systems in the world. Carlsbad Caverns comprise some 80 known caves that snake through the porous limestone reef of the Guadalupe Mountains. Fantastic and grotesque formations fascinate visitors, who find every shape imaginable (and unimaginable) naturally sculpted in the underground— from frozen waterfalls to strands of pearls, soda straws to miniature castles, draperies to ice-cream cones.

Although Native Americans had known of the caverns for centuries, they were not discovered by whites until about a century ago, when settlers were attracted by sunset flights of bats from the cave. Jim White, a guano miner, began to explore the main cave in the early 1900s, and to share its wonders with tourists. By 1923 it had become a national monument, upgraded to national park in 1930.

Two caves, Carlsbad Cavern and Slaughter Canyon (formerly New) Cave, are open to the public. The National Park Service has provided facilities to make it easy for everyone to visit the cavern, with elevators, a kennel for pets, and a nursery. Visitors in wheelchairs are common.

Visitors to the cavern can either walk down through its natural entrance or go by elevator to a point 750 feet below the surface and begin walking there. The paved walkway through the natural entrance winds into the depths of the cavern and leads through a series of underground rooms. This walk is 1³/₄ miles in length and takes about an hour and 45 minutes. Parts of it are steep. At its lowest point, the trail reaches 830 feet below the surface, ending finally at an underground lunchroom whose existence seems to amaze many visitors.

Here, those who have taken the elevator join the tour of the spectacular 14-story-high Big Room, with a ceiling looming 255 feet over the trail. The floor of this room covers 14 acres; a tour, over a relatively level path, is 1¹/₄ miles in length and takes about an hour. Visitors may either join one of the frequent guided tours or simply wander through the cavern by themselves.

Everyone is advised to wear flat shoes with rubber soles and heels because of the slippery paths. A light sweater or jacket feels good in the constant temperature of 56°, especially when it's 100° outside in the sun. The cavern is well lit. Rangers are stationed in the cave to answer questions.

At sunset, a crowd gathers at the cave entrance to watch a quarter-million bats take off for the night, mid-May through October. (The bats, and some of the people, winter in Mexico.) All day long the Mexican free-tail bats sleep in the cavern, then strike out on an insect hunt at night. A ranger program is offered about 7pm. On the second Thursday in August (usually), a "bat flight breakfast" from 5 to 7am encourages visitors to watch the bats return to the cavern.

Slaughter Canyon Cave was discovered in 1937 and was mined for bat guano commercially until the 1950s. It consists of a corridor 1,140 feet long with many side passageways. The lowest point is 250 feet below the surface, and the passage traversed by tours is 1³/₄ miles long, but more strenuous than hiking through the main cavern; there is also a strenuous 500-foot rise hike from the parking lot to the cave mouth. The tour lasts about 2¹/₂ hours. No more than 25 people may take part in a tour, and then by reservation only. Everyone needs a flashlight, hiking boots or shoes, and a container of drinking water. Slaughter Canyon Cave is reached via U.S. 180, south 5 miles from White's City, to a marked turnoff that leads 11 miles into a parking lot.

Spelunkers who seek access to the park's undeveloped caves require special permission from the park administration.

Aside from the caves, the national park offers a 10-mile one-way loop drive to view Rattlesnake and Upper Walnut Canyons, and Rattlesnake Springs Picnic Area, on County Road 418 near Slaughter Canyon Cave, a water source for hundreds of years for the Native Americans of the area. Backcountry hikers must register at the visitor center before going out on any of the trails in the 46,766 acres of the park.

Admission: $5 adults, $3 children 6–15, under 6 free.

Open: Visitor Center daily Memorial Day–late Aug 8am–7pm; rest of the year 8am–5:30pm. **Closed:** Christmas Day.

NEARBY ATTRACTIONS

★ **Guadalupe Mountains National Park,** HC 60, Box 400, Salt Flat, TX 78947. ☎ **915/828-3251.**

Some 250 million years ago, the Guadalupe Mountains were an immense reef poking up through a tropical ocean. Marine organisms fossilized this 400-mile-long Capitan Reef as limestone; later, as the sea evaporated, a blanket of sediments and mineral salts buried the reef. Then just 10 to 12 million years ago, a mountain-building uplift exposed a part of the fossil reef. This has given modern scientists a unique opportunity to explore Earth's geologic history and outdoor lovers a playground for wilderness experience.

The steep southern end of the range makes up the park, while the northern part lies within Lincoln National Forest and Carlsbad Caverns National Park. Deer, elk, mountain lion, and bear are found in the forests, which contrast strikingly with the desert around them. In these isolated basins and protected valleys is a proliferation of vegetation rare elsewhere in the Southwest.

The Visitors Center, 55 miles southwest of Carlsbad via U.S. Highway 62/180, offers a variety of exhibits and slide programs telling the story of the Guadalupe Mountains, as well as ranger-guided walks and lectures. Information, maps, and backcountry permits are also obtained at McKittrick Canyon Visitor Center (10 miles northeast via U.S. 62/180 and a side road) and Dog Canyon Ranger Station (reached through Carlsbad via N.M. 137 and County Road 414, about 70 miles).

McKittrick Canyon is one of the few spots accessible by paved road. Protected by its high sheer walls, with a green swatch of trees growing along the banks of its spring-fed stream, it is a beautiful location. It is a great spot for bird-watching and viewing other wildlife, and an especially lovely sight during fall foliage time, late October to mid-November. Most of the national park's 86,416 acres are reached only by 80 miles of foot or horse trail through desert, canyon, and high forest. Backcountry hikers require water and permits; camping must be in designated areas. There are developed camping areas at Pine Springs and Dog Canyon.

Admission: Free; Pine Springs and Dog Canyon Campgrounds $6 per night.

Open: Visitor center, June–Aug 8am–6pm; Sept–May 8am–4:30pm.

Artesia

In this quiet town of 11,300 people, 36 miles north of Carlsbad on U.S. 285, the principal attraction is the **Artesia Historical Museum & Art Center,** housed in a Victorian home at 505 W. Richardson Ave., Artesia (☎ **748-2390**). Open Tuesday to Saturday from 10am to noon and from 1 to 5pm, it exhibits Native American and pioneer artifacts, traveling exhibits, and art shows.

Visitors looking for a stopover in Artesia might consider the **Best Western Pecos Inn,** 2209 W. Main St. (Highway 82), Artesia, NM 88210 (☎ **505/748-3324**). Further information can be obtained from the **Artesia Chamber of Commerce,** P.O. Box 99, Artesia, NM 88210 (☎ **505/746-2744**).

Hobbs

Located 69 miles east of Carlsbad on U.S. 62/180, on the edge of the Llano Estacado tableland, Hobbs (pop. 29,400) is at the center of New Mexico's richest oilfield. Many oil companies have their headquarters here.

Points of interest include the **Lea County Cowboy Hall of Fame and Western Heritage Center** at New Mexico Junior College, on the Lovington Highway (☎ 392-1275). It honors the area's ranchers, both men and women, and rodeo performers and is open from 10am to 5pm Monday through Friday, and from 1 to 5pm Saturday (closed college holidays). The **Confederate Air Force Museum** (☎ 392-5342) at Lea County Airport, on U.S. 62/180, displays World War II aircraft; the **Soaring Society of America** (☎ 392-1177) has its national headquarters at the Hobbs Industrial Air Park, north of town on N.M. 18. Native American artifacts and pioneer mementos are displayed by appointment at the **Linam Ranch Museum** (☎ 393-4784), located west of town on U.S. 62/180.

Twenty-two miles northwest of Hobbs via N.M. 18, at the junction of U.S. Highway 82, is the town of **Lovington** (pop. 9,500), another ranching and oil center. The **Lea County Historical Museum,** 103 S. Love St. (☎ 396-5311), presents memorabilia of the region's unique history in a First World War–era hotel.

If you plan to stay in Hobbs, try **Hobbs Motor Inn,** 501 N. Marland St. (☎ 397-3251), or the **Zia Motel,** 619 N. Marland St. (☎ 397-3591). You can get a good square meal at the **Cattle Baron Steak & Seafood Restaurant,** 1930 N. Grimes St. (☎ 393-2800), or **La Fiesta,** 604 E. Broadway (☎ 397-1235). **Harry McAdams State Park,** 4 miles north of Hobbs on N.M. 18 (☎ 392-5845), has campsites and a visitor center. For more information, contact the **Hobbs Chamber of Commerce,** 400 N. Marland St. (☎ 397-3202 or toll free **800/658-6291**).

Where to Stay

Most properties are along the highway south toward Carlsbad Caverns. An 11.1875% tax is imposed on all lodging bills (6.1875% state tax and 5% city lodging tax). Parking is usually provided free of charge.

Best Western Cavern Inn, 17 Carlsbad Cavern Hwy. at N.M. Hwy. 7 (P.O. Box 128), White's City, NM 88268. ☎ **505/785-2291** or toll free **800/CAVERNS.** Fax 505/785-2283. 63 rms. A/C TV TEL

Rates: May 15–Sept 15 $59–$75 single or double; Sept 16–May 14 $49–$65 single or double. AE, CB, DC, DISC, MC, V.

This motel and the overflow properties flanking it—the 44-room Guadalupe Inn and the 25-unit adobe Walnut Canyon Inn—suffice as places to rest one's head before or after a visit to Carlsbad Caverns. Guest registration is in the arcade with the western facade on the south side of the highway; the motel is on the north side. Rooms are very spacious, with a southwestern decor.

Most folks dine and drink across the highway at the Velvet Garter Saloon and Restaurant (see "Where to Dine," below). The White's City arcade contains a post office, grocery store, gift shop, Million Dollar Museum of various antiques and paraphernalia, and Granny's Opera House, a theater for weekend melodramas. Between the Cavern Inn and its neighbor properties, there are two swimming pools, two hot tubs, and a court for tennis, volleyball, and basketball. Pets are not allowed.

★
$
Best Western Motel Stevens, 1829 S. Canal St., Carlsbad, NM 88220.
☎ **505/887-2851** or toll free **800/730-2851** or **800/528-1234.** Fax 505/887-6338.
202 rms, 15 suites. A/C TV TEL

Rates: $60–$70 single; $65–$75 double; $65 and up suite AE, CB, DC, DISC, MC, V.

Well-landscaped gardens surround this handsome property, composed of several buildings spread across the spacious grounds. The very attractive lobby and restaurant are located in a central brick building with a tile roof.

Rooms are good-sized, with southwestern decor, and most have two queen beds. All have remodeled bathrooms with large mirrors and spacious vanities. Some units, with peaked ceilings to make them feel even larger, have backdoor patios. A microwave/refrigerator combo is available ($5), and suites have kitchenettes.

There are handicapped-accessible rooms with roll-in shower; nonsmoking and connecting rooms; and pets are allowed.

The Flume (see "Where to Dine," below), open daily from 6am to 10pm, is a beautiful fine-dining establishment specializing in American cuisine. The motel has room service, courtesy car, guest laundry, 24-hour desk, swimming and wading pools, and playground.

Continental Inn, 3820 National Parks Hwy., Carlsbad, NM 88220. ☎ **505/887-0341.**
Fax 505/885-0508. 60 rms and suites. A/C TV TEL

Rates: $32.95 single; $37.95–$42.95 double; $49.95 suite. AE, CB, DC, DISC, MC, V.

This economical motel has all the necessities for travelers on a budget. Rooms have coffeemakers; most have queen-size beds, there are a few kings, and one room has a water bed. Suites are equipped with refrigerators, and the Honeymoon Suite has a heart-shaped tub below a mirrored ceiling, and a shower for two. There's an outdoor heated swimming pool, and connecting, nonsmoking, and handicapped-accessible rooms are available. A 24-hour restaurant is nearby.

★
Holiday Inn, 601 S. Canal St. (P.O. Box 128), Carlsbad, NM 88220.
☎ **505/885-8500** or toll free **800/742-9586** or **800/HOLIDAY.** Fax 505/887-5999.
100 rms. A/C TV TEL

Rates: $75–$85 single; $81–$91 double. AE, CB, DC, DISC, JCB, MC, V.

A handsome New Mexico Territorial-style building houses this first-rate full-service hotel in downtown Carlsbad. Rooms have southwestern decor, and there's a beautiful outdoor heated swimming pool, sauna, and whirlpool, plus an exercise room and playground. Guests have self-service laundry facilities. Nonsmoking, connecting, and handicapped-accessible rooms (some with roll-in showers) are available.

The hotel has two restaurants: Ventanas offers fine dining, serving steaks, prime rib, seafood, veal, and pastas; the Phenix Bar & Grill has sandwiches, burgers, soups, salads, and prime rib.

Stagecoach Inn, 1819 S. Canal St., Carlsbad, NM 88220. ☎ **505/887-1148.** 55 rms.
A/C TV TEL

Rates: $30 single; $40–$54 double. AE, DISC, MC, V.

A large, tree-shaded playground area with a picnic table set back from the highway is the earmark of this motel, which also features an adult pool and children's wading pool separated for safety's sake by a fence. Pets are permitted. Rooms have ample space, and are simply but comfortably furnished. Facilities include a coin-op guest laundry.

The adjacent restaurant specializes in Mexican food, burgers, and barbecue, with meals from $3.95 to $6.95; it's open from 5am to 9pm Monday to Friday, and 6am to 8pm Saturday and Sunday.

Where to Dine

The Flume, at Best Western Motel Stevens, 1829 S. Canal St. ☎ **887-2851.**

Cuisine: AMERICAN. **Reservations:** Recommended for dinner.
Prices: Appetizers $3.95–$7.75; lunch $3.25–$7.95; dinner $7.95–$15.95. AE, CB, DC, DISC, MC, V.
Open: Mon–Sat 6am–10pm, Sun 6am–9pm.

This elegant restaurant has a southwestern feel, with rich wood and upholstery, lovely chandeliers, wall sconces, and candlelight. The menu includes lots of steaks, a New Orleans shrimp plate, and a special teri-yaki chicken breast. Lighter dinners, called "Young and Young-at-Heart" meals, are available.

Lucy's, 701 S. Canal St. ☎ **887-7714.**

Cuisine: MEXICAN. **Reservations:** Recommended on weekends.
Prices: Main courses $3.75–$11.95. AE, CB, DC, DISC, MC, V.
Open: Mon–Sat 11am–10pm. **Closed:** Thanksgiving, Christmas, and New Year's.

Since 1974, Lucy and Justo Yanez's friendly, casual downtown restaurant has made diners—visitors and locals alike—feel right at home. It's dedicated to the words of a Mexican proverb printed on the menu: *El hambre es un fuego, y la comida es fresca* (Hunger is a burning, and eating is a coolness). The food is superb, with Lucy's personal adaptations of old favorites—steak ranchero, caldillo de Miguel (beef stew), Tucson chimichanga, and shrimp fajitas. Finish with a dessert of buñelos, sprinkled with cinnamon sugar. Children's plates are available; diners can choose how hot they like their red or green chiles.

Sirloin Stockade, 710 S. Canal St. ☎ **887-7211.**

Cuisine: STEAKS.
Prices: Main courses $4.99–$10.99. MC, V.
Open: Daily 11am–10pm.

Part of a statewide eight-restaurant chain of family steak houses, the Sirloin Stockade serves a variety of steaks, chicken and shrimp platters. There are several buffet food bars offering soups, salads, hot dishes, and desserts; and children's and senior citizens' menus are available.

Velvet Garter Saloon and Restaurant, 26 Carlsbad Cavern Hwy., White's City. ☎ **785-2291.**

Cuisine: AMERICAN. **Reservations:** Recommended in summer.
Prices: Appetizers $2.95–$3.25; main courses $6.95–$12.95. AE, CB, DC, MC, V.
Open: Daily 4–9pm.

This comfortable coffee shop–style establishment near the Carlsbad Caverns Highway junction boasts two beautiful stained-glass windows portraying the caverns and the Guadalupe Mountains. The menu includes steaks, chicken, and fish. Nearby Fat Jack's caters to fast-food diets with three meals daily; the saloon is unmistakable, with the longhorns mounted over the door.

Index

334

Now Save Money On All Your Travels By Joining
FROMMER'S™ TRAVEL BOOK CLUB
The World's Best Travel Guides
At Membership Prices!

Frommer's Travel Book Club is your ticket to successful travel! Open up a world of travel information and simplify your travel planning when you join ranks with thousands of value-conscious travelers who are members of the Frommer's *Travel Book Club*. Join today and you'll be entitled to all the privileges that come from belonging to the club that offers you travel guides for less to more than 100 destinations worldwide. **Annual membership is only $25.00 (U.S.) or $35.00 (Canada/Foreign).**

The Advantages of Membership:

1. Your choice of **three free** books (any **two** Frommer's Comprehensive Guides, Frommer's $-A-Day Guides, Frommer's Walking Tours or Frommer's Family Guides—plus **one** Frommer's City Guide, Frommer's City $-A-Day Guide or Frommer's Touring Guide).

2. Your own subscription to the **TRIPS & TRAVEL** quarterly newsletter.

3. You're entitled to a **30% discount** on your order of any additional books offered by the club.

4. You're offered (at a small additional fee) our **Domestic Trip-Routing Kits.**

Our **Trips & Travel** quarterly newsletter offers practical information on the best buys in travel, the "hottest" vacation spots, the latest travel trends, world-class events and much, much more.

Our **Domestic Trip-Routing Kits** are available for any North American destination. We'll send you a detailed map highlighting the best route to take to your destination—you can request direct or scenic routes.

Here's all you have to do to join:

Send in your membership fee of $25.00 ($35.00 Canada/Foreign) with your name and address on the form below along with your selections as part of your membership package to the address listed below. Remember to check off your three free books.

If you would like to order additional books, please select the books you would like and send a check for the total amount (please add sales tax in the states noted below), plus $2.00 per book for shipping and handling ($3.00 Canada/Foreign) to the address listed below.

FROMMER'S TRAVEL BOOK CLUB
P.O. Box 473
Mt. Morris, IL 61054-0473
(815) 734-1104

[ ] **YES!** I want to take advantage of this opportunity to join Frommer's Travel Book Club.

[ ] My check is enclosed. Dollar amount enclosed_____*
(all payments in U.S. funds only)

Name _____

Address _____

City _____ State _____ Zip _____

Phone (   ) _____ (In case we have a question regarding your order).

All orders must be prepaid.

To ensure that all orders are processed efficiently, please apply sales tax in the following areas: CA, CT, FL, IL, IN, NJ, NY, PA, TN, WA and CANADA.

*With membership, shipping & handling will be paid by Frommer's Travel Book Club for the three FREE books you select as part of your membership. Please add $2.00 per book for shipping & handling for any additional books purchased ($3.00 Canada/Foreign).

Allow 4-6 weeks for delivery for all items. Prices of books, membership fee, and publication dates are subject to change without notice. All orders are subject to acceptance and availability.

Please send me the books checked below:

FROMMER'S COMPREHENSIVE GUIDES

*(Guides listing facilities from budget to deluxe,
with emphasis on the medium-priced)*

	Retail Price	Code		Retail Price	Code
☐ Acapulco/Ixtapa/Taxco, 2nd Edition	$13.95	C157	☐ Jamaica/Barbados, 2nd Edition	$15.00	C149
☐ Alaska '94-'95	$17.00	C131	☐ Japan '94-'95	$19.00	C144
☐ Arizona '95 (Avail. 3/95)	$14.95	C166	☐ Maui, 1st Edition	$14.00	C153
☐ Australia '94'-'95	$18.00	C147	☐ Nepal, 2nd Edition	$18.00	C126
☐ Austria, 6th Edition	$16.95	C162	☐ New England '95	$16.95	C165
☐ Bahamas '94-'95	$17.00	C121	☐ New Mexico, 3rd Edition (Avail. 3/95)	$14.95	C167
☐ Belgium/Holland/ Luxembourg '93-'94	$18.00	C106	☐ New York State '94-'95	$19.00	C133
☐ Bermuda '94-'95	$15.00	C122	☐ Northwest, 5th Edition	$17.00	C140
☐ Brazil, 3rd Edition	$20.00	C111	☐ Portugal '94-'95	$17.00	C141
☐ California '95	$16.95	C164	☐ Puerto Rico '95-'96	$14.00	C151
☐ Canada '94-'95	$19.00	C145	☐ Puerto Vallarta/ Manzanillo/Guadalajara '94-'95	$14.00	C135
☐ Caribbean '95	$18.00	C148			
☐ Carolinas/Georgia, 2nd Edition	$17.00	C128	☐ Scandinavia, 16th Edition (Avail. 3/95)	$19.95	C169
☐ Colorado, 2nd Edition	$16.00	C143	☐ Scotland '94-'95	$17.00	C146
☐ Costa Rica '95	$13.95	C161	☐ South Pacific '94-'95	$20.00	C138
☐ Cruises '95-'96	$19.00	C150	☐ Spain, 16th Edition	$16.95	C163
☐ Delaware/Maryland '94-'95	$15.00	C136	☐ Switzerland/ Liechtenstein '94-'95	$19.00	C139
☐ England '95	$17.95	C159	☐ Thailand, 2nd Edition	$17.95	C154
☐ Florida '95	$18.00	C152	☐ U.S.A., 4th Edition	$18.95	C156
☐ France '94-'95	$20.00	C132	☐ Virgin Islands '94-'95	$13.00	C127
☐ Germany '95	$18.95	C158	☐ Virginia '94-'95	$14.00	C142
☐ Ireland, 1st Edition (Avail. 3/95)	$16.95	C168	☐ Yucatan, 2nd Edition	$13.95	C155
☐ Italy '95	$18.95	C160			

FROMMER'S $-A-DAY GUIDES
(Guides to low-cost tourist accommodations and facilities)

	Retail Price	Code		Retail Price	Code
☐ Australia on $45 '95-'96	$18.00	D122	☐ Israel on $45, 15th Edition	$16.95	D130
☐ Costa Rica/Guatemala/ Belize on $35, 3rd Edition	$15.95	D126	☐ Mexico on $45 '95	$16.95	D125
☐ Eastern Europe on $30, 5th Edition	$16.95	D129	☐ New York on $70 '94-'95	$16.00	D121
☐ England on $60 '95	$17.95	D128	☐ New Zealand on $45 '93-'94	$18.00	D103
☐ Europe on $50 '95	$17.95	D127	☐ South America on $40, 16th Edition	$18.95	D123
☐ Greece on $45 '93-'94	$19.00	D100			
☐ Hawaii on $75 '95	$16.95	D124	☐ Washington, D.C. on $50 '94-'95	$17.00	D120
☐ Ireland on $45 '94-'95	$17.00	D118			

FROMMER'S CITY $-A-DAY GUIDES

	Retail Price	Code		Retail Price	Code
☐ Berlin on $40 '94-'95	$12.00	D111	☐ Madrid on $50 '94-'95	$13.00	D119
☐ London on $45 '94-'95	$12.00	D114	☐ Paris on $50 '94-'95	$12.00	D117

FROMMER'S FAMILY GUIDES

*(Guides listing information on kid-friendly
hotels, restaurants, activities and attractions)*

	Retail Price	Code		Retail Price	Code
☐ California with Kids	$18.00	F100	☐ San Francisco with Kids	$17.00	F104
☐ Los Angeles with Kids	$17.00	F103	☐ Washington, D.C. with Kids	$17.00	F102
☐ New York City with Kids	$18.00	F101			

FROMMER'S CITY GUIDES

*(Pocket-size guides to sightseeing and tourist
accommodations and facilities in all price ranges)*

	Retail Price	Code		Retail Price	Code
☐ Amsterdam '93-'94	$13.00	S110	☐ Montreal/Quebec City '95	$11.95	S166
☐ Athens, 10th Edition (Avail. 3/95)	$12.95	S174	☐ Nashville/Memphis, 1st Edition	$13.00	S141
☐ Atlanta '95	$12.95	S161	☐ New Orleans '95	$12.95	S148
☐ Atlantic City/Cape May, 5th Edition	$13.00	S130	☐ New York '95	$12.95	S152
☐ Bangkok, 2nd Edition	$12.95	S147	☐ Orlando '95	$13.00	S145
☐ Barcelona '93-'94	$13.00	S115	☐ Paris '95	$12.95	S150
☐ Berlin, 3rd Edition	$12.95	S162	☐ Philadelphia, 8th Edition	$12.95	S167
☐ Boston '95	$12.95	S160	☐ Prague '94-'95	$13.00	S143
☐ Budapest, 1st Edition	$13.00	S139	☐ Rome, 10th Edition	$12.95	S168
☐ Chicago '95	$12.95	S169	☐ St. Louis/Kansas City, 2nd Edition	$13.00	S127
☐ Denver/Boulder/Colorado Springs, 3rd Edition	$12.95	S154	☐ San Diego '95	$12.95	S158
☐ Dublin, 2nd Edition	$12.95	S157	☐ San Francisco '95	$12.95	S155
☐ Hong Kong '94-'95	$13.00	S140	☐ Santa Fe/Taos/ Albuquerque '95 (Avail. 2/95)	$12.95	S172
☐ Honolulu/Oahu '95	$12.95	S151			
☐ Las Vegas '95	$12.95	S163	☐ Seattle/Portland '94-'95	$13.00	S137
☐ London '95	$12.95	S156	☐ Sydney, 4th Edition	$12.95	S171
☐ Los Angeles '95	$12.95	S164	☐ Tampa/St. Petersburg, 3rd Edition	$13.00	S146
☐ Madrid/Costa del Sol, 2nd Edition	$12.95	S165	☐ Tokyo '94-'95	$13.00	S144
☐ Mexico City, 1st Edition	$12.95	S170	☐ Toronto '95 (Avail. 3/95)	$12.95	S173
☐ Miami '95-'96	$12.95	S149	☐ Vancouver/Victoria '94-'95	$13.00	S142
☐ Minneapolis/St. Paul, 4th Edition	$12.95	S159	☐ Washington, D.C. '95	$12.95	S153

FROMMER'S WALKING TOURS

*(Companion guides that point out the places
and pleasures that make a city unique)*

	Retail Price	Code		Retail Price	Code
☐ Berlin	$12.00	W100	☐ New York	$12.00	W102
☐ Chicago	$12.00	W107	☐ Paris	$12.00	W103
☐ England's Favorite Cities	$12.00	W108	☐ San Francisco	$12.00	W104
☐ London	$12.00	W101	☐ Washington, D.C.	$12.00	W105
☐ Montreal/Quebec City	$12.00	W106			

SPECIAL EDITIONS

	Retail Price	Code		Retail Price	Code
☐ Bed & Breakfast Southwest	$16.00	P100	☐ National Park Guide, 29th Edition	$17.00	P106
☐ Bed & Breakfast Great American Cities	$16.00	P104	☐ Where to Stay U.S.A., 11th Edition	$15.00	P102
☐ Caribbean Hideaways	$16.00	P103			

FROMMER'S TOURING GUIDES

*(Color-illustrated guides that include walking tours,
cultural and historic sites, and practical information)*

	Retail Price	Code		Retail Price	Code
☐ Amsterdam	$11.00	T001	☐ New York	$11.00	T008
☐ Barcelona	$14.00	T015	☐ Rome	$11.00	T010
☐ Brazil	$11.00	T003	☐ Tokyo	$15.00	T016
☐ Hong Kong/Singapore/ Macau	$11.00	T006	☐ Turkey	$11.00	T013
☐ London	$13.00	T007	☐ Venice	$ 9.00	T014

*Please note: If the availability of a book is several months away, we may
have back issues of guides to that particular destination.
Call customer service at (815) 734-1104.*